FOR A PAL

GUADALCANAL LEGACY
50TH ANNIVERSARY
1942-1992

TURNER PUBLISHING COMPANY
Paducah, Kentucky

February, 1944. General chasers—A Marine patrol trudges through the jungle in hot pursuit of Jap Major General Matsuda and his forces. (USMC Photo, No. 72, 822. Courtesy of Kenneth F. LeBay)

TURNER PUBLISHING COMPANY

The Front Line of Military History Books
P.O. Box 3101
Paducah, Kentucky 42002-3101
(502) 443-0121

Guadalcanal Legacy
50th Anniversary 1942-1992 Staff:
Author: Mr. Philip D. Birkitt
Editors: Mr. Gene Keller
      Dr. Robert C. Muehrcke
      Mr. Donald W. Peltier
      Mr. Joseph Micek

Turner Publishing Company's Staff:
Publisher's Editor: Mr. Robert J. Martin
Designer: Mr. Trevor W. Grantham

Library of Congress Catalog
Card Number: 91-67155
ISBN: 1-56311-053-9

Printed in the United States of America.

Limited Edition. Additional books may be purchased from Turner Publishing Company, Paducah, Kentucky.

TABLE OF CONTENTS

Foreword 4
Prayer 5
Preface 6
Dedication 7
Medal of Honor 8
Memorial Dedication 9
Board of Directors 10
GCV Past Presidents 11
Guadalcanal Book Committee 12
Guadalcanal Veteran's Tribute 13
Publisher's Message 14

The Guadalcanal Legacy 16
    Panic at Tulagi 17
    An Operation Open to the Gravest Doubts 19
    Follow Me and Run Like Hell 23
    Strange Ships in the Sound 25
    We Are Firing On Our Own Ships 30
    Their Swords were Flashing in the Sun 36
    Ichiki's Folly 37
    The Ridge Should be a Good Rest Area 39
    An Endless Jungle Path 43
    I Must Warn Them in Rabaul 46
    What is this Guadalcanal Like? 47
    Those Sharks Were Real Killers 49
    The Situation is Worse Than I Imagined 52
    Tutsugeki! 55
    Get the Big Ones 57
    Tenacious Tanaka 60
    Tanaka Tries Again 64
    We Can No Longer Send Out Patrols 65
    I Dream of Rice Cakes and Candies 66
    When Will Help Come? 68
    Sunset 72
    Not Just A Distant Land 74
    Bibliography 76

Personal Experience Stories 78
Guadalcanal Reunion 92
Guadalcanal Memorial Museum 98
Guadalcanal War Memorial 99
Guadalcanal Veterans 100
Guadalcanal Index 151

FOREWORD

Eugene L. "Gene" Keller
National President

It becomes difficult for me to express my feelings of honor and pride to represent such an outstanding group of men and women as their president. It's been many years since this young man of 17, who on August 7, 1942, waded ashore on the isle of Guadalcanal. I enlisted November 23, 1941 but it was May 1942 before I joined C Co., 1st Pioneer Bn., 1st Marine Division at New River, NC. I arrived too late to take part in the maneuvers or learn how to go down a landing net, so when it became time to go over the side, I just followed the rest of the men. I recall several sailors wishing us well and we were acting very macho, but in reality, we were some very frightened young men.

When you try to look back some 50 years ago, it becomes difficult to remember so many details of the operation. This just might be a good thing as there still are a lot of memories that are not so pleasant to remember. The comradeship of those days though will never be forgotten or the pride that we shared in serving our country in the Battle of Guadalcanal. This is the same bond that now exists within the Guadalcanal Campaign Veterans even to this day. Who can ever forget those Japanese Battle Wagons, standing off shore and blasting us for two hours . . . those constant air raids and constant hunger. . . your buddies, shaking with malaria or suffering dysentery and you helpless to do anything for them . . . no sleep and Japanese everywhere? These are just a few of the things that bind us together. "'Guadalcanal', the name will not die out of the memories of this generation."— *New York Times*.

I am extremely proud of the Guadalcanal Campaign Veterans for perpetuating the spirit and the history of that island of Guadalcanal. It behoves us all to educate the youth of today and I hope that our National Museum will do just that. I hope that I have contributed to the success of the organization and I am sure that who ever follows me will serve it with the same dedication that I have. I have not taken lightly the honor bestowed upon me and I thank you all for your confidence and trust. *Semper Fi* and may God bless us all.

Gene Keller

PRAYER

Rev. Frederic P. Gehring, C.M.

O' Heavenly Father, whose Legacy promised Eternal Blessings and Happiness to those who serve their country well, look with favor upon this second edition of our publication, *The Guadalcanal Legacy, 50th Anniversary.* Your guidance with its first heartbeat has made it a must to our heroic warriors of Guadalcanal.

The expertise of our editors and those who have contributed touching photos and stories related to their experiences on that war-torn Island of Guadalcanal has attracted hundreds of our comrades who are anxious to look back upon those days and months on that war-torn Island of Guadalcanal.

The Guadalcanal Legacy had become a *"Vade Mecum"* to anyone who has been on that jungle island and experienced the horrors of warfare. Our boys became "men overnight" . . . heroes died in the arms of their comrades.

As age takes its toll and our comrades cling to that faith that gave them the courage to "keep-on keeping on," may this second publication of *The Guadalcanal Legacy, 50th Anniversary* inspire our younger generation who now face new tension, new modification of up-to-date war machines and the possibility of World War Three.

Let Peace be our legacy . . . and not War. Yes . . . we are aware that Peace means Love and Love means Sacrifice, but let it not be the Supreme Sacrifice that our Americans will have to make. O' Heavenly Father, let our legacy be "God Bless America."

Rev. Frederic P. Gehring

PREFACE

Mitchell Paige

During the Persian Gulf War, my thoughts were with those First and Second Division Marines who were the first American ground troops to engage the enemy in combat. Nearly 50 years ago, our First and Second Division Marines launched America's first ground offensive of World War Two in the Solomon Islands. In 1942, Guadalcanal became a household name to all Americans.

With the advent of the 50th Anniversary of that landing, we reflect on the names of that era which were familiar to all who served on Guadalcanal in 1942. Ships that brought us to the island and those that took us away— *Albena, Alchiba, American Legion, Ballard, Barnett, Bellatrix, Betelgeuse, Colhoun, Crescent City, Elliott, Fomalhaut, Fuller, Gregory, Heywood, Hunter Liggett, Libra, Little, McCawley, McKean, Neville, President Adams, President Hayes, President Jackson* and *Zeilin.*

Then there was Henderson Field, the prize of the South Pacific over which the war was all about. The many rivers we crossed—the Langa, Malimba, Matanikau, Metapona, Ilu and the Teneru. Terrain that both sides had traversed— Edson's Ridge, Koli Point, Kokumbono, Kukum, Lunga Point, Point Cruz and Tetere. In the skies we had out valiant Cactus Air Force with their Wildcat's, SBD's, 400's and Cobras while the enemy had their Zero's, Betty's, Kawanishi's and Vals.

The Ichiki, Kawaguchi and Sendai, under the leadership of Furumiya, Huakutake, Kiyotake, Nakaguma, Maruyama and Oka made it rough for all of us. Yes, Guadalcanal, Tulagi, Gavutu, Tanambogo, Florida and Savo were truly household names, together with the ubiquitous "Washing Machine Charlie" and the ever-present malaria carrying Anopheles mosquito.

We can never forget Jacob Vouza with his brave Scouts, Martin Clemens with the dedicated Coast Watches and Father Fred Gehring *"The Padre."* They too shall always be a part of the precious *Guadalcanal Legacy.*

Mitchell Paige, CMH
Colonel
USMC (Ret'd)

DEDICATION

General R. E. Galer

If you mention Guadalcanal today, most people would wonder . . . . Fifty years ago, Guadalcanal was a household word known by all Americans.

Guadalcanal, an island in the British Solomon Islands (approximately 5000 miles southwest of the United States), was discovered in 1568 by the Spanish explorer Alvaro De Mendana DeNeyra. In 1788, Lieutenant Thomas George Shortland, in command of two British transports, landed and examined the island. In 1893, Guadalcanal, with the other Solomon Islands, became a British protectorate. In 1942, Guadalcanal became an American icon, spoken with feeling for the troops who were assaulting the Japanese occupation forces of that island.

On July 5, 1942, a U.S. reconnaissance plane . . . discovered an airstrip under construction by the Japanese on the Solomon Islands and Guadalcanal. The airfield was a potential threat. The Joint Chiefs of Staff were convinced that immediate military action was required.

The JCS directive gave a target date of August 1, 1942 to commence the attack—just one month after the initial discovery of the airfield. The attack was to be executed against Guadalcanal (code named "Cactus") and the island of Tulagi.

"There is no question that Japan's doom was sealed with the closing of the struggle for Guadalcanal."—Japanese Admiral Tanaka. The struggle for Guadalcanal was arduous, dangerous and time consuming. Even today the horrors of that little island in the Pacific haunt its veterans. Even so, many thanks must be given to not only combat personnel, but also non-combat personnel, the Sea-Bees, the Coast Guard and ground crews. Martin Clemens, of the British/Australian Navy, and his crews of coast watchers and native scouts were instrumental in directing attacks against the Japanese on Guadalcanal. Without the aid of these people, without their contribution to the struggle for Guadalcanal, the outcome might have been horrendously different.

We may all be proud for having been a part of this force, many gave their all to accomplish a task under deplorable conditions. Those who "gave their all" and did not return from Guadalcanal should not only be recognized and remembered by all Americans as accomplished soldiers, but also as effecting *the* task which led to the defeat of the Empire of the Rising Sun.

BGen. R. E. Galer
USMC (Ret.)

MEDAL OF HONOR

General R. E. Galer

Mitchell Paige

*BAILEY, Kenneth D.

BASILONE, John

*BAUER, Harold William

*CALLAGHAN, Daniel Judson

CASAMENTO, Anthony

DAVIS, Charles W.

DEBLANC, Jefferson Joseph

EDSON, Merritt Austin

FOSS, Joseph Jacob

*FOURNIER, William G.

GALER, Robert Edward

*GILMORE, Howard Walter

*HALL, Lewis

*KEPPLER, Reinhardt John

MCCANDLESS, Bruce

MUNRO, Douglas Albert

PAIGE, Mitchell

SCHONLAND, Herbert Emery

SCOTT, Norman

SMITH, John Lucian

VANDEGRIFT, A. Archer

These men—Army, Navy and Marine, were presented
the Medal of Honor in memory of their service to the United
States of American during combat action on Guadalcanal.

MEMORIAL DEDICATION

"For A Pal" Dedication is located at the Kalamazoo Aviation History Museum, Kalamazoo, Michigan. The Guadalcanal Campaign Veteran's Museum is also located at Kalamazoo.

In Memorian
For A Pal

At the going down of the sun and in the morning, we shall remember him. For he who fought with us shall be our Brother.

Each of us is diminished by his loss.

**Guadalcanal Campaign Veterans
Gene Keller, President**

GUADALCANAL VETERANS BOARD OF DIRECTORS

E. L. Keller, Sr. - President

Donald Lutes, Sr. - Sr. Vice Pres.

Joseph Micek - Treasurer

Marshal Chaney - Secretary

Fr. Fred Gehring - Chaplin

Harry Horsman - Historian

Rudy Bock - Legal Officer

Jack Brookshire - V. P. S. East

George Jager - V. P. N.Central

Richard Mackie - V. P. S. Central

John Mueller - V. P. Northwest

Tommy Stamos - V. P. S.West

Andrew Brodecki - Director

Richard Henning - Director

Ed Flori - Director

Fred Hitzman - Quartermaster

*** Not pictured:**

William Caroll, Vice President, Northeast
Patrick Neary, Junior Vice President
Mitch Przybycien - Director

William Parker - Director

Don Peltier - Director

GUADALCANAL CAMPAIGN VETERANS
PAST PRESIDENTS

Mr. Mike Zello

Mr. Chuck Breijak

Mr. Graydon Cadwell

Mr. Kurt Ackermann, Sr.

Mr. Ted Blahnik

A TRIBUTE

We, the veterans of Guadalcanal, in gratitude for their leadership and dedication to the Guadalcanal Campaign Veterans Association, would like to take this opportunity to recognize our past Presidents. We, the Veterans and members of the GCV, acknowledge the tireless devotion and labor to our cause given by these fine men. It has been said that the hope of a future rests on the foundation of the past; without the leadership of these men, our organization could not have become all that it is today. We thank you.

GUADALCANAL LEGACY, 50TH ANNIVERSARY BOOK COMMITTEE

Mr. E. L. Keller, Sr., President

Mr. Joseph G. Micek, Treasurer

Mr. Don Peltier, Director

Dr. Robert C. Muehrcke, M.D.

It is the hope of The Guadalcanal Legacy, 50th Anniversary Book Committee that this tribute to the Guadalcanal Campaign Veterans will be one treasured for the rest of your lives. To be sure, we haven't included all the stories or pictures that we would like to see in print, but we have strived to give you the very best of what was submitted. I want to thank Mr. Joseph C. Micek, Mr. Don Peltier and Dr. Robert C. Muehrcke, M.D., who gave me support and much needed advice. I am certain that without their assistance, it would have been impossible to produce a work of this magnitude.

Of course, many, many thanks must go to the Guadalcanal Campaign Veteran's who contributed both stories and pictures to make this family heirloom worthy of being passed on to future generations.

A special "thank you" must go to Mr. Philip Birkitt—his story runs throughout this book. *Semper Fi* to you, Sir.

The Guadalcanal Legacy, 50th Anniversary Edition is dedicated to the men and women who gave so much on the island of Guadalcanal so that future generations may remember what sacrifices were made in the name of freedom. May the world never forget.

GUADALCANAL VETERANS TRIBUTE

Vandegrift, Edson, Paige and Basilone receive the Medal of Honor for their service on Guadalcanal.

We, the veterans of Guadalcanal, in gratitude for the efforts of the following men and their quest for the preservation of the legacy of Guadalcanal, would like to take this opportunity to formally recognize both the men and their works.

We thank Mr. Richard Tregaskis, who wrote the famous *Guadalcanal Diary*. The *Diary* later became a best seller and was eventually crafted into a movie starring Lloyd Nolan and William Bendex. Mr. Tregaskis emphasized the valor of the fighting Marine on the Island of Guadalcanal. Through his efforts, the world became familiar with the struggles faced by those on that horrid island in the 1940s. For his efforts in the preservation of our legacy, we offer him a heartfelt "thank you."

We thank Mr. James A. Michener. He described the destiny of the American Warrior on Guadalcanal. An excerpt of this fine work:

"They will live a long time, these men of the South Pacific. They had an American quality. They, like their victories, will be remembered as long as our generation lives. After that, like men of the Confederacy, they will become strangers. Longer and longer shadows will obscure them, until their Guadalcanal sounds distant on the ear, like Shiloh or Valley Forge."

In addition to this reflection of truth, Mr. Michener wrote the following for the Guadalcanal Memorial Dedication:

"How improbable it was that two world powers, the United States and Japan, should meet in deadly combat here on this island at the end of the world. How curious that the destinies of the two powers should have been decided here, and that the future of the Pacific Ocean area, including even New Zealand and Australia, should have been determined in part by the land battles that transpired on this island and the great sea battle at Coral Sea.

This is land that should be revered, and I was pleased, during my last visit to Guadalcanal, to find that American and Japanese veterans of the furious battles of 1941 and 1942 could return to Guadalcanal as friends, could visit the [battlefields] together and could pay their respects to their fallen comrades, as we are doing today."—James A. Michener

Also, for his efforts in the preservation of our legacy, we offer a heartfelt "thank you."

PUBLISHER'S MESSAGE

From the amphibious assault on August 7, 1942 to 1992 marks the 50th Anniversary of the struggles of the battle on the now famous British Solomon Island of Guadalcanal. "At what stage of the war did you feel that the battle swung against you?" a Japanese Admiral was asked. He answered simply, "Guadalcanal." This turning point in WWII history is commemorated in this volume. It is with great pleasure that we publish "The Guadalcanal Legacy, 50th Anniversary." It is a fitting complement to the first volume containing the story captured in the history as well as the memorable pictures. Both books contain the unique feature of personal "war stories" and biographies, which describes and records this epic incident from the pens and hearts of those who were there. Thank you to Mr. Gene Keller, Mr. Don Peltier, Mr. Joseph Micek, Dr. Robert C. Muehrcke, M.D. and Mr. Philip Birkitt for their outstanding contributions, loyalty, and dedication to the Guadalcanal Campaign Veterans and for their untiring efforts to see their legacy documented. They have indeed exemplified that "It isn't the cost of belonging- it's the price you paid to be eligible." A special thanks to the veterans who participated in the publication of these books by sharing your history with us—it is preserved for generations to come. More importantly, thank you for the many sacrifices, the hardships of combat, disease, malaria, fever and sickness that you endured. And to the families of those who gave their lives for our freedom—we will remember you!

It is Turner Publishing Company's goal to honor all of those who have fought for the peace of United States of America by preserving their history in this personal way where soldier, sailor, or airman can have his story written for all to read and remember.

Mr. Dave Turner, President
Turner Publishing Company

GUADALCANAL LEGACY
50TH ANNIVERSARY
1942-1992

They landed—in pieces—ripped apart by guns and bombs of the US Navy, these Japanese landing boats are scattered all along the segment of the beach where they attempted to debark troops on Guadalcanal in the last stages of battle for the South Pacific stronghold. (USN Photo, No. W-ES-111-51882)

PANIC AT TULAGI

by Philip D. Birkitt

The Japanese fleet, moving through the blue waters off Guadalcanal, was the most beautiful sight Sister Marie Therese had seen. It was May 3, 1942 and she had been walking along the beach near Visale Mission when she looked out to sea and saw more than a dozen sleek, grey warships passing by, no more than two miles off shore. She stood and watched until they disappeared behind Cape Esperance and, as their wash swept along the shore, she wondered how long it would be before Japanese troops landed on Guadalcanal and reached the Mission. For the first time she felt a little fear. Although she was an American citizen she had thought that her work as a missionary would protect her from the Japanese, but now she wondered whether or not it might have been better to have left when she had been offered the chance several weeks before.

An hour later passing Cape Esperance the Japanese ships approached Tulagi, the tiny capital of the Solomon Islands. As the cruiser *Okinoshima* entered the harbor, columns of smoke were rising from burning fires scattered throughout the town and at the marine wharves. The town was deserted. The British had left, and what they could not take with them, they had burned. Rear Admiral Aritomo Goto, flying his flag on the *Okinoshima*, ordered 500 troops of the 3rd Kure Special Landing Force to go ashore and as they quickly spread throughout the town, other ships in his force began landing air force personnel, radio and communications teams, a seaplane base unit and an anti-aircraft unit. By early afternoon the town, and the small island it was on, were secured and 12 Kawanishi, 4 engine reconnaissance float planes landed on the smooth surface of the harbor, followed by 12 Zero float plane fighters. Throughout the rest of the day large quantities of aviation gasoline, ammunition and stores went ashore from transports in Goto's force. Within 24 hours the Japanese had established an important base to expand their conquest of the southwest Pacific.

From Goto's fleet, Mr. Ishimoto stepped ashore at Tulagi. He wore the uniform of a Japanese Naval Petty Officer but was, in fact, a political officer. For several years before the war he had worked as a carpenter in the Solomon Islands while secretly coordinating the movements of Japanese fishing vessels. Between 1937-1939 these innocent looking vessels had drawn up accurate charts of waters around Tulagi and Guadalcanal. Now Ishimoto faced the more difficult task of persuading the Solomon Islanders to support the Japanese expansion.

In early 1942 the Japanese considered that at least ten army divisions would be needed to successfully invade Australia. At that time this number of troops could not be spared when much of southeast Asia had still to be conquered. The Japanese policy thus became one of isolating Australia to prevent American aid getting through to the Australians. In order to do this the Japanese planned to seize Eastern New Guinea then drive through the Solomon Islands to New Caledonia and Fiji.

On February 11th the Japanese had landed on Bougainville. In March they occupied parts of New Guinea and established a large base at Rabaul on New Britain. To the British administration in Tulagi, at that time, the threat from the north was ominous, yet many felt the Japanese would not come any further south. The resident commissioner at Tulagi, William Marchant, began to advise civilians to leave for Australia, to be on the safe side, even though he himself did not think the Japanese would "bother coming this far." He realized there was little to stop them, however, for the only forces at his disposal consisted of 120 trained Solomon Islanders with three European officers. Between them they had just over 100 rifles and three machine guns. In charge of this "Defense Force" was Major Foxstrangways who arrived at Tulagi in January. He was under no illusions as to the capability of his troops.

In February he told Marchant, "the Japanese strength is unknown but must be considered to be unlimited. The morale of our troops is high at the moment but is bound to deteriorate sharply if they are subjected to any form of attack unknown to them, for example dive bombing or naval bombardment." Marchant knew he could expect no help from Britain. Thousands of troops were tied up in Singapore which was about to fall and the British Far East fleet had been driven back beyond India. He decided not to attempt to defend Tulagi, dismissed the Defense Force and made plans to move the government center to Malaita, a larger island, 30 miles east.

Those who wanted to escape to Australia faced the difficulty of getting there. The only regular service was a small steamer, the *Morinda* due at Tulagi on February 8th but already booked up for the few passengers

Jungle foliage near Henderson Field. (Courtesy of Don DeLap)

she normally carried. As the ship entered Tulagi harbor she was attacked by a long range Kawanishi bomber. On board the ship was Martin Clemens, a district officer returning from leave in Australia. "As the Kawanishi circled we were all told to lie down on the deck" he recalls, "it circled twice and then came in; I felt he couldn't miss, but he did, thank God. The captain, peering through his binoculars shouted 'bombs away'; I didn't even bother to look. The plane went over us and so did his bombs, landing 75 yards away with a big splash. The Kawanishi came around again and dropped four more bombs, all of which fell astern. Lukin, the ship's purser, ran to the bridge and opened fire on him with an ancient Vickers machine gun. Useless! The plane was out of range. It circled once more and then cleared off."

The Kawanishi bombers were visiting Tulagi every day and dozens of people were, by then, hoping to get away on the *Morinda*. When Clemens went ashore, he was amazed to find there was near chaos everywhere. The government offices were shut or deserted and everyone seemed to be looking out for themselves. The dock was piled high with baggage and unpacked belongings. The Captain of the *Morinda* at first refused to take anyone who had not previously booked but he was eventually persuaded by a government official to take as many people as his small ship could carry. An arbitrary list of passengers was quickly drawn up but disorder soon developed. There was a rush to get aboard the ship; some passengers were injured in the crush and eventually a fight broke out on the dock between those who had decided to stay and those who, regardless of the passenger list, were determined to get on board. In scenes of near panic the *Morinda* hastily cast off

her moorings and steamed slowly out of the harbor. The last scheduled run to Australia had gone.

Marchant's only knowledge of the activity of the Japanese was supplied by three Australian Catalina seaplanes based at Tulagi for reconnaissance purposes, and serviced by a small detachment of Australian air force personnel. On February 11th they reported the Japanese were at Kieta on Bougainville, 250 miles to the north. Many people in Tulagi began to expect the arrival of the Japanese within days. The Australian troops began blowing up marine stores and Clemens found "a general state of hysteria" developing. The town became deserted and when Marchant dismissed the police force, widespread looting developed. Throughout the town, houses were littered with wrecked furniture and broken crockery whilst anything of value was removed and canoe loads of loot were paddled off to other islands. Clemens was disgusted with the way people were behaving and asked for a transfer to one of the other islands nearby. He had already been to see Marchant who eventually decided to send him to Guadalcanal as district officer. Marchant himself prepared to move to Malaita and Clemens was equipped with a tele-radio set, a broadcast schedule and a code number. Other officers were sent to different islands with similar equipment and instructions to radio information on Japanese shipping, air and troop movements to Australia, in the event that the Japanese occupied their area. As district officer each was also expected to maintain medical aid and law enforcement in their area. Clemens crossed over to Aola, on Guadalcanal, on February 11th. He had with him, 18 local policemen and 12 rifles with 300 rounds of ammunition.

At Tulagi the Japanese raids became more frequent - the main target being the small radio

station. The radio operator, a retired Australian seaman called Tom Sexton, grumbled constantly about his old equipment. "If the Japs come here and ask me where the radio is, and I show them this" he said, "they'll shoot me for concealing the real thing."

Japanese expansion into the southwest Pacific area had been foreseen by the United States Navy. In January, 1942, Admiral King (chief of Naval Staff) expected the Japanese to isolate Australia behind a chain of island bases. King thought it necessary that the United States should themselves occupy islands in the southwest Pacific as rapidly as possible. In January, American troops landed in Fiji and in March, they reached the New Hebrides - 600 miles southeast of Tulagi. The Solomon Islands were seen as the next step towards the Japanese base at Rabaul, but further progress was curtailed because there simply were no more troops available in the area. King then appointed Vice Admiral Robert Ghormley to command a newly created South Pacific force and area. Ghormley was to be responsible for all operations in the Solomons-New Zealand-Fiji area. It was a thankless task.

Ghormley had acquired a brilliant reputation as a planning officer in Washington but in 1941 he had been sent to London as a special naval observer. When King called him back to Washington to take up his new command he knew he was placing Ghormley in a difficult position. In a message to Ghormley on April 17th he told him, "you have been selected to command the South Pacific Force and South Pacific Area. You will have a large area under your command and a most difficult task. I do not have the tools to give you to carry out the task as it should be. You will establish your headquarters in Auckland, New Zealand. In time, possibly this fall, we hope to staff an offensive from the South Pacific."

King gave Ghormley no idea where the offensive would take place within the huge area of his command and Ghormley got no help from the Navy Bureau. Everything was in short supply. Men, ships, aircraft and equipment to build up bases, were simply not available. At Vila, in the New Hebrides, the Marines were clearing the jungle and building an airstrip with picks and shovels only. Ghormley eventually learned that he was to have the 1st Marine Division, but at that time it was at New River in North Carolina, and a division in name only.

At New River on March 23rd General Alexander Vandegrift was given command of the division. Vandegrift had joined the Marines in 1909 and had an outstanding record of service and battle experience in Haiti and Nicaragua against insurgents. Only two days before he took command, the division's 7th Regiment was ordered to embark for garrison duties in Samoa, taking with them the division's most experienced men since it was thought likely the regiment would see action first. Among them was Sergeant Mitchell Paige, at 24 - he had already seen six years of experience with the Marines from Cuba to China. A dedicated professional, his machine gun section had carried out improvisations on their weapons which raised the rate of fire from 500 to 1300 rounds a minute.

When the 7th Marines sailed from Norfolk, Virginia on April 10th, Vandegrift was left with the 1st and 5th Regiments of the division, both understrength. Soon, however, hundreds of Marines began arriving at New River from all over the country. They included sergeants from recruitment centers, gunnery experts with service dating back to the trench warfare of 1918, and privates, with bad disciplinary records, but experts with the rifle, machine gun, mortar and bayonet. From the Paris Island training camp, "green" recruits went into more training under these professionals, and many were sent to the mouth of the Patuxent River, Maryland to take part in amphibious landings on a small island called Solomons Island.

On April 15th Vandegrift was ordered to send the rest of his division to New Zealand. When he protested that his men were not in a combat-ready state, he was assured by Admiral King that there would be plenty of time for further training in New Zealand. It was not expected that the 1st and 5th Marines would be needed for combat before January, 1943.

Hundreds of men were switched to packing, crating and marking the thousands of items needed to set up a base camp in New Zealand. The advance group left Norfolk on May 10th and over the next six weeks, a succession of stately liners and rusty old freighters sailed from Norfolk, New Orleans and San Francisco. Some of the freighters had been hastily chartered from private ship owners, whose main aim was financial gain. The M.V. *John Ericsson* fed the Marines on rancid butter, rotten eggs and spoiled meat. Hundreds of the men developed dysentry. The cramped, crowded quarters allowed no room for exercise and by the time the ship got to New Zealand all the men had lost 10-15 pounds in weight. Marine Signalman Arnold Kaufmann, on the transport *Heywood* remembers it was just as bad on his ship. "My memory of that ship leaves nothing but despair" he recalls, "we were very crowded and there was never enough food. At mealtimes there were always long lines of men waiting to be fed. The crew were selling us sandwiches at $1 each. Many of us lived for days on peanuts and Pepsi in brown beer bottles. A friend and I once stole a case of grapefruit, but we had to dump it quickly over the side when they came looking for it."

AN OPERATION OPEN TO THE GRAVEST DOUBTS

In the Solomons there was a pause in Japanese activity and it was not until March 30th that the Shortland Islands, 200 miles northwest of Tulagi, were occupied. In the Shortlands the Japanese established a naval base and from there the big Kawanishi planes raided Tulagi several times a day. In April, Clemens and the other district officers were ordered to destroy any trucks and move away from the coast. On May 2nd the Australians at Tulagi began to burn their remaining stores and prepared to join Clemens. Late that night Tom Sexton sent a last message on his ancient radio, "steak and eggs, steak and eggs." It was the code meaning Tulagi had been abandoned. Throughout the night the burning of stores at the base cast a fiery red glow in the sky. Just before dawn the Australians reached Clemens' base and two hours later, watching through binoculars, Clemens saw Goto's ships entering Tulagi. He quickly passed this information over his teleradio, to Allied HQ in Australia.

Goto's peaceful occupation of Tulagi proved to be short-lived for the carrier USS *Yorktown* - operating south of the Solomons - sent two strikes against Tulagi on May 4th. The destroyer *Kikuraki* was sunk; two other ships damaged, and numerous large fires started among the newly landed stores. After the last raid the Japanese ships left port, leaving 800 troops isolated on the small island. The fleet sailed for Rabaul but the flagship *Okinoshima* was torpedoed and sunk by the U.S. Submarine *S42* one week after leaving Tulagi.

The main Japanese attacks in May and June were in the Philippines and the Central Pacific. On May 6th, Corregidor, the island fortress in the Philippines, fell. The Japanese then planned to invade Midway Island, a thousand miles west of the Hawaiian Islands. Admiral Yamamoto saw the Midway operation as an opportunity to draw the main U.S. fleet into battle.

U.S. Intelligence had, however, anticipated the Japanese attacks on Midway which began on June 4th. In the ensuing battle, four Japanese carriers were sunk and hundreds of planes and trained pilots lost. The actual invasion of Midway by a 2000 man force under Colonel Ichiki, was cancelled, and these troops returned to their base on Guam.

After this major set-back the Japanese interest shifted back to the Pacific southwest. The island of Tulagi was too small for the construction of an airfield so on June 21st a fleet of 13 transports and cargo ships crossed over to Guadalcanal. They landed engineers, heavy road building equipment and laborers who began to clear a large grassy plain on the north coast as the site for an airfield. From Guadalcanal, the American base at Espiritu Santo in the New Hebrides, would be well within bombing range.

By the end of the month there were a thousand troops and laborers working on Guadalcanal. Many of the laborers were Koreans but the Japanese began to recruit local labor as well. Nicholas Visaona who lived in a village at the mouth of the Matanikau river remembers the first landings of the Japanese there. The villagers welcomed them at first, paddling out to the Japanese transports, hoping to sell bananas and pineapples. The transports were unloading guns, ammunition and stores into small barges and as the villagers approached the Japanese shouted at them and waved them off.

The next day about 200 troops landed at the village and with them was Ishimoto, the Japanese ex-carpenter, turned political officer who was one of the few Japanese who could speak English. Ishimoto called a meeting of the villagers and ordered all men between 16 and 50 to work on road building between the Matanikau and the Lunga river - three miles to the east, where the airfield was being constructed. He told them the British would never return; the American fleet had been sunk, and they should cooperate willingly with the Japanese. The laborers were to receive food but no pay. After a month's work each man would be "rewarded" with a wooden disc stating he was now a Solomon Island citizen. About 20 men from the village started work on the road but gradually the total built up to 200 as men from other villages were recruited. None of them were use to hard physical labor for several hours a day in the hot, humid climate. They were easily tired and soon they began to slip away at night, carrying reports of the Japanese activity to Clemens.

The Japanese knew that Allied radio operators were hidden in the island and in July, a force of 500 men was landed with orders to spread along the

Pilots of VMF-224 at Henderson Field, Guadalcanal. VMF-223 and VMF-224 were the first two Marine Fighter Squadrons on Guadalcanal. (Courtesy of Gen. Galer)

View from Kukum, Guadalcanal with Solomon Islands and Florida Island in the background, Nov. 1942-March 1943. (Courtesy of William F. Dolan)

On the beach at Guadalcanal in 1942. (Courtesy of J. Sumner)

coast, then march into the rugged interior in search of these agents, and to recruit additional laborers. On July 3rd they reached the Catholic Mission at Visale. Sister Marie Therese remembers they behaved quite well, apart from taking whatever they wanted. Nobody was mistreated but all radios were confiscated and food and clothing was taken, even the washing on the lines. All the priests and nuns were questioned for several hours on the wherabouts of the coast watchers, as the Allied radio operators were called, but they could tell them nothing.

The Japanese then ordered them not to leave the Mission compound but apart from that they were to be allowed to continue with their normal activity. "They were civil and polite to us" recalls Sister Therese, "because they knew we had influence with the Solomon Islanders and they hoped we would help them to recruit laborers. Their attitude changed later on after the Americans landed". The Japanese set up a small base at Sapuru, two miles east of Visale, but visited the Mission every day. "They never seemed to do much", remembers Sister Therese, "they would set up a machine gun on the veranda then just sit around chattering and smoking. After a while we took no notice of them."

After the Japanese defeat at Midway, Admiral King looked for an area where Japanese expansion

could be stopped. General Douglas MacArthur, commanding Allied forces in Australia, suggested an attack on Rabaul but King rejected this as too risky and eventually decided to attack in the Solomons, with a view to seizing Tulagi then moving along the islands towards Rabaul. Privately he decided the attack would have to take place in July or August but he said nothing about dates when his staff agreed on that area of operations as the most suitable for their limited resources.

Meanwhile, Ghormley had arrived in New Zealand and advance elements of the 1st Marine Division were setting up their base camp near Wellington. On June 25th, Ghormley flew to meet MacArthur in Australia. The news he received staggered him. He was told to assault the Tulagi/Guadalcanal area with 1st Marines; the invasion date was to be August 1st. It meant he had five weeks to mount the operation. Because 1st Marines had been stripped of their 7th Regiment, Ghormley would be given a regiment from 2nd Marine Division and the 1st Raider Battalion then in New Caledonia. The 1st Parachute Battalion and 3rd Defense Battalion then in Hawaii would also be made available to bring the total force up to 19,000 men.

When Ghormley returned to New Zealand and told Vandegrift, his first question was "Where is

Tulagi?" When he realized how scattered his forces were he told Ghormley it would be impossible to land them all anywhere by August 1st. Ghormley asked King to put the date back, but King refused to consider any change.

Vandegrift's major problem was that the second echelon of his division was not scheduled to arrive in New Zealand until July 11th. Loading of the transports in American ports had been done so hurriedly he was not sure what cargo they were carrying. He did know that whatever their cargo was, it would have been commercially loaded - that is loaded principally for the ships' stability, and when the ships reached New Zealand they would need to be "combat loaded" so that the equipment needed first was loaded last. This could take weeks. Eventually Ghormley decided that the rear echelon would rendezvous with the other units at Koro Island in the Fiji group, nothing would be done about "combat loading" the rear echelon and after two or three days of practice landings, the combined force would then proceed direct to the Solomons.

Vandegrift detailed his intelligence officer Lieutenant Colonel Frank Goettge to gather as much information as he could on the Solomons but it proved to be a difficult task. The only available charts of the area were almost 30 years old and lacked any detail of the possible hazards of beach landings. Goettge flew to Australia in a desperate attempt to contact anybody with personal experience of the Solomons. He managed to talk to a few of Marchant's district officers who had joined the Australian Navy; among them Dick Horton who was detached to serve with the Marines. Using information from ex-planters, schooner skippers and missionaries, Goettge was able to draw up sketch maps of the Guadalcanal-Tulagi area. An appeal for a submarine to be sent to investigate the beach conditions on Guadalcanal was turned down by Ghormley as being too dangerous, and certain to alarm the Japanese if the submarine was caught in the act.

On July 4th an American bomber, blown off course, flew over Guadalcanal. One of the crew idly took a few photographs and when these were developed they showed the Japanese were well advanced with the airfield construction near the Lunga river. This alarming news caused Ghormley to shift the main emphasis of the planned invasion from Tulagi to Guadalcanal and Vandegrift ordered more reconnaissance flights over the island. On one such flight a B-17, flying over Tulagi, saw three Zero float plane fighters take off from Tulagi Harbor. The B-17 flew on to the south end of Guadalcanal then turned to follow the coast up towards Lunga. As they approached the airfield the three Japanese fighters, having gained altitude, fell upon the plane. For minutes the inside of the B-17 was filled with the clatter of machine guns. Two of the Zero's were shot down and the third flew off, but the B-17 was then past the Lunga area; no photographs had been taken and they had insufficient fuel to make another pass over the area.

Later two more flights managed to get good film of the area. The film was processed but lost in an administration foul up. It eventually reached Goettge's office in New Zealand, after the landings took place.

Many other difficulties began to plague Ghormley's plans. It was not until July 10th that the Combined Chiefs of Staff gave him his operational orders. On reading them he was unsure what the principle aim of the operation was. It had been named "OPERATION WATCHTOWER" but he could not decide whether he was to occupy a defensive position on Guadalcanal and Tulagi or whether the invasion was to be the first step in a drive towards the Japanese base at Rabaul. He became increasingly pessimistic of the success of the operation and again flew to Australia to confer with MacArthur.

MacArthur was against the operation from the beginning. He favored a direct attack on Rabaul, and told Ghormley that the Solomons operation was "open to the gravest doubts." The two commanders decided to advise King to postpone it, but in a strongly worded reply, King rejected their advice. "It is necessary to stop the Japanese and stop them at once," he replied.

Ghormley returned to New Zealand more depressed than ever, and found new problems had arisen. The New Zealand dock workers were on strike, refusing to combat load the transports. The Marines themselves-cursing the dockworkers-had to work shifts unloading, sorting and reloading the ships. Many of the stores had been packed in flimsy cardboard boxes piled high on the docks. When it began to rain heavily the boxes broke apart, their soaked contents creating an utter mess everywhere. One Navy officer remembers walking 100 yards through a swamp of sodden cornflakes. To save time and space all personal equipment such as seabags, bedrolls, suitcases and even tents were ordered to be left behind. Fuel and ration supplies were reduced and ammunition supplies were cut by a third.

On the planning side, difficulties arose over evaluating what information was available. Tide tables for Guadalcanal gave conflicting information. Plans for coordinated naval gunfire and air support were difficult to formulate as the warships to be involved were still widely scattered. Desperately Ghormley asked again for a postponement and reluctantly King agreed to putting the invasion date back to August 7th. General Samuel Griffiths, 1st Marines, later summed up the situation by saying "The operation was conceived, planned and launched on a crash basis. The meticulous planning that went into later operations was totally missing on that occasion. In fact, this, the first Allied offensive of World War II was characterized by near frantic, and sometimes near fatal, improvisation." On July 22nd the fleet left Wellington, and four days later met the last of the task force off Koro Island, to begin practice landings and naval gunnery drill.

The practice landings soon showed many problems. Some of the transports never got more than half their boats in the water, while boats from other ships milled around for hours waiting to practice the run into the beach. It was then decided that because of the high coral reef around the island, the boats would not actually make a landing, just practice going in. This change of plans did not reach some of the boat crews and when they attempted a landing several of them ran aground on the coral.

Rifleman Gilbert Dolloff, 2nd Battalion 1st Marines, went into the boats from the transport *George F. Elliott*. He remembers "when we approached the shore we found we were up against a solid wall of coral about 20 feet high, so we turned around and went back to the ship. The first platoon of our E Company had their boat wrecked on the coral and had to wade ashore further north of their planned landing site. Only about one boat in six actually made a landing." Private Robert Corwin on the transport *Barnett* had made only one practice landing during his training in North Carolina. He recalls that "off Koro Island we went into the boats early in the afternoon and spent two hours going round in circles, we were about two miles off shore. The sea was rough with a heavy swell running, and lots of our guys soon became seasick. In the late afternoon we began our run in to the beach but when we had gone halfway we were told the landing had been called off. Too much surf on the beach was the reason given."

Planning conferences on board the carrier *Saratoga* were equally unsatisfactory. Ghormley had decided to remain in New Zealand and execution of the operation had been delegated to Vice Admiral Fletcher. Ghormley had given him no letter of

Pictured here are the Marine Corps officers that map and direct Leatherneck activities against the Japanese. Seated, Front Row (L to R): Lt. Col. O. K. Pressley, Col. M. A. Edson, Lt. Col. H. E. Rosecrans and Lt. Col. R. E. Hill; Second Row (L to R): Lt. E. B. McLarney (MC), Brig. Gen. W. R. Rupertus, Col. R. C. Kilmartin and Maj. William Enright; Third Row (L to R): Captains Ralph Powell, Daryle Seeley and Thomas Philpott. (Defense Dept. Photo (USMC) No. 50506)

Tulagi under bomb attack, August 7.

This Japanese machine gun post was placed on a hill overlooking the coastline at Tulagi.

A Japanese Mitsubishi. The plane was known as a "Betty" bomber to the Leathernecks on Guadalcanal.

instructions and Fletcher did not submit to Ghormley any operations plan until a month after the landings. Fletcher had no previous experience in the type of operation planned. These two commanders had met briefly at Pearl Harbor where Fletcher had been opposed to the whole operation, and felt sure it would be a failure. At conferences on the *Saratoga* he simply stated what he would do and what he would not do. He was not prepared to discuss the plans with Vandegrift or any of the other commanders.

The amphibious landings were to be under the command of Admiral Richard Kelly Turner, while Fletcher would be with the carrier support force 200 miles south of Guadalcanal. When Fletcher asked Turner how long it would take to land the troops and supplies, Turner said five days. Fletcher replied he would only give air support for two days; the carriers would then withdraw from the area. Vandegrift and Turner were both offended by Fletcher's uncompromising attitude. Vandegrift told him "this is not to be an exercise but the landing of a full division on a hostile shore; it needs air cover for a minimum of four days." Fletcher replied that he would listen to no more arguments, then closed the meeting. Turner then attempted to contact Ghormley, to use his influence, but found that the whole operation was already under strict radio silence.

The press was under no such restriction, however. Marine officers had bought copies of the July 4th edition of the *Wellington Dominion* which reported "Operations to seize Japanese held bases such as Rabaul, Wake Island and Tulagi are advocated by a military writer, Major Elliott in the *New York Herald Tribune*. Elliott states that what is needed is to drive the Japanese out of these bases and to convert them to our own use. This can only be done by landing troops on these bases."

Only a few days before this report, the *New York Times* had stated "It is significant that the censor has passed news of the arrival of a completely equipped expeditionary force of American Marines at a South Pacific port recently. Marines are not usually sent to bases where action is not expected."

Incredibly the Japanese 17th Army Headquarters at Rabaul had been warned to expect an American invasion in the Solomons or New Guinea, only six days before the planned invasion. Japanese naval intelligence had picked up two new Allied call signs in the southwest Pacific. Both were on the Commander-in-Chief circuit (4205 kcs) and communicated directly with Pearl Harbor. Japanese intelli-

The USS Enterprise (CV-6), *a* Yorktown *Class carrier, as she appeared in 1939. She earned 20 Battle Stars. (Division of Naval Intelligence, Courtesy of Ted Blahnik)*

gence concluded a new task force had been created in the Southwest Pacific and passed a warning to Rabaul. It was ignored at 17th Army Headquarters.

At Koro Island, difficulties multiplied. Dive bombing practices proved to be wildly off target. Naval gunfire was inaccurate. Many of the landing boats had developed mechanical failure or had been lost due to grounding on the reef or even broaching in heavy seas. One transport had lost half its boats and another had 12 out of service. Many of the officers began to think the invasion would have to be reduced to a hit and run raid. Vandegrift angrily described the Koro Island exercise as "a fiasco". He conferred with Turner and they quickly agreed on measures to improve the landing procedures. Changes were made in the disembarkation procedure, a boat pool was established among the transports to make up for the losses, better methods of ship to shore communication were devised and the planned run-in to the beach was changed to a much quicker and more orderly method.

There were some difficulties they could do nothing about. Admiral Crutchley, in command of the cruiser escort force, arrived in the cruiser *Australia* only after these conferences had ended. He had not, therefore, been able to assess the gunnery exercises for himself. Two transports with elements of the 2nd Marine Regiment did not join the invasion fleet until after the Koro Island exercises.

Eventually on July 31st the combined force, totalling 75 ships, which included three aircraft carriers, turned to the west and headed towards the Solomon Islands. Many of those on board remember it was a hot, cloudless day and as the sun sank towards the horizon ahead of them, it sent out orange and red rays resembling the Japanese flag. The surface of the sea turned gold then blood red in the fading light. An ill omen, some said, as night closed swiftly over the darkened ships.

FOLLOW ME, AND RUN LIKE HELL

One of the most successful of Japan's admirals in early 1942 was Rear Admiral Gunichi Mikawa. After Pearl Harbor he had led a force of battleships and cruisers which roamed freely smashing Allied warships from Ceylon to the Philippines. By nature he was a quiet spoken intellectual but his grasp of naval tactics and his skillful aggressive leadership had brought him quickly to the top ranks of the Imperial Navy. On July 12th he was given command of the newly created 8th Fleet with headquarters at Rabaul. His task was to aid 17th Army Commander General Hyakutake's operations in the New Guinea-Solomons area.

In Tokyo the Admiral met his new operations officer, Commander Ohmae, one of the Navy's best planners. Together the two men sipped tea and discussed possible future operations, then Ohmae left for Rabaul to investigate the facilities available. Mikawa followed at a more leisurely pace in his new flagship, the heavy cruiser *Chokai* which arrived in Truk on July 25th. There, the Admiral met again with Ohmae who flew up from Rabaul with disturbing information. As a naval base, Rabaul lacked a great deal, Ohmae reported. Repair facilities were limited; no thought seemed to have been given to defenses and the only air cover available would have to come from two small airfields still under construction. The operations staff there seemed to have little to do and lacked any sense of planning or direction. When Ohmae had protested, he had been assured there was "nothing to worry about-

Crossing the equator on the Salvo Island. *(Courtesy of George Pelvit)*

A boxing bout aboard the troop transport SS Santa Elena. *She was enroute between the Panama Canal and Melbourne, Australia. February 1942. (Courtesy of William F. Dolan)*

after all, the Americans are shattered". Mikawa was dismayed by the report and immediately called for a conference with Admiral Inoue from whom he was taking over.

Inoue and his staff assured Mikawa there was nothing to fear; there was just no possibility of an American invasion anywhere in his new command. Mikawa officially took over command the next day, July 26th, and reached Rabaul four days later. He found conditions at the base just as bad as Ohmae had reported. Buildings and accommodation were so lacking that only after a great deal of difficulty did he manage to get an old hut near the airfield at Vunakanau, for his headquarters. He found the airfield itself in such bad condition that pilots had been landing on the nearby golf course. So poor were the anti-aircraft defenses of the base that he decided to split his force into two parts. He kept only two light cruisers at Rabaul and sent five cruisers and a destroyer 200 miles north to the base of Kavieng on New Ireland.

When Mikawa met General Hyakutake to co-ordinate their plans, he found the main aim of operations was to be the capture of Port Moresby. Mikawa was concerned about the general's lack of interest about his flank in the Solomons. The Americans were known to be building air bases in the New Hebrides and from there could be a dangerous threat to Tulagi. Hyakutake was not concerned and dismissed any threats to the area as mere pinpricks. Hyakutake had only been at Rabaul a week and considered the Solomons was an unimportant sideshow to the main attack in New Guinea. True the Americans were bombing Tulagi and Guadalcanal almost every day now but an airfield was under construction on Guadalcanal and this would provide adequate cover for the area. The airfield would be finished shortly, he told Mikawa; it would have 60 planes and should be ready for operation on August 7th.

Mikawa was not convinced. Every day Rabaul was receiving messages from Guadalcanal, requesting fighters to be flown in. There were 2,570 men in two construction battalions on the island but most of them were laborers or engineers. The only reliable troops on the island were 150 men of the 84th Infantry Battalion. Intelligence units at Rabaul began to report increased American radio traffic in the Solomons-Fiji area. Hyakutake's staff assumed an American force was moving towards New Guinea and his staff told Mikawa the radio traffic and daily bombing in the Solomons were probably a diversionary tactic.

Despite these assumptions it was decided to increase the Kawanishi reconnaissance flights in the Solomons, but on August 5th the weather took an unseasonable change for the worse. Low, heavy cloud covered much of the area; there were frequent rain squalls and cloud ceilings were often as low as 100 feet. Rabaul reported "all searches canceled because of inclement weather". At Tulagi on the morning of August 6th, three Kawanishi planes got off, but all returned within an hour. The skies were so low they could see nothing. "Result of searches, negative" was the report.

For the invasion fleet the change in weather was the first good luck they had. In the week long run from Koro Island to the Solomons, the Marines were briefed on what to expect, except that the officers themselves did not have much idea what the landings would be like. The Marines were not even told where they were going until after the fleet left Koro Island. Marine Private Robert Corwin remembers that when his platoon leader told them they were to land on Guadalcanal he also admitted he did not know where it was or even how to pronounce and spell the name. "It didn't matter" recalls Corwin, "we were all volunteers anxious to have a go at the Japs. Most of us were 18 or 19 years old and it was all one big adventure."

Goettge's intelligence unit anticipated the landings would be opposed by about 5,000 troops centered around the airfield. Because of this it had been decided to make the landings four miles east of the airfield at what was to be called "Red Beach". The intelligence memorandum outlined the main difficulty expected. "From the landing point our forces will have to cross a stream about 20 feet wide, some 400 yards inland from the beach. This is the Ilu River and runs parallel to the shore. On the south bank of the Ilu is high grass, up to four feet high, which affords possible positions for machine gun and rifle fire with a field of fire extending across the stream towards the beach". Much of Goettge's information had been supplied by pre-war administrative officers in the Solomons, who were with the invasion force to act as guides. They provided rough sketches of the landing area from memories of a few years before, but much of their information contained inaccuracies.

Goettge's memorandum at least prepared the officers and men for the worst. Lieutenant E. Snell, assigned to a beach transport group, thought the landings would be strongly opposed and considered it likely that two-thirds of the boats would be sunk before they reached the beach. He expected a 25% casualty rate on the first day. Lieutenant Colonel Maxwell, commanding officer of the beach landing party also expected a bitter struggle on the beach. He told his officers "we didn't even know about the Ilu until a few days ago but it is too late to change our plans now. It is going to be a difficult matter with that river to cross. Grass four or five feet high and drainage ditches. "The only thing to do" he concluded, "is to get out of the boat fast, shout 'follow me' and run like hell".

On August 5th the airfield on Guadalcanal received its heaviest raid, causing terror among the Solomon Island laborers. None of them had any idea of the destructive power of a 500 pound bomb, or the simplest precautions to take. When the bombing started they ran to look for cover in the jungle instead

"Can Do" is born on Guadalcanal. Note shield on 26th Battalion Headquarters tent. Photo taken in early 1943. (Courtesy of Edward Faber)

USS Bennett (DD-473). Photo taken off the coast of Hawaii, July 7, 1943. She saw combat in Guadalcanal, Bougainville and Maranawa. Destroyers were used for a variety of purposes, especially plucking survivors of sinking vessels from the sea. (Courtesy of Andrew A. Slovinec)

An unidentified US Army troop transport and destroyer (at left) off Guadalcanal. March 1943. (Courtesy of William F. Dolan)

I Co., 3d Bn., 1st Marine, 1st Marine Division, machine gun section. Front Row (L to R): Pollio, Davis, Walsh, Giffier, McCarthy, Brock, Helmerich, Bubanas; Back Row (L to R): Worrick, Griffen, Davis, King, Aurthur, Hopkins, Gryzb (Courtesy of A. J. Worrick)

A US troop transport standing off Guadalcanal; Cape Esperance is in the background (at left). March 1943. (Courtesy of William F. Dolan)

of getting into trenches. One of the laborers, Alan Sio, remembers seeing a bomb explode amongst a group of laborers at the edge of the airfield. Thirty were killed - many through ghastly shrapnel wounds. Others were more fortunate. Two bombs landed amongst a group of laborers from Visale Mission, but both of them failed to explode. Nicholas Visaona from Matanikau village was still working on the road to Lunga but on August 6th one of Clemen's scouts arrived and told him to run away because the Americans were coming soon and anyone who stayed behind would be killed with the Japanese. The word spread quickly and by evening all of the Solomon Island laborers had disappeared. Lieutenant Okamura, in charge of the construction battalions, sent a message to Rabaul. "The local laborers have all run away, but we are not concerned because this sort of thing has happened before."

Throughout August 6th, the invasion fleet prepared for the landings next day. Marines sharpened bayonets and knives, inspected grenade pins and oiled rifle bores while machine gunners carefully folded 250 round belts of ammunition into wooden green boxes. Landing craft were swung out to the ships' sides and Coastguard men tested their engines. Ships' derricks hoisted howitzers out of the holds on to the decks where they were rolled to ships' sides for easy unloading. Boxes of shells, mortars, spare parts, rolls of barbed wire and gasoline cans were stacked on deck.

That evening Vandegrift felt a sense of relief. The overcast skies meant they had not been detected. It seemed possible the invasion would have the element of surprise. In the quietness of his cabin he wrote to his wife-

"Tomorrow at dawn we land in the first major offensive of the war. Our plans have been made and God grant that our judgment has been sound. Whatever happens you'll know I did my best. Let us hope that best will be good enough."

STRANGE SHIPS IN THE SOUND

During the night of August 6th the invasion force passed along the west coast of Guadalcanal and just before daybreak, rounded the northwest end of the island. Here it split into two groups. Transport group Yoke headed for Tulagi and transport group X-Ray headed for an area off Red Beach. They seemed to have achieved complete surprise as day-

USS Neville APA-9, under command of Col. William B. Tuttle, landed more than 1700 GIs of the 147th Inf. RCT at Aola Bay, Guadalcanal, Nov. 4, 1942. (Courtesy of W. Chaney)

Christmas Day on Christmas Hill, Guadalcanal, B Co., 1st Bn., 2d Marine Div., 3d Platoon. (Courtesy of Gordon L. Perry)

Rear Admiral Guichi Mikawa.

light brought no attacks from the Japanese. Many of the men on the transports thought it was some trick, and expected Japanese shore batteries to open fire at any moment.

At 0615 the cruiser *Quincy* opened fire on the Lunga Point area. Correspondent Richard Tregaskis, on board one of the transports, remembers "Brilliant green/yellow flashes of fire from the *Quincy*, and other warships, followed by red pencil lines of shells arching through the sky. Dive bombers from the carriers began to bomb the landing area and there was a sudden gush of red flame near Lunga Point as a fuel dump was hit." The American cruisers catapulted off their float planes which flew low along the beach over orderly rows of coconut trees. The pilots reported no activity on shore was to be seen.

On shore Nicholas Visaona had taken his family to a small creek a mile up river from the mouth of the Matanikau. He had thought that any fighting would be restricted to the beach area. As he looked towards Lunga it seemed the whole area was erupting in red flashes and thick black smoke. Many times fighters roared overhead, machine-gunning the jungle. Some of the planes were so low he could even see the pilots and hear the clatter of their guns.

Further inland Martin Clemens tuned his radio to listen to the talk between pilots over the Lunga

passing information to each other on targets in the area.

On board the transports the Marines lined up to climb down into the boats, as the cruiser fire became concentrated upon the Red Beach landing area. Marine Private Robert Corwin remembers that "we could see a long strip of sandy beach, low-lying palm trees and green hills far inland. It was a beautiful sight, and a bright, clear morning. The cruiser fire was really hitting the beach area: I didn't see how anyone could still be there. At 0800 the transports sent their boats away. We did not spend much time going round in circles this time; before we knew it we were on our way into the beach. There was still no fire from the shore. Suddenly we scraped to a standstill, then it was up and over the sides, into the surf - then up the beach. There was no opposition at all as we ran up towards the palm trees."

Correspondent Tregaskis went ashore with the fifth wave of landing craft. He recalls the heavy cruiser fire to soften up the beaches, "All along the beach a line of blue and black geysers leaped up where the shells landed. After the firing stopped a haze of dirty black smoke hung over the edge of the land and we were heading straight into it. At 0950 we hit the beach. Our landing was leisurely. I jumped ashore from the bow of our boat and walked slowly up the beach. It was hardly the 'hell-for-leather' leap and dash through the surf to the sounds of rattling machine gun fire I had expected."

Surprise had been complete. The Japanese had just started breakfast when the invasion force had been sighted. When the shelling started the Korean laborers fled the airfield and disappeared into the nearby hills. The construction camp at the airfield was hastily abandoned. Okamura sent a hurried radio message to Rabaul. "Encountered American landing forces and are retreating into the jungle." His detachment of troops retreated two miles west to the Matanikau river.

At Red Beach Tregaskis found that by 1030, working parties had begun to unload barges with machinery, equipment and supplies. A tractor was already at work. Walking inland, Tregaskis found Marines crouched behind trees, rifles at the ready. Some had rubbed mud over their faces, others had fastened twigs and branches to themselves for camouflage. There was still no sign of opposition and Tregaskis remembers the only sound of firing came from the cruisers at Tulagi.

Once clear of the beach the Marines found it heavy going through the thick jungle. Private Gilbert Dolloff, 1st Marines was struck by the strangeness of the experience. He had expected to fight his way up

the beach and had been puzzled by the lack of opposition and the quietness when the shelling had stopped. "Once clear of the beach", he recalls, "the air was hot, heavy and humid. The jungle stood out like a solid green wall. We had to cut our way through every step".

By 1100 the Marines had pushed 600 yards inland and had crossed the Ilu. Maxwell's fears about crossing the Ilu were unfounded. It was, in fact, no more than a stagnant creek - almost wide enough to jump across. Beyond the Ilu the Marines cut wide paths through the grass to allow ammunition carts to be taken forward.

The initial objective on this first day was "a grassy knoll" believed to be two miles inland. This objective was in fact Mount Austen which was some ten miles inland. Again the plans had been based on inaccurate information. As the 1st Marines moved inland they spread out and soon the different units became separated from each other in the thick jungle and began to lose contact. Occasionally a few shots were fired at Japanese stragglers fleeing west, but some units mistook this fire for Japanese attacks. In the sweltering heat of the afternoon, the heavily laden men moved slower and slower and the advance became a struggle by scattered units to make their way through the jungle.

While 1st Marines moved slowly inland, 5th Marines sent one battalion along the coast towards Lunga. They too met only scattered resistance from a handful of Japanese. The Marines had, however, expected greater resistance and so their advance was a slow and cautious one.

Difficulties began to develop on the landing beach itself. The 1st Pioneer Battalion had the job of unloading supplies from the boats on to the beach, but many of the Pioneers were still on the transports, with less than 500 available on the beach. Few of the landing boats had ramps so almost every box of stores had to be lifted up and over the boats sides to men standing waist deep in the water. So many men were needed to unload the boats that few were available to carry the supplies inland. The beach soon became piled up with tons of stores hastily put down anywhere. Ammunition boxes were mixed up with cases of C rations; medical supplies with fuel cans. Many of the overworked Pioneers complained about men of 3rd Battalion, 5th Marines who sat around doing nothing or even went for a swim. These men were the rear-guard unit and their officers refused to let them get scattered about unloading boats when they might be called into action at any time. Gradually the situation worsened. By mid-afternoon 100 boats were on the beach waiting to unload, while 50 more were standing off the beach unable to find a place to land. Eventually all unloading from cargo ships was stopped.

Meanwhile at Tulagi that morning, the cruiser *San Juan* and destroyers *Monssen* and *Buchanan* had begun shelling the small island at 0630. Dive bombers also began attacking the small town and dockland area and the Japanese seaplane base centered on the two smaller islands of Gavutu and Tanambogo nearby. Six Kawanishi planes moored near Gavutu were left burning; one managed to take off but was shot down before it gained altitude.

On the transport *Calhoun* Dick Horton, an ex-district officer in the pre-war government watched the naval gunfire landing on Tulagi while he waited with the 1st Raider Battalion to climb down into the boats. He had been assigned to guide them over the island. "As we stood by our assault boats the men reacted in different ways" he recalls, "some yawned continuously; others smoked furiously, while others joked, chatted or wrote hasty notes. I felt nothing but dull fatigue. The appalling crack and blast of the 5-inch guns from *Monssen* and *Buchanan* almost drowned out the order to man the boats. As we approached the beachhead, the boat's coxswain opened fire with a machine gun on the jungle beyond the beach at our landing area. There was no return fire. A few minutes later the boat hung up on the coral about 50 yards from the beach. I jumped over the side and immediately disappeared over my head in the water".

In fact all the boats grounded on the coral between 30 and 100 yards from the beach and the Raiders waded ashore in water which was often up to their armpits. Fortunately their landing was not opposed. The Japanese had withdrawn to the southeast end of the island. The Raiders scrambled ashore then began climbing the 350 feet high ridge that ran down the center of the island. At its widest, Tulagi is no more than 1,000 yards and by 1100 the four companies of Raiders had established a line across the island and begun moving towards the town and docks - meeting only scattered resistance from a few groups of Japanese fleeing before them. Behind the Raiders the 2nd Battalion, 5th Marines landed and moved towards the northwest end of the 4,000 yard long island. They also met no resistance.

At the southeast end of the island the Japanese withdrew to Hill 208 and Hill 281 which were separated by a deep ravine. As Colonel Edson's Raiders approached Hill 208 they came under fire from automatic weapons and rifle fire. Edson halted the advance and called on the *San Juan* for supporting fire. For several minutes the cruiser brought down a barrage of 5-inch shellfire on the hill causing the Japanese to move back to Hill 281 where their positions could not be reached by the naval gunfire. Hill 208 was taken by late afternoon and the advance was then held up by the main Japanese defenses on Hill 281 and in the ravine between the two hills. Meanwhile the 2nd Battalion, 5th Marines had cleaned out the northwest end of the island and two companies were sent to support Edson.

Although the landings at Red Beach and on Tulagi had been unopposed there was no chance of such good fortune for the landings at Gavutu and Tanambogo - two small islands that formed the main Japanese seaplane base half a mile east of Tulagi. The two islands were joined by a 500 yard causeway and defended by 500 troops. Most of these were Air Force and Navy personnel operating the base, but with no escape they were determined to defend their positions to the last.

The attacks on the two islands were to be made by three companies of the 1st Parachute Battalion. Captain Richard S. Johnson of B Company, the second of the three to land, had taken a dim view of the plans for the attack largely because their landing was not to take place until four hours after the landings on Tulagi. There were not enough boats for a simultaneous landing. Johnson felt that the delay would give the Japanese more than enough time to prepare a hot reception for his men. Still the men seemed to be in good spirits. As their landing boats pulled away from the transport *Heywood* the troops gave a big cheer and a whistle for the Captain of the ship, who had issued orders against whistling on the way out from the States.

"I then turned to look towards Gavutu" Johnson recalls. "The *San Juan* was shelling the island heavily, supported by 5-inch fire from a destroyer which passed close by - her decks littered with empty shell cases. Her Stars and Stripes were blowing stiffly in the wind and the men gave a big cheer as she went past. As we approached Gavutu I ordered all my men to keep their heads down when machine gun fire from the beach began to make sharp snapping sounds as the bullets passed overhead. Two of my men at the stern of the boat were killed, however. I looked back towards *San Juan*; she was still firing so heavily that at times the whole ship was hidden by the yellowish-grey smoke from her main gun salvoes. Unfortunately the shelling destroyed the seaplane ramp where we were supposed to land but our boat cox-

A barge landing supplies.

1st Squad, 1st Platoon, A Co., 1st Pioneer Bn., 1st Marine Division. Beach defense at Lunga Beach, Nov.-Dec. 1942. (Courtesy of F. G. Davison)

swain headed for it just the same. As soon as we hit it the ramp dropped and I got out as fast as I could because the machine gun fire from the Japs was very heavy by that time and there were already several dead and injured Marines on the beach. I saw that one of my troopers, Corporal Montgomery, had followed me, but that was all because the coxswain must have panicked. With only two of us ashore he backed the boat away from us and tried to land again a little further along the ramp. He found he could not make it but lowered the boat's ramp again anyway and the rest of my men came ashore in water up to their necks, with bullets kicking up the water all around them. Casualties began to mount quickly. Major Robert Williams, Battalion Commander, was severely wounded early in the fighting and Captain Mason of Intelligence, was killed crossing the beach towards us."

Johnson's company and C Company which came ashore a little later were badly hit by the Japanese machine guns dug into caves on the two small islands. The seaplane landing ramp could also be fired on from both of the islands so the parachutists were caught in a vicious cross-fire. Johnson

recalls "despite the heavy shelling by our warships their shells had little effect on the Japanese positions. The high explosive shells did not have the penetration to knock out the coconut log bunkers covered with sand. Despite the intense fire we managed to work our way towards the center of Gavutu but a three hour bloody fight raged for the little island. Dick Huerth, Commander of C Company got killed. Dick had been a close friend of mine; in fact he had been groomsman at my wedding only three months before. Later on, when the Japanese began firing into the command post, Lieutenant Young, the communication officer, was killed in a single-handed assault against a pillbox, and 2nd Lieutenant Bill Kaiser was killed leading his men up Hill 148, the highest point on Gavutu." The fighting for Gavutu had been so costly that the Commanding Officer of the Parachute Battalion asked for reinforcements before attempting to take Tanambogo, and also called for more fire support from the warships and aircraft. In the late afternoon planes from the carrier *Wasp* and the destroyers *Buchanan* and *Monssen* subjected the tiny island to heavy fire. To Johnson it was another impressive bombardment but he had learned a lot

Platoon 43 at Marine Barracks, Parris Island, SC. Drill instructors were: Sgt. J. Milner and Cpl. Camlin. (Courtesy of Dr. Cesare)

Troops on Guadalcanal advancing. (Courtesy of J. Sumner)

during the day and expected a vicious fight for the island.

Shortly after dusk six overcrowded boats arrived from Tulagi, bringing a company of the 2nd Marines under the command of Captain Crane. The Parachutists Commander, Major Miller, told Crane that Tanambogo was occupied by 'no more than a few snipers' and ordered the Captain to land his men on a small jetty at the northwest end of the island, then work their way towards the causeway pushing the enemy ahead of them. As the boats pulled away from the seaplane ramp one of the boats ran aground but the other five approached the jetty and the leading boat landed Crane and about 30 men. As the next boat approached, a shell from the supporting destroyers blew up a nearby fuel dump. The blazing fuel lit up the men and boats who immediately came under a hail of fire from the Japanese. One boat's crew was wiped out; other men struggling to get ashore were cut to pieces by the fire, or, stumbling in the water suddenly disappeared in a deep pool in the coral. One boat managed to get two machine guns on

to the jetty but the Japanese fire was so intense they were soon driven back to the boats, four of which managed to pull clear. Crane and his 30 men were still ashore but began to suffer casualties so that eventually only 12 men made it back to the boat and got away. Later Crane and one or two others swam back to Gavutu.

At Visale Mission that morning, Sister Marie Therese had watched the invasion forces pass by. She knew there were few Japanese troops on the island and fully expected the Americans would reach the mission in a few days. Shortly after 0700 hours several American planes flew over the Mission and the nearby Japanese camp at Saputo. From there the American planes came under fire but, possibly mistaking the base for the Mission, they turned and bombed the Mission. One of the buildings was destroyed. The planes then made several runs, machine-gunning the area. "They came so low" recalls Sister Therese, "I felt sure they were coming in through the windows. I could see lines of bullets kicking up dust in the compound as they passed

overhead." Although nobody was injured during the attack, the missionaries decided to abandon the Mission. With several Solomon Islanders they set off through the jungle to a small village four miles inland. Later when the Japanese patrol arrived they assumed the missionaries were making for the American lines with information about the Japanese troops in the area. Patrols were sent out to track them down.

At Rabaul the first news of the invasion came in a radio message from Tulagi at 0630. "Strange ships in the Sound, what does it mean?" it asked. Then later "Enemy task force of 20 ships atacking Tulagi. Severe bombing. Enemy landing operations under way. Help requested." Mikawa immediately contacted Hyakutake and asked for troops to be sent to Tulagi, but Hyakutake still believed the assault in the Solomons was no more than a hit and run diversionary raid. The main allied attack was still to come in New Guinea, he believed, and refused to weaken his forces there. He told Mikawa he was unnecessarily alarmed and that he, Hyakutake, was not going to be panicked into hasty action. He had just received a message from Tokyo which showed the Army General Staff were not alarmed either; they believed the invasion force was no more than a 2,000 man reconnaissance in force designed to destroy the airfield, then withdraw.

Unable to get any help from Hyakutake, the Admiral then turned to Commander Tadishi Nakajima of the Tinian Air Base. He told the Commander that he believed the landings were in force and posed a direct threat to the Japanese expansion over the last eight months. The Commander was preparing a bombing raid against Port Moresby at the time and had 24 Mitsubishi bombers ("Betty" type) already loaded and ready for takeoff. He was prepared to send them to Tulagi instead but they would need figther escort, and some of the fighter pilots were too inexperienced to make the 1,200 mile return journey. Mikawa had by then received the last message Tulagi was able to send - "The enemy strength is overwhelming; we will defend our positions to the death, praying for everlasting victory". He showed the message to Nakajima who then agreed to send an escort of 18 Zero fighters flown by his most experienced men.

Among these Japanese pilots few were more experienced than Saburo Sakai. In 1937 he had graduated as the outstanding pilot of the year. He came from a Samurai warrior family background, yet he was warm and good humored. Keen, well trained and fighting-fit, he frequently sharpened his reflexes by catching flies in flight with his fist. In 1938 he had been sent to China and quickly made a name for himself as, with skill and daring, he built up his total number of enemy planes destroyed to 13.

As the Mitsubishis and Zeros flew southeast from Rabaul they crossed over Green Island. Sakai thought he had never seen a sight so beautiful as the horseshoe shaped island covered with green hills and set in a deep blue sea. As they approached Guadalcanal the planes climbed to 20,000 feet then suddenly far below them was the invasion fleet spread out. The tiny ships were turning and twisting in all directions to avoid the bombs. Before he could see much more, Sakai found himself engaged with American fighter planes which had risen to meet the Japanese attack. Most of the American planes were concentrating on the bombers, forcing them to make wild bombing runs almost four miles above the ships. He was surprised at how quickly the Wildcats and Avengers could maneuver and he was soon engaged in a desperate series of dogfights. After a great deal of difficulty he came in on a Wildcat fighter, gave it a long burst and watched it go down. Suddenly his windscreen seemed to explode. He felt a shattering blow to his head then total darkness as he passed out.

A strong, cold wind coming through the shattered windscreen brought him back to his senses. The plane was falling like a stone and he was horrified to find he could see nothing except a curtain of red before his eyes. He groped for the joystick, found it and pulled. With a sigh of relief he felt the plane level out. He found he could not move his left foot - in fact the whole of the left side of his body felt paralyzed. Only his right foot could move and he touched the rudder bar with it. Blinded and half paralyzed he realized the end must come soon. Tears began to fill his eyes and as they did so the red curtain in front of his left eye was washed away. Miraculously he could see with one eye at least.

The compass showed he was heading out into the Pacific, and he slowly brought the course round towards Tinian. With one hand he carefully felt his forehead and touched a wound from which blood still trickled into his eyes. Unwrapping the silk scarf from his neck he slowly pushed it into the wound. The pain was agonizing and he almost passed out again. As he flew northwest he slowly became drowsy. Then a feeling of despair came over him as he wondered if he would ever be able to get back to his base and land the plane safely. Suddenly he saw Green Island below him and became determined to get back. Next, in St. George's Passage between New Britain and New Ireland he flew over a line of warships steaming south. Finally the airstrip came into view. He circled once than came in to land. A bump, a sharp jolt and the plane skidded to an abrupt halt. Moments later, Sakai, unconscious, was lifted from the cockpit. Of the 42 planes which had left that morning, only half returned.

Unknown to the Japanese at that time, the southward flight of their planes had been spotted and reported by Paul Mason, a coastwatcher on Bougainville. Time and again his reports of the number, type and direction of flight of Japanese bombers gave ample warning which allowed the American fighters to gain altitude and meet the Japanese planes before their run in on the shipping. The attack that Sakai escorted reached the invasion force at 1200 but the bombers were so high flying that no damage was done to the shipping. The attack warning, however, caused all unloading to stop and the ships steamed about in the Channel in evasive actions as the bombers arrived overhead. Unloading was resumed at 1300 hours but two hours later was stopped again as a second force of Japanese planes arrived. These included dive bombers which made determined attacks on the transports and escorts, causing damage to the destroyer *Mugford* with 22 dead.

After Mikawa had persuaded Nakajima to send the first raid against the invasion fleet, he quickly made plans to bring his cruiser force into action in a night attack against the congested shipping. Details were sent to Tokyo for approval and meanwhile, he gathered his force together. The heavy cruisers *Chokai*, *Aoba* and *Kako* were on their way to the Admiralty Islands for an operation there. He sent the destroyer *Yunagi* at full speed to intercept and recall them. Two other cruisers, *Kinugasa* and *Furutaka* were already en-route to Rabaul from Kavieng, and two light cruisers, *Tenryu* and *Yubari* were in Rabaul. Mikawa was fortunate because the *Chokai* had picked up signals of the American landing and her Captain had decided to return to Kavieng before *Yunagi* met the three cruisers. By early afternoon these four ships were in St. George's Channel, near Rabaul when suddenly, a low flying Zero roared over the ships. It was Sakai in his desperate flight back to his base.

In Tokyo the Chief of Naval Staff was at first appalled at the risks Mikawa's plans entailed. Cruisers were not meant to fight in narrow, confined waters. His staff officers, however, saw the plan as a bold strike with an opportunity to hit the allied ships hard. Eventually approval was sent and by nightfall Mikawa's force of seven cruisers and one destroyer had rendezvoused and were steaming fast towards their target area. Mikawa was still far from satisfied. Before leaving he had made another attempt to persuade Hyakutake to send troop re-inforcements, but with no success. In desperation the Admiral had scraped together 450 men of the 5th Sasebo Special Landing Force, the nearest Japanese equivalent to Marines. Armed only with rifles and light machine guns these troops were hastily ordered on board the transport ship *Meiyo Maru* with orders for Guadalcanal. The ship would not be able to leave until the 8th and it would take two days to reach Guadalcanal. It was as much as Mikawa was able to do.

On Guadalcanal the 1st Marines became so scattered during the afternoon, as they struggled through the jungle, that before dusk the order was given to halt any further advance so that units could re-establish contact with each other. Three battal-

A soldier provides a drink to a fallen comrade. (Courtesy of J. Sumner)

The Marines used emergency radio equipment for communication with advancing patrol forces. Also, the Leathernecks kept in touch with ships of Fleet this way. First stories on offensive came through these radios. Victor Branch on the radio, Sgt. Harvey Skaugen, third from left, (KIA on Peleliu, awarded Silver Star), Q. Williams on right. (Courtesy of V. Branch)

ions, about 2500 men, had advanced as far as two miles inland and spent the night on both sides of the Tenaru river. The first battalion of 5th Marines, moving along the coast towards Lunga Point, reached Alligator Creek just before dusk and spent the night there.

As darkness fell swiftly over the thick jungle it became a living, fearsome thing to many of the nervous sentries. Raucous bird calls, shrilling crickets and croaking frogs seemed to be all around them. Every tree seemed to hide a Japanese soldier; every movement in the grass became a sniper and every birdcall a signal to send a screaming horde of enemy soldiers charging forward.

For most of the men the main enemy did come at sunset, as brown clouds of mosquitoes rose from the undergrowth with vicious bites on any exposed skin and pumping malaria into their bloodstreams.

Signalman Kauffman, 1st Marines, was on sentry duty that first night. He recalls, "the password that night was 'chesterfield', it was always a word with an l or an r in it because the Japanese could not pronounce those letters properly. We were all nervous and nobody knew what to expect. At one time another sentry and I heard a rustling sound in the jungle nearby. I called out for the password, but there was no answer and the gentle rustling sound seemed to be coming closer. It was very dark and neither the other sentry or I could see anything where the rustling seemed to be coming from, but we both fired towards it. After that there was silence. Next morning we went out and found a dead cow with two bullets in it near where the rustling sound had come from."

Corporal Chuck Breijak, 1st Marines, had found some abandoned Japanese equipment during the day. Amongst it was a diary. "I figured the owner would not be using it anymore", he recalls, "so I started to use it myself". Breijak had got as far as the Tenaru river during the day and his first entry for August 7th read: "Slept in a dry river bed, but in wet clothes. Not much sleep. Everyone seemed to go on a shooting spree during the night and one of our men got killed."

During the first day another man had been injured by a bayonet as he cut his way through the jungle. These were the total casualties among the troops landing on Guadalcanal in the first 24 hours.

WE ARE FIRING ON OUR OWN SHIPS

After the first day's progress Vandegrift realized that Mount Austen was further inland than his inaccurate maps showed. Since the airfield was the most important objective he directed 1st Marines to turn west and sweep towards the airfield on the morning of the 8th. 5th Marines were ordered to continue their advance along the beach towards Lunga Point.

By early afternoon the 1st Marines broke out of the jungle and reached the end of the airfield. They had met no resistance. The main runway of the airfield was 3700 yards long, but it had been started from each end and in the middle was an unfinished strip of a few hundred yards. The strip was surfaced with broken coral, gravel and cement, with an electric light system along its entire length.

Just beyond the airstrip was a large camp with scores of tents showing signs of hasty departure by the Japanese. In one tent, serving dishes, set in the middle of the table, were filled with stew, rice and cooked prunes. Bowls and saucers around the edge of the table were half filled with food. In other tents were also signs of a speedy retreat. Helmets, rifles and clothing were scattered about. Shoes, mosquito

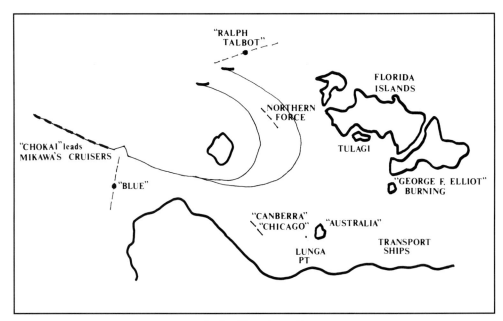

Battle of Savo, August 9.

Aerial photograph of Lunga Pt., July 1942. (USMC Photo)

nets, soap and other toilet articles had been left behind.

At a large bend in the Lunga River at the western end of the airfield, was the Japanese Headquarters camp. Here were wooden huts well stocked with a wide range of foodstuffs and bottles of wine. In the main office was a large drafting board; properly angled up drawing boards; shelves filled with blueprints; drafting supplies and record books. Parked at this camp were 35 trucks and nine road rollers - all of which were undamaged and serviceable.

The 5th Marines moved more quickly along the beach than they had the previous day. Many of the men had begun to feel more confident after finding so little resistance. They reached the mouth of the Lunga during the afternoon and crossed over it then pushed on to the small village of Kukum, a mile west of the river. There they found another Japanese supply center, hastily abandoned. Four field guns and a considerable quantity of small arms ammunition were found along with oil, gasoline, radio equipment and a great deal of rice and tinned food.

On Tulagi the Japanese had twice attacked the Raiders in force during the night. The first attack broke through between A and C companies forcing C Company back towards the coast. The second attack was against the front of A Company but was

stopped 20 yards from the Raiders' line. This was followed by small groups of Japanese sneaking through the lines then making a series of attacks against Edson's command post which was at the onetime residence of Resident Commissioner Marchant.

Dick Horton was at Edson's command post that night as the short sharp attacks began to develop. "The sudden screams of charging enemy soldiers, the whine of bullets and the sudden searing blasts of nearby firing were my first experience of night fighting" he recalls. "I found it frightening but as the enemy came closer, and hand to hand fighting began, there was no time for personal worries, it was too hectic and the firing too heavy until their suicidal rushes ended in suddenly cut off cries and groans that went on for a short time, then died away. When daylight came, the area around the Residency was littered with torn and crumpled dead Japanese. Bones shone whitely through their ragged, bloody clothing. On one man, tendons hung loose with a foot which pivoted round in the breeze. Everywhere the air was heavy with the putrid and sour smell of the dead."

During the morning E and F companies of the 2nd Battalion, 5th Marines moved across the base of Hill 281 then swept round behind it and began to drive the Japanese towards the Raiders. After laying down a heavy mortar barrage the Raiders pushed into the ravine where the Japanese were concentrated - many of them hidden in coral caves. Any movement across the mouth of the cave meant death and the Raiders moved from cave to cave throwing in grenades and explosive charges. Sometimes the resourceful Japanese managed to throw these out again before they exploded. Eventually by evening the last resistance was overcome except for individual snipers and small groups of men flushed from hiding places. Over 200 Japanese died in defending the island. Some managed to get away and swim to the larger Florida Island nearby, only to be tracked down and killed days later by Solomon Islander scouts and a party of Marines.

On Tanambogo the bloody repulse of Crane's Marines compelled Vandegrift to send over reinforcements from the transports at Red Beach. The next morning two companies of 3rd Battalion, 2nd Marines arrived on Gavutu with two tanks. Tanambogo was again heavily shelled by the destroyer *Buchanan* and in the afternoon the two companies were landed, preceded by the tanks, near the causeway on Tanambogo.

On the tiny island among the shell-scattered coconut trees and logs the two tanks found it difficult to maneuver effectively. In one tank Lieutenant Robert Sweeny poked his head out of the turret to reconnoitre. He was immediately shot through the head. The tank then stalled and as the crew clambered out, they were attacked by a large group of Japanese, swinging knives. One of them was even using a pitchfork. The crew escaped as the Marines came up behind the tank and gave them cover. The second tank was less fortunate. It became stuck when a group of Japanese soldiers ran forward and pushed an iron bar in its treads. They then managed to set the tank on fire using oily rags. As the crew struggled out they were attacked by the Japanese using knives. Two of the crew were killed. Two others managed to escape but were badly burned. One man did not escape from the tank but did manage to mow down 42 of the Japanese shouting and screaming within the arc of fire of the tank's machine gun.

The bitter struggle continued throughout the night with a Parachute company crossing the causeway to help the Marines. In the caves, dug-outs, trenches and pillboxes on the tiny island the Japanese fought savagely, often in hand to hand combat. It was not until the next morning that the last of the defenders had been killed, but here again some managed to swim across to Florida Island. In the vicious struggle some 450 Japanese had died over the two days it took to capture the island. Casualties among the Marines and Parachutists were just over 100.

Just before noon on the 8th, the first air raid of the day started. Again a warning had been flashed by Paul Mason on Bougainville so that the fighters from Fletcher's carriers were ready. Forty-five Japanese dive bombers came over and 17 of them were shot down as furious dogfights developed high above the wheeling ships. Damage was restricted to the destroyer *Jarvis* hit by one bomb. In the early afternoon another group of bombers arrived. The 24 year old transport ship *George F. Elliott* was hit by a damaged plane which crashed on board near the bridge. The explosion ruptured a fuel tank and blazing oil cascaded down into the engine room. Soon the fire was out of control. Correspondent Richard Tregaskis saw what happened from the beach. "Suddenly a huge flash of fire, as red as blood, burst along the ship's side, then a cloud of sooty black smoke billowed from the blood red roots and towered high into the sky", he remembers. The ship's crew fought the fire for hours but it became out of control. At 1900 the ship was abandoned and the destroyer *Hull* moved in to sink the transport. She fired four torpedos at the blazing ship, but only one torpedo exploded and this was not enough to sink the ship. She drifted and burned throughout the night - a flaming beacon visible for miles to guide Mikawa's cruiser force moving down from the North.

On the morning of the 8th, Mikawa, anxious to learn of American strength at Guadalcanal, sent off a float plane from each of his cruisers. Only two of these planes reached the invasion area late in the moring and were quickly driven off by anti-aircraft fire. On returning they reported one battleship, six cruisers, 19 destroyers and 18 transports in the target area.

Men and machines "bathing" in the Lunga River, Guadalcanal, December 1942. (Courtesy of William F. Dolan)

Bridge building on the Lunga River.

By mid afternoon Mikawa had drawn up his plans which were signalled to each of his ships "...we will go from South of Savo Island and torpedo the main enemy force in front of the Guadalcanal anchorage. After that we will turn towards the Tulagi area to shell and torpedo the enemy. We will then withdraw North of Savo Island."

Unknown to Mikawa the Allied warships were stationed each night just off Savo Island, some 20 miles west of the transports. Other events, however, began to work in Mikawa's favor on the afternoon of the 8th. Admiral Fletcher's 48 hours of air support were beginning to run out. For Fletcher the greatest fear was the safety of his three aircraft carriers, as there was only one other American carrier in the Pacific. The carrier *Lexington* had been lost in May, and the *Yorktown* in June and these losses now made Flecther cautious. His carriers were operating 200 miles south of Guadalcanal when Fletcher sent a radio message to Ghormley asking for permission to withdraw his ships. He told Ghormley he had lost 21 out of his original 98 planes and that his ships were running low on fuel.

Without waiting for Ghormley's reply, Fletcher recalled all his planes and turned south towards the New Hebrides during the late afternoon. In addition to his three carriers he had one battleship, six cruisers and 15 destroyers. The major threat to Mikawa had been removed.

During the day Mikawa's cruisers had been steaming down 'the Slot' as the waters between the different large islands in the Solomons became known. Shortly after leaving Rabaul his ships had been sighted by the submarine S-38 which sent a report to Turner but at the time, the Japanese force was still so far away it was not seen as a threat. The cruisers were seen twice by aircraft as they passed down the Slot but due to delays and complex communications these sighting reports did not reach Turner until it was too late.

Unaware of these developments Mikawa felt sure he would be reported promptly and to deceive the spotting aircraft he split his ships into two groups during the daylight. At the approach of aircraft the ships altered to courses away from the general direction of Guadalcanal. After dark the two groups rejoined and at high speed approached the Allied warships screening the transports off Tulagi and Lunga.

Between Guadalcanal and Tulagi, Sealark Channel is only 19 miles wide at its narrowest point. The southern entrance to the channel is made hazardous by several reefs but the northern entrance provides unobstructed deep water except for the small island of Savo, lying five miles off Cape Esperance, the northern tip of Guadalcanal. It was here that Rear Admiral Crutchley, in command of the United States/ Australian cruiser force guarding the tranports, placed his ships. They were divided into two groups.

One group called the Southern Force, was made up of the Australian cruisers *Australia* with Crutchley on board, and the *Canberra*, the cruiser USS *Chicago* and the two U.S. destroyers *Bagley* and *Patteson*. This force patrolled a line along the coast of Guadalcanal from Cape Esperance towards Lunga. The second group, the Northern Force, was made up of the American cruisers *Vincennes*, *Quincy* and *Astoria* with the U.S. destroyers *Helm* and *Wilson*. They patrolled a box square north of Savo. To the northwest of Savo, the destroyers *Blue* and *Ralph*

*Talbo*t patrolled across the entrance to the channel. Both were equipped with surface radar and had previously shown their ability to pick up cruiser targets up to ten miles away at night. Crutchley's orders read "Meet the enemy to seaward of the area between Savo and Sealark Channel. In the event that an enemy force is sighted it will be engaged by the cruisers and shadowing destroyers will illuminate with searchlights. It is expected that our extensive air reconnaissance will give warning of approaching enemy surface forces." Unfortunately air reconnaissance reports were taking several hours to reach him.

Turner's headquarters were on board the transport *McCawley* off Lunga point. At 2030 when he received news of the withdrawal of the carrier force, he described Fletcher's action simply as "desertion".

Fletcher had promised at least 48 hours' cover, but had left without Ghormley's permission, after only 36 hours. Turner realized that without air cover the transports would have to leave the next morning but he hoped they could unload throughout the night. He sent for Vandegrift and Crutchley to draw up plans for the next day.

Crutchley decided to save time in getting to the *McCawley* by pulling the *Australia* out of line and steaming down to Lunga Point. Before he left the Southern Force, he handed over command of it to Captain Bode on the USS *Chicago*. This ship was last in line in the Southern Force but Bode expected Crutchley to return soon and so made no change in the disposition of the force. Bode had been Captain of the battleship *Oklahoma* lying in Pearl Harbor on 6 December 1941. He had gone ashore the night before and when he returned the next morning his smashed ship lay capsized in the harbor - the first victim of the Japanese attack that day. The bitter feeling still hurt him, to have lost his ship when absent from it. Yet, for him, an even crueler and more tragic fate lay ahead.

At 2315, 30 miles to the north of Savo, Mikawa's cruisers launched float planes equipped with flares. When these planes passed over the *Ralph Talbot* a short time later the destroyer passed a message over T.B.S. (Talk Between Ships) radio; "plane sighted over Savo, heading east". On board the *Vincennes* Captain "Freddie" Riefkohl saw the planes were showing lights and assumed they were friendly planes - probably from the carriers with a message for Turner. Riefkohl had not been told the carriers had withdrawn. On the *Quincy* radar contact was also made with one of these planes as it flew around for several minutes. Eventually the contact was regarded as being of no consequence.

At midnight the conference on *McCawley* ended but Crutchley stayed on a little while longer to chat with Vandegrift. When Crutchley returned to the *Australia* he decided against rejoining the Southern Force and instead, began to patrol to and from the Guadalcanal coast in a line half way between the transports and the Southern Force. He did not tell Bode of this change in his plans. Had the *Australia* rejoined the Southern Force it is likely she would have reached the cruisers at the same time as Mikawa did.

At 0043 the cruiser *Chokai* led Mikawa's force as it approached Savo. Lookouts suddenly reported the *Blue* five miles away on a course which would cross the Japanese line. Every gun trained on the unsuspecting destroyer as Mikawa altered course slightly to the left, away from the *Blue*. As he did so *Blue* reached the end of her patrol line, reversed course and moved slowly away from the cruisers. Almost immediately the *Ralph Talbot* was seen on the left but she, too, was moving away from the Japanese ships. Mikawa altered course to the right and his line of cruisers slipped between the guard ships unseen by either of them.

At 0136 the Japanese cruisers entered the Channel between Savo and Cape Esperance and lookouts

Marines' Best Friend

reported the Southern Force moving slowly towards them. Incredibly, and despite radar on the *Chicago*, the Southern Force did not see the enemy ships until six minutes after the cruisers had fired a shoal of torpedoes towards them at 0137. Finally at 0143 the *Patteson* sighted the Japanese ships and sounded the alarm over the T.B.S. "Warning, warning, strange ships entering harbor".

At almost the same moment the Japanese float planes dropped flares over the transports, silhouetting the ships of the Southern Force only 4500 yards from *Chokai*. She immediately opened fire, followed by *Aoba* and *Furutaka*. On the *Canberra* the alarm bells had just begun to ring when two torpedoes smashed into the starboard bow. The principal control officer ordered "port 35 degrees" to help bring the guns to bear as three Japanese cruisers were reported. Captain Getting arrived on the bridge as a torpedo wake was seen coming from the port side and passing close down the starboard side. As the ship's stern was swinging out towards it, he shouted "hard a starboard!" Two more torpedoes were then seen approaching and the ship maneuvered desperately as the order to open fire was given. Too late. Two brilliant flares from Japanese planes floated down, bathing the stricken ship in a pale green light. The next instant, several shells smashed into the bridge. The gunnery control officer was killed at once and Getting fell badly wounded. A second salvo of shells hit the bridge and also the engine room. Steam and power were cut off and the ship slowed to a halt. Burning fiercely and beginning to list, she drifted out of the action, her main guns still trained in.

The Executive Officer, Commander Walsh, worked his way through the burning ship to the bridge, where he found Getting mortally wounded and lying in a scene of complete devastation. Walsh bent down to help the Captain who whispered painfully "Carry on;" Walsh laid him down then hurried off to try and save the ship. Getting, drifted into intervals of unconsciousness as the ship's doctor tried to save him. For the Captain and his ship, it was already too late. Both died slowly over the next few hours.

As soon as *Patteson* sighted the Japanese she fired off starshell to illuminate them, then swung round to bring her starboard torpedo tubes to bear. In the noise and confusion the order to fire torpedoes was not heard and the opportunity was almost immediately lost. *Patteson* then fired several rounds towards the Japanese cruisers before they disappeared. The whole action was so brief that the Executive Officer arrived at his battle station just as the firing stopped.

Chicago also fired off starshell when she heard the alarm, but at 0147 she was hit by a torpedo and several shells. On her radar she could see two ships to the southwest, although all the firing seemed to come from the northwest. More starshell was fired but failed to ignite. *Chicago* steamed towards the two ships on her radar.

Mikawa had earlier become concerned about the presence of *Blue* astern of his force and at 0136 had ordered the destroyer *Yunagi* to patrol between Savo and Cape Esperance. On this line *Yunagi* met the U.S. Destroyer *Jervis* - damaged by air attack earlier in the day, and now on her way to Australia for repairs. These were the two ships on the radar of *Chicago* and as she headed towards them, *Yunagi* opened fire on *Jervis*. It was 0200. *Chicago* then fired on *Yunagi* searchlights and after 25 rounds, the lights went out. *Chicago* switched on her lights and swept the sea. There was nothing to be seen, but she continued steaming southwest while heavy shellfire and burning ships were seen to the northwest.

The last ship in the Southern Force, the destroyer *Bagley* was closest to the Japanese cruisers. Like *Patteson* she turned to fire her starboard torpedo tubes but at the critical moment the firing primers

Taking a break from combat, a weary soldier rests. (Courtesy of J. Sumner)

were not ready. Her infuriated skipper, Lieutenant Commander Sinclair, swung the ship to bring the port tubes to bear and fired off eight torpedoes towards the disappearing Japanese cruisers.

As the enemy ships swung north, away from the shattered Southern Force, they split into two columns which trapped the Northern Force between them. On board *Vincennes* Riefkohl had received the warning from *Patteson* and watched the flares, starshell and explosions lighting up the night sky. Because he received no more messages from the Southern he assumed they were probably engaging a Japanese destroyer or some other light craft that may be trying to sneak past them. He never thought for a moment that a large Japanese naval force would have slipped past *Blue* and *Ralph Talbot* without a warning from them.

Riefkohl's latest intelligence about Japanese naval forces had been a message received in the previous afternoon which had placed "three cruisers, three destroyers, two seaplane tenders or gunboats" off the island of Bougainville some 200 miles north of Savo. Riefkohl had discussed this report with his officers and they had decided the Japanese ships were probably preparing to set up an air base at Faisi Island just South of Bougainville. The three cruisers of the Northern Force were all of the *Astoria* class and in each case the weakest point was the well deck near the stern where three fabric covered floatplanes were totally unprotected and had some 130 gallons of aviation fuel in each plane. Most of the crew had been stood down from battle stations after a hectic 15 hour day in action against Japanese planes.

The Japanese cruisers bearing down on the Northern Force had been rigorously trained for night battles over a period of months in realistic exercises in the North Pacific. Lookouts had been trained so that they could identify a ship at night by its silhouette from five miles away. Each cruiser flew a sleeve at

night to help identify it. Torpedo and gunnery control had been brought up to new standards of excellence, but perhaps the most potent weapon was the 'long lance' torpedo with twice the explosive power of the standard American torpedo. Most of the ships in Mikawa's force had trained together for months and had developed a highly efficient night signalling system.

Riefkohl, on the other hand, lacked any awareness of danger even when the Japanese cruiser searchlights suddenly lit up his ship. He assumed the lights were from ships of the Southern Force. Suddenly, to his horror, six tall spouts of water rose majestically near his ship as the Japanese cruisers opened fire. While the alarm bells rang, another salvo from the cruiser *Kako* demolished the bridge. As the crew hurriedly ran to battle stations the bridge was hit again; fire erupted in the airplane hangar, battery No. 2 was smashed, fire control station wrecked and all power to searchlights and phones was lost. Despite the damage *Vincennes* managed to fire off a salvo which struck the *Kinugasa* but at 0155 the *Vincennes* received two torpedo hits. No. 1 fire room was destroyed and everybody there was killed. Steering control became lost and Riefkohl tried to steer the ship with engines. At 0200 she was floodlit again by the *Chokai*, *Aoba* and *Kako* on her starboard side while the other Japanese cruisers fired from her port side. Riefkohl assumed these searchlights were from friendly ships and ordered a large "Stars and Stripes" to be hoisted. On seeing this, the Japanese ships thought they had engaged a battleship and poured even heavier fire into the hapless ship. After being hit by two more torpedoes and numerous shells the ship began to heel over, burning fiercely. At 0215 the Japanese ships broke off the engagement and at 0230 Riefkohl ordered abandon ship. Ten minutes later the *Vincennes* capsized and sank with the loss of 322 lives.

A captured Japanese Field Artillery piece. These guns were similar to the French 75mm guns used by the US Army during World War I. Notice the wooden wheels with steel tires. Initially, these guns were designed to be horse drawn. The American troops captured scores of these pieces at Guadalcanal. (Courtesy of W. M. Chaney)

Next in line to *Vincennes* was the *Quincy* and when General Quarters sounded, Gunner's Mate Byers ran to the starboard airplane catapult and struggled into flash-proof clothing as the bridge ordered "warm up planes". A few seconds later a six-inch shell hit the port catapult and the plane on it suddenly flared up as its fuel tanks exploded. A burning wing from the plane on the catapult, dropped off and fell on to another plane in the well deck, setting it on fire. Burning fuel oil spread across the deck and cut off Byers from the foamite locker. Soon the flames spread across the whole deck isolating those crewmen at the stern. Byers remembers a shell fragment then severed the steam line to the ship's whistle, and scalding water rained down on the men in the well deck and boat deck.

Between the bridge and the well deck, were eight five-inch guns - four on each side. No. 6 gun was hit first, then No. 2 where all the crew were killed or injured except the Gun Captain Bryant. He ran to the other guns to get replacements as another hit wiped out all the gun loaders on No. 3, except one man, Drum. Bryant and Drum tried to man the gun themselves with Drum loading and Bryant pointing, but flames and smoke from the planes in the well deck drove them away from the gun. As they ran past No. 4 gun, Bryant noticed all the crew were laid out around it in an untidy heap; clothes torn, and scalding water from the broken steam line cascading on to them. Behind him Bryant saw that wooden rafts were beginning to burn and as flaming oil spread across the deck towards him he grabbed a floater net and jumped over the side. As he swam away he looked back to see the ship heeling over as ready ammunition at the guns began exploding.

Throughout the *Quincy* in mess compartments and repair stations, men struggled hopelessly with the fires and explosions. At anti-aircracft batteries men and guns were blown to pieces under the intense fire from the enemy cruisers. With all his guns out of action the Gunnery Officer sent his assistant, Andrews, to the bridge for instructions. When he got to the bridge Andrews found it was completely wrecked with dead bodies scattered everywhere. Only three or four people were still alive - one of them, the helmsman. Andrews asked where the Captain was and the helmsman pointed wordlessly to a dead figure sprawled among the wreckage. The helmsman told Andrews that the Captain had told him to steer towards Savo in the hope of beaching the ship there, but by that time the ship was listing so badly Andrews ordered all those on the bridge to abandon ship.

Quartermaster Nathaniel Corwin's battle station was far away from the action, in the after steering station over the rudder. "There were two others with me", he recalls. "The steering station was small and it was cramped with three of us in there. I had the phones on and soon got word from the bridge that *Astoria* had been hit. Then things started popping. Smoke poured in from the ventilator shaft so fast we had to close it but there was still so much smoke it was hard to breathe. Then I lost communications with the bridge and all other stations. Next the lights went out except for one emergency light. The rudder went all the way over to the left and seemed to be jammed. By this time I was sweating buckets of water; I just couldn't think. There was an emergency bell system for steering control from the bridge and I waited for the bridge to use it, but nothing happened, so we went ahead and shifted steering units and brought the rudder amidships. Then someone on the bridge tried to use the bell system but it died out."

He went on - "just about then I noticed the ship was heeling to port and I felt funny as hell. All three of us suddenly knew what was happening and we decided to get out. The hatch above us was so hot we had a hell of a time getting it open and when we got out and on to the deck above, the place was really a mess. Eventually I reached the main deck aft but then lost my footing as the ship heeled over more. I slid right over the side and landed on someone else in the water, then another person landed on me. Boy, I did some tall swimming, for a while, then looked back. The stern had risen high into the air and seemed to be right over me, so I started swimming like hell again. When I looked back again it was just in time to see her slide under. For a while I lay on my back and prayed like I never prayed before. I must have been in the water three or four hours. I found a group of survivors clinging to a raft and I stayed with them. At one time we saw a destroyer moving slowly through the darkness but no one dared say a word in case it was Japanese. We were all scared they might machine gun us in the water or take us prisoner. Eventually we did make contact with a destroyer and were picked up. I was cold, wet and very tired."

Quincy had gone down at 0235 taking 370 men with her, yet despite her terrible fate she scored the most damage against the Japanese. One of the few salvos she managed to fire had struck the *Chokai*, wrecking the chartroom and killing 34 men. Without charts for Sealark Channel, Mikawa was reluctant to go further in to the Channel and attack the now helpless transports.

On *Astoria* Lieutenant Commander Topper felt the ship shudder with an underwater explosion at 0144. He assumed it was caused by a depth charge dropped against a Japanese submarine the destroyers may have found. In fact it was caused by depth charges from the Japanese cruisers to keep off any American submarines in the area. Next a lookout reported "starshell on the port quarter". Topper ran out to the wing of the bridge. Sure enough a string of aircraft flares were falling slowly through the sky over towards Guadalcanal. Topper sent word to call Captain Greenman. Moments later the main battery of *Astoria* fired a full salvo, and General Quarters rang throughout the ship. Greenman ran up to the bridge, amazed to waken and find his ship apparently in action. "Who gave the order to commence firing?" he demanded. Topper replied that he had no idea. "We are firing on our own ships", said Greenman. "Let's not get too excited and act hastily, cease firing", he ordered as a second salvo split the night.

At main battery fire control on *Astoria* Lieutenant Commander Truesdell had come on watch at midnight to find the fire control radar was not working and nothing was being done about it. He was furious, and called out Chief Radioman Datko to get it fixed as soon as possible. By 0145 it was operating again and just then starshell burst in the sky to the southwest. "All stations alert" Truesdell called out and sounded general alarm. A few seconds later he saw columns of water rising near the *Vincennes* and his spotters identified *Chokai*. Truesdell rang the bridge for permission to open fire but could get no answer. Without hesitating he ordered "open fire" and *Astoria* fired her first salvo that had so alarmed Greenman on the bridge.

As Truesdell gave the order to fire a second salvo, the bridge called him, ordering cease fire and asking what he was firing at. "Japanese Nachi class cruiser" he replied, "for God's sake give the order to commence firing". Just then Greenman saw a salvo of shells hit *Vincennes*. "Whether they are our own ships firing at us, or not" he said, "we will have to stop them; commence firing". The confusion caused a three minute delay and it was long enough for *Chokai* to close on the *Astoria* and begin to pound her. Here again the planes on the well deck were quickly set on fire, then No. 1 turret and the bridge and gun deck were wrecked. Power failure caused gun turrets to fire only occasionally - sometimes only one barrel in three on the main turrets firing. Despite this, *Astoria* managed to fire 50 eight-inch shells, one of which damaged a gun turret on *Chokai*.

Continued Japanese shelling caused a series of engine room explosions. Chief Water Tender Smith was in No. 3 fireroom when a tremendous blast wrecked No. 1 fireroom sending splintered metal flying past him. His own fireroom began to fill with smoke and Smith ordered his men out. They found the port exit hatch blocked by smoke and fire, and the starboard hatch jammed shut. Smith managed to push it up a few inches and saw that a grating had fallen on it. He flashed his light in the darkened machine shop above and shouted for help. No one heard him and he fell back exhausted. Others scrambled up the ladder to the hatch, shouting for help. Finally a machinist came and struggled with the grating. He could not move it enough to clear the hatch cover but several men pushing from below got the hatch opened 12 inches. It was enough for all of them to squeeze through. In the machine shop they then found one exit blocked by fire and at the other end, more than 30 bodies were piled up. They quickly climbed over the bodies and eventually escaped through a hatchway on to the well deck where they dodged the flaming oil and gasoline from the burning planes before jumping over the side. On the bridge of *Astoria* most of the men were killed in the initial salvos from the Japanese. Boatswains Mate Young was severely wounded but managed to steer the ship away from the enemy towards Savo Island. Soon, however, he collapsed and another helmsman took over but shortly afterwards all engine room power was lost and the ship drifted helplessly, buring fiercely from the bridge to the stern.

After Greenman had finally given the order to commence firing, Topper had gone to the damaged control station but was soon driven out by smoke and flames. As fires spread throughout the ship he gathered about 300 men at the bows, after the Japanese shelling stopped. Slowly, working their way towards the stern, they began to bring the fires under control despite the constant risk of the magazines exploding. They fought to save the ship throughout the night but after daybreak she listed to port and at 1100 a magazine exploded. By noon the water was at deck level and the last fire fighters were taken off. Fifteen minutes later, *Astoria* heeled over and sank.

The two destroyers in the Northern Force played little part in the action. *Wilson* found that *Vincennes* was between her and the enemy initially and she was obliged to fire over the cruiser, aiming at the Japanese searchlights. Suddenly *Helm* appeared out of the darkness ahead and *Wilson* swung hard left only just avoiding a collision. By that time four of the Japanese cruisers had come up on the same side of *Vincennes* as *Wilson* was, and the destroyer then fired on *Chokai* with no apparent effect, until suddenly the Japanese cruisers were gone.

Helm had been on *Vincennes* port bow and some way ahead of the cruiser. She did not realize the cruisers were under attack until shells started exploding on them. She never did see any Japanese ship but turned south, crossing in front of *Wilson*, then went in pursuit of a ship four miles to the southwest. This turned out to be *Bagley* from the Southern Force but by the time *Helm* identified her the battle was over.

At 0220 the Japanese cruisers turned to the northwest and sped away at full speed. To Mikawa the loss of his charts, lack of torpedoes and the fear of air attack at dawn induced him not to attack the transports. As the cruisers cleared Savo they were seen by *Ralph Talbot* on her patrol line. She fired four torpedoes towards them with no apparent effect but was brought under fire by three of the cruisers as they sped past. The destroyer was rapidly reduced to a flaming, listing wreck and probably only saved by a heavy rain squall that suddenly hid her from view. Powerless and burning fiercely she was left to drift towards Savo.

On Savo itself the islanders had found the night to have been one of absolute terror. The crash and thunder of guns in the Channel, the starshells throwing weird colors and the drifting burning ships, were like a nightmare to many of them who had no idea what was going on. Michael Rapasia, one of the villagers on the island, remembers that the vibrations from the shelling and explosions made the ground shake and coconuts fall out of the trees. He and most of the other villagers fled from their huts and hid in holes in the ground for the rest of the night. The next morning he found an unexploded torpedo more than 100 yards up on the beach and all during the morning groups of sailors struggled ashore. He took one sailor, who was covered in oil, back to his village and spent the rest of the day cleaning the oil off him. The sailor's hair was so thick with oil that Rapasia simply cut off most of it.

To Admiral Turner on *McCawley* the sudden outbreak of shelling, the explosions and the colorful flares off Savo brought confusion and it was not until the brief engagement was ended that he was finally able to send a message to Fletcher. "Surface attack on screen, *Chicago* hit by torpedo, *Canberra* on fire." The Northern Force was not in a position to answer Turner's call for information.

When Fletcher received Turner's message his carrier force was 200 miles southwest of Savo. He had still not received Ghormley's permission to retire from the area so he turned his ships back towards Guadalcanal. On the carrier *Wasp* there was in fact an air group which was specially trained in night operations. The ship's Captain F. Sherman asked the commander of air support group for permisison to fly off this group against the Japanese cruisers. Sherman suggested that the *Wasp* and a few destroyers could be detached to make a high speed run to Guadalcanal. Three times he asked for permission but each time he was told 'no'. At 0330 Fletcher finally received Ghormley's permission to withdraw and so turned his ships back again towards the New Hebrides.

When the Japanese cruisers cleared Savo they left more than 1,000 men struggling in the oil and debris covered water. For many of them their greatest ordeal was just beginning. Those who were badly wounded did not long survive the struggle to keep afloat. Many were saved by the care of their shipmates. Marine Corporal Chamberlain, who was wounded in five places, was weakening rapidly in an attempt to stay afloat when Seaman Caryl Clement swam over to him. He removed the laces from Chamberlain's shoes and used them to tie the Marine's hands to a floating ammunition drum. As the night wore on an added terror developed as groups of survivors were attacked by sharks. At first light in the morning rescue boats moved among the swimmers while seamen in the boats drove off the sharks with rifle fire.

At 0800 it became obvious that the crippled, burning *Canberra* would not last much longer. The crew were taken off by destroyers and the ship was then sunk by torpedoes from the destroyer USS *Ellet*. This brought to four the number of Allied ships sunk. The *Chicago* was also so badly damaged that she was out of action for many months. The *Ralph Talbot* eventually made sufficient repairs to enable her to get under way and make towards Tulagi late in the morning.

Why did Mikawa not go on to attack the transports and other warships off Lunga and Tulagi as his original plan had called for? Apart from the Southern and Northern cruiser forces there was an Eastern force made up of the cruiser USS *San Juan* and the Australian cruiser *Hobart* with two destroyers off Tulagi. The *Australia* was still patrolling between Savo and the transports and there were 11 destroyers and four destroyer/transports guarding the 19 cargo ships and transports, among them the still burning *George F. Elliott* It would have taken less than an hour for Mikawa's cruisers to be among these ships after he had attacked the Northern force.

It was 0220 when the Japanese ceased firing on the Northern Force ships, but by then the Japanese were split into two groups. To have gathered the ships together, issued new orders and gone on to attack the transports and then escape clear of Savo would have taken perhaps two hours. Mikawa knew that the longer he delayed his departure from the area the greater was the chance that daylight would find his ships within range of U.S. carrier planes. This seems to have been the principle reason for his withdrawal from the area, plus the fact that after the damage to his chartroom he no longer had charts for the area.

After the war Commander Ohmae, Captain Kato of the *Chokai* and Rear Admiral Matsuyama of the *Tenryu* all agreed that the objective of the attack had been to destroy the transports. When Mikawa returned to Japan he faced an enquiry board. He told the board that he had considered that the main function of cruisers was to attack other similar enemy warships and that soft targets such as transports could be attacked by lighter warships. In his view he had defeated the enemy warships and left the transports to be finished off by other Japanese warships. The board considered that he had missed an opportunity to do much more damage than he had done. He lost command of the cruiser force.

There was also an enquiry by the U.S. Navy. Admiral Hepburn took months to make his findings before he submitted a report to King. The report was immediately classified, and few of the details of it are available even today. The main criticism it contained was an apparent lack of awareness of the danger that the Allied ships were in and the failure of individual ships to communicate fully with each other once the fighting had started. On the Allied warships many had noted the presence of the planes overhead but none had considered they posed any threat, assuming they were friendly aircraft.

Among the destroyers *Blue* was unaware of the Japanese ships until the action started. She remained on her patrol line throughout the action, and her radar which had not detected seven large warships later picked up a small island schooner passing a mile away, and at 0210 she detected another ship near the Guadalcanal coast. She went over to investigate and found the destroyer *Jarvis*. This ship had been

Japanese skulls chained to a Marine jeep on Guadalcanal. This was a common sight.

Along the Lunga. (L to R): Stewart Marty (deceased), Francis (Pudge) White (deceased) and Orein G. DeLap. (Courtesy of Donald DeLap)

damaged by bombs earlier and had left Lunga at midnight heading towards Australia for repairs. *Jarvis* was also detected by *Yunagi* which fired a few shots at her then reported the escape of *Jarvis* to the southwest. Next day the luckless ship was found by Japanese planes and sunk with the loss of all hands.

Among the other destroyers *Helm* did not fire a shot and saw the Japanese searchlights only briefly. Yet there were seven minutes between the attack on the Southern Force and the attack on the Northern Force where *Helm* was ahead of *Vincennes*. Some warning had, however, been received. At 0143 the *Patterson* had radioed "Warning, warning, strange ships entering harbor." At that time the cruisers in the Northern Force had been engaged in a routine course alteration which had been delayed for two minutes in order to keep all ships on station. Thus the message from *Patterson* was never received on the bridge of *Vincennes* or on *Astoria*, while on *Quincy* it was not relayed to gunnery. The *Australia* could not receive it either since she did not have the T.B.S. system.

On *Australia* the flares and gunfire convinced Crutchley that a surface action was underway. He radioed this to Turner who could see the gunfire himself. Crutchley then decided to wait, convinced that his five cruisers and four destroyers could handle any surface ships sent against them. He also thought that if he steamed into the action it would only confuse matters and it would be better to stay where he was and guard the transports. Crutchley thus became a helpless spectator to the action.

THEIR SWORDS WERE FLASHING IN THE SUN

At Guadalcanal on the morning of the 9th, while rescue boats were still picking survivors out of the water, Turner called another meeting with Vandegrift and Crutchley. With no air support, and very few escort ships left, they decided the transports would have to leave that day. Turner expected the Japanese warships to return at any time and wipe out the shipping.

Unknown to him Mikawa's only thought was to get far away from the area before he was caught by American air strikes. By noon the Japanese were 200 miles northwest of Guadalcanal and Mikawa split his

force up. The cruisers *Aoba*, *Kako*, *Kinugasa* and *Furutaka* were sent to Kavieng while Mikawa led the rest of his ships towards Rabaul. On the morning of the 10th as the Kavieng ships approached their base they were sighted by the American submarine S-44. From a range of 700 yards she fired four torpedoes - two of which struck *Kako*. Within minutes the cruiser broke up and sank. Some consolation for the losses at Savo.

Among the merchant ships at Lunga none had discharged more than a quarter of their cargo. Turner ordered any essential items to be landed during the day but all ships were to leave at 1800 that evening. It was an impossible task. In order to land food, ammunition and a few pieces of artillery, boats had to be taken from the transports landing Marines so that when the ships left at the end of the day they took with them 1400 Marines as well as the bulk of the food, ammunition, artillery, tanks, tools and fuel. The cargo ship *Fomalhaut* had discharged only 15% of its heavy equipment and only one bulldozer had been put ashore.

Ten thousand Marines were left on Guadalcanal to watch the invasion fleet sail away to the south that evening. Not a single ship was left in Sealark Channel. The Marines had been left with enough ammunition for four days of normal use and with food for two or three weeks. They were also left in no doubt that the Japanese now controlled the seas around the island and that they could expect an enemy landing at any time. Among the Marines, feelings ran high. Many remembered what had happened at Bataan and Corregidor a few months previously where American troops, with no chance of evacuation, had been left to fight towards a hopeless end. Private Robert Corwin, 1st Marines, remembers "I had a feeling, and I'm sure most of the others had as well, that none of us would ever get off that damned island. We had stuck our necks out and now it was just a case of where the Japs were gonna chop it".

Corwin was particularly concerned when he noticed the *Quincy* was not among the warships that were leaving. His brother was Quartermaster Nathaniel Corwin who had escaped from the steering flat on the cruiser just before she sank. After he had been rescued Nathaniel was put ashore at Lunga but later in the day he was sent out to one of the transports which left that evening. It was to be several months before the brothers knew what had happened to each other.

The only Japanese troops ordered to be sent to

the island were the 450 men that Mikawa had put on board *Meiyo Maru* just before he left Rabaul. The ship cleared Rabaul on the afternoon of the 8th but when only 50 miles away from the base, she was torpedoed by the submarine S-38 and quickly sank with a heavy loss of life.

Thinking that Japanese landings were imminent Vandegrift drew his Marines into a defensive perimeter central around the airfield bounded to the east by the Tenaru River, and to the west by the Lunga. He ordered all supplies moved off the beach and scattered widely. The Marines were put to digging beach defenses and the 1st Engineer Battalion was ordered to get the airstrip ready for use as quickly as possible. They immediately set to work using the abandoned Japanese trucks, road rollers and tractors.

In his diary for the 9th, Marine Corporal Chuck Breijak wrote, "Marched back to the beach today, strung some wire and set up our machine guns. We are only 30 yards from the beach and if the Japs land they will be on top before we know it. Food is short and we ate only coconuts today until we raided one of the Jap warehouses near the beach. In the afternoon, five Jap planes came over and machine gunned the beach. They were here and gone before anyone could fire a shot."

The next day Vandegrift sent out patrols to find out where the Japanese were and to test their strength. Correspondent Tregaskis joined one of these patrols towards the Matanikau River. "We followed a trail towards the river and found several dead Japanese who seemed to have died of wounds probably suffered from the shelling on the day of the landing" he recalls. "At one time I looked along the trail with my field glasses and saw three or four men, several hundred yards away, looking in our direction. I was not sure if they were Japs or not. 'Those are our men said a Marine nearby. 'I don't think so' replied another. In a flash we were all certain. 'Take cover' someone shouted and I hit the ground as the Japanese vanished into the jungle at the side of the trail." Similar confusion arose elsewhere because the Japanese Navy field uniform was similar to the Marines' utility suit. On another patrol Marine Lieutenant Gateby saw a figure in the jungle aiming a rifle at him. "Hold your fire" he shouted, thinking it was a Marine. Suddenly he realized it was an enemy soldier; he raised his rifle to fire but found the safety was still on. As he fumbled desperately to release it he looked up at the Japanese and saw that he too was releasing his safety. Both men fired at the same instant. Gateby received a flesh wound in the side of the chest and the Japanese staggered back and fell into the undergrowth. Cautiously Gateby approached and found the man had been shot through the lungs. He was leaning back against a tree, his legs drawn up; there was a shocked and mute expression on his face. His breathing was slow and faint and in a few minutes he died quietly.

This patrol activity brought in a few prisoners. "Most of them were a measly lot", Correspondent Tregaskis recalls. "None were more than 5 ft. tall, they were puny and had sallow skins. The first two I saw had shaved heads and were bare from the waist down; the Marines had been diligent in their search for weapons. A third prisoner had been allowed to keep his khaki colored trousers. He wore a scraggly beard which made him look even more wretched, and on his head he wore a visored cap of cheap cloth with an anchor insignia. The prisoners blinked their eyes like curious birds as they looked at me. The first in line gaped - a gold tooth very prominent in the center of his mouth".

One of the prisoners was a Naval Petty Officer. He was questioned by Lieutenant Colonel Goettge, of the Intelligence Section, and told Goettge there was a group of Japanese on the west bank of the Matanikau who wanted to surrender. What seemed to be a white flag had, in fact, been seen there, and on the night of the 12th, Goettge, with a 25 man patrol, landed by barge near the mouth of the river. Sergeant Charles Arndt was with the group as they walked up the beach. "It was real dark" he remembers, "no moon or stars but I could see a few huts at the edge of the jungle. It was so quiet - we were all surprised when the Japs started firing. We hit the ground but Sergeant Custer, near me, got hit in the arm and gave his pistol to me. After a while the firing stopped and we tried to dig into the sand, then find Goettge. Someone near me whispered 'Goettge, Goettge'. There was no answer". Another Sergeant, Few, then crawled forward and found Goettge. Few remembers when he reached Goettge he felt a hole in the Colonel's head, "I knew he must be dead" he recalls. "Just then someone appeared close by; I challenged him but he came at me. My gun jammed and he struck me in the arm and chest with his bayonet. I pushed his rifle away and knocked him down then stabbed him with his own bayonet." Arndt remembers there was no cover on the beach - "We all lay as quiet as we could except for touching each other now and then".

After a while the firing started again. Commander Pratt got it first, in the back then in the chest. After a while he died. Next Lieutenant Cory got hit in the stomach and Captain Ringer was hit as well." About one the next morning Ringer asked for a volunteer to go back and try to get help. Arndt volunteered. He crawled across the sand on his stomach until he reached the sea then swam along the coast towards Lunga Point which was four miles away. Often he hit coral outcrops which badly cut his legs, body and hands. Eventually he found a canoe and although there were numerous bullet holes in it he pushed it into the sea and paddled towards Lunga with a broken plank.

Shortly after Arndt got away from the beach, the Japanese fire resumed and continued intermittently throughout the night. Another man, Sergeant Spaulding, managed to get away and just before dawn Sergeant Few also began to crawl into the sea. As dawn broke he swam straight out to sea before planning to turn and follow the coast. A few shots threw up the water nearby and when he turned to look at the beach he saw the Japanese "Had closed in on those who were left and were hacking them to pieces". Few remembers, "I could see their swords flashing in the sun". Of the 25 man patrol only Arndt, Spaulding and Few survived. Two days later a strong patrol was sent along the coast to investigate. The Japanese had gone, and there was no sign of what had happened to Goettge or the others who had died with him.

ICHIKI'S FOLLY

On August 13th, Army High Command in Tokyo ordered General Hyakutake to make the capture of Guadalcanal a priority over all other operations within his command. Hyakutake still believed there were no more than 2000 American troops on Guadalcanal. He was initially puzzled at the absence of Allied shipping in Sealark Channel after Mikawa's raid, then he decided that the Marines had been abandoned and he could therefore wipe them out at any time. The first problem was to contact any surviving Japanese troops on Guadalcanal and find out where they were centered. On August 15th he ordered the fast destroyer *Oite* to Guadalcanal with 200 troops and a radio communications detachment. It would take only a day to reach the island and in the meantime he sent over reconnaissance flights to look for Japanese camps and bombers to drop basketloads of ammunition and supplies.

That morning Coast watcher Martin Clemens, with several Solomon Island Scouts, left his base in the jungle behind Aola and set off along the coastal plain towards the American lines 30 miles away. "Suddenly three planes came flying low toward us", Clemens recalls. "We all stood like stupid fools, waving and cheering as they approached. Then through my field glasses I saw red balls on the wings of the planes. I shouted a warning to the others and we quickly took cover. The planes circled once then dropped containers of ammunition and rations. We decided to leave the area as quickly as possible before the people they were intended for arrived on the scene."

Hyakutake had only recently taken command of the 17th Army at Rabaul and, as was usual in the Japanese Army, he was expected to put together his 50,000 man force from units assigned to him from other commands. These included the 2nd Division, then in the Philippines; the 38th Division in Java; the 35th Brigade in the Paulus Islands; an anti-tank regiment in Manchuria and a detachment of 2000 men on Guam under the command of Colonel Kiyono Ichiki. It was this detachment that Hyakutake ordered immediately to Guadalcanal. Hyakutake told Ichiki that the American Marines on Guadalcanal had been abandoned, that there was no activity among them and that it was thought that their morale

would be low. Ichiki's orders read "...quickly recapture and maintain the airfield. If this is not possible wait until the arrival of more troops".

Colonel Ichiki considered that the task of wiping out what he thought to be 2000 demoralized, abandoned American Marines, presented no problem and he welcomed the opportunity to display his well known tactical skill. He left for Guadalcanal confident that he would not need the extra troops Hyakutake had said would be available. Ichiki's troops were divided into two groups. Nine hundred men were put aboard six destroyers under the command of Admiral Raizo Tanaka. These troops landed at Taivu Point, 20 miles east of Lunga, on the night of 18th August. Tanaka, one of Japan's ablest admirals, was pessimistic about the whole operation. "In my opinion this is the most difficult operation in war", he wrote, "a landing in the face of the enemy without rehearsal or any preliminary study, is dangerous. Expediency is taking precedence over prudence - there must be a lot of confusion at 8th Fleet Headquarters." The remaining 1100 men of Ichiki's force were to follow later in a transport ship and four converted destroyers.

From Taivu Point, Ichiki sent strong patrols towards the American lines at Alligator Creek. At

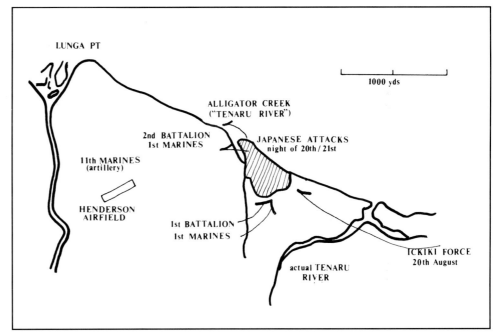

Battle for the Tenaru River, August 21.

Massacre near the Matanikau, Oct. 25, 1942. (Courtesy of Irv Reynolds, No. MA1Rad10D)

Martin Clemens directing Solomon Island scouts.

Marine legend MGYSGT Lou Diamond of the 1st Marine Division.

the same time, from within the perimeter, Martin Clemens was sending out patrols of Solomon Islander scouts and police. On the 20th one of the patrols led by Sergeant Major Jacob Vouza, met one of Ichiki's patrols near Taivu Point. Vouza had met many Japanese troops before this, but they had usually been wearing forage caps. Ichiki's men wore helmets which Vouza mistook for American. With Vouza was his nephew, Saki, who warned Vouza that the approaching patrol was Japanese, then ran off.

Vouza believed Saki was wrong, and waving cheerfully, approached the patrol. He was quickly captured. At the time he was carrying a small American flag and, suspecting him of working for the Americans, the Japanese tied him to a tree and began questioning him. "I remember the tree was covered with ants" Vouza recalls. "The Japanese asked where the American positions were but I told them I was just a laborer and knew nothing. They didn't believe me and one of the soldiers stepped forward and drove his bayonet into the left side of my chest. When he raised the bayonet again I tried to push it away but it went through my hand, under my chin and into my mouth, cutting off part of my tongue".

Vouza collapsed and the Japanese left him for dead. Later Vouza recovered consciousness; he

freed himself and began to walk slowly through the jungle towards Lunga. At times he collapsed again but recovered a little and went on again, constantly fearing he would run into more Japanese.

The Marines also sent out patrols looking for the Japanese. One patrol led by 1st Marines Captain Charles Bush, ambushed a 30 man Japanese group east of the perimeter. At the approach of the Japanese, Bush split his force into two groups, sending a platoon under 2nd Lieutenant John Jackym to cut off the Japanese rear. Jackym recalls "We came across the Japanese quite suddenly; they were all cleverly camouflaged and hard to see until they seemed to pop up out of the bush only yards away. It was horribly frightening, uncertain and confused; they seemed to be all around. I just fired furiously whenever one of them came into view". There was heavy firing on both sides for several minutes during which time, 27 of the Japanese were killed. Three U.S. Marines died and four were wounded.

Among the dead Japanese, Bush found several officers with detailed maps of the American positions. All the Japanese wore helmets with the army star as against the white chrysanthemum and anchor of the naval landing forces they had already seen on Guadalcanal. Bush hurried back to warn Vandegrift of the likelihood of an attack.

Vandegrift hastily strengthened his defenses on the west bank of Alligator Creek (generally known as the Tenaru River by mistake at the time), with 2nd Battalion, 1st Marines. They dug defensive positions along the river bank and covered them with logs. Artillery was brought up to register on the east bank, and a single line of wire, all that was available, was strung across the narrow spit at the mouth of the creek.

At 0120 on the morning of the 21st, a brilliant green flare rose from the east bank and hung over the river mouth, bathing it in ghostly light. A Marine sentry fired a single shot then 200 shouting and screaming Japanese rushed across the shallow river towards G Company, 2nd Battalion. The single strand of wire checked them momentarily but as machine-gun fire opened up on them they surged forward into G Company positions.

There then followed a confused melee of savage hand to hand fighting. Corporal Dean Wilson remembers his rifle jammed as three Japanese charged his foxhole. He grabbed a long bush knife and slashed the nearest one across the stomach so hard that the man fell back screaming, and clutching his entrails. Wilson then jumped out of the foxhole and

killed the other two with the knife. Nearby Corporal John Shea moved into a foxhole to clear his tommy gun. As he did so a Japanese soldier rushed forward and bayoneted Shea's left leg. With his right leg Shea swung and kicked the Japanese soldier in the stomach then having cleared his gun he shot the Jap five times in the chest.

As the Japanese attack faltered the Marines counter attacked and drove them back across the river mouth. Ichiki's men then brought the west bank of the river under heavy fire from light artillery, mortars and machine guns. A second attack was then launched against the Marines by a large group of Japanese who waded into the sea, crossed the river mouth and came ashore a few hundred yards west of the river.

Rifleman Gilbert Dolloff, E Company, 2nd Battalion, remembers this Japanese attack up the beach. "It was a dark, moonless night and difficult to see very far. Bill Wallace had a position to my left and on my right was a machine gun post and a 37mm gun beyond that. Suddenly all hell broke loose as Wallace started firing towards the surf. Directly in front of me was a dead tree - maybe 18 ft. long and partly in the surf. Wallace shouted to me that the Japs were hiding behind it, so I began firing at each end of it. I thought the Japs were landing from boats and never imagined that they had been walking through the surf".

Meanwhile the Japanese artillery fire continued and Dolloff recalls "the artillery fire seemed to be wounding quite a lot of our guys and the machine gun near me got knocked out. The only survivor brought me some ammunition. It was a godsend because I was getting low on ammunition. Most of the firing was coming from the river with artillery, mortars, machine guns and rifles. We kept on firing until Jap artillery started to land among us. One hit Wallace's position directly and he got hurt bad. Then Ray Roberts got killed nearby, another hit on an emplacement behind us and killed Ray Edlin and two others, all guys I'd been through training with".

"About daybreak the firing died down and we went on to the beach to mop up. Lieutenant Colonel Pollock was with us and was only a few feet away from me when a Jap officer, who seemed to be dead, suddenly got up and fired his pistol towards the Colonel. I finished off the Jap and got his pistol while the Colonel took his sabre".

Just before daybreak the badly wounded Vouza had managed to get through the lines to Pollock's headquarters about 100 yards behind the west bank. He asked to speak to Clemens and when the coastwatcher arrived he remembers "Vouza was in an awful mess, he had a gaping wound in his throat and I thought he did not have long to live. He gave me a lot of valuable information which I phoned back. He had lost a lot of blood and expected to die. He gave me a message for his wife and children then collapsed and we carried him back to the hospital".

When daylight came the 1st Battalion, 1st Marines moved downstream along the west bank of the river then crossed over to the east bank and began pushing the Japanese into a small area of jungle near the river mouth in a steady advance through the trees and thick undergrowth. Private Robert Corwin remembers "as we approached the area where the Japs were concentrated, a Jap soldier hiding in the jungle, suddenly stood up and fired. Down went poor Bob McCarthy a few yards away from me as another Marine shot the Jap. We had a good look at the Jap because it was the first enemy soldier most of us had seen. He was obviously an officer, tall in size, with some gold teeth. Our platoon was then ordered to flush out some Japs believed to be hidden in some foliage about 100 yards on our left. The platoon commander ordered "fix bayonets", then yelling wildly we ran towards it while the commander shouted "go get 'em, men". To the relief of everyone there were no Japs there".

Throughout the morning the Japanese were subjected to heavy shelling and by mid afternoon had been compressed into an area 1,000 yards deep and running along the beach for about 1,000 yards. In the afternoon the Marines sent four light tanks across the river mouth, scattering the Japanese hidden in the undergrowth. Correspondent Tregaskis watched from the west bank. "It was fascinating to watch the tanks pivoting, turning and spitting tongues of yellow flame, or to see them knocking down palm trees from which snipers fell. Groups of fleeing Japanese, flushed from the undergrowth seemed to rise from beneath the tank treads before being cut down by the tanks' machine guns". Tregaskis was about 150 yards from the river bank and in the undergrowth itself many Japanese were wounded and unable to get out of the way quickly enough, and were crushed under the treads of the tanks.

The Japanese fought back with grenades, as Tregaskis also remembers "The explosions of the grenades were throwing fountains of black earth and showers of dirt near the tanks. I hadn't realized so many Japs were hidden in the grove; group after group were flushed out and shot down. Suddenly I saw a bright orange flash amidst a cloud of black smoke - bursting under the treads of one tank. It stopped, crippled, but its machine gun kept firing".

Most of the American casualties occurred when Marines followed the tanks. Japanese wounded pretended to be dead until a Marine passed by, then they would suddenly run at him from behind with a bayonet or throw a grenade at him.

Private Robert Corwin's group pushing up the east bank of the river arrived when most of the action was over and a few prisoners had been taken. "They were sitting in a circle; some were half dressed; some of them smiled a little but most them didn't" he recalls. "When we got near the beach there were dozens of dead Japs all over the place. A few hundred yards off-shore some of the Japs were swimming out to sea and Marines on the beach were firing at them".

Later in the afternoon Rifleman Gilbert Dolloff also crossed over to the east bank - "there was already a putrid smell of death in the air" he remembers. "I could hardly believe so many could be killed in such a small area, it seemed suicidal. The artillery, mortar and 37mm. cannister had simply blasted many of them apart". Before nightfall more than 800 dead were counted. Fifteen prisoners had been taken and about 30 of the Japanese managed to escape through the jungle or by sea. Among these were 1st Lieutenant Sakakibara and Private Tadashi Suzuki. They got into the sea and stayed there with their noses just above water level until nightfall when they crept quietly along the beach to a small company Ichiki had left at Taivu Point.

The final defeat of the Ichiki force was helped by the arrival of the first planes at the recently completed airstrip, which was named Henderson airfield. On the afternoon of the 20th, 19 fighters and 22 dive bombers arrived as Marines jumped out of their foxholes and dugouts to cheer and wave wildly. Some of these fighters were in action the next day - machine-gunning the shattered Ichiki survivors fleeing to the east. More planes flew into Henderson on the 22nd and by the end of August there were 64 planes operating from the airfield.

The Marines supply position was also improved when three destroyer transports brought in rations, ammunition and fuel supplies on the 15th and again on the 20th. It was not enough, however, and for days the Marines were restricted to two meals a day and a quart of water. Corporal Breijak in his diary for the 19th wrote, "We have enough food for two days but the Japanese stores left behind would last another five days. Tonight for supper I had rice and Japanese fish-heads - never tasted anything so lousy in my life".

The impure water taken from the rivers soon led to an outbreak of dysentery which swept rapidly through the perimeter. Men forced to visit the latrines 20 or 30 times a day became so weak they had to be helped to get their pants down. Malaria was also beginning to spread and those unable to wash or change their clothes became afflicted by painful, itchy fungus infections particularly between the legs. Cuts and scratches rapidly became infected and the ever present humid heat sapped men's energy.

THE RIDGE SHOULD BE A GOOD REST AREA

The remaining men of Ichiki's regiment were on their way to Guadalcanal in the transport *Kinryu Maru* and on four converted destroyers. This group was escorted by Admiral Tanaka himself in the cruiser *Jintsu* with seven destroyers. As an additional screen, and to lure the American carriers into battle, Admiral Yamamoto, Chief of the Imperial Navy, had dispatched a force of three carriers with a screen of cruisers and destroyers. On the 24th and 25th August this force clashed with Fletcher's carrier support group in an area 200 miles northeast of Guadalcanal in what became known as the Battle of the Eastern Solomons.

At the approach of American planes, Tanaka was ordered to take his transports back towards the north but four hours later this order was cancelled and he resumed his course for Guadalcanal. On the morning of the 25th his ships were caught by bombers from Henderson. The cruiser *Jintsu* was hit squarely between her two forward turrets and the blast wrecked the bridge throwing Tanaka to the deck where he lay unconscious for a short time. When he recovered he found the *Kinryu Maru* had also been hit and was burning fiercely. He ordered the destroyers alongside the transport to take off the troops but as this operation started, a flight of B-17 bombers appeared overhead and dropped a pattern of bombs. One of the destroyers alongside the transport was hit and sunk. Shortly afterwards hundreds of men leapt into the sea as the *Kinryu Maru* also heeled over and sank. The remaining destroyers picked up the burned, wounded and soaked survivors from the water then turned north towards a base in the Shortland Islands 250 miles northwest of Guadalcanal.

Tanaka was disgusted with the way the whole

1943—Ensign John F. Kennedy, USNR, and his P-T Boat 109 crew, in lower Solomon Islands.

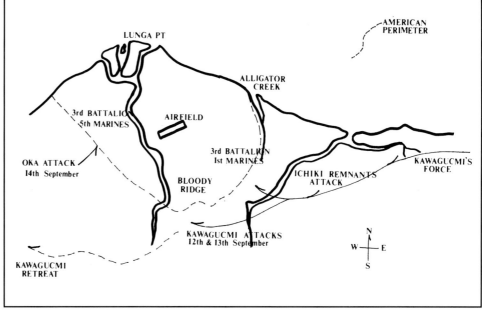

Troop movements during September 12-14.

Kawaguchi's staff in a jungle clearing, planning the attack against Henderson Field.

operation had been planned and executed. He told Mikawa "The operation gave no evidence of careful, deliberate study; everything seemed to be so completely haphazard". Although Mikawa was commander of the 8th Fleet within whose area Tanaka had been operating, Mikawa himself was subordinate to the overall Area Commander Admiral Tsukahara. They operated from different bases, interpreted intelligence differently and gave conflicting orders to Tanaka, who often wondered if they knew what they were doing. Tanaka also told Mikawa that land operations on Guadalcanal would have to be planned a lot better. "I knew Ichiki was a magnificent leader but his defeat showed that infantrymen armed with bayonets and rifles have no chance against an enemy equipped with modern heavy weapons." It seems more likely, however, that Ichiki was the victim of his own over-confidence. As an experienced field commander he must have known what machine guns and cannister fire would do to a massed infantry attack. He had failed to reconnoiter the American defenses or correctly determine the size of the force he was attacking. For Colonel Ichiki's rashness, 800 men had been slaughtered.

After his talks with Tanaka, Admiral Mikawa sent a report to Tokyo. He argued that "Large naval units should be sent to the Solomons" and went on to say "We have been underestimating the enemy and over estimating ourselves. Enemy resistance on the island has been extremely stubborn and unless future operations are carried out with careful and deliberate planning based on accurate information, our probability of success is slight". In reply Tokyo instructed Hyakutake to suspend all operations in New Guinea and make the recapture of Guadalcanal his first priority.

At Henderson the recently arrived aircrew and ground staff were operating under primitive conditions. Damaged planes were kept operational by stripping bits and pieces from wrecked planes. Fueling of the planes had to be done by hand pumps from 40-gallon drums. There were no machines to belt the ammunition for anti-aircraft guns and no spare tires, wheels or propellers. When it rained the airstrip became a mud bath and when it dried out clouds of choking dust filled the air at each take off and landing. Pilots spent the night in foxholes losing sleep as the Japanese began to bomb the airfield day and night. The pilots were constantly tired out; many of them became ill with dysentery and all of them complained of gas pains when flying on a substandard diet of hash, beans and rice.

At the end of August a detachment of Seabees (Construction Battalion) - 392 officers and men arrived to take over maintenance of the airstrip. In command of them was J.P. Blunden who recalls the difficulties they had to work under. "We found a hundred Seabees could repair the damage caused by a 500 lb. bomb in 40 minutes. We had to work that fast because at one time after a Jap raid there were 13 craters in the airstrip and our planes circled overhead for an hour while we filled them in".

At Rabaul Hyakutake ordered Major General Kiyotake Kawaguchi to Guadalcanal with a force of 6,000 men, which included the remainder of Ichiki's force then in the Shortlands, the 128th Infantry Regiment under Colonel Oka and a battalion of the 4th Infantry Regiment supported by artillery, engineers and anti-tank gunners. The advance force of 3,500 men arrived off Guadalcanal on the afternoon of August 28th on six destroyers which were attacked by planes from Henderson. One of the ships blew up and sank and two others were damaged as they turned back towards the Shortlands. Tanaka recognized that the American command of the air made further daylight landings impossible so the destroyers returned the next night and landed 1,000 men at Tasimboko near Taivu Point.

Kawaguchi arrived at the Shortlands on August 29th and immediately disapproved of the use of destroyers to ferry his troops to Guadalcanal. He argued with Tanaka that the destroyers could not carry heavy equipment and that barges should, therefore, be used. "If Ichiki had taken heavy equipment, he might have succeeded" he added. Tanaka was not convinced and felt sure American planes would destroy any barge traffic. Unable to agree the two commanders put off any further argument until the next day.

When the talks resumed Tanaka finally persuaded Kawaguchi to use the destroyers, but Colonel Oka remained unconvinced. Kawaguchi agreed to let Oka use barges and land his 1,100 man force at Kakombona, ten miles west of Henderson field, while Kawaguchi's 2,400 man force would land at Tasimboko, east of the airfield.

Before they parted, Kawaguchi proposed a toast - "Gentlemen, I think our faith is our strength. I swear to all of you, we will smash the enemy. On to Guadalcanal! "

"To Guadalcanal!" the assembled officers shouted.

Among the group was the correspondent Gen. Nishino. A small frail man, yet an accomplished war reporter with three years' experience following the Army in China. Later Nishino joined Kawaguchi in his small cabin on the destroyer *Umikaze*. He found the General was not as confident as he had seemed to be earlier.

"The Americans are well dug in" he told the correspondent. "They have endless supplies and it seems an extremely difficult task for a small unit like ours to retake the airfield. Wouldn't you think the destruction of the Ichiki detachment would be a lesson to us?" he asked. "Headquarters belittles the enemy on Guadalcanal" he went on without waiting for a reply. "They declare that once we land successfully the Marines will surrender". He stopped suddenly, alarmed at what he was saying, then added hurriedly - "This is not a problem for us to discuss here".

A few hours later the *Umikaze* and seven other destroyers, with soldiers crowding their decks slipped out of Faisi Harbor, in a high-speed dash to Guadalcanal. When night fell Nishino stood out on deck watching the sparkling phosphorescence of the ships' wakes. "An endless display of fireworks" he thought.

Just before midnight the destroyers edged slowly in towards the coast at Taivu Point. Nishino half expected the landing boats to be met by American fire, but the only sound was the soft splashing of the troops as they waded ashore. As they ran up the beach a few darkened figures cautiously emerged from the jungle. They were the half starved remnants of Ichiki's rear guard. "Don't leave your footprints in the sand" they urged. "We are always being attacked by American planes". They began to sweep the beach with palm leaves as Kawaguchi's men disappeared into the dark jungle.

Between August 29th and September 2nd these destroyer runs, which became known as the "Tokyo Express", landed all of Kawaguchi's men and considerable quantities of ammunition and supplies at Tasimboko and at Tassafaronga, a small village five miles west of the Matanikau, where the original troops on Guadalcanal had, by then, established their headquarters.

On the night of September 4th, three Japanese destroyers running supplies to Tasimboko also shelled American positions near the airfield. Shore batteries returned fire and a Catalina plane flying overhead dropped flares to illuminate the destroyers. To the surprise of the Japanese the flares showed two American destroyer transports off Lunga Point. These ships were the *Little* and the *Gregory*. Both were old destroyers which had been stripped of most of their guns in order to carry troops and supplies.

The Japanese ships immediately turned their fire on the two ships both of which returned fire from their inadequate armament. On the *Little* Chief Boatswain's Mate Ralph Andree remembers "We got three or four rounds off then the Japanese shot through us like paper. They couldn't have been more than 2,000 yards away. Their first shot hit a fuel tank and set us on fire then they kept shooting until we were on fire over the whole ship." On the bridge Lieutenant Commander Lofberg tried to run the ship aground but a shell hit, in the steering gear, jammed the rudder. He ordered "abandon ship" just before he and everyone else were killed when a shell hit the bridge.

On *Gregory* the situation was soon just as bad. Lieutenant Heine recalls "Our 4" put out one of the Jap searchlights but we received a number of hits on the bridge. When I got up there only one man was still alive. I went to the boat stations and lowered No. 2 and No. 3 boats into the water then collected about 20 men and launched a life raft. The Japanese ships moved in closer and directed machine gun fire among the crew. I told the men to jump overboard and get to the life raft. As we got into the water the Japs swept past only 100 yards away, still shelling and machine gunning."

Men struggling in the water were killed by the shellfire and in some cases sucked under by the propellers of the Japanese ships as they closed in. Lieutenant Kelet, engineering officer on the *Little*, remembers one of the Japanese ships passed within 30 yards of him. After the burning ships sunk the survivors clung to damaged lifeboats and life rafts until rescued the next morning. Thirty-three men were lost with the two ships.

The next morning planes from Henderson flew over Skylark Channel looking for survivors but also found 48 of Colonel Oka's barges only 20 miles north of Guadalcanal. Oka had planned on reaching the island before dawn but had been held up by heavy seas. A destroyer escort had left the barges at sunrise and the helpless little craft, only 47 feet long and with a maximum speed of seven knots were then subjected to repeated bombing and machine gunning.

For the troops crowded in the open well deck of each barge, there was no protection. Only a simple steel shield protected the helmsman. The barges scattered. Some headed towards Savo; others towards Cape Esperance but under the constant air attack many of them sunk and on others the troops were slaughtered by machine gun fire.

By noon some 300 men, among them the shattered Colonel Oka, managed to get ashore at Cape Esperance. Another 300 landed on Savo and crossed over to the Cape after nightfall but almost 500 had died at sea during that murderous morning.

It took Oka's men several days to recover and march the 30 miles from Cape Esperance to the Matanikau. They arrived with little food or ammunition and an effective fighting force of about 450 men. It was only half of what Kawaguchi was counting on to support his attack against Henderson airfield.

Kawaguchi's plan called for Oka to cross the Matanikau and attack towards Lunga while Kawaguchi himself would lead his men to an area south of Henderson before attacking towards the airfield.

On September 2nd Kawaguchi's force began cutting a path inland through the thick jungle towards the distant hills. Unwilling to break radio silence to contact Oka he sent a 4-man patrol, under Lieutenant Nakayama, ahead of the main force with orders to circle round towards the Matanikau, contact Oka and give him details of the Kawaguchi plan. Kawaguchi left considerable supplies at Tasimboko with a 300 man-guard force.

Meanwhile Martin Clemens' scouts had reported the Japanese build up at Tasimboko and Vandegrift called over Colonel Edson's 1st Raiders from Tulagi to attack the Japanese camp. Dick Horton was still acting as a guide with the Raiders and remembers the attack on the camp on 8th September. "The engines of our Higgins boats produced a loud roar in the stillness of the pre-dawn darkness as we approached the beach" he recalls. "Every Jap for miles around must have been alerted, and we all cowerd down in the boat expecting to be shelled at any moment, but nothing happened. We beached, then rushed up the shore without any opposition. I couldn't understand it because we soon found some 47 mm. cannon in the jungle which could have made mincemeat of us."

At the time of the landing two transports with destroyer escort passed by heading towards Lunga. The Japanese mistook these for ships supporting the Raiders' landings. They sent a hurried message to Rabaul reporting a large American landing at Tasimboko then fled into the jungle. Horton continues "We began to move along a path going inland whilst other companies moved along the beach, with no sign of the Japanese, until suddenly there was the hot blast of an explosion nearby, a rushing, searing

wind, and I dived for cover. The Japanese were firing on us from almost point blank range. A shell landed close behind me and the explosion sucked the air out from my lungs. As I panted to get my breath back, 3 high-pitched mosquito-like whines passed over my head. Japanese snipers in the trees were getting our range. I crouched low and then ran back along the path we had taken."

It was a brief rearguard action as most of the Japanese disappeared but it held up the Raiders for two hours and was not overcome until the 1st Parachute Battalion was also sent from Lunga to help. By the afternoon the Japanese resistance was overcome - many escaped but left 27 dead. They also left large amounts of food and ammunition, several of the 47mm field guns and some radio equipment. From signs around the camp, Colonel Edson of 1st Raiders, suspected about 4,000 Japanese had been in the area. Later the Raiders returned by boat to Lunga after destroying most of the supplies.

Unaware of the attack on his base, Kawaguchi was still leading his force through the jungle. With them was Gen. Nishino, the newspaper correspondent. Small, even by Japanese standards, he found it hard to keep up with the troops. Because of the fear of American planes they moved only by night and Nishino remembers, "The jungle seemed to get thicker all the time; we had to cross numerous rugged ridges then scramble down deep ravines to cross shallow swamps thick with rotting vegetation. I found myself constantly tripping over tangled roots and creepers in the dark. Sometimes it took hours to cover only a few hundred yards".

Many of the men had malaria, others had dysentery and they were constantly attacked by myriads of mosquitoes with bites as sharp as needles. By day they could not light any fires because the smoke may be seen by the American planes, so the men subsisted on dried fish, crackers and candy. Ahead of them the Nakayama patrol sent earlier by Kawaguchi, had pushed on to find Oka. Time and time again they became lost beneath the dark umbrella of the rain forest. They ran out of food and became exhausted by the constant scrambling up and down one ridge after another.

Once they were attacked by three or four vicious dogs belonging to a Solomon Islander. On another occasion they met a small group of starved Japanese sailors who had been driven into the jungle the day the Americans landed. They told the patrol they had eaten nothing since then except berries and now everyday at least one of them died from disease

or malnutrition. The four men, unable to help them, struggled on for two more days before they reached the Matanikau river on the 13th September, the day planned for Kawaguchi's assault. It was afternoon before the exhausted Nakayama found Oka and passed on Kawaguchi's orders, only six hours before the time for the co-ordinated attack.

The last message that Kawaguchi's rearguard sent to Rabaul, before they abandoned Tasimboko, caused considerable alarm to Hyakutake. His staff had already revised their estimate of American strength at Henderson to 5,000 men and they now believed a large force had landed at Tasimboko and that Kawaguchi would be trapped between there and Lunga. Hyakutake immediately alerted two more divisions for service on Guadalcanal - the 2nd Division and the 38th Division. The 2nd Division was still being assembled under 17th Army Command after its transfer from the Philippines and Hyakutake was only able to send the division's 4th Infantry Regiment immediately. He ordered fast destroyers to land the Regiment on Guadalcanal on the 18th September. As an immediate measure planes were sent to bomb the Americans he believed were at Tasimboko. The only damage done by these planes was to the Japanese who had returned to Tasimboko after Edson's Raiders had left.

On the 10th Kawaguchi's force reached the Tenaru River and several hundred men from the original Ichiki force were detached, with light artillery, to cause a diversionary attack towards the airfield, when Kawaguchi made his main attack.

After two more days cutting their way through the jungle the main force reached their assembly area two miles south of Henderson airfield. Kawaguchi had planned to attack that night but as most of his force was still strung out along the jungle trail he postponed the attack until the next day and only sent probing patrols towards the Americans positions on the night of the 12th. They reported that a large ridge obstructed a direct attack against the airfield. Kawaguchi decided it was too late to look for another area to attack; the ridge would have to be occupied first.

After Edson's Raiders returned from their attack on Tasimboko and reported a large Japanese force in the area, Vandegrift prepared for an attack against his seven mile perimeter. He placed the 1st Marines to the east near Alligator Creek, and the 5th Marines to the west at Kukum village. In the center he had only engineers and pioneers to place west of the Lunga, while east of the river he sent Edson's

Solomon Island scouts lead a Marine patrol near Henderson Airfield.

Marine ingenuity—Floyd E. Bowen, M.M., 2/C, with his ice cream freezer. It made 60 gallons when fully loaded. It was the envy of the island. (Courtesy of Edward Faber)

The still. (Courtesy of Seibert)

Raiders and the 1st Parachute Battalion to occupy a ridge one mile south of the airfield and overlooking it. Vandegrift told Edson the ridge would serve as a suitable rest area for his men after their raid on Tasimboko; it was a quiet area and well away from the daily bombing that Henderson airfield was receiving.

Edson's men moved on to the ridge in the afternoon of the 12th. It was 1,000 yards long with steep sides overlooking the jungle on three sides. At the southern end the Raiders and Paratroopers began to dig defensive positions and that evening several small attacks were made against them by Kawaguchi's patrols. Edson realized that the ridge could become the main area of the Japanese attack and that the skirmishes were possibly only the prelude to a major attack. During the 13th he ordered his men to improve their defensive positions and he got artillery batteries between the ridge and the airfield to zero in on the southern approaches to the ridge. By evening on the 13th Edson thought he was ready to receive a major attack.

Kawaguchi also thought he was ready. In a rain soaked jungle clearing he gave his officers a final briefing. "We will take the enemy by surprise," he

told them, his thick mustache dripping water . "As you know, gentlemen, the Americans have been strongly reinforced with men and supplies. Perhaps they are stronger than we are, and our troops must overcome difficult terrain before we even reach the enemy lines. We face an unprecedented battle so you and I cannot hope to see each other after the battle. This is the time to dedicate our lives to the Emperor". He took out a small bottle of whisky and added "Shall we drink to success?" He poured a little into each officers' canteen cup. "You, too", he smiled at the correspondent Nishino.

As the officers dispersed to their units Kawaguchi took Nishino over to the maps and showed him the American positions on it. Kawaguchi seemed depressed. "No matter what the War College says", he said quietly to Nishino, "it is extremely difficult to take an enemy position by night assault. If we succeed here it will be a wonder in the military history of the world".

As Kawaguchi's force of over 2,000 men assembled near the ridge, Colonel Oka broke radio silence to report that Nakayama had reached him and that he was now moving forward to attack the 5th Marines at Kukum.

At the ridge the night was so dark men could hardly be seen a few yards away and Kawaguchi's officers marked large white crosses on their backs for their soldiers to follow. One officer even sprinkled a bottle of perfume, intended for his wife, over himself then told his men to follow their noses. As the men approached the ridge one of them stumbled over a small black object. It was a listening device - one of many set by Raiders.

At 2100 Ichiki's men to the east of Alligator Creek opened artillery fire against the 1st Marines and simultaneously a rain of Japanese mortars fell on the ridge. Then, as red flares rose from the jungle, 2,000 of Kawaguchi's men surged towards the ridge with shouts of "tutsugeki" (charge). They were met by intense machine gun fire from the Raiders and Paratroopers, but in the glare and flash of exploding grenades the Japanese charged forward over their own dead. Within minutes they reached the Paratroopers' lines and forced them back in savage, hand to hand fighting. A Paratroop company commander ordered smoke pots to cover their withdrawal and as the smoke was lit up by exploding mortars someone shouted "gas attack". Confusion arose on all sides. Some paratroopers jumped out of their foxholes and withdrew along the ridge. Their commander, Captain Torgerson was furious, and charged everywhere cursing and rallying his men. Slowly they moved back again just in time to meet another wave of screaming Japanese.

Captain Richard Johnson, commanding C Company of the paratroops, remembers that the confusion over the fall back of the paratroopers B Company probably arose because they became disorientated by the smoke. "I recall they moved back along the ridge towards my position at one time but seemed to recover and then went back. We were busy anyway, as the fight was in full swing by then, but we were firing at sounds more than visible targets. A little later we were ordered to move along the east side of the ridge as the Japs were working their way round us. When we started to move we suddenly ran into a large group of Japs. A grenade exploded so near I was momentarily blinded by the flash then I saw one of my platoon leaders, Roy Smith, go down. I ran over towards him and found he was not hurt but stunned. As I bent over him another group of Japs came up the hill towards us. I raised the Johnson automatic I was carrying but in the excitement of trying to get the Japs, I found I had not released the safety. It was like a bad dream as I hastily released it and fired towards them. Some went down; the rest scattered, but I then found others had infiltrated behind us and were actually between us and the battalion aid station. We climbed up to the top of the ridge and some desperate hand to hand combat took place. One of my men was bayoneted seven times, yet he survived. The Japs just kept coming and didn't make their last charge until dawn".

On the west side of the ridge the Marines had also moved hastily back along the ridge, to regroup. Edson got on the phone to the artillery commander, Price, asking him to lower the range and shell the southern end of the ridge, which was now swarming with Japanese. Price brought the shellfire down to within 200 yards of the Marines' positions each time the red flares warned of another Japanese attack. In blind rushes through the shellfire and despite a barrage of grenades, mortar and machine gun fire, the Japanese attacked again and again.

The correspondent Nishino remembers the end of the ridge erupted continually in the glare of exploding shells and the night was made hideous by the storm of firing above the screams and shouts of the attackers. Gradually successive attacks became less fierce and before dawn they were reduced to small suicidal groups. Daybreak showed the sides of the ridge cratered with shell holes and littered with over 600 dead Japanese, while the Marines had lost

143 dead and wounded. Thereafter the ridge became known as Bloody Ridge.

The attack by Ichiki's men against the 1st Marines was sent across a flat, open area of grassland where the Marines had burned the grass and hung empty tins, with stones in them, on wire in front of their machine gun posts. After the initial artillery fire Ichiki's men charged across the open field to be met by machine gun fire. The attack was made by about 500 men, many of whom were cut down within minutes. The survivors took cover and kept up a spasmodic fire on the Marine positions for the rest of the night. Corporal Breijak remembers "we put up a lot of flares that night to show us where the Japanese were. At one time I had just lined up a Jap with my rifle but the flare went out before I could fire. Later another flare set fire to the grass on the other side of our wire. In the light from the burning grass I could see dozens of Japs running back from the wire into the jungle. By that time I was on a machine gun and sent arcs of red tracer through the flames after them. The firing kept up until about 5:30 in the morning".

After daybreak the 1st Marines sent six tanks across the field to clean out the Japanese positions. They were met by accurate anti-tank fire which knocked out three of the tanks. A fourth rolled down a bank and the other two then withdrew. Breijak's battalion later gave covering fire to the 2nd Battalion which was then sent across Alligator Creek to patrol. "It seemed to be a very dangerous thing to do" Breijak recalls, "but they came back, and told us the Japs seemed to have gone back into the hills and all they had found were numerous dead Japs and abandoned mortars and machine guns, most of which were damaged". In fact, the remnants of Ichiki's men made their way back in scattered groups to Kawaguchi's camp at Tasimboko, leaving nearly 200 dead scattered in the jungle, along the river banks and in the fire scorched grass.

Colonel Oka's attack from the west towards Kukum in support of Kawaguchi was delayed by the difficulty the Colonel's men found in crossing the ridges to their jump off position. It was not until the afternoon of the 14th that they finally launched their attack with 1,100 men against the 5th Marines a mile west of Lunga. Here again the Marines were in well-prepared defensive positions backed up by artillery which broke up each successive attack by Oka's men. Against the heavy machine gun and rifle fire, Oka could make no progress, and when he fell back to re-group, the shellfire broke up his formations.

Three miles to the south of Oka's position, Kawaguchi heard the intensity of the artillery fire die down towards evening and there seemed to be no answering fire from Oka's troops. Sadly he realized Oka had failed and would be no further help. Another attack on Bloody Ridge seemed suicidal but he decided success may still be grasped from defeat. His men had, after all, succeeded in pushing the Americans back to within half a mile of the airfield the night before. With great difficulty he managed to gather together 800 men who had been scattered in the jungle by the constant machine gunning from American planes during the day. After darkness he led them back towards the ridge but directed the attack slightly to the east of the ridge through a fold which led directly to the airfield.

In the darkness of the night again the red flares rose from the jungle, but once more Price's artillery loosed a barrage of shellfire among the charging troops. It was even worse than the night before. Lit by the green light of flares and the orange shell bursts among them, the ghostly looking mass of men surged forward against a hail of fire cutting through them like a scythe. Correspondent Nishino again followed the men forward. "The artillery fire seemed to be a never ending earthquake", he recalls. "Trees toppled over and red hot shrapnel whistled through the air". Eventually the shelling forced the Japanese to take cover in small groups; some managed to set up machine guns, but all remained pinned down for the rest of the night.

At daybreak the machine gun posts were wiped out one by one by mortar fire, but dozens of men lay concealed among the shell craters and smashed trees at the approaches to the ridge. In one group Nishino lay and looked out on a devastated wasteland that had been jungle. Once a mortar shell, exploding nearby, lifted him into the air. As he clung to the ground he began to shiver with malarial fever even though the hot sun was high in the sky. When the bout of fever passed he felt drowsy and thought perhaps he was dying. His thoughts drifted back to his family, friends and his editor who had told him to be careful not to get killed on Guadalcanal. When the sun began to set he revived a little and raised his head slowly to look around. There, only half a mile away, he saw the busy airstrip. So near, he thought, and yet ... When darkness had covered the ridge again he crawled slowly back across the charred landscape towards Kawaguchi's camp - a mile south of Bloody Ridge.

Beneath the jungle canopy Kawaguchi viewed the shattered remains of his brigade. More than half his men were dead on the slopes of Bloody Ridge or now, badly wounded, lay in the jungle with no medical attention available to them. Kawaguchi, like Ichiki before him, had found the futility of fanatical "banzai" charges against massed firepower.

Unsure how many American troops had landed at his Tasimboko base and not even aware that they had left the base, Kawaguchi decided to make his way through the jungle towards the Matanikau River to join up with Colonel Oka. He faced a formidable task. There were 400 wounded to carry and stretchers had to be constructed for these. To save time, stretchers large enough to carry four men were made. Supplies were also very short. A lot had been left at Tasimboko and Kawaguchi had planned to be using American rations after capturing Henderson airfield. Fortunately water was not a problem as his planned route closely paralleled the upper reaches of the Lunga River. After a day of preparations, the able, the sick, and the walking wounded began their painful journey through the jungle carrying the burden of their wounded. It is uncertain how many started down the narrow trail - what is certain is hundreds did not live to see the end of it.

AN ENDLESS JUNGLE PATH

With radio communications difficult in the jungle covered ridges and valleys, Kawaguchi was unable to keep Rabaul informed. On the 14th Hyakutake sent four transport planes to Henderson expecting the airfield to be in Japanese hands. The planes came back riddled with bullets. Plainly the airfield had not been captured, and the airforce 25th Flotilla on New Britain was ordered to increase their attacks on Henderson.

"Line 'em up and squeeze them off." Lt. Col. Pollock's orders to his men at the Tenaru. Note the 03 rifle.

The raids became a regular event, the first arriving every day at about noon with advance warning from Mason and other coastwatchers which allowed the fighters to meet the bombers high over Guadalcanal. Correspondent Tregaskis remembers one such raid - "A large squadron of Mitsubishi 96 bombers moved in slender white threads across the blue sky towards Lunga Point. The planes were set against an almost cloudless sky and had a long course of blue to cover before they reached the bombing zone. This gave the anti-aircraft guns an unusually good opportunity. At first the puffs of ack ack smoke were too high and ahead of the Japanese planes, then they came within range and the flashes of shellbursts came in front of the slowly moving planes. Then one bomber on the left side of the squadron was hit. I saw the orange flash of an explosion under his wing, below the starboard motor, which began to trail a stream of white smoke as the plane pulled out of the squadron and began to lose height. Just as it did so another shell burst right underneath the belly of another plane in the formation. A tongue of yellow flame spread across the middle of the plane, followed by a cloud of black smoke. In an instant the plane began nosing straight down towards the ground. Then one of its' wings was torn off, as if it was made of paper, and fluttered down after the more swiftly falling fuselage, which then suddenly began to fall apart - chunks of metal fluttering and falling away in all directions."

One of the other damaged planes came down in the lagoon near Visale Mission. Although the missionaries lived in a village inland, they visited the mission at regular intervals. After the plane ditched, the pilot got out and waded ashore. He was bleeding badly from a cut in the head and was taken to the Mission by a group of Solomon Islanders. Sister Marie Therese and another nun were at the Mission that day and because the pilot was bleeding profusely they cleaned and dressed the wound. The Solomon Islanders then took the pilot to the nearby base at Sapuro, while the nuns returned to the village.

When the pilot reached Sapuro the Solomon Islanders with him were arrested and questioned about the whereabouts of the missionaries and when no one would tell them, the Japanese threatened to shoot one of the Islanders, Peter Keko, an 18 year old youth. Keko then promised to take the Japanese to the village and he led a small patrol off through the jungle. Keko told the other islanders he would try and lose the patrol in the jungle then escape. After Keko led the patrol in aimless wandering for two hours the Japanese N.C.O. in charge of the patrol became suspicious and began shouting insults and threats at Keko. A scuffle then developed and Keko ran off through the long grass. He had only gone a few yards, however, before the N.C.O. shot him through the head.

The shot that killed Keko echoed through the hills and was heard at the village where the missionaries were staying. After briefly discussing the danger of the situation to themselves and the villagers they decided to leave and walk around the coast to another Mission at Tangarare, 35 miles away. When they left that night there were ten missionaries and 20 Solomon Islanders in the group. The Islanders followed the missionaries and when they came to a stretch of sandy beach the Islanders, who were barefooted and had wide open toes, carefully placed their footprints in those of the missionaries to cover their tracks.

In the early hours of the next morning, as they approached a beach, they heard scraping sounds and the voices of a party of Japanese. Approaching quietly they saw a large Japanese submarine just off shore with several small boats landing supplies from it. For two hours they lay hidden in the jungle near the beach until it was safe to move again, and the following day they reached Tangarare Mission, run by a Dutch priest, Father de Klerk.

Other missionaries on Guadalcanal were not so lucky. At Ruavatu Mission near Tasimboko the Japanese had asked two priests, Duhamel and Engebrink to go to the Americans at Lunga and ask them to surrender after the battle of Savo when the Marines had been abandoned. The two men both refused at that time and also later when the Japanese asked again. Eventually Duhamel, who was an American himself, did go to Lunga and shortly after he returned to Ruavatu the Japanese base at Tasimboko was raided. The Japanese believed Duhamel had told the Americans about the base and after the raid, Duhamel, Engebrink and two nuns at the Mission were taken out and bayoneted.

The Japanese not only turned against the missionaries, who had hoped to remain neutral, but also against the Solomon Islanders who they hoped would help them. Even before the American landings the Japanese had alienated the Islanders by desecrating churches, enforcing unpaid labor and stealing the few possessions they had.

After the struggle at Bloody Ridge many of the Japanese, half starved, dug up the villagers' gardens for food and thus endangered the livelihood of the local people themselves. Clashes began to occur between small groups of Japanese soldiers and villagers. The Japanese in some cases shot villagers on sight and soon an increasing number of small villages between the Tenaru and Matanikau River became abandoned as the villagers moved further inland. Among them was Nicholas Visaona who had worked for the Japanese on the Lunga road. In mid September he left his village a mile up-river from the mouth of the Matanikau and walked across the island to where he expected to find some peace and quiet. After four days he reached the mission at Tangarare, adding to the refugees from Visale, and the problems of Father de Klerk.

After the struggle for Bloody Ridge, Vandegrift's men had a quiet period which they used to strengthen their defenses around the perimeter. Splinter proof foxholes were dug. Gun emplacements and machine gun posts were strengthened with log roofs then covered with soil into which fast growing creepers and grasses were placed for natural camouflage. Large areas of grass, beyond the wire perimeter, were burned to give better fields of fire. On the barbed wire, Marines hung tin cans and grenades with the pin partly removed. Large patrols were sent out every day - sometimes up to 200 men in a group. Their faces smeared with dirt and their clothing hung with foliage, they moved slowly and cautiously along narrow jungle trails, exploring every turn and searching the trees overhead for snipers. Despite every care they met frequent ambushes from cleverly concealed Japanese positions often dug in the ground so deeply only a firing slit showed. In other cases the Japanese set up machine guns inside the hollowed out trunks of large trees.

On September 16th, Marine Jack Morrison did not realize his ten man patrol had been ambushed until a burst of fire cut through the group. Morrison fell with a bullet in the shoulder and crawled partly off the track to seek cover in the undergrowth. Several yards ahead of him another Marine had fallen, wounded, and lay groaning by the side of a log. The rest of the patrol seemed to have vanished. After a few minutes of ominous silence Morrison saw a Japanese soldier appear out of the jungle. He was covered in foliage and so well camouflaged, Morrison did not see him until he moved. The Japanese ran down the track, jumped over the log and jabbed downwards with his bayonet at the wounded Marine who lay there. The groaning stopped and the Japanese disappeared into the jungle again.

Morrison pulled himself further into the undergrowth for cover, clenching his teeth to stop himself crying out in pain. Nearby he saw another Marine, who he recognized as Harry Dunn, sprawled out and apparently dead. A heavy silence fell over the area but after several minutes the Japanese soldiers began to emerge from the jungle and move among the dead Marines, stripping them of their personal belongings, while laughing and calling to each other. After they had left, Morrison remembers he passed into a semi-conscious state and felt himself becoming weaker as the blood oozed from his chest wound.

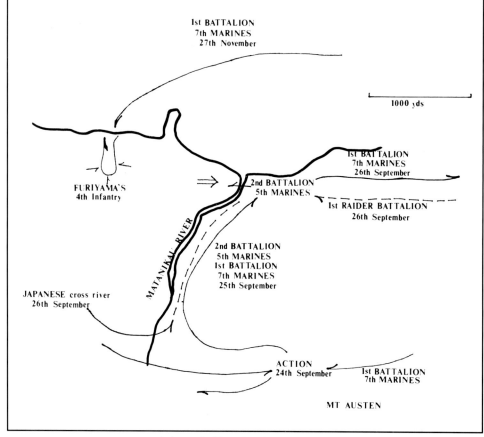

Action at the Matanikau, September 24-27

Even after the Japanese left he dared not make a sound and he felt too ill to move.

When night fell he drifted off to a tired sleep then suddenly awoke in terror as a heavy hand fell across his mouth. "Don't move", a voice whispered, "It's me, Harry Dunn". Dunn pulled Morrison further away from the trail and tried to dress his wound. He then crept among the dead looking for water canteens, but found none. Leaving Morrison he then crawled several hundred yards to a stream to get some water, but before he got there he saw a group of Japanese soldiers sitting on the bank. After he crawled back to Morrison the two spent the rest of the night and all the next day hidden in the undergrowth. As the sun got hotter the increasing stench of the dead brought hundreds of flies around them whilst on the ground were dozens of ants. Morrison weakened throughout the day and at dusk, Dunn left him again to crawl back to the stream. The Japanese had gone and Dunn went back to half drag Morrison to the stream where they drank for the first time in two days.

Throughout the rest of the night Dunn staggered towards the Marine lines, half carrying Morrison. Sometimes he passed out from sheer exhaustion then regained consciousness to crawl on a few hundred yards more while watching and listening for any signs of the Japanese. Just after dawn they finally reached a Marine outpost.

Private Robert Corwin also remembers a similar patrol along the east bank of the Lunga on September 17th. "Charlie Debele and I went," he recalls, "Charlie was a B.A.R. man (Browning automatic rifle) and I was his assistant, though I had never fired one in my life. I remember it was a clear, warm and sunny day like you get on Long Island in July or August. Perhaps half a mile south of our lines our platoon was ordered to cross the Lunga to a small island in the river. Debele was just ahead of me when we stopped at the edge of the river to refill our canteens. I was watching two Marines on the other bank come down towards the water's edge when the stillness was broken by a burst of fire. One of the two Marines just collapsed like a sack of wheat. The other hesitated for a moment, the machine gun spat again and then he went down too. Neither of them made a sound."

Some shouting and rifle shots then broke out and we got orders to comb the island in the river from one end to the other. We were about half way along the island, pushing through the shoulder high grass, when another Marine and I suddenly stumbled on two Japs. One was lying under a blanket and the other was kneeling beside him. Neither of them seemed to have any weapons. I shouted 'stand up, you're under arrest' or something equally as silly, and motioned them with my bayonet to stand up and go to the rear. The one under the blanket didn't move. I figured he was dead, or near it, and we left him. When we got to the east bank of the river again, I could still hear the Jap machine gun firing but by that time we had got a mortar up. It was the first time I'd seen a mortar team in action. There were several swooshes and bangs and I could see smoke and dirt being thrown up where the mortars landed. After a while the machine gun didn't fire anymore".

Corwin continues, "Captain Brush of A Company then said some of his men had been trapped in the jungle by some Japs and a squad was detailed to go and help them. Debele went with them but the rest of us were told to go back to our lines. The rescue squad hadn't been gone long when they came running back, led by a sergeant, his face hot and flushed with fear. He reported they had run into an ambush and some of the squad had been hit, including Debele. Volunteers were asked to go back and help and I went along with them.

There was no sound as we made our way cautiously through the thick green foliage, and after

The Bloody Ridge after the battle. (USMC Photo)

about 15 minutes we came to a small clearing maybe 20 feet in diameter. In the clearing, several Marines lay, apparently dead. I thought one of them was Debele. I called out 'is that you, Charlie?' He lifted his head a little and he looked very pale but managed to say 'yeah'. I walked towards him and said, 'don't worry, we'll get you out of here', then knelt down beside him. Suddenly WHAM, and I was laid out on my back with a bullet in my shoulder. My helmet fell off and I dropped my rifle.

The bullet had gone through my shoulder, near the neck and out below the shoulder blade. Suddenly the war, which had seemed a great adventure before we landed, didn't look that way any more. I managed to turn and look round. There was no sound but I saw Ralph Ingerson, his face half hidden by the foliage, beckoning to me to get up and run out of there. I didn't need to be told twice. I quickly jumped to my feet and had taken maybe three or four steps when a second bullet got me in the leg and I fell down again. There was silence again and this time I didn't dare make any move for a while. When I did look up again I saw Ralph in the same place, but now he was kneeling down with his head on the ground, and softly coughing. The bullet that had got my leg had gone through it and then gone on to get Ralph in the throat. After a while he stopped coughing. Now the silence was total, nothing stirred or made a sound in the heavy, humid air.

I began to think that if I stayed where I was the Japs would be coming along soon to use me for a little bayonet practice. I thought that if I stayed still until it got dark I could perhaps slip away. Then I realized I didn't have the courage to lie still until then since the Japs may be coming along at any time. My right elbow was beginning to give me a lot of pain and I wondered what had happened to it. I found I could not move the fingers on the right hand either. I wriggled my toes and flexed my leg muscles and they seemed to be working. I knew the second bullet had gone through inside my right leg just below the crotch, without touching a bone. I decided to go. I lay motionless for a while longer then scrambled quickly to my feet and took off down the trail so quick a jackrabbit would not have passed me. I shouted, 'B Company, B Company' and after a few minutes I caught up with the last of our group. The corpsman shot me full of morphine and a stretcher was produced. I made the rest of the trip on my back watching the stars coming out as night fell".

These scattered groups of Japanese were the last of Ichiki's men. Many were wounded and left to die alone, or in small groups, deep within the jungle. All of them became starved and wandered aimlessly in search of food at the gardens of the small villages

within a few miles of the coast. Martin Clemen's local police and scouts were constantly employed in tracking down these roving bands. Skilled at moving quickly and quietly through the jungle the scouts could even detect the Japanese by their smell. Constable Saku, one of Clemen's most reliable men, remembers the Japanese had a smell rather like that of dry hay and that they were remarkably careless when foraging for food in the villages.

He recalls, "Once we got a message from the people of Mambulo village that the Japanese were raiding their gardens. There was a group of about 80 of them and we finally found them near a river. They had piled up their arms on a large rock and were busy getting nuts to eat. They had no guards. We cut across the river, took their rifles and hid them, then closed in on them. Without arms they picked up stones to defend themselves and as we did not want to make too much noise we finished them off with axes and spears". American intelligence officers had asked the scouts to bring in Japanese prisoners for questioning. "Sometimes we did" recalls Saku, "but most of the time we spared no one".

Beyond Bloody Ridge Kawaguchi was meanwhile making his way slowly towards the Matanikau. The strongest men were employed in cutting a path through the thick jungle; others carried machine guns, mortars and boxes of ammunition, while with each of the large stretchers, several men struggled along. The path led across swampy valleys and seemingly endless ridges each of which seemed steeper than the last as the heavily loaded men scrambled and slipped, looking for a foothold while dragging along the large bulky stretchers.

By the second day progress was reduced to a painfully slow crawl. Many of the walking wounded collapsed along the side of the trail and were abandoned. The stretcher bearers covered only a mile or two. Nishino found that the whole column became split into groups of about 20 men, with each group setting its own pace. During the day the heat and the humidity and the lack of medical facilities led to gangrene in the wounds of the stretcher cases. By evening when they stopped, they were plagued by flies and the putrid smell of poisoned wounds was so overpowering that the stretcher bearers left the stretchers in a clearing a few hundred yards away from the main group.

The following morning the helpless men on the stretchers presented a ghastly sight and foul stench. Their festering, gangrenous wounds oozed putrid yellow pus on to the stretchers. Those with dysentery had only added to their appalling, filthy condition. Nishino recalls the whole area, around the clearing containing the stretchers, hummed with countless flies. So revolting was the sight that the stretcher bearers abandoned them. Many of the men on the stretchers asked for a knife and with one quick thrust escaped a lingering death. Others, perhaps with more courage, hobbled off along the trail in a pathetic attempt to keep up with the column, but soon collapsed. Kawaguchi's retreat through the jungle was becoming a corridor of death for hundreds of his men.

On the fourth day, food supplies were exhausted. Many of the non-wounded were already weakened by malaria and dysentery and could no longer carry the burden of the heavy weapons. Mortars were left by the trail, then machine guns and next, men threw off all excess weight, boxes of ammunition, packs and helmets. Nishino, wracked with bouts of fever, followed the long column. "Day after day" it seemed to him, "I walked along the endless jungle path, past scores of blood-soaked dead, dying and wounded for whom there was no longer any hope. The trail was littered with abandoned equipment of all kinds. The men had thrown away everything, it seemed, except their rifles. Despite the hardship I knew I had to keep up with the tail of the column at least; if I got left behind I knew there would be little hope for me either".

I MUST WARN THEM IN RABAUL

On September 18th the advance party of the 2nd Division that Hyakutake had ordered to Guadalcanal, landed near Cape Esperance. It was the 4th Infantry Regiment under Colonel Nomasu Nakaguma. The 2nd Division was one of the finest in the Japanese Army and prided themselves on being considered the Emperor's own troops. The division had a distinguished record going back over 70 years. After a day spent in organization at Cape Esperance the 4th Infantry moved off along an old Government trail that hugged the coast and brought the regiment to the Matanikau river on September 22nd. On that day Kawaguchi and his wretched survivors also began to drift into Oka's camp by the Matanikau. Nakaguma was horrified by their appearance. He found it hard to believe that Japanese troops could be reduced to such a deplorable state. Not only were they in shocking physical condition

but their whole attitude to the war was completely defeatist as they spoke of their bitter experiences on Bloody Ridge; the intense American fire and their grueling march through the jungle.

Nakaguma immediately ordered his own men not to mix with those of Kawaguchi and, in fact, felt very relieved when Kawaguchi himself decided to arrange transportation back to Rabaul in order to make a personal report. With his survivors, Kawaguchi took the trail towards Cape Esperance. Nakaguma had assured him that there was food and medical supplies along the trail which the 4th Infantry had established on their march. Unknown to both of them, however, those supplies were rapidly exhausted by the near-starving Marines and laborers who, having fled into the jungle on August 7th, had only emerged again when Nakaguma established the supply posts. After a brief stay at Oka's camp, Kawaguchi's men faced the ordeal of a 35 mile walk to Cape Esperance with little help along the way.

Five miles east of Oka's camp, Vandegrift also received reinforcements in men, stores, weapons and equipment. On September 18th 4,000 men of the 7th Regiment, 1st Marine Division arrived. This unit was the first one sent abroad from Norfolk, Virginia in March with the Division's most experienced men, in the expectation it would see action first. They had garrisoned Samoa since May and were shipped to Guadalcanal in response to Vandegrift's appeal for more troops after Kawaguchi's assault. Sergeant Mitchell Paige who landed with the 7th Marines was glad to join up again with some of his old friends in the other units of the division but he was shocked by their appearance. "They all looked thinner and their hair was long and unkempt. In many cases the expressions on their faces and the way they kept glancing up at the sky told us that our friends had been going through hell" he recalls. The constant glancing to the sky was not without reason as Japanese bombing raids on the airfield had become heavier and more frequent.

At the airfield Martin Clemens remembers they had a primitive air raid warning system. He recalls, "There was a shaky bamboo mast up which they hauled a Japanese flag for 'Condition Yellow' which meant enemy planes in the area. 'Condition Red' meant that enemy planes were overhead, then they ran out, hauled down the Japanese flag and ran up a black flag, if they had time." It seemed a bit confusing because 'Condition Black' was the code for "invasion imminent."

For J.P. Blunden and the Seabees maintenance of the airfield often became almost impossible due to the constant bombing. It became even more nerve wracking when the Japanese began to drop delayed action bombs on the runway. Exhausted pilots, many with malaria, led to a high accident rate. On September 8th alone, eight planes had crashed on take off; one of them hit a bulldozer and exploded in a huge orange fireball. Only two days later, Corporal Breijak from his defensive position at Alligator Creek near the end of the runway, remembers watching as a fighter prepared for take off on the airfield. "As he came down the runway he bounced a couple of times in some holes. I could see he wasn't going fast enough to get off as he approached the end of the strip, but he just kept going and ploughed into the trees. The plane was a wreck and I heard later the pilot was hurt real bad".

By the middle of September only 11 of the 38 planes flown in at the end of August were still serviceable. After a desperate appeal from Ghormley every carrier in the southwest Pacific flew any plane it could be made to spare, direct to Guadalcanal and in three days 60 more planes reached the airfield. Still 'Condition Red' existed almost every day from late morning to nightfall and the Japanese planes added 250 pound "daisy cutter" bombs to their arsenal. These bombs exploded to send jagged metal scraps whipping through the air in all directions. While Ghormley strained to keep up his air force strength, the 25th Air Flotilla on Rabaul was built up even more rapidly. On September 12th it received an additional 140 planes to increase the attacks against Henderson.

After receiving fresh troops, Vandegrift made plans to attack the Japanese on the west bank of the Matanikau. Lieutenant Colonel Chester Puller, in command of the 7th Marines, was ordered to cross the river two miles from its mouth then swing in towards the coast. Two days after Puller's attack the 1st Raiders were to cross the river mouth and move along the coast squeezing the Japanese between them and Puller's Marines.

Puller set off on 24th September but while moving inland, ran into a strong Japanese patrol that had crossed the Matanikau. The 2nd Battalion, 5th Marines, were sent to help. The vicious fire fight that developed on the slopes of Mount Austen lasted until sunset and Puller had to send back two companies of men carrying their wounded over the steep ridges. The next day he pushed on towards the river but the

Marines on Guadalcanal.

Cleaning out Japanese trenches.

The supply line takes to the hills—a Raider battalion hikes over rugged terrain during operations on Guadalcanal. Note native guides. (USMC Photo, No. 51, 728)

timetable was now upset so instead of crossing the Matanikau, Puller moved down river on the east bank. He reached the mouth of the river on the 26th and joined up with Edson's Raiders. An attempt to cross was met by heavy fire from Oka's men in thick jungle on the west bank, and the 7th Marines were flung back with numerous casualties.

The next day they went into reserve and another attempt to cross the river two miles inland was made by Edson's Raiders, while the 2nd Battalion, 5th Marines, attacked across the river mouth. During the night, however, a small Japanese unit had crossed to the east bank and effectively stopped any progress by the Raiders. When the Raiders notified Edson by radio, the message was misunderstood and Edson thought they had crossed the river. He then ordered three companies of 7th Marines to land behind the Japanese lines just west of Point Cruz. These units were led by Major Otho Rogers and they landed without opposition then moved slowly inland through the thick jungle. Suddenly a storm of fire hit them from three sides. They had walked into an ambush by 2,000 men of Nakaguma's 4th Infantry.

Major Rogers was killed almost at once and the Marines fell back towards the beach. Their radio had been left behind and there was no way of calling for help as the Japanese moved in. On the beach some of the Marines pulled off their white tee shirts and arranged them on the ground so as to spell out the word 'help'. This simple message was seen by a plane from Henderson and the word was passed to Puller. He boarded the seaplane tender *Ballard* and directed it to steam to a position off the beach where the Marines were gathering. The *Ballard* then directed heavy fire on the Japanese positions. Higgins' boats were sent in to get the Marines away, but when they went in a second time they were met by heavy fire from Japanese positions on Point Cruz, several of the boat crews were killed or wounded and it was late afternoon before the last of the Marines had been evacuated from the beach.

After this action it seemed to Nakaguma that the Americans were attempting to gain control of the trail that ran along the narrow coastal plain from the Matanikau to Point Cruz. In many places this plain is no more than a quarter of a mile wide before it runs into steep coral ridges rising to 300 feet. Nakaguma centered his defenses in the gullies between the ridges from where he could then pour enfilading fire on to the plain and across the trail.

More Japanese troops were arriving nightly on the Tokyo Express and landing between Cape Esperance and Tassafaronga, a small village half way between the Matanikau and Cape Esperance. The destroyers in the Tokyo Express left the Shortland Islands in mid afternoon with each ship capable of carrying 150 men and their light equipment. By midnight they were off the coast of Guadalcanal and landing the troops using rubber boats and small landing craft. Wounded and sick soldiers were ferried out to the destroyers which then left for the return to the Shortlands in sufficient time to be beyond the range of American aircraft at dawn.

On one of these return trips the destroyers took the Kawaguchi survivors and the correspondent Nishino. Kawaguchi discussed the fighting with Nishino as the two men stood on the beach. "It has been a tragedy for us", Kawaguchi said, "because of the devilish jungle my men were scattered all over the area and completely beyond my command. When I get back to Rabaul I will have to tell Hyakutake that our traditional methods of attack are of no use against the Americans and their fire power". To Nishino the General suddenly seemed to be a pathetic figure, standing in his tattered uniform on the beach. He felt a wave of sorrow and pity for him and reached forward to shake his hand. As he did so the General's hand felt hot and wet. Nishino realized, with a sudden shock, that Kawaguchi had malaria.

WHAT IS THIS GUADALCANAL LIKE?

In Rabaul the news of Kawaguchi's defeat caused a wave of shock. Two attempts to drive the Americans out had failed disastrously and more than 4,000 men had been lost. Hyakutake decided he would go to Guadalcanal himself to direct a new offensive and would take with him the 17th Army's heavy artillery which included huge 150mm howitzers, capable of hurling an 80 pound shell six miles. The 38th Division was scheduled to reach Guadalcanal in mid October and most of the 2nd Division were already in the Shortlands and being ferried to Guadalcanal on the *Tokyo Express*. With these troops, Hyakutake would have a force of almost 30,000 men.

Transporting such a large force with artillery and supplies led to bitter arguments between the Army and Navy. The Navy favored using the Tokyo Express and barges but the Army felt that would be too risky and argued for a large transport group with a powerful Naval escort. The Navy, however, had been suffering heavy losses in the southwest Pacific. Between August 7th and October 7th they lost one carrier, a cruiser, three destroyers, two transports and numerous barges. Tanaka insisted that heavy bombing be used to knock out Henderson airfield before he would escort Hyakutake's transports to the island. The question was eventually passed to Admiral Yamamoto, Naval Commander in Chief, who promised the support of three carriers and two battleships for an intense bombardment of Henderson airfield.

In the Shortlands, Major General Nasu, a Brigade Commander in the 2nd Division, met Nishino on his way to Rabaul. The two were old friends but Nasu did not recognize the correspondent at first. "Nishino", he said, "you look so terribly ill; tell me what is this Guadalcanal like?" Nishino hesitated to reply. After the speedy victories of the first few months of war, few of the Japanese entertained any thoughts of defeat. The survivors of Kawaguchi's force, with their stories of American supremacy, were looked on as defeatists; a disgrace to the samurai fighting spirit: men to be avoided, and, if they talked too much, to be reported. Nishino was, therefore, cautious but eventually he told Nasu about the Americans' firepower; endless supplies, and their fighting spirit. "If we send our forces in piecemeal they will be destroyed," he added. "Our soldiers are being asked to give their lives without proper equipment or supplies". Nasu nodded slowly - "You may be right" he said, "I will soon see what Guadalcanal is like myself".

On Guadalcanal one of Vandegrift's problems was the increasing number of refugees and downed United States airmen who made their way to Tangarare Mission. He felt that as the campaign continued, the Mission was in increasing danger from the Japanese patrols that were moving along the south coast. On September 22nd, Vandegrift's staff sent a message to Father de Klerk at the Mission, advising him that two PBY float planes would arrive on the 28th to evacuate everybody there. The priests and nuns buried all but essential luggage but on the evening of the 28th, the rescue attempt was cancelled. The planes were not available but may be able to try again on the 30th. When that date came only one plane was available but it was agreed it could make two trips. Then, at the last moment, the rescue was cancelled again and no future date was given.

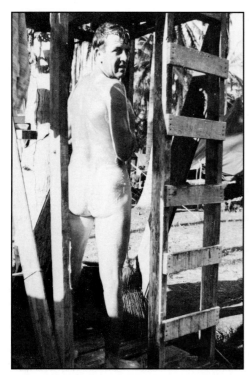

Bob Kennedy takes a shower in the rest area. He served with Co. F, 182d Inf., Americal Division. (Courtesy of William F. Dolan)

Jack Crimlisk, Co. F, 182d Inf. Americal Div., visits the latrine at the Jungle (Perimeter) Line. (Courtesy of William F. Dolan)

At Henderson the coastwatchers' center became more alarmed at the increasing activity near Tangarare and feared the possibility that the murder of the priests and nuns at Ruavatu would be repeated on a larger scale. Plans were quietly made to bring a small ketch, the *Ramada*, over from Malaita and on the night of October 3rd, Dick Horton, without any official permission; boarded the little ship at Lunga anchorage and set off for Tangarare. After steaming along the enemy-held coast for several hours the *Ramada* cleared Cape Esperance, before the nightly *Tokyo Express* arrived, and at dawn the next morning, reached Tangarare. The local inhabitants ran excitedly up and down the beach as the little ship anchored off shore. Within an hour or two the priests, nuns, rescued airmen and about 15 Islanders were on board and Horton began the hazardous return journey in daylight. Among those on board was Bishop Aubin and Sister Marie Therese from Visale, and the Solomon Islander, Nicholas Visaona, who had decided to return to the battle area and go to work for the Americans. Father de Klerk was left at Tangarare and began to build up a group of armed Islanders who drove the Japanese patrols away from the area, killing more than 60 in a month.

On the overcrowded little ketch, Sister Therese remembers the return journey was uneventful. "In the afternoon" she recalls, "we passed Visale Mission on our way back to Lunga. All the mission buildings had been destroyed and there was smoke rising from two or three of the wrecked buildings. For those of us who lived there for so many years it was a desolate sight and I wondered if I would ever see the place again". When the *Ramada* reached Lunga anchorage all the nuns and priests were sent over to a nearby transport ship which left that evening for the New Hebrides. Nicolas Visaona got ashore and within a few days was attached as a guide to American patrols probing the area near his abandoned home on the Matanikau river.

On October 7th, Vandegrift made another attempt to force the Japanese back from the Matanikau river. His plan was similar to that used in fighting between 24th-26th September but this time he was determined to push a stronger force over the river. When the Marines approached jump off positions on the east bank, they found a force of about 150 Japanese had established a camp a few hundred yards

from the mouth of the river on the east bank. They engaged the 1st Raiders in a fierce struggle and after nightfall, in heavy rain, made a desperate attempt to escape. After fierce hand to hand fighting in the darkness the camp was taken while fleeing Japanese, illuminated by flares, were shot as they swam back across the narrow river.

During the 8th there was a continual heavy downpour. The steep sides of the ridges were too slippery for any movement and no action was possible on either side. When the hot sun rapidly dried out the ground on the next morning, 2,000 Marines crossed on a log bridge a mile up river. They then split into groups and moved along three ridges towards the sea, taking Nakaguma's defensive positions from behind. On the western most ridge, Puller's 7th Marines suddenly topped a rise to find hundreds of Nakaguma's men encamped in a ravine between two steep ridges. Puller immediately called for artillery fire from the east bank.

The jungle filled ravine quickly erupted in an inferno of shellbursts, sending thousands of steel fragments into the milling Japanese. Trees were splintered and crashed to the ground; earth, stones and bodies were thrown into the air. When the Japanese scrambled up the sides of the ravine to escape, they were cut down by machine gun fire from the Marines on top of the surrounding ridges. By noon, more than 600 Japanese lay dead in the devastated ravine with hundreds more wounded. Colonel Nakaguma's 4th Infantry regiment was virtually wiped out. The Marines lost 65 men, and twice as many wounded, but the advantage they gained was short-lived.

Vandegrift's intelligence unit had warned him of the approaching transports carrying Hyakutake's main force, so the Marines moved back across the Matanikau to strengthen the perimeter around the airfield.

Vandegrift was also concerned about numerous small landings the Japanese had made east of the perimeter. It seemed likely that the Japanese were planning to build up on both sides of the perimeter and force Vandegrift to fight on two fronts. On October 7th, Martin Clemens was sent to Aola, 30 miles east of the perimeter to make preparations for a Marine landing against the Japanese in that area. Clemens was met by some of his local scouts who

reported the Japanese were at two villages - Gurabasu and Koilotumaru, about six miles west of Aola.

The next day three companies of Marines were sent to Aola from Tulagi; among them was Sergeant James Sorenson. "We were told there were about 200 Japs with artillery near Aola" he recalls. "On the afternoon of the 8th we left Tulagi in Higgins' boats towed by two tugs. Each tug was pulling about eight boats. We got to Aola the next morning but the other tug arrived late. They had met a Japanese destroyer in Sealark Channel during the night and when they maneuvered to avoid it, one of the boats got badly damaged and 30 Marines were thrown into the sea. The tug had spent a long time looking for them in the dark but only managed to pick up 15 of them".

Two companies of the Marines were sent towards Koilotumaru by way of a long trek inland to avoid being seen by the Japanese. The third company, led by Martin Clemens and the commander of the force, Captain Stafford, left Aola at midnight to attack Gurabasu village which was four miles away. Clemens remembers; "It was such a dark night and so difficult keeping contact in the dark that eventually I got all the Marines to put a piece of rotten wood in his belt at the back. The wood was luminous and could be easily seen by the man behind. By 5:30 a.m. we had reached the outskirts of Gurabasu but the mortar men had difficulty getting into position and we did not attack until 8:30 a.m. Our attack was met by very little return fire and we began to close in. Unfortunately Captain Stafford, who was next to me, stood up too soon and received a bullet straight between the eyes. I immediately ran forward and the others followed. There was a brief struggle in the village then the remaining Japs ran off. We had obviously caught them by surprise because some of them were still in bed". Twenty seven Japanese were killed and a large quantity of stores, charts and maps were found as well as a radio. Captain Stafford was the only American casualty.

The two companies sent to attack Koilotumaru were meanwhile making their way through the rugged interior. Sorenson remembers, "We seemed to be climbing one razor back ridge after another and were finally forced to halt at a 40 foot high, sheer cliff wall which took half an hour for the detachment to scale. Next we came to a swamp where the local people had constructed a floating log bridge. The logs were about 10" in diameter and laid end to end. At about every ten feet along the "bridge" a pole had been driven into the swamp and vines had been tied between the poles to serve as a hand rail. It was a very difficult crossing for us, wearing combat boots and carrying machine guns and boxes of ammunition. With the logs bobbing and swaying under foot it took a lot of time to get across". That night the two companies stayed in a local village surrounded by a high woven fence of poles. The next day the march resumed. "It was like a nightmare," Sorenson recalls. "We went down the side of a 60 foot cliff clinging to tough green vines strung from the brush. Another cliff, less steep, was descended by our sliding on our backsides down a muddy trench and only topping when you hit the guy in front. There seemed to be no real trail to follow and as the day wore on, the detachment began to spread out into widely spaced groups as many of the men were unable to keep up. Some of us had malaria and a lot had recently had dysentery. Others walked painfully along with blood sloshing in their boots from stinking jungle rot and open sores that never seemed to heal. Then we came to a river that was chest deep and running between high, slippery banks. This was soon followed by another stream-so fast flowing, it almost took you off your feet. After that we spent the rest of the morning cutting our way through thick, clawing jungle before we came to an endless mangrove swamp. It was knee deep in water and black oozing mud with a horrible tangle of mangrove roots everywhere. When we got through the swamp we hit a good trail directly towards Koilotumaru and moved along it.

After a while two other sergeants, Denley and Burgess stopped and we figured the trail was just made for an ambush so we moved into the jungle for about 25 yards then walked along parallel to the trail. After a while, Burgess, Denley and I went on to the trail again and suddenly saw a single Japanese soldier on the trail; his back towards us, looking out to sea with a pair of binoculars. Burgess whispered he was going to fire at the man. Now Burgess had been in the Marines for years and was a good sergeant but probably the worst rifle shot in the entire Marine Corps. When he took aim, Denley and I stood behind him ready to fire straight ahead if Burgess missed. He fired once and the soldier fell. I guess no-one was more surprised than Burgess, who then ran along the trail and bayoneted the Jap just to be sure. We searched him and found a few maps on him, by which time the Solomon Island scouts who were with us came up, looked at the Jap and started shrieking, jumping around and throwing their arms about excitedly. Apparently the Jap was Ishimoto, a political officer sent to recruit labor for the Japs and was perhaps the most hated of the Japanese soldiers on Guadalcanal.

After that we soon came to Koilotumaru. The village was fenced in by a broken-down stockade. We circled it carefully then moved in. There was no sign of the Japanese and the scouts told us it looked like they had left that morning".

When Vandegrift heard of the results of these actions he ordered a large Marine patrol to continue along the coast from Koilotumaru and make their way towards Lunga, cleaning out any Japanese units or supply depots they found. It meant a three day march through the jungle which many of the Marines, afflicted with malaria, dysentery and jungle rot, were not capable of. Those who were thought incapable of making the march were shipped back to Tulagi and a composite patrol of 70 men from the three companies set off under Lieutenant Lineweber, for Lunga on October 12th.

As they moved slowly west along the trail a few hundred yards inshore from the beach, they began to find numerous small Japanese supply depots, arms, ammunition and a few pieces of artillery all of which were destroyed. Several times they cautiously surrounded villages which the Japanese used but each time the enemy had moved out ahead of them. By the 14th the patrol reached Tasimboko, the site of Kawaguchi's base wrecked by the Raiders earlier. "There was nothing but havoc and destruction" Sorenson recalls. "Shell holes and bomb craters were everywhere; trees were splintered and the under brush shredded from gunfire. Along both sides of the trail were uniforms containing the skeletal remains of long-dead Japanese soldiers: some in groups of three or four, but elsewhere there were groups of 30 or 40 uniformed skeletons. The whole desolate, wrecked area extended for almost half a mile".

It was not until that afternoon that the patrol caught up with the fleeing Japanese. "We were crossing a river which was almost waist deep" Sorenson remembers. "Suddenly a squad of Japanese soldiers appeared on the back about 50 yards away. There was a B.A.R. man with me and he fired off a couple of shots while struggling to keep his footing in the swiftly flowing river. Then his gun jammed. The Japanese also fired a few rounds then turned back into the jungle. Another Marine fired and hit one of them who staggered, fell and clutched at his comrades who dragged him off into the jungle. We hurriedly took up firing positions in a group of weeds by the river's edge while Burgess took a squad to try and circle round the Japs. Just then a flight of our planes went over, flying very low.

The last plane seemed to be having trouble - its motor coughing and spluttering, then it went into a long curving glide and hit the ocean about 100 yards from the beach. A squad raced down to the beach and Corporal Rogal, who was with them, pulled off his boots, dropped his equipment and swam out to the plane. It was taking water and sinking slowly but Rogal managed to reach it and drag out the unconscious pilot then tow him back to shore. When the pilot came to he told us the Japs had landed a large force west of the perimeter and it looked like we were in for a rough time. When Lieutenant Lineweber heard this he had a talk with the non coms and it was decided we should get back to the perimeter as soon as possible. We did a quick march for the rest of the day and reached the perimeter just before dark".

THOSE SHARKS WERE REAL KILLERS

The large Japanese troop landings that the pilot had reported were Hyakutake's main force brought to the island on the night of October 11th. Ghormley's intelligence had reported the approach of this force and he had sent a cruiser force under Rear Admiral Norman Scott to intercept the Japanese ships. Scott had learned a lot from the lessons of the defeat at Savo in August and for three weeks he had drilled his ships in night tactics. As his ships approached Cape Esperance that night the cruisers flew their float planes off with orders to track and report on the enemy ships. He had no wish to repeat the illumination provided by the burning planes on the cruisers that night off Savo. Most of Scott's ships catapulted their planes off safely but on the Salt Lake City a float plane crashed and burned on take off. Fortunately it fell into the sea but in the darkness of the night the burning plane was visible for miles and was, in fact, seen by the approaching Japanese ships, which reported it as "A distant fire on Guadalcanal", shortly before they split into two groups.

The transports carrying Hyakutake's heavy artillery and 700 troops headed towards Sealark Channel, with a destroyer escort, whilst a screen of three cruisers and two destroyers patrolled to the west on a course directly across the path of Scott's approaching ships, which were in line astern of each other. The last cruiser in this line was the Helena which at 2325 detected the Japanese cruiser force on her radar when they were 14 miles away. Unsure of the contact, however, Helena made no report to Scott and at 2330 his ships reversed their course as they patrolled off Cape Esperance. With each ship in line turning as they reached the same position it took several minutes for the line to reverse its course and while this was going on, Captain Hoover on Helena finally decided to report his radar contact of the Japanese ships which were then only six miles away.

The cruiser Boise also reported "five bogies bearing 295 degrees". The phrase "bogies" usually meant "aircraft" but Scott took it to mean ships. He believed the ships may be his own destroyers and checked over the T.B.S. (talk between ships radio). One of the American destroyers was, in fact, leaving the formation. It was the Duncan and she headed towards a radar contact four miles away. Meanwhile, on the Helena, Captain Hoover was getting impatient as the Japanese came to within 5,000 yards. Over T.B.S. he asked Scott for permission to open fire. Scott replied "Roger" in the course of his conversation with the destroyers over the crowded T.B.S. For Hoover it was enough and at 2346 he ordered "open fire". Ahead of him, Salt Lake City fired almost at the same time and threw starshell to

illuminate the confused scene.

The Japanese cruisers were also in line astern with Aoba, Furutaka and Kinugasa - all of which had been in the Savo action. On this occasion they were caught by surprise themselves; unaware of Scott's ships until 6" shells hit Aoba, where Admiral Goto believed he was being fired on by the destroyer escort sent with the transports. He immediately ordered a reversal of course, which actually brought his ships swinging round closer to the Americans, as the other two Japanese cruisers opened fire. Seconds later a shell wrecked the bridge on Aoba and Goto fell mortally wounded. Still believing he was being fired on by his own ships, he muttered "stupid bastards!" a moment before he died.

Scott also believed his cruisers were firing on his own destroyer escort and ordered "cease firing", but the T.B.S. confusion was, by then, so great the order had to be repeated several times for the benefit of ships which were sure they were engaging the enemy. The brief pause that followed when Scott told his destroyers to flash recognition lights was the break that the Japanese needed. Furutaka was on fire and Aoba was badly damaged as they turned away to the northwest. When Scott gave the order to resume firing the San Francisco made out the shape of a nearby ship without recognition lights. She switched on her searchlights and bathed the Japanese destroyer Fubuki with light. Immediately the destroyer was ripped apart by shells from every American vessel nearby and in three minutes Fubuki exploded and sank.

Scott then turned his ships to the northwest and paralleled the course of the fleeing Japanese ships. The burning Furutaka was by then sinking, but Aoba and Kinugasa both fired on their pursuers and obtained several hits on Boise. Suddenly a massive orange blossom of flame rose from Boise as a shell exploded in a forward magazine. Blast swept throughout the forward part of the ship followed by flames which cut off whole sections. The order to flood all forward magazines was given but by then the crew at the flood control panel were all dead. Just as it seemed the ship would explode, the sea flooded in through an underwater shell hole, quickly putting out all fires near the magazines. With more than 100 dead Boise staggered out of the line and made off to the southwest.

Perhaps the most unfortunate of Scott's ships was the destroyer Duncan, partly the cause of the confusion, she had approached to within 2,000 yards of the Japanese ships at the start of the action when the other ships had been completing the reversal of their course. As the shells began to fly, Duncan was hit repeatedly by fire from the American cruisers. Her topsides were soon smashed and a shell in the engine room released a cloud of scalding steam which drove out the fire room crew. Another shell killed everyone in the chartroom. Radio; gunnery control; communications, and steering were all quickly lost. The ship's skipper, Lieutenant Commander Taylor, ordered the burning bridge abandoned but there was only one way to go - over the side. The ship was still steaming at 15 knots when Taylor got the wounded and able-bodied over the side, then got into a life raft himself. As he drifted away the helpless skipper watched his ship steam on erratically, burning fiercely and throwing out explosions as ammunition was ignited. Below her decks some of the engine room crew were still fighting the fires and continued to do so for almost two hours before they, too, were forced over the side. Still the burning ship drifted for hours - eventually sinking at noon the next day.

Despite the loss of Duncan and the damage to Boise, Scott had achieved the first United States Naval victory around Guadalcanal. He had not, however, stopped the Japanese transport group getting through. While he had been engaged in his confused Battle of Cape Esperance, six destroyers landed 1,000 troops and two transports put ashore eight six-inch guns and others of smaller caliber, 16 tanks, several tractors and large quantities of stores were also landed.

On the morning of October 13th the airfield received two unexpected raids. Coastwatcher Paul Mason who had given warning so often before, was on the run from Japanese patrols on Bougainville and Henderson airfield's recently installed radar system was not working as 24 Japanese bombers suddenly flew over. In minutes the airfield was blasted by numerous bombs. Parked planes were destroyed; large holes knocked in the runway, and 5,000 gallons of fuel went up in flames. A few fighters managed to get into the air from a nearby fighter strip which had recently been completed. A short time later these planes returned to Henderson for refueling and halfway through the operation, a second flight of Japanese bombers appeared. Again several planes were destroyed on the ground and large fires started.

For the Seabee Commander J.P. Blunden, the worst was yet to come. No sooner were the fires brought under control when a new noise was heard "Like the sound of an express train coming towards you", Blunden remembers. "The next moment a huge geyser of stones and earth erupted on the runway". Hyakutake's heavy artillery was in position and ranging on the airfield. Blunden remembers "fifty bombs and shells hit Henderson that day. Shell craters are a lot worse than bombs. With bombs you feel they will not hit the same place twice but with shells what are you going to do? You know, just as the Jap artilleryman knows, that if he leaves his gun in the same position and fires a second shell, it will hit in almost the same spot as the last one did. So a good old Jap trick was to fire one shell, give you just enough time to start repairing the hole it made, then fire a second shell. All we could do was hope we would hear it coming soon enough to get out of the way before it exploded".

Many thought the long range fire came from one gun which became known as "Pistol Pete", but actually the Japanese had several of them. "Pistol Pete" kept up a steady barrage until nightfall, but most of the shells hit one end of the runway only. That evening another raid occurred which did little damage, then at just after one the next morning, "Washing Machine Charlie" came over. "Washing Machine Charlie" was the name given to the nightly Japanese reconnaissance plane. The sound of its engine sounded very like that of a washing machine motor. The plane flew slowly over the length of the airfield. At one end it dropped a red flare; in the center, a white one; at the other end, a green one. The parachute flares were watched by many as they slowly descended - bathing the whole area in light.

Those few who were looking out to sea saw a long flicker of fire erupt in the dark sky near Savo Island. Moments later, sounds like a fleet of trucks came through the air and huge explosions broke out over the whole airfield. The 31,000 ton Japanese battleships *Kongo* and *Haruna* had come down from the north with special bombardment shells as evidence of Yamamoto's intention to wipe out the airfield. Each shell was five feet long and weighed 1,400 pounds. A broadside from the two battleships sent 16 of these shells each time while between them they could also fire 32 six-inch guns and 16 five-inch.

For two hours the ships steamed slowly up and down Sealark Channel and subjected Henderson to a barrage unlike any other since World War I in France. More than 900 of the huge shells were hurled against the airfield, where planes, trucks and trees were flung cartwheeling into the air. Ammunition and fuel exploded while burning oil and petrol spread across the airfield. On the battleship *Kongo*, Captain Koyangi recalls, "It seemed that Henderson had been

The destroyer USS Duncan *(DD-485), Oct. 7, 1942, before the Battle of Cape Esperance, Oct. 11-12, 1942. (Courtesy of Andrew A. Slovinec)*

Highway One, Guadalcanal. (Courtesy of Bill Shields)

(L to R): Henry Giconda, "Shadow" Perrault and Frank Holloran. They served with Co. F, 182d Infantry, American Division at Guadalcanal. (Courtesy of William F. Dolan)

changed into a lake of fire and the explosions on the airfield were better than any fireworks display. Among the crew there were spontaneous cries and shouts of excitement".

For the Marines on shore it was, for many, the most terrifying night of their lives. The ground repeatedly heaved and shook; the constant roar of the shells passing overhead and exploding with shattering impact and the fear of being blown to pieces was too much for some who broke down and wept openly. Martin Clemens, living in a tent near the airfield, remembers the sound of incoming shells as "like a hundred steel doors being clanged shut". Sergeant Mitchell Paige remembers "huge trees being cut apart and flying about like toothpicks sailing through the air, while the whole ground constantly shook as if there was an earthquake".

Dawn the next morning showed the airfield was a complete shambles. Wrecked planes, some upside down, littered the area. Martin Clemens counted six huge craters within a hundred yards of his tent. Steel matting on the runway was reduced to twisted scrap. Bits of clothing and equipment, flung about by the shell-bursts, dangled from telephone lines. Forty-one men had been killed; 55 planes wrecked, and 24 damaged.

The recently completed Fighter Strip No. 1 - a mile west of Henderson was, however, virtually undamaged and 11 planes were still operational there. By removing serviceable parts from wrecked planes, a further ten planes were also made operational during the day, despite another bombing raid and a renewed shelling from "Pistol Pete". Desperate attempts were made to get these planes into the air as quickly as possible after an early morning reconnaissance flight reported six Japanese transports steaming towards the island with a destroyer escort. Henderson was able to send 11 bombers against the convoy but it was so well protected by Zeros that only slight damage was done to one of the destroyers.

That night the cruisers *Chokai* and *Kinugasa* steamed into Sealark Channel and again shelled the airfield with over 700 eight-inch shells. The terror of the night before was repeated on a slightly lesser scale and the next morning, only one bomber was in operation at the airfield. Dawn also showed the six Japanese transports had reached the island, and were calmly unloading at Tassafaronga, only ten miles west of Lunga while several Japanese destroyers patrolled in Sealark Channel and numerous Zeros flew fighter cover over the landings. Morale at Henderson and among the Marines at Lunga sank to its lowest. Through binoculars the Japanese could be clearly seen unloading tanks and artillery and yet there was virtually nothing anybody could do about it. Sergeant Mitchell Paige remembers, "there were so many Jap planes in the air, you would have thought they had captured Henderson. Time and time again they flew over our beach area machine gunning it".

By 11:30 that morning, the ground staff at the airfield got two more bombers operational and they made the first strike against the Japanese transports. Three of the ships had unloaded and left and the three bombers escorted by a few fighters from Fighter Strip No. 1, were able to make short repeated attacks on the other three which were all set on fire by the planes and then run aground by their crews, but three of the fighters were lost to the Zeros.

By noon the situation became even more desperate when the airfield ran out of fuel for the planes. Some fuel was obtained by draining it from the tanks of damaged planes and this allowed another strike against the Japanese ships at Tassafaronga with fighters strafing their newly-landed supplies. After an urgent appeal from Vandegrift, several C-47 cargo planes flew in from the New Hebrides with 55 gallon drums of fuel and B-17 bombers also attacked the Japanese transports before nightfall.

The night brought no relief for the battered forces in the perimeter. Shortly after midnight, "Washing Machine Charlie" flew slowly over and lit up the airfield once more as, for the third successive night, an intense naval bombardment erupted. This time it was the Navy cruisers *Maya* and *Myoko* which, in two hours, poured 1,500 shells into the airfield area and Fighter Strip No 1. The fuel flown in the previous day went up in a fiery holocaust with blazing drums thrown spinning into the air. Yet again the ground staff, pilots and Marines, spent a sleepless night in their fox-holes while red hot shell fragments whipped through the air above and the ground heaved and shook with every shellburst.

The extent of destruction the next morning made the situation seem hopeless. The three bombers and 12 of the fighters had been destroyed. Ammunition was dangerously low and fuel was exhausted. Vandegrift felt the tide had turned against him and expected heavy Japanese infantry attacks. In a message to Nimitz he said, "Our troops are in no condition to undertake the prolonged campaigning needed to secure the island. Steps must be taken to gain control of the seas around Guadalcanal to prevent enemy landings and the bombardments we have experienced in the last three nights".

In the United States the depressing news was used to prepare the public for the possible evacuation of Guadalcanal, or if that was impossible, a determined fight to the last. On October 16th, Secretary of the Navy, Frank Knox, told a press conference - "The situation is not yet hopeless and I am sure every man will give a good account of himself".

On Guadalcanal there was little left to give an account. Rifleman Gilbert Dolloff remembers, "we all expected a landing on our beaches after the shelling, but we were so low on ammunition that we were given 20 rounds each. The feelings we had then are hard to describe - one of utter abandonment and despair. I know every man in my platoon immediately put one round in his pocket because none of us wanted to become a Japanese prisoner". Sergeant Mitchell Paige remembers he was told to report to the Battalion Command Post. "When I got there I was given my allotment of ammunition and food rations. They then told me to use it sparingly because that's all there was". Signalman Kauffman thought at the time, "if the Japs had followed up the shelling with a landing against us, it would have been all over".

Later that day, 16th October, Kauffmann was in the Command Post area of 1st Marines when the usual bombing raid came over at noon. A fragmentation bomb landed nearby killing two Marines, while the blast threw Kauffmann several yards. When he came round he was bleeding from both ears and had back injuries. "At the time of the blast" he remembers, "I had a submachine gun in my hands but it was later found 20 feet away from me with the barrel twisted like a pretzel. I was lucky to come out of that". Three days later he left the island on a transport plane for the New Hebrides.

These transport planes were put on a continual shuttle service to try to keep essential supplies brought in, yet each load of fuel they brought in was enough to keep 12 fighters in the air for only an hour. The submarine *Amberjack* was quickly converted to carry 9,000 gallons of gasoline and ten tons of bombs but when she arrived in Sealark Channel, there were several Japanese destroyers patrolling and she had to remain submerged for 12 hours before coming in at night to unload.

Despite Japanese control of the seas around Guadalcanal, an attempt was made to run a convoy through to the island and on the 15th October two transports and two tugs towing barges loaded with gasoline and bombs left the New Hebrides with a destroyer escort. The next morning the ships were sighted by a Japanese reconnaissance plane and, expecting an attack to follow, they turned back. The tug *Vireo* was considered too slow to clear the area so she was abandoned and her crew transferred to the destroyer *Meredith*. While this was being done a force of 27 Japanese planes attacked the destroyer.

In a hail of bombs, torpedoes and machine gun fire, the destroyer was sunk within minutes. The survivors tried to swim back to the *Vireo* but the tug drifted away too quickly and they were forced to cling to the life rafts and debris from the *Meredith*. Before they left, the Japanese planes flew low over the survivors and machine gunned many in the water. Machinist 2nd Class Lyle Webster from *Meredith* remembers, "dozens of men shot while swimming, just threw up their hands and disappeared below the water". For most of the survivors there was not enough room on the life rafts but during the day, many of the badly burned and wounded died and were pushed over the side to let some of the swimmers get on board.

Webster remembers it was the second day when the sharks began to gather. "There were about 50 or 60 of them" he recalls. "They came up close and brushed against the men clinging to the sides, who kicked out against them. Those sharks were real killers though, and they started taking the guys in the water one by one. A man would suddenly scream and then disappear in a bloody flurry of water. Some of the men began to climb on to the overloaded rafts which started to sink so they were pushed off again shouting, fighting and cursing. It was ghastly. Some men went crazy and just swam away; others fainted, slipped into the water and disappeared. The worst came when there were no more men left in the water. The sharks then flipped themselves on board the rafts and debris in order to get at the men there. One sailor had his buttocks ripped off and another lost an arm - snapped off clean at the elbow.

For the terrified men on the rafts there seemed to be no escape from the horror as the sharks attacked hour after hour and one by one the men continued to disappear. On Webster's raft, which originally had 40 men on it, there were only 13 left at daybreak on the third day after the sinking, when two destroyers were seen to be approaching. "Even though we were all desperate for help," Webster recalls, "we dare not signal to them in case they were Japanese ships, but as they approached we could see the stars and stripes. They came up slowly and we got picked up, but later when we checked, we found that only 77 of the original 237 crew on the destroyer and tug, had survived".

On October 16th the seaplane tender *McFarland* got through to Guadalcanal with 40,000 gallons of gasoline, torpedoes and ammunition. As she unloaded off Lunga she took on board about 100 injured Marines, from the previous three days bombardment. The ship's captain, John Alderman, kept glancing nervously up at the sky as the cargo was hurriedly unloaded. His worst fears were confirmed when a string of Japanese bombers appeared overhead. Alderman quickly got the ship under way in order to maneuver and dodge the bombs in Sealark Channel, but a bomb struck the stern of the ship, starting a fire, and knocking out the steering.

Some of the crew were switched to caring for the wounded and for hours the rudderless ship, leaking by the stern, with no engine power and burning, drifted helplessly in the Channel. After the fires had been put out it took several more hours before enough engine repairs could be made to get the ship under way again. Eventually at midnight the ship reached Tulagi with 27 dead and 28 wounded among her crew.

In three days almost 300 men had died at sea in the attempts to keep Guadalcanal supplied.

THE SITUATION IS WORSE THAN I IMAGINED

Hyakutake's supply position was not greatly improved after his six transports unloaded at Tassafaronga. Many of his stores had been destroyed by the American planes that had managed to get into the air, but 4,000 men, 16 tanks and over 100 artillery pieces had been landed. Over the next few nights the Tokyo Express landed more troops without opposition and by October 18th, Hyakutake had more than 20,000 well-equipped, healthy troops. He was, at last, in a position to mount a major offensive against the Americans and he turned to Colonel Masunobi Tsuji for the plan.

Tsuji was regarded as perhaps the most brilliant and original planner in the Army. In 1941 he had been assigned to Unit 82 of the Japanese Army engaged in planning the conquest of S.W. Asia. On the day he was appointed, he wrote in his diary - "I vow to the gods that night and day I will abstain from wine and tobacco; forget instinctive desires and worldly passions, to say nothing of loss, appetite and even life and death. My whole mind is concentrated on gaining victory".

He flew over British airfields in an unarmed reconnaissance plane taking pictures with a hand held camera. The pictures he obtained were not clear enough to be of any value but Tsuji told his diary, "there is no need for photographs - the image of everything I have seen is so clearly printed on the retina of my eye and on my mind". For months he labored over analysis of British strengths and weaknesses and on the basis of his reports the Army developed new combat techniques which allowed them to sweep through S.E. Asia in three months.

When war started in December, 1941, Tsuji distinguished himself by his daring, unconventional, but highly successful tactics. He was always where the action was, never hesitating to disobey orders to take full advantage of unforeseen developments at the front.

A small, frail looking man, wearing large glasses - he was impatient with those who did not share his untiring, endless devotion to the extension of Japan's empire. To many of his more easy-going superiors he was frequently insubordinate and rude. Others he reported to the political police for apparent lack of devotion to duty. He made many enemies. In Malaya his commanding officer once said of him, "the extermination of such poisonous insects should take precedence over all other problems". Yet the admiration of many junior officers, and Tsuji's undoubted brilliance, protected him.

In August, 1942, he had been on the General Staff in Tokyo but when the Guadalcanal campaign started he quickly got himself transferred to Hyakutake's staff. In Rabaul, Tsuji met Kawaguchi and took an instant dislike to him. The man was a loser, a complainer and probably a Liberal, thought Tsuji. He was disappointed when Hyakutake insisted that Kawaguchi should return with him to Guadalcanal, where Kawaguchi's local knowledge would be useful.

On October 9th, Hyakutake and his large staff arrived on Guadalcanal. Tsuji's opinion of Kawaguchi fell even lower when he saw the sick and emaciated survivors form Kawaguchi's force. "Their hair was long and filthy, and it could be pulled out in handfuls", Tsuji recalls. "Their uniforms were torn and dirty and they were in such poor health that their teeth were falling out. I was appalled at what I saw on Guadalcanal."

As the Staff Officers made their way along the

A Japanese prisoner behind barbed-wire in the POW stockade. In captivity, they looked rather harmless. Nevertheless, they were treacherous.

The old Prisoner of War Stockade at Guadalcanal as it appeared in December 1942. (Courtesy of Joseph L. Kiwak)

trail towards the Matanikau, they passed numerous primitive leaf-roofed hospitals where the sick and wounded lay with little or no medical attention. Dozens of others lay dead along the sides of the trail. In the fetid heat their bloated rotting bodies lay unburied, or half buried as the survivors were too weak to dig graves.

When Hyakutake reached Nakaguma's headquarters near the Matanikau river he was stunned to learn of the virtual loss of the 4th Infantry Regiment after it had been shelled in the ravine. He, too, had been shocked by the sight of Kawaguchi's survivors and in a radio message to Rabaul he ordered, "Send more supplies and equipment; the situation here is far worse than I imagined".

Four days later, however, after the naval bombardment of Henderson airfield, Hyakutake felt the situation had improved sufficiently for him to launch an attack. He called his staff officers in and a battle plan, largely the work of Colonel Tsuji, was drawn up. It consisted of four points: -

1. Lieutenant General Maruyama would cross the Matanikau then lead 5,600 men of his 2nd Division around Mount Austen, two miles inland, for an attack against the airfield from a point just south of Bloody Ridge. Since Kawaguchi knew that area, he was to accompany Maruyama.

2. A battalion of the 38th Division would land at Tasimboko and attack the American perimeter from the east as soon as Maruyama's attack was successful.

3. From the Matanikau River, the Commander of 17th Army Artillery, Major General Sumiyoshi, would lead a combined attack of tank and infantry with 3,000 men.

4. Colonel Oka would lead a mixed force of 500 men in an attack from Mount Austen area towards Kukum.

It was agreed that the attacks would all take place on October 22nd except that Sumiyoshi would attack a day or two before that, to force the Americans to transfer troops, defending the airfield, towards the Matanikau. Maruyama immediately dispatched a group of engineers under Captain Oda to cut a path through the jungle behind Mount Austen for the light artillery he planned to take with him, then two days later he led his men into the jungle. With Maruyama was Tsuji, Kawaguchi and Major Gen-

eral Nasu who was soon to find out the truth of what the correspondent Nishino had told him. Nasu commanded the 2nd Division's 29th Infantry Regiment, one of the crack units of the Japanese Army. The regiment had many dedicated and skilled officers in its ranks - among them Captain Jiro Katsumata.

At 25 years of age, Katsumata had already had extensive combat experience in China, Manchuria and Java. Because of his experience and training, many replacements had been put into his 11th Company. He felt fortunate that he still had several long serving N.C.O.s and he was sure they would soon get the replacements into shape. Their first task was the 35 mile march through the jungle, along what became known as the Maruyama Trail, before their attack on Henderson. In addition to his own equipment every man carried a shell, a part of a machine gun, or a box of ammunition. The average load on each soldier was 60 pounds. Each man had also been provided with rations for five days. After which it was expected they could be using captured American supplies.

The first days march was easy; even pleasant, as the force moved off through coconut groves then over a range of hills that led inland towards Mount Austen. On the second day they entered dense, hilly forest and the trail became so narrow they had to move in single file. Soon they came to a succession of steep hills made slippery by heavy rain and covered in thick undergrowth. Progress became slower as the day became hotter and more humid. The greatest difficulty was faced by the ten man teams assigned to each of the 70 mm. Howitzers they were taking with them. Each gun weighed nearly 500 pounds and the ridges soon became so steep that the gun carriers had to use ropes, blocks and tackle, to get the guns up. The artillery section began to fall behind. On the third day the terrain became even worse. The ridges were several hundred feet high and covered in undergrowth, will tall tress that kept out any wind that may have cooled the hot, damp, heavy air. The top of one ridge showed only a succession of similar ridges ahead. The heavily loaded men, sweating profusely as they scrambled up the slopes became exhausted.

Katsumata found his inexperienced replacements getting further behind all the time and sent some of his N.C.Os back to lash the men with thin canes. Further back along the column the artillery men lay exhausted on the trail and finally abandoned their guns. As the march got behind schedule, Maruyama put his men on half rations and sent a radio message to Sumiyoshi, postponing the attack until the 23rd October. Sumiyoshi had, however, already started making probing attacks across the Matanikau to test the Marine defenses.

On October 2, two tanks supported by infantry attempted to cross the sand pit at the mouth of the river. Corporal Breijak's battalion from the 7th Marines had been moved to the east bank of the river several days before and he remembers: "It was all quiet until that afternoon when a Jap tank suddenly appeared on the other side of the river."

"We got the shock of our lives because none had any idea the Japs had tanks. It opened fire with its main gun and machine guns then came across the sandpit. Our 37mm guns replied, hit it twice and knocked it back into the trees where another hit finished it off. The Japs hit back with artillery and mortar and kept it up all through the next day. Shell bursts among our positions caused concussion in several men and three were killed by shell pieces."

On the Maruyama Trail, progress slowed to a crawl. Continual heavy rain made the steep slopes so slippery that ropes had to be rigged to help the men scramble up. Many of them had developed malaria and the skimpy half rations of rice balls and fish, could no longer carry their heavy loads. After the artillery was abandoned, mortars were left behind, then the heavy machnine guns and the boxes of ammunition for them. On the morning of the 22nd, the original date for the attack, the exhasuted column was still nine miles from their attack positions. Once again Maruyama sent a message to Sumiyoshi, postponing the attack a further 24 hours, but Sumiyoshi received only a garbled version of this message and launched his attack on the 23rd.

The assault began with heavy artillery and mortar fire on the Marines on the east bank of the Matanikau, then nine tanks moved across the river mouth. They were immediately brought under fire by Marine artillery and eight of the tanks were quickly destroyed. The last tank got across the river and moved among the Marine foxholes firing on machine gun posts, one of which was defended by Corporal Breijak.

He remembers: "We had been firing the machine gun when it jammed. We did everything we knew to clear it but it didn't work. While we were working on it, I looked up the trail quickly, then had another look because I couldn't believe what I saw. There was no mistake, however. A huge tank was coming straight towards us. We had nothing to hit it with and we decided to make a run for it when the tank was closer. There were three of us in the gun nest, Bellow, Kline and myself. Bellow went first, then me, then Kline. I don't know how I ever got out of it because I could hear the tank firing all the time as I ran up a slope towards a dugout. Bellow and I both made it but Kline got hit in the back, arms and legs. A real mess."

The tank wandered around for several minutes then stopped close to Private Joe Champagne's foxhole. Champagne threw a grenade which damaged the tank's treads so when it moved off again it was no longer under control. It got to the sandpit in an attempt to get back across the river but was then knocked out by artillery fire. The artillery then shifted fire to the east bank where Sumiyoshi's infantry were massing. The guns had previously zeroed in on that area and each battery was assigned a narrow strip along which the range was stepped up and down to cover the area in depth. The effect on Sumiyoshi's infantry was murderous. Shell splinters created havoc in the massing troops among which 600 died. The attack groups fired up in disorder and the assault was called off as Japanese artillery fired on the Marine positions.

Meanwhile, Corporal Breijak had gone back to the command post and had been sent to work carrying ammunition up to other machine gun posts. When the Japanese artillery fire began he recalls: "We took cover in a shell hold but another Marine nearby got hit and I gave a hand to get him back to the aid station. Then I got more ammuniton and started going forward again. Suddenly I heard the whine of a shell, then the whole ground seemed to come up and hit me and everything went black. The next thing I knew it was the next morning and I was in a hospital bed, with concussion and injuries to my back and chest. I guess I was lucky not to have been hit by any of the splinters from that shell".

Deep in the jungle Maruyama was still struggling along the trail when he heard the distant sound of gun fire from the Matanikau. Realizing Sumiyoshi had attacked prematurely he urged his men forward the last few miles to launch his attack towards the airfield as quickly as possible, but it was the afternoon of the 24th before they reached their positions two miles south of Henderson. Here Maruyama divided his force into two groups. On the left, Major General Nasu would lead 2,500 men across a range of hills near Bloody Ridge and Kawaguchi with an equal force would attack a mile further east.

When the force split up, Colonel Tsuji accompanied Kawaguchi who told the Colonel he was far from happy with the area he was supposed to attack from. He suggested an attack even further east would be more successful in an area where the American defenses seemed lighter and his men would only have to cross a few rolling hills rather than steep ridges. Tsuji agreed and promised to return to Maruyama and get approval for the change in plans. Privately Tsuji disapproved; to him it seemed typical of the lack of drive and forcefulness he so hated in Kawaguchi. When he returned to Maruyama's headquarters he said nothing about the change in plans.

Kawaguchi's progess was again held up on the jungle covered slopes and he called Maruyama to ask for a 36 hour postponement of the attack, assuming Maruyama knew by then, of the cahnge in his plans. Maruyama did not know and was furious with the suggestion of any more delay. It seemed that Kawaguchi, who had himself failed so miserably in his own offensive, would now risk the success of Maruyama's attack. It was an impossible situation, Maruyama decided. He called Kawaguchi on the cable phone again. "Major General Kawaguchi" he spoke severely - "report immediately to Divisional Headquarters." He was then ordered to hand over his command to Colonel Toshinari Shoji. On hearing of Kawaguchi's dismissal, the cunning Tsuji immediately telephoned 17th Army Headquarters. "Kawaguchi refused to advance," he reported, "the Divisional Commander has relieved him of his command." He did not elaborate.

Opposing Maruyama's offensive were two battalions of 7th Marines under Colonel Puller, and soldiers of the recently landed 164th Infantry Regiment. On October 23rd, however, Sumiyoshi's attack at the Matanikau created a serious threat and Puller sent one of his battalions towards the river. Maruyama's strategy had worked but he had not moved quickly enough through the jungle to take advantage of the position.

On the afternoon of October 24th, Puller's Marines spotted a Japanese officer at the edge of the jungle observing their positions through binoculars. The Marines hastily dug additional defensive positions while the 164th Infantry cut new fields of fire in the tall grass facing their positions.

One mile to the south, Nasu's men gathered slowly in the thick jungle as heavy rain began to fall. Two companies were ordered to reconnoitre the American positions - the 9th Company under Lieutenant Makita and the 11th under Captain Katsumata. In the slippery rain-soaked jungle, the two compa-

nies made slow progress and as night fell they had made no contact with the American positions.

Katsumata and Makita discussed the situation. They decided Makita's company would lead and Katsumata's would follow. It soon became so dark, however, that the two companies lost contact with each other. In order to keep his men together, Katsumata ordered them to place their hands on the shoulders of the man in front.

As they stumbled on, they suddenly tripped over an American telephone cable. They cut the line then moved along it in the hope of wiping out an American observation post. They were already too late. The outpost had been manned by a group of men under Sergeant Ralph Briggs. Earlier he had phoned Puller. "Colonel", he spoke softly, "There's about 3,000 Japanese between you and me."

"Are you sure?" asked Puller.

"Positive" replied Briggs, "they've been all around us, singing and smoking cigarettes. Now they're heading your way."

"All right, Briggs, but make damn sure" the Colonel urged. "Take your men to the left, go down and pass through our lines near the sea. I'll call them to let you in. Don't fail and don't go in any other direction. I'll hold my fire as long as I can."

Briggs and his small group crawled away on their stomachs through the undergrowth. Hours later, after they had become split up, most got back to their own lines, but four were caught and killed by the Japanese.

As Katsumata's group followed the telephone line a voice in the jungle suddenly called "Katsumata, Katsumata!" It was the lost Makita with only a small group from his company. Makita told Katsumata that his men had found an open field with a line of barbed wire across it. One of his Lieutenants, Nakagome, had wanted to send a patrol across the field but Makita had said no, as it may alarm the Americans and jeopardise the regiment's attack later.

Makita led Katsumata and his men towards the wire where Katsumata sent small patrols to follow the wire to the right and left. Shortly afterwards, machine gun fire suddenly broke out on the right and one of the patrols came running back. Fire also broke out on the left and Katsumata then withdrew his men into the jungle, and watched the red tracers arching through the sky. Realizing the two machine guns would have to be destroyed he sent word back to a squad of engineers to bring up some dynamite. They told him there was none available. Like so much else it had been abandoned on the Maruyama Trail. Katsumata recalls that his men who had shed so much of their equipment had only a rifle, bayonet and 15 rounds each. He ordered one squad to the right to deal with the machine gun there, and decided to take the rest of his men across the field then swing to the left to get the machine gun from behind.

Katsumata realized his men were by then, tired, wet and hungry. He thought the recent replacements in his company would also be scared at the thought of their first engagement with the enemy. "It seemed to me" he recalls, "that some of the men may panic or get lost in the darkness, so I decided to lead them across the field in short rushes in the hope that this would keep us all together." The rain had by then stopped, the coulds were beginning to break up and occasionally the moon broke through. Across the field, Katsumata could see a distant tree and told his N.C.O.s that it would be their initial target. They then went forward, in a rush across the field, for about 30 yards before hitting the ground. From the ground, Katsumata could no longer see the tree, so he told his N.C.Os to wait with the men while he went forward to locate the tree again. Having done so, he turned to make his way back to his men but was horrified to see them get up and charge over to the left, shouting wildly.

Post exchange on Guadalcanal. The exchange is well stocked the day after a supply ship arrives, but word travels fast and stores are soon drained. Business is at a standstill until the next supply ship arrives. (USMC Photo, No. 51,731)

In a moment the American machine gun fire broke out and dozens of Katsumata's men fell screaming with chest, arm and leg wounds. Katsumata ran quickly after them shouting, "Lie down and keep quiet" repeatedly, but above the shouting; screaming, and firing, he could not be heard. One group of the men then ran into a mine field. A line of explosions erupted among them throwing men into the air. From the flashes of the explosions the rest of Katsumata's men could be seen and the machine gun fire switched to them as Katsumata caught up with them and got them to lie down. For several minutes the men lay quietly in the grass while machine gun fire continued all around them, then one of the men whispered he had found a barbed wire fence.

Katsumata crawled towards the wire then moved along it to the right until he found a part that was only about two feet high. He shouted to his men, "The wire is not high, jump over it, come with me". He then got up and jumped quickly over the wire. He was immediately hit by two bullets. One grazed his right cheek bone, broke his helmet strap then tore off the lobe of his ear. The other bullet grazed his right knee, but as he ran forward he hardly felt either of these. After a 20 yard dash he fell to the ground and called to his men to join him, despite the noise of continual firing and the screaming of the wounded. Out of the darkness 2nd Lieutenant Shirai joined him and then two privates. They lay still until the firing stopped a few minutes later and the only sound was the low moaning of wounded men around them. Katsumata sent Shirai back to the wire to bring the rest of the men forward but the Lieutenant returned after several minutes and told Katsumata he had found noone alive. Katsumata could hardly believe it; there had been 140 men in his company.

A few minutes later he heard men moving through the grass about 50 yards to his left and beyond the wire. He thought it was probably men of the 9th Company with Lieutenant Makita who Katsumata had told to support him. Then he heard the voice of Nakagome, one of Makita's lieutenants, shouting "Attack, attack!" followed by the rush of men through the grass towards the wire. Katsumata shouted "I am here, Nakagome, watch out for the wire" but could hardly even hear himself above the sound for firing that broke out again. Ahead of Katsumata, more machine guns started firing as a flare rose in the sky to show the 9th Company struggling with the line of coiled wire. Man after man fell back or collapsed across the wire.

The firing continued for several minutes but gradually the groans and screams of the wounded died away and when the firing suddenly stopped Katsumata was struck by sudden silence. "After so much noise," he recalls, "the sudden quietness was awesome; even the insect noises of the night were stilled." As the moon drifted between the clouds he looked at his watch. Nearly midnight, and only 30 minutes since, he had led his company into the field. Then the shelling started.

Most of the shells exploded in the field or in the jungle behind but a nearby shellburst brought down the top of a tree which fell with a rendering crash about ten yards from Katsumata's group. The four men crawled towards it and took cover beneath its branches. A short time later a number of shells fell near the wire and shell pieces whipped through the air into the group of men. Katsumata was wounded in his right ankle and Shirai in the left leg. One of the Privates was hit in the hip. Another shellburst, a few minutes later, sent a jagged piece of metal that buried itself in the chest of the second Private. He died a short time later.

As Katsumata's group clung to the ground, the rest of his regiment launched an attack several hundred yards to his left, led by the regimental commander, Colonel Furimaya. Their furious charge, shortly after midnight, was met by a hail of fire from Puller's 7th Marines. Despite the intensity of the fire, Furimaya's men scrambled up the slopes and within minutes burst through the Marines' line in fierce hand to hand fighting.

Sergeant John Basilone remembers the confusion and bitter fighting. "When the first wave came at us we drove them back but they came again and started to get through. My ammunition was getting low and I ran over to the next outfit to get some more. Soon after I got back, a runner told me the Japs had got through on our right and had killed two Marines and wounded three at a machine gun that had jammed. I grabbed one of our guns and told the crew to follow me. When I got to the post with the dead Marines, I fixed the jammed gun. By that time we were really pinned down with bullets smacking the sandbags all the time. The Japs were still coming through and I moved from one gun to the other, firing as fast as they could be loaded. It was pretty bad at times because the Japs sometimes came up behind me and I would have to turn and fire at them with a pistol."

Meanwhile the desperate Puller had been phoning Colonel del Valle, in charge of artillery, to request all the available artillery support.

"I'll give you all you call for," del Valle replied, "but God knows what will happen when the ammo we have is gone."

"If we don't need it now, we'll never need it" said Puller, "if the Japs get through here tonight, there will be no tomorrow."

As Puller hung up, the phone rang again. It was Captain Fuller, a company commander in 7th Marines. "I'm just about running our of ammunition" he reported desperately.

"You've got bayonets, haven't you?" Puller retorted.

"Sure, yes sir."

"All right, then hang on."

Having penetrated the American lines, Furimaya signalled his success to Maruyama who misunderstood the message and reported to Hyakutake that the airfield had been captured. The next stage of the attack plan was put into operation and three destroyers, carrying troops of the 38th Infantry, headed into Sealark Channel, planning to land the troops at Tasimboko.

As the fierce fighting continued near Bloody Ridge, Vandegrift hastily sent forward troops of the newly landed 164th Infantry to plug the gaps in the Marine defenses. Slowly the line was restored and Furimaya became isolated behind the Marine lines. At 3:30 in the morning Maruyama sent a third wave of troops to relieve Furiyama. This time the line held as the Japanese attack lacked the momentum of the earlier charges.

Throughout the long night Katsumata's group hugged the ground as the shelling continued. He hoped that Furimaya's attack would sweep past his position, but as the night wore on the Japanese attacks became fewer and weaker and Katsumata realized that if he stayed where he was he would be shot as soon as it got light. He decided to get back across the wire and try to contact the squad he had sent to attack the machine gun post. "Shirai said it was impossible," Katsumata remembers, "and that we should commit suicide before the Americans found us." He put his pistol to his head but I laid my hand on his shoulder and said "Don't be a fool, we can do that anytime, but we must first make another attack." Shirai's and the Private's wounds were too severe to allow them to move fast so Katsumata went back alone. When he got to the wire he found four or five of his men hanging there lifelessly. Climbing over the wire he dashed across the field but stumbled and fell. When he picked himself up he found he had tripped over a dead soldier and on looking round in the early morning light, saw a group of almost 50 dead nearby.

Just after dawn he reached the edge of the jungle and moved slowly to the right calling out repeatedly, "This is Katsumata, gather here, we will make another attack soon." Slowly, one or two men emerged from hiding and in an hour he gathered 15 survivors around him in from his own and Makita's companies, then, hearing Japanese voices in the jungle nearby, he left them and moved towards the approaching sounds.

He found Lieutenant Colonel Watanabe with about 50 men. Katsumata began to tell the Colonel what had happened to his company then suddenly someone shouted, "The Americans are coming!" Immediately everyone scattered to take defensive positions. Katsumata raced towards a small hill with about 20 men. They had a machine gun with them and quickly set up a small perimeter. Katsumata remembers how confused it all was. "It seemed nobody in my group had actually seen any Americans," he recalls, "and I was not sure what was going on. A few scattered shots were heard in the jungle nearby, followed by several shouts, but we saw no one until after an hour, a runner arrived with orders for me to report to Nasu's headquarters."

When Katsumata got to the headquarters he found nothing but confusion there as well. "Nobody seemed to know what was going on and, in fact, they were surprised to hear my company had been in action." He recalls, "They had, however, now learned that Furimaya had not actually captured the airfield, but no one knew what had happened to him or where he was. Nasu told me another attack was to be planned for that night and I was ordered to join Maruyama's staff in the planning of it."

Colonel Oka's part in the offensive was delayed by his own timidity. He had not even crossed the upper Matanikau on the evening of Maruyama's planned attack. In a report to Hyakutake, Oka claimed, "The regiment endeavored to accomplish its objective of diverting the enemy, but they seemed to be planning a firm defense of this region." Actually it was true. 7th Marines were still taking up their positions and Hyakutake, not satisfied with Oka's weak excuses, went forward himself to tell the Colonel to make a more determined effort.

7th Marines found great difficulty in reaching their new defensive positions. Sergeant Mitchell Paige remembers, "After transferring from the Bloody Ridge area it took us a day to reach our new position one mile east of the Matanikau. To get there we had to clamber up one ridge after another carrying heavy machine guns, ammunition and supplies. We finally reached the position at dusk in heavy rain. Everyone was bone weary, wet and chilled. It was so dark visibility was zero and I wasn't sure we were in the right position so I left the men and crawled along the ridge on my hands and knees, groping my way forward until I reached out and felt the ridge falling away on all sides. Then I went back and got the men up to that point. We then ate our meager ration of spam, scooping it out of the can with our fingers. I thought we were going to get some peaches as well but Leiphart, who had been carrying a big can of peaches, told me he had dropped it and it had gone bouncing down the side of the ridge. The little guy stuttered and trembled when he told me about it, so I felt sorry for him really."

Paige's squad had reached the ridge just before Oka's advance party, which, early the next morning, approached the Marines' position. Paige remembers, "It was 0200 when I was startled into wakefulness by low mumbling sounds. I woke up 'Smitty' Smith who was next to me and we listened carefully. The sounds came again - low voices in Japanese 'damare' (keep quiet) and 'yoko ni nare' (lie down). I quickly and quietly crawled around and woke up everybody, warning them to stand by for action. I knew that if we opened fire we would betray our position but on the other hand we couldn't let the Japs infiltrate our perimeter. Maybe they were already getting ready to charge our lines. I pulled a pin from a grenade and pitched it over the side of the ridge. As soon as the rest of the men heard it click they threw grenades as well. There were numerous muffled explosions followed by screams of pain and we let them have some more grenades. Then there was silence over the ridge and the jungle and that was the end of it. It must have been a small patrol but somehow I felt we had not seen the last of them."

In Rabaul, the realization that Furimaya had not got to the airfield, caused consternation and confusion. A message was quickly sent to the three destroyers heading towards Tasimboko but was not received by the ships.

At 1020 that morning, October 25th, the destroyers were passing Lunga Point when they sighted the two American minesweepers *Zane* and *Trevor* leaving Tulagi. After a brief exchange of fire the minesweepers fled towards the reef-strewn southern entrance of Sealark Channel and the destroyers then fired on the tug *Seminole* and a converted fishing boat which was ferrying fuel from Tulagi to Lunga. The small fishing boat was quickly sunk and *Seminole* turned back towards Tulagi as the Japanese shells began to land around her. Shopfitter Ed O'Neill remembers - "We were carrying 400 drums of gasoline on the foredeck and although we managed to avoid 15 shells, one eventually hit the engine room, knocking out all generators. Flames then spread rapidly through the ship and the drums of gasoline began to explode as the skipper ordered

abandon ship". Getting off the blazing ship was a problem as four of the life rafts had gone up in flames but most of the crew got away in the last raft, paddling through the burning fuel which spread over the sea.

O'Neill remembers he did not get to the raft in time and searching for some means of escape could only throw over the side, the charred remains of one raft. It barely floated - being half submerged - but he threw a couple of planks on to it then climbed over the side on to it and paddled off with a short piece of plank. Once clear of the ship he watched it move away, blazing fiercely until a fiery explosion erupted and it quickly sank. O'Neill then recalls, "I was several hundred yards away from the other raft and after the ship sank the destroyers came nearer. I felt for sure they were going to fire on us but then several spouts of water rose among the destroyers and they turned away and headed towards Savo."

The survivors were rescued form a possible untimely end by shore batteries at Lunga which brought the destroyers under fire. One of them was damaged. They then left the area under a smoke screen and were attacked shortly afterwards by planes from Henderson. The planned landings at Tasimboko were abandoned. Phase two of Hyakutake's plan never got started.

The few planes that attacked the Japanese destroyers had been lucky to get off the airfield. Heavy rain during the night had made the airstrip a vast quagmire, so deep in mud in some places that some planes could not be moved until the afternoon when the hot sun dried out the field. Just in time, as 16 Japanese bombers with fighter escorts bombed the area during the afternoon. Twenty fighters managed to get off the ground at Fighter Strip No. 1 and tangle with the Japanese fighters. Of the three United States' planes lost, one was flown by Lieutenant Jack Conger. After being damaged in a dogfight with a Zero, Conger's plane got out of control and went into a vertical dive. As the plane screamed towards the sea, Conger reached up to slide back the cockpit hatch. It was jammed. In desperation he made a supreme effort and magaed to get it open just wide enough to climb out, only 150 feet above the sea. His parachute opened up just in time to check his fall before he hit the water. After he had undone his parachute harness he looked around to see a Japanese pilot also parachute into the sea and land about 20 yards away. Conger was soon picked up by a rescue boat which he then directed towards the

swimming Japanese. As the boat approached the man, Conger leaned out to help the Japanese get on board, but instead the pilot pulled out a pistol, pushed it against Conger's head and pulled the trigger. Click! The gun misfired. Conger fell back into the boat in shock and surprise while the Japanese put the pistol to his own head and again pulled the trigger. Click again. Conger then grabbed an empty water can and brought it crashing down on the pilot's head again and again until the man was unconscious - after which he was dragged into the boat.

The Japanese pilot's attitude towards his capture was typical. For a Japanese serviceman to surrender or allow himself to be captured was everlasting disgrace to himself and his family. He was expected to fight to the end, and, when all else had failed, to make a suicidal charge, or commit suicide directly. Because surrender or capture was unthinkable, the Japanese soldier was never told his rights as a prisoner or warned about what not to say. Consequently when captured he was often very talkative, particularly when he found he was not going to be shot and was, instead, given a decent meal. On Guadalcanal about 200 Japanese prisoners were taken during the campaign and many of them gave useful information. Conger later became quite friendly with the pilot who had tried to kill him.

TUTSUGEKI!

The Japanese attacks near Bloody Ridge on the 25th had not been made in full force. The Shoji/Kawaguchi attack in support of Nasu had been made by only a few hundred who had managed to struggle through the jungle in time. Most of this force never reached their attack positions. They wandered around all night in the dark jungle, eventually became lost, and just before dawn found themselves at the rear of Nasu's troops. The confusion was so great that they were then retained by Nasu for his new attack that night. Maruyama, at Divisional Headquarters, was furious when he learned during the day what had happened. The whole offensive was falling apart. The endless delays in getting through the jungle; the confusion over whether the airfield had been captured during the previous night, and finally to find the attack had only been made with half the force he had expected. For this he blamed the miserable Kawaguchi. It seemed the only person who had

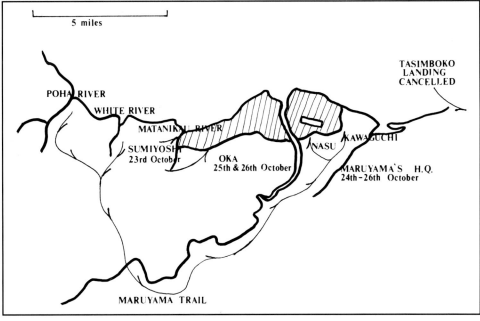

Japanese attacks, October 23-26.

distinguished himself was Colonel Furimaya.

After Furimaya's men had broken through the American lines, however, they became scattered and the Colonel found himself with only Captain Suziki and seven other men. Unable to get back through the lines they lay hidden under vines and leaves during the day. Furimaya spent the time making notes on the defenses that the Americans were constructing all around him. He felt confident Nasu would make another attack that night which would rescue him.

Nasu himself was ill with malaria and running a temperature of 104 F but he decided to lead the attack personally that night. He had available the survivors of 29th Infantry; the Shoji/Kawaguchi force and the reserve regiment, 16th Infantry - a total force of almost 3,000 men. Shortly before nine that night, without any preliminary shelling or mortar fire, this force suddenly surged out of the jungle towards the American lines. They were met by a storm of machine gun and rifle fire. Nasu had gone up with the forward troops and, weakened by malaria, was using his sword as a cane to help himself across the ground. When he reached the first line of American wire, a bullet tore into his chest. All around him his men were being decimated by the furious fire from American positions, from which 37 mm. cannon fired cannister shot into the masses of charging men. Whole sections of the Japanese were swept away and within ten minutes of the initial attack, every commander, down to company level, was dead or wounded. Still the men reformed and charged again, scrambling and stumbling over their own dead. Successive charges continued for three hours but gradually became weaker, until, after three hours, sheer exhaustion and ghastly losses brought an end to the slaughter shortly after midnight.

Nasu was found among the dead and wounded. His breathing was painful and shallow as his men placed him on a stretcher and carried him back to Maruyama's headquarters. When he arrived there, and was carried in to see Maruyama, he was only half conscious. He roused himself in an attempt to say something, but failed and fell back dead.

While Nasu's men had been swarming towards the American lines, Colonel Furimaya led his trapped men towards the front line. Time and again they were pinned down by American fire and two of his men were killed. Towards midnight, as the Japanese charges grew weaker, the group hid again in the underbrush and although they tried again in the early hours of the morning, there seemed to be no way of getting through.

At dawn on the 26th they faced another day of hiding behind enemy lines. Towards evening Furimaya ordered the men to split up and make their way individually through the lines. The Colonel watched them crawl off one by one until only he and Suziki were left, then they also moved off slowly from one shellhole to the next. They were repeatedly fired on and Furimaya, exhausted by hunger and thirst, eventually told Suziki he could go no further. He admitted to the Captain that he had failed; there was only the honorable way out now left. He wrote a letter to Marayama saying he had no excuses for his failure or the loss of his regiment, then gave it to Suziki, asking him to try to get the letter through. The two men then shook hands and, as Furimaya stood erect, Suziki put his pistol to the Colonel's head and fired.

Four miles to the west, Colonel Oka, with three battalions did not manage to take his part in the offensive until Nasu's second attack on the night of the 25th. At 2130 that night Oka's men made several charges against the 7th Marines but each attack was driven back by heavy fire. There then followed a long pause and Oka tried again at two in the morning.

Sergeant Mitchell Paige remembers, "After all the noise earlier in the night it was then so quiet you could hear the men breathing. Everybody was awake and alert and then we saw small lights flickering in the jungle at the bottom of the ridge. During the day we had strung wire on the ridge and fixed empty cans with empty cartridges in them, on to the wire. I moved along our line warning the men not to fire yet, to let the Japs get close then give them everything. Manning the No. 2 gun next to me was Corporal Gaston, and little Leiphart and they both whispered they could hear some rustling in the undergrowth. Everyone was straining to see and hear, but there was nothing to be seen although we could hear soft mutterings down in the jungle. Then I thought I could see a dark figure approaching Gaston's position. I grabbed a grenade, pulled the pin but held down the lever, waiting for a moment. Next the tin cans rattled, somebody shrieked, then all hell let loose. We threw grenades over the ridge and as they exploded, Japanese rifle and machine gun fire opened up on us."

"The first wave of enemy troops then swarmed into our positions. Immediately it was a confusing struggle lit up by flashes from machine fun fire, grenades and mortars. Dark shapes crawled across the ground. Struggling men fought on the ground with bayonets and swords shouting curses at each other. In the flickering light I saw a fierce struggle taking place at No. 2 gun. Some Japs were running towards Leiphart who was kneeling down,

apparently hit. I managed to shoot two of them but the third charged at Leiphart and ran him through with his bayonet. Leiphart was the smallest guy in the platoon - he weighed barely 125 lbs. The Jap ran him through with such force he lifted Leiphart into the air. I took careful aim and shot Leiphart's killer. The other guy on the gun, Gaston, was also having trouble. He was flat on his back and a Jap officer with a two-handed sword was hacking at him. One of Gaston's legs had already been cut up and he was warding off the sword with a rifle. The rifle was soon splintered then Gaston wriggled round on the ground and swung up his good leg, kicking the Jap under the chin so hard it must have broken his neck. The other Japs ran on to the next machine gun which was manned by Corporal Grant and privates Scott and Hinson. The Japs swarmed in to the gun post. Scott was killed and Hinson got hit in the head. Then I saw Pawlowski get killed and Stansberry go down hit in the shoulder but still firing his tommy gun. There seemed to be an endless wall of Japanese coming up the slopes and about 75 men had broken through our platoon. One of them lunged at me with a bayonet but he must have been off balance. I put up my left hand to bar the bayonet which got me between two fingers but enough to ward off the blow. As the Jap went past me he dropped dead, then suddenly the enemy seemed to just melt back down the slopes and before I knew it they were out of sight."

Several of the machine gun posts had been knocked out of action and there were numerous wounded in Paige's platoon. Although the Japanese had been driven back, many of them climbed the trees in the jungle and brought the ridge under continual sniper fire. Paige was clearing a jammed machine gun when the next wave of Japanese overran the ridge 50 yards from him, then swept towards another ridge which sheltered the Command Post. Fox Company holding that ridge was driven back with heavy losses but Paige got to the abandoned No. 2 gun, where Gaston lay injured, swung the gun round and opened fire on the rear of the Japanese.

Paige had adapted all the machine guns in his section to increase their fire rate considerably above the designed rate and the No. 2 gun poured out 1,300 rounds a minute until the ammunition was exhausted and the gun was steaming. It caused havoc on the Japanese clambering up the ridge with their backs to Paige, who remembers "I then ran along the ridge to other gun posts trying to keep them firing but at each position I found only dead bodies and I realized I must be the only one on the ridge. As I ran, I kept bumping into enemy soldiers running around aimlessly in the dark and it seemed they did not know they had almost complete possession of the ridge. I then ran on until I got to George Company on our right flank where I found two men I knew. I told them I wanted some ammunition, grabbed it then shouted at them to fix bayonets and follow me.

By then it was just beginning to get light and I knew that once it did get light and the Japs saw how well they had done, they would send another wave to occupy our ridge. When I got back to the No. 2 gun I quickly loaded it and emptied a full belt of 250 rounds into the Japs still on the ridge behind me. I was getting low on ammunition when three guys from my platoon, Star, Heilly and Joncek, started running along the ridge bringing more ammunition. It was almost daylight and we came under a lot of Japanese rifle fire when they realized what was happening. Star got to me first with a belt of ammunition but almost at once he got hit in the stomach. Then Reilly arrived and he got hit in the groin. Joncek was doing well because he had been wounded earlier but when he reached my gun he got hit in the neck again. I was looking right at him when it happened. A piece of flesh just disappeared from his neck. It was getting too unhealthy so then I dashed from gun to gun, fired a few bursts then moved off before the grenades the Japs were throwing could get me".

On the ridge behind Paige the Japanese attack weakened after Paige's fire into their rear and gave Major Odell Conoley, in the Command Post on the other side of the ridge, the chance to gather a small force of runners, signallers and headquarters personnel. With this mixed group, Conoley led a charge over the crest of the ridge and forced the Japanese back to the ridge where Paige was running from gun to gun. Paige himself then called on the men he had gathered from George Company. "I told them I was going over the top of the ridge and I wanted them behind me" he recalls, "then I set off and they followed me, shooting and yelling. At one time I almost ran in to a Japanese field officer - he had emptied his revolver and was reaching for his two-handed sword. He was no more than four or five feet away when I cut him down. The men from George Company followed me all the way down the ridge and on to the edge of the jungle where the last of the enemy disappeared. The shooting and yelling quickly stopped and then there was that strange quietness that always seems to follow".

Four miles away, Maruyama listened to the sounds of Oka's attack fade away, and in the silence that followed he realized the Colonel's attack had also failed. Nasu's attacks on the previous two nights had cost over 2,000 dead on the devastated ridges near the airfield. Hundreds more were wounded or sick with malaria. There was nothing more to be done but gather the survivors together and make the trek back to the Matanikau. Colonel Shoji argued that it would be quicker to get to Koli Point and Maruyama agreed to let him take his group in that direction.

On the afternoon of the 26th the survivors split up. In Maruyama's group was the Kawaguchi, miserable in disgrace, and Colonel Tsuji, stunned by the bloody defeat his planning had led to. For all of them the misery of defeat was made worse by the exhausting march back along the endless Maruyama Trail. The ghastly retreat Kawaguchi had made in September was now repeated. Again the sick and wounded who could go no further were left to die along the narrow track. Once more, food supplies were exhausted and the men were reduced to eating roots, the bark off trees and even chewing the rifle slings.

As Tsuji walked slowly along the trail, subdued by his first experience of defeat, he recognized a battalion commander, Minamoto, lying with the wounded by the side of the trail. The lower half of Minamoto's body was wrapped in blood-soaked rags. Tsuji hurried over to him, "Hold on," he urged the commander, "we'll send someone back for you." "I haven't eaten for two days," Minamoto whispered weakly. Tsuji gave him a little rice and when Minamoto pointed feebly towards other wounded men lying nearby, Tsuji fed them until the last of his food was gone.

It took Tsuji five days to reach the Japanese lines at the Matanikau River. He hurried to Hyakutake's headquarters near Point Cruz where he quickly arranged for help to be sent back along the Maruyama Trail then sat down to compose a telegram for dispatch to Army Headquarters in Tokyo.

"I must bear the full responsibility for the failure of the 2nd Division which courageously fought for days and lost more than half their men in desperate attacks," he wrote. "They failed because I underestimated the enemy's fighting power and insisted on my own operations plan which was erroneous."

As he waited for the radiogram to be sent, the sound of heavy firing from the Matanikau river area was heard. The Americans were making a major attack across the river.

GET THE BIG ONES

After the defeat of Maruyama's offensive, Vandegrift planned to take advantage of the situation by pushing the Japanese back from the Matanikau towards Hyakutake's headquarters at Kokumbona, three miles west of the river. Before doing so, Vandegrift sent small groups of intelligence officers across the river, under cover of darkness, to locate the Japanese artillery posts and obtain an estimate of troops in the area.

This work was largely done by two intelligence officers from 1st Marines - Taylor and White. In the early morning hours of October 29th Taylor crossed the river with six men then crawled through the jungle towards a suspected artillery post on a ridge overlooking the river. They moved with deliberate caution to avoid even snapping a twig when they passed Japanese sentry posts. After several hours they found two 75 mm. guns hidden under large piles of kunai grass. In a few minutes they had removed the breech mechanism from each gun, but as they did so a dog started barking nearby. Looking towards the dog, Taylor also saw 40 Japanese soldiers asleep under a grass and bamboo shelter. The dog, barking noisily, began to run around the sleeping Japanese until one of them woke up. Taylor's men quickly hid near the guns. The Japanese soldier who had awoken shouted angrily at the dog and then threw a stone at it. The dog ran off and stopped barking while the Japanese soldier went back to sleep.

Moving quietly through the jungle past the sleeping men, Taylor then found two more 75 mm. guns. He began to remove the breeches from the guns when he suddenly had a feeling somebody was watching him. He looked around and saw two Japanese soldiers sitting in front of a hut, 100 yards away, watching him silently. Another soldier came out of the hut and the two men pointed towards Taylor and began arguing with the third man. Taylor decided to try to bluff. He waved to the small group and finished removing the gun breeches, then nodded towards the three men and slowly walked off.

On the night of October 31st, Vandegrift's engineers put several floating bridges, made of planks on empty drums, across the Matanikau and the next morning two battalions of 5th Marines crossed, supported by units from 7th Marines. Resistance was initially slight as they moved towards Point Cruz but it stiffened rapidly as the day wore on.

With one company of Marines was Correspondent John Hersey who recalls, "We had just reached the river bank when we came under heavy mortar and machine gun fire from the other bank. The Japs were so well hidden it was as if the trees and vines were firing at us. Even if we had been able to see the enemy, there is not much we could have done as our men were getting killed and wounded all the time."

USS San Francisco *(CA-38), a* New Orleans *class cruiser. (Division of Naval Intelligence photo)*

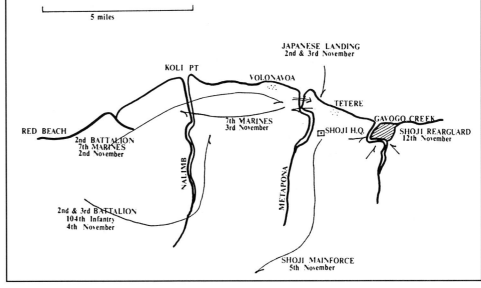

Actions in the Koli Pt. Area, November 2-12.

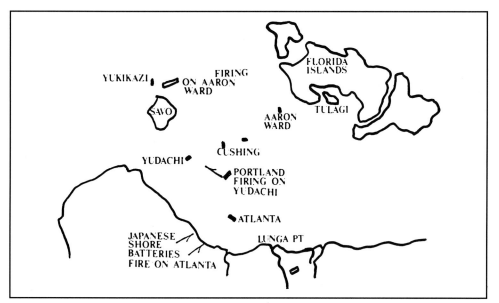

Daylight positions of US and Japanese ships on November 13.

Hersey found the mortar fire was terrifying. "They were landing about every ten seconds, now 50 yards away, now 20 feet away. One of our machine gun crews did manage to get their gun set up by the river but almost immediately a mortar landed near them, scattered the crew and knocked the gun over. The gun sergeant managed to crawl back to the gun and he got it right just as another mortar landed nearby. When the smoke cleared I could see the sergeant face down on the ground - a large hole in his back. He started to get up at one time then fell again as a continual hail of machine gun fire hit the area and slashed through the jungle where the rest of the company was concealed."

Meanwhile other Marines had crossed the river and began to push the Japanese back. Hersey recalls the Japanese fire on the Marines he was with gradually slackened as the Japanese pulled back towards Point Cruz to avoid being cut off by the Marines on their flanks.

At Hyakutake's headquarters Tsuji was still writing his report when a Colonel Sugita arrived exhausted, and in a tattered uniform from the front line. Excitedly he told Tsuji that the Americans had crossed the river in several places and were pushing towards Point Cruz. He added that the regimental commander was planning a last attack with about 150 men, "I shall go with them," he concluded. "Don't be rash, Sugita," replied Tsuji, "tell the men to dig in, it is only a matter of holding out for a few more days until our re-inforcements arrive."

Substantial Japanese re-inforcements were indeed on their way to Guadalcanal. After news of Maruyama's defeat reached Imperial Headquarters in Tokyo, they immediately ordered the 51st Division and a mixed brigade in China, to be shipped to the island. The build up of 38th Division was accelerated and hundreds of its troops were arriving nightly on the Tokyo Express. On November 2nd, as the 5th Marines fought their way towards Point Cruz, the Express landed 1,500 men at Koli Point where they joined up with several hundred survivors that Colonel Shoji had brought there after splitting away from Maruyama's forces following the fighting near the airfield.

Vandegrift had been aware that Shoji was gathering at Koli Point and on November 1st he sent the 2nd Battalion, 7th Marines under Colonel Henneken, to clean them out. For the 7th Marines it meant a forced march from their positions near Kukum. Sergeant Mitchell Paige remembers the long march through the thick jungle along the coast. "It was an awful long and hot day, with a break of ten minutes in each hour. During one such break someone suddenly shouted 'watch out!' then there was a loud crash as a big log crashed down on the path. It killed two men and injured four others; it had been a ingenious bobby trap set by the Japanese and released by a man tripping over a vine."

By darkness the battalion had reached a position on the Metapona river, a mile west of Shoji's camp and eight miles east of Lunga Point. Paige remembers, "We dug in deep enough so only our guns were above the sand and then we used debris from the beach, logs and foliage to camouflage our positions. About 2230 when it was raining very hard we peered out to sea and saw ghostly looking ships creeping silently in towards the coast. We counted six ships altogether. The famous Tokyo Express was unloading right on our doorstep. Because of the rain, our radio was out of action so we could not call Henderson. Our heaviest guns were 30 calibre machine guns and if we had fired on the Japs as they came ashore, the guns on their warships would have wiped us out. The first Jap boat landed only 300 yards up the beach from us. They took about three hours to unload about 1,500 men. There was nothing we could do, not even talk in whispers, but pray to God nobody accidentally fired his gun. I heard later that Colonel Henneken had sent back two runners to the perimeter but neither of them got there as both were killed by roving Japanese patrols. About two in the morning the Jap ships left as quietly as they had come."

These new landings brought Colonel Shoji's force up to 2,300 men and he prepared to move west against the perimeter. On the banks of the Metapona, Henneken, realizing he now faced a superior force, waited for the Japanese to approach. Mitchell Paige remembers, "As we suspected, they came along the beach towards us the next morning and it looked like they were going to walk right through our positions. As we crouched down waiting for them to come a little closer, some kncklehead of a rifleman let loose with a single shot. The Japs scattered fast but our machine guns got a lot of them before they got into the jungle. After that, the Japanese laid mortar on us. We could hear them coming through the air like a box car, then crashing into the trees behind us. The handle and wheels of one of our machine gun carts went sailing up through the trees. Then the mortars started falling around us. Word came to fall back to the perimeter but it was fire and move all day and by nightfall we had got only as far as the Nalimbu river, three miles back, where we dug in for the night."

During the day, Colonel Henneken managed to get a radio message to Vandegrift who interpreted the new threat from Shoji as being of more importance than the offensive in the Matanikau/Point Cruz area. These attacks were halted and the Marines moved back across the Matanikau into the perimeter while three battalions of outer troops were forced marched to help Henneken at the Nalimbu. They moved against an empty threat, as that day, Shoji was ordered to march his troops into the jungle, travel south of Bloody Ridge and Mount Austen, and join up with Hyakutake's forces at the Matanikau. Shoji left only a rearguard to face the reinforced Marines at the Nalimbu when they attacked on November 6th. Unaware of this, the Marines moved forward slowly, expecting the scattered resistance was the prelude to a trap. The Japanese fell back slowly to Gavago Creek, a mile east of Henneken's original line on the Metapona. At the Creek, the rearguard held out during two days of confused, bitter fighting in tortuous mangrove swamps. Many of the Japanese managed to slip through the encircling Marines and soldiers to escape into the interior, but 450 fought to the last and died around the muddy creek. The Marines lost 40 dead and 120 wounded but Shoji's diversion had also lost Vandegrift the advantage he had briefly gained of crossing the Matanikau, where Hyakutake began a rapid build-up.

On November 7th the Tokyo Express landed 1,300 men of the 38th Division, among them Lieutenant General Sano, the Divisional Commander. Three nights later another group of 600 men landed but the main part of the 38th Division was in the Shortlands were 12 transports were loading to take them to Guadalcanal. Rear Admiral Tanaka, who had previously been angered at his failure to land the main Ichiki force in August, was put in charge of this transport group and its escort of 18 destroyers. Tanaka, like Mikawa before him, insisted that Henderson airfield must be heavily attacked before he would risk his transports near the island. On the night of November 12th, a bombardment force of the battleships *Hiei* and *Kirishima* together with the cruiser *Nagara* and 11 destroyers under Rear Admiral Hiroaki Abe, approached Savo from the north.

Large American re-inforcements were also beginning to reach Guadalcanal. On November 12th, seven transports brought in nearly 6,000 infantrymen, airmen, Marines and engineers as well as large quantities of stores, ammunition and materials. Among the new army infantrymen arriving that day was Corporal James Jones of the 25th Infantry Division. He remembers his first impression of Guadalcanal was, "How beautiful the island seemed with the clear, blue sparkling sea; the long sandy beach; palms trees waving in the breeze with the dark green band of jungle behind. None of it looked like the pestilential hellhole that it was."

As the transports began to unload they were attacked by numerous Japanese torpedo and dive bombing planes. The transports had been escorted by five cruisers and 13 destroyers, which, at the approach of the enemy planes put up a wall of fire against them. It was undoubtedly the most intense anti-aircraft fire put up by ships during the whole campaign. The sky was filled with dirty brown shell bursts and even the cruisers main batteries joined in - firing short so that their shell splashes threw up huge waterspouts in the path of low-flying Japanese torpedo planes. On the shore, Shopfitter Ed O'Neill, one of the survivors from the sinking of *Seminole* three weeks before, stopped his work with a beach party to watch the torpedo planes. He remembers "they seemed to come in groups of three or four, flying only 20 or 30 feet above the water. Then the cruisers guns threw up waterspouts and twice I saw a plane fly into a waterspout then crash."

Corporal James Jones, 25th Infantry Division, had only just gotten ashore from the transports when the air raid started. He remembers, "The approaching bombers seemed like little black specs but with smaller specs of fighters moving in among them. One or two of the bombers then began to trail black smoke and fell fluttering and twisting to the sea. As the planes passed overhead the sounds of gentle sighing came through the air then the first bombs fell among the transports. I remember seeing three bombs walking towards a ship. The first landed, some distance in front of it; the second closer, and the third fell right alongside the ship into a barge that was loading. Across the water I heard a clear, high scream from some luckless individual on the barge, followed immediately by the sound of the explosion. When the debris and waterspout had fallen back into the water there were only a few heads bobbing about in the water where the barge had been."

The warships and transports turned skillfully and uniformly at right angles to avoid the numerous torpedoes released against them so that none of the torpedoes struck the ships. A damaged Japanese bomber, however, crashed on board the cruiser San Francisco causing considerable damage and killing 24 of the crew. Jones remembers the wounded being brought ashore after the raid. "A few could walk but all were suffering from shellshock and blast. Blood-stained, dazed and staggering, they came slowly up the beach to the arid station. Some were so badly wounded the doctors did not spend much time on them. The doctors would give them a pat on the shoulders and they stared back with deep, incomprehending looks."

Before his company moved off Jones remembers three of the wounded sailors died. "Two of them died quietly," he recalls, "but one of them roused himself from his dazed condition and began to shout and swear at the war, the generals, the doctors and everything else that had led to his being there then and at the point of death. Eventually he sank back, into semi consciousness and doped with morphine, passed away quietly." To the men in Jones company, unused to the harsh reality of war, it was a sobering introduction.

After the raid Turner received information about the approaching Japanese naval bombardment force, and although the transports had not finished unloading, he decided that they must leave that evening. As an escort he ordered five of the destroyers to go with them but the five cruisers and the remaining eight destroyers were to remain and engage the Japanese ships that night.

The American ships were commanded by Rear Admiral Daniel Callaghan, a one time naval aide to President Roosevelt, but with little experience of co-ordinating a fleet in night battle exercises. There was an added disadvantage since Callaghan's ship the cruiser San Fransisco had lost her radar when a Japanese plane had crashed on board earlier in the day. The cruiser Atlanta with Rear Admiral Norman Scott on board, had radar and so Callaghan decided that would use its radar and the T.B.S. system to communicate to Callaghan the approach of any Japanese ships. Scott was against the idea because he himself had commanded the American ships at the Battle of Caper Esperance a month earlier and knew the confusion that could arise over the T.B.S. if an engagement started with enemy ships.

Callaghan had arranged his ships in line astern with destroyers Cushing, Laffey, Sterett and O'Bannon followed by the cruisers Atlanta, San Francisco, Portland, Helena and Juneau. Behind them came destroyers Aaron Ward, Barton, Monsson and Fletcher. Throughout the night they patrolled steadily up and down a line from Lunga towards Savo and at 0125 on the morning of the 13th, the radar on Atlanta picked up Abe's approaching bombardment force between Savo and Cape Esperance. Callaghan's ships were approaching Savo and so he ordered a slight turn to the right to bring his ships across Abe's path, then asked for a string of information on range, bearing, course and the composition of the enemy ships as seen by radar on other ships in his force. The T.B.S. immediately became crowded since it was also used for tactical control between the

ships. Speed, range, and bearing information clashed with inquiries as to whether the bearings were true or relative.

Meanwhile the Japanese ships approached at almost 30 knots and well within range. They were led by destroyers Yudachi and Harusame which at 0140 altered course to the left and while doing so found the leading American destroyer, Cushing suddenly appear out of the darkness. So close were the ships that Cushing immediately altered hard left to avoid ramming Yudachi. The ships following Cushing altered to the left as well. Confusion. When Atlanta altered course, Callaghan asked why. "Avoiding our own destroyers." replied Atlanta, so San Francisco and the rest of the line altered also. This alteration brought the American ships on a course directly opposite to that of the Japanese and one which led directly between the Japanese battleships and their destroyers' escort. Cushing asked for permission to open fire on the Japanese lead destroyers but Callaghan was still trying to decide what was happening so by the time he gave permission, Cushing's targets had disappeared.

At 0150 the Japanese battleships flashed on their searchlights and fired brilliant white starshell that turned the night into day. The leading American ships were all clearly seen. Callaghan realized his ships had already penetrated the Japanese formation and at once ordered "open fire, odd ships fire to starboard, even ships to port". Cushing opened fire on a Japanese destroyer, then as the battleship Hiei bore down on her, Cushing altered course to the right to bring her torpedoes to bear. She was hit by numerous shells and reduced to a flaming wreck within minutes, although she did fire six torpedoes towards Hiei which forced the battleship to turn sharply to the left, followed by Kirishima.

Behind Cushing the Laffey also received heavy fire from Hiei with which she narrowly averted a collision. The two ships sped past within 1,000 yards of each other - so close that Laffey poured machine gun fire into the bridge of Hiei where several fires were started. The ship's Captain was killed and Abe himself was wounded. Hiei replied with 14" shellfire which destroyed the engine room in Laffey. Ruptured fuel lines caused a fire and after the ship was also struck by a torpedo, the order to abandon ship was given. As the stern sank, the depth charges exploded in a shattering blast which killed most of the crew struggling in the water.

Stertet next in line fired several salvoes at the Japanese searchlights before she was hit in the stern by shellfire and lost steering control. Her skipper also found Hiei heading towards him and swung out of the way using his ship's engines. Four torpedoes were fired at Hiei but none were seen to hit. Further shell hits on the Stertett knocked out most of her guns and caused widespread fires, but her engine room was undamaged and she got through the action battered but in one piece.

O'Bannon, fourth in line, fired on Hiei as soon as the battleship switched on searchlights, and continued to do so until forced to alter course to avoid Stertet. This brought O'Bannon so close to Hiei that the battleship could not depress her guns sufficiently to engage the destroyer. As O'Bannon brought her guns to bear, Callaghan, on the T.B.S. ordered "cease firing, own ships". On O'Bannon the skipper hesitated briefly then ordered two torpedoes fired at Hiei. They sped straight to the target - but failed to explode. By that time the battleship had been the target of numerous ships and shell bursts were breaking out along her whole length. The huge battleship was burning fiercely as she turned away from Callaghan's ships and headed out of the Channel. After O'Bannon fired her torpedoes she altered course rapidly to avoid the sinking Laffey but as she passed the stricken ship it exploded so violently that O'Bannon was almost lifted out of the water. By that time the scene was so confused that O'Bannon's skipper pulled

away from the area to sort things out. He then decided Japanese transports may be slipping past so he headed down the coast towards Lunga in search of them.

The first cruiser in the American line was Atlanta, with Admiral Scott. Japanese searchlights fixed on her from the start and she came under intense fire. A salvo hit the bridge, killing Scott and almost everybody else there. A torpedo then exploded in the engine room and the disabled ship drifted off the right into the line of fire from San Francisco whose 8 inch shells caused havoc on the Atlanta. Callaghan, realizing what had happened called "cease fire, own ships". He meant it for gunners on his own ship but the message went out on the T.B.S. causing momentary confusion on several ships. It was also too late to help Atlanta. Wrecked by 50 shell hits and two torpedo hits, she drifted helplessly down the Channel towards Lunga.

San Francisco had brought one of the Japanese destroyers under fire as soon as the action began. She then engaged a second target and while doing so, she hit the Atlanta as she drifted out of the line. After he had given his "cease fire" order, Callaghan spotted the Hiei and called out "we want the big ones, get the big ones" as he then ordered "commence firing" again, Hiei swept past San Francisco on an opposite course and the two ships fired at each other at what was virtually point blank range, causing extensive damage to each other. The bridge on San Francisco was wrecked and Callaghan was killed there with many others. The other Japanese battleship Kirishima and the cruiser Nagara then added to the damage on San Francisco. Perhaps the only thing that saved the ship was that the Japanese shells, designed to bombard Henderson, were not armour piercing and although the ship was hit by 45 shells, none caused any engine room damage.

The cruiser Portland had opened fire when the Japanese searchlights came on and continued to do so even when she heard Callaghan's "cease fire" order because her targets were quite definite. The skipper on Portland asked Callaghan, "What's the dope, do you want to cease firing?" Callaghan replied, "Yes." The Portland ceased firing, while she made an alteration, then resumed firing but was almost immediately hit by a torpedo in the stern. The damage was such that the ship could only steam in a large circle. The battle then moved away from the disabled cruiser and she was still steaming slowly in circles the next morning when at daybreak, she sighted the abandoned Japanese destroyer Yudachi also disabled during the battle. Portland commenced firing on the destroyer and after her sixth salvo the Japanese ship suddenly blew up.

The Helena, next cruiser in line behind Portland, engaged in rapid fire with various targets throughout the savage battle. At one time her guns were firing on three different targets while her skipper dodged the numerous torpedoes streaming though the sea. Helena received only slight damage and continued firing until the Japanese ships broke off the engagement at 0225.

The last cruiser in line was Juneau which shifted fire from one target to another for 15 minutes until she was hit by a torpedo in the forward fireroom. She limped away with a damaged propeller shaft and probably a broken keel. The actual extent of her damage that night is unknown because she met a sudden, terrifying end the next day.

The first of the destroyers in the rear was Aaron Ward. She engaged an enemy ship but was forced to cease firing when friendly ships got in the way. Her skipper then decided to leave the line and close with the enemy ships. In doing so she almost collided with Helena and had to go full astern. Eventually she fired on a ship showing unfamiliar lights (it was probably the Monsssen) and was then hit herself in the stern engine room.

She lost power, as the engine room became flooded, and then drifted away to the east.

The next destroyer in line was *Barton*. She fired four torpedoes at the destroyers screening the Japanese battleships, but then was forced to stop to avoid collision with another ship. While stopped, she was struck by two torpedoes. She broke in two almost at once and sank within minutes amid a sea of blazing oil. Only 25 of her crew of 250 survived. The ship had been commissioned only five months before and her first, and last, action had lasted seven minutes.

Astern of *Barton* the *Monssen* fired five torpedoes towards *Hiei* then five more at another Japanese ship. None of these torpedoes were seen to hit the target, or if they did, failed to explode. Suddenly, just ahead *Monssen* saw *Barton* explode and sink. *Monssen* was so close she almost immediately passed through the wreckage, burning oil and survivors. Next a green starshell burst over the ship and her commander, thinking it had been fired by an American ship, ordered recognition lights switched on. Immediately she became the target of numerous ships and was hit by heavy shells which caused havoc on board. A five inch turret was blown over the side, her bridge was wrecked and fire rooms and engine rooms damaged. She was abandoned at 0220 but drifted, burning fiercely until noon when she exploded and sank. half of the crew were lost with her.

The last destroyer in line was *Fletcher*. By skillful use of radar she shifted fire from one target to the other starting a fire on one of her targets. When *Barton* blew up and *Monssen* was caught in a storm of shell fire, *Fletcher's* skipper realized complete disorder existed so he took his ship away to the north, assessed the situation, then returned and launched torpedoes at *Kirishima*. If the torpedoes hit the battleship, none of them exploded. *Fletcher* was the only American ship to survive undamaged that night.

In the Japanese flotilla the sudden appearance of Callaghan's ships among his own ships caused confusion in Admiral Abe, because a reconnaissance flight over Sealark Channel the previous day had reported no enemy warships in the Channel. The action with the American warships developed so quickly into a disorderly melee that Abe decided to withdraw from the area. His ship, however, had been the target of so much American fire that her officers later counted 85 shell hits. Her tall, pagoda-like bridge was badly damaged and fires raged throughout the ship. The ship's rudder was jammed and her engines were damaged but her main armament was still working. The only other casualty among the Japanese ships was the destroyer *Yudachi* which became so badly damaged she was abandoned by her crew. Other Japanese ships received only negligible damage and were clear of Savo, northbound, by 0230 except for *Hiei*.

Built before World War I, the 31,720 ton *Hiei* sacrificed armour for speed and the eight inch shells from Callaghan's cruisers had penetrated deep before exploding, causing extensive damage. Her damaged engine room allowed only a very slow speed and by dawn she was only just north of Savo. The fires burning inside the ship were out of control and even the hull itself had begun to glow red. The destroyer *Yukikaze* stood by to take off the battleship's crew.

At dawn United States airmen flying off from Henderson found the whole area south of Savo was littered with burning, listing, damaged ships; vast amount of debris; oil and hundreds of survivors. Off Tassafaronga the *Atlanta* was barely afloat. Two miles north of her, *Portland* was steaming in circles firing at the burning *Yudachi* six miles to the west of her. The *Cushing* and *Monssen* were both drifting and burning fiercely, and further away still was the uncontrollable *Aaron Ward*.

For *Aaron Ward* the battle was not yet over. Far way to the northwest, just off Savo, lay the *Hiei*. the range was over 20,000 yards, 11 and one-half miles, far outside that of the five inch guns of *Aaron Ward* but comfortably within that of *Hiei's* big guns. As the men on the *Aaron Ward* watched helplessly, the great turrets of the battleship trained slowly towards them, the guns elevated and a ripple of fire flashed from the battleship's eight 14 inch guns. On the destroyer the officers started their stop watches. Time hung heavily as they waited for the 12 tons of shells to reach them. The first salvo hit 500 yards short - the shells ricocheted off the water and passed overhead with a crash like thunder. The next salvo landed over the ship. One salvo short: one salvo over, so the third salvo seemed likely to be a hit. The destroyer's officers watched as the big guns came down to load position, then elevated and fired again. The range was perfect but the deflection had crept off a little and the shells landed just ahead of the destroyer. Just when it seemed a fourth salvo must be the end for *Aaron Ward*, planes from Henderson began to bomb the distant *Hiei*. There was no fourth salvo.

The battleship was repeatedly bombed throughout the day. Extensive damage was caused on her superstructure and new fires started. The ship began to burn from stem to stern and in the late afternoon her crew gave up the struggle. They transferred to the destroyer *Yukikaze* and Abe gave the order to scuttle the battleship. Eventually she went down five miles northwest of Savo - the first Japanese battleship to be sunk in the war.

Desperate efforts were made to save *Atlanta*, drifting towards Japanese shore batteries on the Guadalcanal coast. She was taken under tow and reached Lunga during the afternoon, but could not be kept afloat and eventually sank three miles offshore in the early evening. *Portland* finally reached Tulagi with aid of a tug pushing strongly against her bows to keep the cruiser's course straight. *Cushing* and *Monssen* both went down during the afternoon and *Aaron Ward* was towed to Tulagi.

Admiral Turner expected another Japanese naval force to attempt to bombard that evening and ordered the damaged cruisers and destroyers to leave for the New Hebrides as soon as possible. As they steamed south they were seen by the Japanese submarine I-26 which fired a spread of torpedoes towards the *San Francisco*. On board the cruiser Lieutenant Commander McCandless saw the torpedoes pass ahead of his ship then go on to hit the cruiser *Juneau*. McCandless remembers, "The *Juneau* didn't sink - she blew up with the force of a volcano. There was a terrific thunderclap and a plume of white water which was quickly blotted out by a huge brown hemisphere a 1,000 yards across, from within which came the sound of more explosions. A twin five inch gun turret rose slowly into the air above the cloud and then dropped back out of sight." Debris rained down on the *San Francisco* and other nearby ships. When the huge brown cloud had drifted away there was nothing to be seen of the *Juneau* or her 600 man crew. Incredibly 100 men did survive the shattering explosions and clung to debris.

One of the survivors was Signalman L. Zook who remembers many of the survivors were wounded and hardly able to hang on to the debris. "As time went by," he recalls, "the rafts and debris drifted apart; some of the wounded just let go and drifted off. On larger rafts, when the wounded died, they were pushed off into the water so that others in the water could get onto the rafts. We had no food or water and under the hot sun some guys drank sea water. Within hours they were reduced to dangerous madness and began fighting with the same ones among us. They had to be pushed off the rafts." The men on the scattered rafts drifted for days. Three men eventually paddled to an island and were cared for by a plantation owner. Six more men, including Zook, were picked up when sighted by a Catalina float plane. Several days after this the destroyer *Ballard* picked up a lone survivor. A total of ten. Of the 590 men lost with the ship five of them were brothers - the Sullivans.

Never again did the United States Navy allow brothers to serve on the same ship.

TENACIOUS TANAKA

Before Abe had clashed with Callaghan at what became known as the Naval Battle of Guadalcanal, the 12 transports carrying the bulk of the 38th Division had left the Shortlands. Tanaka had been confident that Abe would have destroyed Henderson airfield sufficiently to let the transports get to Guadalcanal without interference by American planes. When he heard that Abe had not bombarded the airfield, Tanaka turned the transports back to the Shortlands while new arrangements were made to shell Henderson.

The loss of *Hiei* came as a shock to the Imperial Navy and Abe was reprimanded then transferred to a shore job later in the year. The next bombardment of the airfield was under the command of Mikawa and he arrived in Sealark Channel on the night of 13th November with four cruisers. There were no American ships in the channel and for two hours the airfield was subjected to another heavy shelling. In the morning 18 wrecked planes littered the airfield and 32 others were damaged, but ground staff managed to get together 20 serviceable planes which flew off to look for Mikawa's cruisers. They were found 140 miles to the northwest and attacked several times throughout the morning by planes from Henderson and the carrier *Enterprise* which was operating south of Guadalcanal. The cruiser *Kinugasa* was sunk and a second cruiser badly damaged, then attacks were diverted to Tanaka's transport group which was spotted during the morning - 120 miles northwest of Guadalcanal. The determined Admiral had decided to run 11 transports through in day-light, confident that Mikawa's bombardment the night before had immobilized Henderson airfield.

Throughout the morning and afternoon of the 14th, the transports and their screen of 11 destroyers were attacked repeatedly by torpedo bombers and dive bombers despite a curtain of fire put up by the destroyers. Tanaka remembers "Bombers roared down on their targets as though they would plunge into the sea, releasing their bombs barely in time to pull out. Every hit raised a sheet of fire and clouds of smoke as the transports burst into flame and took that sickening list that spells their doom. When the planes left, hundreds of soldiers were jumping overboard from the burning, sinking ships". By late afternoon, six of the transports had been sunk and a seventh had turned back towards the Shortlands. The destroyer screen picked up hundreds of burned and wounded men from the water, but for 3,000 soldiers and seamen for whom the run to Guadalcanal ended in a watery grave that afternoon.

At last night fell and hid the remaining transports as they steamed on towards the island. "A sorry remnant," Tanaka recalls, "in six attacks the enemy sank six transports; the crews were near exhaustion and the remaining ships, after zigzagging all day were scattered in all directions." He hoped that another shelling of the airfield would save him from any more attacks the next day. Admiral Kondo in the battleship *Kirishima* and with a force of cruisers and destroyers were ordered to shell the airfield again before Tanaka's ships reached the island.

Over the previous few days American submarines and planes, and Australian coastwatchers had given Turner a fairly clear picture of the gathering Japanese naval units. Rear Admiral Willis Lee in the battleship *Washington* with a second battleship *South Dakota* and four destroyers had been ordered to

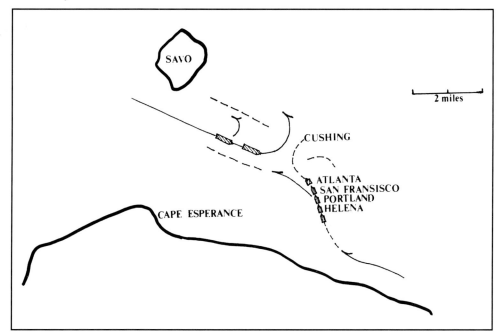

Battle of Guadalcanal, November 13.

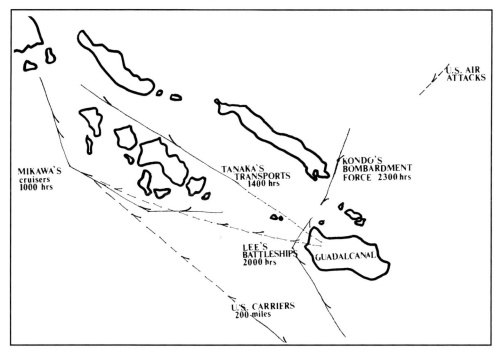

Positions of US and Japanese Naval Forces, November 14.

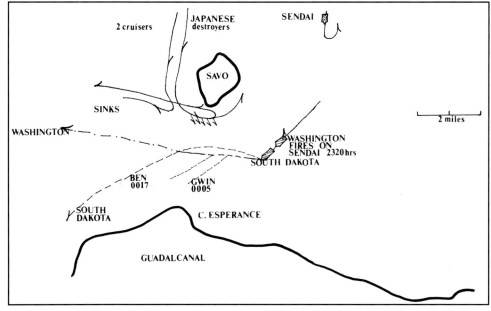

Battle of Guadalcanal, November 14-15.

Guadalcanal to stop the nightly shelling of the airfield. Lee had not been able to get there in time to stop Mikawa's cruiser force on the night of the 13th but he was waiting, just south of Savo Island, when Kondo's group approached the next night. Kondo split his force into two groups near Savo Island, sending the cruiser *Sendai* with a destroyer to the east of the island while the main force of *Kirishima*, three cruisers and seven destroyers went between Savo and Cape Esperance.

At 2320 *Washington* and *South Dakota* both fired on *Sendai*. The Japanese cruiser made smoke and reversed course and *Washington* fired a few parting shots at her. While Lee's attention was thus engaged, his four destroyers, *Walke*, *Benham*, *Preston* and *Gwin*, were two miles ahead and making contact with Kondo's main force as it entered Sealark Channel close against the shore of Savo Island. *Walke* immediately opened fire, followed by the other three destroyers. It was such a dark night that the gunners themselves could hardly see the Japanese warships and many of the crew on the destroyers thought they were firing on Japanese shore batteries on Savo Island. The Japanese ships replied with torpedoes, one of which struck *Walke* in the forward magazine, with an ear splitting roar. Everything from the bridge forward disappeared. As the stern began to settle the depth charges, previously reported to be on 'safe', blew up one by one among the survivors in the oil covered waters.

Next in line the *Benham* was the victim of a torpedo which blew off her bow. Reduced to a speed of five knots she limped away in the direction of Cape Esperance.

On *Preston*, Lieutenant McKee recalls the ship was hit repeatedly by shellfire which demolished superstructure over most of her length. He remembers "she began to sink by the stern in less than two minutes. I stepped off a ladder into the sea and began swimming. After a while I found a damaged raft, most of it had been shot away but there was enough room left to support me. All around me in the darkness I could hear men calling for help or directing shipmates to rafts. Japanese shells were still landing among the men in the water but what worried me was that we were right in the path of *South Dakota* and *Washington*."

Both of the United States battleships had been dogged by problems at that time. Just as *Walke* had opened fire, the *South Dakota* had a power failure. Gyro compasses, radars and gun turrets were all out of action for three vital minutes; the crew felt helpless as their own destroyers ahead exploded and burned. To avoid these destroyers, *Washington* altered course to the left, but *South Dakota* altered to the right and so was silhouetted by the burning destroyers, to the main force. The *Kirishima* and two Japanese cruisers immediately poured heavy fire into her, even as *South Dakota* got her power restored and replied with every gun. So intent was the main Japanese force in directing their fire on *South Dakota* that *Washington* was not noticed until she poured a heavy concentration of shellfire into *Kirishima*. In just seven minutes, the old Japanese battleship was torn apart by nine main battery shells of a ton each and over 40 five-inch shells from a range of 8,000 yards. She lost steerage, and began to burn throughout her wrecked superstructure.

When *Kirishima* was knocked out of action, *Washington* continued on a course which was in the general direction of Tanaka's transports coming down from the northwest. This sudden threat to the transports led the Japanese warships to reverse course and follow the *Washington*. It gave the damaged *South Dakota* a chance to slip away, for with over 100 dead or wounded and with communications destroyed, she had little more to contribute to the engagement.

Tanaka's group of four transports and 11 destroyers had been 25 miles northwest of Savo when he had seen the distant flashes of gunfire and the glare from burning ships. He sent two destroyers ahead to help Kondo and shortly after midnight they met the *Washington* speeding towards them. Both destroyers launched torpedoes - some of which exploded in the turbulence of *Washington's* wake - others were spotted by lookouts and Lee conned the ship along the direction of the torpedoes, none of which hit his ship. Having drawn the main force of Japanese warships away from the surviving American ships, he then turned to the southwest and left the area at high speed.

Off Savo the battered *Kirishima*, burning fiercely, was further wrecked by a number of internal explosions and three hours after the engagement, Kondo ordered her abandoned, and scuttled. At the cost of three destroyers sunk (*Benham* was ordered scuttled the next day) and one battleship badly damaged, Lee had thwarted yet another attempt to knock out Henderson airfield, and it was the planes at Henderson which prevented the Japanese build-up on the island.

In the early hours of the 15th, Tanaka knew that Kondo had failed to hit the airfield. He also realized that his transports could not reach the island, unload and get clear before dawn, so he decided to run them aground at Tassafaronga to ensure that they would at least not be sunk before they could unload. When daylight came on the 15th, pilots from Henderson were amazed to see the four transports, firmly aground, unloading thousands of troops and tons of supplies. With little or no aircover during the day, the Japanese transports were hit repeatedly by planes from Henderson which ran a shuttle service over the 20 miles from the airfield to Tassafaronga, loading up with bombs and machine gun bullets time and again. All four ships were quickly set on fire; hundreds of men going ashore from the ships were slaughtered by machine-gunning fighters. By afternoon the sea around the ships was turning red as countless dead floated amid the wreckage. So ghastly was the widespread bloody carnage that many of the airmen were physically sick at the sight. By nightfall only 2,000 men were safely ashore and from the bombed and burning supplies, only 5 tons of ammunition and 1,500 bags of rice could be salvaged. Most of the troops loaded on to the destroyer had not been landed but were carried back to the Shortlands when the destroyers fled from the area before dawn. Despite the grim determination of Tanaka to get the transports through, he had landed only one man in six of those who had left the Shortlands. It had been at the cost of two battleships, a cruiser, three destroyers and 4,000 lives lost in two days.

It was a bitter blow to Hyakutake's plans. He could still expect the Tokyo Express to bring a few thousand of the troops taken back to the Shortlands but without supplies, the condition of his troops on Guadalcanal was deteriorating so fast he no longer felt capable of making a major attack until the 51st Division arrived from China. In the meantime he ordered his men to prepare defensive positions from the Matanikau, inland along the ridges, as far as Mount Austen.

The positions were soon tested. United States re-inforcements had continued to build up and on November 18, the 182nd Infantry Regiment crossed the Matanikau. They soon ran into strong resistance. On the series of hills overlooking the river, the Japanese were in well camouflaged dugouts covered with logs and earth. Between each dugout were interlocking fields of machine gun fire and the whole area had been zeroed in by Japanese mortars and artillery. Little progress was made by the United Sates soldiers - most of whom had only been on the island a week and found the hot, humid climate and steep hills quickly sapped their strength. The next day, part of the regiment moved along a narrow

The battleship USS Washington *(BB-56). She earned 13 battlestars. (Courtesy of Ted Blahnik)*

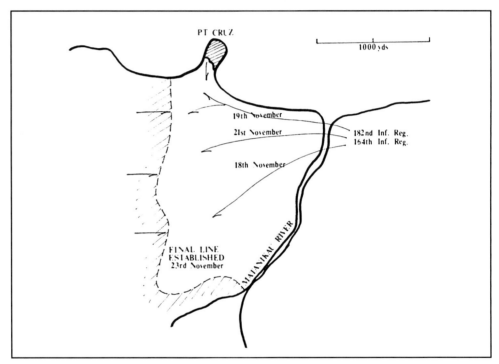

Matanikau Offensive, November 18-23.

Japanese troop transport, Kinugawa Maru. *She was bombed and beached in mid November at the mouth of the Bonegi River. The area was under the command of Col. William B. Tuttle.*

coastal plain from the Matanikau towards Point Cruz. They got about half a mile before they were pinned down and forced to dig in for the rest of the day. At dawn on the 20th, Hyakutake brought up troops form Kokumbona and in several charges, forced the men of the 182nd Infantry back, until United States artillery and planes stopped the Japanese charges. During the rest of the day the Japanese were pushed slowly back until they were just west of Point Cruz, although on the Point itself the Japanese held out.

On the 21st, the 164th Infantry Regiment of the Americal Division took over the offensive and over the next two days, fresh assaults were made against the Japanese positions. No progress was made except to clear Point Cruz - a promontory 500 yards long and 400 yards wide. Elsewhere the Japanese showed grim determination to fight for every yard. From the hills and gullies just south of the narrow coastal plain, they poured enfilading fire from cunningly concealed positions. At dusk on the 23rd the attacks were called off and the line then held, running south of Point Cruz, inland one and a half miles, to the west fork of the upper Matanikau, was to be unchanged for almost two months.

The stiff resistance the Japanese offered owed more to their tough discipline and training, rather than their well-being. By the end of November, after the disastrous failure of Tanaka's transports, their supply position was becoming critical. Many units had been on half rations for weeks and in mid-November, they were reduced to one-third rations. Men supplemented their meager diet by eating coconuts, bamboo shoots and wild potatoes, or taro.

Despite the advice of some Solomon Islanders the Japanese could not distinguish between cultivated and wild taro and the wild taro they ate caused irritation in their throats. With some 25,000 men in an area of less than 20 square miles, the Japanese soon exhausted the local food supplies and then began to eat grasses, ferns, river weeds and the bark off trees. Their medical arrangements were also hopelessly inadequate; little was available in the way of drugs and medicines; bandages had to be re-used, or wounds bound up with cloth. In the hot, fetid air of the jungle, the slightest wound, attacked by numerous flies, became infected within a day. Blood poisoning and gangrenous wounds multiplied rapidly, condemning the half-starved and weakened men to a sure, if slow, death.

The incidence of malaria was almost 100% and the huge black flies covering the unburied dead, later contaminated food so that thousands of troops contracted dysentery and enteritis which weakened them still further. Many of the soldiers became too weak to go out on patrols and simply stayed in their foxholes or dugouts for days - emerging only to search for food and water. In a report to Tokyo, Hyakutake told Army Headquarters, "The force at the front lines consists of three types. First there are those who are too weak to walk - they are confined to static defense positions. Second there are those who can walk with the aid of a stick - they are responsible for cooking. Third, there are the comparatively healthy ones who can still engage in patrol activity".

Nicholas Visaona, the Solomon Islander who had once worked on the Japanese road to Lunga was, by then, working as an army scout for the Americans. On one patrol, in late November, Visaona was several yards ahead of an army sergeant when he saw a group of Japanese soldiers lying on the ground, apparently resting - 200 yards ahead. Visaona called out to the sergeant behind him but the sergeant replied "Keep quiet, just make hand signals". Together they cautiously approached the Japanese, then the sergeant told Visaona to go forward and see if they were armed, while he, the sergeant, kept him covered. Visaona found the Japanese arms were all stacked off to one side away from them. As he approached he saw that the soldiers were awake but they all seemed too tired to even get up. When he got nearer he found the Japanese were all very thin and looked ill. In some cases they were suffering from dysentery and being too weak to defecate properly, their clothing smelt disgusting. Some of them called out for water as Visaona approached and he gave them what he had from two water bottles. When the sergeant came he sent Visaona back to camp for some laborers and when they arrived they carried the Japanese back to the American lines.

Hyakutake's daily messages to Rabaul became increasingly desperate. At the end of November, with regular food supplies exhausted, he sent a message asking for immediate help, adding that the starved and wounded were dying at the rate of 100 a day. He concluded "...if food supplies are not sent at once, then by the time re-inforcements arrive it is doubtful how many troops will still be alive here".

Disease was also an increasing problem within the American lines. The rate of malaria cases were running at 700-900 a week in November and the men also found that malaria brought on a form of secondary anemia which led to a rapid decline in resistance to other diseases. In late November a Naval doctor, Lieutenant Commander E. Smith reported that in the 1st Marines there had been an average loss of weight of 20 pounds in every man since August. In some cases individuals had lost as much as 45 pounds in the three months. Smith found that the rain, sticky heat, swarms of insects and mosquitoes, malaria and dysentery all contributed to a rapid rundown in health which led not only to blood stream infections and gastrointestinal diseases, but a more ominous, damaging long-term disorder in thinking and even the will to live.

Around Bloody Ridge, the Tenaru river and the Matanikau, many men had, by late November, spent almost two months in the same foxhole or dug out and associated it with survival. They could not then be persuaded to leave their foxholes without threats from their officers. Others weakened by jaundice, dengue fever or festering tropical ulcers which oozed a cupful of pus every day, simply could not make the effort to walk back to a kitchen for hot food. In isolated foxholes, the darkness of the jungle at night, with the endless noises of countless insects and squawking birds, began to prey on men's minds. Each bird call could mean a signal to send a group of Japanese soldiers snaking through the grass to silently cut the throat of someone in a foxhole. Almost every night somewhere round the perimeter there would be a sudden rush of feet towards an American outpost, a scream, a few shots, then all quiet again, but with one or two men left dead or injured.

In a few cases the endless struggle to survive against the enemy, disease and apathy, pushed men's minds too far and grim, hideous habits began to develop. In one unit leg bones were cut off dead Japanese. The bones were then cut into sections, the marrow scraped out and the bone cut to form a ring. In another case the ears of Japanese were cut off and hung on a grizzly "clothes line." Another soldier, regularly inspected the mouths of dead Japanese and wrenched out any gold teeth with a pair of pliers. The teeth were then kept in a bag hung around his neck.

The most severe strain was felt by the pilots at the airfield. Doctor Victor Falk, a flight surgeon at Henderson, arrived with a group of 40 pilots on September 28th. He recalls "Many of them had less than ten hours experience in dive bombers before they arrived for combat at Guadalcanal." Over the next two months Falk recorded what happened to each of the pilots. "Within a week three of them failed to return from missions and a fourth was evacuated with combat injuries. During the heavy shelling on October 13th, four more from the group were killed and the next day another pilot crashed on landing and was evacuated with severe injuries. On October 15th three more pilots were lost in attacks against the Japanese transports beached at Tassafaronga. The day after that, two pilots were killed in combat. A week later another pilot suffered injuries after an emergency landing; he was evacuated along with a pilot who had suffered a concussion from a bomb blast. On November 6th we evacuated two more pilots from the group, with severe malaria."

Falk remembers that the pilots, like everybody else, never had decent food and suffered from constant lack of sleep caused by the nightly bombing. This led to exhaustion among the pilots and contributed towards further losses. Falk continues, "On November 7th one of the pilots went missing shortly after take-off and the next day another man was lost in bad weather. Two days after that a pilot received a broken jaw when forced to land at sea and on the 13th we lost two more pilots in the attacks against the battleship *Hiei*. The following day a relief squadron arrived and the remaining 17 men, in the original group of 40, were evacuated to the New Hebrides." Falk recalls also, "During the time we were on Guadalcanal the squadron's losses were so high we had ten commanding officers in six weeks." He goes on, "when the 17 survivors reached the New Hebrides I found that 13 of them had malaria. They recuperated for several weeks but at the end of that time, only one man was considered fit for combat duty and was sent back to Guadalcanal". Falk concludes "I heard later that when he got to Henderson he just refused to fly combat again and was put on ground control."

Captain Joe Foss was America's top fighter pilot on Guadalcanal - being credited with 26 enemy planes destroyed during two six weeks tour of duty. Foss also remembers that the food was continually awful; sleep was only possible for brief periods and he was on alert everyday. Frequently he put in ten to 12 hours flying a day. "The usual routine," he recalls, "was to get up at almost five in the morning in order to be ready for a possible dawn patrol and if you did not have to do that, you were on standby duty in case the Japs came over later, which they usually did. Once that happened you would probably be flying for the rest of the day with two or three missions."

Foss had a healthy respect for the enemy. "The Jap pilots were good," he recalls, "they had a good plane in the Zero with superior speed and better maneuverability than any of our planes, but I thought their tactics could have been improved. They should have stayed further away from our more heavily armed fighters instead of coming in so close to engage us. All the same, every time I went into action against them I came back with holes in my plane and I got shot down once."

For others, well removed from the turmoil at Henderson, this period of the campaign with so little action, became boring. At Point Cruz, Corporal John Weiss, with an artillery unit, had been on the island two months and had seen the action from artillery bombardments only. At the end of November, in search of a little more action, Weiss and three others from his unit volunteered to join a patrol which was sent to clear out some Japanese believed to be hiding in a cave inland from Point Cruz. While moving slowly through the thick undergrowth, Weiss suddenly saw his first enemy soldier. "He was running through the trees," Weiss recalls, "I was surprised at how small he seemed. I fired one shot in his direction then he disappeared behind some trees. The next thing I knew there was a shattering blast very near which knocked me over and I felt a sudden pain in my leg like somebody had just kicked me."

The Japanese soldier had thrown a grenade which had landed so close that not only was Weiss injured but another man nearby fell screaming with a grenade splinter in his belly. When Weiss recovered a little from the initial shock, he saw that his leg had been almost severed by the grenade, yet it did not seem to be bleeding too much. He thought perhaps the hot grenade splinter had cauterized the blood vessels it had severed. He recalls, "I knew I was in a bad way though and after a few minutes I began to feel weak and dazed. I half remembered being lifted onto a stretcher a little later but when they lifted the stretcher, the canvas sheet below me tore and I fell on to the ground. Eventually I had to hobble back to our lines with a makeshift crutch and when we got there, I passed out."

Weiss recalls that the days and weeks which followed were spent in only a semi-conscious state. "I recovered consciousness only at irregular intervals. Once when I came too, I seemed to be in a dugout that was being shelled; occasionally the ground shook and a shower of dirt fell on to me from the roof but I felt too weak to brush if off my face. It seemed like days later when I came round again and examined my wound. It was infested with white maggots, yet I was not alarmed because I remembered that in World War I they used to put maggots on wounds because maggots ate diseased flesh". Sometime later, Weiss recalled being on a ship and when he finally recovered full consciousness he was in a hospital bed in New Zealand. "I had no idea how long I had been there or even what day or month it was" he recalls, "but my leg still hurt a lot. A nurse passed by and I called her over to ask how my leg was. She told me that they had taken it off. It took me a long time to get over that".

TANAKA TRIES AGAIN

The loss of so much shipping in Tanaka's determined but futile attempts to re-enforce Guadalcanal, led to the adoption of different Japanese tactics in late November. Tanaka's new plan was that his destroyers would arrive off the beaches at night and cast off long lines of drums containing supplies. Each destroyer was considered capable of carrying 250 drums which would be hurriedly pushed over the side to be collected by small boats operating from the beach. To make it easy to collect all the drums they were tied together in long chains of 40-50 drums. A boat would pick up a rope attached to the first drum and take it ashore where a beach patrol would then haul in the whole line of drums. Tanaka planned the first attempt for the night of November 30th.

American Naval forces had, meanwhile, been re-organized. After the extensive damage suffered by the *South Dakota*, battleships were no longer to be committed to the restrictive waters of the Solomon Islands. On November 28th Admiral Carleton Wright took command of a cruiser force at Espiritu Santo in the New Hebrides, with orders to intercept Japanese night landings on Guadalcanal. Wright was given little opportunity to familiarize himself with the tactics required, as the next day he received word of a Japanese group of destroyers and transports heading towards Guadalcanal. He immediately put to sea with his five cruisers and four destroyers.

As Wright's ships approached Guadalcanal on the afternoon of the 30th they met an American convoy southbound with a destroyer escort. Wright ordered two of these destroyers to join his force. They were the *Lamson* and *Lardner*. On the *Lamson* Commander Abercrombie became the senior destroyer officer present, but Wright found it impossible to send him any operational plan and, in fact, did not even pass to Abercrombie the recognition signals that the cruisers were using. Abercrombie was simply told to fall into line behind the cruisers.

Shortly after Wright's force anchored off Lunga

Point a Japanese reconnaissance plane passed overhead and later reported to Tanaka that there were several enemy cruisers and destroyers in Sealark Channel. Anticipating trouble, Tanaka only loaded six destroyers with drums and assigned two unloaded destroyers as a screen. He told the destroyer captains that if they were attacked while unloading they were to cease unloading and engage the enemy immediately.

As Wright's ships patrolled from Lunga to Savo that night the leading destroyer *Fletcher* sighted one of Tanaka's screening destroyers, *Takanani*, at 2316. She was 7,000 yards away and speeding past on an opposite course, inshore near Tassafaronga. *Fletcher* called Wright, who was on the cruiser *Minneapolis*, over the T.B.S. for permission to open fire. In reply Wright only asked *Fletcher* for more details of the sighting and gave the order to open fire four minutes after *Fletcher* had asked for it. The Japanese destroyers had, by then, passed by. However *Fletcher* and the other three leading destroyers in Wright's force fired off 20 torpedoes at the Japanese ships.

During those four minutes Wright had begun to get good radar contacts on the Japanese ships using radar on the *Minneapolis*. When the enemy destroyers were five miles away Wright ordered "commence firing" as the four leading destroyers loosed off their torpedoes.

All five United States cruisers immediately brought the Japanese destroyers under intense shell fire. Soon the lead destroyers joined in while the *Lamson* and *Lardner* with poor radar and unsure of where the target was, fired starshell. The crescendo of firing from the 11 warships of Wright's force was staggering even to those on Guadalcanal who had endured the shelling of the airfield in October. Off Tassafaronga the quiet moonless night was shattered by the combined fire of nearly 120-eight-inch, a six-inch and five-inch guns among the cruisers and destroyers.

The target for much of this fire was the screen destroyer *Takanani*. Tanaka's orders had been that if they were attacked, all ships should fire torpedoes then withdraw quickly, but under no circumstances should they use gunfire. *Takanani* followed these instructions but came under such a hail of fire that she eventually replied with five-inch shellfire which served only to concentrate American fire on her. Within minutes she was reduced to a flaming wreck and the cruiser fire shifted to the other Japanese destroyers. Among these ships, the well trained crews followed Tanaka's instructions, even though

some ships were still clearing away drums from the deck. Within a few minutes they had all reversed course and put on full speed as they launched about 20 torpedoes towards Wright's cruisers.

Minneapolis had just fired her ninth salvo when the first of these torpedoes struck her. At 2327 two huge explosions against her side thew wreckage and flames to mast-head height. Fuel oil began to burn and from the bridge, Captain Rosendahl was horrified to see about 60 feet of his ship's bows had been torn downwards forming a huge scoop which washed the sea up to the forward gun turrets. *Minneapolis* managed to fire three more salvos before she lost all power.

Behind *Minneapolis* the *New Orleans* quickly altered course to avoid her, but was herself almost immediately hit by a torpedo with such a devastating explosion that the 600 foot cruiser was simply torn in half just in front of the bridge. The forward section, with eight-inch guns pointing skywards, drifted past the rest of the ship, bumping and scraping its way towards the stern. It all happened so quickly that men on the stern section thought they were passing the sinking *Minneapolis*.

Next in line was the cruiser *Pensacola* which swung hard left to avoid the burning ships ahead of her. In doing so she moved in the direction where the Japanese torpedoes were coming from and received a torpedo amidships. Her engine room flooded so quickly only one man was able to escape. All communications were knocked out and from a ruptured fuel tank, a sheet of flaming oil burst skywards and enveloped her large tripod mast where gunnery control crews were burned alive.

The fourth cruiser *Honolulu* altered course to the right and so passed the damaged ships ahead of her, keeping them between her and the Japanese. With rapid course alterations she passed through the area safely and at maximum speed, firing repeatedly, she followed the retiring Japanese destroyers towards Cape Esperance.

The last of Wright's cruisers was *Northampton* and she attempted to follow *Honolulu* but at 2347 was hit by the last torpedoes fired from the Japanese destroyer *Oyashio*. Here again the cruiser's engine room was hit and ruptured fuel tanks led to extensive fires which, at one time, burned from the bridge to the stern. *Northampton* also developed a dangerous list and eventually the ship stopped to control flooding from sea water pouring into her engine room. For three hours the ship burned like a huge torch just south of Savo, and became the target of Japanese shore batteries on Guadalcanal. The list increased

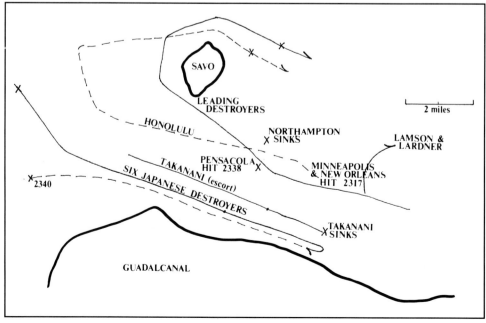

The Battle of Tassaforonga.

Members of 147th Inf. RCT Service Company. They were stationed in the interior of the Carney Field perimeter in the vicinity of Koli Point/Volinavau. They were general trouble shooters. The 147th Inf. RCT was the only company or detachment within the 147th to be awarded the Presidential Unit Citation at Guadalcanal. (Courtesy of Sgt. Chris Seibert)

and her skipper, Captain Kitts, ordered "abandon ship", at 0150. Kitts and a small salvage crew remained behind to fight the fire for another hour, but they too were forced off the ship shortly before she sank.

The *Lamson* and *Lardner*, astern of the cruisers could contribute little to the action. They were not aware of the presence of the Japanese ships until the engagement started. Their main concern then was to keep clear of the burning cruisers. Having no battle orders from Wright these two destroyers fired off starshell to illuminate the battle scene, then switched to shellfire when the Japanese destroyers were illuminated. At one stage *Lamson* hurriedly displayed recognition lights when it was thought the cruiser fire was directed towards the ship. This only brought heavier fire towards her so she turned her lights off and steamed off towards Lunga to search for Japanese ships close in towards the shore.

Among Wright's cruisers only the *Northampton* was sunk but *Minneapolis*, *Pensacola* and *New Orleans* were out of action for almost a year. Only the *Honolulu* was undamaged, and none of the destroyers had suffered any damage.

One of Wright's problems had been poor illumination of the Japanese ships by the American starshell. Wright had, however, planned for better illumination because during the day he had ordered the cruisers to fly off her float planes to Tulagi. The pilots had been instructed to wait until dark then fly over the Savo area while awaiting orders from Wright concerning the illumination he wanted the planes to supply from flares.

Late that night the waters in Tulagi harbor were mirror smooth without even a breath of wind. Several times the planes roared across the waters before they finally managed to lift themselves slowly into the air. When they arrived off Savo they saw three burning ships below them and imagined them to be Japanese transports. The pilots circled the area awaiting instructions from Wright, unaware that one of the burning ships was in fact *Minneapolis* with Wright on board with shattered communications. Since the pilots did not receive any orders to drop flares they did not do so.

Continuing to circle the area the pilots saw the streaming phosphorescence wake of a large ship off Cape Esperance, heading northwest. It looked like a long green pencil on the inky black sea. It was in fact the undamaged *Honolulu* moving at high speed after the Japanese destroyers. This pursuit was, however, short. *Honolulu* made no further contact with the enemy that night and circled north of Savo looking for other Japanese ships before joining the four U. S.

destroyers that were picking up survivors from the *Northampton*.

On Guadalcanal the starving Japanese had received few drums that night but Tanaka, persistent and determined as ever, was back again two nights later with seven destroyers which unloaded 1500 drums of supplies. A week later he made another attempt with 11 destroyers - Tanaka himself in the new commissioned *Teruzuki*.

After the destruction of Wright's cruisers a small group of P. T. boats was built up at Tulagi and was given the role of disrupting the Japanese supply system. As Tanaka's destroyers approached Tassafaronga on the night of December 11th, three of the torpedo boats suddenly roared towards them out of the darkness. The Japanese met them with a storm of machine gun and shellfire while searchlights swung across the sea to pick out the fast, nimble boats. As quickly as they had come, they were suddenly gone but moments later the *Teruzaki* was hit by two torpedoes. The shattering double blast threw Tanaka to the deck and when he regained consciousness his ship was burning fiercely. He ordered an immediate withdrawal as the crew fought to contain the flames.

The burning ship guided another torpedo boat P. T. 44 towards the destroyers but as she approached she was hit by a shell in the engine room. Most of the crew went aft to launch a liferaft but as they did so a fuel tank exploded. Of the 11 man crew only two survived - one of which was Lieutenant Charles Melhorn who immediately dived overboard. He recalls that as he did so another shell hit the boat and he felt the concussion from it as he swam under water. Almost immediately afterwards the boat blew up with a tremendous roar. "The concussion paralyzed me from the waist down," recalls Melhorn, "and the water around me seemed to be red. My lifejacket brought me up to the surface but I came up in a sea of fire with flaming wreckage falling all round me. I started to swim feebly but I thought the game was up when the water which had shot up in the explosion came raining down again. It put out the fires all round me." "It had all happened so quickly," he added, "that from the first hit in the engine room to the final explosion, it had taken less than 15 seconds."

On the *Terazuki* the struggle to save the ship went on for four hours but finally the dazed Tanaka ordered "abandon ship" and when the flames reached the depth charge magazine, *Terazuki* blew up. Tanaka had finally had enough. When he returned to the Shortlands on the 12th, he ordered no more destroyer

runs were to be made - "because of the moonlight nights," as he put it.

A few days later he left to take up an appointment with the General Staff in Tokyo. He had decided the struggle to supply Hyakutake was lost and that the only thing to do was to evacuate Guadalcanal.

WE CAN NO LONGER SEND OUT PATROLS

When Tanaka got to Tokyo he found that Colonel Tsuji had managed to get the Central Staff to adopt another of his plans to drive the Americans off Guadalcanal. Despite his own bitter personal connection with Maruyama's defeat, the colonel still exercised great influence in Tokyo. His plan called for the establishment of a new army command at Rabaul, 8th Army, under General Hitoshi Imamura, with 50,000 troops to be sent to Guadalcanal. Tanaka and other naval officers pointed out the severe strain this would place on available shipping. "At great cost the Navy carried successive waves of confident troops and over-confident generals to Guadalcanal" Tanaka said "not only have they failed to defeat the Americans but they were themselves on the verge of starvation and defeat." The Army replied that defeat was due to the Navy abandoning them. With strong naval support around the island they felt success could still be obtained. Throughout December the two sides argued-neither wanted to be blamed for defeat. At Army Headquarters a succession of war games were held to try to predict the outcome of sending more troops. Eventually after these 'games,' the Army was convinced that they would probably lose up to three-quarters of any troops which tried to reach the island.

Sending supplies to the island became increasingly difficult, and the Japanese and naval headquarters turned to novel methods of trying to get around this problem. During November and December, 38 submarines ran an under-water shuttle service between the Shortlands and Kamimbo Bay near Cape Esperance. Some of these submarines were the I-15 class of over 2,500 tons, equipped with a catapult and plane hangar. All of them were stripped to the bare essentials except for one deck gun and two torpedoes. It was a four day round trip, submerged at six knots, and even then each submarine could only carry about fifty tons - enough supplies to last the 30,000 troops on Guadalcanal for only two days. Losses soon began to mount once the P. T. boats found the Kamimbo Bay terminal. On December 9th, P. T. 59 torpedoed the submarine I-3 unloading on the surface near Cape Esperance. The submarine was simply blown to pieces and only one man of her crew survived to scramble ashore.

In Tokyo Bay the Navy experts tried numerous methods of unloading the submarines which remained submerged. Attempts were made to eject stores from the torpedo tubes, but little success was obtained. Bags of rice were found to burst when ejected from the torpedo tubes. Next, biscuit tins were tried, but they too broke open. An attempt was then made using rubber containers which were also found to burst easily. Throughout December, rice became scattered all over Tokyo Bay as a result of these tests, but eventually a method using metal drums was found to work.

Still the losses in submarines continued to mount. On January 29th, the I-1 was approaching Kamimbo Bay on the surface when the New Zealand corvette *Kiwi* spotted the submarine's wake. The corvette's skipper, Lieutenant Bridson, realized the submarine was bigger and more heavily armed than his small

A native and Bill Dolan (Co. F, 182d Inf.) at Guadalcanal. (Courtesy of William Dolan)

Christmas Day Mass at Guadalcanal. December 1942. (Courtesy of Joseph L. Kiwak)

ship but he opened fire with his four-inch gun and machine guns. The I-1 immediately submerged to 90 feet but *Kiwi* dropped depth charges which forced it to the surface again. Bridson then brought his ship in close to rake the submarine with machine gun fire, killing the I-1 commander and everyone else on the bridge except the navigator. *Kiwi* then scored a direct hit on the I-1's deck gun, killing the gun crew. Bridson then rang for full speed and the corvette rammed I-1 near the conning tower. As the submarine heeled over, soldiers on her deck shouted with alarm and jumped overboard with full packs on.

The *Kiwi* pulled clear and as she was veered away the submarine's navigator ran along the deck shouting and waving a sword, then tried to clamber on board the corvette. He had one hand on the *Kiwi's* deck rail while his feet were on the deck of the submarine. As the two ships parted he fell, still shouting, into the sea. The two ships then exchanged furious machine gun and rifle fire as a second corvette, *Moa*, steamed up to join in the battle. Later an American P. T. boat also opened up with machine gun fire on the submarine. Eventually the submarine's steering gear was damaged and as she steamed erratically in Kamimbo Bay, Bridson rammed her once again while the Japanese raked the corvette with rifle fire. The bows of the *Kiwi* ran right up onto the deck of the submarine and ruptured her fuel tanks. Thick oil poured out on to the sea as the *Kiwi* pulled away again. The corvette's guns had, by then, been firing for more than an hour and had become too hot to operate further. *Kiwi* steamed out of range of the submarine while the *Moa* moved in to finish off the I-1.

As the submarine began to sink she was run ashore. The crew scrambled over the sides into the shallow water and ran up the beach pursued by machine gun fire from *Moa*. More than 30 of the submarine's 100 man crew had been killed in action. The survivors gathered on the shore and found they only had two swords and three rifles between them, plus a small amount of explosives. Suddenly they remembered important code books which had been left on board the partly submerged submarine. An officer and three men waded out together and used the explosives to blow up the bows of the submarine in an attempt to sink her. The ship was, however, firmly lodged on a reef so they were not successful

and later the wrecked submarine yielded important information to United States Intelligence.

The submarine freight service was a futile attempt to supply Hyakutake. At best it could only bring in less than 500 tons of supplies a day and showed a Japanese admission that the control of the seas around Guadalcanal had passed to the Americans. Neither Tokyo Express nor the submarine freight service could bring Hyakutake the heavy artillery or tanks he called for to push the Americans back. On the other hand, if the submarines had been used against American shipping, they could have exercised a stranglehold on Guadalcanal. In the months between November 1942 and February 1943 more than half of the submarines on the freight service were sunk.

As the number of submarines reaching Kamimbo Bay became fewer, the difficulties of Hyakutake's force worsened rapidly - from a peak of 30,000 men, the Japanese strength had dropped to 25,000 in mid-December but thousands of these were useless for they included ragged, half-starved and wounded survivors of Kawaguchi's and Maruyama's defeats in the months before. Malaria and dysentery ran unchecked throughout the weakened troops.

Along the 30 mile trail from Point Cruz to Cape Esperance, numerous leaf huts, hidden in the jungle, served as primitive hospitals, but the acute shortage of medical supplies meant that little could be done for the sick and wounded. Dirty, infected bandages were used time and time again. In the humid heat the injured rapidly developed blood poisoning and their septic, putrifying wounds attracted hordes of fat bluebottle flies. Other skeletal figures lay helpless and weakened by dysentery, continually fouling themselves and adding to the revolting stench while they waited for death.

The deaths from sickness, starvation and injury ran at more than 100 a day in late December and the able-bodied were so weakened by malnutrition that they were too weak to bury such large numbers of dead. The putrid smell of rotting corpses, moved to the edge of the jungle, only added to the loathsome stench from the hospitals. A grim fatality guide was drawn up by men. The sick who could still sit up were given 20 days. Those too weak to speak would be dead in two

days and those to weak to even blink their eyes would be dead in 12 hours.

In radio messages to Rabaul the desperate Hyakutake appealed repeatedly for help. On December 23rd he reported "... no food is available and we can no longer send out patrols". None the less he asked Imamura for permission to launch a final attack, pleading, "It is better to die an honorable death than to die of hunger in our own dugouts."

Rabaul was quite aware of Hyakutake's desperate position but was getting frantic in new efforts to ship supplies to him. As Japanese submarine losses began to mount, a new method was tried in December. Twin engine Mitsubishi bombers, which normally carried up to a ton of bombs, were loaded with bags of rice and ammunition. The bombers that managed to escape the American fighters then roared low along the coast from Cape Esperance to Tassafaronga while crewmen threw out the bundles. Frequently these planes were being followed by American fighters and as the bombers made erratic course alterations to dodge their pursuers, the bundles of supplies ended in the sea or deep in the jungle. So little actually reached the Japanese troops that this method was soon stopped.

Other attempts were then made using barges, and even sailing vessels which worked their way down from the Shortlands by night, stopping at daylight to hide along the coast of one of the many islands in the group. A lot of the traffic passed near Segi on the island of New Georgia 50 miles northwest of Guadalcanal. There, a coastwatcher, Kennedy, kept a close watch on the traffic and gradually built up a small fleet of canoes, manned by Solomon Islanders, who armed themselves by taking the guns from Japanese patrols they occasionally wiped out. One of the Solomon Islanders, Bill Bennet, would then lead his men against small Japanese barges and boats carrying supplies.

Bennett remembers, "On one occasion a scout brought word of a barge that had landed on a small island near our camp. I took two canoes and 20 men armed with rifles and a machine gun. We paddled round to the other side of the island and approached the Japanese from overland. As we crept towards the barge it was evening and the crew was preparing a meal while chatting and joking. There did not seem to be any guard. When I gave the word we fired with everything we had into the barge. One of the crew managed to reach a machine gun near the bow and got off a few rounds before he was hit, pitched forward and fell into the water. When the firing stopped there was complete silence and no sign of life on the barge. I picked up a submachine gun and went forward alone. As I crossed the deck of the barge a hatch nearby suddenly lifted and the head and shoulders of a man appeared. I shot him at once, then ran over to the hatch, dropped a grenade down it and closed it. From below there was muffled explosion and a high-pitched scream. Later we took the dead ashore and buried them, then we took whatever was useful off the barge before we sank it."

I DREAM OF RICE CAKES AND CANDIES

Hyakutake ordered his starved, emaciated troops to dig in and to stay in their foxholes even if the Americans passed them by. Each foxhole was to become a fortress and the occupants, too weak to attack or to retreat, were to fight to the last.

On Mount Austen extensive defenses had been dug but food supplies ran out in December. Lieutenant Yasuo Obi of the 124th Infantry remembers many of his men began to eat lizards, worms, beetles and any insects they could catch. "They had reached the limit of their endurance" he recalls, "their shrunken faces had become the color of the earth, and their hair was falling out. Those who had always been thin were reduced to skin and bone while those who had been fat became swollen with the effects of beri-beri. The fillings and caps in men's teeth began to fall out and every morning one of two men would not wake up from their night's sleep". Obi found that even the living began to give off the same stench as the dead.

In the dugouts overlooking Henderson Field the emaciated men sat behind their machine guns with blank expressions on their faces, wracked with dysentery, squirting their yellow liquid excrement around the dugout. Here too, the smell was overpowering - attracting hordes of flies. The few who were strong enough to converse found they could estimate how soon a man would die by the number of flies gathering around him. As a man's life ebbed away, in the last few days he could not find the strength to brush off the flies which settled on his stinking body.

On the American side there was a big build-up during December. By the middle of the month the 13,000 men of the Americal Division had arrived including 3,000 men of the 132nd Regimental Combat Team and another 3,000 men of the 182nd Infantry Regiment. the 18th Naval Construction Battalion (Seabees) were also landed to improve the fighter strips and roads and by the end of the month the Air Force strength had been built up to 200 planes. On December 9th, General Patch (Commander of the Americal Division) took over command of land operations. Elements of the 25th Army Division were also beginning to arrive and from that date onwards it was planned that the Army should do the fighting on Guadalcanal.

The 1st Marine Division which had been on the island since the landing date was gradually withdrawn during December. All of them had thought at times that they would never leave what they had come to regard as a hellhole of a place, and for hundreds of them the island had, in fact, become their last resting place. By the time the Division was withdrawn from the line on December 5th they had suffered 774 killed and 1,962 wounded. Almost everyone else in the Division had succumbed to malaria or dysentery a number of times and the troops had been so weakened that many of them could not find the strength to climb the cargo nets up the sides of the transports carrying them to Australia. Corporal Al Bonner who had come ashore with the first waves almost four months before managed to climb almost as far as the ships' rail before he lost the strength to go any further. As he hung on to the cargo net he began to feel his hands losing their grip on the ropes: he thought for a moment he was going to fall into the boat but just then a sailor leaned over the side and pulled him up. Before he went below he took one last look at Guadalcanal and quietly prayed to God he would never see the place again.

With his troop strength building up towards 40,000 men, General Patch planned a new offensive against the Japanese. His first target was Mount Austen. At 1,514 feet above sea level, it was not really a mountain but the highest of a series of steeply-sided, thickly-wooded ridges about six miles south-west of Henderson. On Mount Austen the Japanese observation posts had reported daily on traffic at the airfield and shipping off Lunga. So important was the Mount Austen position to the Japanese that they heavily fortified it with two battalions under the tireless command of Colonel Oka, supported by a regiment of mountain artillery. This position was also protected by pillboxes from another ridge called the "Gifu" (named after a district on the main island of Japan). Here there was a 1,500 yard line of pillboxes manned by 500 men of the 38th Division. These strongpoints were made of layers of logs with earth on top and with walls two feet thick. They had been dug into the ground so deeply that only narrow firing slits were above ground. Often hidden by thick grass and with all pillboxes having overlapping fields of fire they were to be tough nuts for the troops of the Americal Division who had no previous combat experience. Although Oka's men were starved, diseased and short of ammunition they were still determined to fight.

On December 17th, Patch sent a company from the 132nd Infantry Regiment "to occupy Mount Austen". There seems to be no reason why he did not know it was strongly fortified because a Marine patrol earlier had reported that it was. As soon as the company contacted the Japanese defenses they were driven back by machine gun fire from dugouts they could not even see. The next day the regiment's third battalion (800 men) were sent forward. These inexperienced troops had been on Guadalcanal only ten days and were not then acclimated to the humid heat that rapidly sapped a man's energy and made any hill climbing with combat equipment a major task in itself, leading to streams of sweat from every pore in the body.

This assault was quickly stopped by the steep terrain and by Japanese fire which seemed to enfilade every approach. On the 19th the regiment's first battalion joined in another attempt, but the total force, now of 1,600 men, could make no progress. Casualties began to mount at an alarming rate. Colonel Wright, of the 3rd Battalion, was killed and Japanese infiltration teams cut the supply lines, brought 3rd Battalion headquarters under fire and shot up medics carrying the wounded back. For three days the attacks continued. Each night Japanese patrols worked their way through the American lines creating as much noise and confusion as possible as they moved swiftly from one point to another.

On December 22nd a new tactic was tried by Colonel John Arthur, commanding the operation. All American troops in the Mount Austen area moved back 1,000 yards while the area was subjected to the heaviest shelling of the campaign. Thousands of shells exploded on the two ridges from early morning to afternoon. Dozens of planes ran a shuttle service from Henderson, unloading 500 pound bombs. When the bombardment ended, 3rd Battalion moved forward again, but the ground was so pitted with shell holes and bomb craters that by nightfall the battalion had only regained the 1,000 yards it had given up before the shelling started.

Even this intense shelling had little effect, mainly because the Japanese positions were so well dug in and camouflaged that artillery spotters could not give adequate information regarding the positions of the targets. When the troops went forward again on the 23rd, some progress was made against the highest point on Mount Austen and this was taken by 3rd Battalion on Christmas Eve, depriving the Japanese of their main lookout over Henderson. Christmas Day was spent in probing patrols while other men ate cold beans under the cover of rocky outcrops often only a few hundred yards from the Japanese strongpoints.

On the 27th the battered, tired and depressed 3rd Battalion moved 1,000 yards to the west to try to envelope the Gifu ridge. Here again they met heavy machine gun fire from Oka's strongpoints. The following day the 1st Battalion was also moved up to help with an attack against the Gifu from the south. Progress was slow as each of the Japanese pillboxes were protected by overlapping fields of fire from other strongpoints. The regimental commander, Colonel Nelson, was, by now, exhausted with the pressures on him. He was in a malarial fever and increasingly concerned about his mounting casualties as well as the loss of dozens of his men who had to be moved back to base hospitals suffering with malaria and dysentery. He asked to be relieved of his command and on December 29th Colonel Alexander George took over the command.

George was more successful than Nelson in so far as he managed to get the regiment's 2nd Battalion, previously on beach defenses, transferred to the attack on the Gifu so that all of the regiment were available when George resumed the attack on December 31st. In the next four days of careful probing attacks and the gradual elimination of the Japanese pillboxes, the regiment had surrounded the Gifu on three sides. In just over two weeks the regiment had lost 182 dead and wounded with another 130 evacuated with illness.

Conditions in the Japanese defenses in the Gifu had worsened continually over the Christmas - New Year period. 1st Lieutenant Okajima had landed on Guadalcanal on November 5th and was, therefore, in better condition than most of Oka's men who had been on the island for three months. On the Gifu, Okajima joined a platoon where most of the men already weak from starvation, were diseased. He started a diary on December 24th as the Americans ended the first week of the assault against the Gifu. Okajima recorded that of the 62 man platoon, ten had died of illness before he started his diary. He went on-

December 25th: Two more men died today of malaria and over-work. At the end they could not lift a hand.

December 26th: Another man died today with malaria. His mind had become effected. We have now lost 13 men. The men's minds are always on food and when asleep I dream of food - the rice cakes and candies I used to know. At

Gun positions close to Henderson Field, November 1942.

A Japanese Transport grounded and destroyed at Tassafaronga.

ST. LOUIS BRIDGE
Minneapolis Ave.

"St. Louis bridge" (Courtesy of Joseph L. Kiwak)

other times my mind is on re-taking Henderson.

December 27th: One more died today.

December 28th: 1st Lieutenant Tanai died this morning; my tears overflow.

December 29th: Syoychi died of slight wounds. Why does it happen? His wounds were no more than scratches, they did not even bleed, yet tonight he is dead.

December 30th: A new attack has been planned for January 15th. We shall sweep the Americans into the sea in two months. Our navy will wipe out the Americans off Tulagi. Victory in the Spring of 1943!!

January 2nd: Two officers died today, one of them on patrol. Now I have no rival for the post of company commander.

Other Japanese diaries at the time, record the news of a large offensive against the Americans planned for mid-January. At Rabaul, 8th Army Commander General Imamura had 50,000 men ready for shipping to Guadalcanal. At the end of December, United States reconnaissance planes reported over 100 transports, and warships gathered at Rabaul. Unknown to Imamura, however, the Army/Navy arguments continued in Tokyo all through Decem-

ber. The Navy pointed out that to transport the 8th Army to Guadalcanal would place an impossible strain on available shipping. American submarines had sunk 600,000 tons of Japanese merchant shipping in 1942. The Imperial Navy had lost six aircraft carriers during the year and around Guadalcanal alone, had lost two battleships, three cruisers and five destroyers. Even if they did succeed in getting Imamura's force to Guadalcanal, the Americans there were now so strong it was unlikely Imamura's troops would affect the final outcome, the Navy argued.

On Christmas Day the Army and Navy leaders held an emergency meeting at the Imperial Palace. It was no longer a question of whether to withdraw from Guadalcanal, but which service was to be blamed for defeat. Admiral Fukudome, Chief of Naval Operations, favored withdrawal but hesitated to make a final decision. "What do you think of joint tactical map games before we decide?" he suggested to Marshal Sugiyama, Army Chief of Staff, and Colonel Tsuji. Of all the men in the room only Tsuji had personal experience in Guadalcanal. "You are all well posted on the battle situation and you can't even reach a decision," he replied hotly, "you had better all resign!" He went on to deride them, "the naval commanders I met at Guadalcanal all told me the big shots in the Naval General Staff and Combined Fleet should come out to Guadalcanal and see what we have to take, then they might understand."

Navy Captain Tomioka stepped forward angrily, "Are you trying to say destroyer commanders are all faint of heart - take that back," he demanded. Tsuji turned on him, "Have you ever been to the fighting front; do you know what's going on there?" Tomioka suddenly made towards Tsuji but Fukudome stepped between them. "I am sorry Tsuji-kun he said, "what you say is true."

Eventually new map games were agreed on. They proved what everyone knew—hardly one transport would get through to Guadalcanal.

On December 31st, Sugiyama and Admiral Nagono sought an audience with the Emperor to seek Hirohito's approval for the withdrawal. After a brief discussion, the Emperor reluctantly signed the orders. He was increasingly concerned at the way the war was developing. From the beginning he had cautioned the General Staff against a war with America. He had not been excited by the easy victories of the beginning of the war, and now only a year after Pearl Harbor, he realized the tide was turning against Japan.

On New Year's Day a special Army courier, General Ayabe, left Tokyo by plane for Imamura's headquarters with top secret orders for the with-

drawal from Guadalcanal. Three days later he reached Rabaul and met hurriedly with Imamura and his naval commander, Vice-Admiral Kusaka. Both of the commanders were appalled when they read the orders Ayabe had brought with him. They argued that withdrawal would undermine Japan's whole strategic position in South East Asia and demoralize the armed forces. "A withdrawal would allow the Americans to take the initiative" Imamura pointed out, "it would give them the confidence to strike against any vulnerable Japanese island outpost". He went on to tell Ayabe that when the 50,000 troops he had were landed on Guadalcanal, then with Hyakutake's forces, they would d have a two to one superiority over the Americans. He had, in fact, already sent Hyakutake the plans for a new offensive in mid-January.

For several days the arguments went on, with Imamura on the edge of refusing to carry out the orders. Ayabe tried to console him by pointing out that the withdrawal would make troops available for intensified operations in New Guinea. In the end he told Imamura that the orders came from the Emperor himself and such supreme authority must be obeyed. Imamura finally agreed to plan the evacuation and Kusaka was persuaded to supply a fast destroyer group to give cover to the evacuation fleet. Imamura insisted, however, he would have to send a strong force to the island to act as an aggressive rearguard while the main force was withdrawn. The evacuation was planned for the first week in February.

WHEN WILL HELP COME?

On Guadalcanal General Patch had received all of the 25th Army Division by the first week in January and on the 10th he resumed his offensive against the Japanese dug in on the Gifu and a range of hills near the Matanikau river, called Galloping Horse and the Sea Horse. At the Gifu the 132nd Infantry Regiment were replaced by the 35th Infantry while the 27th Infantry were sent forward to clear Galloping Horse.

The Matanikau river splits into a fork, running southwest and south, a mile from its mouth. The Galloping Horse area is between these two tributaries and consists of a ridge rising steeply to 500 feet, topped by an uneven plateau with a line of small hills. The whole area overlooks the Matanikau and it was strongly fortified by several hundred Japanese troops of the 228th and 230th Infantry Regiments. The attack began on the morning of the 10th with an intense artillery bombardment of the area. To surprise the Japanese the artillery fire was co-ordinated so that although guns from different positions fired at different times, all shells landed at the same time. This was called "time on target" fire. The guns poured in nearly 6,000 shells in less than an hour and this was followed by 24 planes dropping bombs and depth charges on Japanese positions protected from the shelling by the steep slopes. The stunned Japanese offered only light resistance and by nightfall more than half the area had been taken. The remaining resistance was centered on Hill 53 at the end of the ridge.

On the 11th the 3rd Battalion, 27th Infantry attacked the hill but in a series of assaults against cleverly camouflaged Japanese machine guns, were driven back each time. Corporal James Jones' company was in reserve and from the distance he watched men of the 3rd Battalion in one of their assaults. As men ran up one of the smaller hills at the base of Hill 53 they began to drop one by one. Near the top of the hill they faltered, hesitated, then began running back.

Two men who appeared to have been injured could not keep up and fell as several Japanese appeared over the top of the hill and dragged these two men back. When the small hill was finally taken later in the day, the Americans found the bodies of these two men savagely mutilated, with one of them beheaded.

Towards evening Jones' company was sent in to replace the company that had taken the worst losses of the day and which then held a small hilltop position. After Jones' company took over the positions a gentle breeze coming up the hill brought with it a putrid smell which had already become familiar to them all. Jones walked down the hill a little way and remembers, "I found the dead soldier curled up in the grass. It looked as if he had been killed the day before. Rigor mortis had set in but there was little swelling. There was no sign of how he had died; he lay on his side with his knees pulled up, his hands clenched and bent up beside his face, but not touching it. Already he seemed to have become part of the ground on which he lay, his grimy green fatigues and olive drab helmet were not easy to see. Although his features were undamaged there seemed to be a haziness about them. Instead of being an individual - a human being - he seemed to have become a small insignificant object like a rock or a broken branch of a tree littering the ground."

Jones remembers there was always a vague feeling of dislike and annoyance towards the dead and wounded, "They became instantly strangely different from the rest of us," he recalls. "As far as the dead were concerned there was an instinctive dislike of touching them, as if they would contaminate you in some way. It was somewhat similar with the wounded, you made them as comfortable as possible and did all you could for them but there was a feeling of slight distaste, guilt or irritation and when they were taken away you heaved a silent sigh of relief." Jones also remembers his own attitude towards possible death or injury. "You had to accept the fact that you were probably going to die. It was part of the process of becoming a soldier, because only by accepting that possibility could you function properly as a soldier."

The next day Jones' battalion was sent into attack Hill 53. He remembers there seemed no alternative but for a frontal attack. On the left side of the hill the ground fell away sharply to the river and on the right it ran into dense jungle which was strongly held by the Japanese. At the base of the main hill were a series of small rises in the ground which could offer some cover but the whole area had been zeroed in by Japanese mortars and was covered by numerous widely spaced machine gun posts dug into the ground. Covered by logs, and largely hidden by brown kunai grass, the posts were difficult to see from even 20 or 30 feet. Each position was manned by two or three emaciated, starved or diseased men for whom retreat was impossible, and surrender unthinkable. They became determined and tenacious defenders.

After a brief initial shelling of the slopes of the hill, two platoons of Jones' company went forward. At first there was no resistance and in a series of short rushes the men reached the lower slopes. As they then rose to rush forward again they were fired on simultaneously from several positions. The lieutenants in both platoons were immediately killed and within seconds Jones' platoon had lost a quarter of its strength in dead and wounded scattered among the knee-high grass. Everybody else hurriedly sought cover behind the nearest rocky outcrop or in a shellhole. A man near Jones, suddenly hit in the throat, cried out "Oh my God" then clutched at his throat and sank slowly to the ground as blood spurted from a severed artery. The bursts of fire, and the sudden death that had struck all around him, terrified Jones. "I remember lying on my belly and looking at the other sweating, scared faces all around me,

wondering which of us was going to die next" he recalls.

Then the Japanese mortars began to fall among them. Each shell threw up a fountain of black earth and stones and sent steel splinters cutting through the air. Men hiding behind large rocks found mortars falling behind them and made quick dashes for better cover as machine gun fire kicked up the dirt around them. Slowly the casualties began to mount. Here a man died quickly with a mortar splinter buried in his chest or back. Elsewhere a man bled slowly to death while medics were unable to reach his exposed position. At one time Jones remembers, another man lay on the exposed hill for what seemed like hours, screaming in agony as he attempted to hold in his intestines after his belly had been ripped open.

Later in the morning the Japanese fire slackened and the mortar fire was reduced to an occasional round. When the hot sun rose high in the sky the men trapped on the exposed foothills, with little or no water, sweated not only from the unbearable heat but

also from the constant fear of being blown to bits at any moment. Some men simply passed out with heat exhaustion as they lay terrified at the edge of shell craters. Later in the morning men who were surprised to find themselves still alive began to gather in small groups and seek out the hidden enemy machine guns. Rifle fire was directed against a few Japanese seen moving about higher up the hill, but whenever a group of men from Jones' company collected and seemed to be moving forward, the Japanese observation posts on the hilltop brought in more mortar fire.

The machine gun fire and mortars kept the Americans pinned down for most of the day but towards late afternoon one squad managed to work round to the left of the Japanese positions and destroyed four machine gun posts. Later another group found a gap in the Japanese positions and worked their way along a ridge to a position where they could overlook the main Japanese defensive positions.

The following morning the 2d Battalion Executive Officer, Captain Davis, led a group of four men

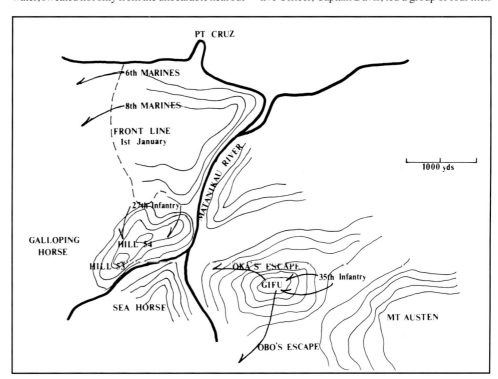

The Japanese Offensive, January 10-22.

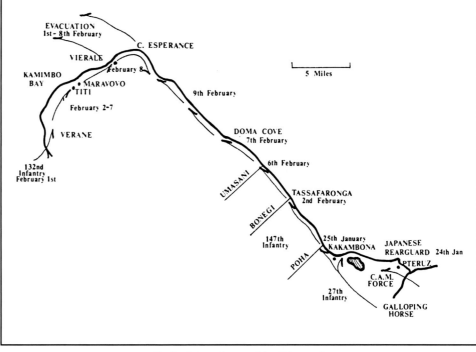

The final phase, January 24 to February 8.

along this narrow ridge. As they drew near the Japanese defenses they were seen by enemy soldiers who threw grenades at them. Fortunately only one of these grenades exploded and no one was injured. Davis and his men replied by throwing several grenades into the Japanese defenses before they charged. In a savage, brief struggle against sword waving Japanese officers and men, 17 of the defenders were killed with no losses among Davis's men. This attack broke the back of the Japanese defenses on Hill 53 and was to earn Davis the Medal of Honor. The top of the hill was then heavily shelled and this was followed up by an attack by 2nd Battalion which swept the Japanese off the hill by mid-day.

At about the same time a Japanese squad carrying supplies got through to Oka's men still holding out on the Gifu. They had managed to work their way through the lines of the 35th Infantry and carried with them Hyakutake's orders to Oka to abandon the position and fall back to the west. By that time the Gifu had been under attack for three days by the 35th Infantry. Heavy shelling had begun to reduce Oka's defenses which by then consisted of about 40 machine gun posts. Time and again these defenses had been broken up the attacks by the 35th Infantry and Patch, completely frustrated by the lack of progress, relieved the 2nd Battalion's commander.

The new commanding officer tried psychological warfare by bringing up loud speakers and urging the Japanese to surrender, promising food, water and medical treatment. To the starved and sick embattled defenders this was a strong appeal and about half a dozen made their way to the American lines. It seems likely many more would have done so if they had had the strength to do so, but to other defenders, the appeal drew only contempt. Sub Lieutenant Obi in his diary for the 13th wrote "General Patch is determined to get rid of us by all means and does not understand why the Japanese continue with absolutely hopeless resistance. Towards evening the American broadcast started. The men listened in silence, they know that speaking will greatly exhaust their bodily strength. The broadcast went on "All personnel of the 124th Infantry, how are you? How many days more do you think you have to live? You have already done well enough your duties as the soldiers of the Japanese Army. You need not hesitate to come towards us. Throw down your arms and come to us with your hands held up with a piece of white cloth in your hand. Come down the hill. We have an abundant supply of medicine and food. We will broadcast again tomorrow. Have a good sleep and think it over. Good night."

The message was broadcast several times and American planes also dropped leaflets over the area. Obi told his diary he would rather die than to be taken prisoner but he also wrote that the constant reference to "plenty of medicine and food" had an effect on everyone. "Plenty of medicine and food", the phrase ran through his mind time and again- "almost like the chorus of a song" wrote Obi.

The final broadcast came on January 17th and ended with a warning, "An hour's notice. If you do not come down we will repeat the life-destroying bombardment". It had no effect, and the main Japanese defenses were subjected to an intense shelling for an hour. Again the American troops had been pulled back to clear the area for the artillery bombardment, but once again it was dark before they could re-occupy their original positions so there was no infantry to follow up the shelling.

In their dugouts and pillboxes the Japanese endured the shelling silently but suffered very little from it. Obi remembers the shelling uprooted many trees but only occasionally was damage done to the defenses. "Officers and men had long forgotten their fear of American bombs and they sat thinking about a search for food in the abandoned American foxholes before the Americans returned." When the

GIs of Co. B, 147th Inf. RCT try to free a jeep at Carney Field perimeter.

2d Battalion, 182d Infantry Div. leaving Guadalcanal, March 1943. (Courtesy of William Dolan)

The 1942-43 section of the American military and naval cemetery at Guadalcanal. Buried here are soldiers, sailors and Marines who made the supreme sacrifice for the Island of Death.

fighting resumed on the 18th it was a bitter struggle from one pillbox to the other. "When the Americans came again" Obi recalls, "the officers and men forgot their fear of death; the hunger and disease, and they fought desperately in defense of their positions. There were no more supplies of ammunition or food and many men did not even have the strength to stand up. Others, weak with dysentery, clung to their foxholes desperately while frequently spilling bloody excrement."

When Oka had received Hyakutake's orders to abandon the Gifu he knew most of his men were too weak to escape with him. After discussions with his staff, Oka handed over command of the Gifu to Major Inagaki who had refused to abandon the sick and wounded. Oka and most of his staff, together with about 100 able-bodied troops, managed to get through the American lines on the 17th as the encirclement of the Gifu was completed. After escaping Oka realized he had left the regimental flag with Inagaki and he turned back determined to take the flag with him before the Gifu fell. As he made his way back with a small group of men, he ran into an American patrol. In a short, fierce firefight, Oka and all his group were killed.

For three days more Inagaki's wretched sick and wounded kept up a desperate defense against American attacks. Time and again they managed to drive back the attackers, defeated by the interlocking fields of fire from the machine gun posts.

Major Nishiyama was another of the defenders who kept up his diary and on the 17th recorded, "The situation has become very difficult and there is nothing now left but to make up our minds to die. I have shared my last cigarettes with my friends and I was very touched when Lance Corporal Fujiwara came to me and said, 'Sir, this is the final stage, I would like to give you a farewell present but all I have is a little rice, would you please take it'. Nearby Lieutenant Okajima's position has apparently been overrun. Earlier in the day he was badly wounded but was still fighting with grenades. Now all is quiet from his position. Captain Fukada has also died. At least they will suffer no more and I envy them that. In all my years as a soldier I have never known such a tragic battle".

On the next day Nishiyama wrote, "The enemy is now getting closer, we have only three sub-machine guns, a rifle and a few grenades. We have no water. How can we survive in this heat without water, yet we must struggle on. I hear we have now lost over 400 dead here and only 200 of us are left. Some of my men talk about trying to escape but I cannot allow it as it would only weaken our resistance to the enemy". Two days later there was a final entry in Nishiyama's diary. It read simply "Oh God!"

On January 21st the Americans managed to get a tank up the steep ridges and it moved methodically from one pillbox to the other destroying each one. That night Inagaki led a wild banzai charge against the Americans with every man who could be persuaded to get to his feet. In a furious struggle Inagaki and 85 other defenders were killed. The next day only scattered resistance was met as the Americans overran the whole area, but some small groups of Japanese slipped between them and escaped to the jungle. Among them was Obi, specially entrusted with the regimental colors that Oka had died for. Obi had a pistol and two grenades and he told himself that rather than let the colors be captured he would destroy them with one grenade and himself with the second.

In the jungle, Obi, with about half a dozen other men, found new enemies - heat, and above all, thirst. "Water" he recalls, "the thought of finding it was the only thing that kept us going. Men's throats burned like fire as the hot sun shone with its glare. Death from hunger would bring sleep but death from thirst

would be like death in madness. On Guadalcanal I saw men eat human flesh and terrible as it was, it was not so terrible as to see men dying of thirst. They writhed in agony and when they opened their mouths a wave of heat came out."

The group staggered westwards through the jungle as the sounds of firing on the Gifu became fainter. A day later they came to a small stream. Together the men tumbled down the slope and plunged their heads into the cool waters. Obi had wrapped the regimental colors around himself and this hampered his movements a little so that he was the last to reach the stream. When he was only a few feet away from it the laughing and shouting of the men in the stream was shattered by a burst of machine gun fire from the American soldiers hidden in the jungle on the other side of the stream. In an instant the men in the stream were wiped out. Obi remembers he had one brief picture of horror as they screamed and fell into the water, before he turned and ran. Bullets cut through the jungle around him. Once he turned and fired his pistol, uselessly he realized, "then I ran on like someone in a dream and tore myself away from the American pursuit". When he finally stopped, exhausted, he realized he was now alone. The picture of the slaughter at the stream kept going through his mind and he thought how senseless it all seemed. "Strangely, I did not feel any anger" he remembers, "as I sat resting in the jungle I began to wonder what the meaning of it all was - a man suddenly alone like this does not feel hate". When he got to his feet he knew he was lost. He was not even sure what day it was. Fortunately he had a small compass and with this he began to work his way slowly towards the west.

While the Gifu and Galloping Horse were being slowly reduced, the quietest part of the front was around the Point Cruz area. There had been no action in that area since November but Patch had strengthened his forces there by moving up two batteries of artillery from the Americal Division. Sergeant Bill McLaughlin remembers space was so limited on the small peninsula that the large 155 mm. howitzers were placed only 30 feet apart. "The area had been bitterly fought over several weeks before" he recalls, "and everywhere there was the stench of rotting bodies. There was no depth to the ground and the dead had been hastily buried in shallow graves or simply left in foxholes that had blown in on them. Arms, legs and parts of bodies protruded from the ground and were covered with white maggots feasting on the rotting remains. Near our gun a booted foot stuck out of the ground and no matter how many times we covered it with soil, someone would stumble over it and it would be uncovered again the next morning."

On January 14th, when night fell, McLaughlin remembers "Condition Black" (invasion imminent) was set. Several Japanese destroyers had been reported coming south from the Shortlands and it was thought they would make landings near Point Cruz. "We got the word that there were no infantry re-inforcements available," recalls McLaughlin, "so we were told that if the Japanese landed we were to fight as long as possible then retire into the hills and sell our lives as dearly as possible. When I heard that I can tell you I never felt so low in all my life and felt sure I was never going to see my home again." Later that night, "Washing Machine Charlie" appeared and dropped a few brilliant flares over Point Cruz. Japanese mortar and rifle fire began to hit around the artillery and the order was given to commence firing against the Japanese lines. Before this could be done, "Condition Red" (air raid) was sounded and the executive officer at McLaughlin's battery protested that if his guns fired they would give away their position to the bombers overhead. "Fire anyway," he was told and shortly after the first few salvos, the gun positions were bombed. McLaughlin recalls, "We

heard the roar of a divebomber building up to a hair raising crescendo as it dived towards us, then came the unnerving, sinister swish of approaching bombs which made us grovel helplessly in our foxholes. A stick of four bombs exploded right across our front. The second and third bombs straddled our position and blew up our tents. One man who had not bothered to get into his hole until too late, was blown 40 feet through the air and was badly injured. Fortunately, after the bombing, the Japs did not make any landings near us."

During this time the 2nd Marine Division had begun to push the Japanese from the Point Cruz area towards White River, a mile to the west. Here the ridges ran to within a few hundred yards of the beach leaving only the narrow coastal strip along which a track led westwards towards Hyakutake's headquarters at Tassafaronga. Advance along this track was held up by Japanese machine gun posts on the ridges and in the ravines which could pour enfilading fire onto the track. In dugouts and foxholes, cunningly concealed, the Japanese, following Hyakutake's order, allowed the Marines to pass by, then opened fire on them from behind. On the 15th the Marines brought up tanks to reduce machine gun nests and eventually flame throwers were used to burn out the last bitter defenders in the bunkers. So intense and slow-moving was the fighting that in four days the Marines advanced only 650 yards, but in so doing killed over 600 Japanese. With such slow progress, Patch realized it would take many months to drive the Japanese back to Cape Esperance. He became even more alarmed when his intelligence unit reported that ten Japanese destroyers had landed several hundred more troops at the Cape on the night of January 14th.

Unknown to Patch these Japanese troops were, in fact, the 600 men rearguard that were to cover the withdrawal. Imamura had sent his Chief of Staff, Colonel Imoto with the group, carrying the evacuation plans to be given to Hyakutake personally. Imoto had landed just before midnight with a handful of staff officers. Each man carried a 100 pound pack of food as they set off along the trail towards Tassafaronga. Along the trail Imoto became increasingly alarmed at the conditions the troops were enduring. When he had stepped ashore at Cape Esperance the first thing he saw was an emaciated dead Japanese soldier lying unburied near the beach. Now, as his party moved slowly eastwards they repeatedly came upon groups of dead and dying soldiers, starved, feverish with malaria, too weak to help themselves or make any further progress towards the relief supplies they expected to find at Cape Esperance.

Imoto recalls, "Even those soldiers who were not ill were very pale and thin. Most of them had thick beards and their eyes were sunk into skulls on which the skin was drawn tight over the protruding bones. Many wore torn and dirty uniforms and I was shocked to notice that their rifles, in many cases, were rusty and dirty. When I inquired why this was so, I was told the men were too weak to clean their weapons." Some of the soldiers were, in fact, so weak they could no longer even carry the standard Arisaka rifle which weighed nearly nine pounds.

Late that morning, Imoto's party reached a field hospital and camp at the Segilau river, seven miles east of Cape Esperance, "I was also shocked at the deplorable conditions I found at the hospital" Imoto recalls. "There were simply a few huts with coconut tree leaves for the roof. No mosquito netting. No food. All the patients were very ill with dysentery and there was a disgusting smell everywhere. The only help available came from several soldiers who themselves hardly seemed strong enough to walk about. Numerous dead had been buried at the roadside in graves so shallow that body parts were sticking out of the ground."

To Imoto it seemed unbelievable that conditions could have been allowed to become so bad. "At the hospital I met some officers who asked when they could expect help from our planes," he remembers. "They told me that they had been promised help for three months but the only planes they ever saw were American and they seemed to machine gun the area every day." Imoto tried to comfort them, "I could not tell them of the evacuation plans but I told them to be patient a little longer and that help would soon be here."

At the camp a truck was found and the tired men in Imoto's group gratefully unloaded their packs onto it, before it drove off towards Tassafaronga with Imoto and some of his staff. At eight that evening they reached the Bonegi river and after a few questions they were told Hyakutake had his headquarters nearby. For some time they wandered in the dark jungle but eventually found the headquarters 500 yards from the river.

In a blacked out tent, with only a spluttering candle, Imoto discussed the plans first with Hyakutuke's senior staff officers, General Miyazaki and Colonel Konuma. Konuma lay on a bed of twigs and listened quietly to Imoto's reasons for the withdrawal. In the flickering light of the candle Imoto could see the stunned surprise the two staff officers felt, both of them thought he had come with plans for a new offensive. "Withdrawal is impossible," said Miyazaki eventually, "with so many sick and wounded a withdrawal would become a disaster once the Americans realized what was happening. If re-inforcements and a new offensive are not possible," he went on, "then we must cut our way into the enemy lines and bring back at least one last bit of glory." Throughout the night the three men discussed the issue until at daybreak they were forced to seek shelter when American planes again strafed the campsite. Away to the east the sounds of heavy firing could be heard as the fighting near Point Cruz resumed.

Imoto was taken to see Hyakutake, he remembers "I found him sitting on a blanket in a cave which he had dug beneath the roots of a large tree. I handed him the withdrawal order. He listened to my explanations with closed eyes. When I had finished he said very slowly, "The question is very grave, I want to consider the matter quietly and alone for a little while. Please leave me until I call for you."

Throughout the morning Hyakutake sat alone in his cave, deep in thought. At noon he sent for Imoto and told him, "It will be a very difficult task for the army to withdraw under existing circumstances, but the orders of the Emperor must be carried out at any cost". Imoto then went to face the senior and junior staff officers to explain the evacuation orders. Again he met a hostile reaction, with most of the staff in favor of an honorable death in an attack against the American lines. Others stated frankly that the men in the front line having accepted their fate of fighting to the last in the foxholes simply would not now quietly retreat. Major Hosokawa, the planning officer of the 38th Division staff, suggested that the men be told they would be sent on board ships at Cape Esperance then make a new landing behind the American lines. He thought this would be the only way to persuade them to leave the front lines.

Eventually it was agreed that the rank and file would not be told what was really happening, they were to be allowed to continue thinking that the offensive planned for the 15th was merely postponed and that meanwhile troops would be repositioned. The 600 men rearguard was sent to take up front line positions and this seemed to confirm what the men thought was true. Officers and men who were in fairly good condition working in rear echelon groups were sent to replace front line men who could hardly walk. Emergency food supplies were set up at Kokumbona, Tassafaronga, Cape Esperance and Kamimbo Bay, a few miles west of the Cape. Movement of the sick and injured along the trail towards

the evacuation center at Kamimbo Bay was improved and hundreds of patients began to gather there to await the arrival of fast destroyers schedules to evacuate them. As they were collected they were also sorted into two groups, for some reason that was not explained to them. The two groups were actually those who were considered worth saving and those not worth saving. For many of the chronically sick, the diseased, the wounded who had endured months of starvation and abject misery the "evacuation centre" was to be no more than a final cruel bitter irony.

From Hyakutake's headquarters detailed instructions were sent out for last minute burial or destruction of artillery guns, trucks, tractors. All ammunition except that needed for rifles, machine guns and mortars was to be sunk in the area or buried in the jungle.

In the Point Cruz area the Americans had meanwhile continued to push the Japanese back yard by yard towards White river. On the 18th January the 8th Marines were replaced by the 147th Infantry Regiment and this Composite Army-Marine (CAM) force crossed the narrow White river two days later. At that stage Japanese resistance began to weaken and by the 22nd the Americans were within a mile of Japanese Divisional Headquarters at Kokumbona. Two miles inland the men of the 27th Regiment, 25th Division had also broken the back of Japanese resistance after the struggle at Gifu, Galloping Horse and another ridge called the Sea Horse. These troops moved slowly westward from one ridge to the other, becoming increasingly surprised at the lack of any serious resistance.

By the 22nd the advance had become so rapid that forward companies began to lose walkie-talkie communication with their battalion headquarters. Company commanders were given "independent commands" to push ahead as quickly as possible exploiting the local situation as they saw fit. They swung in towards the coast and reached Kokumbona on the 23rd trapping hundreds of Japanese still facing the CAM force on the coastal strip between Kokumbona and White river. Kokumbona itself had been held by only a small Japanese force in two defense lines. After a heavy mortar attack on the defenses they were rapidly overrun as the American troops ran hard but cautiously low through the short grass between the orderly lines of coconut trees. They leapt over dugouts and emplacements which at Galloping Horse had held them up for three days. Here and there the odd running figure fell, as the Japanese fired a few shots, but suddenly they were in the village itself and found the scattered Japanese were killing themselves with grenades, guns and knives. Those who did not were quickly shot or bayoneted, but about 15 skinny and dejected prisoners were taken.

The main Japanese force had, however, escaped to the west but several hundred still opposed the Marines at White river. Incredibly these Japanese troops were not aware that their line of retreat had been cut. On the night of the 23rd a large group of Japanese infantry, hauling a 37 mm artillery piece, made their way noisily along the track from White river towards Kokumbona. They were talking loudly and using lights as if the Americans were miles away. One company of men from the 27th Regiment in Kokumbona blocked the trail and waited silently as the Japanese approached to within 100 yards then poured heavy fire into them, accounting for more than 50 of the Japanese.

Between Kokumbona and White river the Japanese were compressed into an area which ran for a mile along the coast and no more than a mile inland. From White river they were under attack by three regiments of the CAM force and from Kokumbona by the 27th Infantry Regiment. Pressure against them was increased by shelling from American destroyers but throughout the 23rd the Japanese fought bitterly for every yard, foxhole and machine gun

post. On the 24th they were finally overwhelmed and besides 400 dead they lost several artillery pieces, machine guns and their last tank. Anxious to follow up as quickly as possible Patch sent two battalions of the 27th Infantry in pursuit of the main Japanese force. By the 25th the Americans reached the Poha river, two miles west of Kokumbona, and were then stopped by the first of Hyakutake's skillful rearguard actions.

SUNSET

On Guadalcanal several fast flowing, shallow rivers empty into the sea between Kokumbona and Cape Esperance. Most of these rivers are no more than 50 yards wide and in dry weather seldom more than knee deep. In heavy rain the river levels rise rapidly but most of the time all of these rivers are fordable over most of their length. The banks of the rivers are several feet high and covered with thick jungle to the very edge of the river. It was at these several rivers that the Japanese began to fight a series of delaying actions.

Captain Kurosaki, fighting with the rearguard remembers, "at each river bank we constructed log emplacements which were covered with grasses and vines, and overlooking 40 or 50 yards of river crossing. We would wait until the Americans had begun to ford the river then lay down small arms fire on them." The Americans then withdrew back from the river banks and their artillery pounded the Japanese positions, for an hour or two before the troops went forward again.

The shelling of Japanese positions along the coast was also done by destroyers. Commander F. Bell of the *Grayson* remembers when his was one of the several destroyers engaged in the bombardment. "We slipped along the coast" he recalls, "only about 3,000 yards off the beach, keeping a careful watch through our glasses. Our targets were enemy ammunition dumps near the Umasami river which was a thin coppery thread almost hidden by overhanging branches. We were just off the mouth of the river when control reported a target on its west bank. We began firing our five-inch to a depth of 2,000 yards. This was exploratory shooting, we walked the salvos along the river bank then spread them out. Suddenly from deep in the undergrowth there was a heavy detonation, flames and smoke curled through the trees. We had found a target and for five minutes we gave it a thorough going over until we felt certain no supplies of any value would be left to the Japanese. We repeated this procedure for four miles along the coast until we got to the Segilau river". Bell also remembers that "On Guadalcanal the main east-west mountain range is buttressed by ridges that run off at right angles down to the sea. On these ridges the Japanese were clearly visible as we steamed past and we would lay our shells among them and on gun emplacements."

The gun positions on the ridges near Cape Esperance had been placed by the Japanese to cover the stretch of water between Cape Esperance and Savo Island and give supporting fire to their barges moving along the coast to Tassafaronga. Frequently these batteries replied to destroyers like *Grayson* and raised columns of water around the ships forcing them to steam out of range.

The distant sounds of artillery fire and Naval shelling served as a guide to Sub Lieutenant Obi struggling through the jungle clad hills after his escape from the *Gifu*. He had soon lost track of the days of the week. Each night he gathered sticks and leaves to cover himself while he tried to sleep. Everyday was a hot, exhausting struggle to make his way west, to search for water and to catch a few lizards and insects for food.

He killed the lizards by scrambling after them on the rocks and slashing them with his sword but as each day passed he noticed it became harder to chase them and he missed them more often when he swung his sword. "I told myself," he recalls, "that I had been a fencing expert and I should not miss, but I knew it was because I was becoming weaker. I began to think that I would soon be too weak to chase the lizards and then die of starvation. I decided that before that happened I would kill myself."

One night he became so depressed that he drew his pistol and put the barrel in his mouth, but as his finger tightened on the trigger he thought of the men who had fought and died on the *Gifu*. "It had seemed hopeless to them, I knew" Obi recalls, "but they had still fought to the end, proud of their regiment and of its colors. The colors had been passed to me and so I knew I had to keep trying as well". As he listened to the far off shelling and bombing he thought he could distinguish the sounds between Japanese artillery and American bombs. He remembers "I knew that the Japanese must be where the American bombs were falling so I took a compass bearing of the sounds and moved off in that direction."

Along the coast the advance was slow. Patch began to despair at the lack of progress and reorganized his troops twice in an attempt to get ahead faster. He asked his commanders for "a more aggressive and offensive action" to defeat the Japanese before they could land more troops. His own troops at the front line were largely the 147th Infantry Regiment which had arrived in November. With no previous combat experience and untrained in jungle warfare, they moved cautiously and methodically through the jungle where every treetop could hide a sniper waiting until they had passed before firing on them from behind. The jungle itself was turned against them by the cleverly camouflaged snipers that Kurosaki left behind to cover his slow retreat. The snipers, thickly covered with leaves and branches seemed to become part of the foliage, hardly visible until they moved.

Progress was reduced to several hundred yards a day and stopped altogether when light resistance was encountered, until the area had been devastated by shellfire. It took six days to cover the four miles from the Poha to the Bonegi river and there the advance was halted for three days. Attempts to cross the river on January 30, 31 and February 1 were all stopped by Kurosaki's determined rearguard. For three days the artillery searched for Japanese positions on the west bank. Two destroyers *Wilson* and *Anderson* between them poured in more than 1,000 five-inch shells. Eventually on February 2, the 147th Infantry got across the river. In their four attempts they had suffered 69 casualties. Hyakutake had gained an invaluable three days to gather his ragged army at Cape Esperance and begin its evacuation.

On February 1 a force of 20 Japanese destroyers was spotted 150 miles north of Guadalcanal, moving quickly towards the island. Patch still believed the Japanese were re-inforcing and he ordered an all out attack on the destroyers. Forty planes from Henderson found the ships just before sunset but there was a cover of 30 Zero fighters over them. A bitter air battle took place with the destroyers firing furiously on the American bombers that managed to get through. One destroyer was damaged and forced them to turn back, while four American planes were destroyed.

After darkness three American minelayers laid 300 mines off Cape Esperance and 11 P. T. at Tulagi were alerted. Just before midnight the P.T. boats met the 19 Japanese destroyers three miles west of the Cape. In a fierce, fast battle four of the P.T. boats were lost, usually exploding whenever a Japanese shell penetrated their paper thin hulls and exploded among fuel tanks. The P.T. boats acted independently of each other, each boat taking advantage of any opportunity which suddenly presented itself. In the general melee burning P.T. boats were sometimes mistaken for Japanese destroyers and the confusion was heightened when American and Japanese planes joined in.

P.T. 123 approached to within 500 yards of a Japanese destroyer when suddenly a Japanese plane glided in and released a bomb which landed near the stern. The boat quickly burst into flames and the crew took to the water. The sea around Savo has always been notorious for the many sharks there and they were there that night. While the terrified wounded clung to damaged rafts the able bodied survivors fought off the sharks as best they could. During the long night two men were lost but dawn brought rescue for the remainder.

As the Japanese destroyers maneuvered swiftly to avoid the torpedoes fired by the P.T. boats they ran into the edge of the minefield laid earlier that night. The destroyer *Makigumo* struck a mine and became a blazing wreck which attracted further attacks by American planes. The burning destroyer was eventually scuttled by her crew.

Despite the various attacks made against the destroyers they managed to get close inshore at Cape Esperance and began to pick up Hyakutake's troops. Within a few hours a shuttle service of barges and other small boats had taken 5,400 men out to the waiting destroyers. Many of the men were the sick and wounded who had spent months on Guadalcanal. Among them was Private Tadeshi Suzuki, one of the few survivors of Ichiki's force after the battle of the Tenaru river from which he had escaped only by standing in the sea with just his nose above water. Now, an emaciated physical wreck, he was so weak he had to be lifted onto the deck of a destroyer.

Long before dawn the destroyers had completed loading and were far to the north the next morning when American planes found them. The ships threw up a curtain of fire as the aircraft attacked and little or no damage was done to the destroyers.

With the Japanese falling back slowly before him Patch had been trying to scrape sufficient L.C.T. (land craft, tank) barges together to land a force behind the enemy lines and force them to fight on two fronts. Eventually, on February 1, six L.C.T.'s landed the 2nd Battalion, 132nd Infantry at Verahue, a small village ten miles southwest of Cape Esperance, with orders to push along the coast towards the Cape. The battalion landed just after dawn and met no opposition but the barges and their destroyer escort became split into two groups and were attacked by Japanese planes on the return journey to Lunga. The destroyer *De Haven* was hit almost at once by three bombs and sunk within minutes with the loss of 167 men. A second destroyer *Nicholas* was damaged while one of the barges shot down a single enemy plane.

At Verahue the battalion of infantry moved off towards Cape Esperance and on February 2 They reached the village of Titi, six miles from the Cape.

The battalion was then frequently pinned down by enemy rifle and machine gun fire while each night Japanese barges ferried thousands of troops to waiting destroyers in Kamimbo Bay. They reached the village of Titi six miles from the Cape. There they stayed for four days engaging in no more than a little patrol activity, while four miles away dozens of Japanese barges were ferrying thousands of troops to the waiting destroyers at Kamimbo Bay. Meanwhile Patch's troops, halted at the Bonegi river for three days, had finally got across on February 2nd. Further progress was still slow, it took another four days to cover the three miles to the next river, the Umasami.

On February 4 another large group of Japanese destroyers, with the cruiser *Maikaze* left the Shortlands to evacuate more men from Guadalcanal. Again the ships had a strong fighter escort which tangled with 30 bombers sent against them from the Henderson. Repeated attempts by the planes to get through to the destroyers were driven off, but the cruiser and one destroyer were damaged for the loss of ten bombers. That night the few P. T. boats at Tulagi which were operational made another sweep off Cape Esperance while Catalina flying boats dropped flares on the area. Nothing was seen. The Japanese destroyers were two miles further away along the coast at Kamimbo Bay and during the night they lifted almost 5,000 men off the beaches. Among them was Hyakutake and his staff. The general climbed wearily up the ladder against the side of the destroyer *Hamikaze* and stopped on deck for a few quiet words with the ship's captain. He then went below to rest and when the destroyer slipped away from the coast he did not look back as the darkened outline of Guadalcanal faded in the night.

Two days later Hyakutake reached Rabaul and immediately met Imamura to give a report. "I have lost two thirds of my men on that wretched island," he told Imamura bitterly, "it is the first time a Japanese army commander has been defeated in this war." He went on to say that he had already considered committing suicide as a means of apologizing for his disgrace but he felt he still held a responsibility towards the men who had been evacuated. Imamura hastened to console him. "I understand how you must feel", he told Hyakutake, "and it would be understandable if you did kill yourself. I admire your feelings of responsibility to your men but you have another responsibility as well." He went on, "You alone can explain to the Army High Command the difficulties we now face in fighting the Americans." In an effort to ease Hyakutake's conscience Imamura pointed out that Hyakutake was not solely responsible for the defeat. He drew a parallel with the traditional Japanese Sumo Wrestling, saying that if the yokozuna,

Company E and F, 182d Infantry Regiment, Americal Division leaving Guadalcanal, March 1943.

or leader, of a wresting team was defeated because he had not eaten enough to maintain his great weight then he was responsible for his own defeat. "In your case, however, he reminded Hyakutake, "we lost control of the air and the seas so it was not your fault you did not get the supplies you needed, therefore you are not wholly responsible for what happened."

With only a few thousand Japanese left on Guadalcanal the rearguard under Kurosaki redoubled their efforts to convince the Americans that they faced a much larger force. As Patch's troops crossed the Umasami river on February 7 and pushed slowly towards the Segilau river, Kurosaki's men moved quickly from one position to another, stopping only to fire off a few shots and generally make as much noise as they could. The constant crackle of rifle fire was heard by Lieutenant Obi sill struggling through the jungle two weeks after being driven out of the *Gifu*. He recalls, "As I approached the coast I heard a great deal of rifle fire which I recognized as coming from our Arisaka rifles. I was anxious not to get caught in the middle of a battle and I knew the Americans must be near. I turned away from the coast again. As I cautiously worked my way through the jungle I head two or three voices nearby. I listened carefully and then was overjoyed to recognize them as Japanese."

Obi ran towards the patrol calling out his name and regiment, then, weakened by starvation and his ordeal in the jungle he collapsed as the patrol approached. A short time later he recovered consciousness in a Japanese camp. He was given some shoes and a few rice balls, then, so relieved at having found his countrymen again he broke down and wept. Around his waist he still had the colors of the 124th Infantry Regiment. "I unwrapped it" Obi recalls, "then folded it neatly. As I did so I thought of all the men who had fought and died under that flag and now I alone was left with it; it made me very sad."

That night 17 Japanese destroyers made the run to the evacuation beaches at Cape Esperance and Kamimbo Bay. The Japanese were doubtful if a third evacuation could be accomplished and felt sure the Americans must know what was happening. Ten of the 17 ships were therefore, detailed to patrol off Cape Esperance to engage American warships which

were expected to attempt to stop the evacuation. Yet there was no opposition. Patch still believed the ships were bringing in re-inforcements and 15 dive bombers had attempted to attack the destroyers before nightfall. They had little success largely because low cloud and heavy rain hid the ships. The P. T. boats at Tulagi were still not operational but a few Catalinas and dive bombers from Henderson made attempts to hit the Japanese ships as they began to load off Kamimbo Bay.

By midnight the last few thousand men gathered quietly on the beaches, waiting patiently for the numerous small barges to ferry them out to the destroyers. Some of the wounded were carried onto the barges on stretchers but hundreds of other wounded and sick were left behind. The rearguard troops passed among them handing out grenades to enable the wretched men to at least avoid capture. The sick who were too weak to even pull the pin from a grenade were carried on their litters to those who were able to do so. Thus three or four men were able to share together in a final act of comradeship when the grenade exploded.

By 0230 on the morning of the 8th the evacuation was completed and as the destroyers steamed off towards the Shortlands, the dozens of barges they had used were cast off to drift in Kamimbo Bay. In the three nights of the evacuation nearly 12,000 men had been pulled out of Guadalcanal. It was an impressive performance and when he heard of it later even Admiral Nimitz admitted, "Skill in keeping their plans disguised, and boldness in carrying them out, have enabled the Japanese to withdraw their garrison."

Near the village of Titi, four miles west of Kamimbo Bay, the battalion of the 132nd Infantry who had landed in the hope of preventing the evacuation had begun to move slowly towards the Bay on the 7th. Throughout most of that night, they were subject to Japanese rifle and machine gun fire but they could also hear the motors of the Japanese barges. The next morning the battalion found there was no resistance. They had met only very light resistance but moved cautiously expecting a determined final stand by the Japanese. Their casualties were light but included the regimental commander Colonel George,

shot and wounded, when he went forward to urge a faster pace. After a quiet night, in which the evacuation was completed, the battalion started forward again the next morning. By mid-morning, meeting no resistance and seeing dozens of empty barges drifting off shore, they suddenly realized what had happened and then moved forward quickly, reaching the bay at noon. The shoreline was littered with abandoned weapons, helmets and ammunition boxes and in the hot humid air hung the stench from the grenade shattered remains of the wounded and sick Japanese.

The next morning the 132nd reached the Mission at Visale, long since abandoned, most of its buildings burned to the ground and its priests and nuns by then scattered throughout the Pacific from Australia to Fiji. At Sapuru the Japanese base was deserted. Abandoned equipment was found in empty huts and a few barges were washed up on the shore. Before noon the 132nd Infantry joined up with Patch's main force pushing along the coast from the Segilau river and the campaign for Guadalcanal was over. For a few days a handful of Japanese, who had missed the final evacuation, harassed the Americans with scattered sniper fire but were either tracked down or fled deeper into the hills to die of starvation or disease.

It had been almost six months to the day since the initial landings at Red Beach and for the Japanese army it was the first defeat in five years of war throughout Asia and the Pacific. At Guadalcanal the red sun began to set.

NOT JUST A DISTANT LAND

For the Americans the Guadalcanal campaign led to a lesson book on island invasions which they successfully followed over the next two years throughout the Pacific. Although conceived in haste with faulty intelligence and inadequate training the campaign succeeded partly because of the skill and determination of American field officers such as Edson, Torgeson and Puller. The widespread coastwatchers service which so often informed on Japanese air and naval movements and the invalu-

USS President Hayes *(APA-20) (Courtesy of Joseph F. Sprock)*

able help given by the Solomon Islanders to the Americans were also factors in the defeat of the Japanese.

For the American Navy the close action, the ship-to-ship Naval battles during the campaign were often a bitter lesson obtained at high cost. The United States Navy had not fought a ship to ship action since the Spanish-American War 45 years before. Even then the action was largely confined to an inefficient Spanish squadron trapped in Manila Bay. Since that time the Navy had not maintained adequate levels of training, tactics or armaments to meet the threat of a superbly efficient Japanese navy.

Too often, in the battles around Guadalcanal, American communications, recognition signals and equipment readiness were inadequate to deal with the swiftness and stunning ferocity of Japanese attacks. The greatest problem for the American warships lay in their torpedoes. The Mark 10 torpedo had one third of the explosive power of the Japanese torpedoes. Furthermore, the Mark 10 quite simply did not work most of the time. It either ran too deep or its contact explorer malfunctioned on striking a target. On the night of November 12 more than 20 torpedoes had been fired, at close range, at the battleship *Hiei*, yet none had exploded. The "improved" Mark 14 torpedo, with a magnetic exploder, caused just as many problems and missed opportunities. So unreliable was the magnetic exploder that it was ordered not to be used, but that decision was not made until March 1944. On the Japanese side the highly efficient "long lance" torpedoes had wiped out Wright's cruiser force in ten minutes at the Battle of Cape Esperance.

Despite the Japanese advantages in training and armaments the struggle for control of the seas around Guadalcanal was won by that side which could replace its losses the most readily. Both Mikawa and Tanaka were conscious of this and cautioned Tokyo that American shipping losses could be made good rapidly whereas Japanese losses could not. Japan simply did not have the resources, or the inventiveness at that time, which allowed American shipyards to turn out an 8,000 ton "Liberty" type cargo ship in as little as a week, from huge pre-fabricated parts.

On land too, the battle became one of supply as American planes made the area too hazardous for Japanese cargo ships to reach the island. More Japanese troops were lost at sea on their way to Guadalcanal than were actually killed in fighting on the island. Of the 12,800 men of the 38th Division 5,173 were lost at sea and among the 11,790 men of the 2nd Division, 7,671 were lost in a similar way. The hopeless struggle to supply their force also cost the Japanese innumerable lives in the submarines, barges and planes that were lost in these attempts. As Hyakutake's supply position became increasingly desperate his force's strength simply withered away so that no really decisive land battle was necessary to gain control of the island.

At the battle front the superior American supply position, which was never seriously threatened after the November naval battles, allowed them to use a level of firepower that stunned many of the Japanese. At Bloody Ridge and later in Maruyama's attacks, the outnumbered Americans put down such intense and sustained fire that the initial Japanese charges were decimated while subsequent heavy shelling made regrouping for further attacks almost impossible.

For the American front line soldier Guadalcanal wiped away the myth of the invincibility of the Japanese soldier. Before August 1942 as Japanese troops swept through China, Southeast Asia and the western Pacific, the image of the Japanese soldier became grossly exaggerated. He came to be regarded as a master of rapid, skillful movement. Cleverly camouflaged, superbly trained, a small but tough jungle fighter he used the terrain to its utmost advantage. He was seen, and feared, as a man who

could creep quietly through the jungle, kill soundlessly and as silently withdraw to merge into the dark foreboding forest. He could march for 24 hours in full combat gear; run the last few miles and immediately go into combat. The 2nd Division did, in fact, pride themselves on this ability.

On Guadalcanal, however, the Japanese soldier was often seen to be foolhardy, reckless, even suicidal in hopeless frontal assaults against massive firepower. Much of his attitude owed itself to the ancient Japanese warrior tradition based on overwhelming assaults that carried all before them. Even in the jungle the Japanese troops were often careless and noisy on patrols, seldom using men on their flanks.

The Japanese did, however, make better use of the jungle terrain. Deadly booby traps devised from jungle materials, treetop snipers and defensive positions which merged completely with their surroundings made them a cunning and skillful enemy. In defense the Japanese soldier was tenacious, holding out for weeks against odds of ten to one even though reduced to a physical wreck by disease and starvation. Such men deserved better leadership than they got, far too often they paid a high price for a basic weakness in the commanders.

The lack of flexibility and the rigid adherence to preconceived plans based on faulty intelligence shown by some of the Japanese commanders was a major cause of their defeat. Hyakutake held to his initial belief that the landing on Guadalcanal was no more than a hit and run raid when plainly it involved a fleet of 80 ships. Ichiki's force was wiped out largely because of his own over-confidence based on Hyakutake's faulty analysis of the situation. It also

seems hard to believe that Hyakutake could ignore the lessons of Kawaguchi's defeat at Bloody Ridge and subsequent death march for 30 miles over some of the most formidable landscape imaginable. Yet he sent Maruyama, with artillery, over the same path to attack at almost the same place only six weeks later, with equally disastrous results.

Was the Japanese command structure so rigid, so impersonal that advice from junior officers based on bitter personal experience was ignored? Such stupidity - there can be no other word for such a futile exercise - cost the lives of almost 3,000 men at Bloody Ridge. Thirty-five years after the event the jungle trail they hacked out could still be followed by the numerous items of rusty equipment they abandoned - guns, shells, helmets and whitened, sun-scorched skulls.

On the American side the fighting cost the lives of 1,600 Marines and soldiers with a further 4,250 wounded. Many more lives were lost at sea defending the area and keeping it supplied. At the Battle of Savo on the night of August 8 more than 1,200 lives were lost, the sinking of the *Juneau* in November took 700 lives, while over 300 men were also lost in attempts to get supplies to Guadalcanal in September. The casualty lists do not number the thousands of men struck with malaria, dengue fever and dysentery who somehow had to keep going although at times almost immobilized by pain. Sergeant Mitchell Paige remembers at least 20 malaria attacks. "At times the pain was so intense I could not move my limbs." he recalls. "I had to look down all the time because when I looked up, intense stabbing pains went through my head. Throughout it all, I had to stay in the firing line."

1st Raider Battalion, A Co. Officers—Top, (L to R): Clinton Haines, ? Pettit, Dan Heslin; Bottom (L to R): Joe Broderick, Frank Kemp and Tom Pollard.

For thousands of Marines and soldiers, on both sides, disease, added to poor food and lack of sleep meant constant physical exhaustion when desperate efforts often had to be made to dig defenses in the hot sticky climate. Sweat streamed from every pore in the body, ran down the legs and gathered in boots so men often sloshed around in their own sweat. In such conditions the feet rapidly developed jungle sores and fungal infections which, impossible to keep dry, developed into large festering and bleeding wounds so that any walking became an agonizing experience.

For most of the campaign the Americans were confined to a perimeter seven miles long and about two miles deep at the most. Almost all of it was within range of "Pistol Pete" and bombed almost daily. There was no "rear area" away from the constant shelling and bombing, although some areas were considered safer than others, so the physical hardships were shared by all and today are best remembered by all. Marine Gene Keller, when he thinks of Guadalcanal, remembers not so much the Japanese but the hardships of day to day living. Most of the Marines, soldiers and airmen rarely, if ever, came into physical contact with an individual armed Japanese soldier, but the exhaustion, oppressive climate, mosquitoes, the new and strange diseases that never seemed to be cured or the revolting jungle sores that never seemed to heal; these are remembered by everyone who was there. "Guadalcanal took years off the lives of us all" Keller recalls, "I could see it in the hollow eyed, thin and exhausted men who left when I did. Most were in their early 20's but they all looked middle-aged, were worn out, and silent. To me, Guadalcanal is not just the name of a distant island somewhere in the South Pacific, it is - well . . . it's more like a very deep and personal emotion."

BIBLIOGRAPHY

Bell, J. *Condition Red.* Longman, Green & Co., London. 1949

Bennett, B. Interview. 1977

Bonner, A. Interview & Correspondence. 1976-80

Breijak, C. Correspondence. 1976

Buckley, J. *A History of Motor Torpedo Boats.* Combat Forces Press. 1953

Clemens, M. Unpublished diary. Australian War Memorial, Canberra.

Coggins, J. *The Campaign for Guadalcanal.* Doubleday & Co. 1957

Congdon, D. *Combat: Pacific Theatre.* Dell Publishing Co. 1958

Corwin, N. Correspondence. 1976

Corwin, R. Correspondence. 1976

Dolloff, G. Correspondence. 1977

Feldt, E. *The Coastwatchers.* Bantam Press. 1946

Griffith, Samuel B. *The Battle for Guadalcanal.* J.P. Lippincott. 1963

Hersey, J. *Into the Valley.* Knopf. 1963

Horton, D. *Fire over the Islands.* Reed Publishers. 1962

Hough, F. *Guadalcanal: The Turning Point.* J. P. Lippincott. 1947

Hoyt, E.P. *Guadalcanal.* Jove Publications. 1983

Jackym, J. Interview & correspondence. 1977

Johnson, R. *Follow me: The story of the 2nd Marine Division in World War II.* Random House. 1948

Johnson, R. S. Corerspondence. 1977

Kaufmann, A. Correspondence. 1976

Katsumata, J. Interview. 1976

Kurosaki, C. Interview. 1976

Laracy, H. *Marists & Melanesians.* University of Hawaii Press. 1976

Leckie, R. *Challenge for the Pacific.* Hodder & Stoughton, London. 1966

Lord, W. *Lonely Vigil.* Viking Press. 1978

McLaughlin, B. Correspondence. 1976

McMillan, G. *The Old Breed: A History of the 1st Marine Division in World War II.* Infantry Journal Press. 1949

Masanori, I. *Men of the South Pacific.* Bungei Shunju Shinsa. 1962

Miller, T. G. *The Cactus Air Force.* Harper & Row. 1969

Morison, Samuel E. *History of U.S. Naval Operations in World War II Vol. 5.* Little, Brown & Co. 1959

Muehrcke, R.C. *Orchids in the Mud,* J.S. Printing 1985

Newcombe, R. *Savo.* Holt, Rinehart & Winston. 1961

O'Neill, E. Correspondence. 1976

Paige, M. *A Marine named Mitch.* Vantage Press. 1975

Paige, M. Interview & Correspondence. 1976

Potter, J. *Admiral of the Pacific.* Heinemann. 1952

Rapasia, M. Interview. 1976

Royal Australian Navy in World War II. Australian War Memorial, Canberra. 1957-58

Sakai, S. *Samurai.* New English Library. 1966

Saku, G. Interview. 1976

Sharrod, R. *History of Marine Corps Aviation in World War II.* Combat Forces Press. 1952.

Sio, A. Interview. 1977

Sorenson, J. Correspondence. 1976

Theresa, M. Interview. 1976

Tolland, J. The Rising Sun. Cassell & Co. 1971

Tregaskis, R. *Guadalcanal Diary.* Blue Ribbon Books. 1943

Visaona, N. Interview. 1976

Vouza, J. Interview. 1976

War History Department of the Japanese Defense Ministry. *Army Tactics in the South Pacific War Vol. I* Asagumo Press Ibid. Vol. 2.

Webster, L. Correspondence. 1976

Weiss, J. Correspondence. 1977

Zimmerman, J. L. *The Guadalcanal Campaign.* United States Marine Corps Historical Division. 1949

E. L. Keller, Sr. playing the bass drum in a parade at Melbourne, Australia, February 1943—after leaving Guadalcanal.

Many Americans died on Guadalcanal. Bill Dolan visits the cemetery located on Guadalcanal.

GUADALCANAL LEGACY
50TH ANNIVERSARY
PERSONAL EXPERIENCE STORIES

December 1942, west of Henderson Field. A native work party. M. Gross and Corp. Wood, truck driver and mechanic.

VMSB-131
FIRST US MARINE TORPEDO BOMBER SQUADRON ON GUADALCANAL

Marine Air Squadron VMSB-131 was stationed at Quantico, VA, on December 7, 1941, when Pearl Harbor was attacked. A few days later, it transferred to San Diego and provided antisubmarine patrol along the California coast until it transferred to Ewa Airfield, Territory of Hawaii, in September 1942. The squadron trained with SBD dive-bombers for three weeks and then exchanged the SBDs for TBF Avengers to become the first Marine torpedo bomber squadron in Naval Aviation History. Three weeks later, on October 24, 12 TBFs were loaded aboard the Merchant Marine troopship *Jane Adams*. Three days later, the remaining 12 were loaded aboard the Escort Carrier USS *Nassau*, a "Baby Flattop."

On November 11, from a point about 75 to 80 miles south of Espiritu Santo Island in the New Hebrides, all on-board squadron TBFs took off and landed safely on Bomber Strip #1. The *Jane Adams* had arrived on November 7 but the ship's crew would not unload the TBFs due to a dispute over 'hazardous pay.' So the VMSB-131 personnel aboard locked the crew in their rooms and unloaded the aircraft themselves four days later.

Welcome to Guadalcanal

The crews worked all night. The next day six aircraft, with Lt. Col. Pat Moret in command, were flown to Guadalcanal. They were escorted by an R4D (DC3) transport. As the flight approached the shoreline at 800 feet and 130 knots airspeed to land at Henderson Field, a cruiser was spotted ahead and on the right flashing a recognition signal toward the TBFs. None of the flight crews were prepared or in a position to respond because they knew the ships were friendly and the R4D crew would certainly acknowledge the challenge. However, the transport crew failed to respond and, suddenly, "all hell broke loose." Flak began exploding all around the TBFs with the resultant concussions rocking and rattling the planes. the crews quickly realized that they were being fired upon and then heard the transport pilot telling to the base control tower, "Cactus Control, Cactus Control, tell those SOBs they have friendly aircraft over head." The flight was still in formation, taking no evasive action when the firing began but scattered like quail not knowing if the Japanese had control of the island or if the Marines did. Later they were told that a flight of Japanese dive-bombers had flown in on the same flight path the day before and the Navy had shot down half of them.

Early in the afternoon on the same day, a large Japanese naval force was sighted north of Guadalcanal and proceeding at a speed to position itself to bombard Henderson Field that night. The naval force included the battleships *Hiei* and *Kirishima*, a cruiser, and 15 destroyers. That night there ensued, a great naval battle, and bright flashes were sighted in the northern sky and loud booming sounds were heard by those ashore at Henderson Field.

Shortly after daybreak on November 13, the *Hiei* was located heavily damaged, out of control, and running in circles ten miles north of Savo Island. At 6:15 a.m. Captain Dooley took off with all six squadron TBFs to attack the *Hiei* but two aircraft returned to the field because of mechanical failure. Just before the attack was to begin, an enemy fighter attacked the formation and T/Sgt. John Dewey was credited with downing the squadron's first Zero. During the night, the *Hiei* was scuttled.

Prelude to Disaster

On the night of April 6, 1943, the Japanese had attacked Henderson Field and the surrounding area with wave after wave of bombers and fighters, and had sprayed Henderson Field with fragmentation and antipersonnel bombs. Many fellows complained that they had been kept on-the-hop all night between their

Henderson Airfield with Lunga River in the background.

tents and foxholes, and one pilot reported that he had taken off and put on his shoes eight times. The next afternoon, the Japanese attacked the area again but at least half of the estimated 150 enemy aircraft were downed along with a few of our own fighters.

In response to these two attacks and reports from reconnaissance aircraft of a vast increase in the number of enemy aircraft on airfields in the Bougainville area, a torpedo bomber attack with 100 pound bombs was ordered to takeoff beginning at 2:00 a.m. on April 8. This decision proved to be a fatal one for the aircrews of VMSB-131 assigned to this mission, and to the three Navy squadrons that also participated.

Returning fighter pilots on patrol up The Slot had reported rapidly deteriorating weather in the vicinity of the Russell Islands. As the six squadron TBFs formed into two sections, they soon encountered heavy turbulence. As they approached the Russell Islands area, the turbulence became so violent that the order was given to return to base. Lt. Bill Ritchey's plane was bouncing around so much he could not complete the turn. So he banked away opposite from the other planes to avoid a collision and successfully returned to Henderson Field at 4:30 a.m. Apparently, as the other planes turned, at least two planes collided; one eventually went down in the ocean; and nothing is know about the fate of the other two. With three crewmen in each plane, it was believed that 15 men had been lost. This was the worst disaster the squadron had ever suffered since it was formed in 1920.

South Sea Island Rescue

Later that day and all of the next, squadron planes combed the areas up The Slot searching for lost aircrew men. The search planes flew in pairs and, suddenly, two days later on April 10, Lt. Tom Reese and his turret gunner, Sgt. Bill Bolan, were sighted on the beach on Lamon Island. In the typhoon, as their plane skimmed the surface of the ocean to fly below the turbulence, the engine quit and their plane dropped into the ocean. After they retrieved the rubber raft, it sank before they could rescue their radio gunner, S/Sgt. Paul Moyer, from the radio compartment. Then, as Lt. Alvin Clark dropped supplies on the beach, his engine sputtered and the crew of three now made it five stranded on the beach.

A few minutes later, Captain George Dooley, squadron CO, found turret gunner T/Sgt. Bill Lares frantically waving his arms in the air on a small island just over the horizon. He had been in one of the two

planes that apparently had collided and, fortunately, he came up in the water near a rubber raft. He had drifted all day on April 8 and landed on the unnamed island that evening. He had spent the previous day patiently searching the skies for a rescue plane. Dooley's radio gunner, Sgt. George Bobb, immediately contacted a PT boat in the area and Dooley led it first to the five on Lamon Island and then to pick up Lares. On the way back to Guadalcanal, a Marine pilot, Lt. Connelly, bailed out from his damaged fighter plane in the path of the PT boat. The seven airmen were all very happy to be safely "home" on Guadalcanal.

Medal of Honor Recipients

Throughout the long history of VMSB-131, General Christian F. Schilt was the only individual to be awarded a Medal of Honor while a member of the squadron. The event took place on January 6, 7, 8, 1928, at Quilali, Nicaragua. He served on Guadalcanal in 1942-1943 as CO of MAG-11, Chief of Staff of the 1st MAW, and CO of the Strike and Search Patrol Commands, Solomon Island. Three other former VMSB-131 pilots were awarded the Medal of Honor for events in the area of Guadalcanal; Maj. John L. Smith, August-September 1942, CO VMF-223; Lt. Col. Harold W. Bauer, May 10 to November 14, 1942, CO VMF 212, posthumously; and 1st Lt. Kenneth A. Walsh, August 15-30, 1943, VMF-124.

THE WAY HOME

Across the land last week, for six warm days and nights, a troop train rumbled. It was an old train, with no fancy name. To the engineers and switchmen, it was No. 7452-C. The men on board dubbed it the "Home Again Special," and wrote the new name in chalk on the sides of the old Pullman cars. In another war there might have been brass bands at every stop. But in this pageantry-less, slogan-less war, the train just rumbled on toward New York, through the big towns and the whistle-stops.

The men aboard were 370 members of the 1st Marine Division -survivors of Tulagi, conquerors of Guadalcanal; the men who mowed down the Japs like hay at Bloody Ridge, and crossed the bloody Matanikau River; the invaders of Cape Gloucester, the rain-drenched fighters of Talasea, the men who took Hill 660 when they should have been annihi-

lated halfway up; the unnamed defenders of Nameless Hill, the survivors of Coffin Corner.

These men on the troop train, already famed in communiqués and the war's best-sellers were heading home for a 30-day furlough after 27 months of battle.

NO. 3 BOMBER RECON. SQUAD ROYAL NEW ZEALAND A. F.

A Summary of Operations from Henderson Airfield Guadalcanal 23 November 1942 to 10 February 1943

No. 3 Squadron RNZAF entered the campaign on 23 November when a flight of six aircraft and eight crews was detached from the Squadron at Santo and sent forward to operate from Guadalcanal. The aircraft had been preceded by a small servicing party, which moved by sea three days earlier and had set up camp in a jungle-clad gully close to Henderson Field.

As with all other aircraft on Henderson at that time the unit came under the operational command of the Senior Naval Aviator, Guadalcanal (SENAVCACTUS), then Brigadier-General L. E. Woods, USMC, of the 1st Marine Air Wing.

The Hudson was essentially a reconnaissance aircraft, lightly armed with machine guns for self defense and always carried bombs for use if a suitable target came along. In its primary role of reconnaissance the squadron was asked to conduct day and night searches of the approaches to Guadalcanal, and daily low-level searches along the coastlines of islands which might be used as staging points for enemy movements of supplies and troops.

The Hudson flight began operations the day after it arrived at Guadalcanal, and during the first week aircraft sighted enemy ships four times, enemy aircraft three times and were twice attacked by enemy aircraft. On the first day of operations a Hudson captained by Flying Officer George Gudsell saw a tanker and two transports, escorted by a destroyer, to the south of Vella Lavella. The Hudson was attacked by three Nakajima float planes which were circling above the convoy, but they did not press home their attacks, being deterred by the Hudson's turret and side guns. After an engagement which lasted about twenty minutes the Hudson escaped without either side having scored any hits.

A more severe engagement occurred three days later on 27 November when a Hudson again captained by Gudsell sighted an enemy task force to the southwest of Vella Lavella. Gudsell reported the composition and position of the force and then closed in to make a closer inspection. As he was doing so he was dived on by three land-based Japanese fighters. In their first attack they put the Hudson's top turret gun out of action and then concentrated on attacks from astern. Gudsell directed the Hudson from the astrohatch while the second pilot Flying Officer McKechnie piloted the aircraft. After an action which lasted 17 minutes the Japanese aircraft broke off and retired, having scored only three hits and without having injured any of the Hudson's crew.

This early action contributed to the high morale which prevailed in the squadron throughout its tour of operations. In the previous month a number of American search planes had been lost to enemy action and, after seeing the comparatively light armament of the Hudson it was considered we would be sitting ducks for Japanese fighters. The proof that the Hudson could repel odds of three to one when properly handled and resolutely fought was comforting to all the aircrews. Gudsell was awarded the U.S. Air Medal.

Until the middle of December the Hudsons flew on four, five or six patrols daily over New Georgian, Santa Isabel, Choiseul and the surrounding waters. An average flight extended about 400 miles from base and lasted up to five hours. When enemy shipping was located it was usually too strongly defended for the Hudson to attack and the appropriate action then was to radio back to base giving the position of the ships so that strike forces of SBD's and TBF's could be sent out to deal with them. Only occasionally did the Hudson's find targets which they could profitably attack themselves.

On 2 December a Hudson captained by Sergeant Page on a routine patrol to the west of New Georgia spotted a fully surfaced submarine of about 500 tons and with a lookout on the conning tower. Page made a bombing run out of the sun and dropped two 250-pound anti-submarine bombs and two 325-pound depth charges as the submarine crash dived. Three of the bombs fell short and one just over the target. A large patch of oil came to the surface over the position where the last bomb had landed. The submarine was probably damaged, but in the absence of definite proof no claim was made of its destruction.

From about the middle of December the daily programme for Hudsons was changed to two morning and four afternoon searches as this seemed to fit in better with the routine of the *Tokyo Express*. Twice in the first week of December the *Tokyo Express* ran down from the northern Solomons to Guadalcanal. On the 3rd two heavy cruisers, two light cruisers and six destroyers left Buin and made a dash down the 'Slot'. They were successfully tracking coastwatchers and search planes from the time they left Buin. At half past three in the afternoon an RNZAF Hudson sighted them moving south near Vella Lavella and shadowed them for about two hours. Radio contact with Guadalcanal was difficult as the Japanese attempted to jam the Hudson's signal, and then asked for the message to be repeated and immediately afterwards sent a message cancelling it. Nevertheless a strike force of dive-bombers, torpedo-bombers and fighters was sent from Henderson and attacked the Japanese force at 1830 hours in the channel opposite central New Georgia. Four of the enemy ships were hit by bombs and ten enemy aircraft were shot down.

The afternoon dash by the *Tokyo Express* down the 'Slot' to Guadalcanal became a regular occurrence by the Japanese who were attempting to reinforce and supply their garrison there. On six occasions in December and ten in January the Hudsons became involved. Also during December photographic reconnaissance confirmed that the Japanese were building an airfield at Munda under a camouflage of coconut plantations, leaving the trees standing until they were ready to begin the final surfacing of the runway. One of the first attacks on this was made by an RNZAF Hudson on the morning on 9 December. It bombed the strip from 7000 feet and scored a hit on the runway and set fire to buildings and tents.

Air operations in January and February were hampered by bad weather. The rainy season had started by the end of December and for the next few months there were frequent heavy rainstorms throughout the area. Japanese shipping took full advantage of the cover they provided, and which enabled it on many occasions to escape detection by searching aircraft.

After a relatively quiet period towards the end of December the Japanese in January again started large scale attempts with destroyers to reinforce their garrison on Guadalcanal. This made for a very busy time for the Hudsons of No. 3 Squadron and an average of almost seven sorties a day were flown. Most of these were routine patrols, but individual Hudsons were occasionally used for special missions. On 8 January a Hudson was sent to bomb a village near Kieta on Southern Bouganville where the natives had been supporting the enemy. Another Hudson bombed Munda on 11 January and on 24 January a Hudson patrol attacked a Japanese tanker in Vella Gulf, 215 miles from Guadalcanal.

The latter half of January and early February were particularly hectic in terms of Japanese air

Company Headquarters, Co. F, 182d Infantry, Americal Division. Rear (L to R): Dave Thalheimer, Al Palladini, Gordon May, Bob LaRosse, Dewey Taylor; Front (L to R): Manny Correia and Bill Dolan.

attacks on Guadalcanal and movements of their shipping to embark their troops. In addition to the actions described there were numerous occasions when the Hudsons located, reported and then shadowed enemy shipping moving to Guadalcanal and when they were retiring to their bases in the northern Solomons. The last run of the *Tokyo Express* involving the Hudsons took place on the night of 7 February. First reported about 1400 hours by a coastwatcher, 19 destroyers moving south at high speed in an area of low cloud, were located by a Hudson 20 miles east of Ganonga Island and again at 1615 hours south of Ganonga. SBDs attacked at 1730 when the enemy were 20 miles south of Rendova Island and scored hits on two ships. This was the first time the *Express* had come round the south of New Georgia instead of taking the more direct route down the 'Slot'.

While the air operations were never boring, life on the ground at Guadalcanal had its moments also. On the nights early in January when the *Tokyo Express* visited Cape Esperance small forces of enemy bombers carried out diversionary raids on Henderson Air Field. Later in the month nuisance raids at night became more frequent. 'Washing Machine Charlie' with his engines de-synchronized could be relied upon to make regular calls and keep everyone awake. Although Guadalcanal was being bombed almost nightly and bombs fell in and around our camp there were no New Zealand casualties from these actions.

The New Zealand camp consisted solely of tents set on muddy ground. The absence of dugout accommodation meant that the men had to tumble out of their beds into foxholes whenever enemy planes were overhead. For some weeks the efficiency of the unit was threatened, although it was never impaired, by fatigue caused by broken nights and lack of sleep.

PFC. "HARDROCK" GERKIN MEETS THE COMMANDING GENERAL

by Ted Blahnik

The ear-banging, newly promoted buck sergeant has just been ordered to take half of the Platoon to the Lunga River to bathe, wash the utilities on their backs (the only clothes they have on Guadalcanal), to shave - but mainly to get the stink off their frames - which have been attracting numerous flies that seem to disturb the sensitive guys in-the-rear-with-the-gear.

There are about eight of them from the 1st Platoon, L-3-5, including Curley Woods, Zega, Miller, Hap Poloshain, Yogi, and Pfc. Lawrence (Hardrock) E. Gerkin. They arrive at the Lunga at a spot where a long, fallen tree extends half-way across the river. The tree trunk has been bleached to wash clothes as well as bodies. After grounding their weapons on the river bank, they walk into the sweet, clean water and the sergeant sees a short, older, thin-haired guy on the other side of the tree, bathing alone. They pay no attention to this other guy until Hardrock pipes up sayin, "Jeez, this guy's got a bar of soap." "Hey, Mac," he says, "Where the hell did you ever get that soap? Do you mind letting me use a little of that soap?" This older looking guy half turns, arm extended with the soap in hand and says, "Here, help yourself." Gerkin grabs the soap without a thanks or by-your-leave, however, the sergeant, standing waist deep in the water, sees what Pfc. Larry E. Gerkin apparently did not see. The guy with the bar of sweet-smelling soap is none other than our Commanding General, A. A. Vandergrift!

This story actually starts out in early November, 1942, on a sun-baked ridge, about 100 yards or so beyond the MLR (Main Line or Resistance), where two understrength platoons of L-3-5 are partially dug in to supposedly play the roll of delaying the slop-heads in case they decide to attack the Matanikau end of the perimeter. In those days, we were just told to dig in and hold your position to the last man. Under our breaths or to each other, we would usually mutter, "Who the hell does the last man report to?"

At first, captured Jap rice was brought out to the ridge by small patrols, once a day, however, after a week or so, some days, we got our two spoonfuls of rice, but other days, it didn't arrive and the raggety warriors got to the stage where they didn't care about anything anymore. The men were becoming lethargic and that was serious because, in combat, once you get to the "I don't care stage," somebody will be "separating your dog tags" real soon; that's if you are still wearing your dog tags.

On the morning before they are unexpectedly relieved off the ridge, a platoon size patrol, protecting a bird colonel, comes up the ridge. The newly promoted sergeant and his runner/telephone cranker are lying in the shade when this colonel with pressed riding britches, shine boots, neat brush-cut, looking like he is ready for the parade ground, approaches and asks, "Who's in charge here?" The sergeant says that he is. The man struts around the two reclining figures, all the while sniffing and looking down in disgust. The colonel makes his second mistake (the first one was coming out there) by asking, "When's the last time you people washed yourselves?" The sergeant doesn't answer right away and before he can, the little 17 year old runner/telephone cranker speaks us and says something like, "Colonel, that's the dumbest question I heard in a long time." "Now, why don't you ask another stupid question like, "When's the last time you people had a drink of water?" Without answering, the colonel takes out his canteen and hands it to the sergeant and tells his pistol patrol to break out their canteens, also. With that, the young runner yells, "WATER!!!", and the dozen or so men in the platoon came out of their positions where they had been sleeping, (sleep days - stay awake at night) resembling wide-eyed, haunted looking zombies, with dirty, tattered clothes, long overdue shaves, needing haircuts, sick with malaria and dysentery, gaunt and thin from the lack of food and thirsty as hell. It was honestly a mess of raggedy-ass Marines.

Early the next morning, they are relieved and sent to the Lunga River to bathe, wash their clothes, etc., where the 1st class BAR man, Pfc. Lawrence E. Gerkin, is bumming soap from the commanding

general, shooting the breeze, and not knowing who this guy is.

As the men wash themselves and their clothes, the sergeant is trying to get Hardrock's attention because it is obvious he doesn't know who this man is that he is talking to. Pretty quick, Gerk says something like, "Boy, what a hell of a way to fight a war! No chow, very little drinkable water and not enough ammo to start a firefight." The general replies with "yes, it's not the best way to fight a war." Gerkin asks, "What outfit you in, Buddy?" The general says, "Headquarters." The sergeant is calling - "Hey, Gerk! Come over here," but Gerk pays no attention. Then Hardrock says, "Jeez, you Headquarters guys must be getting all the chow and good supplies and us guys on the line get what's left over." "Well, it's not exactly like that," the General says. The sergeant is easing out toward his number on BAR man when Hardrock pipes up with, "Well, you guys in Headquarters must be getting some pretty good chow because you still have a small puss-gut going, buddy."

The sergeant is glaring at Hardrock. He is along side of Gerk, now. The general is on the other side of the tree. The sergeant looks over and says, "Good morning, General. How are you today?" A. A. says, "I'm fine - how are you men today?" Hardrock has now disappeared under water. The general is smiling (his laugh for the day?) We are making small talk when Gerk surfaces, hands back the general's bar of soap, which is mostly gone by now, and soberly says, "Jeez, I'm sorry general, but if you have to beat your gums, it's best to start at the top!" The general is laughing and says, "You make a good point, young man."

And so it went. Just another average day in the life of Pfc. Lawrence E. Gerkin - the aforementioned being the story of how he met and took a bath with General A. A. Vandergrift on Guadalcanal.

THE GUADALCANAL STRUGGLE ENDS

by Robert C. Muehrcke, M.D./Joseph G. Micek

On 31 December 1942 the Japanese Imperial General Headquarters accepted an unforgettable defeat on Guadalcanal and cancelled all proposed counter offensives to retake what they called the "Island of Blood and Death." On 4 January 1943 the Imperial General Staff ordered General Hitoshi Imamura and Vice-Admiral Jinichi Kusaka to evacuate any survivors from Guadalcanal. This message

Memorial Service for 1st Marine Division on December 31, 1942. (Courtesy of Ted Blahnik)

Five veterans of Guadalcanal. (Courtesy of Herbert B. Huffman)

was personally delivered to the Rabaul Headquarters by a senior army officer from the Imperial Army Headquarters.

Gen. Hyakutake realized the difficulty of holding his line in the Kokumbona area as a result of the strong XIV Corps offensive starting in mid-December 1942 at Mount Austen (Phase I). In December, Gen. Hyakutake ordered his front line troops to hold their Mount Austen position until the last man was killed.

When the XIV Corps pressed the Phase II of the offensive in January 1943, Gen. Hyakutake changed his plans. The Japanese troops were to withdraw westward to the Cape Esperance area. There they would make their final, and desperate stand. On 15 January 1943 Gen. Hyakutake explained the evacuation "as a change in his disposition of troop(s) for future offensives."

On 1 January 1943 Gen. Alexander Patch Jr., started the final all-out offensive to "secure" Guadalcanal. On 5 January Gen. Patch assumed command of the newly organized XIV Corps which consisted of the Americal and the 25th Divisions and the CAM (Composite Army Marine) division. On 6 January the 25th Division, commanded by Maj. Gen. J. "Lightning Joe" Lawton Collins, began moving westward to the Matanikau.

On 9 January 1943 the Second Battalion 25th Infantry had completely relieved the tired, worn down, and depleted in strength 132nd Infantry from the Japanese Gifu stronghold. As part of Phase II offensive, other units of the 35th Infantry swung south of Hill 27 and attacked Hills 43 and 44, a pair of hills resembling a seahorse on the serial photo map.

The Beginning of The End

Phase III started when the 27th Infantry moved its attack southwest from the lines below Point Cruz toward a large hill known as the Galloping Horse. On 21 January 1943, "I" Company of the 147th Infantry moved west from Koli Point and was transported around to Beaufort Bay in southwestern Guadalcanal. The reinforced rifle company, commanded by Lt. Fred Flo of the 164th Infantry Regiment marched

north, up and across the 5,000 foot mountain range to the village of Tapananja some 3,000 feet above sea level on the Kokumbona-Beaufort Bay Trail. There a defense trail block was set up to prevent the enemy from using this strategic trail to evacuate Guadalcanal.

The Composite Army Marine (CAM) Division commanded by Brig. Gen. Alphonse A. DeCarre USMC advanced along the coastal road. The Marines attacked south of Point Cruz while the CAM Division continued their pursuit of the "retreating" Japanese. On 1 February 1943 the CAM Division was at the Bonegi River just below Tassafaronga. Here were recently landed, 600 fresh troops; their mission was to cover the Cape Esperance exodus. This Japanese rear guard made a heroic stand covering Lt. Gen. Hyakutake's westward withdrawal.

The 182nd Infantry secured the famous "waterhole" and moved up the coast toward Cape Esperance. On the nights of 22-23 January 1943 the Japanese XVII Army started it's withdrawal to Cape Esperance. The Japanese resistance was stubborn, and aggressive. The Marines killed 1,200 Japanese and gained 3,000 yards of ground to reach Kokumbona on 23 January. Two days later, the Marines occupied Kokumbona, and held positions along the Poha River.

The Second Battalion to Cape Esperance

Following the Mount Austen Campaign, the Second Battalion 132nd Infantry had two and one-half weeks rest and recuperation along the relatively inactive airfield perimeter of defense. The morale of the entire battalion was high. They had their baptism by enemy fire at Hill 27. In spite of high casualties, they did not lack the spirit to fight and win. The officers and men were proud of their accomplishments.

The XIV Corps General Staff also highly rated the Second Battalion as a fighting organization. In fact, Gen. Patch stated several times that the battalions fight at Mount Austen earned him his "third star."

By the latter part of January 1943 it was evident that the Japanese were carrying out a delaying action to cover a retreat to Cape Esperance. Simultaneously the Japanese were massing naval strength at Rabaul

and air strength in the mid-Solomon Islands. The General Staff of XIV Corps believed the Japanese were planning a full scale attack to retake Guadalcanal.

The Cape Esperance pursuit was extremely exhilarating to the American infantrymen for several reasons. It was short- nine days. Two amphibious landings were involved. The American casualties were low. Four men were killed ("F" Company) and the regimental commander was wounded. The Japanese loss in killed ratio was 36 for every American killed. For the American infantryman each day was action packed. Their joint efforts climaxed in ending the battle for Guadalcanal. The civilian soldiers were no longer amateurs, but now professionals. They could accurately criticize the professionals and this they did. For example the "virgin innocence" of the general staff caused their failure to recognize the tactical significance of the successful massive exodus in three nights of approximately 13,000 Japanese fighting men.

The Tokyo Express

The Tokyo Express's main mission on 1-2 February 1943 was to evacuate the Japanese 38th Infantry Division, including Col. Oka, some native personnel, hospital patients, and others, totaling 5, 394 men. Also, unknown and embarrassing to Americans, especially to the Island's general staff and to Admiral William F. Halsey, the Japanese evacuated the first of three groups of Japanese fighting men which eventually totalled 12,940 soldiers and sailors. The Japanese were making plans for their Dunkirk to evacuate troops the nights of 4-5 February (4,972 men) and the nights of 7-8 February (2, 638 men) from the Village of Marovov and Kamimbo Bay. Each Japanese destroyer took on at least 600 men.

Surprising A Japanese Patrol

At 1300 hours, just south of Titi, a Japanese patrol was observed on one of the grassy, hilly fingers overlooking the beach trail. While the enemy patrol concentrated on the main Task Force body moving along the beach trail, Lt. Quast was able to work the flanking squad to within 150 yards of the Japanese. The squad surprised the entire patrol and "killed" 15 Japanese soldiers. The Task Force suffered no casualties. Maj. Butler believed the Japanese were the same who fired on the ship Kocorana on 31 January 1943.

At 1415 hours the main body reached Titi. The narrow, flat strips along the beach gradually gave way to foothills rising into the interior to higher mountains. There were fewer coconut groves than on the Lunga side of Guadalcanal. A stream coursed around the southern end of the coconut grove and flowed into the ocean. The coconut grove extended inland for approximately 1500 yards to the valley from which the small mountain stream flowed. This was the location of the Task Force's bivouac perimeter. One flank tied in at the ocean. The formation of a perimeter of defense was "standard operating procedure" (SOP) at all times.

The remainder of the Second Battalion Task Force passed through a beautiful area of banana groves and cultivated fields. Many men picked and ate papaya during the advance. Col. George was constrained to moving cautiously forward. He believed fresh Japanese troops landed on 1-2 February. At night the Second Battalion was prepared for a surprise banzai attack. Col. George kept the main body close together at all times. the future advance was to be slow. No information from Division Headquarters reached the Task Force that the Japanese were either planning to reinforce Guadalcanal or to evacuate the island.

The Last Guadalcanal Banzai Charge

Our dug in infantry was a mile in front of the Village of Marovovo. It was shelled by Japanese 90mm mortars and artillery fire. Following the barrage the Americans could hear loud screams from the Japanese in their final Guadalcanal banzai charge on the "empty village." The shooting and artillery continued for more than an hour. There was an extremely large Japanese force in the attack. If "G" Company or the entire Task Force had positioned themselves to defend the village, they would have been decimated.

Capt. Prewitt heard the motors of the Japanese small boats. He and others thought the Japanese were landing tanks and getting into position to attack the Americans. Early the next morning this information was radioed to Col. Ferry. In addition, Col. Ferry received a message from regiment that 20 enemy destroyers were expected to reach Cape Esperance on the night of 7-8 February and a Japanese attack would follow. the entire Task Force was alerted.

The nights of 3-4 February were quiet; by the afternoon of 4 February the entire Task Force was within the perimeter. All ammunition and supplies were now at Titi; Battery "B" of the Marine artillery was in position. Not very much patrol activity occured. At midnight 4-5 February the Japanese were extremely active at Cape Esperance; the men heard loud noises of a large surface Naval battle. They saw flashes from both American and Japanese Naval guns.

The night of 4-5 February, flares were gain observed in the direction of Cape Esperance. The sounds of distant bomb explosions were heard across the mountain range at the airfield.

Unknown to the Americans the Japanese had evacuated 4,972 men by Adm. Tanaka's "Tokyo Express" via the "slot" to Bougainville. No enemy contacts were made since 2 February. Although Japanese aircraft detected our landing it was of concern to Col. George that the enemy did not

Guadalcanal, 1942. (Courtesy of J. Sumner)

Wading ashore. Guadalcanal, 1942. (Courtesy of J. Sumner)

On Guadalcanal, 1942. (Courtesy of J. Sumner)

respond t our presence. Our 105mm howitzers had not fired since the landing.

The Marine artillery usually "zeroed-in" initially by firing a round with an overhead burst until a man from Company "F" was killed. Then Lt. Wojik fired a round into the ocean and "walked" the subsequent rounds onto the target. The American Navy vessel may have suspected the round fired into the ocean was Japanese fire directed at them.

Company "F" Patrol Ambushed

On the afternoon of 5 February 1943 a patrol from Company "F" led by platoon Sgt. Ramirez made a reconnaissance of Marovovo. On their return they engaged a Japanese "ambush"" patrol. The encounter took place only a short distance from the Company "F perimeter. In the head-on confrontation five Americans were killed by fire from a British McVicker heavy machine gun. On contact, the Japanese dropped the machine gun and firing started. The Japanese lost 11 men killed. The ambush was very close to the Task perimeter, therefore individual patrol members attempted singly to reach their lines. Unfortunately, two men were cut off; they along with Guadalcanalese scouts were taken prisoners. Sgt. Ramirez was unable to estimate the exact number of Japanese they encountered. The presence of these Japanese verified the Guadalcanalese report of seeing Japanese in the area, north of Marovovo.

A few days later and 12 miles farther north, the Japanese left one of the captive infantrymen of "F" Company to die. He was shot through the abdomen. The bodies of the other prisoners were later found, stripped naked, and bayoneted in the legs and abdomen.

A man from "F" Company was killed when the Marine artillery "zeroed" in. A short round exploded; the very next second the infantryman was an unrecognized remains of protoplasm; he was killed by "The Demonical Ghost of Friendly Fire." The 75mm howitzer shells continued to shoosh overhead toward the Japanese. All men of the Task Force were saddened by the first casualty from "F" Company.

Artillery support was from Battery "F" 10th marines. The Marine forward field artillery observer, Lt. Michael Wojik, was assigned to Capt. Prewitt. Wojick was a second lieutenant not yet 19 years old. He reported to Capt. Prewitt with his fatigues above the elbows and knees. On the back of his fatigues jacket, in red paint, were lettered the words, "Tojo eats S—t." Wojik's "Gung-Ho" attitude continued throughout the movement toward Marovovo.

While directing artillery fire, Lt. Wojik was also seen firing his rifle; he personally killed a Japanese soldier. In 1961-63, Wojik and Prewitt, both lieutenant colonels, accidentally met in Taiwan while assigned to MAAG. Unfortunately, this spirited and extremely professional artilleryman, Wojik, never received the Silver Star Award recommended by Capt. Prewitt.

The Pincers Join

On the morning of 9 February 1943, Col. Ferry's combat team started around Cape Esperance for the Village of Tenaro. A site was selected by Col. Gavan for the pincers to meet. The advance point pushed beyond the range of 75mm pack howitzers. When supporting fire was needed, both Capt. Prewitt and Lt. Giesel used their 60mm mortars or the heavy mortars of "M" Company and "H" Company.

At approximately 1630 hours with Company "E" leading and Company "G" next in column, the Second Battalion moved into Tenaro. There, on the east bank of the Tenamba River, they met the First Battalion of the 161st Infantry. Major Butler shook hands with their battalion commander Col. James A. Dalton of Burlington, VA. Col. Dalton remarked "Boy am I glad to see you." Both men congratulated each other.

That night the Guadalcanal radio announced the termination of organized Japanese activities. This marked the end of the fierce battle for Guadalcanal - an island the Japancsc referred to as "the Island of Blood and Death." There since August 1942 the Japanese lost 32,926 men. However, they displayed unusual courage and cunning, especially in their well organized evacuation of more than 12,000 soldiers and sailors.

Gen. Alexander M. Patch, Jr. sent the following message to Adm. William F. Halsey: "Total and complete defeat of the Japanese forces on Guadalcanal effective today. Am happy to report this kind of compliance with your orders because the Tokyo Express no longer has terminals on Guadalcanal."

Adm. Halsey replied: "When I sent a Patch to act as tailor for Guadalcanal, I did not expect him to remove the enemy's pants and sew it on so quickly. Thanks and congratulations."

Japan Admits Its Defeat

On 9 February 1943 a Tokyo broadcast was transmitted by the German radio. The report admitted the evacuation of Japan's armies from Guadalcanal. "After an intense six months battle against U.S. forces, approximately 13,000 Japanese survivors were rescued. Many of the Japanese survivors appeared sick and starved." This was the first information reported by the Japanese General Staff about the Cape Esperance withdrawal.

For the weary and anxious Marines and Army infantrymen, it was great to enjoy their most expensive luxury, and as an aftermath, a clean bath and a good night's sleep.

Days later Gen. Sebree, "John the Baptist" still could not realize the Japanese evacuated Guadalcanal in large numbers. He demanded of Lt. Col. Casper, now commanding the 132nd Infantry, an explanation as to why radio silence was not broken by an American officer, Lt. Giesel of the 132nd Infantry the night of 7 February 1943. Had Gen. Sebree witnessed the withdrawal of 2,500 Japanese aboard 19 Japanese destroyers, he too would have been frustrated, for he in any manner did not relish the thought of later fighting the same Japanese in Bougainville or the Philippines.

GUADALCANAL AND THE "CACTUS AIR FORCE"

by R. E. Galer

If you mention Guadalcanal today, most people would rather if this was a new fast food or some distant land. Fifty years ago it was a household word known by all mature Americans. Today it is familiar to the Social Security set, their families and their grandchildren who remember "Guadalcanal".

Guadalcanal, an island in the British Solomon Islands (approximately 5000 miles southwest of the United States), was discovered in 1568 by the Spanish explorer Alvaro De Mendana DeNeyra. In 1788 Lieutenant Thomas George Shortland in command of two British transports landed and examined the island. In 1893, Guadalcanal with other Solomon Islands became a British protectorate. In 1942 it became an American household word spoken with feeling for our troops who were assaulting the Japanese forces occupying the Island.

For the middle-aged and young a brief review of history, of our (USA) participation in World War II.

On December 7, 1941, in a "Day to Live in Infamy" the Japanese Fleet made a surprise attack on the U.S. Pacific Fleet based at Pearl Harbor (Pearl Harbor is the port for Honolulu, Oahu, Hawaii). The Japanese, for all practical purposes, destroyed the Pacific Fleet and by afternoon President Roosevelt declared the U.S. at war with the Japanese and their allies and we became allies initially with the Australians, British and the French for our entry into World War II. We were ill-prepared and ill-equipped to fight but the entire population of the USA were mad, ready and eager to engage the enemy. In the next few weeks we had serious set backs at Wake Island (which fell) and the Philippines which later fell. On April 18, 1942, Jimmy Doolittle brought home to the Japanese people that they were in for a real fight, when he countered with an air raid on Tokyo, leading his squadron of Army Air Corps B-25s from a Navy carrier and delivering the message to Tokyo. The next real Japanese move, apparently motivated by the Doolittle raid, was the attack on the Island of Midway. Midway held and the Japanese fleet was very heavily damaged. This was the first time the Japanese had actually been stopped and they lost four carriers in the operation. In the next months there were several Naval actions at sea with both sides suffering major damage. On July 5, 1942, a U.S. reconnaissance plane and the British (Australian) coast watcher discovered an airstrip under construction by the Japanese in the Solomon Islands on the Island of Guadalcanal. Admiral King immediately recognized the potential threat and convinced the Joint Chief of Staffs (JCS) that immediate action was required. The JCS directive initially gave a target date of August 1, 1942 - just a month off - for the attack (code name "Watch Tower") on Guadalcanal and the nearby Island of Tulagi. The code name for Guadalcanal was "Cactus."

The landing would be made by the 1st Marine Division commanded by Major General Vandegrift and Marine Aircraft Group 23 providing air support. The transports and their screening and fire-support ships were under Rear Admiral Kelly Turner. The senior admiral, Vice Admiral Fletcher was theoretically the tactical commander and he had the carriers *Saratoga*, *Enterprise* and *Wasp*, and their support ships in Task Force 61. (It later appeared that his only concern was for his carriers and their support ships). D-Day was changed to August 6 for Tulagi and August 7, 1942, for Guadalcanal - exactly eight months after Pearl Harbor.

On "D" Day the inexperienced 1st Marine Division stormed ashore and captured both Tulagi (the capital of the Solomon Islands) on August 6th, and the airfield under construction on Guadalcanal (this island 20 miles from Tulagi) on August 7th.

The two battalions landing at Guadalcanal (code name "Cactus," the source of the name Cactus Air Force) were virtually unopposed as there were only some 400 Japanese, including natives, working on the construction of the airfield (the airfield to be named by the Marines, Henderson Field, after Major Lofton Henderson, a Marine pilot killed at Midway).

The runway under construction was only 2600 feet long. The division's 1st Engineers Battalion immediately began to lengthen it to 3500 feet using any material available plus steel landing mats. These engineers were soon reinforced or replaced by a Navy Cub Unit (Sea-Bee's).

To put this "Watch Tower" operation in the proper perspective so that our readers will fully appreciate the efforts and accomplishments of the 1st Marine Division with its Air, the Army and the Army Air Corps and the Navy plus its Air Groups, one must understand some of the command, communication, and logistic problems our troops and our allies had to contend with as well as the enemy and surrounding jungle. From Washington (JSC) to Australia (Gen. MacArthur) to the combat area the Senior Commanders (our theoretical friends) fought each other for supplies, troops and aircraft - each with what appeared to be different goals. The Army wanted to send everything to Europe (planes, man and equipment), the Navy, principally Adm. King fought them all to get support for operation "Watch Tower" (code name that included Cactus) and Gen. MacArthur wanted everything under his control in Australia. A famous Adm. King quoted to his Admirals prior to the operations, "I don't know what the hell this logistical this is that General Marshall keeps talking about, but I want some of it."

Our force was put together for the operation without ever really getting together or ready. Elementary things like combat loading the ships was not really accomplished because "in New Zealand where the ships were being loaded the 'unions' would not work on weekends or in inclement weather." Combat Marines did their best to load in a very short period. There was no "Beach Crew" in the attack force to handle the equipment on the shore. It just piled up and there was no equipment unloaded to move the bulk of the first supplies, i.e. bulldozers, trucks, fork lifts, etc.

Only one conference, supposedly of all the commanders, was held on Saratoga before the operation. Adm. Ghormley, Commander South Pacific, was so busy setting up his quarters and office in New Zealand that he failed to attend. He in short, abdicated his command responsibility and paved the way for several tragic events that almost caused failure of the Watch Tower operation, i.e. Adm. Fletcher asked Rear Admiral Turner how many days it would take to unload troops and equipment. He answered, five days. Fletcher stated he would leave after two days. R. Adm. Fletcher stated that the troops could not be landed in two days. General Vandegrift objected vigorously to Adm. Flecther's declaration and argued it was imperative that air support be available a minimum of four days. Interestingly enough, no record was kept of the meeting and Adm. Ghormley's Chief of Staff remained quiet and he should have made the necessary decision to keep air support in place.

Rehearsal for the invasion, in General Vandegrift's words, was a "fiasco," a "complete bust."

Intelligence photos of the Guadalcanal beaches prepared by MacArthur's intelligence officer were improperly addressed and mailed July 20, these photos were located in December, four months after the invasion, in Melbourne, Australia.

Communication was strange, i.e. message from coast watchers on movement of Japanese was picked up in Townsville, Australia, relayed to Melbourne, then to Pearl Harbor and back to Fletcher and Turner, and then possibly to Guadalcanal.

In short, the first allied offensive in the Pacific of WWII was a complete fiasco and was nearly fatal to the whole Pacific War operation.

What made it work was the real effort, personal sacrifice, courage and perseverance of those on the beach - Marine, Army, Navy, Coast Guard and Australian Coast Watchers and their native scouts who combined and worked together to make it a success. An "all for one and one for all" dedication probably not equaled in any other WWII operation.

Working for the success of our operation, strangely enough, were the Japanese who apparently had the same command, communication and logistic problems that the Americans had, i.e. the Army (and the Japanese public) did not know the extent of the Japanese Navy losses at Midway or that the Navy was building an airfield at Guadalcanal. Consis-

tently during the entire operation misinformation and communication was provided and seriously crippled the effectiveness of all combat decision, i. e. two or three times Henderson Field was reported as "retaken."

With that background back to the highly successful landing virtually unopposed on August 7 and the occupation of the airfield including the capture of some Japanese equipment and supplies (fortunately including some of their food). The troops are ashore and supplies are coming in or piling up on the beach.

Imagine Adm. Turner's "surprise" at dinner on "D" day, in that he had anticipated several days of air cover while his ships were unloading (remember he asked for four days air cover) when his communication center intercepts a message on August 8 — Adm. Fletcher to Adm. Ghormley —that Adm. Fletcher began to pull out his air cover forces 12 hours before he received any authorization from Adm. Ghormley to do so. Adm. Turner called it "desertion" of the vital part of the assault force.

Thus began the approximately 120 day struggle of the "men on the beach" against the enemy, the elements (very unfriendly), and shortages of food, supplies, ammunition, gasoline and reinforcements. With our position being bombed every day and shelled every night, by both land artillery and ship bombardment up to battleship size. On August 31 - Adm. McCain to CincPac - "If requested reinforcements are not made available Guadalcanal cannot be supplied, hence cannot be held." Only three top commanders, Gen. Vandegrift (ground), Gen. Geiger (air) and Adm. Nimitz, had confidence that the air field could be held and the island taken, the enemy defeated. Gen. MacArthur and the JCS in Washington thought it "a lost cause".

On August 20, the first two squadrons, one fighter (F4F's) and one dive bomber (SBD's), Capt. Smith VMF-223 and Maj. Mangrove VMSB -232 of Mag 14 landed to the wild cheers of all the troops who had been experiencing daily (weather permitting) air attacks from the Japanese. On August 22 five P-39 aircraft of the Army 67th Fighter squadron and one dive bomber (SBD's) equipped squadron arrived to become the home based "Cactus Air Force". All visiting pilots, regardless of service, with or without their own aircraft, were inducted and put on the flight schedule. This included B-17s from MacArthur's area, SCAT transport planes as well as complete carrier air groups. All of the personnel and equipment of MAG-14 never did reach Henderson Field.

For the next three months, as the Washington, D. C. brass and media continued to say, "the issue was in doubt."

September was highlighted by both air and sea battles. Reinforcements arrived in the form of Mag-14 and the 7th Marines. The U. S. Navy controlled the sea area during the days and the Japs controlled at night. Bombing and shelling at night was the normal activity. The most famous ground battle during this period was the Battle for Edsons Ridge named after the Edson's Raiders. All available air provided air-ground support for this operation which took place within sight of Henderson Field.

October brought on two large-scale Navy actions with the Japs trying desperately to reinforce their troops and by bombing and shelling to destroy our forces at Henderson Field. On October 12-15, these attacks succeeded in destroying many of our aircraft, our fuel supplies and our communication capabilities. These were dark days. Fortunately we were reinforced with the 163 Army Division. The next all out Jap effort (land, sea and air) was October 25-26, when the ground attack almost penetrated Henderson Field and pilots armed with hand guns came to a full ground alert on the edge of the runway. The sea battle for Santa Cruz Island resulted in the *Hornet* being sunk and the *Enterprise* being badly damaged. Their air squad-

rons were a welcome badly needed addition to the Cactus Air Force.

November is identified as the Month of Decision. On the 4th, the 8th Marines plus two batteries of 155mm guns came aboard so we finally had the capability to conquer "Pistol Pete," the Jap artillery piece that disturbed our sleep almost every night. Then on the 11th and 12th, Mag 11 arrived to replace Mag 23 who were in bad shape. Also the 182 Infantry Division arrived. November 15th turned out to be the last air/sea major battle. For five days there was almost unrelieved air/sea/land combat that fundamentally settled the Battle for Guadalcanal.

On December 9, the final U.S. land offensive was launched and completed the securing of the island.

October and November, 1942, was probably the most critical time for Cactus and its supporters. Japan mounted a strong attack on October 12, using ground troops, air and Navy to route the defenders from Henderson Field. They threw everything - battleships - betty (bombers) fighters - and thousands of troops in the attack. General Geiger could count six SBD bombers and five F4F fighters in operating condition, ready and able to meet the threat. Adm. Ghormley, excused as exhausted, relinquished command of the area to Adm. Bull Halsey, a much needed replacement. The Secretary of the Navy, Knox, described the situation as seen from Washington, D.C. "Everybody hopes that we can hold on." On November 12 to November 15, the Japanese made another major effort to dislodge the defenders; once again they were repulsed with large losses to both sides. It is believed that this battle signified the eventual victory of the Cactus defenders. Adm. Tanaka recorded "the last large scale effort to reinforce Guadalcanal had ended." During this period the Cactus Air Force - be in two aircraft or 20, depending on what was available and flyable, rose to engage any and all enemy aircraft (usual flights of 24 bombers with a similar number of fighters) and to bomb and strafe enemy ships from battleships to landing craft - never mind the relative strength. On one day, 25 October, 22 enemy air-craft were shot down by our fighters with the loss of only three F4F Wildcats.

One would be negligent if they did not relate the statements attributed to the two Japanese leaders on or about December 1, 1942.

Quote: Adm. Tanaka, "There is no question that Japan's doom was sealed with the closing of the struggle for Guadalcanal."

Quote: M. Gen. Kawaguchi, Commander of Japan's counter offense, "Guadalcanal is no longer merely a name of an island in Japan's military history. It is the name of the grave yard of the Japanese Army."

No account of the Battle for Guadalcanal could be written without reporting on the major contribution made by Captain Martin Clemens, of the British/Australian Navy, and his crews of coast watchers and native scouts. They were the eyes and ears for the Cactus Air Force. Without their input there is little doubt on my mind that the Cactus Air Force would have succeeded. It is difficult to appreciate and put into proper perspective the contribution these few brave and creative men made to this operation. All our pilots will always be grateful that they were there, to warn us, to help us and rescue those of us who were shot down.

Also the so-called normal non-combat personnel deserve special mention. The Sea-Bees, the Coast Guard, the ground crews all pitched in and no effort, including being under fire, stopped them.

We all can be proud for having been a part of this force, many of whom gave their all to accomplish an impossible task under awful conditions and who succeeded in accomplishing their goal. Those in fact who "gave their all" and did not return from

October 16, 1942. American Marines following the Battle of Tenaru on Guadalcanal found this wounded Japanese soldier on the battlefield and immediately rendered first aid. Dead Japanese littered the battlefield after the fighting. (USMC Photo, No. W-SOL-21-13335)

this action should not only be recognized and remembered by all Americans as brave men who made the supreme sacrifice with their lives, but also accomplished their task which led to the defeat of the Japanese.

WHEN THE BOMBING AND SHELLING STOPPED

by C. A. Buser

There was always that delicious time just after the bombing and shelling stopped. That brief moment had all the elements of wonder and beauty collected in a lifetime, seemingly tightly compressed then suddenly released like the instant blossoming of a flower or the sudden burst of a sunrise. It did not last long — but it was marvelous.

Now, as each issue of the GVC *Echoes* arrives, I read the names in "TAPS,"glancing time and again at the accompanying picture of our "For A Pal" statue, and think that, for those fellows, the bombing and shelling have at last completely stopped.

I remember when Ted Blahnik first wrote to me of the statue. He said there would not be a dry eye in the crowd at the time of the unveiling. For once my old friend was wrong. I, who always seem to have a tear duct at the ready, did not feel like weeping. For me, the noise stopped for just a little while.

As you all remember, Guadalcanal was a terribly noisy place, both day and night and whether you were in the air, on land or on the nearby seas. There were the planes and the jeeps and trucks and landing craft and mortars and rifle fire and the Brownings and grenades and artillery bursts and mess gear and birds and ack-ack and torpedoes, bombs, depth charges

and strafing runs. There seemed no end to it. The October shelling in particular just about pushed us all over the brink.

My, how we prayed and promised and pledged. And how we thought of that special handful of really special people back home and of the that other special handful of guys close enough to hear our every thoughts. It all boiled down to just that. And we felt so helpless and tired, yet strangely exhilarated and more than a little scared. Would it ever end?

For me, and probably for many, war is not a moving picture. Rather, it is a sequence of very vivid still shots, images burned into the brain, never to be forgotten. "For A Pal" personifies many of those images. It contains elements of so many enduring parts — part corpsman, part chaplain, part SeaBee, part soldier, part sailor, part airman, part coastwatcher, part Marine and part native constabulary man. One gets the feeling that that same knife will next be scratching a name under a Star of David. "For A Pal" says so much: "Soul and sacrifice, patriotism and peace, faith and friendship."

We are indebted to the inspiration that guided the hand of the sculptor, Kirk H. Newman, and to O. L. "Bud" Turner, himself a SeaBee, who financed it all. We feel that Mr. Newman and "Bud" too would understand when we acknowledge a yet deeper debt to those many, many fallen comrades, our band of brothers, for whom the bombing and shelling have stopped and for whom that magic "after moment" will continue through eternity.

THE CANAL

By Robert C. Muehrcke, M. D.
Author of Orchids in the Mud

The men who fought on the beaches, in the jungles, the rain forest, and the palm groves, never

called Guadalcanal anything but the Canal. William Manchester never heard Guadal- used. To the Japanese who fought there, it was *Gadarukanaru*, or the "Island of Death."

James A. Michener, author and a former Naval officer, to describe the Canal used harsh derogatory words such as "God Forsaken." To other servicemen, the Canal had an exciting beauty as a tropical island.

Jim Jones, author of *The Thin Red Line* and *From Here to Eternity*, from the 25th Infantry Division, wrote some strong words about what the Canal meant to our generation.

Finally, William Manchester OPTS for the Canal. In his words, "It is simple, it is sanctified by the men who fought there, and it would be instantly recognized by the survivors."

THE JUNGLE FIGHTERS
The Story of the Americal Division

Submitted by Joseph G. Micek, 132d Inf. Regt., Americal Division. (Source: Saga Magazine, July 1957. Original article by Bruce Jacobs)

The Americal Infantry Division is a division of distinction. It is the only modern Army division with a name instead of a number, and the only Army division to receive the Navy Presidential Citation for gallantry in action. The jungle fighters who wore the blue and white Southern Cross shoulder patch fought the grinding, wearing battles of the Pacific— Guadalcanal's Henderson Field, the jungle trail to Numa-Numa, the tangle of ancient vines and cogon grass in Cebu.

The only Army division formed for combat at an advance base in wartime, the Americal was the first United States Army Division to take part in offensive action in any theatre of operations in World War II. Rarely, however, did its exploits make the papers back home, and then it was usually incorrectly identified as the "American" Division or the "Miracle" Division.

It would be difficult to imagine more dramatic circumstances than those under which the Division went into combat. Its advance elements reached bloody Guadalcanal just in time to help the Marines save Henderson Field. Like the Minute Men of old, they raced into battle to fight for what appeared to be a lost cause. Though inexperienced in the arts of war, they helped swing the balance of victory to our side at a time when the Marines, who had carved the beachhead and established the perimeter, were weak from battle losses and malaria.

The Americal soldiers were Minute Men in the real sense. For the most part, they were volunteers; National Guard soldiers from the states of Massachusetts, Illinois and North Dakota. How they came to be assembled under the Americal banner in the far reaches of the Pacific is a story that begins with the departure, from New York Port of Embarkation, of Army Task Force 6814—headed for parts unknown. The date was January 23, 1942. It was 47 days after Pearl Harbor; the day the Japanese invaded the Solomon Islands. Japanese aggression was at its high tide in the Far East. Wake and Guam, key islands in the Pacific, had fallen. The Japanese had won Malaya and Hong Kong and were bulling their way into Bataan. In the "hot corner" of the Southwest Pacific, they streamed down through New Guinea and the islands of Melanesia to menace Australia.

Task Force 6814, commanded by Brig. Gen. Alexander "Sandy" Patch, was a conglomeration of what the Army calls "miscellaneous units." There was the 51st Infantry Brigade, whose two principal elements were the 132d Infantry Regiment and the 182d Infantry Regiment. There were old-style field and coast-artillery regiments, assorted ordnance, quartermaster, medical, signal, aviation and light-tank units. They had been assembled on a moment's notice and had come from training camps in half a dozen different states.

The infantry regiments of the task force were units that had been cut adrift in the 1941 "streamlining" of the National Guard divisions. The Guard divisions had come into federal service as "square" divisions but were eventually "triangularized." In the process, each lost one regiment. The 182d Infantry, for example, had been "squared out" of the 26th (Yankee) Division, to the great disgust of the Bay Staters. Its antecedents dated clear back to 1636, and its regimental colors were decorated with streamers from the Revolutionary War, the War of 1812, two campaigns of the Civil War and the Meuse-Argonne in World War I. Similarly, the 132d Infantry had lost its place in the Illinois 33d Division. The old "Second Illinois," as the 132d was known prior to World War I, traced its ancestry to 1861 and six campaigns of the Civil War from Tennessee to Atlanta. It carried World War I streamers for Picardy, the Somme Offensive, Lorraine and the Meuse-Argonne.

The convoy steamed south from New York, cleared through the Panama Canal and headed into the vast blue waters of the Pacific. It raced southwest to Melbourne, Australia, then north and east, until the soft, shimmering outline of New Caledonia appeared off the port bow one day. The handful of Aussies and French Foreign Legion troops stationed there breathed a sigh of relief as the Task Force moved ashore with its impressive array of trucks, jeeps and weapons. The GIs were stunned to find the city of Noumea a "little Paris" out in the middle of the Pacific. Few, except the stamp collectors, had ever heard of *Nouvelle Caledonie.*

Gen. Patch garrisoned the sprawling island and readied it against the day of attack. He dispatched outposts to the New Hebrides and put the engineers to work building new airfields to stretch its wings. Soon, the Task Force was reinforced by the arrival of more artillery and another infantry regiment—the 164th, a North Dakota National Guard outfit that formerly belonged to the 34th (Red Bull) Division. The old First North Dakota's regimental colors had seen the Far East four decades earlier, during the War with Spain and in the Philippine Insurrection.

Church bells tolled in thankfulness from Australia and New Zealand to New Caledonia when the Japanese were defeated in the Battle of the Coral Sea. Less than a month later, US naval and air forces again triumphed in the Battle of Midway. Suddenly Task Force 6814 was in the backwash of the war. New Caledonia was no longer under pressure, and the task force soldiers feared they would become garrison troopers, doomed to spend the war far from the thunder of the guns.

Their destiny was dictated in a secret letter from the War Department to Sandy Patch, who had acquired the second star of a major general. Out of the forces then under his command, he was to form a brand-new infantry division. And, in view of the unusual circumstances—the activating of a division outside the United States—it was to be given a name instead of a number. Washington proposed "Necal" Division, since "Necal" was an early code name for New Caledonia. It was decided, however, that the men themselves should have the final say in the selection of a name. General Patch cast his vote for "Bush" Division, but in the final balloting, he was outranked by a private first class, David Fonseca of Roxbury, Massachusetts. PFC Fonseca came up with the name that was to become so meaningful in the campaigns that lay ahead—*the Americal.* After

A dead Japanese lies to the right of a foxhole. (Courtesy of Al Schuster)

all, reasoned Fonseca, the division was to be formed from American troops stationed on New Caledonia. Fonseca's nomination for the new division's name was forwarded to Washington, and on May 27, 1942, the American Division became a going concern. Most of the units of Task Force 6814 were absorbed into the new organization; a few were transferred to the island command and remained behind when the Americal moved out of New Cal and plunged into jungle war.

On Guadalcanal where the Marines had landed in August, there was real trouble. As commanding general of the Army forces in the South Pacific, Maj. Gen. Millard F. Harmon urged upon Vice Admiral Robert L. Ghormley, the South Pacific commander, the immediate dispatch of a regimental combat team to Guadalcanal. Ghormley concurred, and within a few hours, the Americal's 164th Infantry RCT, under the command of Col. Bryant E. Moore, was placed on the alert. It moved down to the Nickel Docks on October 8 and began loading into the Zeilin and the McCauley for the boat ride to the north. It was an uneventful trip, until the convoy dropped anchor near Lunga Point. Then the Japanese rolled out the welcome mat. As their bombers roared overhead, the 164th Infantry went about the business of unloading and setting up shop in the beleaguered perimeter. Colonel Moore reported to the commanding general of the 1st Marine Division, Maj. Gen. Archie A. Vandegrift, and Vandegrift ordered Moore's regiment of American soldiers into Sector Two, the longest infantry sector in the 22,000-yard perimeter. The new arrivals were inexperienced, but at least they were fresh and eager.

Back on New Cal, meanwhile, Admiral William F. Halsey was named South Pacific commander. The 59-year-old "Bull" Halsey put it straight to Vandegrift: "Can you hold Guadalcanal, or do you expect to have to pull out?" he radioed.

"I can hold it," Vandegrift assured him, "if I get more active support than I've been getting."

"You'll get it," Halsey replied. Once more, orders began streaming into the American Division Headquarters. Now the Bay State 182d Infantry was alerted to move out.

On Guadalcanal, the 164th was going through its baptism of fire. It had already withstood fierce naval bombardment and had been under air attack. But now Bryan Moore's soldiers got their taste of the infantryman's war. On the night of October 24-25, they took the full brunt of a Japanese ground assault. It came on a black, moonless night following a day of heavy rainfall. It was clearly the enemy's intent to recapture the vital strips of Henderson Field. The heaviest blow fell upon the sector defended by the 1st Battalion of the 7th Marines, and a "fire call" went out for the 3d Battalion of the 164th Infantry, which was then in regimental reserve about a mile from the front. As the Marines fought valiantly to hold back the enemy tide, Lt. Col. Robert K. Hall marched his American Battalion through the dense jungle, and slipped into position alongside the Marines. With the added firepower of the Army, a series of Japanese attacks was thrown back.

At the height of the battle, Cpl. Bill Clark, a Nebraskan, and two privates set out to recover a pair of light machine guns that had been damaged when their crews were wiped out. The men with him were killed, but Clark kept advancing under intense fire. By the time he reached the guns, he was less than 15 feet from the muzzles of the Jap guns. But Clark coolly tied up the two damaged guns with his belt and hauled them back to his own lines. He stripped them down, and by salvaging the usable parts from each, he managed to assemble one machine gun in good working order—all in the dark. Clark's gun spit into action just in time to help hurl back a Jap foray.

At dawn on October 25, the Japs melted away into the jungle, giving the Army and the Marines a chance to realign their battered forces. The lineup, as night fell, found the 1st battalion, 7th Marine Regiment, on the right; the 3d Battalion, 164th Infantry, in the center; and the 2d Battalion, 164th Infantry, on the left. Reinforced by fresh troops delivered to Guadalcanal by the "Tokyo Express," the Japanese launched another series of attacks, and continued to hurl themselves at the approaches of Henderson Field on the morning of October 26. After some of the most savage fighting of the campaign, the Japs broke and retreated toward Koli Point and Kokumbona. It was a clear-cut triumph for the Americans and Marine General Vandegrift singled out the 164th for special praise.

Elements of the 182d Infantry now began to arrive in force. Brig. Gen. Edmund B. Sebree, the Americal's assistant division commander, was given command of a sector, as the 164th took part in an offensive across the Mataniakau River in November. When an attack of dengue fever kayoed Brig. Gen. William H. Rupertus, assistant division commander of the Marines, General Sebree took full charge of the march to Koli Point. It was the first time in the Guadalcanal Campaign that a senior officer of the Americal bossed a combined force of Army men and Marines. Soon the assault battalions of Col. Daniel W. Hogan's 182d Infantry joined the push.

The Marines provided covering fire as Lt. Col. Bernard B. Twombley took his 2d Battalion across a footbridge over the Matanikau, toward Hill 66. The battalion pushed forward, but advance elements were pinned down near the Water Hold. Led by Lt. Col. Francis F. MacGowan, the 1st Battalion crossed the Matanikau on the following morning and fought a series of brisk skirmishes as it moved toward the objective at Point Cruz. The 182d attack was momentarily slowed by the terrible heat, but it resumed when Gen. Sebree sent the 164th forward to help out. The 182d stormed the Point Cruz defenses, but the 164th ran into a hornet's nest. Mortar fire in the 3d Battalion area, for example, killed the battalion surgeon, four lieutenants and a first sergeant.

As plans were prepared for the full relief of the 1st Marine Division by the Americal, a small group of American soldiers embarked upon an unusual adventure, setting out in a schooner from Lunga Point under the command of 1st Lt. Frederick T. Flo of the 164th Infantry. In the group were 13 soldiers from the North Dakota regiment, two Marine radiomen, a pair of Marine Navajo "talkers" (the Japanese were never able to master the Navajo language, and it provided a "code" that was never broken) and a member of the native police. The schooner swept out to sea. and went west around Cape Esperance. The first stop was at the Tangarare settlement in Beaufort Bay, where Lt. Flo chatted with the Rev. Henry De Klerk of the Society of Mary. Father De Klerk, who had remained at his mission on the southern coast of Guadalcanal when the Japanese invaded the Solomons, assured the 164th Infantry soldiers that there were no enemy soldiers between Beaufort Bay and Tiaro Bay. The next stop was Tiaro Bay. Here the patrol went ashore and began a thorough reconnaissance of the area. Finding no trace of the Japanese, Flo and his men moved on to Marovo, then Kamimbo Bay and Aruligo Point, in the eight days that followed. From the report turned in by Flo when the patrol returned to Lunga Point in the waning days of November, Division intelligence officers correctly reckoned that the main strength of the enemy lay east of Visale on Guadalcanal's northern coast.

In December, most of the remaining elements of the Americal arrived at Guadalcanal. The 132d RCT, under the command of Lt. Col. LeRoy E. Nelson, was almost immediately hurled against Japanese positions on strongly defended Mount Austen. Another welcome arrival was the Americal's Mobile Combat Reconnaissance Squadron, under the command of the dour Scot, Lt. Col. Alexander M. George. This colorful unit (later to be redesignated as the 21st Cavalry Reconnaissance Troop) had been formed by Col. George on New Cal as a mobile striking force, and it now numbered more than 500 troopers, equipped with jeeps and armed to the teeth. For all its proud mobility, the squadron was destined to fight on foot in the mud of Guadalcanal.

With the Americal at full strength, Gen. Patch became the commander of all forces on Guadalcanal. The first order of business, he decided, was the capture of Mount Austen. The Illinois regiment marched into the lines and swung into action. Lt. Col. William C. Wright's 3d Bn. battered away at the approaches of the heights of Mount Austen, but were stopped in their tracks. When Wright moved out in front, trying to search out a trail that wasn't covered by Jap guns, he was killed by machine gun fire.

During the battle, the Illinois soldiers of the 132d came up against the Gifu, the Japs' stoutest defensive. It consisted of a horseshoe-shaped line of about 45 interconnecting pillboxes between Hills 31 and 27. The pillboxes were made of heavy logs, and their roofs were three feet thick. Each pillbox contained one or two machine guns plus two or three riflemen, and they were flanked by riflemen and machine gunners dug into the bases of mahogany and banyan trees. The GIs of the Americal were staggered by this seemingly impenetrable jungle fortress, where mortar fire made no impression, and where even howitzer fire was ineffective unless there was a direct hit. The 2d Bn. of the 132d made the principal assault against the Gifu. Under the command of Lt. Col. George F. Gerry, it moved southwest from Hill 11 toward the slopes of Hill 27, shortly after daybreak on New Year's Day.

"This is a helluva way to spend New Year's Day," a corporal from Joliet, IL, growled.

"At least," on of his buddies declared, "we won't have a hangover tomorrow."

By four p.m., the battalion had reached the top of Hill 27, without a single casualty. During the day, however, the regimental commander, who was suffering from malaria and fatigue, was relieved, and Col. Alexander M. George left his beloved Mobile Combat Recon. Squadron to take over the old "Ever Ready" Regiment. Col. George at once proved a tonic for the tired soldiers of the 132d. Arriving at the regimental front in mid-morning, clad only in shorts and a fatigue cap and armed with a brace of .45 caliber pistols and an M1 rifle, he casually commenced an inspection tour.

"Lookit that silly damfool," a GI jeered, "he's asking to get his ass shot off."

Some sergeant, who did not know the new regimental commander, bellowed out, "Hey, fella! You better get to hell away from here!"

George, however, was out to prove to his men that Japanese small-arms fire was generally ineffective against moving targets. He calmly completed his Cook's tour of the front, while the Japs peppered away at him without coming close.

On the following morning, the regiment again attacked. The 1st Battalion advanced to the west and the 3d Battalion struck at the northern approaches. But once again, it was Ferry's 2d Battalion that enjoyed the greatest success, overrunning its objective a little after nine in the morning. As the assault troops reached the summit, they spotted a three-inch mountain howitzer out in the open, its crew sprawled carelessly in the shade. The Japs raced toward their gun, but they were swiftly cut down by the fast-shooting Americal soldiers.

The Guadalcanal Campaign drew to a close as elements of the Americal, along with elements of the 2d Marine Division pushed toward Koli Point. During the advance, when the American soldiers of the 182d Infantry were under brutal mortar fire, 1st Sgt. James J. Gaffney of Lowell, MA, raced 200 yards through the impact area to rescue one of his officers. He brought the officer out on his back, lugged him to an aid station and then sprinted back through the exploding shells to repair broken communications lines.

The important enemy stronghold at Kokumbona fell in late January. As the main U.S. force pushed toward Cape Esperance along the northern coast of the island, Gen. Sebree (Sebree had become Division Commander January 3, 1942, when Gen. Patch was named XIV Corps Commander) dispatched a reinforced battalion to the south coast, to land in the enemy's rear. A battalion of the 132d, under the command of Lt. Col. George F. Ferry, was dispatched to make the end run.

Col. George of the 132d was in command as Ferry's reinforced battalion moved ashore February 1, covered by U.S. Fighter planes. Although Jap bombers roared overhead, none made any passes at the beachhead as Col. George led his command along the southern coastal trails toward Titi. On February 7, George was wounded and Ferry took command. Maj. H. Wirt Butler, the exec, took command of the battalion as the landing force continued its march to Marovo . . . Kamimbo Bay . . . around Cape Esperance . . . to Tenaro . . . and the long awaited linkup with the troops who had marched along the northern route. With the juncture of these two forces, the organized resistance of the Japanese on Guadalcanal came to an end. America's first offensive campaign in the Pacific was in the bag, and "Bull" Halsey jubilantly wrote to the first commander of the Americal Division; "When I sent a Patch to act as tailor for Guadalcanal, I did not expect him to remove the enemy's pants and sew it on so quickly . . . Thanks and congratulations."

Out of the mud and misery of Guadalcanal— the Americal's first baptism of fire—came the Navy's Presidential Unit Citation, and a few weeks after the conclusion of the campaign, the tired malaria-ridden Americal troopers were relieved. Everyone half-expected, half-anticipated a return to New Caledonia, but instead the convoy headed southeast to the fabled island of Fiji. The Division set up camp upon Viti Levu, the principal island of Fiji. It regained its health, trained its replacements and enjoyed the niceties of civilization in the crisp, friendly "liberty city" of Suva. The Fiji interlude came to an end in mid-December, 1942. The rear echelon of the Division was dispatched to Guadalcanal, until such time as it could join the bulk of the Americal in a new forward area.

THE SCOUTS WE LEFT BEHIND

By Gary Bousman

In August 1942, after winning the battles of the Coral Sea and Midway, the U.S. began turning back the Japanese tide on land with the assault on Guadalcanal and later on New Georgia. The writer of this article visited two natives who gained fame for their exploits against the occupiers. (Source: Veterans of Foreign Wars Magazine, August 1988 Edition)

They beat him with rifle butts, stabbed him in the chest and throat and left him to die. But they underestimated Jacob Vouza's strength and determination to help the U.S. Marines, whom he had only recently met and learned to admire.

Had the Japanese known that this large, brown-skinned, former constable would crawl three miles through the jungle to the American lines, they might not have been in such haste to leave him. They had no idea, in spite of his wounds, he would gnaw through the ropes they had used to tie him to a tree.

Vouza was leading a patrol of natives on Guadalcanal on the night of Aug. 20, 1942 when he remembered he was carrying a small U.S. Flag given to him by a Marine. Having this on his person was not smart, he reasoned. Leaving the patrol, he turned off aloe to hide the Flag in a nearby village.

He was too late. He walked right into the path of an enemy platoon. The Flag was all the evidence the platoon leader needed. Vouza could not deny that he had been with the Americans, but the interrogation that followed was no help to the Japanese. The man who was later knighted by Queen Elizabeth II for his bravery shook his head every time a question about American troops strength was put to him.

Jacob Vouza had lost a lot of blood by the time he dragged himself into the Marine lines west of the Ilu River. In spite of the gaping wound in his throat, his report on Japanese numbers and weapons was of great help to the 2d Battalion, 1st Marines. On the basis of his reconnaissance, a Marine detachment crossed the river, outflanked the enemy and added to the difficulties Col. Kiyono Ichiki was having in his attempt to capture Henderson Field from the Marines.

Completing his report and thinking he was dying, Vouza dictated a final message to his wife and children. For a time it was touch and go, but with the help of doctors and new blood, the man who had once tracked pig rustlers and chicken thieves in the jungles of Guadalcanal lived to lead many more patrols as the Japanese were driven westward toward Cape Esperance.

For this heroic action, Gen. Alexander A. Vandegrift awarded Vouza the American Silver Star and made him a sergeant major in the Marine Corps. The British government honored him with the George Medal, and he was made a member of the Order of the British Empire in 1957.

Vouza was a colorful character. When he walked through the Marine lines and volunteered his services, an Australian coastwatcher, Martin Clemens, was hesitant to add this former constable to his team of native scouts. Clemmens knew the islands, and he knew Vouza had been reprimanded several times for taking the law into his own hands. Would the other scouts work with this headstrong man? But Vouza rose to the occasion. He knew the country, and he feared neither the jungle nor the enemy.

In the spring of 1983, I revisited Guadalcanal. Though my involvement on this island was with the Army on the hills west of the Matanikau River, I was determined to visit, photograph and salute the man who, during the previous 40 or so years, had been a symbol of pride to the people of the Solomon Islands.

Sir Jacob, now an old man, lives in a small village about 20 miles east of Honiara, the capital of the Solomon Islands, an independent nation since 1978. Finding his home was a challenge to me and my driver. The driver had trouble locating the village, and I had trouble holding on to the seat as he dodged the potholes. The last four miles were over a one-lane road surrounded by tall blades of Kunai grass so close to the car I had to keep my elbows away from the window. I had no idea what we would have done if we had encountered a car coming from the opposite direction. I concluded that any veteran who visits Jacob Vouza also should be given a medal.

But the Journey was worth it. Attired in a colorful lava-lava, Vouza stood tall as he lifted his sunglasses upward until they rested on his grey hair. A faint smile revealed the dentures presented to him by TV celebrity Jack Parr, when he revisited Guadalcanal in 1962. His natural teeth were damaged when he gnawed the ropes with which to

free himself from the tree he had been tied to.

A U.S. Flag flies in front of his home. At the base of the flagpole, a bronze tablet reads:

In Dedication to Sergeant Major Jacob Vouza and his Solomon Island Scouts For supreme intrepidity and valor in the face of the enemy during the struggle for Guadalcanal, 1942-1943 Presented by U.S. Marine Raider Association

Finding William Bennett was not so difficult. He lives near the village of Kokambona, the site of the Japanese command until late January, 1943. My first visit to this village was a few weeks after the enemy began retreating toward Cape Esperance. The houses at that time were built with coconut fronds and bamboo poles. Today, most of the houses are frame cottages.

William Billy Bennett, as he was affectionately called by fellow scouts, served behind enemy lines on New Georgia Island. The son of a New Zealand father and a Melanesian mother, Bennett was second in command of a small army of natives under the watchful eye of coastwatcher D. C. Kennedy. In canoes they prowled the bays and inlets, and on the hilltops they scanned the seas. Messages concerning Japanese movements were sent by runners or signal fires along the coast.

Coastwatchers, who radioed valuable information concerning Japanese fleet and air movements, were often on the run as they dodged enemy patrols. It was different with Kennedy and the natives he recruited. Known as "The Kennedy Boys," they started as a small army with only six rifles. As raids were made on enemy patrols, rifles, bayonets, grenades and machine guns were added to the arsenal of this rugged force. Japanese barges or patrols that ventured too close to their base at Segi, on the southern tip of the island, were attacked and destroyed. Many Japanese scouting parties simply disappeared, with no trace of their fate.

For example, in November 1942, two Japanese barges stopped for the night in a lagoon five miles north of Segi—too close for the comfort of Kennedy or Bennett. When darkness came, the little army of 23 men opened fire using captured rifles and machine guns. They were greeted with a brief burst of fire from a machine gun on one of the barges.

Bennett boarded one of the barges and was jumped by a Japanese sailor, who proved no match for William Billy. With this assailant out of the way, Bennett threw a grenade down the engine hatch. That ended all resistance. The next step was to salvage all weapons and equipment, bury the enemy, and sink the barges in deep waters. Another patrol had disappeared, leaving the enemy command at Munda puzzled and frustrated.

Very few Japanese soldiers or sailors survived an attack by these determined Melanesians, but a few did. Now and then a downed enemy pilot was picked up, confined to the Kennedy Stockade, and eventually sent to Guadalcanal on a submarine or PBY.

As the little army won more skirmishes, its arsenal of weapons increased and so did the number of recruits. All were subject to strict discipline, and disobedience often led to an "across the drum" lashing.

Ships were added to the force. A 57-foot diesel barge was captured while the Japanese patrol was ashore foraging for food. Two more were added after U.S. planes shot holes in the batteries. While the crews were on foot seeking help from the base camp, Kennedy's Boys towed the barges to Segi where repairs were made.

155mm Howitzer Gun emplacement near Henderson Airfield on Guadalcanal, December 1942. (Courtesy of Malsch)

The pride of this small "navy" was the 10-ton schooner, *Dundavata*, a two-master that had previously belonged to the Seventh-day Adventist mission. Its wheezing engine needed a lot of coaxing, and William Billy Bennett was the man to do it. He was an experienced sailor and a competent mechanic. In April, 1943, armed with machine guns and several canoes in tow, the *Dundavata* set out for Marova Lagoon. Scouts had reported a whaleboat loaded with Japanese. They boat was probing every inlet, apparently looking for the Kennedy camp.

When it was discovered that the crew had gone ashore on one of the islands, the *Dundavata* dropped anchor behind another island. Lookouts were posted in palm trees, and the crew waited for the Japanese to make the next move.

It was dark when word came that the whaleboat was heading their way. With Bennett at the wheel, and Kennedy manning a machine gun— one taken from a downed plane—the *Dundavata* headed straight for the enemy boat. Guns were soon firing from both vessels, and in the scrap, Kennedy was nipped in the thigh. When the enemy firing stopped, Bennett was ordered to ram. That ended the encounter, and again Kennedy's base was saved from detection. More weapons were collected, and another patrol vanished from the Japanese roster with no clue as to what happened.

(Author's note: While serving a short tour on Tulagi Island in the spring of 1943, I saw a schooner fitting the description of the *Dundavata* come into the harbor. The decks were covered with palm fronds—obviously camouflaging weapons. I did not have the presence of mind to make inquires about the ship, but now I wonder if it could have been the *Dundavata*—possibly bringing Kennedy to the Navy hospital to be treated for his wounds?)

Kennedy did well to choose William Bennett as his second-in-command. In addition to his skills as a mechanic and sailor, he had been a cook, medical assistant and school teacher. Often before a skirmish, he would give the scouts a pep talk like a coach in the locker room before a game.

William Bennett is a modest man. It was not until after my visit that I learned from other residents, and from my driver, of his heroism during the war. He showed me the copra he was drying in front of his home, but never mentioned the fact that he was awarded military medals, or that after the war, he was the government information officer in charge of its news and radio station.

Not all Japanese mistakes in the Solomon Islands were tactical. One of the greatest errors was their failure to win the friendship of the Melanesian people. They landed on the islands with a contemptuous attitude toward these friendly people. They raided their gardens, drove many from their villages, pressed them into service without pay and at times beat or shot them. One wonders what historians would have written about the Solomon Islands campaign if the Japanese had employed native guides, scouts and burden bearers.

Often I saw long lines of islanders carrying weapons, food and water to positions far up in the hills. Now and then I would see an American soldier give a cigarette to a native or stop and talk. No wonder men like Jacob Vouza and William Bennett gave so much to the Allied cause.

A native Guadalcanalese family searches for a new home. Their old residence was destroyed during combat action on the island of Guadalcanal.

Hot showers that were built by Battery B on the road to the front. Water was pumped into barrels from a well. Fire built under the barrels heated the water. Gravity then delivered the hot water to the showers.

GUADALCANAL CAMPAIGN VETERANS REUNION

Top left: *Guadalcanal Campaign Veterans National Reunion at Omaha, Nebraska. August 24, 1991. (L to R): Joseph Zimmerman, Terry Zimmerman, Mary Ann Quinlan and Gene Keller. Luau Banquet.*

Top right: *Regional Reunion, Chicago, IL, 1983. (Clockwise) Rita and Gene Keller, Jack and Edna Brookshire, Gene and Ida Ballentine, Vern and Ann Smith.*

Middle left: *The GCV Reunion at the Sheraton Inn, Anderson, IN. July 1986. Maurice "Shady" Eggers of Indianapolis, IN and George W. Wyatt of Tulsa, OK. Both served with the 1st Pioneer Bn., 1st US Marine Div. on Guadalcanal. Eggers died Sept. 15, 1987. Mr. Wyatt is the author of <u>Super Breed</u>, a story of the contributions of the USMC's 1st Pioneer Bn. and 1st Marine Division during World War Two.*

Middle right: *The Pensacola, FL, Regional Reunion, November 1986. (Clockwise, seated): Jean Blahnik, Jack Brookshire, Julian Bay, Lottie Hartnig, Rita Keller and Ida Ballentine. (Clockwise, standing): Ted Blahnik, Gene Keller and Sid Hartnig.*

Lower right: *1987 Guadalcanal Campaign Veterans Reunion at Norfolk, VA. Army Nurses.*

GUADALCANAL CAMPAIGN VETERANS REUNION

Top left: *Memorial services at Ft. Bragg, NC for the National Reunion, October 1990. President Keller is speaking from the podium.*

Middle left: *At Denison Stadium, Winter Haven, FL, August 1987. US Army, Navy, Air Force and Coast Guard, plus delegations from the United Kingdom, New Zealand, Australia and veterans groups assemble for the 40th Anniversary Memorial Tribute to the fallen Guadalcanal Veterans. Following the memorial service, there was a 21 gun salute.*

Middle right: *Ida Ballentine and past President Graydon Cadwell tripping the light fantastic at the dinner dance. August 12, 1988 at the dedication of the GCV memorial museum.*

Lower left: *8th National Reunion, October 1989. The Alamo.*

Lower right: *USAF Academy at Colorado Springs, CO, August 1985. The Academy's Protestant Chapel: the site of the GCV 6th National Reunion Memorial Services.*

GUADALCANAL CAMPAIGN VETERANS REUNION

Top right: *(L to R): Marilyn Paige, Ed Pollard and Mrs. Pollard at the Ontario, Canada, Regional Reunion October 4, 1990.*

Top left: *(L to R): John Mueller, Chuck Briejak and President Gene Keller. Regional Reunion, Portland, Oregon, May 5, 1990.*

Middle left: *President Gene Keller speaking at the 1992 regional reunion, Portland, Oregon.*

Middle right: *Memorial service at "For A Pal"— August 7, 1989.*

Lower right: *(L to R): William Coysh, President Gene Keller, Jerry Mohn and Stan McDonald. 1992 Regional Northeast Reunion at Valley Forge, Pennsylvania. These men were members of C Co., 1st Pioneers, 1st Marine Division*

GUADALCANAL CAMPAIGN VETERANS REUNION

Top left: (L to R): Brookshire, Bird Dog, Keller, M. Crabtree, Carrol, Kermish, Mohn, Zimmerman, Lt. Frank Turner, (seated) Hartnig. At the Fayetteville, North Carolina National Reunion, September 1990. Members of C Co., 1st Pioneers—A mini reunion of their own.

Bottom: Guadalcanal Campaign Veterans 1992 Regional Reunion, Valley Forge, Pennsylvania.

GUADALCANAL CAMPAIGN VETERANS
1992 REGIONAL REUNION
VALLEY FORGE, PA.

ABS VISUALS, INC.

GUADALCANAL CAMPAIGN VETERANS REUNION

Top left: *William Carroll, Vice President, North East and Gene Keller, President, at the Saturday Night Luau, August 1991 Omaha, NE reunion.*

Top right: *At the Colorado Springs Reunion in 1985, four place settings symbolize MIAs from the Navy, Coast Guard, Army and the Marines.*

Middle left: *This monument stands near the Alamo in memory of those who gave their life for God and Country in 1836 at the Alamo. This is the GCV 8th National Reunion in October 1989 at San Antonio, Texas.*

Middle right: *The Guadalcanal Campaign Veterans state reunion in Memphis, Tennessee, May 1991. Everyone was there and had a great time.*

Lower right: *At the 1985 National Guadalcanal Campaign Veterans Reunion in Colorado Springs, Colorado. The entire group at the foot of stairs in front of the Air Force Academy Cadet Chapel.*

GUADALCANAL CAMPAIGN VETERANS REUNION

Top left: *During the First National Reunion of the Guadalcanal Campaign Veterans, H. C. Peterson, USN 26th Naval Construction Battalion (Seabees), is flanked by two USN Veterans of the Guadalcanal Campaign. Norfolk, Virginia, August 1975.*

Middle left: *August 1978, Greenwood, Indiana. Hoosier GCV Semi-annual reunion banquet. Good food and comradeship born of wartime experiences abound throughout the evening.*

Middle right: *Marine Colors at Atlanta, Georgia, May 1986. Regional reunion.*

Lower left: *Members of C Co., 1st Pioneer Bn. (L to R): Duane Moore, A. J. Thompson III, G. Riopelli, Jack Brookshire, G. Mohn, Russell Cummer, Gene Keller, Joe Zimmerman.*

Lower right: *Colorado Springs, Colorado, August 1985. Australian Maj. Martin Clemens, who served as a "Coastwatcher" during the Japanese Occupation of Guadalcanal. He was the principal speaker at the GCV Association 6th National Reunion Banquet. At the right of Maj. Clemens is Ms. Virginia Schafer, former US Ambassador to Papua, New Guinea and the Solomon Islands.*

GUADALCANAL MEMORIAL MUSEUM

A cherished dream for a few of us, a place of pride for all of us was dedicated on Aug. 7, 1988 with the dedication of the Guadalcanal Memorial Museum. Here in the United States is a monument and museum dedicated to the ultimate sacrifice at Guadalcanal of over 7,000 young American men. Men who participated in the first American land offensive of World War II. Men who literally "turned the tide" in the Pacific Theatre of War.

Museum curator, Gene Keller, agrees that we can all be justifiably proud of what our organization has done without asking the government to contribute one red cent to its construction. Built with funds from the men "who were there." Planned, organized and reverently put together by "men who were there." It is our precious gift to the people of our country and to those men we "left behind."

Within its confines, you will find diorama's of the Battle of the Tenaru, the Battle for Mount Austen and the Sea Battle for Guadalcanal (Third Savo) along with a narration of each. Pictures, models, artifacts and even dirt from Red Beach adorn the walls, cabinets and show cases. Too, our Wall of Honor displays each of the men who earned the Medal of Honor during our campaign along with their citations.

It is hoped that each of you will have the opportunity to visit our museum while bringing your sons, daughters or grandchildren to see what we have done.

Ted Blahnik

GUADALCANAL—SOLOMON ISLANDS WAR MEMORIAL

Original artwork by Donald Moss. (Courtesy of J. Micek)

The Guadalcanal, Solomon Islands War Memorial Foundation was founded in January 1987 as a joint venture with the American Battle Monuments Commission. The Commission raised more than $750,000 to construct three memorials on Guadalcanal. The Foundation purchased the sites and transferred legal title to the US Government. It is with this same spirit of cooperation that these organizations sponsor their memorials on the Island of Guadalcanal.

In conjunction with the 50th Anniversary of the invasion of Guadalcanal by American Forces, a formal solemn dedication of the memorials on the Island will be held August 1992. The Foundation will mediate the activities of the dedication in cooperation with the United States Government and other participating governments. The memorials on Guadalcanal that are scheduled for dedication are: the main memorial on Skyline Drive, the American-Allied (Vouza) Memorial in Honiara, the capital of Guadalcanal, and the Edson Memorial, constructed on the western edge of Henderson Airfield.

Joseph Micek

GUADALCANAL LEGACY
50TH ANNIVERSARY
VETERANS BIOGRAPHIES

Survey Party on Cape Esperance, Guadalcanal. They were to establish gun positions for the troops.

*Editor's Note: All members of the Guadalcanal Campaign Veterans organization were invited to write and submit biographies for inclusion in this publication. The following are from those who chose to participate. The biographies were typeset exactly as received, with a minimum of editing. As such, the Publisher is not responsible for errors or omissions.

HAROLD P. AARHUS, was born April 17, 1916 Mayville, ND.

Inducted into Federal Service Feb. 10, 1941 for one year training, from Fargo, ND. Also trained at Ft. Benning, GA.

His regiment the 164th Infantry left the U.S. March 1942 aboard the USS *President Coolidge*. Spent several months in New Caledonia before sailing to Guadalcanal. They were warmly greeted by Marines and Japs.

The 164th Infantry was the first Army unit on the offensive in WWII. Besides Guadalcanal, he participated in the Bougainville Campaign.

Awards: Combat Infantry Badge, Bronze Star, Presidential Unit Citation.

He remembers being lost in the jungle, recon patrol and arriving at the perimeter at midnight.

Discharged from Camp McCoy, WI with rank of 1st sergeant in August 19, 1945 and returned to the States.

He participated in the 7th War Bond Drive—*Here's Your Infantry*.

Aarhus has five children and nine grandchildren. Enjoys gardening, golfing and some traveling.

KARL R. ADAMS, was born May 18, 1921 in Alma, MI. Entered service on Feb. 5, 1942. Attached to the 2nd Marine Div. Trained at Camp Elliott, San Diego, CA.

Participated at Guadalcanal, Wellington, New Zealand, Solomon Island. Was stationed at California Naval Hospital, Marine Headquarters, Jacksonville, FL.

Awarded the South Pacific Combat Theater Ribbon. Discharged as a private first class on Dec. 8, 1944.

Remembers that while on patrol, a friend "Treo" sighted their first enemy contact and killed 50 caliber duty on Maui line of defense with good friend the "Swede". Remembers acquaintances: Gunnery Sergeant Homer, Hal Schumaker, Johnson from Illinois, Cusenberry from Texas.

Married Clara Henderson of Melbourne, FL in 1945. They have two children Patty and Karla, grandson Karl and granddaughter Stacey.

He is retired lieutenant colonel from Florida Highway Patrol and also retired from staff of Florida legislature.

RAYMOND J. ADAMS, was born Nov. 17, 1914 in Decatur, MI. Enlisted in U.S. Navy March 26, 1942. Boot camp at Great Lakes, IL. Assigned to USS *McCalla* (DD-488) May 23, 1942.

Participated in night engagement off Savo Island - Guadalcanal (Battle of Cape Esperance). Several Jap ships of the "Toyko Express" were destroyed. USS *Duncan* was the only U.S. ship lost. October 11 and 12, 1942 *McCalla* remained in area and rescued 197 men of the *Duncan* crew and took three Jap prisoners. November-December 1942 Task Force 62 and 67 operating about Guadalcanal, sunk Jap sub. Repelled two dive bombing and torpedo plane attacks, and bombarded beach positions - 40 landing boats destroyed. June 30, 1943 attacked by 24 torpedo planes and later eight dive bombers. *McCalla* destroyed two and possibly three. Rescued 97 men from USS transport *McCawley* that had been torpedoed. September 29, 1943 action against evacuation barges - Kula Gulf collided with USS *Patterson* lost about 50 foot of bow. While en-route to Mare Island for a new bow, rescued 868 survivors of the torpedoed troop transport USS *Cape San Juan*.

May 14, 1944 transferred to Com. Des. Pac. Pearl Harbor. August 3, 1945 transferred back to USS *McCalla*.

Awards: American Area Service Medal, Asiatic Pacific w/one Silver Star and one Bronze Star.

October 4, 1945 received discharge at Naval Reserve Armory, Chicago, IL yeoman 1st class.

JOHN P. AMBROSE, was born in Butte, MT on Aug. 10, 1921. Raised in San Francisco, CA. Enlisted in the Navy December 1941.

After one month in boot camp in San Diego was sent to Pearl Harbor and aboard USS *Seminole* at 65. Operated in and out of Pearl for five months.

Ordered to Suva, Fiji to operate with the fleet. October

1942 sent to Guadalcanal area to pick up a barge that was adrift after the sinking of USS *Meridith*. Towed the barge to Talagi. While off-loading drums of Av. gas and ammo at the canal, the *Seminole* was sunk Oct. 25, 1942.

After some months on the canal was sent to the USS *Whipstock* an Av. Gas tanker. Operated between Espiritu Santo and Guadalcanal.

Returned to the States December 1943, and assigned to USS *Salamua* (CVE-96). Took part in Philippines invasion and was in Tokyo Bay for the signing of the Japan surrender. Discharged October 1945 in San Francisco.

Married Josephine Kuhn in 1946. They have two sons, Michael and Steven and a daughter, Kathleen and five grandchildren.

Retired from Pacific Telephone Company in 1981 after 35 years service in San Francisco. Now reside in Napa, CA.

ALBERT C. ANDERSON, SR., was born in Marion, SC Aug. 22, 1924. Enlisted in U.S. Navy in August 1941, graduating boot training at Norfolk, VA October 7.

Was then assigned to the battleship USS *Washington* (BB-56), which was soon escorting convoys from the British naval base at Scapa Flow, Scotland to Murmansk, Russia.

After several months convoy duty the ship returned to the States and after overhaul at New York Navy Yard, got underway in August for the South Pacific via the Panama Canal with a stop at Tongatabu, arriving Noumea, New Caledonia in early October 1942.

In one of the many battles for Guadalcanal (Third Savo), the night of Nov. 14, 1942, the *Washington* sank the Japanese battleship *Kirishima*, without taking a single hit.

After this and other Pacific actions, the ship returned to the States for repairs in March 1944. After going on leave and to trade school, Albert and his fiance, Frances McBride, of Shenandoah, VA were married. He was then assigned to the destroyer *Farragut*, also in the Pacific, there completing his enlistment.

After the Navy, in September 1945, he went to work for Merck & Company, Inc., a manufacturer of pharmaceuticals, retiring Oct. 1, 1983 after 38 years. After retirement, Albert and Frances moved from Harrisonburg, VA to their present home in Burleson, TX. They have two children and three grandchildren.

JOSEPH ANDERSON, was born in Ossing, NY July 11, 1921 and enlisted in the Marines on Jan. 24, 1942 at New York City.

He did his boot training at San Diego and sailed from San Francisco on board the USS *Wharton* the first part of April, arriving Pearl Harbor ten days later.

He joined VMSB-232 and departed the latter part of July on board *William Ward Burroughs*, arriving at Guadalcanal August 25. Disembarked to Tulagi, three days later moving to canal on USS *Little*. He left the canal the middle part of October on board the USS *Vireo* (picked up as stranded on the way). Went to Efate, then arriving New Caledonia end of December to Santos. A few days later went to the canal for six more months, then back to the United States.

Departed from States February 1944 with VMO-251 arriving Santos, then Bougainville, then Phillipines. Returned to the States June 1945.

Discharged as master sergeant at Cherry Point in September 1945.

Married March 1946 to Claire Dean and have two children one son, Bobby and one daughter, Margery.

RODNEY C. ANDERSON, was born Dec. 15, 1920 in Flint, MI. Enlisted USMC Sept. 26, 1941.

Trained at Parris Island, SC then to Quantico, VA and AMM School Navy Pier, Chicago, IL.

Assigned to VMSB-141 at Camp Kearny, CA. Embarked SS *Lurline* San Diego, transferred USS *Matsonia* at American Samoa. New Caledonia aboard USS *Jackson* flown out Dec. 13, 1942 to Espirito Santo.

USS *Jacob Zieland* to New Zealand to train New Zealand pilots in SBDs.

Wartime marriage to Violet E. Schroeder of Skokie, IL. They have two sons and a daughter.

Second tour of duty included Iwo Jima and Okinawa. Discharged Camp Perry, Great Lakes Naval Station Nov. 4, 1945 as master sergeant.

Graduated General Motors Institute and worked for Buick Motor Division Flint, MI.

Recalled to Korea in 1951.

Retired Grumman Corp. 1985. He and his wife reside in Kalamazoo, MI.

FRANCIS ARCIAGA, JR., was born Nov. 10, 1924 in Chicago, IL. Enlisted in the Marine Corps Jan. 2, 1942 taking boot camp in San Diego.

Joining A-1-1 1st Marine Div., on Guadalcanal November 1942, and on to Cape Gloucester, hospitalized before Peleliu, went on to the Okinawa Campaign.

Back over-seas in June 1946 were he was a M.P. and criminal investigator in Tsingtao, China until November 1948. Picked up nick-name "Ace".

As a criminal investigator until he retired when chief investigator and as a master sergeant October 1961 at San Diego.

For over 25 years since retiring, he has been the historian for law enforcement in the Marine Corps, and custodian of the archives located at Camp Pendleton.

He resides with his wife of 40 years, Jeanette, in Huntington Beach, CA. He has two sons.

EDWIN L. ARMSTRONG, was born May 13, 1921, Sioux City, IA. Enlisted in the regular Navy, October 1941. Boot camp in San Diego. On Nov. 29, 1941 transferred to DesBase San Diego for instruction on operating Landing Boats. January 12, 1942 transferred to USS *President Jackson* for duty, Portland, OR.

Made landings at Tulagi, Solomon Islands, landing

Marines in the initial waves, Aug. 7, 1942. On August 9, left Tulagi and ordered to temporary duty with 2nd Marine Div. when the *Jackson* left the area due to enemy action. Until boarding the USS *Heywood* late in December, landed Marines in many areas of Guadalcanal, rescued sailors and pilots downed in the many battles, and once with other Higgens boats, tried to pull a crippled destroyer into Tulagi Harbor. Contacted malaria fever and laid for many days on a cot on Tulagi with fever of up to 107. Participated in six more invasions, and transferred to States in April 1945, Shore Patrol duty, Washington, DC.

Armstrong went to UCLA after discharge from the Navy in 1947. Received masters degree and worked as an engineer until retirement in 1985. Presently lives in Fox River Grove, IL, where he is village trustee and is active in photography. He is married to Evelyn and they have three sons and one daughter, all now married.

MARVIN V. AYERS, was born Lebannon, OH near Cincinnati Feb. 23, 1919. Enlisted 147th Infantry, Ohio National Guard 1937. Federalized Oct. 15, 1940, Sergeant, Camp Shelby, MS.

Commissioned second lieutenant Dec. 8, 1940.
Met wife Biloxi, MS: five children, eight grandchildren. Three sons: one USMC, one US Army, one USAF.
Overseas April 7, 1942 Tongan Islands. Departed November 11 for Guadalcanal (layover at Espirito Santos due to naval battles). Arrived Nov. 29, 1942. Security for Carney Field area. Front lines January 20th La Sage Trail area. Problems at Bonegi River. Received additional fire support from destroyer. Used pack mules from 97th FA to supply troops in foothills. Relieved February 6 but remained on island until May 12 total of 165 days.
Overseas 43 months. Attached to Marines often, and on nine different ships. After Guadalcanal: Western Samoa, New Caledonia, Emirau, New Caledonia again, Iwo Jima, Okinawa.
Iwo Jima March 21, 1945; relieved Marines northern sector, commendatory letter from Marine General Erskine. Promoted to lieutenant colonel age 26.
Management Proctor and Gamble Cincinnati until retiring March 1976 on the beautiful Mississippi Gulf Coast.

CHARLES E. BARNARD, was born at Ferndale, MI April 9, 1925. Schooling in Ferndale.

U.S. Marine Corp April 9, 1942 - 1948. Boot camp Marine Corp Depot San Diego, CA. Sent to NASN. Island July 1942 then to Camp Kearney. From 1942-1945 served USMC with VMSB-132 1st Marine Air Craft Wing. From 1945-1948 USMC Reserves.
He joined U.S. Army May 1948 with 11th Airborne Division ARCT. He made two jumps behind enemy lines in Korea. Returned to Ft. Bragg, NC June 1957.
At Pope AB, North Carolina joined USAF June 1957. Served 18 months in England making classified flights through out Middle East until 1959. Returned to Pope AB, North Carolina.

In 1960 sent to Vietnam with operation "Mule Train" flying C-123s dropping supplies. Returned Pope AB, North Carolina 1962. Retired 1964 as E5.
Awards received: one Air Medal, Combat Infantry Badge, Senior Aircraft Member Badge, two Master Parachutist Badges, three Air Force Longevity Service Award Ribbons, Presidential Unit Citations, Army Good Conduct Medal w/ four Loops, American Campaign Medal, two Asiatic Campaign Medals, World War Two Victory Medal, Army Occupation Medal w/Japan Clasp, National Defense Service Medal, Korean Service Medal w/five Stars two are w/Heads, United Nations Service Medal, Republican Vietnam Campaign Medal.
His wife is deceased. He has three living children and one son and daughter that were murdered. He has ten grandchildren.
Barnard is retired from the autopart sales (25 years) and the Highway Patrol (16 years). Was volunteer police captain for three years. Barnard is a member of the VFW.

HENRY E. BARTON, was born Oct. 2, 1919, Elgin, IL. Selective Service April 23, 1941, and inducted in service at Chicago, IL, armory same day. Camp Grant, IL for processing. Basic training Camp Forrest, TN, Co. L. 130th Inf. to Medical Det. 130 Inf. Volunteered to 132nd Inf. Med. Det., Co. G. aid man in South Pacific Campaign. Guadalcanal, Bougainville. Sent back to States on rotation, assigned to Hq. Det., 1234th Convalescent Hospital, Camp Upton, New York. Rank held: Sgt. Tech., Med. Tech.

Awards: Presidential Unit Citation, CMB, Combat Infantry Badge, Bronze Star Medal. Separation date August 23, 1945.
Married Aug. 8, 1945 to Lucille Garrett, who was a surgical technician in service.
Three daughters. Retired from printing, Oct. 31, 1984. Resides in Elgin, IL.

WILBUR T. BAUGH, was born Sept. 4, 1914 in Llano, TX. Enlisted in Army Aug. 6, 1941 and received basic infantry training at Camp Roberts, CA. Transferred to Tacoma, WA and joined 161st Infantry Regiment.

Served 44 months overseas in Hawaii, Guadalcanal, New Georgia, New Zealand, New Caledonia and the Philippines. Discharged at rank of technician fourth grade.
Awards: Asiatic Pacific Medal w/three Battle Stars, Combat Infantryman Badge, Bronze Star, Philippine Liberation Ribbon, Good Conduct Medal and Phillipine Presidential Unit Citation Badge.
He remembers nightly visits from "Washing Machine Charlie" and a large, 120 Jap plane air raid on Guadalcanal.
After the war, married Betty Pernetti. They have two children and five grandchildren.
Worked in construction as a carpenter, superintendant and state building inspector. Is now retired.

JESSE A. BEANBLOSSOM, born in Litchfield, IL on Nov. 21, 1921. He enlisted in the Marine Corps, August 1942.
After training at San Diego Marine Base, he was assigned to the First Marine Aircraft Wing, North Island, San Diego, CA. They shipped out in November 1942, bound for the South Pacific on the Dutch Motorship *Bloemfontein*.

Arrived Noumea, New Caledonia late in December 1942. Embarked aboard USS *Hunter Liggett* to Guadalcanal, Solomon Islands. Was assigned to MABS - 1 on arrival and served there until September 1943. Sailed on M.S. *Island Mail* to Purvis Bay, Tulagi and then to Undine Bay, Efate, New Hebrides.

Embarked on USS *Pinkey* and sailed to Pallikulo Bay, Espititu Santos and then back to Guadalcanal October 1943. From here to Hawthorn Sound, Ondongo, New Georgia on a USNLCT. Returned to the States, August 1944 and was stationed at the El Toro Marine Base until discharged in October 1945.
Married Verna Rull in 1955 and they have on son Todd. Have resided in Springfield, IL for the past 35 years.

KENNETH RICHARD BECKMAN, was born July 20, 1923 in St. Paul, MN. He attended public schools in Mason City, IA. He attended the University of Northern Iowa (then Iowa State Teachers College) 1947-1950, B.A.; University of Iowa, M.A. 1955; University of Illinois S. Ed., 1966.

He enlisted in the Navy Dec. 8, 1941 and was inducted on June 7, 1942. Graduated U.S. Naval Training Center Great Lakes, Co. 435, on June 25, 1942. Assigned USS *Jenkins* (DD-447) in July 1942. Participated in the Landings on North Africa; became a shellback Dec. 14, 1942. Asiatic-Pacific duty until 1945. Ship was damaged twice-Lingayen Gulf, Phillines and Borneo. Acquired 14 Battle Stars on European-African and Asiatic-Pacific Theater Ribbons.
He was married Dec. 31, 1943 to Eleanore H. Gaffri of Mason City, IA. They graduated from high school together. He has two children Suellyn Brewster, Bloomington, IL and Greg A. Beckman, Normal, IL. There are four grandchildren and two great grandchildren. He taught in Special Education at Illinois State University for 25 years.
He is a member of the USS Jenkins organization, Guadalcanal Campaign Veterans, and American Legion. Life member National Education Association, Council for Exceptional Children.
He is a collector (you name it), likes to travel and fishes every chance he gets.

FREDERICK JULIAN BECTON, Rear Admiral, USN, retired, was born May 15, 1908, in Des Arc, Arkansas. He was commissioned an ensign upon graduation from the U.S. Naval Academy in June 1931.

He served in battleships, destroyers and a Yangtze River gunboat. Off Guadalcanal he was executive officer of the destroyer *Aaron Ward*. She was disabled by three 14 inch shells on Nov. 13, 1942. After becoming captain of the ship she went down April 7, 1943, following a dive bombing attack. Returning to the U.S. he commanded the new destroyer *Laffey* (DD-724). She participated in the Normandy Invasion; in the Ormoc, Mindoro and Lingayen Gulf assault landings in the Phillipines. At Okinawa she withstood an attack by 22 Kamikazes. Although five Kamikazes crashed into her she survived.

Awards include the Navy Cross and four Silver Medals. In 1956-1958 he commanded the battleship *Iowa*.

He married Elizabeth Hilary Reuss in March 1949. They have two daughters, Julie Becton and Mrs. Joseph Wagner, in addition to two grandsons.

JOHN H. BEEM, was born on Sept. 4, 1921 in Iowa Falls, IA. Entered service on Sept. 1, 1940. Served on board USS *Hunter Liggett*.

Was at Coral Sea Battle, two years in the Solomons, landings at Guadalcanal and Bougainville.

Received three Battle Stars. Discharged as BM 1/c.

Married and has three children and five grandchildren. He is a retired buyer.

FRED BEJECK, was born Aug. 4, 1916 in Cleveland, OH.

Drafted by Selective Service Feb. 8, 1941. He trained at Camp Shelby, MS (made corporal) and Indiantown Gap, PA. Left USA from New York April 1, 1942, through Panama Canal to Tonga Tabu. Arrived May 10, 1942, was made sergeant then staff/sergeant. Left Tonga Oct. 20, 1942 and landed on Guadalcanal Nov. 29, 1942. He went to Beaufort Bay on a special mission and was called back to be first sergeant of Co. M.

May 1943 left Guadalcanal to British Samoa with 3rd Marine Brigade. February 1944 went to New Caledonia, April 11, 1944 landed on Emirau Island NW of Bougainville. Left Emirau July 8, 1944 back to New Caledonia. Left New Caledonia and went to Iwo Jima March 20, 1945. He was one of the last men to leave the original Co. M. Left Iwo Jima June 9, 1945 to Hawaii, to Portland, OR, to Camp Atterbury, IN. Discharged June 25, 1945.

He married Agnes M. Majewski Aug. 4, 1945. They had three children, Joanne, Janice, Fred Paul. They now have four grandchildren. He is retired and resides in Bedford Heights, OH.

ALFRED PETER (BENNY) BENEDETTO, was born in Wakefield, MA on Jan. 16, 1923. He attended Wakefield High School and soon enlisted in the Marine Corp in 1941. He trained at Guantanamo Bay, Cuba for the South Pacific Campaign.

He served in the Asiatic-Pacific Theatre with the 1st Marine Amphibious Corps. F.M.F., 9th Defense Battalion, Special Weapons 30 Caliber Machine Gun attached to the 1st Marine Div. and 2nd Marine Div. on Guadalcanal. Later his unit was attached again to the 43rd Inf. Div. He landed on Rendova on D-Day with the Army Ranger Bn. and the 27th Infantry. After Rendova he landed on Munda taking the air field, still attached to the 43rd Army Div. Served 27 months in the Pacific and later was transferred to the Boston Naval Ship Yard. While at the ship yard he was transferred aboard the USS *West Point* as a gunner and security duty. His travels took him into the North Atlantic European Theater waters.

He earned the Presidential Unit Citation (Guadalcanal) attached 1st Marine Div. and 2nd Marine Div. Two Navy

Commendations: Guadalcanal and Rendova - New Georgia area. One Army Commendation with the Rendova-New Georgia Group from the 43rd Army Inf. Div. The Asiatic-Pacific Campaign Medal w/three Battle Stars, The European-African-Middle Eastern Campaign Medal (USS *West Point*), The American Campaign Medal, The Victory Medal World War II, The Good Conduct Medal.

He was honorably discharged in 1946 with the rank of corporal.

He married Agnes C. Meuse of Reading, MA. He has seven sons. He has lived in Wakefield, MA all his life. He owned a construction company (S. Benedetto Sons Inc.) and is now retired.

He is a Life Member of the 1st Marine Div. Association, the Guadalcanal Campaign Veterans Association, and the Veterans of Foreign Wars Post #2346. He attends Marine Corps reunions.

DALLAS R. BENNETT, was born near Bassett, NE, March 6, 1920. The youngest of four boys, growing up in Bassett and graduating from Rock County High School in 1937.

Served two years in the CCC at Valentine, NE, Lakes Refuge before enlisting in the U.S. Marine Corps, July 1940. Boot camp in San Diego with the 70th Platoon. From private to platoon sergeant, on the last promotion list from headquarters Marine Corps, Washington, DC 1942 assigned to-2-6, K-3-6 and Hq. -2-2 at the base in San Diego and at the building of Camp Elliott. Left the USA aboard the *President Hayes* making the initial landing on Tulagi, and the consolidation of Guadalcanal with Hq. 2-2, after six months to McKay's Crossing, New Zealand. Promoted to gunnery sergeant, and evacuated to the States with malaria. Served at Kodiak, AK, Camp LeJeune, Parris Island, Army Intelligence School, Camp Ritchie, MD, the Hastings Nebraska Naval Ammo Depot, returning to the 2nd Marine Division Recon Co., on Saipan. The occupation of Japan and promoted to first sergeant, of Hq. Co., Hq. Bn., 2nd Div., at Nagasaki and Sasebo, returning to the States and discharged at Treasure Island, CA, July 1946.

Returned to Bassett, NE, where with a brother spent over 25 years in our construction firm, Bennett Bros., Inc., also serving as Mayor, Master of the AF & AM Lodge, and as assistant fire chief before entering the postal service as an assistant, postmaster, clerk and retiring as a rural letter carrier in 1985.

Married to Lois Krause in 1945 they have two married daughters, Faye and Jacalyn, and four grandchildren.

HOWARD E. BENNINK, while on defense at the Tenarn River, and a member of Lt. Weiss's platoon, he and another Marine decided one dark night to have some fun, he threw logs into the river until Cpl. Marino woke up and gave the order to Fire Away. He worked the bolt on his Springfield rifle along with the rest of the squad like they were semi automatic's. The next day, Lt. Weiss complimented the 4th Sqd. for being on the ball.

He left the First Division at Cape Gloucester, and joined the 5th Division and landed on Iwo Jima in 1945 where he received a Purple Heart.

Bennink was born July 25, 1922, Ottowa, CO. Entered the service Jan. 6, 1942. Discharged Oct. 25, 1945 with the rank of sergeant. He is a retired barber. He married Elizabeth April 26, 1942. They have three children, six grandchildren.

ROBERT O. BERGER, JR., was born March 5, 1917 and inducted in April 1941 after unsolicited "Greetings" from President Roosevelt. Trained as buck private at Selfridge Field near

Detroit; he attained the rank of Chief of Garbage Collection. When that job became nauseous, he went to Mather Field in Sacramento as a Navigator in the US Army Air Corps. After Hawaii and Midway, his crew landed on Henderson Field in the first B-17s to arrive. Next six months, they operated out of Guadalcanal (bombing mainly Bougainville and Munda) and search missions out of Esperitu Santo. February 1943 he was sent back to the US for reassignment; their beloved *Galloping Gus* stayed behind and eventually crash-landed in swamp in New Guinea where today the plane is still in exceller shape. All of which earned him a Distinguished Flying Cross an an Air Medal and ultimately the rank of captain. And furthe ultimately, a great family of six children and numerous grandchil dren who might read this and understand Grandpa a little better.

MIKE BERNARDO, was born Jan. 17, 1922 in Staten Island NY. He enlisted in the Marine Corps. Jan 27, 1942. He wer through Parris Island and was assigned to B-1-5, First Marine Div and shipped out to New Zealand. He participated in the landing on Guadalcanal Aug. 7, 1942, then went to Melbourne, Australia, and then on to Cape Gloucester.

He returned to the States and served time in the Annapolis MD. Shipped to San Diego and discharged in September 1945. He met his wife (Virginia) in Santa Monica, CA. and they have one son (Gary) and two grandchildren (Amy and Brian).

He was in business 26 years (Fabri-Tron, Inc.) and eventu ally sold his business to a Marine Corps buddy, George Waselinko

He resides in Palm Desert, CA and also in Coeud 'Alene, ID.

MARIO BERRY, was born Jan. 23, 1920 and spent childhood in West New York, NJ. Enlisted in the Naval Reserves in Hoboken, NJ in early 1938. Reported for active duty Nov. 2, 1939

Served on the following vessels: USS *Helena*, USS *Ranger*, USS *Arizona*, USS *President Hayes*, and the USS *Fuller*. Served at NAS Jacksonville, FL and in the Pacific area from Guadalcanal to Okinawa. He returned to civilian life in 1945.

Enlisted in the Naval Reserves in Jersey City, NJ in June 1947 as QMQ1C. Ordered to active duty in October 1950 and served in Europe and Iceland until he was discharged in 1952. He is active in Veterans Affairs, and hold office as Cheminot Alt Nationale in the 40/8, also serves as a volunteer in the local hospital also Veterans Memorial Home. He served one term as commander of his American Legion Post.

WILLIAM A. BEST, was born in Westfield, NJ, Aug. 17, 1920. Enlisted April 24, 1939, in the PLC program at Dartmouth College. Called to service and commissioned as second lieutenant at Basic School, Philadelphia, communications training at Quantico, VA and Fort Benning, GA. Joined HqSq MAG-11, and shipped out Oct. 15, 1942 from San Diego for Noumea aboard SS *Lurline*, and was sent to Guadalcanal as a replacement to HqSq MAG-14. On April 12, 1943, the group went to New Zealand to recuperate.

Sept. 11, 1943, after two bouts of malaria, making

captain and becoming engaged to a Kiwi, went with MAG-14 to Ondonga, New Georgia to establish fighter strip for Bougainville support. Rotated home Christmas via New Zealand where he married Marian Punch Jan. 21, 1944. Duty with 9-MAW at Cherry Point, Kinston and Congaree until shipped out to MCAS Ewa, HI, June 25, 1944. (Inactive at Brooklyn, NY Thanksgiving, 1945.)

Six children, Kerry, Warwick, Michael, Jeffery, Peter and Leslie. Worked 41 years for AT&T Co. Retired and living in Kill Devil Hills, NC.

ANTHONY J. BETCHIK, was born in Cleveland, OH April 13, 1921. He enlisted in the Marine Corps in April 1942. He served in boot camp at Parris Island, SC on to Quantico, San Diego, CA then to Kearny Mesa to join VMF 121.

He left San Diego in August 1942 for Guadalcanal aboard the SS *Matsonia*, disembarked Noumea, New Caledonia. Relayed to Cactus aboard a R4D in early October. "121" kept the Cactus Air Force flying from Fighter 1 while undergoing heavy shellings from Jap battleships, cruisers and countless air attacks.

Evacuated in mid-December to Efate, New Hebrides due to bouts with malaria, fungal infections and a critical session with amoebic dysentery. After a hospital stay, rejoined "121" on Espiritu Santos. Malaria and problems persisted. Sent to Auckland, New Zealand on the hospital ship USS *Rixey*. After three months, boarded the SS *Lurline* and landed at Treasure Island Naval Base at the end of 1943. Discharged at Cherry Point at the end of 1945.

Using the GI Bill, he spent 11 years completing high school and college with a B.E.E. Degree. Five more years to become a licensed Professional Engineer. Operated his own construction and consulting firm for 35 years.

Married Mary Olive Garry in January 1944 at St. Joseph's Cathedral, San Diego. Have three boys and two girls, four grandchildren and two great-grandchildren. They remain in the Cleveland area.

ANTHONY J. BEYERS, he was born in Perth Amboy, NJ Feb. 13, 1919 and was inducted into the Army October, 1941.

Processed at Fort Dix, NJ and sent to Camp Croft, SC for training. Shipped to Camp Edwards, MA. Assigned to the 182nd Inf. Regt. Anti-Tank Co. He left Brooklyn, NY, January 1942 aboard the USS *Argentina* as part of Task Force 6814-A.

Reached Melbourne, Australia in February. Left there aboard the USS *Santa Rosa* and arrived in Noumea, New Caledonia in 1942 where they became the Americal Div. Arrived in Guadalcanal in 1942 aboard USS *Crescent City*. Welcomed by a group of 27 Japanese torpedo bombers. Higgins boat reached the beach and they were on their way to the hell of jungle fighting and surviving.

He was went to the Fiji Islands where he spent a good deal of time in the hospital with continuing attacks of malaria.

He rotated to the States in 1944 and discharged from Governors Island in September 1945.

Married Helen Wagerik in 1944. Currently reside in Hopelawn, NJ. Retired from Raritan Copperworks, Perth Amboy.

RALPH L. BIGELOW, born in Sedwick County, KS, July 30, 1921. Graduated from North High School in Wichita and attended Kansas State. Enlisted into the service Jan. 27, 1942.

He served in the Asiatic-Pacific theater with the Thirteenth Air Task Force. He served 2 years, 9 months and 19 days in a Jungle environment.

For his military service he earned the following: Good Conduct Medal, WWII Victory Medal; he received campaign stars for the Bismarck Archipelago, Central Pacific, China Offensive, Eastern Mandates, Guadalcanal, Leyte, Luzon, New Guinea, Northern Solomons, Southern Philippines and Western Pacific Campaigns. He also received the Distinguished Unit Emblem with one Oak Leaf Cluster, Philippine Republic Presidential unit Citation Emblem, Philippine Liberation Ribbon with two Bronze Service Stars.

He married Dorothy N. Atherton of Sedwick County, KS on Jan. 9, 1946 at Maize, KS. He has two children, Mark Lauren Bigelow and Cynthia Jean Stiverson. He has three grandchildren. They all reside in Kansas State. He has lived in Maize, KS since 1948. He worked in construction until 1957, when he started his own construction company and is now retired.

He is a member of the American Legion, Veterans of Foreign Wars, Guadalcanal Campaign Veterans and the 307th Bomb Group.

TED BLAHNIK, joined the Navy in August 1940 and after "boots" was sent directly to the USS *Helena* (CL-50) aboard which he served until it was sunk in July of 1943. He was later transferred to the USS *Wisconsin* and was a "plank owner" of that ship. From there he was sent to the Demobilization Pool at Great Lakes and finished his six years as a Shore Patrolman in Chicago.

Married his wife, Jean, on Christmas Day, 1943. They have three children.

He attended Western Michigan University and later taught school for 22 years as teacher, athletic director and assistant principal. He retired in 1981 and is currently involved with the Guadalcanal Campaign veterans having acted in the capacity of president for six years and editor of their newspaper for 10 years.

RUDOLF KARL BOCK, was born in Garrett Twp (Arthur) IL May 17, 1920. To Cedar Rapids, IA to join Navy, but came back with obligation to be a Marine. Enlisted Nov. 25, 1941, USMC off to San Diego and the shortest "ever" boot camp, 2 1/2 weeks, and failing the "dit-da-dit" test, after telephone school joined 1st Marine Div.-Hq Co-1st Pioneers in NC early March 1942, went to New Zealand and to Guadalcanal Aug. 7, 42, attached to several units on Canal, Tulagi, Gavutu.

To Australia in December and back up to New Guiena, over to New Britain (Cape Gloucester, Iboki and Talasea). After rest in Pauvuvu, to Peleliu with Hq-1-1, where he received a BS and PH. Last year 1945 at Camp Lejeune, and to Lincoln NE to pick up a BA & JD.

Married to Virginia Pyle in Lewiston, NE, May 26, 1946. Two sons, Shelley (law) and Karl (GE) in Kansas City area, daughter, Kim, Colorado Springs, CO. Four grandchildren.

Admitted to practice in Nebraska and Federal Court in 1950 just in time to go on active duty in North Carolina during Korea. With a major insurer in Claims and as House Counsel with top playground equipment manufacturer. Retired from the Reserve in 1973 as first sergeant. Present interests: travel space available, jazz music appreciation and trial preparation. He lives with his wife, Virginia, at Overland Park, KS.

JACK W. BONDS, was inducted into the Marines on Dec. 14, 1941 at Dallas, TX. He trained in San Diego and shipped out on the USS *President Hayes* in the summer of 1942. He was a scout assigned to E Co., 2nd Bn., 2nd Marine Div.

He landed on Tulagi on Aug. 8, 1942. That night he stood on the beach in the rain and watched the second battle of the Coral Sea between Tulagi and Guadalcanal. After Tulagi was secured, the Japanese sank a YP boat in front of his foxhole. The next night they came back and shelled it and burned it to water level. The enemy planes chased all supply boats away and they nearly starved. After approximately three months, he went to Guadalcanal. The same hardships existed there. Very little food and water. One day he was assigned to scout a ridge for signs of the enemy. He didn't see a thing and reported this to his unit. His company advanced over the ridge and encountered heavy enemy fire. He found out later it was called Bloody Ridge. After three months on Guadalcanal, his unit was sent to Paekakariki, New Zealand for six months R & R.

For his service during World War Two, he received the following: Asiatic-Pacific Campaign Medal, Good Conduct Medal, Presidential Unit Commendation Ribbon. He married Jean R. Bonds. He is a retired elevator mechanic.

JAMES WILLIAM BOWLES, was born at Musella, GA March 13, 1924 and enlisted in the Marine Corp Oct. 28, 1941. After boot camp at Parris Island, SC he was sent to New River, NC where he was assigned to A Co., 1st Pioneer Bn.

Participated in original landing at Guadalcanal on Aug. 7, 1942, and remained there until Dec. 9, 1942. He was discharged on Nov. 13, 1945, with the rank of corporal. He retired after 40 years in pipe line construction. He is married, with one daughter.

VICTOR F. BRANCH, (Nee Victor Bianchi) was born in Rochester, NY on Dec. 26, 1920. He enlisted in the Marine Corp Nov. 16, 1939. After receiving training at Parris Island, SC, he was sent to radio school in Quantico, VA. After completing a high speed radio course, he was transferred to H&S 5th Marines, 1st Marine Brigade, Quantico, VA.

He left Quantico with H&S 5th Marines for Guantanamo

Bay, Cuba. He returned to Quantico with H&S 5th Marines, 1st Marine Div. in April 1941 and transferred to headquarters 1st Amphibious Corps until December of 1941 when he transferred to 1st Signal Co., 1st Marine Div. Headquarters New River, NC.

In May 1942 he left Norfolk, Virginia with 1st Signal Co., Hq. Bn., 1st Marine Div.aboard the USS *Wakefield* for Wellington, New Zealand. He left there aboard the USS *McCawly* to participate in action against the enemy on Guadalcanal from Aug. 7, 1942 until Dec. 14, 1942. September 1943, he left Australia for further action in the Solomon Islands. He left Cape Gloucester for Pavuvu in 1944 and left there for the States in August of 1944.

After attending Naval Gunfire School at the Naval Base in Coronado, CA, he was transferred to the 1st Assault Signal Bn.in Hawaii. He received an honorable discharge from the Marine Corp as a technical sergeant on Jan. 4, 1946.

After being discharged from the Marine Corps, Victor Branch attended Syracuse University, were he attained a BA Degree. He also attended Law Schools at the Syracuse University and the University of Houston.

He became a member of the State Bar of Texas in June 1954 and is the senior associate in the firm of Branch and Lambert, Attorneys at Law, in Houston, TX. He is a member of the Texas Trial Lawyers Association, the State Bar of Texas, the Houston Bar association and the Phi Delta Phi International Legal fraternity.

He remains active in the affairs of the 1st Marine Div. Association as a National Director. He is a former President of the Houston Chapter of the 1st Marine Div. Association and is presently Reunion Chairman for the 1993 Reunion. He is also a director of the Marine Corps Coordinating Council of Houston, Inc.

He is married to Evelyn C. Tull. He has one daughter, Angela Branch Jones, from a previous marriage. He also has two steph-children, Terry Williams and Melody Buntrock.

WALTER CHARLES BRATTEN, was born in Edwardsville, IL on April 10, 1922. He graduated from Liberty Prairie School. He enlisted in the Navy Jan. 2, 1942 and went to boot camp at Great Lakes IL. He served in the South Pacific and was on the USS *Cushing* when it sank at the Guadalcanal Battle in 1942. He spent 13 months at Espiritu Santo.

He received three campaign stars and a Presidential Unit Citation. He was honorably discharged March 6, 1946 at Norfolk Naval Hospital, Norfolk, VA, with the rank of Storekeeper 2nd Class.

He married Ruby E. Lambert of Charles City, IA on Oct. 30, 1945, who he met at Norfolk, VA, where both were serving a tour of duty. He has three children: Michael Alan Bratten, Patricia Ann Bratten Stanley and Bonny Agnes Bratten Ladd. They have eight grandchildren (one set of twins). They all reside in Edwardsville, IL. He has lived in Edwardsville all of his life. He worked as a mechanic and then worked for the Federal Government in Quality Control and now is retired. He is a member of the Edwardsville Lions Club, Masonic Lodge, American Legion, Disabled American Veterans, Tin Can Soldiers and Veterans of Guadalcanal. His hobby is taking care of the grandchildren.

CHARLES CHUCK BREIJAK, was born Nov. 1, 1920 at Detroit, MI. As Pearl Harbor erupted on Dec. 7, 1941, a friend and he made an important decision to get into a fighting unit to help defend the flag. They were both thinking the same thing—join the Marines. They had their goodbyes and somehow managed to make the journey on an old train that Abe Lincoln must have travelled on—pot bellied stove, gas lantern and all. At the time, they had never heard of Parris Island. It somehow appeared to be the end of the world, bad food, strict discipline, and one rough, tough D.I. But now, he thanks God for its training.

On to the Boondocks of New River, NC. As a raw recruit, he was assigned to M-3-1 water cooled Browning Machine Gun Company. They later, in time, debarked, by train for San francisco, CA. They boarded the ship, *John Ericson* for a 30 day voyage to Wellington, New Zealand. Everyone had the duty, upon arrival, four hours on, four hours off to sleep. Purpose, transfer of cargo, weapons, personnel to a combat ship, USS *McCauley*. Come to find out, it was the flag ship of their convoy.

Next thing they knew, they were headed out again, for another unknown. First to Fiji for a practice run, then the big unknown Guadalcanal.

There are a few good memories of the island. But, if one were to ask what was most haunting . . . it would be the night of Oct. 23, 1942. They were on the beach spit, confronted with a tank attack. There is nothing worse than haveing that monster looking down your throat, firing point blank. Seconds before, their gun had jammed—red hot. For some of them, it was the end on Guadalcanal. Casualties were flown to a naval hospital in the New Hebrides. Some time later, they were shipped to Silverstream Hospital in New Zealand and then to Oak Knoll naval hospital, Oakland, CA.

He did light guard/patrol duty thereafter. He was married in 1945. He can remember saying that he would never go back to that hell hole . . . but he has since twice returned to pay respects to the people and search sites. It is no longer the same place as he knew it. He served with M Co., 3d Bn., 1st Marine Regt., 1st Marine Div.

JOHN W. BROZEK, was born Feb. 11, 1920 and enlisted in the Marine Corp on Jan. 20, 1942. He graduated from boot training in San Diego, CA. He participated in action against the enemy with the First Div., 7th Regt. at Guadalcanal. The Division regrouped in Melbourne, Australia. Most suffered with malaria. He was engaged in battles at Oro Bay, New Guinea, Cape Gloucester, and New Britain. On Sept. 23, 1944, he was wounded on Peleliu Island and sent to Caledonia Hospital. He was moved to Pavuvu, in the Russell Islands.

He was discharged in 1945 at Camp Lejeune, NC.

He was awarded three Battle Stars and a Purple Heart.

Wartime marriage to Violette Lazarewicz. They have two children and five granddaughters. He retired in 1982, after 36 years as a tool and die maker. He enjoys golf, gardening and square dancing. He resides in North Tonawanda, NY.

MICHAEL J. BUGLIONE, was born in Methuen, MA of Feb. 25, 1919 and entered the U.S. Army on March 14, 1941.

He was assigned to the 180 F.A. 26th Yankee Div. at Camp Edwards, MA. He participated in the Fort Devens and Carolina Maneuvers in 1941. He sailed out of Brooklyn, NY with Task Force 6814-C aboard the *Santa Elena* via the Panama Canal arriving in Australia Feb. 26, 1942. He participated in operations with the 221st F.A. Bn., Americal Div. in New Caledonia, Guadalcanal, Fiji Islands, Bougainville, Leyte, and Cebu Philippines.

He was evacuated from Guadalcanal due to injury in March 1943. He was transferred to Navy "600" Hospital in Efate, New Hebrides. His most memorable experience was the day a lone Japanese plane, flying low, straffed their gun position at the base of Point Cruz, Guadalcanal. He returned to the United States in August 1945 and was discharged at Fort Devens, MA in September of 1945. He married Mary S. Forte in Sept. 1, 1945. They have no children. He is widowed.

He has resided in Haverhill, MA for 44 years. He retired from Raytheon Co., working on both the Hawk and Patriot.

MITCHELL BUJNOWSKI, was born Jan 8, 1921 in Lowell, MA. He joined the U.S. Navy on Dec. 17, 1941 and was stationed on the USS *Alshain* (AKA-55), USS *San Diego* (CL-53) LST840, LST503.

His most memorable experience was crossing the equator and tying up to the dock at Yokuska, Japan at war's end. He was honorably discharged as a boatswain mate chief. He received a Good Conduct Award, American Campaign, National Defense, Asiatic, Pacific, Occupational, Korean Service, Korean, Victory.

He married Margret Hinkley, Snohomish, WA. They have a daughter, Maryann, and a son, Michael. They also have two grandsons. He is retired, enjoying fishing and working his own hobby shop.

RUSSELL B. BURCH, he entered the U.S. Army, Aug. 6, 1941. He took basic training at Camp Wolters, TX. He was assigned to Co. "B" 147th Inf., 37th Div. at Camp Shelby, MS. in October 1941, as a rifleman in a rifle squad. Within weeks he attended Cooks and Bakers School and was transferred to Pennsylvania's Indianatown Gap Military Reservation, with the 37th Div.. He boarded the USS *Hunter Liggett*, and sailed for TongaTabu via the Panama Canal. He landed at Nukulofa, Tongatabu, with the 147th Inf.Regimental Combat Team. This unit was assigned to Task Force 0051, along with elements of the 3rd Bn. and Service Co. He boarded the USS *President Hayes* on Nov. 11, 1942. On Nov. 29, 1942 he landed at Koli Point, Guadalcanal. During the Guadalcanal Campaign, he worked as a cook. He was very restless on his off days. On those days, he made mail and supply runs to the forward areas as a volunteer on Service Company trucks. He also volunteered for numerous patrols.

He was evacuated from Guadalcanal to Australia with chronic malaria. He later joined his unit in British Samoa, and between training cycles he spent periods of hospitalization in the Fourth Separate Naval Hospital. In early 1944, his unit transferred to New Caledonia. In March 1944, the unit sailed for Emirau Island. In July 1944, the unit was relieved by a USA Colored Inf. Regiment, later the 147th Infantry-RCT was returned to New Caledonia.

In January 1945, Burch returned to the states on a 30-day furlough. He married the girl of his dreams: Edna Mae Chaney f Somerset, KY. They met while he was on furlough, December 1941. He returned to the Asiatic-Pacific, first to Saipan, then Iwo Jima, where the 147th Inf. RCT was accredited with killing 1602 Japanese and capturing 867. He was then sent to Tinian.

Eventually, he was returned to the States. He was mustered out of the US Army, at Fort Lewis, WA on Sept. 25, 1945. He received the following awards/medals: six overseas bars, habsmark, the Combat Infantryman's Badge, a Bronze Star Medal, Asiatic-Pacific Theater Medal with six Campaign Stars, National Defense Service Medal, and the World War Victory Medal, and a Presidential Unit Citation, which his Service Company earned at Guadalcanal.

He temporarily settled in Butte, MT, but like the dragonfly he was, he didn't light long. He and Edna moved briefly to Ohio/Kentucky; then to Idaho and Oregon. In 1960, they planted their roots in indiana and resided there until he and Edna retired. They spent their winters at Lake Wales, FL and their summers at Lake Monroe, near Bloomington, IN.

Burch and Edna were blessed with a son, Maj. Phillip R. Burch, and a daughter, Judy Mae Wolny. They have two grandsons and two granddaughters. Maj. Burch has served in the US Army in Korea, Vietnam and Germany, as well as in the States. Maj. Burch also served in the USA-R, Indiana, Idaho and Oregon National Guards. He has been employed by the VA and currently is employed by HUD at Boise, ID.

JACK BURKARD, was born in Jersey City, NJ on June 7, 1924; he enlisted in the Marines Dec. 8, 1941. He attended boot camp at Parris Island, SC. The training battalion was divided in half at graduation, half went to Dunedin, FL to attend Amphibian Tractor School. After tractor training, C Co., 1st Bn., 1st Div. bivouacked at New River. The unit shipped out of Norfolk, VA in early June 1942.

Four troop transports escorted by five destroyers to the Panama Canal, here were those Balloon Barrage Marines that left the boot camp when the training battalion was broken up. After passing from the Atlantic to the Pacific Ocean, the naval escort was now one destroyer and one cruiser. The trip lasted almost 60 days, then New Zealand landfall in early August, within two hectic days, they were again at sea.

Guadalcanal, August 7, third wave. Later on, he went to New Caledonia. Returned to the US aboard the USS *President Taft* which landed at San Francisco, CA.

He married Doris Zimmerman of Philadelphia and had eight children: Janet, John, Judith, James, Jennifer, Jeffrey, Jerry and Jason. They reside at the Jersey Shore.

ROBERT J. BURKHEAD, was born in Bethany, IL on Aug. 20, 1922; enlisted in the Marines on Jan. 3, 1942. He was in boot camp in San Diego, CA. He was a charter member of the newly formed B.1.2. of the 2nd Div.

His unit was attached to the 1st Division that was sent to Guadalcanal. B Co. was the Contingent that landed first, 20 min. before the others on Florida Isles. He was sent to help the Paratroopers and was wounded twice attempting the landing on Gavutu. Hospitalized in New Zealand and then returned to B Co. on Guadalcanal. He was wounded wading in at the Tarawa landing. He made the initial landings on Saipan & Tinian Isles. He returned State side from Tinian, after 26 months overseas. He was discharged in California in 1946. He married Dorothy Bowlby in 1949. They have six children. He is now retired in Gainesville, GA.

JAMES W. BURNS, was born in Long Branch, NJ on Feb. 4, 1922 and enlisted in the U.S. Marine Corp. Jan. 19, 1942. After boot camp in San Diego he was stationed at Mare Island and Alameda Naval Air Station.

He was transferred to VMF 121, MAG 14, Kearney Mesa, CA. His squadron shipped out of San Diego aboard USS *Matsonia* arriving at Noumea, New Caledonia Sept. 22, 1942. He flew into Guadalcanal Sept. 25, 1942 with five pilots and eight enlisted aircraft mechanics. Dec. 5, 1942, sent to Esprito Santo for rest period and then to Auckland, New Zealand. He returned to the States in October 1943 and was stationed at El Toro, CA.

He married Gloria Aschettino on Jan. 1, 1944 at St. Joseph's Roman Catholic Church in Santa Anna, Ca.

Gloria and Jim have three children and five grandchildren. He was discharged a Master Tech Sgt. at Cherry Point NC. He is presently retired from the New Jersey State Police as a detective sergeant, first class.

BENNIE F. BURNS JR., was born in Whitman County, WA on May 3, 1920; enlisted in Co. E, 161st Inf., Washington National Guard Oct. 17, 1939 at Pullman, WA. He was mobilized into federal service Sept. 16, 1940; his unit trained at Fort Lewis, WA with the 41st Div. Dec. 6, 1941, his unit was on a troop train headed for San Francisco when they heard of the attack on Pearl Harbor. He served in the Asiatic-Pacific Theater with Co. E, 161st Inf., 25th Tropical Lighting Div. He was section leader of the 60MM Mortar Section of the Weapons Platoon. He earned the Combat Infantryman's Badge, the Bronze Star and the American Defense Ribbon. He was honorably discharged from Hammond General Hospital at Modesto, CA in 1943 with the rank of sergeant.

On December 22 at Lewiston, ID, he was married to Lillian M. King of Moscow, ID. He has three stepchildren, three children (two from a previous marriage). He has eight grandchildren. He has lived in Moscow, ID since 1950. He has worked as a gardener, assistant grounds supervisor and plumber for the University of Idaho for over 29 years. He retired in November 1983.

He is a member of the Moose Lodge, VFW, and Guadalcanal Campaign Veterans. His hobbies include bowling, travelling, stamp collecting and model railroading.

J.D. BYARS, was born in Runge, TX on Feb. 18, 1920; enlisted in the Navy in 1937. He was stationed on the USS *Bristol* escorting convoys to England when WWII occurred.

He was stationed on the USS *Fomalhaut* when the Marines landed on Guadalcanal in August 1942. He made four different trips to Guadalcanal with Marines and supplies until October 1942. He served on numerous ships in Admiral Wright's Flag. He saw action in the Aleutians on the USS *San Francisco*, and was three days out of Guam on the USS *Saginaw Bay* enroute to Japan, Aug. 15, 1945, when the Japanese surrendered.

He retired a million dollar salesman for Proko Industries, Dallas, TX. Published two books of peoms, *Moods of a Sailor*, 1942, (out of print) and *Dusty Memories* (1987). These are "mini" stories in rhyme, mostly written during WW II. An accomplished commedian at age 70. He taught communication for 12 years before retiring from the Navy. He has been married to June since 1944. They have one son.

DENNIS E. BYRD, was born May 8, 1921 at Brown County, TX and enlisted in the USMC June 21, 1941. He had boot camp at San Deigo. He had almost completed Aviation Radio School and helped load VMF-221 aboard the USS *Saratoga* at North Island NAS the night of December 7th.

He joined VMSB-232 at Ewa, T.H. Jan. 12, 1942. He sailed on the USS Long Island and was a rear seat gunner for Major Richard C. Mangrum in SBD MB-21, the first Marine aircraft to land on Henderson Field. He flew with Major Mangrum on all his Guadalcanal missions. He was awarded an Air Medal. He was evacuated from Cactus Oct. 13, 1942 aboard *Zeilin* and arrived in the first truck convey of Marines assigned to new El Toro Marine Air Station. He received a special order discharge to enlist in Navy V-5 Aviation Cadet Program Feb. 4, 1943.

He received his Navy Wings and Marine Commission from Colonel R.C. Mangrum at NAS Corpus Christi, TX Jan. 15, 1944. He was a Marine F4U fighter pilot with VMF-523, VMF-115, VMF-225, and MGCIS-6. He was awarded a DFC with Gold Star, two Air Medals and 8 stars, PUC with 2 stars, NUC and A.P. with 4 stars. He resigned regular commission May 16, 1950.

THOMAS S. CALLAGHAN, born June 8, 1920 and enlisted in the Marines Dec. 8, 1941 and went active Jan. 2, 1942. He had boot camp at Parris Island with platoon 13 and then went to Telephone school in Quantico.

Joined the 3rd Bn 1st in May 1942. Left San Francisco June 22, 1942 for 58 days on a ship to Guadalcanal. Maintained Camp Lejune's telephone system and volunteered to return to FMF. A-bomb was dropped just before boarding the ship to invade Japan.

Discharged Oct. 12, 1945. Married Mary Alice Britt in 1949. They have five children: Mary, Steven, Betsy, Maureen and Amy. He worked 35 years for AT&T, retiring in 1978 at Marathon, FL.

WILLIAM J. CANNON, was born in 1924 and enlisted in the Marine Corps in 1941. He went through boot camp at MCRD San Diego, with Platoon 206. He trained at Camp Elliot, C Company, 1st Bn., 2nd Marines, landed on Florida Island to the left and right of Tulagi respectively, at about 07:40, Capt. E.J. Crane, skipper of B Co., was the first American ashore in a W.W. II offensive, a fact very seldom mentioned in any of the books on the Solomons Campaign; it was supposedly a 1st Div. show.

His most memorable experience was on his eighteenth birthday, when they were given word of a counter invasion. They were pulled back from a drive west of the Matanikau River and positioned around Henderson Field. Having had no time to dig foxholes (they were moved in after dark) a group of the men from C Co. were clustered around a large banyan stump. He stretched out under a shelter half to keep out of the drizzling rain. Leaning on one elbow, he was listening to the off-beat engine of a Japanese artillery-spotting plane and looking up at the greenish flares it was dropping. After a little bit, large shells started coming in. Suddenly something hit him hard, right between the shoulder blades, and he could feel flesh ripping and blood flowing. Startled, then stunned for a couple of minutes, he finally figured that if he could still see the flares and hear the planes, he must not be dead. Finally he worked up the courage to try to feel the gaping wound. Reaching over his shoulder, he stretched to feel the wound but found nothing. Then he reached around his side. No break there either! The fact was that a ball of mudd off a 14 inch shell had hit him! Although they lost several men that night, some of the men in C Co. were saved by the soft ground.

He has served in New Zealand, Paekakariki, Tarawa, Saipan and Tinian. He came back to the States in 1944 aboard the President Jackson. He married Dorothy Hillin in 1946 and worked in sales and resort ownership/management, chiefly in California. They moved to Australia in 1969 where Dorothy died in 1970. He returned to California in 1971 where he married Ann Alderson in 1979. He now lives on ten acres near Sacramento raising ducks, fruit and several other kinds of trees, and enjoying their cats and dogs.

ERROLL J. CANTLIN, was born in 1920 and enlisted in the U.S. Navy in 1941. He was in boot camp in San Diego. He was assigned to the USS *Helena* in 1942 and served aboard until it sank in 1943. He later served on the USS *Kasaan Bay* (CUE 69) and Hedron Fleet Air Wing Two at Kaneohe Bay, Hawaii.

He was discharged in 1945 at Bremerton WA. He served in the Naval Air Reserve for 21 years. He spent 20 years in Aircraft and Missle Mfg. He retired from the U.S. Postal Service in North Hollywood, Ca. in 1980. He has lived in Sydney, Australia since 1980.

He is presently employed by overseas Telecommunications Commission. He travels extensively in the Pacific and Malaysia area.

He is presently the Commander of the Yanks Down Under Post of The American Legion in Sydney.

SAMUEL A. CARLISLE, was born in 1916 and enlisted in the USNR, 22nd Division in Chicago in 1933. He mobilized as Quartermaster Second Class, Assigned to USS *Neville* (APA 9) at Portland, Oregon. While attached to Seventh Amphibious Force, Participated in landings at Tulagi, Guadalcanal, Sicily, Makin, Kawaj Lein, and Eniwetok. He was Commissioned Ensign and Transferred to USS LSM 65 as Executive Officer and Navigator. While attached to Flotilla Seven, participated in six landings in the Philippines, and one in Borneo.

He separated from active duty at Great Lakes with the rank of Lieutenant. He earned Naval Reserve Medal, Good Conduct Medal, American Defense with Fleet Clasp, American, European and Pacific Theater Medals and Philippine Liberation Ribbon. Awarded seven Bronze Battle Stars. He was Honorably discharged at age 65 after 48 years of Naval Service.

He has lived in Houston, TX since 1948. Entered the Insurance Business and retired in 1985 as President of a local Insurance Agency. He is a lifetime member of Guadalcanal Campaign Veterans.

EDWARD J. CARPENTIER, was born in 1921 and enlisted in the Navy in 1942. After training at San Diego, he was shipped to Pearl Harbor to board the USS *Minneapolis* (CA-36). We participated in the Battle of Coral Sea, the Battle of Midway, also in the expedition for the occupation of Guadalcanal, Tulagi Area, Solomon Islands.

Participated in expedition for reinforcement of Guadalcanal. Participated in expedition occupation of Funafuti & Ellice Island. Participated in Battle of Tassafaronga when we got hit with two Torpedoes in November of 1942. Transferred to the USS *Heywood* then to Guadalcanal boat pool then over to Tulagi. Transferred again to the USS *Bellatrix* went to the Invasion of Sicily, then the Invasion of Tarawa. Transferred again to USS *Curb*, then on to USS *Vermillion*. Made B.M. second class. Discharged October 1, 1945 and remained in reserves unitl 1955.

Married Jeanne Wilson in 1944, had a daughter and two sons, eight grandchildren, four great grandchildren, has been married for 46 years, living in Salinas, CA.

RONALD C. CARROW, SR., born in Orchard Park, NY Oct. 13, 1922. Attended Manlius School, Manlius, NY 1941 went to work for father at Carrow Chevrolet in Orchard Park, N.Y. On Dec. 8, 1941 informed father I was going to join the Army. He wasn't happy about this and said, "If you think you are so tough, why don't you join the Marines." I joined the U.S. Marines Dec. 13, 1941.

After Parris Island, saw duty at Lakehurst, N.J. Air base, Philadelphia Navy Yard and Dan Diego, North Island. December 1942, boarded a Liberty Ship at San Diego for parts unknown. 30 days later after transfer to a Navy ship, we stopped at Tulagi to unload ammunition and then the 1st Marine Repair and Salvage Sq. arrived on Guadalcanal. The idea was to salvage damaged planes and repair for use again. A good idea, but not too practical. Our claim to fame - I-F4F named *Miss Fit*.

Returned to the states in 1944 and stationed at the new El Toro Marine Base. Married to home town gal (Naomi) in Santa Anna, CA. the same year. 42 years later, have three boys and one girl. Discharged as staff sgt. in 1945 and returned to Orchard Park, NY to go back to work in fathers Chevrolet dealership. Called back in Korean War with 6th 105 Howitzer Battalion, USMC. Became President of Carrow Chevrolet Corp. Have never missed a Memorial Day parade as drill sergeant for our local VFW post.

WILLIAM M. CHANEY, was born in 1922 in Pulaski County, KY. He enlisted in the U.S./Ohio National Guard, in 1940. Mobilized into Federal Service Oct. 15, 1940. He served in the Asiatic-Pacific Theater with the 147th Infantry Regimental Combat Team, United States Army, from April 7, 1942 - Dec. 31, 1944. He earned the Combat Infantryman's Badge and three Bronze Campaign Stars (for Guadalcanal, Northern Solomons and the Bismarck Archipelago Campaigns). He was honorably discharged on June 23, 1945 at Camp Atterbury, IN with the rank of Staff Sergeant/Infantry.

Married the former Mae Marie Smith of McCreary County, Kentucky, December 1, 1945 at Meece, Kentucky. He has three children and seven grandchildren.

He resides in Indianapolis, IN and is a retired Coach Operator, for the Indianapolis Public Transportation Corpora-

tion. He is a member of the Shriners, The American Legion, VFW, DAV, Guadalcanal Campaign Veterans Association, the 37th Infantry Division-USA Veterans Association, and the U.S. Army Non Commissioned Officer Museum Association, Americal Division Veterans Association, and the Society of the First Infantry Division, USA.

He is an Honorary Lt. Col. Alabama State Militia. Commissioned Kentucky Colonel.

SAMUEL M. CHARLES, JR., born Matewan West Virginia June 17, 1918. Enlisted United States Marine Corps at Baltimore, MD as did his brother William Mack Charles, on Sept. 28, 1938. Served with Marine Air Group 14 on Guadalcanal. Returned stateside January 1944.

Married Irene Bedford at Vista, CA. They have one son, three daughters, and six grandchildren. Continued service in the Marine Corps., at El Toro, Cherry Point and Korea until 1958. Transferred to Fleet Reserve and retired Oct. 1, 1968 with 30 years.

Employment with Tustin Elementary School District, Tustin, CA with the maintenance department until 1974 second retirement. Moved to beautiful northern Idaho for the good life of a snowbird.

HARRY C. CHILTON, was born July 20, 1920 Watertown, New York. Enlisted July 27, 1938. Boot Camp Newport, RI. New York Worlds Fair Detachment. 6/40 - 9/41 USS *Curtis*. 9/41 - 10/42 VP-14. 12/7/41 at NAS Kaneohe Bay. 3/42 Plane Captain of 14 -P-7 part of three plane detachment of VP-14 to patrol SO PAC. Reenlisted 8/7/42 VP-14 at Noumea.

Took part in early Guadalcanal night patrolling operations. Early September 1942 flight crews of VP-14 formed Pat Su 1-1 under CMM Perry Gregg. The 20 man crew maintained the PBY's of VP-11,12,51,54,& 91 at Henderson Field. Evacuated late November 1943 through Noumea to NAS Jacksonville, FL. Routine Navy Air Group assignments until July 1958 when he transferred to the Fleet Reserve.

Attended Jacksonville University. B.S. Fla. A&M. M.S. FSU. Have been vocational teacher until present time.

Happily married to Betty J. Musselman of Watertown, NY since April 25, 1941. They have one daughter, Kristina J. Holden & one grandson, Jonathan E. Holden, both of Jacksonville, FL.

HERSCHEL B. CHIPP, born Missouri, 1913. Enlisted V-6 Office Training Program, Los Angeles, 1940; assigned USS *Prairie State*, New York. commissioned and assigned USS *San Francisco* (CA-38), Pearl Harbor, 1941. Served this ship 1941-45.

Major actions: Pearl Harbor, Wake, Guadalcanal, Aleu-
ans, Gilberts and Marshalls, Truk, New Guinea, Saipan, So. 'hina Sea, Leyte Gulf, others. Guadalcanal actions: landing, August 1942; escort, supply and bombardment missions; 1ajor battles; Cape Esperance; Battle of Guadalcanal, 12-13 .ov. 1942. Shore duty, Operational Training Command, acific Fleet, San Diego, Jan. 1945.

Professional career, 1945-81; Columbia University, NY; Jniversity of British Columbia; University of California, erkeley. Advisor, Spanish Ministry of Culture. Author, articles nd books on the war in the Pacific, the Spanish Civil War.

Resides in San Francisco and Madrid. Member: Pearl Iarbor Survivors, Guadalcanal Campaign Veterans, USS San 'rancisco Association, Veterans of the Abraham Lincoln Battalion, International Brigade, Spanish Civil War, Navy .eague, others.

ALFRED SALVATORE CIARDI, was born in Boston MA on July 11, 1915. He graduated from Beebe Jr. High in Malden. He enlisted in the Navy on Sept. 26, 1942. He went o the Great Lakes for training. After his stay at the Great .akes, he was transferred to Treasure Island in California. He vas then shipped to North Caledonia. Two weeks later he was lrafted on the USS *Libra* (AKA-12).

He earned the American Theater Medal, Asiatic Pacific Theater Medal w/seven Stars, Philippine Medalw/one Star. He was honorably discharged on Feb. 8, 1946 at Boston, MA, n with the rank of boatswain mate 1/c on Feb. 8, 1946.

He married Anna A. Constantino of Boston, MA, on June 23, 1946. He has two children Paula Ciardi and Steven A. Ciardi both of Randolph, MA, and three grandchildren. He has lived in Randolph for ten years.

He worked as a finisher in a rolling mill and then worked at the Post Office for 31 years. He retired in 1975. He is a member of the Elks in Randolph and a member of the Italian American Veterans club in Malden MA.

LESTER W. CLARK, was born October 27, 1918 in New York City. He graduated from Jamaica High School. Pearl Harbor drove him to a Marine Corps recruiting office. Seven months after his arrival at the Parris Island boot camp, he hit Beach Red at Guadalcanal on Aug. 7, 1942. As a member of H-2-1 1st Marine Division, he saw major action at the Teneru where the Ichiki Detachment was obliterated. After R&R in Australia, he saw further action at Cape Gloucester before being rotated home.

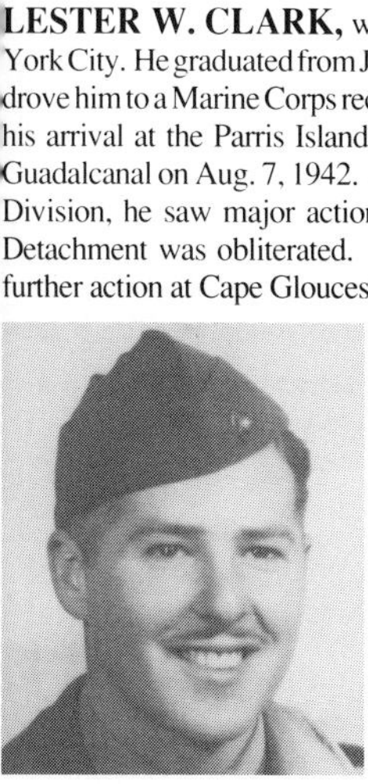 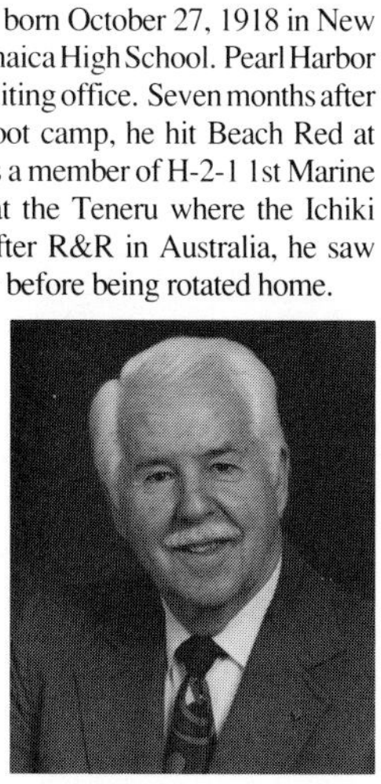

Severe malaria attacks prevented more overseas duty and the PFC was honorably discharged in September of 1945.

Marriage to childhood sweetheart Dorothy Anne Florin produced 49 wonderful years, two fine sons, Bruce and Randall. He served 20 years, in the NYPD without a day of sick leave. Retired in Florida, he authored a book *An Unlikely Area* and keeps busy with six grandchildren and bowling. Unfortunately, his dear wife lost a two year battle with cancer this past July.

RAYMOND W. CLARK, SR., was born June 3, 1922 and enlisted in the U.S. Navy Jan. 22, 1942. He was taken to Buffalo, NY to the main recruiting station for his physical. From there he was taken to Newport, RI training station for three weeks. From there he went to Boston South Station to await assignment.

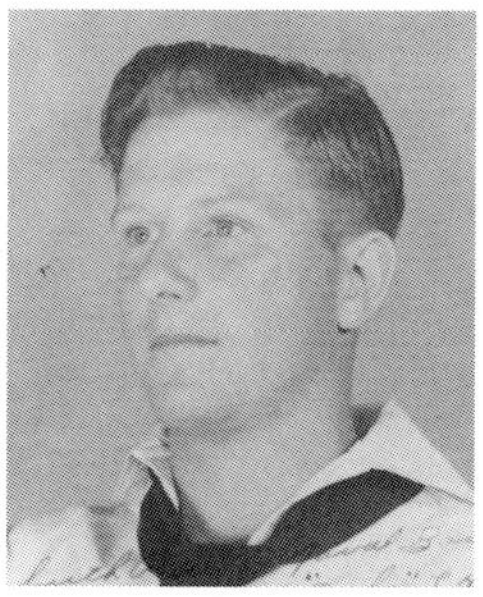 

A short time after arriving at Boston he was assigned to the USS *Quincy* (CA- 39) a Brooklyn Heavy Cruiser. After receiving supplies, small repairs and test we set sail for the Panama Canal. Went through the ditch to San Diego, CA. While at San Diego, we had gunner practice with the USS *North Carolina*. Our next stop was the Fiji Island of Tango Tabu. After leaving there, we were told where we were going. From then on we had all kinds of drills. We arrived at Guadalcanal on the morning of August 7. Everything went smooth, no mishaps. Action was light for the two days, then the night of the 8th and 9th hell broke loose. After hell broke loose, they were sunk and he was in the water for about 6 hours before being picked up by the destroyer USS *Elliot*. Being a seaman second class he was brought back to Pearl Harbor. After receiving a new sea bag and records, he went up to Naval Air Station Barbers Point. Oahu, Hawaii. He spent two years duty at that station. After leaving Barbers Point, he went to San Francisco and home on a 30 day leave. After returning off leave, he went to San Pedro small craft training school. After completing the training, he was assigned to an APA. USS *Arenac*. After completing shake down and the necessary things we headed for the South Pacific. Made several stops such as Guam. Got into the fighting at Okinawa. Was under many air attacks. From the APA., he went to mine sweepers and L.S.T.'s.

Was discharged at Orange, TX in October of 1945 as a chief boatswain mate.

Upon returning home he went back to his job on the railroad. Completed his 30 years there and retired. Since retiring from the railroad, he has operated a hobby greenhouse. He earned four awards during his enlistment. He is married and has five children and four grandchildren.

WARREN FREDERICK MARTIN CLEMENS, was born in Aberdeen, Scotland on April 17, 1915. He studied at Christ's College, Cambridge and was then appointed to the Colonial Administrative Service in Solomon Islands Protectorate in 1938, serving as a Cadet on Malaita for three years where he carried out various development schemes. Mr. Clemens then took charge of San Christoval District until November of 1941, when having offered himself for war service without avail, he went to Australia to endeavor once more to join the armed forces.

But Colonial Service officers were not accepted, and he returned on the steamer sent to evacuate Europeans. Although bombed by the Japanese, he volunteered to stay behind with the Resident Commissioner.

Posted to Guadalcanal, he soon became District Officer. As Coastwatcher, reported enemy movements by radio. After helping RAAF personnel to evacuate, he evacuated the Government Station at Aola Bay and 'went bush' where he set up headquarters and continued gathering information. The Japanese arrived on Guadalcanal in May 1942 after prolonged attacks. After the landing by US Marines in August 1942, Mr. Clemens walked down and was appointed British Liaison Officer. He continued operation his scouting and intelligence team (all Solomon Islanders) in cooperation with Marine combat units, and involved the islanders in rescuing pilots, guiding patrols, carrying ammunition and rations, and unloading ships; he was awarded the Military Cross in December 1942. When the Marines were relieved by XIV Corps, US Army, Mr. Clemens became their British Liaison officer in the last stages of the battle, commanding the Solomon Islands Defence Force, mostly Solomon Islanders with British officers and an attached group of the Fiji Commando.

The rest of 1st Commando (Fiji) was later added, and the two units took part in landings on the Western Solomons in August 1943. Awarded the American Legion of Merit, Mr. Clemens remained District Commissioner, Western Solomons until peace with Japan was declared in August 1944, and was also Liaison officer with 2nd Australian Corps on Bougainville.

With the longest combat service of any officer in South Pacific Command, he went on UK leave in time to march in the London Victory Parade in May 1946, and was posted to Palestine in July.

Deputy District Commissioner in Samaria for some months, he then became District Commissioner in Gaza until February 1947, he became District Commissioner in Nicosia & Kyrenia, Cyprus (1948-49, 1952-57) and was awarded the OBE (Officer, Order of the British Empire) in 1956. He studied at the Imperial Defense College (1958) and returned to become Defense Secretary (1959-60); he was made a Commander of the British Empire (CBE) in 1960, received a tribute from the City of Philadelphia, USA in 1968, and elected an honorary member of the Naval Order of the USA in 1985. Married to Anne Turnbull in 1948. Mr. Clemens now lives in Australia where he manages family grazing properties and other business interest; he also has various charitable and cultural interests, including the Red Cross Executive, Australia-Britain Society (chairman), Navy League, International Social Service, etc. He has four children, all leading successful careers.

WILLIAM M. CLEVELAND, was born Oct. 18, 1917, in Cleveland, OH and grew up and went to school in Akron, He joined the U.S. Army Air Corps in 1939 and was sent to Wheeler Field, T.H. to the 6th Pursuit Sq. and then to Like Field in Pearl Harbor. Later he was sent to Hickam Field. His recruit training was completed at Wheeler and he took mechanics training on the P-26E.

At Hickam Field, he was assigned to duty at the Motor Pool as a school bus driver and attended the University of Hawaii during 1940-41 until school was canceled for the military.

He was assigned to HqSq 5th Bomb Gp(H) on the day of the Attack and used his school bus to haul the injured and dead from around the parade ground and the big barracks. Transferred to the 431st Bomb Sq of 11th Bomb Gp(H) and moved to Kahuku Air Base where he assisted in preparing LB-30s for Pacific flights. Went to Midway battle in B-17 and returned June 5, 1942 with Lt. Col. Sweeney.

With 431st Bomb Sq, went to Fiji in July and saw squadron B-17s searching and bombing in Southern Pacific and Solomons. Lost several good friends on D-Day, August 7, 1942, at Guadalcanal, and soon moved to Espiritu Santo in the Hebrides Islands. From Santo staged in and out of the 'Canal' in B-17s and lost a few to shelling by warships of Japan. Sent to Hawaii and home in April 1943 with malaria and dengue fever. Recovered at Salt Lake City Air Base.

Discharged as M/Sgt at Gowen Field, Boise, ID, in October 1945 and re-enlisted in the AF through 1960, when he retired.

After service, he was appointed an Education Officer in Civil Service and completed 13 years with the DOD at bases and overseas locations in the Far East. Has earned a number of Service and campaign medals and was awarded the Air Force commendation Medal for Korea and the Distinguished Civilian Service award for Vietnam. He is New Hampshire State Chairman in PHSA and appointed their National Historian.

STAN COLEMAN, joined U.S.N.R. 21st Div., 5th Bn. at Chicago, IL Oct. 8, 1940, 21st and 30th Div., Peoria, IL, activated Dec. 14, 1940. Transported to Philadelphia NRS. Thence to Baltimore Shipyard and boarded SS *George F. Elliot*. Armed in Norfolk, proceeded to Guantanamo Naval Base, Cuba. Detached temporarily to USS *Denabola* as ship's bugler. Returned to *Elliot* and amphibious training with the 4th Marines in the Virgin Islands.

December 7, 1941 ship was in dry-dock Portsmouth Navy Yard. Sea ready Jan. 3, 1942. Transported troops from New York to Belfast, Ireland via North Atlantic and American refugees from Grennoch, Scotland back to the States.

Deployed to southwest Pacific and August 7, 1942 invasion of Guadalcanal, Solomon Islands. August 8th the *Elliot* was hit by a Mitsubishi torpedo bomber amid ships and became the first ship casualty of the first land and sea offensive against Japan. Abandoning ship we were picked up by USS *Hull* and later to USS *Hunter Liggett*. Morning of August 9 ringside seat to sea battle off Savo Island. Left for Noumca, New Caledonia and Wellington, New Zealand and four more runs to Canal during which was transferred to USS *Neville* and radar gang. Subsequent campaigns-Sicily, Mediterranean-Makin-Kwajelien-Enowetoc and Saipan.

Attained rate of Radarman 3/C. Honorable Discharge, Great Lakes, IL. October 1945.

Married October 1946. Four children and nine grandchildren.

BILL H. COOKE, was born in Gastonia, NC on Jan. 22, 1922, moved to Kannapolis NC at age one where he grew up and graduated from Cannon High School. Was an All-State Football player and Golden Glove Boxing Champion.

He enlisted in the Marine Corps 07-26-40 and completed boot camp at Parris Island, SC. He served in peace time at Quantico, VA., Parris Island, SC, New River, NC., and British Somoa.

He participated in action against the enemy at Guadalcanal, Sept. 18, 1942 to Jan. 4, 1943. Oro Bay, New Guinea, Oct. 9, 1943 to Dec. 19, 1943. Cape Gloucester Dec. 26, 1943 to May 3, 1944. All combat action with the 1st Marine Division (B-1-11). He was a Section Chief and SGT. of a 75 mm Battery.

He returned to San Diego July 7, 1944 and discharged from Quantico, VA. Sept. 15, 1945. Returned to College, graduated from the University of North Carolina Charlotte and received his PH.D., from Oxford Graduate School. He is presently pastor of The First United Methodist Church in Davis, Oklahoma.

He married Thelma Lee Blalkwelder in 1944, and has 2 children and 4 grandchildren. He also served in the North Carolina Air National Guard. Taught in the public schools and was Professor of Criminal Justice at the University of North Carolina at Charlotte.

He is a member of the Guadalcanal Campaign Veterans, The Marine Corps League, and The First Marine Division Association.

ROBERT E. COUCH, was born Sept. 2, 1919 and enlisted in the service on Sept. 20, 1940, had boot camp at Chanute Field with the 72 Bomb Squad, 11th Bomb Group.

He was stationed at Hickham Field as a Flight Engineer on B-17's. His most memorable experiences were Hickham Field on Dec. 7, 1941 at Midway Battle, Battles off Guadalcanal and the bombing missions in the Solomon Islands.

He received Distinguished Flying Cross, Air Medal and Cluster Campaign Medals.

He married Helen Nellis, and has three children and four grandchildren.

JOHN F. COWLES, was born May 20, 1922 in New London CN. He enlisted in the Marine Corps in July of 1940. Participated in the Guadalcanal invasion from August 7 until Dec. 22, 1942, with Headquarters Company, 1st Battalion, 1st Marines, 1st MarDiv. Participated in the Okinawa invasion from April 1st to July 18, 1945, with Signal Company, III Marine Amphibious Corps. Following the Japanese surrender, he served in North China with the 1st Marine Division from August, 1945 to November, 1946. He was discharged as a Technical Sergeant in July, 1947.

His awards include the Bronze Star Medal and the Commendation Medal for Bravery.

He married his high school sweetheart, Mary Ellen Sheldon, on July 9, 1943. They have nine children and (presently) twenty-two grandchildren.

He was employed by Western Union Telegraph Company for 40 years in microwave and satellite communications; retiring as a Senior Director of the Company. They reside in Falls City, Nebraska.

LEON GUS CRAWFORD, was born April 3, 1918 and entered the service October 14, 1938. He was a member of Company D, 1st Battalion, 5th Marines. He was stationed at Parris Island, then Quantico, VA., Guantanamo Bay, Cuba, Camp Pendleton, Portsmouth N.H. and Camp Lejune.

He was discharged as a Sergeant in January of 1946.

His most memorable experience was the Matanica River tank battle. He received the Presidential Unit Citation, WWII Victory Medal, American Campaign, Service America Defense, and the Marine Good Conduct, twice.

He married Medora Sawyer in Exeter, N.H. and had 3 sons. His wife died in May of 1951. In 1954, he married Rebecca Rhyne in Mt. Holly, N.C. They had one daughter and have six grandsons. He retired in 1980, after laying brick for 40 years. They reside in West Pelzer, SC.

PETER CULTRERA, was born in New York City, NY on Aug. 4, 1921. He enlisted in the Army on March 2, 1942. Arrived Oahu, Hawaii, May 8, 1942.

Assigned to 8th Field Artillery Battalion, B Battery, Communication section and Forward Observation Team of the 25th Tropic Lightning Division. In the third week of May, 1942, B Battery set up positions for shore defenses on The Punch Bowl and his Forward Observation Team on the roof of The Royal Hawaiian Hotel. During June 4 to 6, 1942, they sweated-out the outcome of The Battle of Midway.

Arrived on Guadalcanal on Jan. 1, 1943 to reliev some of the Marine units. Guadalcanal was secured on Feb 17, 1943. Arrived in Auckland, New Zealand, Nov. 1(1943 for rest and recreation. Arrived New Caledon around the beginning of March 1944.

Arrived in Lingayen Gulf, Luzon, Philippines, an established a Beach Head. From San Fabian, we went ea to The Barrio of Rosaldo, into Belete Pass, all the way t Santa Fe, our prime mission. It was Tropic Lightnin Division 165 days in combat. Was awarded The Bronz Star.

Was discharged Oct.12, 1945 with the rank of Pfc.

Married his wife Antoinette Rawluk of New Yor City, NY on Dec.15, 1945. Have two daughters and tw grandchildren.

Employed as supervisor for Exquisite Form Bras sieres and Botany 500, and is now retired.

He is a member of the Guadalcanal Campaign Veter ans, 25th Tropic Lightning Division Association, D.A.V and V.F.W. His hobby is loving his wife, daughters an grandchildren.

BILL CUMMINGS, was born Feb. 2, 1919 in Bienville GA. He entered the service August 17, 1935 in Dallas, TX. H was a Co. L 35th Inf. 25th Inf Div. and was stationed at F Benning, GA.

When he retired in June of 1959, he held the rank o Captain.

His most memorable experience was Christmas Dinne below Henderson in 1942.

He has received the Silver Star, Bronze Star, Battle Fielc Commission, and the Combat Inf. Badge.

His wife's name is Lee, and they have five children and eleven grandchildren.

JAMES L. CURLEY, was born in Pawhuska, OK on Oct. 17, 1919. He enlisted in the Marines in Springfield MO. in June of 1940. He had Marine training at San Diego to North Island N.A.S. Joined Marine Aircraft Repair and Salvage, Sq. 1; USS *Walter Colton* to Espiritu Santo; USS *Titania* to Guadalcanal Feb. 14, 1943. Main job aircraft engine mechanic; also filed priority papers for CO.; made criminal investigations. Had malaria. Memories: Dayligh raid, nearly 100 Japanese planes, nearly all shot down. Watched sup periscope running parallel to our ship at 50 yds. Saw one of two torpedo near misses fired at us near Espiritu Santo. Arrived San Francisco May 18, 1944.

Left Marines as Master Technical Sgt. June 27, 1946, Quantico, VA. Was never outshot on qualification day with 30-06 rifle during 6 yrs. as a Marine. Was inventor of light armor plate used during WWII.

Has one son Arlie G.

Married Elwanda Bearden formerly FBI and school teacher. Resides Hutchinson, KS, since war.

THEODORE P. DAL DON, was born in Millbrae, CA June 29, 1916. Entered service Aug. 4, 1941. Completed basic training at Camp Roberts, CA. Then sent to Ft. Lewis, WA. Assigned to M Co., 161st Inf. After nine days left for San Francisco. Scheduled to sail for the Philippines, Nov. 28, 1941. Finally left December 16. Arrived Schofield Barracks on the 21. Next day moved to Hickam Field, assigned to Hq.

Co., 3rd Bn., 161st Inf. Then to Guadalcanal, New Georgia, New Zealand, then to New Caledonia where he was selected on the first rotation to return to the States.

Arriving in San Francisco May 4, 1944. Assigned as Cadre at Camp Roberts until his discharge with rank of sergeant Sept. 23, 1945.

Returned to the family business as a nurseryman in Millbrae. Married March 28, 1949, has a daughter and a grandson. His wife passed away after 35 years of marriage. He is now retired and is active in the American Legion and the Forty et Eight. Elected to serve as Grand Chef de Gare 1986-1987 in the Gran Voiture du Calif. In 1989 was appointed Aide de Camp Nationale to the Chef de Chemin de Fer.

C. W. DAVIS

JESSE E. DAVIS, was born in Abita Springs, LA on Oct. 6, 1922. Enlisted in the Marines June 15, 1939. Boot camp in San Diego, CA. After Sea School went aboard USS *Argonne* and then to Pearl Harbor where they were bombed on Dec. 7, 1941. From there to the carrier USS *Yorktown*, participated in Coral Sea battle and Midway with the 3rd Defense Bn., 1st and 2nd Marine Div. Then went to the Navy Yard at Portsmouth, NH and the Navy Yard at Washington, DC.

Went aboard USS *Independence* at Okinawa. Ended the war at the Navy Yard in Yokasuko, Japan, landing there Aug. 30, 1945 and leaving there Sept. 6, 1945.

After discharge went to work for the Louisiana State Police in Baton Rouge, LA in 1946. Met Lucia Covey, they were married Jan. 20, 1947. They are the parents of four children and four grandchildren.

Retired as a lieutenant with the Louisiana State Police in January of 1966 and immediately went into the heavy equipment business where he has been employed by the same company for 25 years.

FREDERICK G. DAVISON JR. (DAVE), was born in Pottsville, PA Aug. 15, 1924, moved to Bridgeton, NJ. Enlisted U.S. Marine Corps Dec. 18, 1941 but was not sworn in until Jan. 5, 1942 at the Philadelphia Navy Yard and shipped to Parris Island the same day.

After boot camp he was assigned to A Co., 1st Pioneer Bn., 1st Marine Div., and shipped to New Zealand.

He not only did the electrical work on the lights that were built in the machine shop of the American Legion but landed with them on Guadalcanal Aug. 7, 1942 and maintained them at night as well as working 48 hours straight unloading the ships on Red Beach. These lights had the same marking colors as did the banners used to mark for food, equipment, ammunition, etc., during the daylight hours. The lights were almost useless as the men working at night kept knocking them down.

Dave also made the landing on Cape Gloucester December 1943, and did a tour in Vietnam 1965-1966. Retired USMC Oct. 31, 1972.

Dave and his wife Ginger own and operate the Old Store in Pearce, AZ which is an old gold mine ghost town with a population at one time 3700 and now only 11.

The Old Store was placed on the National Register of Historic Places, Nov. 16, 1978.

HERBERT H. DEIGHTON, USMC SERGEANT, was born in Park City, UT Sept. 9, 1923.

Lived 1925 to 1936 in Los Angeles, CA 1936 to 1942 La Habra Heights, CA. Graduated Whittier California High School. Enlisted USMC July 3, 1942: attended boot camp in San Diego. Camp Elliott, shipped out to Wellington, New Zealand Oct. 20, 1942 with G Co. 6th Marines. Arrived Guadalcanal Jan. 4, 1943 on the USS *President Jackson.* Left on the same ship Feb. 19, 1943 for Wellington. Nov. 20, 1943, Tarawa with 2 Section, Headquarters Co. 2nd Bn. 6th Marines, Saipan June 15, 1944 with Hq.-2-6. Tinian July 26, 1944 with Hq.-2-6. Returned U.S. Jan. 4, 1945. Duty MCRD San Diego and North Island NAS, Feb. 12, 1945 to discharge July 2, 1946.

Three years college, then four years Northwestern University Dental School. Dental practice 1953 to 1989, Escondido, CA. Married 25 years and has two daughters. He is single now and enjoying every minute of single retirement.

DONALD D. DELAP AND OREIN G. DELAP

(Donald born on Feb. 20, 1920 at Crookston, MN, Orein born on July 24, 1921 at Crookston, MN.) They both enlisted in the Medical Detachment of the 164th Infantry Div., North Dakota National Guard at Bottineau, ND.

Donald D. Delap

They were inducted on Feb. 10, 1941. The regiment was a part of the 34th Red Bull Div. They trained at Camp Claiborne, LA and took part in the infamous "Loosiana" maneuvers. Immediately after pearl Harbor, they were detached from the 34th and moved to San Francisco and to Northwest States, where they were on guard duty on railroads and various strategic installations.

In February 1942, they sailed from San Francisco on the SS *President Coolidge* for Melbourne, Australia and from there to New Caledonia. On that island, they became a part of the newly formed American Division. Donald was promoted to technical sergeant and Orein was promoted to sergeant. They left New Caledonia in October and on the 13th, they landed on Guadalcanal to reinforce the 1st Marine Div. They immediately received their baptism of fire with air raids and naval shelling. They fought on that "bloody" island until the end of February 1943. They were sent to the Fiji Islands for rest, etc. Both Orein and Donald were hospitalized with malaria. Because of complications, Donald was evacuated to the States on April 30, 1943, and was hospitalized at an Army Hospital in Temple, TX. While there, Donald participated in War Bond drives by speaking at civic organizations in that area of Texas until his was discharged on Sept. 1, 1943. Orein continued to serve with the 164th in the battles for Bougainville and the Philippines. He was enroute home on a lousy, broken down liberty ship when the war ended. He was discharged Aug. 26, 1945 with the rank of staff sergeant.

Orein G. Delap

They both received the Combat Medics Badge, the Bronze Star, the Presidential Unit Citation (Navy), for having served with the 1st Div. Marines. They also received various other campaign medals.

Donald was also given a commendation for meritorious service during the Battle for Koli Point.

They are both proud to have served with the Marines under the command of Gen. Vandegrift. The Americal Division, commanded by Gen. Patch, and especially with the 164th Inf., under Col. Bryant E. Moore.

After discharge, Donald served 33 years in the US Customs Service, first on horse patrol, then in various capacities. Orein graduated from the University of North Dakota, taught school for a short time and held executive positions with the Parker Pen Company. He also spent 22 years with the Matthey Bishop Company in Malvern, PA.

Donald has been happily married to his wife, Eleanor, for 47 years. They have a lovely daughter, Kathleen, and a son-in-law, John Kennedy, and grandson, Jason. Orein has also had a happy marriage with his wife of 44 years, Marianne, and their two sons, David and Daniel. They are both retired, still great friends and live in Cape Coral, FL.

LESTER E. DELAVERGNE, was born April 23, 1922 in Belvidere, IL. Enlisted USMC December 1941 at Rockford, IL. Sworn in at Chicago, IL Jan. 26, 1942. Boot camp at San Diego. S/N 363262 Platoon 188.

After boot training, went to North Island, to San Francisco, left on USS *Wharton*, April 20 in a eight ship convoy to Pearl Harbor. Arrived April 28, went directly to EWA field and was assigned to Squad 232, one of oldest dive bombing squadrons in Marine Corp. known as "The Red Devil Squad." Departed Ewa, Hawaii Aug. 2, 1942, on *William Ward Burroughs*, under sealed orders, destination unknown, traveling alone with no escort, at maybe eight to ten knots. Crossed equator August 10 arriving at Tulagi, the ship ran aground. He was aboard when two Jap float planes came from other side of Florida Island and each plane dropped a bomb a near miss. He became very sick with dysentery, and lost 30 pounds. After a short stay on Tulagi, went over to Guadalcanal by Higgins Boat. VMSB-232 and VMF-223 were first planes to arrive on Guadalcanal, Aug. 20, 1942. Left canal October 22, arrived California November 18. Was given a 30 day furlough. He went to El Toro Jan. 1, 1943, his squadron got torpedo bombers trained until July 4, 1943. They went out again to South Pacific, Noumea, Efate, Espiritu Santos, Munda, Bougainville Campaigns. Then back to the States. On Sept. 15, 1944 on to

El Toro, El Centro, Mojave Desert, to Santa Barbara and was about to go out to Okinawa on converted carrier with TBF Squadron when the war ended.

Discharged Sept. 21, 1945 as technial sergeant. with 1st group of Marines under the point system at Miramar, CA.

Married Jackie F. Morgan, May 2, 1943 Fullerton, CA and is proud to be married to her still. He has one daughter and son-in-law and two grandchildren and one great-grandchild and had a son who died at birth.

Retired May 1, 1987 after 37 years with Sundstrand Corp. Aviation Div. He resides in Rockford, IL.

WILLIAM A. DERRYBERRY, was born in Columbia, TN on Aug. 4, 1918. Enlisted in the U.S. Navy on Oct. 10, 1940. After training at Norfolk, VA, was assigned to the USS *Moffett* (DD-362) doing convoy duty in the North Atlantic. Transferred to USS *Morris* (DD-417), flag staff of Destroyer Sqdn. TWO in May of 1941. Continued convoy duty to Newfoundland, Iceland, Greenland, England and into the Arctic Circle until the attack on Pearl Harbor. Transit to the Pacific through the Panama Canal and joined Task Forces 16 and 17 (USS *Lexington* and USS *Yorktown*). Lost the USS *Lexington* in the Coral Sea Battle in May 1942, and the USS *Yorktown* in the Midway Battle in June 1942. Transferred to the USS *Trevor* (DMS-16), a high speed mine sweeper in July 1942. On Aug. 7, 1942 swept Sealark Channel for the invasion of Guadalcanal, Tulagi and other islands in the Solomons area.

After the Kula Gulf Battle in July 1943, cut a deck of cards for transfer to new construction in September 1943. Transferred to Miami, FL to Sub Chaser Training Center, met and married A WAVE in November 1945. Was then assigned to new construction and put a fleet tug, USS *Salinan* (ATF-161) in commission in 1945.

Discharged in Charleston, SC on Dec. 6, 1946, as a yeoman first class.

Retired from Union Carbide Corp. with 40 years service. (Military service counted as company retirement time).

CARL M. DE VERE, SR. (BUD), born in St. Peter, MN, Aug. 2, 1923. Enlisted in the Marine Corps June 6, 1942.

After eight weeks at San Diego, a week at Camp Elliott and North Island, he joined VMSB-141, a new dive bomber squadron and sailed for Espirtu Santos and final forming of the unit. He arrived at Guadalcanal on Oct. 13, 1942, "The Night the World Blew Up."

He was the first control tower operator on Henderson Field. After 223 Naval shellings, artillery shellings, aerial bombings, and multiple strafings, he was rotated to Espiritu Santos where he joined SCAT as chief operations clerk. As SCAT offices opened in the central Solomons to Bougainville, he trained enlisted clerks to man the new stations.

Stateside he married Estelle Saunders, April 1944. Four children, Carl Jr., Dani Lee, Craig and Mark. Korean service in the 50s, he retired July 1968. Spent 30 years as illustrator/ museum designer for the Corps, retired again in December 1988.

ELWIN H. DEWEY, was born in Hamilton, NY. Enlisted in USMCR Dec. 15, 1941 and attended basic training at Parris Island, radio operator at Quantico, and communications at San Diego. Foreign service areas were New Zealand, Solomon Islands, Australia, Goodenough, New Guinea,

New Britain, Pavuvu, Peleliu, Hawaii, and Sasebo, Japan. During the Guadalcanal campaign was assigned to H & S Btry., 1st Special Weapons Bn., 1st Marine Div. In 1945 was assigned to the 5th Marine Div. and was discharged Nov. 15, 1945.

Returned to Melbourne, Australia July 1946 and married Betty as planned since the Ballarat Campaign. Work for Commonwealth Aircraft and later joined Merchant Navy (oil tanker) to work way back to New Yori.

In 1951 became career Civil Service working at Rome, Dayton, and Newark Air Force Base where retired and currently operate a jewelry and lapidary shop.

Organizational interests are NARFE, National Waco Airplane Club, Rock & Mineral Society, Archaeology Society, Air Force Association, Union of Concerned Scientists, World Federalists, and Planetary Society.

Revisited Auckland, Melbourne, Ballarat (old tent camp area in Victoria Park), Geelong, Canberra, and Sydney during 1989.

SALVATORE DICESARE, was born in Rochester, NY on Nov. 8, 1917. Enlisted in the USMC on Oct. 10, 1939. Attended boot camp at Parris Island, SC. After boot camp, he was stationed at Ft. Mifflin NAD near Philadelphia, PA. He transferred to the Fleet Marine Force and went to Guantanamo Bay, Cuba in the 1st Marine Brigade, E Co., 2nd Bn., 5th Regt. After a few months in Cuba, he went back to Quantico, VA. Around July 1941, the 1st Marine Brigade went to New River, NC which was to be their new base. They then were called the 1st Marine Div.

When Pearl Harbor was attacked on December 7, 1941, the 1st Div. went through intensive training at New River and at Chesapeak Bay, VA. Then in May 1942, they boarded a troop ship at Norfolk, VA and rode through the Panama Canal to the Pacific Ocean, heading for Wellington, NZ, arriving there about the middle of June 1942. After more training, they were on their way to Guadalcanal, Solomon Isles. They left Dec. 9, 1942, for Australia. After getting replacements and training, the Division left for Cape Gloucester. He was temporarily assigned to M.P. duty to 1st Marine Div. Brigade. He rejoined A-1-5 in Pavuru, Russell Isles.

After more training and replacements, they landed on Peleliu, on the Palau Isles. After that campaign, he returned to San Diego, CA. When he was in Australia, he re-enlisted for two more years.

While he was stationed in New River, he met a girl, Emily L. Cox, of Winterville, NC. They were engaged before he left the U.S. They were married Jan. 20, 1945. They lived in Beaufort, SC while he finished his re-enlistment at Parris Island, returning to make their home in Rochester, NY.

He was appointed to the Rochester Fire Department, serving 32 years, and retired at age 62. On Jan. 20, 1992, they will have celebrated 47 years of married life. They had three children; two boys and one girl, all married. So far, they have two grandsons and their daughter was expecting another child in February of 1992. They have been vacationing in North Carolina just about every year since they were married.

He is a Life Member of the 1st Marine Division Association, Guadalcanal Campaign Veterans, and the Cooper Marine Post 603 of the American Legion.

JOHN J. DIPIPPO, was born in Torrington, CT Dec. 6, 1916. Drafted March 13, 1941 sent to Camp Devens. Then to Camp Wheeler, Macon, GA for basic training after basic sent to Co. L, 102nd Inf. at Camp Blanding, FL. This was a hometown National Guard Unit. In the summer of 1941 they took part in the Louisiana Manuevers. Then back to Camp Blanding in time for maneuvers in November 1941 up to North and South Carolina. Returned back to Blanding Dec. 1, 1941. Left the last week in January 1942 across country to San Francisco. Spent a few days at the Cow Palace. Boarded the USS *President Taylor* for their boat trip Feb. 1, 1942. Arriving at Canton Island Friday Feb. 13, 1942. Spent five months there, then sent to Oahu as replacement Co. H, 161st Inf. After manning a beach position for a couple of months received jungle and amphibious training. Left on the Republic and arrived at canal on December 30, taking part in final drive up to Cape Esperance. After continuing attacks of malaria evacuated to New Caledonia Naval Hospital Mob. #5.

Returned to States via San Francisco Letterman General Hospital then to O'Reilly General Hospital in Springfield, MO. Then sent to duty Camp Croft, SC. Infantry Replacement Training Center March 1944.

Awards: Combat Infantry Badge, Bronze Star Medal, Good Conduct Medal, National Defense Medal, and Asiatic-Pacific Campaign Medal.

Discharged June 15, 1945 as a technical sergeant.

WILLIAM F. DOLAN (BILL), was born Stoneham, MA Feb. 20, 1916. Drafted into Co. F, 182nd Inf. Regt., Yankee (26th) Div., March 20, 1941 at Camp Edwards, MA. On Jan. 23, 1942 the 182nd was withdrawn from the Yankee Div. and sailed from the Brooklyn, NY Army Based on the USS *Santa Elena* headed for the Panama Canal and the Southwest Pacific. Landed in Melbourne, Australia on March 3, 1942. Billeted in the home of two wonderful Aussies, Alan and Beth Robinson in Ballarat, Australia for a short time and then sailed (USS *Argentina*) to New Caledonia. There they trained and did outpost duty for eight months. The 182nd, 132nd and 164th Infantrys now became the Americal Division. Company F landed on Guadalcanal on Nov. 12, 1942. Saw action on the canal until Island was secured.

Married to Margaret (Midge); they have one daughter, Geri; one son, Tim; and two grandchildren, Paul and Kim. He is retired from U.S. Postal Service after 40 years of service.

CHARLES E. DRAPER, was born Oct. 3, 1924 in Fairmount, IN. Enlisted in Navy Dec. 8, 1941. Went through Great Lakes NTS like "exlax" and was aboard the USS *Betelgeuse* (AKA-11) on Jan. 2, 1942.

Went to Ireland and Scotland before heading for the South Pacific, took the Army to Tonga that later was on Guadalcanal. Went to Pearl Harbor and picked up a bunch of 1st Marines and dumped them off on Guadalcanal on Sept. 7, 1942 at 4:30 a.m. Made countless trips in and out until Dec. 25, 1942 and headed back to the States. Back to the Atlantic, took part in the invasion of Sicilia and Southern France. All this time on the *Betelgeuse*. Left the "Goose" Jan. 27, 1944 to the Panama Canal. Went on to Japan after the war and got home for good Nov. 21, 1945.

Married to a 1939 classmate Ada Druck on November 5, and they have one son, a daughter and four grandchildren. Their son and son-in-law were both in the Navy in Vietnam and both got home safely.

Has been in the Guadalcanal Campaign Veterans since 1975 and has only missed one national reunion since 1977. His wife and he both retired from General Motors and their son now works for them. His son in law is a "Paws" VP better known as "Garfield" and his brother is Jim Davis.

DAVE DRISCOLL, was born on Oct. 31, 1925 in Boston, MA. Joined the Navy exactly one month before Pearl Harbor was bombed. His father told him there was a war coming. He was put aboard the USS *Atlanta* (CL-51) at Brooklyn. He says that people threw money at them. He was attached to the 3rd Div. During the battle of Guadalcanal (3rd Savo) on Nov. 13, 1942, he had just turned 18 years old and said many "Our Fathers and Hail Mary's" as the *Atlanta* was bombarded by Japanese and "friendly fire". Captain Jenkins called for a scuttling party after all night in water.

Married to Carmen MacLaughlin of Boston, MA, and has four sons. One has joined the Navy and another son who was in the Marines died in 1988. He is retired from the Boston Police Detectives after 33 years service.

JAMES F. DRUGGAN (JIM), was born Feb. 17, 1924 W. Broad St. Columbus, OH. Enlisted U.S. Navy October 1941 USNRS Cincinnati, OH. NTS Great Lakes, IL, December 1941 R. S. Bremerton, WA. By troop train with window blinds pulled down. USS *Zeilin* (AP-9) later retagged (APA-3). While still in dry dock, being fitted for assault transport. Trained Marines and their crew for amphibian landings on West Coast until partly skilled at landing men and equipment on the beach. August 7,8,9, 1942 Tulagai Solomon Island's. They made the first American offensive. October 1942 transferred to Naval base Cactus Lunga Boat Pool Guadalcanal with Higgins Boat, there he served as troop transfer, ship unloading, and rescue and recovery until some time after Thanksgiving November 1942. Transferred by hospital cargo plane to base hospital #2, Naval Base Roses Espirito Santos, New Hebrides. Naval Base, Iriki, New Hebrides, USS *Talamanca* (CUB-13) New Caledonia, Fleet Air Command South Pacific. Boat Cox for Admiral Marc Mitscher Ilee Nue, New Caledonia. Dates are lost in his memory. From October 1942 to October 1943 USS Perida, Treasure Island, San Francisco R. S. May 1943, USNTS Great Lakes, IL June 1, 1943 USNH Great Lakes, IL until October 1943 transfer to U.S. Naval Air Facility Columbus, OH for duration on limited service, there he became a shore patrol. His home town, Columbus, OH he had some good duty, master at arms, and prisoner runner for 9th Naval District.

Discharged boatswain mate second class September 1945. Disability 50% pension.

Retired tool and die maker, machinist after 40 years. He now plays golf with wife Annie of 45 years, and travels to ship reunions. Has one daughter, one son and five grandchildren, and one great-granddaughter.

HAROLD L. DUBICK, S/Sgt. was born Oct. 4, 1919, Cleveland, OH. Inducted Feb. 8, 1941, U.S. Army.

Trained at Camp Shelby, MS with Co., M, 147th Inf., 37th Div. Shipped overseas on *American Legion* April 1942, Landed Tongatabu in May. Sent to Guadalcanal November 1942, then in May 1943, to British Samoa. Later to New Caledonia and Emirau. Back to New Caledonia where was hospitalized and sent back to States in November 1944. Spent time in Moore General Hospital, NC, until transferred to Ft. Sheridan, IL for discharge Aug. 22, 1945.

Most memorable experiences - ride on LCT at night around the canal from Koli Point to Mission at Beaufort Bay during violent storm in raging sea! Also the time spent with Padre de Klerk, the Catholic Missionary at Beaufort Bay.

Retired 1980 from General Motors as tool and die superintendent after 42 years service.

Married May Lou Bucanelly 1955. Five children - Diane, Joan, Jill, Dan and Mike. Has resided in Pittsburgh, PA since 1950.

IRVINE L. DUNNINGTON (BUD), was born on Aug. 8, 1920 Farimont West VA. Enlisted USMC January 1942, from Lancaster, OH. After Parris Island boot camp assigned to M-3-5 1st Marine Div. New River, NC. May 1942 sailed from Norfolk aboard USS *Wakefield* arriving Wellington, New Zealand June. Boarded USS *Fuller* and landed Guadalcanal Aug. 7, 1941. Four months later, 40 lbs. lighter and ranks sadly depleted left the canal for Brisbane, Australia. Brief hospital stints at Melbourne and Adelaide. June 1943 surveyed Stateside with malaria. Assigned to guard detachment MCAS El Toro, CA. May 1945 assigned to Marine detachment USS *Santa Fe* (CL-60). Battle stations quad forties and was at Okinawa at wars end. *Santa Fe* accepted surrender terms from Japanese at Sasebo, Japan.

Married to former Bette Rock, has six children, twelve grandchildren. Retired from Anchor Hocking Lancaster, OH in 1983. Now enjoying retirement in Mesa, AZ.

JOHN DYER, was born March 29, 1924 Albany, NY. Was on board USS *Sangamon* (VGS-26). Stationed at Henderson Field and Guadalcanal.

Remembers invasion French Morocco Nov. 8, 1942. Bombed Port Lyautey, Rabat, Casablanca from Sangamon. Turned around and arrived Solomons area January 1943.

Bombed Monda, Bougainville from Henderson aboard SBD's and TBF's.

Awards: Naval commendation Medal, Presidential Unit Citation.

Married to Elaine Courts. Has eight children and 11 grandchildren.

Retired from Milliken and Company Textile Manufacturers. Enjoys doing hospital volunteer work.

CHARLES EBERSOLE, was born Aug. 9, 1919 in Conoy Township, Lancaster County, PA. He graduated from Bainbridge High School, in 1936 and Elizabethtown High School, in 1937 both in Pennsylvania. He enlisted in the U.S. Navy in April of 1941; Navy Trade School, Pensacola, FL., in August, 1941. Following Pearl Harbor, PBY Squadron airlifting military and dependents from Pacific to San Diego, CA. area.

Received two months Marine Combat Infantry Training; immediately assigned to South Pacific. Waded ashore on beaches of Guadalcanal. After Guadalcanal was secured, served in Navy's first Land Plane Unit (LPU-1), which was a squadron of B24's. Served 37 months in Pacific. Squadron changed from LPU to VB-101 to FAPS-1 (a special Fleet Air Photographic Squadron). Awarded the Bronze Stars and Battle Stars for various Island Campaigns. Also awarded Presidential Citation for a Guadalcanal incident.

Spent 24 years in Navy. Additional duties in Caribbean, Mediterranean, North Atlantic, Guantanamo Bay, Arctic Circle and various shore bases. Honorably discharged from VT-25 in Beeville, TX with the rank of AMHCS. Married Brady Lois Smith of Hollandtown, near Jay, FL in June, 1942. Had three children, two boys and a girl, only one of which is living: Michael J. Ebersole, a Pilot/Park Ranger with the National Park Service in Grand Canyon AZ. Grandchildren reside in Logan, Utah.

After Navy retirement, Chuck Ebersole walked the entire length (2,051 miles) of the Appalachian Trail twice. Once with older son John, non-stop from Georgia to Maine in 1964; 2nd time with younger son Mike in 1965 and 1966.

Entered Utah State University in January, 1965. Earned Bachelor of Science degree in two years and two quarters. Summer work in Idaho with U.S. Forest Service and back to university in winter. Earned a Master of Fine Arts degree in 1969. Finished requirements for doctoral degree in Ecology. Taught General Ecology and Color Photography at Utah State.

Permanent appointment with U.S. Forest Service in Stanley, Idaho in Sawtooth National Recreation Area. Retired from USFS in 1985; managed a Western Ranch with his wife for 11 years. He presently resides in Ada County, Boise, Idaho. Member of Fleet Reserve and Guadalcanal Veterans Organizations. Hobbies include hunting, fishing, photography, writing, gardening, and traveling.

EDWARD A. ELDRIDGE, Edward started out on the USS *Day Star* on his was to the Pacific Zone and the Guadalcanal.

He served on the 46th Pine F. Henderson Navy General Admiral Commander 46th SeaBee.

LEWIS N. EPPIHIMER, was born in West Chester, PA on March 14, 1926 and enlisted in the USMC at Philadelphia on Dec. 8, 1941 at the age of 15.

He trained at Parris Island and was assigned to F-2-7-New River, NC as company runner. Left Norfolk on April 7, 1942 for British Samoa. He spent 31 days on the *Heywood*.

Landed on Guadalcanal Sept. 18, 1942, participated in three battles, quite exciting for a 16 year old kid. His most memorable event was during a battle on October 25 and 26. He lobbed two grenades on a Japanese machine gun directly above him. The next morning, taking dog tags to Bn. Headquarters on beach, encountered three Japs on trail, could have won a Gold that day.

Left canal on Feb. 5, 1943 - six men left in 1st Plt. Attended Scout - Sniper School in August. Sent Stateside, due to yellow jaundice, encephalitis, and malaria.

Received medical discharge on Oct. 25, 1945 at Camp LeJeune.

Married Ruth Speier in 1944 and they have two daughters. He has been Master of the Masonic Blue Lodge twice. He is active in investing and charity work for the Lodge.

CARL W. ERMEL,

was born Dec. 7, 1919 and enlisted in the Marine Corps in August of 1940. After training at Parris Island, SC, he was assigned to Guantanamo Bay, Cuba for 1 1/2 years. Returned to the States and was stationed at Parris Island; New River, NC; Quantico, VA; then back to New River and on to San Francisco in June 1942 where he boarded a ship for New Zealand and then on to Guadalcanal in early August.

His most memorable experience was when they arrived, he was assigned to help load ammunition onto trucks. As trucks were loaded and put on Higgins Boats, they proceeded to shore. When the last truck was loaded and in the Higgins Boat, the Captain gave him a map and showed him where to deliver it. They proceeded to shore and found there was no one on the beach to hinder them. However, since it was now very dark, they unloaded the truck, hid the ammunition, and spent the night on the beach. Early in the morning, a party of Japanese came through but they were able to stay out of sight. When the enemy were gone, the truck was reloaded and they proceeded to the air field.

He was evacuated to Australia in January of 1943 and returned to the States in August 1943 where he was reassigned to Camp LeJeune and Panama.

He was discharged in February of 1945 at New Orleans, LA. He married Lorraine Edelen in 1942. They have five children and have resided in Huntington Beach, CA the past 34 years.

ROBERT J. EVANS, SR.,

was born in Bradshaw, WVA. on June 3, 1920. He enlisted in the USMC in January of 1940. Marine Corp travels include, Parris Island, Quantico, Indian Town Gap, Culebra, Cuba, Ft. Belvoir, New River, New Zealand, Guadalcanal, Australia, Good Enough Island, New Guinea, Cape Gloucester, Pavuvu, Court House Bay, LeJeune, Pendleton, Hawaii, Tinian, Saipan, Guam, Okinawa, Tientsen, Shanghai, Oak Knoll, Quantico. Also Stationed at Orlando FL., as assistant I and I HQ. 8th MCRRD New Orleans. Jacksonville, FL., Air Reserve.

Evans assignments included - rifleman, machine gunner, engineer, pioneer, MC Schools and VMF 111 and 144 as administration officer. CAC officer during Korean Conflict, reverted from WO USMC to WO USMCR and went on to retirement as a CWO-4 USMCR.

Living in Arkansas and in the process of establishing

a museum of Evans Family in which Marine Corps exhibits will form a part.

Had two sons, one USMC and one Air Force, two daughters, one RN, one CPA living in Phoenix area.

EDWARD FABER,

was born in Chicago, IL, Feb. 17, 1911. Learned trade in welding shop 1931 through 1936. Inspected heavy construction which entailed inspection of welds, rivets, re-bars and qualifying welders 1937 into 1941. Joined Iron Workers in 1941 specializing in welding. Joined the Navy CB's in June of 1942. Called to active duty Aug. 21, 1942 and started boots at Camp Allen, Norfolk, VA where the 26th Bn. was formed. After several camps they shipped to New Caledonia and then Guadalcanal where they landed Dec. 26, 1942. Here their Battalion motto "Can Do!" was born, he's sure the first for the CB's. Of his many duties, welding on the pipe lines was his main job. The 26th Battalion left the Canal on Dec. 11, 1943 and landed in San Francisco Dec. 31, 1943 and was based at Camp Parks, CA.

At Camp Parks in September 1944, he entered a new battalion being formed, the 124th N.C.B. They shipped out to Adak in the Aleutians where he was in charge of the welding, radiator repair and blacksmith shop at N.O.B. He returned to the States in December 1945 where he was discharged Dec. 16, 1945 at Great Lakes.

He returned to his civilian job as an Ironworker in 1946. He also returned to his old stomping grounds at the Aragon Ballroom and met his wife, Bernice Kolbe, marrying in July 1947. They have a daughter Carole Sachen and a grandson Tommy born in 1981. Retired from the Ironworkers in 1978 and have resided in the Western Chicago suburb of North Riverside, IL for 33 years.

DAVID FALB,

was born in New York City on Feb. 8, 1922. He was in the service from Aug. 22, 1940 to April 9, 1944. He was with the 5th Regt. 1st Div. F.M.F. H&S Co. Eng. 2A-1-17 Eng. He was stationed at Guantanamo Bay, Cuba from Sept. 30, 1940 to April 4, 1941 and Guadalcanal from Aug. 7, 1942 to Dec. 15, 1942.

His most memorable experience was serving with the 1st Marine on Guadalcanal. From the day he enlisted to the day of discharge were the best days of his life.

He has been married to his wife for 45 years and they

have one son, two granddaughters, and two great granddaughters.

EDWARD CAMPBELL FARMER, JR.,

was born in Muskegon, MI on Aug. 20, 1918 and enlisted in the 2nd Bn., USMCR, in 1939. He was commissioned second lieutenant, in 1942. On Aug. 7, 1942, he landed on Red Beach, Guadalcanal, with HQ-3-5, 1st Marine Div., from USS *Fuller*.

Battalion moved West from ILU, crossing Airfield to KUKUM. Transferred to Captain Spurlock's L-3-5 as platoon leader, 3rd Platoon. 1,000 yards W of KUKUM and 200 from L Hq., set up platoon defensive position from beach across

coconut grove up ridge to right flank of K Company Platoo (Lt. Davies). Patrolled daily to Matanikau and beyond. Hit b OKA force September 14 . Wounded in action as the successfully repelled attack. Evacuated by air September 1 to U.S. Naval Mobile Hospital, EFATE', New Hebride Achieved the rank of Captain.

Graduated Northwestern University Law School, J.D 1951.

Married Kim Harrington, 1955. They have four childre District Judge (Michigan) 1969 to date. Member VFW, DAV Guadalcanal Campaign Veterans.

ARCHIE J. FERGUSON,

was born on April 8, 1919 i Seattle, WA. He joined the U.S. Navy on June 6, 1940. H served on the USS *Yorktown* (CV-5), *Wasp* (CV-7), *Range* (CV-4), *Norfolk* NAS, *Saratoga* (CV-3), Guadalcanal, Ba bers Pt., Palmyra Island. His rank was AOM 1/C.

His most memorable experiences were at North Atlanti Patrol, *Yorktown* CV-5, *Ranger* CV-4, & *Wasp* CV-7. Ra into boot camp in VB-6 along with Major Galer o October 16th at Henderson. Lived next door to him in Seattle Guadalcanal on Henderson Sept. 11, 1942 to Oct. 16, 1942.

He received a defense award with A. Presidential Uni Citation from Guadalcanal.

JOHN D. FERGUSON,

was born July 31, 1918 in Wash ington, D.C. and enlisted in the U.S. Navy on Nov. 17, 1936 i Wilmington, NC. Assigned to USS *Atlanta* (CL-51) on Sept. 15, 1941 as Ensign. *Atlanta* sank on Nov. 13, 1942; two weeks on Guadalcanal; to MO135 Noumea, New Caledonia; to USA, assigned to USS *Mobile*, thence to USS *Miami*. Commissioned ensign and assigned as staff engineering officer for the group of LCI's. Stationed aboard LCI 420.

Seven Battle Stars, President Unit Citation. Reverted to CEM & was discharged on August 25, 1945.

Now retired, registered professional engineer in the Electrical Discipline in the State of Florida.

He is married to his wife, Harriet and they have two children, six grandchildren, and six great grandchildren.

WALTER FINN,

was born Aug. 11, 1917 in New York City. Enlisted in the Navy right after Pearl Harbor. Landed on Guadalcanal, August 1942 a Phm, Cub 1, Lunga Point. After six months of combat, malaria and wounded; spent one year at (Mob Hospital 4) in Aukland, New Zealand.

He returned to the Marine Corps base, San Diego at the end of WWII and was offered a commission but chose the civilian challenge. Walter started selling vacuums knocking on doors. In 1958, he resigned from Hub Vacuum as vice-president to go on his own. Walter founded a giant sales organization, Bed City, which is today the largest bedding chain with 28 stores on the East Coast; annual sales $11,000,000.

1981, Walter was elected president of National Associa-tion of Sleep Merchants. 1983, Leukemia Society of America honored Walter Finn for his contributions and named him a "Corporate Star". 1984, elected board member of the Better Business Bureau. 1986, Walter sold his business, and semi-retired. In November 1986, Walter was appointed by the Office of the Mayor of the City of New York as representative of Corporate Resources.

In May 1987, Mayor Edward Koch honored Walter Finn in the gardens of Gracie Mansion for his many contributions and efforts to the homeless and clothing bank under New York City's Voluntary Action Program. "Walter will offer his services as an arbitrator for the New York Stock Exchange Wall Street, New York, NY." 1991 Walter is now retired and resides with his wife Gertrude in New York City, Fort Lauder-dale, FL and Nice, France.

ARTHUR FISCHER, was born in Jeannerette, LA, on Jan. 16, 1918. He enlisted for one year in the U.S. Army and was stationed at Fort Dix, NJ. He enlisted in the U.S. Navy, in January of 1942 at Newport RI. He was assigned to the USS *Duncan* (DD-485), Brooklyn Navy Yard.

His most memorable event was a ship destroyed in the battle of Cape Esperance on Oct. 11 and 12, 1942. Scuttled next morning. Battle station #2 gun mount-trainer. Received direct hits in #2 Handling Room. Ordered to abandon ship. Last to leave foscle after kapock jacket burst into flames. Spent 14-18 hours floundering and swimming towards Savo Island. Rescued by two natives, in dugout canoe, from Savo as he was being swept by the Island.

Eventually taken from island and transferred to the USS *McCalla*, then to the USS *Solace* to New Zealand. Two months in MOB 4 Hospital, Auckland. Remained in New Zealand until August of 1944.

Married New Zealander, Alison Peter in 1946. They have two sons, Ross Captain (retired) carrier pilot and Ian, geologist. They reside in Brielle, NJ.

AUTHUR FISH, JR., born May 14, 1921 in Gillingham, WI and enlisted in the USMC on Aug. 3, 1942. Attended boot camp at San Diego with Platoon 628. Arrived New Zealand in November of 1942 with 2nd Marine Div.

Guadalcanal Jan. 4, 1943. Back to New Zealand after battle. Stationed at Camp Tarawa Hawaii after Tarawa Battle. Returned to Camp LeJeune, NC in March of 1944 and joined 13th AAA Bn. In January of 1945, was sent to Klamath Falls, OR with malaria. After V.E. Day, did guard duty at the Marine Supply Depot in San Francisco and was discharged from there on Nov. 2, 1945.

Married Betty Lash from Ferndale, MI in 1947, and they have one daughter.

Was a Florida park ranger in Hillsborough River State Park from 1948 - 1959. Located seven miles from the Hills, where his home has been for 43 years. He owned and operated Art's Tree Service from 1959 - 1986 in the Hills.

Retired in 1986 due to his wife's health. Betty passed away in January of 1990. Has been active supporting high school sports.

JACK FOLMER, born March 23, 1917 in St. Charles, MO. Joined 123rd F.A., Illinois National Guard January 1941. Unit Federalized and sent to Camp Forrest, Tullahoma, TN in March 1941. Left Brooklyn, NY in January 1942 for Australia, then to New Caledonia. Became member of HQ Btry., 247th F.A. Bn., Americal Div., when it was formed. Later served in Guadalcanal, Bougainville, Leyte, and Cebu.

Discharged July 6, 1945, and returned to Alton, IL.

Married wife, Virginia in 1951. They have three sons, one daughter, and three granddaughters, Laura, Krista, and Anny. Was a professional photographer until retirement in 1982. Since then have had time to renew contact with quite a few old buddies from the 247th.

ROY E. FORS, was born in Chicago, IL July 25, 1915. Enlisted in the Illinois Naval Militia on April 9, 1935. Division federalized into active service, November 1940. Served aboard the USS *George F. Elliot* (AP-11) in North Atlantic duty, and, until she was sunk Aug. 8, 1942 at Guadalcanal. Transferred to the USS *Zeilin* (APA-3) for further activity at Guadalcanal until she was badly damaged on Armistice Day, Nov. 11, 1942. *Zeilin* sent back to Terminal Island for major repairs.

Remained aboard *Zeilin* for the Attu, Kiska, Tarawa, and Kwajalein landings. Promoted to Warrant Bos'n January 1944. While at Guadalcanal, April 1944, was transferred back to the States and assigned to harbor defense training. Took part in the Iwo Jima invasion and remained there until the war ended. Awarded eight Pacific Battle Stars and two Naval Unit Commendations.

Graduated with a B.A. degree from U.S.C., then married his wife, Derith and has one son, Greig. Now residing in San Francisco. Remained associated with the Navy until July 1975 attaining the permanent rank of CWO-4 USNR.

A. C. FOX, was born Sept. 12, 1911 at Hawaii, T.H.. He joined the Naval Reserve in 1932 as radioman third class. Commissioned ensign in 1935 at the Naval Reserve. In San Francisco, joined the Merchant Marines and began active duty. In April 1942, he was at the Naval Academy for a post graduate course. Served aboard the USS *Boise* (CL-47) for two years.

Was in Guadalcanal Oct. 11-12, 1943 also at CapeEsperance and Iwo Jima while aboard the USS *Saratoga* (CV-3). Then transferred to the Naval Supply Depot at Oakland as communications officer.

Retired in 1972 out of the Naval Reserve. Was in the Reserve for 40 years. Went into Civil Service for two years, retired in 1968.

Married Edna Fox Dec. 4, 1939. They have no children. He resides in Lake of the Pines, CA. He is a "plank owner" of the Naval Memorial.

WILLIAM J. FOX, was born in Trenton NJ on Dec. 23, 1897. Enlisted in Army 1919, buckprivate World War I. Switched services commissioned first lieutenant USMCR Aviation.

County engineer, and Director Regional Commission Los Angeles County, 1926-1955. Recalled to active duty Oct. 1, 1940. C.O. Fighting Squadron 4, USMCR, Long Beach Naval Aviation Base - to 2nd Marine Aircraft Wing, San Diego Naval Air Station. (Lt. Col. Fox selected sites and designed plans Five Marine Corps Air Stations, West Coast 1942). Commanding officer, Henderson Field, Guadalcanal 1942-43. C.O. Marine Air Station El Toro, 1943-44. Strike coordinator, 4th Marine Aircraft Wing 1945, (participated attacks Wotje, Mille, Maloelap and Jaluit, Marshall-Gilbert Islands). CO, MAG-25 Bougainville and Philippine Islands 1945.

Retired Dec. 1, 1946. Brigadier General Oct. 27, 1948. Legion of Merit with Combat "V".

Awards: Distinguished Flying Cross, (5) Air Medals, Purple Heart, Presidential Unit Citation, World War I Victory Medal, World War II Victory Medal, Philippine Liberation Medal, Asiatic Campaign Medal with five Bronze Stars.

He trained horses in Mexico 1949 - 1981. Home Fillmore, CA.

EUGENE J. FULLER, born in rural McHenry, IL on June 4, 1924. Enlisted in Marine Corps Jan. 26, 1942 in Chicago, went to San Diego for boot camp with Platoon #188. Then was stationed at Camp Elliot (2-2-D).

He went aboard the *President Jackson* on June 1, 1942, left the States on July 1 and landed at Florida Island 7:40 a.m. on Aug. 7, 1942. At this time he was listed as M.I.A. He was on shore at Tulagi and then Guadalcanal until the end of January 1943. He was then sent to New Zealand, where he became ill and returned to the States. After hospitalization, he was in Okinawa with the 5th Marines, then on to China. Returned to the U.S. and was discharged on Feb. 14, 1946.

He married Carol Norton on Jan. 18, 1947. They have seven children and ten grandchildren and have resided in Woodstock since their marriage. He was in construction work, then building inspector for the City of Woodstock, retiring in 1987.

LUIE R. FULLER, was born Feb. 18, 1924, in Atlanta, GA. Enlisted in the Navy in August of 1941. He was a aviation metalsmith third class assigned to Cub One detachment Aug. 15, 1942 to Nov. 5, 1942 on Guadalcanal.

Worked with the Aviation Ordnance crew on Henderson Field. Then Nov. 5, 1942 to Jan. 6, 1943 at Tulagi working on PT boats and fueling transient seaplanes in the harbor.

He retired from the Navy in 1961 as a senior chief aviation structural mechanic.

Went to work for the Naval Aviation Depot at Jacksonville, FL, in 1961 retiring after 29 years civil service as a aircraft progressman October 1990.

Married Myrtice Hair August 1956 and they have one son. They reside in Jacksonville, FL.

FRANK J. GADO, was born in Manchester, CT, May 12, 1917. Enlisted in the Navy, April 1936. After training at Newport, RI, attended Woodworker's School in Norfolk, VA. He was assigned to USS *Vincennes*, February 1937 and discharged April 1940.

He re-enlisted March 1941, and entered active duty May

1941. He was assigned to USS *American Legion* (APA-17) and took part in first landing at Guadalcanal, Aug. 7, 1942 and also Bougainville.

He was responsible for hull repair of the ship's 35 landing craft and for C&R damage control bill. He received a citation from Admiral Halsey for performance during a landing operation where a landing craft capsized in New Zealand.

He was discharged chief carpenter's mate, September 1945, Camp Elliott, CA.

He married Helen Meyer in 1944 and has two daughters, Susan and Nancy. He owned and operated San Leandro Pattern Works for 21 years and now resides in Fremont, CA.

ROBERT E. GALER, born Seattle, WA Oct. 23, 1913. Graduate University of Washington, in 1935. Joined from Navy ROTC, the Marines - Pfc. or aviation cadet June 1, 1935. Assigned *Pensacola* for flight training, commissioned 1937 as second lieutenant and received wings of Gold. Various aviation assignments - Fighter Squadron initally at Quantico, VA. 1937 - 1938, Scouting Squad Virgin Islands 1938 -1940. Then Fighting Squad at San Diego, Sq. transferred to Ewa, Hawaii for Pearl Harbor.

Participated in WWII operations at Pearl Harbor, Guadalcanal, Palau, Iwo Jima, Lingayen Gulf, Okinawa. Participated in Korea. Graduated during service from Marine Basic School, Army Command and Staff, Armed Forces Staff College, Air Command and Staff and masters degree from George Washington University.

Received MOH as fighter squad commander at Guadalcanal - citation - reads "Shot down 11 1/2 enemy aircraft in 29 days". Various assignments as group commander in Korea, staff of commander Air Craft Pacific, Staff of 1st Marine Air Wing and final assignment as Direct Guided Missile Division - Buffer.

ALBERT N. GARBARINO, was born in Flushing, Long Island, NY on November 16, 1917. His father served as a Marine, under the command of Admiral George Dewey in the Battle of Manila Bay, in 1898. Albert attended Flushing High School, and graduated from Long Island City Trade School. He enlisted in the Marine Corps on March 5, 1941.

After recruit training at Parris Island, SC, he transferred to the Lighter than Air School, Lakehurst, NJ, where he qualified as a parachutist. He served in the Asiatic-Pacific, attached to the First Marine Parachute Bn., First Parachute Regt., First Marine Div. He was wounded in combat on Guadalcanal, on the Island of Gavutu, British Solomon Islands on Aug. 7, 1942.

He received the Purple Heart, and the Presidential Unit Citation. He was honorably discharged from the Marine Corps on Nov. 13, 1945.

After discharge he attended evening college in San Diego, CA. He worked for Civil Service as a production control resource center requisitioner in conjunction with the Uniform Automated Data Processing System. After 30 years Civil Service, he retired.

He is married to Leora Law of Lone Wolf, OK. He is stepfather of four sons, two of which are now deceased. In 1964, he was elected president of the Association of Survivors, a group of former Marines who hold reunions every year.

HUGO VICTOR GENGE, was born in Lodi, WI on Feb. 10, 1918. In 1932, he moved to Chicago, IL to live with his father and two brothers. His mother had died when he was just two years old. In Chicago, he attended Lake View High School, was a member of the Reserve Officers Training Corps and played a saxaphone in the high school band. In 1934, he enlisted in the Ninth Bn. United States Marine Corps Reserve

so he could have an opportunity to fire the 1903 .30 caliber rifle. In those days one of the requirements to enlist was to be able to afford to buy a pair of regulation shoes. He went on to qualify as an expert rifleman.

After graduation from high school in 1937, he became an employee of the F.W. Woolworth Company in their Traffic Department and remained in their employ for 45 years and ten months until he retired as traffic and private fleet manager of their Denver, PA. Distribution Center. In 1940, the Ninth Bn. was called to active duty and went by train to San Diego, CA and Hugo became a member of Headquarters Co. 2d Defense Bn. When the 2d Marine Div. was formed on Feb. 1, 1941 he was transferred to Hand S-2 as a clerk in the Quatermaster Office.

He sailed aboard the USS *President Jackson* on July 1, 1942 with Hand S-2 headed for Guadalcanal with a stop at Tonga Tabu and Fiji where he was transferred, along with other Hand S-2 people, to the USS *Crescent City*. After landing at Guadalcanal on Aug. 7, 1942, he was back aboard the *Crescent City* when the Unholy Four, along with other ships were sent to Espirito Santo. On Feb. 1, 1943, he was sent to the Silverstream Hospital in New Zealand with malaria and jaundice. He returned to duty with Hand S-2 and went on to Hawaii. Upon being promoted to warrant officer, he was assigned as Assistant Post Maintenance Property Officer at Camp Pendleton. In December of 1944, he was sent to the Third Pioneer Bn. on Guam and after a short tour there was transferred back to the 2nd Marine Div. on Saipan where he was assigned as Division General supply officer. He remained in that position and went with the 2nd Marine Div., FMF to Nagasaki, Japan, where they landed Sept. 25, 1945. In May 1946, he was returned to Camp Pendleton, CA and as his tour of enlistment was complete was discharged as a quatermaster sergeant.

In 1946 upon return to Chicago, IL he met Clarinda Mary Dobson and they were married in 1947. They have two sons, Hugo Victor Genge II (who served in the U.S. Air Force in Vietnam) and George Dobson Genge who is now an executive with AmTrack.

Hugo has served his community by holding the office of Trustee on the Village Board of Trustees of the Village of Willow Springs, IL. He is also a member of the Lions Club, D.C. Cregier Masonic Lodge (past master and now secretary), The Scottish Rite and Medinah Temple Shrine.

GRANT A. GIBSON, was born July 9, 1921 in Cumberland MD. Enlisted in the U.S. Marines Jan. 12, 1942.

After training at Parris Island, he was assigned to Portsmith VA for guard duty. Then to Camp Elliott, shipped out to Guadalcanal, arrived Nov. 12, 1942, joined M-3-7 1st Div.

Most memorable event was their stay in Australia, from Australia to New Guinea then New Britain, then to Peleliu, wounded on Peleliu, returned to States Nov. 17, 1944.

Discharged at San Francisco, CA, Jan. 24, 1946. Married Joyce Pratt of Melbourne, Australia Oct. 20, 1947. They have one boy Mark, two daughters Vickie and Gail. Resides in Painesville, OH for 60 years. Retired Painesville Police 1960. Retired U. S. Postal Service 1977.

ROBERT F. GREENWALD, was born Feb. 17, 1921 in Sappington, MO, St. Louis County. Enlisted in USMC July 3, 1942. Basic training (Boot Camp) at MCRD San Diego, CA, and Camp Matthews and Camp Elliot, San

Diego. Assigned to H-2-6 6th Marines, 2nd Div. USMC as a machine gunner. Served overseas, Pacific area, Oct. 20 1942 until May 17, 1943. Duty stations in Wellington, New Zealand and Guadalcanal. Returned to San Diego Naval Hospital in May 1943. Returned to duty at MCRD and Navy base 32nd St., San Diego. Returned to combat duty with the 11th Marine, 1st Div. Sept. 12, 1944 to Feb. 1, 1946. Made the April 1, 1945 landing on Okinawa. Engaged the enemy until June 21, 1945. Participated in the occupation of China, at Tinsen China Sept. 30, 1945 to Jan. 14, 1946.

Discharged at Great Lakes Naval Station Feb. 15, 1946.

Married to Marie Goedecke in San Diego, CA. on July 14, 1946. Have two children Robert and Rose. Also have four grandchildren. Was an auto mechanic and shop owner until retirement in 1943.

JOHN R. GRICE, was born in Corry, PA April 20, 1923. Enlisted in Marine Corps, Dec. 18, 1941 sworn in in Buffalo, NY Jan. 8, 1942. Discharged Jan. 16, 1946. Trained at Parris Island, shot expert on 45 pistol. Assigned to C Btry. 1st Special Weapons Bn., First Regt., 1st Marine Div., at Tent City, Camp Lejeune, NC.

Shipped out of San Francisco, June 1942 on USS *John Ericson*. Arrived Wellington, New Zealand July 11, 1942. Practice landing Fiji Islands, then participated in the invasion and defense of Guadalcanal from Aug. 7, 1942 to Dec. 15, 1942 as a member of a machine gun crew. Contracted malaria October 1942. Shipped from Guadalcanal to Brisbane, then to Ballarat, Australia. After several major attacks of malaria was evacuated to U.S. Naval Hospitals in Corona, CA. and Philadelphia, PA.

Most memorable event has to be the night of Oct. 13, 1942. Anyone who underwent the shelling of the Jap battleships will never forget it. They had been shelled and bombed by cruisers, destroyers, and submarines countless times but the 13th was supposed to be the knockout punch.

Married Jacquelyn Howard in 1947. Have two sons, John and Stephen. Have resided in Fort Myers, FL since 1974.

MURRAY M. GROSS, was born in New York City on March 15, 1916. Inducted into Federal Service as a member of the 244th Coast Artillery, a National Guard Unit, as of late September 1940. Sent to Camp Pendelton, Virginia Beach, VA for maneuvers and training. (rank-private). Shipped to the South Pacific with a newly formed Americal Div. as artillery support. This occurred in January 1942, one month after the Pearl Harbor attack. (rank-sergeant).

Landed in Melbourne, Australia, after spending 45 days at sea aboard a Grace Line ship converted to transport duty. Two weeks later, in March 1942, they landed at Noumea, New Caledonia with the Americal Div. They were to act as artillery protection for the harbor at Noumea. (rank-sergeant).

Late October 1942, their battery, now known as Btry. "B" of the 259th Coast Artillery, and its four 155 mm cannon, were shipped to Guadalcanal to reinforce and be attached to the 1st Marine Div. as Artillery Support for Henderson Field. (rank-staff sergeant). In March of 1943, they were set-up with 2 guns at Cape Esperance protecting Savoy Channel, and helping to wipe out the last of the Japanese resistance. He was then a

staff sergeant, acting platoon commander and acting first sergeant. Orders came through channels returning them to the States to attend Coast Artillery school at Fort Monroe, VA.

He became a commissioned officer at Fort Monroe, VA in October 1943. After serving at various posts, he finally arrived at Seacoast Artillery Headquarters, Fort Rodman, New Bedford, Massachusetts. At this post he proceeded to blow himself up, experimenting with defusing mines, booby traps and infiltration courses. He was primarily a platoon officer for an anti-aircraft battery. (rank-second lieutenant). After five months hospitalization for his injuries and five or six recurring attacks of malaria, contracted at Guadalcanal, he was assigned inactive duty as executive officer for a replacement outfit at Fort Meade, MD. There he was given a disability retirement as of January 1945. (Acting first lieutenant and executive officer).

FRED J. GUARINO, JR., was born in Clearfield, PA on Sept. 25, 1920. Enlisted in the USMC shortly after Pearl Harbor. Boot camp at Parris Island, then to 1st Div. at Tent City, New River, NC. Left New River in June and arrived in Wellington, New Zealand in July. He remembers the long-shoremen being on strike and how they worked unloading their convoy ships, then loading the ones for the attack on Guadalcanal. Theirs was the Wacky Mac. Landed on the Canal on Aug. 7, 1942. Left in mid December 1942 for Australia.

Stayed in the 1st Div. for New Guinea, New Britian, and Palau. Wounded on Peleliu and returned to San Diego Naval Hospital December 1944.

Discharged from the hospital in February 1945 and went into Infantry Training Regiment at Camp Lejeune, serving under Chesty Puller once again. Stayed there until discharged.

Married Emma Errigo, June 1955. They had three children, one daughter and two sons. Both boys served in the Navy Seabees. He guesses the stories he told about the Seabees on the Canal impressed them more than what their father did. He has resided in Curwensville, PA for the past 35 years.

JOSEPH A. GUSHINSKI, was born Oct. 24, 1920 in Moosic, PA (just outside Scranton, PA). Enlisted in the U.S. Navy in Scranton, PA, July 2, 1942. Boot Camp Newport, RI. Was assigned to the SS *Montpelier* (CL-57) which was at Philadelphia Navy Yard.

Served his whole wartime duty aboard *Montpelier*. He was assigned at Subic Bay, (Phillipines) when ordered to report to Philadelphia, and duty aboard the *F.D.R.* (carrier). Had 30 day leave and returned to Philly, to board the flattop. This was July, 1945. Atomic bomb was dropped on Japan and the war was over at the time the Navy was discharging people who had at least 16 points. After spending almost three years in the Pacific, he almost had double that amount, and qualified for discharge. Rank at honorable discharge was radarman first class (RDM1c). Never reported for duty aboard the *F.D.R.*

Received an honorable discharge Oct. 6, 1945 in Philadelphia Navy Yard.

RICHARD R. GWILLIAM, was born Orange, NJ on April 28, 1920. Enlisted in Marine Corps Feb. 1, 1939. Parris Island then Aircraft One Quantico. September 1942 Aircraft

Repair and Salvage Squadron One. *Lurline* and *Hunter Liggett* to Guadalcanal arriving Feb. 1, 1943. Disembarked under enemy fire and *Liggett* left with all supplies and equipment still aboard. Took detail to Espiritu Santo in belly of TBF, located gear, loaded it on Navy liberty ship and got it to canal. November, 1943 promoted to warrant officer. Joined MarAirSoPac. Ordered to USA February 1944.

Served at El Toro until March 1946. Joined 21st Inf. Bn. Organized Reserve, Lake Denmark, NJ. Activated August 1950 and joined Marine Ground Control Intercept Sqdn. Three. In Korea all of 1951. Home Christmas night 1951. Joined 5th Truck Co., Newark NJ.

Retired as CWO-4 in 1958.

Married Helen Knapp in 1942. Had son Richard, Jr. (deceased); daughter Pamela, and two grand-daughters.

Resides in Hackettstown, NJ. Worked in chemical sales until retirement in March 1985.

ARNOLD HAGIE, was born on April 15, 1917 was selected June 28, 1941. Trained at Camp Wallace, TX July 17, 1941.

Sent to Ft. Bliss November 1941 for departure to Seattle, WA. Here was transferred to the Army Transport Guard Detachment on Dec. 15, 1941. Arrived in Siska, AK, Dec. 23, 1941. Attained the rank of sergeant in Hawaiian Islands April 2, 1941. When getting back to San Francisco, was transferred to 214th Army Anti-Aircraft Arty. and was sent to New Zealand on Oct. 4, 1942. In New Caledonia by Nov. 2, 1942. Jan. 28, 1943, arrived at Guadalcanal and by January 30, was stationed at Henderson Field, Strip No. 1. Left Dec. 22, 1943, leaving behind the mosquitos and contracted malaria on boat to New Zealand for R&R.

Went to New Guinea June 19, 1944. Departed Dec. 11, 1944, for furlough. Arrived in States Dec. 28, 1944. Married Jan. 23, 1945. Reported back to duty in the Philippines at Clark Field and discovered he had enough points for a discharge.

Arrived home Oct. 5, 1945. Has been happily married 45 years. They have four married children and eight grandchildren.

JESSE E. HARE, was born in Philadelphia, PA Nov. 11, 1917. Inducted into Army of the United States Nov. 11, 1941.

After Basic Training at Camp Croft, SC, assigned to Anti-Tank Co., 147th Infantry, Indiantown Gap, PA.

Sailed on USS *Hunter Liggett*, April 9, 1942 for advanced base at Tongatabu, South Pacific. November 11, 1942, sailed on USS *President Hayes* for Guadalcanal where participated in battles for Kokombona and Tassafaronga earning Infantry Combat Badge and Bronze Star Medal. Contracted recurrent malaria but remained in South Pacific serving on Islands of Apia, New Caledonia, and Emirau.

Rotated Stateside arriving San Francisco, May 30, 1944. Subsequently assigned to Quater Master Detachment at Carlisle Barracks, PA where achieved the rank of Tech. 5. Honorably discharged, with Good Conduct Medal, Sept. 21, 1945.

Married to Freda Stackhouse, has three children and four grandchildren with another expected.

Currently employed since 1946 as general manager of a ball bearing distribution company and resides in Morrisville, PA.

GROYDON K. HARTMAN, born in Prescott, WI Sept. 2, 1918, moved to Flint, MI in 1933, and went into the Army in April of 1941. He remembers being in North Carolina maneuvers Dec. 7, 1941 when Japs hit Pearl Harbor.

Shipped out of New York Jan. 22, 1942 on the *Thomas H. Berry*, through the Panama Canal to Australia, on to New Caledonia during battle of the Coral Sea, then to Guadalcanal in 1942. Received the Presidential Citation with Bronze Battle Star, while serving in combat with First Marine Div. Reinforced. A short rest in Fiji Islands then left for Leyte in the Philippines. From there to Cebu, then after three years and seven months in the jungle he was headed home. They stopped in Pearl Harbor for water, that's the day they announced the war was over. "Thank God!" the day it ended, he was where it started. He was in the 721st Armored Bn. Americal Div.

Recieved the Pacific Ribbon w/three Bronze Battle Stars and a Good Conduct Medal.

Discharged from Ft. Sheridan August 1945. On his way home, he met his wife Eleanor on a Greyhound Bus to Flint, MI. They had one daughter, three sons, and seven grandchildren.

Retired from General Motors in 1987. Life membership in VFW. Likes hunting, fishing, wood carving, and retirement.

CHARLES O. HAYNIE, was born Oct. 16, 1920 in Grant Co, IN. Entered U.S. Navy December 1941, served on the USS *Fuller*, Guadalcanal Boat Pool, USS *Alhena*, N.O.B. Iceland and N.A.S. Mayport FL boatswain mate, first class. He remembers the bombers coming in August 7 and the sight of them hitting the water, parachute flares just before the battle at sea on August 8. The APA still burning when the big guns started firing. A Jap bomber landed on her deck. He remembers the feeling when he heard that they had lost all their heavy cruisers. He remembers picking up survivors and burying the dead at sea. The float plane coming in with its lights on and dropping its bomb at the *Fuller* while she was unloading in Tulagi Harbor. He remembers the *Fuller* not picking up her boat crews and weeks later finding they are part of the Guadalcanal Boat Pool. And will never be picked up, 16 months later they go aboard another ship. Unloading ships at Lunga Point and looking up at Cape Esperance and seeing the Japs unloading.

He remembers the bombardment from the Jap battlewagons and no air cover; the taking of men off the *Atlanta*, the torpedo missing the AKA and sliding up on the beach at Lunga Point; the fighter passing down spam sandwiches for Christmas dinner and making sure that from that time on she would be the last ship to be unloaded. The Japanese submarines and ships being used as landing crafts at the battle of Tenaru and orders to stand by to take the Marines of Guadalcanal. The Japanese planes coming in with their landing lights and dropping bombs on the APA and AKA. Laying on the beach in a fox hole waiting for the Japs to land.

He is married to Kathleen Cooper and they have four children and several grandchildren and great grandchildren.

LEROY W. HAZEL, born in Cicero, IL April 6, 1922. Worked at Kraft Cheese Co. in 1939 with Bill Mueller (G.C.V. of Atlanta, GA) who convinced this kid of 17 yrs. that the U.S.N.R. was the place to be. Two weeks cruise, parades, etc., etc. Sounded great! Enlisted in the U.S.N.R. on March 11, 1940 in the 23rd Destroyer Div. in Chicago, IL. Was called to active duty on Dec. 10, 1940 and started the longest two weeks cruise of my life. (Reunited with Mueller at G.C.V. in 1985).

Commissioned USS *Heywood* (APA-6)—(one of the first in it's class). Transported Marines to and from Iceland until early 1942. On Aug. 7, 1942 landed the first Marine Paratroops on Gavatu Island. Was assigned to Tulage Boat Pool until Dec. 15, 1942. Sent to the USS *President Adams* (APA-19). Rotated to U.S. in June 1944 for a 30 day leave. Sent to Landing Craft School in San Diego. Commissioned the USS *Pickens* (APA-190) Sept. 18, 1944. Landed Marines on Iwo Jima, Okinawa, and the U.S. Army to Magoya, Japan.

Discharged from Great Lakes, IL Nov. 28, 1945 as Bos'n 2/C.

Married childhood sweetheart Julia, on Aug. 4, 1946. Raised three sons and has one grandson. All reside in Lake County, IL.

Retired from American Airlines - O'Hare Field, Chicago in October 1984.

PAUL HAMILTON HEALEY, was born in Newburyport, MA, on Sept. 5, 1922; Graduated from Newburyport High School, June 1941. He enlisted in the U.S. Navy on Oct. 2, 1942, and assigned to the light cruiser, USS *Montpelier* (CL-57), which was flagship, and served with shipmate, James T. Fahey, who wrote the best-seller *Pacific War Diary 1942-1945*. USS *Montpelier* operated with Admiral Arleigh "31-knot" Burke and his destroyers in the Guadalcanal - Solomon Islands Campaign. First battle was Rennell Island in which the USS *Chicago* was sunk.

Put into commission the destroyer, USS *Yarnall* (DD-541), also flagship and which operated with Admiral Mitscher's famous Task Force 58, which struck Mindanao, the central Philippines, Luzon, Formosa, Palau and Okinawa. The *Yarnall* also took part in initial landings of Saipan and Tinian, then Guam, and in the first and second Battles of the Philippine Sea.

Medals earned are American Theater of War, Good Conduct, Asiatic-Pacific Area with seven Stars, Philippine Liberation with two Stars, World War II Victory. (Could have more?)

Discharged on Jan.2, 1946, Boston MA, as radioman third class. Graduated from Burdett Business College, MA and attended Loyola University, Chicago, IL.

Single, retired, have lived in South Florida for 35 years. Member of the VFW, DAV, American Legion, and Guadalcanal Campaign Veterans.

ENOCH W. HENDERSON, was born in Beggs, OK on Nov. 21, 1917. Enlisted March 9, 1942. Served with the 14th NCB B-6 all the way until discharge in October 1945.

RICHARD R. HENNIG, was born in Cicero, IL, Oct. 20, 1923, joined the Navy, November 1940. Was a plank owner on USS *Fuller* (APA-7). Their ship took Marines to Iceland in 1941, transported troops to Ireland and Scotland in 1942. They then cruised to the South Pacific to make the invasion of Guadalcanal. Three years on the *Fuller* and 28 months in the Pacific he was transferred to Vella La Vella, Assistant Master at Arms. After four months duty he was shipped to New Caledonia for shore patrol duty, skipper of USS *Georgina*. Returning to Treasure Island after 38 months overseas he was given the option of shipping over for warrant officer or leaving the service.

He was in the glass business and in 1959 sold out to open a mobile home mfg. plant in Florida. In 1975, he sold out to retire and spend more time with Mert, his wife of 38 years. They have a married son and a married daughter with four grandchildren and two great-grandchildren. He has been with the Canal Vets for 14 years and is national director.

WILLIAM H. HENRY, was born March 5, 1921 in Macon, GA. Enlisted in Navy Feb. 21, 1940, trained at N.O.B. in Norfolk, VA, and left Norfolk, VA, in June 1940 for the West Coast aboard the USS *Pyro* and went aboard the USS *San Francisco* in July 1940 at Bremerton Navy Yard. Stayed with *San Francisco* until August, 1941. Transferred to USS *Indianapolis* Dec.5, 1941. *Indianapolis* went back to seas with USS *Portland* when Japs bombs struck Pearl Harbor.

Indianapolis was then making a simulated bombardment of Johnston Island. Immediately joined Task Force 12 and searched for Japs carrier reportedly still in the vicinity. She arrived Pearl Harbor on Dec. 13, 1941; entered Task Force 11 for operations.

Her first action came in the South Pacific deep in the enemy dominated waters about 350 miles south of Rabaul, New Britian. Late in the afternoon of Feb. 20, 1942, the American ships were attacked by 18 twin-engined bombers flying in two waves, in the battle that followed, and 16 planes were shot down by accurate anti-aircraft of the ships and fighter planes from *Lexington* (CV2).

No ships were damaged. They splashed two trailing seaplanes. On March 10, the Task Force reinforced by the carrier *Yorktown* (CV-5) attacked enemy ports at Lae and Salamaua, New Guinea where the enemy was marshalling amphibious force, carrier based planes achieved complete surprise by flying in from the south, crossing the high Owen Stanley Mountain Range, striking Japanese harbor shipping.

They inflicted heavy damage on Japanese warships and transports. The American flyer knocked down many enemy planes. Their losses were light. After June 9, 1942, went aboard the USS *Colhoun*. She arrived at Noumea, New Caledonia on July 21, 1942. She carried units of the 1st Marine Raider Bn. in the initial assualt landing on Guadalcanal on Aug. 7, 1942, and continued to serve as transport and anti-submarine vessel in support of the invasion. At 1400 on Aug. 30, 1942, while on patrol off Guadalcanal, she was struck in a Japanese air raid. She was hit with four direct bombs. Killed all the men in the after deck house. 51 men were killed and 18 wounded. *Colhoun* sank in three minutes. *Colhoun's* last battle.

Returned to U.S. December 1944. Was stationed at Pensacola, FL. One year, discharged March 1, 1946.

HERMAN J. HERDT, born Nov. 16, 1919, Merrill, WI. Joined U.S. Navy April 23, 1941. Military locations include Henderson Field, Gaudalcanal. Flew PBY-5, and PBM. Awarded Distinguished Flying Cross. Achieved rank of AOC. Discharged Nov. 7, 1961.

Married to Freida, three children and one grandchild. Retired from Civil Service NAS North Island, San Diego, CA., on June 31, 1975. Currently employed as an usher at San Diego Stadium and Sports Arena. Was a bombardier of BSVB-101 operating from Henderson Field on Guadalcanal, a bombing raid was flown on Feb. 12, 1943.

Named in most history books as the "Saint Valentine's Day Massacre". The losses for both sides were very heavy for that one day. One week later two more planes were lost on a night raid.

ROBERT E. HILLSTRAND, born Sept. 7, 1922 in Chicago, IL. Entered service Jan. 2, 1942. Assigned to C Btry. 1st Bn. 11 Marines, 1st Div. and stationed in Quantico, VA. His rank was corporal, and his most memorable experience was in Guadalcanal, Camp Glouscester, NB, and Parris Island.

He received the Presidential Technicial Award, and was issued the Navy Unit Commendation bar, World War II Victory, Asiactic Pacific with four stars, American Campaign, and Good Conduct Medal.

He has two sons and one daughter. He retired from Essex Wire Compamy.

OLIVER P. HINES, was born April 24, 1919 in Oakland, CA. Enlisted in the USNR Golfen Gater Sqdn VO-8MR, NAB Oakland AS. June 1937, graduated from high school and transferred into USN. Boot Camp at San Diego. USS *Lexington* (CV-2), X, 1st and K Divs. S2/c, S1/c and SM 3/c. Ens. Howard and Lt. French authorized his request for a Combat Air Patrol round trip ride in a SBD. Will never forget that thrill. Discharged June 1941, at Camp Shoemaker. December 1941, married Louise Oller, best friend's sister, both still hanging in there. Worked as shipwright and Joiner at Kaiser's Shipyard 3, Richmond, CA. December 1941 USNR volunteer for two year enlistment. Called for duty Jan. 28, 1942, enroute to SS *Jean Likes* being converted to USS *Libra* (AKA - 12). Ship commissioned May 1942, at Staten Island NY. June 2, 1942, Norfolk VA. load 200 1st Div. Marines and their combat equipment including: LCVPs; LCTs, tanks, jeeps etc. July 22, 1942 depart New Zealand to Koro Island, Fiji for practice landing. September 7, 1942 debark troops and cargo on initial landings at Guadalcanal and on Tulagi. The Libra shot down 13 Jap planes and was awarded the Navy Unit Citation. Their Captain, Cdr. Wm. B. "4.0" Fletcher, USN, was awarded the Navy Silver Star for outstanding bravery and performance during their 16 months of amphibious operations including six battle star major engagements with the enemy. December 1943, 40 days R&R at home, and promotion to CQM. Assigned to USS *General S.D. Sturgis*, (AP-137), new construction at Kaiser #3 Shipyard Richmond former employer. Really enjoyed seeing his old friends and fellow workers, Supt. Gibson and Supt. MacDonald. July 1944 ship commissioned by Capt. Duncan Scott Baker USNR. Hauling fresh troops to replace 18 month over seas troops. June 16, 1945 enroute San Francisco to Marseilles, France. Hauls U.S. Army troops to Honllandia, NG via Panama Canal. Dump Army troops ashore in Finchhaven, President Truman announced war was over, enroute empty to Manila. Load Allied Generals and Admirals. Haul them to Tokyo. The Luxury Hotel *Sturgis* tied up, port side to, on USS *Missouri* for Allied witnessing and signing of the Unconditional Surrender of Japan Treaty.

Enroute to Seattle, discharged Oct. 28, 1945 one year and nine months after enlistment expired.

November 1945 - November 1950 Civilian Shipwright and Joiner, San Francisco Naval Shipyard. 1950 - 52 Civilian Navigation specialist, USN Hydrographic Office, SF; 1953 Civilian, U.S. Treasury Storekeeper Gauger, Fresno; 1954 - 1972 Trainee, U.S. Treasury Alcohol Tax Unit, Criminal Investigator - Supervisory Criminal Investigator; San Diego; Special Agent ATF in Chg., SLC, Utah; Area Supervisor - Acting Chief Alcohol Tobacco & Firearms, Enforcement Branch, 10 Western States. 1972 -

74 on loan to U.S. Attorney General's, Organized Crime Drive, Strike Force, San Francisco. Will finish his 50 years marriage probation with Louise this December. Have two lovely daughters, two grandsons and two lovely granddaughters.

REDERICK C. HITZMAN, was born in Chicago, IL Aug. 14, 1920. Enlisted 132nd Inf. Regt., Co. I May 13, 1936. received Bronze Star, Combat Infantry Badge, and Navy residential Unit Citation on Guadalcanal. Federalized March 4, 941 as communication sergeant. Went overseas as Naval Task Force. First ground troops to Land Australia and New Caledonia. Participated in Coral Sea Battle. Returned Stateside after Guadalcanal ended as commander to form new jungle raider bn. The command decided that another raider bn. was not needed. nded up as training commander Fort Walter, TX. Trained approximately 15,000 soldiers for duty overseas. Upon release rom Federal Service, reverted to National Guard Status. Re-ained in the National Guard until Sept. 21, 1973.

Retired as Army Major. Promoted to lieutenant colonel the National Guard.

Married Mary Streit Oct. 4, 1940. Left her stranded at Camp Forrest, TN when sent overseas. Has three sons, one daughter, two grandsons and two granddaughters.

WILLIAM B. HOECHNER, was born Dec. 10, 1917 in Glendale, NY. Entered the U.S. Army on March 28, 1941 with the 754th Tank Bn. He was stationed in 1941 at Fort Knox, KY, and Camp Drum, in New York State. He was sent overseas in January 1942 to Australia. He served on Leyte, Guadalcanal, New Caledonia, and the Philippines. His rank was technician fourth grade tank driver.

Last assignment was the liberation of Manila in the Philippines--he was still there when Gen. MacArthur "Returned".

He was awarded the American Defense Service Medal, Asiatic-Pacific Service Medal, and the Philippines Liberation Ribbon.

He married Ruth Glatz in 1947 and was a lifelong resident of New York. He was living in Southold, Long Island, NY at the time of his death. He died Aug. 6, 1988. He was retired from the U.S. Postal Service in 1973.

MARVIN OTTO HOLZHEIMER, was born March 6, 1921 at Hancock, MN. He entered service with the USMC on Dec. 15, 1941. He served at the following military stations and locations: San Diego, CA, Tulagi, Guadalcanal, Klamath Falls, OR and Wellington, New Zealand.

He sailed on the SS *President Jackson*. He recalls spending six months behind a machine gun and returning alive! He was discharged with the rank of corporal on Dec. 16, 1945.

Married for 45 years, has seven children, 12 grandchildren and one great-grandchild. Worked as a logger, truck driver and heavy equipment operator. Retired in 1978 due to a back injury.

ELBERT R. HORTON, was born in Bushy Fork Township, Person County, NC on Feb. 17, 1916. He grew up on a farm and attended Bushy Fork School.

He was selected for service in December 1940. He was inducted on April 5, 1941. He trained at Ft. Bragg, NC (FARTC) and was assigned to the 72d Field Artillery Regiment. He went to the South Pacific in March 1942. (Task Force 6814) and he became part of the Americal Division, Hq. Brty., 246th FA Bn., which participated in the Guadalcanal, Bougainville and Philippine Islands Campaigns. He served four years, three months and 18 days. He was discharged on July 22, 1945.

He worked in textiles for 31 years, retiring in Feb. 1, 1978. He was married on Sept. 1, 1959 to Mattie Hines, RN, PHN, and they now reside at their country home in Mt. Tirzah Township, Person County, NC.

HARLAN J. HOXIE, was born in May 28, 1915 Willmar, MN. At age one, he moved to Worthington, MN, where he grew up and attended school.

He was drafted into the Army Aug. 1, 1941. He took basic training in Radio Communications at Ft. Bragg, NC. He was sent as a replacement to HQ Battery, 180th FA Bn. at Camp Edwards, MA. He was shipped overseas Jan. 23, 1942, part of Task Force 6814 to Australia, then to New Caledonia. At New Caledonia, they became HQ Battery, 247th FA Bn., Americal Division.

They landed at Guadalcanal in November 1942, where they fought until March 1943—then on to Fiji, then to Bougainville until it was secure. Then they travelled on to Leyte to stage for an assault landing on Cebu, Philippines.

He was discharged at Camp McCoy, WI Aug. 30, 1945. After four years in the service with 43 months overseas.

Received the Purple Heart, Bronze Star Medal, Asiatic Theatre Service Medal, Philippine Liberation Ribbon with Bronze Star, American Defense Service Medal, ASR Score and seven Overseas Bars.

He was in the sound, intercommunications, television and radio business for 38 years. He and his wife are retired and spending lots of their time traveling.

BRUCE MCKINLEY HUBBARD, was born Aug. 16, 1923 at Wilkes County, NC. He entered the USMC on Feb. 19, 1942. He served at the following military stations and locations: Guadalcanal, Cape Gloucester, New Britian, Peleliu, Palan Island Group.

He was in the South Pacific Area from June 1942 to November 1944. He was in Special Weapons Battery, 11th Regt., 1st Marine Div. when he participated in action against the enemy at Guadalcanal, BSI on Aug. 7, 1942 to December 1942. He was then sent to Melbourne, Australia, where he joined WPNS Co., 7th Regt. He recalls Edson Ridge. He attained the rank of private first class. He was honorably discharged Sept. 12, 1945 at Camp LeJeune, NC. For his service during WW II, he received the following: two Unit Citations, two Silver Stars and four Bronze Stars.

He married Joyce Hege Hubbard. He has two children by a previous marriage, Connie Hubbard Reece and Kathy Hubbard Mendenhall. He and Joyce have one child, Carl Hubbard, and Bruce also has a step-daughter, Tammy Brendle. He has nine grandchildren. He retired March 1987. He was a self-employed upholsterer.

WALLACE C. HUEBNER, was born March 10, 1916 at Hay Creek. He enlisted in the US Marine Corps on March 24, 1942 and served at San Diego, CA and Camp Pendelton.

He landed on Tulagi Aug. 8, 1942. It was on Tualgi that

he manned a captured Japanese AA gun. He was taken to Guadalcanal the first part of September. He left the canal on Feb. 9, 1943 bound for New Zealand and six months of R & R. From there he was sent to Bougainville.

After 27 months overseas, he was sent back to the States. He got the first leave to go home in September 1944 and reported to Camp Pendleton. He remained there until being discharged in October 1945. He received three Battle Stars for his service on Guadalcanal.

He married Frances Albers on Oct. 23, 1947. They have two girls and four grandchildren. He retired from raising registered Angus cattle in March 1981.

HERBERT HUFFMAN, JR., was born May 24, 1921 in Dayton, OH. He graduated from Stivers High School in 1939. He joined the USMC Feb. 2, 1942 and attended boot camp at Parris Island, SC.

He joined I-3-5, 1st Div., March 1942. He served in the Asiatic-Pacific Theatre from April 1942 until December 1944.

He remembers Guadalcanal, Milnes Bay, NC, Cape Gloucester, Peleliu and Negasebus. He received four Battle Stars. From December 1944 to August 1945, he served aboard the USS *Honolulu*. He was discharged in 1945.

He is married, with three children: Mikaelyn Shields, Patric Huffman and Shannon Long.

He has worked as a social worker for Lutheran Social Service of Miami Valley and is now retired. He received the Silver Beaver from Boy Scouts of America. He is an All-State Commander VFW and member of the American Legion, 1st Marine Division Association and Guadalcanal Campaign Veterans Association.

He will never forget Aug. 7—1942, he landed on Guadalcanal, Aug. 7, 1952 his daughter was born and Aug. 7, 1985, his wife died.

HAROLD E. HURD, was born Aug. 10, 1919 at Wellsville, NY. He entered service with the U.S. Navy on June 28, 1939.

He served aboard the USS *Helena* (CL-50) and was discharged as ship fitter, first class.

He recalls the attack on Pearl Harbor, Battles of Guadalcanal and Cape Esperance and Kula Gulf. He received a Letter of Commendation from Admiral Halsey.

His wife passed away in 1979. They had one daughter, one son and six grandchildren. He is presently retired, doing nothing that he can get out of doing.

JOSEPH H. HURD, JR., was born June 28, 1923 in Aurora, IN. He enlisted with the U.S. Navy on Sept. 10, 1941. He served aboard the USS *President Polk*.

He remembers "Washing Machine Charlie," Tokyo Rose and the full moon bigger than the Japanese Zero's. He remembers dengue fever and turning "yellow as a Jap." He recalls having malaria and the Guadalcanal trots. He remembers the chapel on Santos, one of the reasons he became Catholic (Auckland). Another special memory from Auckland was drinking real milk, not chalk water. He was discharged with the rank of PHM2/c on Feb. 5, 1945.

He is twice married, with five children and five grandchildren. He retired in 1974.

ROBERT L. HUTCHINS, was born Feb. 7, 1924 at Lansing, MI. He received a high school education.

Entered service on Feb. 2, 1942 with the U.S. Marines. He fought on Guadalcanal and Okinawa. Wounded Nov. 3, 1942 at Guadalcanal. At Guadalcanal that they trained for the Okinawa Invasion. He served with E Co., 2d Bn., 7th Marines, 1st Div. and with HQ Co., 3d Bn., 29th Marines, 6th Div. Returned to Guadalcanal a third time on Aug. 6, 1992 for the memorial dedication. Attained the rank of corporal—discharged on Feb. 1, 1946.

He is married, with six children and six grandchildren. Employed as a mortician, state trooper and magistrate, retired in 1975. Member of GCV, 1st Div. Assoc. and 6th Div. Assoc.

HARRY K. HUTTON born in Edinburgh, Scotland Dec. 15, 1921. Emigrated to New Zealand in 1924. Joined the Navy (New Zealand Royal Navy). Basic training at Philomel at Stoker, 2d Class. Joined *Achilles* Oct. 1, 1940, left *Achilles* in November 1940 in Sydney, Australia. Overnight trip to Melbourne by train then on to Bombay, India to join HMS *Leander*. Convoy duties in Red Sea.

Returned to Wellington in September 1941 and then on to Auckland. After re-fit, their ship joined the American Fleet—Task Force Convoy Duties. Met Convoy off Tahiti—took it to Brisbane, Australia. Joined force to take 1st U.S. Marines to Guadalcanal—landed safely. Later they went on to stop the Tokyo Express at Kula Gulf in New Georgie where they were torpedoed. Had 17 and one-half hours below during the trip back to Tulagi.

Returned to Auckland and was drafted to HMNZS Tamaki Training Establishment at ships convoy. After three and one-half years there, he was drafted to Black Prince as Care and Maintenance. Discharged April 2, 1947 as Acting Leading Hand.

He has a son in the New Zealand Navy—Petty Officer (Electrical) and a daughter who is a resident in London, United Kingdom.

ALVIN W. JOHNSTON was born in Roanoke, VA on Dec. 22, 1925. Enlisted in Marine Corps in January 1942. After training at Parris Island, was assigned to Headquarters Co., 1st Bn., 7th Marines at New River, NC.

Shipped out for Upolu, British Western Samoa from Norfolk, VA in early April 1942 aboard USS *Fuller* (AP-7). Departed Samoa on September 2, and arrived at Guadalcanal on Sept. 18, 1942.

Most memorable event: The green flares and sudden bombardment by warships of the Imperial Japanese navy their first night ashore. Departed Guadalcanal Jan. 2, 1943 for Melbourne, Australia. Treated in hospitals in Melbourne and Adelaide for malaria. Participated in Cape Gloucester, New Britain Campaign from Dec. 26, 1943 to April 1944.

Arrived in San Diego, CA on July 9, 1944 aboard USS *General John Pope* on July 9, 1944. Assigned to guard company, Naval Air Station, Pensacola, FL.

Discharged January 1946 from Barracks Detachment, NAS Pensacola, FL.

Married Dorothy E. Teaster on Feb. 6, 1945. Has one daughter, Linda and grandson, Andy. Resides in Roanoke, VA.

WILLIAM G. JOHNSTON, was born in Johnstone, Scotland on March 15, 1919. Came to the U.S. at an early age. Enlisted in U.S. Navy Aug. 20, 1940. Served in the North Atlantic on Neutrality Patrol aboard the USS *Simpson*, four piper destroyer.

Was of the original crew of the attack transport, USS *President Adams*. This ship successfully repelled a torpedo attack by a Nazi submarine on Christmas Day, 1941 in the Caribbean, was disabled and towed to Key West, FL.

Participated in the August 7 invasion of Guadalcanal and the subsequent enemy action in the Solomons campaign. Transferred at Townsville, Australia to run landing craft for a combined operation strike force to invade and occupy the island of Murua, at the time the most advanced position to enemy-held Rabaul. Served nine months in the jungles of Murrua and New Guinea.

Rotated back to the U.S. for leave and assignment to a new ship. Participated in the invasions of Guam and Saipan.

Most memorable event was hitting the beach under fire with the Marines in the Tulagi landings.

Discharged Oct. 30, 1945 with the rank of BM 1/c. Married Lee Kreitler Nov. 17, 1945. They have a son, a daughter, four grandchildren.

Retired after 35 years in administrative positions with Sears, Roebuck & Co.

He enjoys woodcarving and has won many honors in shows throughout the U.S. and Canada, including a blue ribbon in world competition. He is the author of the book entitled *The Beginners Handbook of Woodcarving*.

He now resides in Langhorne, PA.

ARVIL LORAN JONES, was born in St. George, UT, May 23, 1916. Enlisted United States Navy Sept. 23, 1941. Upon completion of basic training, was assigned to Cub 1, a unit of 450 men. Arvil, along with 119 other Cubs, was ordered to Guadalcanal on the USS *Colhoun*, landing there Aug. 15, 1942, bringing aviation gasoline, bombs and ammunition.

Cub One set up living quarters for pilots of first two Marine squadrons, prepared Henderson Field for aircraft, and installed air raid warning system. They serviced these squadrons until Marine ground crews arrived. Then, until Feb. 5, 1943, Cub One performed the dangerous fueling of

---

all aircraft. For this duty, Arvil and the rest of his unit received the Presidential Unit Citation.

Arvil married Lulu Walton June 9, 1946. They have three children and four grandchildren.

Arvil retired from Lockheed 1982. He and Lulu have written a book about his experience at Guadalcanal, titled *Forgotten Warriors: Challenge at Guadalcanal.*

FRANKLIN J. KARAL, was born in Cedar Rapids, IA on Sept. 30, 1920. Enlisted Marine Corps Jan. 6, 1942.

Boot camp San Diego, CA, Rifle Range San Louis Abispo, CA. Assigned to 3 L2, 2nd Div. Left San Diego June 5, 1942 on *President Adams*. Landed Aug. 8, 1942 on Gavutu and Tanambogo. Spent much time on Guadalcanal and surrounding islands. Left for New Zealand about Feb. 1, 1943.

Memorable event: A squad of Marines from 3L2 with a sailor from the USS *McFarland* sailed on the Missonary Bishop's yacht to a coral reef named *Praie Piles* four miles southwest of Jap infested Guadalcanal in uncharted waters. The reef was 15 yards wide and 50 yards long. They had a radio and lights. They helped guide Adm. Willis A. Lee for the November 13-14 battles. Then went on to Tulagi.

Evacuated from Silverstream Hospital, New Zealand to San Diego Naval Hospital with attacks of malaria. Served in guard companies Marine Base, SD Destroyer Base SD Marine Barracks, Washington, DC Annapolis, MD and 4th Marine Division. He was discharged as a corporal.

Married Marie E. Neuhaus 1947. Had four children; Michael, Suellen, Karen, and Elizabeth. Lived at Fairfax, IA all his life.

JOHN M. KEANEY, was born in New York City, NY on June 25, 1918. Moved to Ireland and attended school there. Returned to New York and joined the regular Navy in 1940. After training at Newport, RI was assigned to the USS *Boise*. December 15, 1941, put USS *President Hayes* (APA-20) in commission at the Brooklyn Navy Yard.

January 6, 1942, she sailed for San Diego, CA via Panama Canal.

July 1, 1942, along with sister ships, *Adams* and *Jackson*, the *Hayes* sailed from San Diego, CA in convoy with Marines aboard for the South Pacific. August 7, 1942 made the initial landings on Guadalcanal.

Took part in the occupation of Rendova on June 30, 1943. He was assigned to Navy Base #250 at Munda.

He returned to the States in January 1944 for school and new construction. Put the USS *Bougainville* (CVE-100) in commission on June 18, 1944. July 1944, the *Bougainville* departed from San Diego, CA for the Pacific.

Participated in Iwo Jima and Okinawa Operations. The USS *President Hayes* was awarded the Navy Unit Commendation and seven Battle Stars for WWII service—USS *Bougainville* received two Battle Stars.

In 1946, he was discharged as chief machinist mate. He married Julie Quayle at St. Matthias Roman Catholic Church, Huntington Park, CA, in 1947.

Julie passed away in 1967. He retired from employment with the Federal Government, San Francisco, CA, in 1981.

W. JACK KEEFE,

was born April 27, 1921 in Chicago, IL. Enlisted Naval Reserve Oct. 31, 1941. Assigned attack transport USS *Neville*. During invasion of Tulagi was engineer in Higgins Boat transporting Marines to beach. Had ring side seat for the naval battle of Savo Island when transports had to have boats behind when they left before the battle. Transferred to boat patrol on Guadalcanal October 1942. Transferred to Naval Hospital Auckland, New Zealand wtih malaria January 1943. Sent back to States and assigned to USS *Mascoma* (AO-83), a tanker. Transferred to U.S. Naval Hospital Shoemaker, CA.

Discharged Dec. 12, 1944 with rate of mm second class. Married Virginia Beunz of Chicago, IL September 1944. They have four children and nine grandchildren.

Retired as commercial real estate broker October 1990.

ROBERT J. KELLEHER,

was born in Quincy, MA Nov. 1, 1922. Enlisted 182nd Inf. Dec. 9, 1940. Inducted federal service Jan. 16, 1941.

Trained Camp Edwards, MA and NC maneuvers. Left New York for South Pacific Jan. 23, 1942, via Panama Canal, as Task Force 6814 (later Americal Div.), aboard USAT *Argentina*. Took 35 days to Melbourne, Australia. Month later shipped to Noumea, New Caledonia. Arrived Guadalcanal November 1942.

Awards: Bronze Star, Naval Presidential Unit Citation and Combat Infantryman's Badge.

Evacuated by air, because of malaria, to Espirito Santos, New Hebrides, CUB 1 Naval Hospital, March 1943, and then via hospital ship to 39th General Hospital, Auckland, New Zealand. Returned to U.S. Oct. 26, 1943, Torney General Hospital, Palm Springs, CA. More training, then to European Theatre with 1259th Engineering Combat Bn., late 1944. Returned to U.S. Oct. 15, 1945. Discharged Nov. 5, 1945, Ft. Dix, NJ. Rank: corporal.

Graduated Northeastern University, Boston.

Married Katherine Duhig, Aug. 12, 1967. They have resided in Lincoln, MA since 1971.

EUGENE L. KELLER, SR.,

was born in Bend, OR Oct. 4, 1924, moved to Muskegon, MI. Enlisted in Marine Corps Nov. 23, 1941 but not before his father tried to talk him into joining the Navy. Gene would not hear of it as he wanted to wear those blues that the Marines were wearing. It was not until he was boarding the train for Parris Island that he found out the only Marines wearing blues were the recruiting duty Marines.

After boot camp he was assigned to C Co., 1st Pioneer Bn., and shipped out to New Zealand. He landed on Guadalcanal Aug. 7, 1942 and proceeded to work many hours, unloading equipment, food, ammo and etc. The Japanese navy was on its way so our Navy told Gen. Vadegrift that they were leaving, unloaded or not.

Gene also made landings on Cape Gloucester, Iboki and Tallocia on New Britain and Peleliu. He returned to the States and was stationed at Great Lakes as a prison guard. He suffered bouts with malaria and was sent to Klamath Falls, OR until the wars end.

He met his wife, Rita, sister of his best buddy, Joe Zimmerman, together they shared many experiences. They were married at Poor Souls Chapel May 12, 1945 Great Lakes Naval Base.

Gene and Rita have five children and ten grandchildren. He retired from Western Michigan University where he had worked for the previous 20 years as food service supervisor. Gene is a real ham at heart. He has been active as a song and dance man for 30 years and if you ask him, even now, he will give you a song.

Gene had been the National Secretary of the Guadalcanal Campaign Veterans for the past six years and is presently serving as National President which he considers to be the *highest* honor ever bestowed on him.

BURTON KELLEY

was born March 20, 1918 at Chatham, MA. He enlisted Oct. 30, 1937. He joined the U.S. Navy Feb. 12, 1941 and served aboard USS McCauley. He served at Boston, MA, Norfolk, VA, Chicago, IL and in the Solomon Islands. He was honorably discharged for USN Personnel Separation Center, Boston, MA with the rank of quartermaster, second class.

He received the following medals: WW II Victory Medal, Asiatic-Pacific Ribbon with one Silver and one Bronze Star, Good Conduct Medal, American Theatre Ribbon and the American Defense Medal.

Prior to his enlistment he worked as an apprentice shipfitter with Massachusetts. He married Sarah G. (Nelson) Eldredge on Oct. 12, 1963. He has two step-daughters and four step-grandchildren. He worked with New England Telephone and Telegraph Co. until retirement March 21, 1980.

JESSE L. KELLER,

was born in Orange Heights, FL April 16, 1925. Enlisted in Marine Corps December 1941. Attended boot camp in San Diego, CA. After boot camp was assigned 1st Div. BI-5, landed on Guadalcanal 0900, Aug. 7, 1942. Left the canal in December 1942. Jesse also made two other landings on Cape Gloucester and Peleliu.

Returned to the U.S. December 1944 and was stationed at the Philadelphia Navy Yard.

Married to Jan, has two daughters and two sons. Attended the University of Miami until Korea conflict occurred, was then recalled to active duty. Is now the Chairman of the Board for Fat Boy's Bar-B-Q Franchise Systems, Inc.

ROBERT P. KELLER,

was born at Newark, OH on Sept. 24, 1922. Enlisted in the U.S. Marine Corps on Jan. 16, 1942 at Cincinnati, OH. Went through boot camp and Telephone School at the Marine Base, San Diego, CA. In April 1942 was transferred to New River, NC and was assigned to E-2-11 of the 1st Marine Div.

In May sailed on the USS *Wakefield* from Norfolk, VA. Went through the Panama Canal and on to Wellington, New Zealand. In July went aboard the USS *Neville* and went to Koro, Fiji Islands and then on to the Solomon Islands. On Aug. 7, 1942 landed on Tulagi and about a month later moved to Guadalcanal. Was a forward observer for E Btry. 11th Marines.

On Dec. 9, 1942 went aboard the *President Adams* and went to Brisbane, Australia. In January went aboard the USS *West Point* and sailed to Melbourne, Australia. Was stationed at Ballarat, Australia. Had numerous attacks of malaria during this period and was sent back to the States because of these attacks in September 1943. Was at Oak Knoll Hospital Great Lakes, IL and Klamath Falls Marine Barracks at Klamath Falls, OR. Was discharged at Klamath, Falls in Oregon. Discharged at Klamath Falls on Oct. 27, 1945.

While at the Klamath Falls Marine Barracks met and Married Peggy Yost of Weed, CA on April 16, 1945. Bob and Peggy have four children, two boys and twin girls. Bob is retired from the Morton Thiokol Corporation after 27 years of employment with them. Bob and Peggy live in Brigham City, UT.

THEODORE S. KEPNER,

was born Nov. 6, 1921. He was assigned to CUB 1, USN from Treasure Island, San Francisco to Advanced Base Lunga.

He was a passenger aboard the USS *Wharton* July 20, 1942, to Epirito Santo Base, Half-Moon Bay, then passenger on USS *Fuller* to Tulagi and landed on Guadalcanal Sept. 30, 1942. He was a courier to GC with USN secret codes, and assigned to operate the captured Japanese Navy radio station at Kukum Beach, next to fighter strip No. 2, with five other CUB 1 Navy personnel until February 1943. Station NGK was moved near Henderson fieldl in February 1943. In May 1943, he shipped out of the Canal to the hospital ship USS Pinkney, thence to NOB 6 hospital in New Caledonia for three months, and finally to NOB USN transmitter station at New Zealand.

After his military service, he was commissioned as communications officer in the Hawaii National Guard in Hilo, HI.

He spent his years after the war as an engineer in Europe, Africa, Sydney and Melbourne, Australia, as well as the United States.

His Australian wife is deceased and his three children are now adults. His children were born in Australia, Spain and Hawaii.

J. P. KIDD

was born May 28, 1921 at Ft. Worth, TX. He joined the Army Air Force on Feb. 13, 1942. He served 35 months in the South Pacific, from Guadalcanal to the Philippines. He served with the 68th Fighter Squadron and 347th Fighter Squadron with Group HQ's.

He remembers the beautiful, muddy, sometimes ugly islands on which they were fighting, the first time bomb, first time he was shelled, straffed and the first time he lost a buddy. He remembers a 10 day leave in Australia and 10 more in Auckland, NZ.

He was discharged Feb. 25, 1946 with the rank of captain.

He has been married to Joanne (Briggs) Kidd for 46 years. They have two children and four grandchildren. He worked at a petroleum engineer and was senior vice president in charge of 30 land rigs in the United States. He has worked all over the US, South American and even spent two years in Palermo, Sicily. He retired in 1987 and works part time in his own company.

WILBERT P. KILVINGTON, was born July 5, 1917 at Detroit, MI. He entered the service with the Navy on Jan. 8, 1940. He served aboard the USS *Atlanta* and the USS *Tennessee.*

He remembers his good friends and the horrors of war. He received the Good Conduct Medal, WWII Victory Medal, the Asiatic-Pacific Campaign Medal, Purple Heart Medal and the Presidential Unit Citation. He was discharged June of 1946 with the rank of Chief/CMM.

He retired from General Motors (building engineer) in July 1982. He has four dogs and stays busy gardening, playing stocks and fishing.

MICHAEL KINAL, born in Buffalo, NY, July 1917. Enlisted in the Army June 28, 1941. Arrived at Ft. Totten, Bayside, Long Island, NY. To Ft. Slocum, Brooklyn, NY Army Base.

He went on to Schofield Barracks, arriving October 31, 1941. He served with Medical Battalion, 25th Division. He is a Pearl Harbor Survivor, received his medal March 10, 1992.

January 1942, left for Guadalcanal, six months and then on to the Fiji Islands, New Caledonia, New Zealand and the Philippines. Left there April 1, 1945 bound for the United States.

He was discharged June 28, 1945. He is a lifetime member of the 25th Division, member of the Guadalcanal Campaign Veterans and VFW.

He is married, has one daughter, and is retired. He attends various conventions and reunions. He just returned from the 50th Pearl Harbor Survivors Reunion, Dec. 7, 1991. In 1984, he attended the 25th Division Reunion in Honolulu for 20 days. He plans to attend the Guadalcanal Reunion on Sept. 13, 1992.

EDWARD KIRCHNER, grew up in Hunterdon County, NJ and there graduated high school. He enlisted in the regular Navy, Sept. 16, 1941 and went to boot training at Newport, RI. He went to trade school at Jacksonville, FL. Next to Treasure Island, CA and then to New Caledonia.

From there to Guadalcanal on Nov. 15, 1942. He remained there approximately six months with the so called Acorn Red (One).

Returned to the States approximately December 1943 to squadron NAS Alameda. He remained there until discharge June 24, 1946. He received Aviation Medal, 1st Class. He returned to Hunterdon Farm and started an appliance business  that he operated until retirement. He raised three boys and seven grandchildren.

He enjoys talking about his Navy career.

HARRY E. KISOR, was born Dec. 7, 1919 at Portland, OR. He entered the service with the US Navy on Dec. 11, 1941.

He served aboard the USS *President Jackson,* USS *Cresent City* and several other vessels. Twenty minutes after an air raid, the gunner above him (still white as a sheet), said a torpedo went under the bulkhead (their station). He said it was either set too deep or dropped to close. He will never know. He was discharged with the rank of CM1/c on Nov. 11, 1945.

He has been married for more than 45 years. He has one

child and two grandchildren. He has been employed in the civilian sector as a carpenter, carpenter foreman and construction superintendent.

He retired Nov. 7, 1980 from Bary Hess Construction. He was also employed at the Portland International Airport.

PAUL Z. KISTLER was born May 13, 1918 at Lincolnton, NC. He enlisted in the United States Army on April 5, 1941. He served at Fort Bragg and Fort Sill.

He remembers thinking he was going to be shipped to New Guinea, but was shipped instead to Guadalcanal. He says he is proud to have served his country.

He made a lot of friends in the service, some he still sees at the reunions. He served with the 245th Field Artillery Bn., C Battery.

He was discharged Dec. 29, 1944 with the rank of private first class.

He is married and has three children, plus four grandchildren. He retired in July 1977 after working for the city of Gastonia, NC.

JOSEPH L. KIWAK

SAUL H. KNIGHT, was born Dec. 1, 1921 at Braxton Co., WV. He entered service with the US Navy on June 7, 1942. He went through boot camp at Norfolk, VA then to Diesel School at Richmond, VA. He then had some amphibian training at Little Creek, CA and from there to San Francisco, CA to the receiving station.

From there, he went to Noumea, New Caledonia, where he volunteered for duty at the boat pool on Guadalcanal. He was in the boat pool at Lunga Point on Guadalcanal for six months (1942 to early 1943).

Then went aboard the USS *George Clymer* (APA-27); while aboard, he made initial landings at Bougainville, Guam and Leyte in the Philippine Islands.

He then boarded a minesweeper—USS YMS-197. They operated between Bataan and Corregidor, at Balikpapin and Borneao, where they lost two YMS's.

He was discharged at Bainbridge, MD on Nov. 3, 1945, having attained the rank of motor machinist mate, first class.

He married Annie Grace Bowes July 10, 1947 and they are still together after 45 years.

He has one daughter, Beverly K. Littleton, and one granddaughter, Kristen M. Bell, both of Salem, VA. Kristen is a student at Roanoke College of Salem, VA.

He worked at the plumbing and pipe-fitting trade until retirement in 1980.

He is a member of VFW, American Legion, Guadalcanal Campaign Veterans, Naval Mine Warfare Association, L.O.O.M. and Plumbers and Pipe-fitters Local #645 of Charleston, WV.

His most memorable experience was the six months on Guadalcanal, in particular, while delivering rations and ammo to the front.

He was engineer on a tanklighter (LCM). They failed to make their delivery on the first try for a very good reason, dut did make it the next day. This was later in the campaign and the delivery was to some of the Americal Division boys.

JOSEPH J. KOSSUTH, was born Dec. 1, 1920 at New Jersey. He entered the US Marine Corps on Dec. 8, 1941. He served at Parris Island, SC, New River, NC, Auckland and Guadalcanal.

He was reported as KIA and was severely wounded in a Japanese Air Raid. When he was transported via hospital ship to New Zealand, he had to convince them that he was not KIA, just wounded. He then spent one year in the hospital. He was discharged as a private first class in October 1942.

He married Genevieve A. McCahill 50 years ago. They have three children, five grandchildren and two great-grandchildren. He was a marketing representative. He retired in July 1985.

JOHN E. KRUEGER, JR., enlisted in the U.S. Navy and was assigned to the USS *San Francisco,* 2d Division. Highlights were Pearl Harbor attack, Guadalcanal Campaign, Battle of Esperance, Battle of Guadalcanal and Aleutians Operation. Promoted to gunners mate, second class.

He was transferred to Advanced Gunnery School, Washington, DC, 1943. Commissioned USS *Bryant* (DD-665). While aboard, he was promoted gunners mate first class and later chief.

While serving aboard the USS *Bryant* he participated in the invasions of Palau, Saipan, Tinian and Leyte.

He also saw action during the torpedo runs during the battles of Suriago Straits, Luzon, Mindoro, Lingayen Gulf, Iwo Jima and culminating at Okinawa when their ship was attacked by six Kamikaze planes while steaming alone on picket duty.

Awarded the Silver Star Medal for organizing firefighting operations and rescuing unconscious seaman in ammunition storage locker.

Participated in 14 major engagements. *San Francisco* awarded the Presidential Unit Citation. *Bryant* awarded Navy Unit Commendation. Discharged in 1946.

Married to Florence, they have two daughters, Bonnie and Kim.

He is a retired deputy chief, New Brunswick Fire Department. Presently residing at Lavallette, NJ.

JOSEPH R. LACOY, was born on Oct. 25, 1921 in Penacook, NH.

Graduated Penacook High School in 1939.

He joined the Marine Corps on Jan. 6, 1942 and was discharged on Jan. 6, 1946. His first landing was on Guadalcanal on Aug. 7, 1942, as a forward observer for 81 mm mortars with M,

1. Awarded a Silver Star Medal. His second landing was New Britain in December 1943; again as a forward observer for the 81 mm mortars with M, 3, 1. His third landing was on Peleliu on Sept. 15, 1944; this time with K, 1, as a forward observer and sergeant in charge of 60 mm mortars. He was always on initial landings and made them their entirety with each company.

After he returned to the U.S., he met and married Mary Clancy on April 11, 1945. After he was discharged from the Marine Corps on Jan. 6, 1946, he went to work for the Boston and Maine Railroad in January 1946 and retired 8 years later.

They have a son and a daughter; both of whom live in the South not too far from them.

Shortly after retiring, they sold their home in New Hampshire and moved to the small town of Lillian, AL on Perdido Bay. They both are happy there and are enjoying their retirement years. He plays tennis, does some sailing and enjoys down-hill skiing, he likes the outdoors, wood-working, games and people.

FLOYD LADD, was born May 24, 1926 at Princeton, KY. Enlisted in the U.S. Navy at Denver, CO in December 1942.

He took his training at San Diego, CA.
Served aboard the USS *President Jackson*, Naval Boat Pool at Lunga Point, USS *Algorab* (AKA-8) and USS LCI 227. USS *President Jackson* was first ship to land troops during Guadalcanal Campaign.

Awards: National Defense, American Area, Good Conduct, Navy Occupation, World War II, Navy Unit Commendation, Asiatic Pacific w/five Stars.

Married after WWII and raised one son and has one grandson.

Retired from Navy Nov. 1, 1962 after 20 years of service. Went to work for the Navy and completed 22 years service and retired on Dec. 1, 1986. He is now enjoying the good life.

THOMAS J. LARSON, was born April 10, 1917, Kerkoven, MN. Joined Co. B, 135th MN National Guard at Aitkin when 15. After two years at the University of Minnesota made a vagabond journey as a Rover Scout through the U.S. and Europe for two years. Got out of Europe just before Germany invaded Poland. Graduated as Ensign, USNR, V-7 Program, Northwestern University September 1941.

Arrived Pearl Harbor on YP-109 as Executive Officer on Dec. 5, 1941. Assigned to CinCPac Staff as a communicator Dec. 6, 1941. Sent to Noumea on USS *Aragonne* in July 1942 to serve on ComSoPac Staff. Flown to Guadalcanal on Thanksgiving Day, 1942. Assigned as Com Officer Naval Base Tulagi (Hell's Kitchen) until Nov. 15, 1943. Was liason officer HMNZS *Leander* enroute to Boston December 1943. After service at Naval Air Station, Livermore, CA, served on USS *Lexington* as a deck officer. Ended WWII in Tokyo Bay with the 7th Fleet as a lieutenant commander.

Graduated from University of California, Berkeley, 1947 with a degree in anthropology. Became a member of University of California Africa Expedition for three and one half years in 1947. Attended Cape Town University on GI Bill. Has anthropology degrees from American Univer-

sity - MA, University Oxford M. Litt, Ph.D from University of Virginia. Active as a professor, USAID, explorer, writer for 12 years in 25 countries of Africa. Also carried out anthropological research in Guatemala, Mexico, Peru, Bahamas, and French Polynesia. Taught anthropology at University of Maryland, University of Witwatersrand in Johannesburg, University of Virginia, and Northern Virginia Community College at Annadale for 20 years.

Married Carolyn Collier they have had three weddings (Hamburg, Weisbaden, and Geneva) in Europe and have three children, Laurel, Tom, and Janet.

In early 1992 he planned to carry out the study of social change in Guadalcanal, Tulagai, and Florida Islands. Hopes to meet some of the fellow members down there. Also plans to give lectures to the Japanese tourists at $200 a ticket and tell them where their grandfather met his glorious end. One of his nephews went to Japan and came home with a lovely Japanese princess. Soon he will be a great uncle to a half Japanese boy. Larson says: "C'est la vie".

RICHARD T. LATTIN, was born in Humboldt, IA June 2, 1920. Enlisted Naval Reserves April 1942. Graduated Midshipman School, Columbia University, New York, NY Dec. 2, 1940.

Sailed from San Diego to Noumea, New Caledonia and assigned to USS *Rail*. Went aboard off Guadalcanal February 1943. The *Rail* was engaged in rescue and salvage duty along with towing barges of torpedoes to forward island bases. Here he met John F. Kennedy, which had minor significance in that situation.

After ten months, assigned to USAT H-4. Following Bougainville Campaign was given leave with orders to Diving School, Pier 88, New York City. This was followed by duty in the Asian Theatre as commanding officer aboard the USS APL-29.

Discharged to inactive duty at Great Lakes Naval Base March 1946, rank lieutenant s.g.

Dick and Donna Runft were married May 29, 1948, Cedar Falls, IA. They have five children and three grandchildren. He completed Ph.D in 1952.

Retired June 1986 after 39 years in administration and teaching at the University of Northern Iowa, Cedar Falls, IA.

KENNETH F. LEBAY, was born in Tiffin, OH Sept. 2, 1923. Enlisted Marine Corps Oct. 20, 1940, 8th Bn., USMCR, Toldeo, OH. Activated Nov. 9, 1940, Quantico, VA.

8th Bn. shipped Guantanamo Bay, Cuba, 1st Marine Brigade Signal Co., then Hq. Co., 2nd Bn., 7th Regt. Returned to New River, NC tent camp under construction. 7th Regt. shipped British Samoa April 2, 1942, Guadalcanal Sept. 18, 1942.

Wounded Nov. 2, 1942 at Matanikou River. Rejoined Hq. Co. 2-7 from field hospital, 2-7 moved to line position on Bloody Ridge, a ring side seat for Naval Battle in the Pass 2-7 received a Presidential Unit Citation for this action.

Shipped R&R Melbourne, Australia January 1943, New Guinea Oct. 10, 1943, landed Cape Gloucester Dec. 26, 1943. Was a member of Puller Patrol from Sag Sag to

Araway linking with U.S. Army then over the mountains back to U.S. perimeter. Was assigned responsibility of leading Australian correspondent Nowel Ottaway back to beach perimeter, encountering Japanese Gen. Matsuta's abandoned headquarters en route, then returned to Puller's Patrol.

Returned to States from Russell Islands May 3, 1944, discharged Camp Pendelton. Sept. 22, 1945.

Married Thomasina 1966, they have four children all married, Thomasina and Ken reside in Toledo, OH.

C. J. LINDSAY, was born on June 28, 1922 in Calagary Alberta, Canada. Enlisted USN Div. 13-6 Oct. 24, 1940. Served on board USS *Neville*, USS *Audabon*. Participated at Guadalcanal, Sicily, Kawajelin, Eniwetok, Saipan, Tinian, Guam, Makin, Okinawa, Philippines. He was discharged as BM 1/c.

Awards: Presidential Unit Citation, European-Theatre, Good Conduct Medal.

Married Connie, and they have four daughters, Kate, Mary, Ann, Patty and one son, Dave.

He is still in the sales field.

HERBERT H. LIVINGSTON, was born in Boston, MA on Oct. 15, 1922. He enlisted in the United States Marine Corps on Jan. 13, 1942.

He successfully completed boot camp at Parris Island, SC March 1, 1942. He was then assigned to H Co., 2nd Bn., 5th Marines, 1st Marine Division.

Departed for Wellington, New Zealand May 1942. Departed New Zealand aboard the USS *Neville* and made the landing on Tulagi, BSI on Aug. 7, 1942. August 21, 1942 moved to Guadalcanal. Participated in two battles at the Matanikau River, Edson Ridge, and was ambushed on the East West Trail where he helped carry out a wounded sergeant. Left Guadalcanal on Dec. 15, 1942 for Australia. Participated in the landings on Cape Gloucester, New Britain and Peleiu in the Palau Islands.

Returned to the United States in December 1944. After Navy yard duty went on sea duty aboard the USS *General R. M. Blatchford*.

Awards: Presidential Unit Citation, Good Conduct Medal w/four stars, Pacific-Asiatic Medal w/four stars, American Theatre of Operation Medal, European Theatre of Operation Medal, World War II Victory Medal, Korean Service Medal, Armed Forces Expeditionary Medal, Vietnam Service Medal.

Retired from the U.S. Marine Corps as a first sergeant April 1, 1969.

Married to Christina Scanlon June 8, 1947 in Boston, MA. Has two children, Robert and Donna and two grandchildren. All are now living in Montana. Presently retired from Hines Motor Supply as a salesman.

WILLIAM LOGAN, was born on Oct. 22, 1921 at Sag Harbor, NY. Joined the Navy February 1942, soon after, became a crew member of the *Libra*. While being a coxswain on the *Libra's* Higgins Boats participated in the entire Guadalcanal Campaign. Also, he landed Marines ashore at Ellis Islands, Rendova, Russells and Bougainville.

At Guadalcanal Dec. 27, 1943, Bill transferred to the *Fuller*. Became a gunners mate in charge of 3-inch .50 caliber on the port stern. Took part in the invasions of Pelelieu, Leyte, Lingayen Gulf, Saipan, Tinian and Okinawa.

Discharged November 1945 Bill returned home and married Elaine, his high school sweetheart. They have two children, Barbara and Ronald. He retired from the Southampton Police Department after 24 years of duty. Whenever Bill is not fishing or goose hunting he operates his security guard agency.

KENNETH L. LOVE, was born Sept. 3, 1921 at Benzonia, MI. He entered the service with the US Marine Corps on July 1, 1942. He served Stateside at San Diego, CA, Washington, DC and Hagerstown, MD.

He shipped out of California on the SS *Lurline*, was transferred to a troop ship and entered Guadalcanal around Sept. 20, 1942. He was assigned to G Co., 2d Bn., 7th Marines, 1st Marine Division. Capt. Robinson was their G Co. Commander. His lieutenant was Lt. Walzack. He had a corporal rating.

They moved off Guadalcanal Jan. 5, 1943, going to Australia for nine months to recuperate and train. Spent four months in the hospital with malaria and yellow jaundice. Next he sailed for the Palau Islands, landing on Peleliu. He fought there for 17 days and was wounded in the back and groin. The Marines flew him to Epritiu Santo where he received the Purple Heart while hospitalized for three months before sailing home. At this time, he received a sergeant rating also.

Married and has four childran and six grandchildren. He is a self-employed builder and in real-estate sales.

DARYL A. LOVGREN, was born in Goodhue County, MN on Aug. 6, 1919. He enlisted in the US Naval Reserve on Feb. 9, 1942 at Baltimore, MD. He served aboard the USS *Fuller* (APA-7) from March 27, 1942 to October 22, 1945. He was discharged as chief petty officer on Nov. 21, 1945 at Minneapolis, MN.

He participated in the initial invasion of Guadalcanal on Aug. 7, 1942 and several months of reinforcement activity. Continued to serve on the USS *Fuller* during the invasions of Bougainville, Saipan, Tinian, Peleliu, Leyte, Luzon and Okinawa. He participated in the initial occupation of Japan. He received the Asiatic Pacific Medal with nine Campaign Stars and the Philippine Liberation Medal with two stars. He has a wife, Helen, two sons and two step-daughters. He also has six grandchildren.

He is retired from Prudential Insurance Company. He is a member of Zumbro Lutheran Church, Elks, VFW and the Guadalcanal Campaign Veterans Association.

ROBERT A. LOWERY, was born Feb. 14, 1916 at Malden, MA. He entered the service with the US Navy in February 1941. He served aboard ship on the USS *Texas*, *Alchiba* and *Alhena*. He served at Guadalcanal and Siapan.

He helped set-up visual communication from shore to ship, directing landings. He remembers watching more than 2,000 natives jump off a 2,000 foot cliff into the rocks below. He was discharged with the rank of signalman, first class.

He has been married for 49 years. He has four children and six grandsons. He worked as a salesman and sales manager until his retirement in 1990.

He says that he and his wife have had a good life. Six fine grandsons, all of them are excellent students, four of them are in college and two to go! They enjoy excellent health. He plays golf frequently and travels once or twice a year. His wife is a gem!

CHRIS A. LUCERO (deceased), was born July 24, 1919 at Tucumcari, NM. He entered the service with the USMC on Aug. 28, 1940. He served at the following military stations and locations: San Diego, Camp Elliott, Iceland, New Zealand, Guadalcanal and Hollbrook, CA.

He served on a Kaiser Concrete Ship. He recalls going on liberty before the war with his younger brother, Lea. They would ask Chris for identification, but they never asked Lea. He also remembers talking Lea into lending him some money to go on leave at Christmas, 1941. Payday was the first and 15th of the month. Discharged with the rank of sergeant in 1945.

He married Lucille Lucero from St. John, AZ. They have six children. He was a painter. *(Submitted by Lea B. Lucero)*

DONALD K. LUTES, Sr. was born in Chicago, IL on Aug. 15, 1919. Enlisted in Naval Reserve October 1940. Assigned to the 20th Division, Ninth Naval District. Called into active duty January 1941 and sent to Naval Receiving Station, Bremerton, WA. Boarded the USS *Fuller* (APA-7) April 1940. *Fuller* took part in training exercises and delivered the 6th Marines to Iceland.

After Pearl Harbor, USS *Fuller* was sent to the South Pacific. Participated in Guadalcanal and other campaigns.

Served as a seaman for a year, then transferred to the Medical Dept., rated pharmacist mate, 2d class. Left the *Fuller* in October 1943 for duty at Mare Island, CA and six months duty at San Diego Naval Hospital. Sent to Okinawa with Lion 8-Naval Marine Base Hospital. Discharged October 1945. He married Dorothymae Kummelehne in 1943. They have five sons, Randal, Charles, Kevin, Donald Jr. and Jeffrey, and four grandchildren.

After the war, he continued his education in chemistry at the Illinois Institute of Technology. His career embraced 36 years with Sherwin-Williams Paint Co. during which he held several administrative positions. Since retirement in 1981, he and Dottie reside in Tucson, AZ. He is senior vice president of the GCV Association.

GEORGE C. MACGILLIVRAY, was born in Boston, MA on Nov. 1, 1922. Enlisted in the USMC March 10, 1941. After boot camp at Parris Island he was assigned to 7th Marines, Weapons Co. The summer of 1941 was spent aboard ship doing amphibious exercises at Onslow Beach, NC. Then on to New River, NC prior to Pearl Harbor on December 7.

Early in 1942 the 7th Marines went to Samoa and arrived at the time Corregidor was captured by the Japanese. In September 1942, the 7th Marines rejoined the 1st Marine Div. on Guadalcanal. Four months of bombings, naval shelling and combat while attached to Lt. Col. Puller's (Chesty) bn. during the October 24 battle for Henderson Field and again with Puller at Koli Point in November.

Corporal MacGillivray departed Guadalcanal early January 1943 for rest and hospitalization for malaria in the 4th General Hospital in Melbourne. While in Australia he received a meritorious promotion to sergeant and soon went to New Guinea and Cape Gloucester, New Britain for the December invasion.

After the Battle for Hill 660 and patrols in the area of the airfield, the 7th went to Pavuvu Island in the Solomons. The company commander sent MacGillivray to Officer Candidate Bn. at New River, NC and later in November 1944 to Dartmouth College, Naval V-12 program. By the time four required semesters were completed, the war was over.

He left the Corps after six years and went on to finish college under the GI Bill. In 1950 he joined the Central Intelligence Agency and retired in 1982.

Married to Gloria Manter in 1950 and they had three children Jeffrey, James, and Kathleen. He lives in Bethesda, MD and has had several offices in the 1st Marine Division Assoication.

NORMAN C. MALLETT, was born Nov. 7, 1917 in the Bronx, NY. He was inducted into the U.S. Army in June of 1941 at Camp Upton, Long Island, NY.

After his completion of basic training in Camp Whelling, GA, he was assigned to the 37th Div., 147th Inf., Co. M, Camp Shelby, MI. He disembarked from New York through the Panama Canal into the South Pacific in 1942 on the *American Legion*. It took 33 days to arrive on Tonga Island. They then processed on to Guadalcanal.

His most memorable event was when Admiral Halsey toured the Pacific area and his unit was picked for Honor Guard.

He was rotated on points to the U.S. and stationed at Ft. Knox, TN. After serving his country he was discharged in 1944.

Returned home to marry his childhood sweetheart, Aileen Moran, in 1945. They have four beautiful daughters and five wonderful grandchildren.

Upon retiring as regional manager from Cerco Products, Norman and his wife enjoy traveling and being with their family in Scarsdale, NY.

KENNETH V. MALSCH, was born Nov. 21, 1915 in Waterbury, CT. He graduated from Crosby High 1933 and worked for Swift and Company. He joined the USMC in September 1941. Went to boot camp at Parris Island for two months, was assigned to 4th Bn., 11th Marines, 1st Marine Division.

Was promoted to sergeant in fire direction in April 1942. Was shipped to South Pacific in June 1942. Stationed at New Zealand and participated in Guadalcanal campaign.

He suffered injury and severe malaria. Had attacks en route to Marshall Islands in 1944. He spent several months in hospital, then received a medical discharge in September 1945 as gunnery sergeant. Married to Eileen Murphy of Dracut, MA on Dec. 30, 1944. They have four daughters, Karen, Julie, Eileen, Maureen, one son Kenneth, and eight grandchildren. After discharge, he attended Boston College and received B.S. degree in 1950. Worked for Bridgeport Brass Co. and retired as VP Sales in 1980.

SALVATORE MARCHISELLO born July 3, 1919 at Philadelphia, PA. Joined the U.S. Army on Sept. 17, 1941. He served at Ft. Meade, Camp Croft, Guadalcanal, Bougainville, Camp Robinson, Camp House and Ft. Benning. Discharged Oct. 18, 1945 with the rank of corporal.

He recalls many battle experiences. They landed in Australia, only to be shipped out to New Caledonia for jungle training. They landed on Guadalcanal November 12, 1942. That evening they saw a big battle from the beach. They were also bombed by Jap planes that evening. They were attached to the 1st Marine Div. He was with the Americal Div., 182d Inf. Co. H (Heavy Weapons) as a machine gunner. Every night they had visits from "Washing Machine Charlie." He recalls seeing Japanese troop ships beached on Nov. 12, 1942. At Bougainville, they were outnumbered (20,000 vs. 7,000). The supply lines were cut off by the Japs. They were told they might be driven out to sea by the Japs and were given demolition grenades to destroy their weapons if that happened. They survived because of help from the Navy and Air Force. Flame-throwers were used to get the Japs out of their foxholes.

He received the Combat Badge and Presidential Unit Citation. He is married with two children, five grandchildren. He worked for Shirtmanu Tailoring and General Electric Co. until retirement in July 1983.

JOHN E. MARINKO, was born at Sharon, PA. On May 19, 1937. He entered the service with the US Marine Corps. He served in the Southwest Pacific Theatre of the war. He was discharged with the rank of CWO.

He remembers Hell's Hole, Guadalcanal. He remembers the landing, Aug. 7, 1942, 3:30 a.m. He was known as a Jungle Fighter by Gen. Vandergrift, USMC. Joe Foss and Luke Diamond were his friends.

He has a wife and four sons. He is presently retired, enjoying his wildlife birds and squirrels.

EMIL E. MATULA, born April 4, 1918 at West, TX. He entered the service on Jan. 3, 1937 and served with the 25th Inf. Div. Stationed at Ft. Sam Houston, TX from 1937 until 1940.

He saw action in the battle of Guadalcanal from Dec. 17, 1942 to Feb. 13, 1943. American forces invaded New Georgia, Vella Lavella and Luzon, Philippines. The intense fighting with the Japanese on Luzon, Philippines continued for 165 consecutive days and nights. He was twice wounded and twice returned to battle. He was battlefield commissioned on March 1, 1945 in the Battle of Lupoa. Subsequently discharged Aug. 15, 1945 with the rank of second lieutenant.

He married Evelyn A. Motloch. They have four children and nine grandchildren.

He worked in sales with Dr. Pepper Company and Jewel Tea Company from 1949 to 1980. He retired in July 1980.

He received the following decorations: Good Conduct Medal, American Defense with Bronze Star, Combat Infantry Badge, Asiatic-Pacific Campaign Ribbon with four Bronze Stars and Bronze Arrow, Philippine Liberation Medal with Bronze Star, Purple Heart with two Oak Leaf Clusters and Bronze Star with three Oak Leaf Clusters.

Emil is active in civil affairs of the community. He is past president of Pearl Harbor Alamo Chapter, San Antonio, TX, 1988; past president of SPJST, K.J.T, Highland Hills Assoc., past second vice president of the 25th Inf. Div. Assoc., he has served as chairman of the 1970 KJT state convention, SPJST state convention in 1980 and as chairman, 1981, 25th Inf. Div. Assoc.

BILL MCCABE, was born Oct. 1, 1921 in California. He finished high school in 1940. He worked and started college in Alaska, staying until War was declared.

Returned to California and joined the Coast Guard in February 1942. He had 21 days of boot camp and 14 more days in Marine Combat Training. A tour at Shore Station and then to USS *Hunter Liggett* (APA-14) and the USS *Brewster* (AP-155).

He served in the Pacific Theatre from the Solomons to the Philippines with the exception of one trip to Europe.

He was one of the lucky ones who went where they were sent, did the job they were told to do and came home safe. He was discharged in October 1945.

In 1947 he joined the US Navy Reserve and served mostly as an instructor for 12 years.

In 1992, he was lucky enough to return to the Pacific for the 50-year reunion at Guadalcanal, paying tribute to those who didn't make it home. A wonderful experience and tribute.

DENNIS R. MCCARTHY born in Bronx, NY on June 19, 1919. Moved to Nutley, NJ at the age of five. Raised in Nutley, joined Marine Corps in January 1942, and still resides in Nutley.

Went to boot camp at Parris Island and thence to Tent City, New River at Camp LeJeune, where he joined the 1st Marine Div. in I (Item) Co., 3d Bn., 1st Marine Regt. as a machine gunner. Left Tent City by train for California where they boarded the merchant ship *John Ericcson*, bound for Wellington, New Zealand. Shortly after arrival, they boarded the USS *McCawley* (APA-4) for Aug. 7, 1942 invasion of Guadalcanal.

Was at the battle of Alligator Creek on Aug. 21, 1942, stationed on the beach, just west of Tenaru (Ilu). He remembers that in October 1942, Battle of Matanikau, Jap tanks crossed the spit. One of them veered off the spit into the lagoon about 50 feet in front of his machine gun. During the battle, he remembers a mortar explosion and watching his buddy, Peter Davis, go flying through the air. We got to him and asked him how he was. He said, "OK, but gee, I felt just like a boid flying through the air." After the Canal, they went to Australia and then Goodenough Island, New Guinea, Cape Gloucester, Peleliu, Pavuvu (rest camp?) and finally back to the U.S. in 1944 on the USS *West Point* (APA-23). At one time he was a Corporal. He was discharged as Pfc, Sept. 1945.

He has been retired for several years after working with the Railway Express in New York for 35 years.

He is now a widower, having lost his wife in 1989. He belongs to the West Hudson Det., MCL and NJ Chapter, 1st Marine Div. Assn.

JAMES R. MCCARTHY, JR., was born June 5, 1924 at Waterbury, MA. He entered service with the Marines on Dec. 11, 1941. He served at Parris Island, SC, New River, NC, Wellington, New Zealand, Brisbane and Melbourne, Australia, Finchhaven, New Guinea, Guadalcanal and New Britian.

Of his experiences during service, he recalls one night, around November 12-13, when the Japanese battleships came down the slot. It was horrendous. Their big guns blazing—it lit up the night (even though it was raining cats and dogs.) The Japanese blew out all of their communications. At the time, he was with the 2d Bn., 11th Marines, 75mm Artillery Fire Control. Maj. Foley asked for a volunteer to go with him to the gun battery (about one-half mile) so that they could direct the gun fire.

The shells were still coming in and they were knee deep in mud. It was pitch black after the explosion, but they made it to the gun battery. They completed the mission, holding off a Japanese counter-attack. He can remember the whole incident as it occured yesterday.

Maj. Foley received the Silver Star and he was awarded the Bronze Star, of which he is very proud. He also received four Battle Stars, two Presidential Unit Citations and their unit received a Navy Commendation. He also received a four year Good Conduct Medal.

He says, "At that time [the young] . . . would stick together all the time. Unfortunately, the young of today don't respect the action taken by all of the services in WWII. They don't even know where Guadalcanal was or the significance of the battle."

He was discharged December 1944 with the rank of corporal. He is married to Maria and has three children and two grandchildren. He is the owner of Jim McCarthy Dodge, he retired June 18, 1988.

A. B. MEADOR, born in Araret, AL Nov. 25, 1918. US Army Field Artilley, Aug. 1, 1939 to Sept. 19, 1945. He was discharged with the rank of staff sergeant.

He is married with six children and three grandchildren. He owns a construction company.

He received the following awards: American Defense Service Ribbon and one Star, Asiatic-Pacific Campaign Medal, Good Conduct Medal, four Bronze Stars.

He participated in the following battles/campaigns: Guadalcanal, North Solomon Islands, Central Pacific, Philippines.

He served with the 25th Division, 64th Field Artillery Bn.

RAY A. McDERMED, was born in Chicago, IL on April 22, 1918. He graduated from Harper High School and attended Purdue University.

He enlisted in the Marine Corps Reserve in September 1940 and was mobilized in December 1940. When the 1st Marine Brigade was reorganized in February 1941, he was assigned to the 1st Marines.

After training in Parris Island, SC, he was sent to New Zealand for further training and after maneuvers off Koro, Fiji, landed in Guadalcanal on Aug. 7, 1942, where he remained until December 1942 and he subsequently served at Cape Gloucester, Pelilu and Okinawa.

For his participation in those campaigns, he received a Purple Heart and Bronze Star. After a short assignment on train escort duty in Tietsin, China, he returned to the US. He was discharged from Camp Pendelton, CA in July 1946 with the rank of staff sergeant.

He married Angeline Pantazelos of Chicago on July 29, 1962. They have no children, but are devoted to their five god children and all live in Chicago. He was accepted as a Chicago Policeman and retired on pension as sergeant after 37 years of service.

He is presently supervisor for the Joseph Kennedy Foundation.

He is a member of Guadalcanal Campaign Veterans, Marine Corps League, American Legion, Devil Dogs and Special Agents Association.

His hobbies are Ancient Archeology, travel to the Mid East and financial investments.

JOHN A. McDERMOTT, was born in Albany, NY on Nov. 2, 1921. He enlisted in the Marine Corps Jan. 24, 1942.

After training at Parris Island, he was assigned to Weapons Company, 5th Regt., 1st Marine Div. at New River, NC and shipped out on USS *Wakefield*, May 20, 1942 to Wellington, New Zealand.

He arrived on Guadalcanal Aug. 7, 1942 and was stationed on the beach. He was assigned to a 37mm anti-tank gun squadron. His most memorable events were seeing a torpedo come up on the beach and watching the Japanese unloading ships on the other side of the island.

He was stationed at Cape Gloucester from Dec. 3, 1943 to May 5, 1944. Then to Peleliu Island from Sept. 15, 1944. He returned to the States in November 1944. He was discharged at M.B. Navy Yard, NY. He married Anna C. Bertram in 1966. They have two sons, Jack and Walter, and two daughters, Brenda and Linda. He has resided in New York for 70 years and presently resides in Niverville, NY.

JOHN J. MCDOWELL born Christchurch, New Zealand on Sept. 27, 1917. Enlisted in the Royal New Zealand Air Force (Territorial Air Force) April 1938 and mobilized Sept. 4, 1939. Trained as Radio Operator/Air Gunner and later as Navigator. Commissioned November 1940. October 1942, assigned to No. 3 Bomber Recon. Squad., RNZAF (Lockheed Hudsons) as Nav. Officer. On Nov. 23, 1942, moved from New Hebrides to Henderson Airfield, Guadalcanal with this unit and worked from there under operational command of U.S. 1st Marine Air Wing.

In absence of an air meteorological officer at Henderson, he assumed those duties and at the request of U.S. Air Authorities, made special night forecasts that were used exclusively in the determination of the feasibility of night bombing missions.

Awarded MBE (British Decoration) after Guadalcanal Tour. Following war service, re-trained as pilot and served in RNZAF until May 1973 when retired with rank of Air Commodore (one star).

Married Leah Punch March 30, 1943 and they have four children and 10 grandchildren.

GERALD P. McHALE, was born Nov. 16, 1922 at Binghamton, NY. He entered the US Marine Corps on Jan. 2, 1942.

He landed at Guadalcanal on Aug. 7, 1942. He remembers the landing, Matanikau and Lunga Point. He served as a 60mm mortarman. They left Guadalcanal on Dec. 9, 1942.

He spent 31 months overseas. He was with H and S, B Company, 1st MT Bn., Guard Detachment, MCAS Cherry Point, 1st Casual Company, Camp LeJeune, Marine Discharge Center, Great Lakes. He was discharged Jan. 3, 1946 with the rank of corporal.

He married Marion Hull (deceased) on July 19, 1945 at Jacksonville, NC. They have three children and two grandchildren.

He was a scout executive with BSA. He also worked as a project manager with the reactivation commitee regarding the battleships *New Jersey* and *Missouri*. He retired in 1987.

JOSEPH G. MICEK, enlisted in the Illinois National Guard, 132d Inf. Regt., in 1939 at the age of 15 and one-half years.

The regiment was federalized into active service in March 1941. He is recognized as the youngest US Army Platoon Sergeant at the age of 17 and one-half years.

While in Lane Technical high School, ROTC Program, left as Cadet Captain into active service.

Trained in Camp Forrest, TN. Regiment they sent to the South Pacific in January 1942, via Panama Canal to Melbourne, Australia and into New Caledonia, March 1942.

The regiment became part of the famed Americal Division formed on New Caledonia which participated in the Guadalcanal, Bougainville and Philippine Islands Campaigns, plus the occupation of Japan.

He served as a base correspondent in New Caledonia. He received an appointment to West Point on the island of Guadalcanal, but failed the medical exam due to severe malaria illness.

He graduated college in 1953 with a BSC Degree in accounting. Later, he attained an MA Degree in Health Administration.

He has been a practicing tax-accountant and corporate controller for 20 years. Since 1974, he has worked as Finance Officer of the Hine Veterans Administration hospital, from which he retired in 1990.

He is past national secretary and senior vice-president, current national treasurer of the Guadalcanal Campaign Veterans organization: 4,000 members.

Also currently treasurer of the Guadalcanal-Solomon Island War Memorial Foundation in a joint venture with the US American Battle Monuments Commission, construction WW II monuments on Guadalcanal.

He has visited Guadalcanal five time in the last four years. As monument project manager, he will visit again in August 1992 for dedications.

He is an active member of VFW Post 3579, former member of the National 1976 Bicentennial Commission, former President of the Norridge Youth Activities (receiv-

ing a commendation from the White House in August 1962), secretary of the Norridge Zoning Board of Appeals. Co-author of *Orchids in the Mud*, exploits of the 132 Inf Regt. in WW II. He travels extensively in Europe and the South Pacific. He served on the book committed for the original *Guadalcanal Legacy* and is on the current book committee for the *Guadalcanal Legacy*, 50th Anniversary Edition. He married Marie Tomasiewicz in 1946. They have two daughters, Marilyn and Debra.

LAWRENCE J. MICHIELS, was born in Chicago, IL on April 26, 1922. He joined Div. 9-23, USNR on Jan. 8, 1940. Cruised Lake Michigan on USS *Sacramento* in summer of 1940.

Active duty Dec. 17, 1940 to put USS *Heywood* (AP-A6) in commission in Portland, OR. Attended Higgins Landing Craft School, April 1941. Landed Major Torgerson on Gavutu Island on Aug. 7, 1942.

Spent four months on Tulagi Island in boat pool with Leroy Hazel. Crossed frequently to Lunga Pt. or Guadalcanal. Bunked with Samuel B. Roberts while there. On Dec. 9, 1942 boarded USS *President Adams* (APA-19) off Lunga Pt. Left Adams Jan. 10, 1944 (BM1/c) for Northwestern V-12 program. Left in March 1945 for Cornell University Midshipman School. Commissioned ensign June 7, 1945; joined pre-commissioning crew of USS *Meridith* (DD-890) at Norfolk, VA. Returned to inactive duty in October 1945.

Various USNR billets in San Francisco Bay Area. Released to inactive status June 1972. LCDR-USNR. Retired in 1978.

Married to Anne Bowen in 1947 and has five children: Matthew, Marc, Meighan, Monica, and Mary.

GLENN W. MILLS, was born May 26, 1922 in Jefferson City, TN. Entered the service in September 1941. Assigned to 1st Marine Div. Stationed at Parris Island, SC; Quantico, VA; Melbourne, Australia; Guadalcanal, and the Solomons.

His memorable experiences include finishing boot camp day before Pearl Harbor was bombed and being with the 1st Marine Div. landing on Guadalcanal.

Discharged with rank private first class, he was awarded the Purple Heart, Presidential Unit Citation, Asiatic-Pacific Theater with two stars.

Married and has three sons, two daughters, eight grandsons, and one granddaughter.

He is retired, captain of Honor Guard VFW, member of DAV, and American Legion.

GEORGE MITCHELL, was born Jan. 21, 1913 in Cambuslang, Scotland. Entered the service Aug. 8, 1934, Royal Navy, Stoker II Class. Stationed at United Kingdom, New Zealand, Treasure Island, and San Francisco, CA.

His memorable experiences include Guadalcanal; torpedoing of *Leander*; Yalu, Han Gang; and Tokyo Bay.

Discharged with the rank Commander RNZN.

Married to Constance Neville Mitchell and has one son and two daughters: George, Muriel, and Pauline.

He is a retired Marine surveyor. Now enjoys golf and computers.

JACK STEPHEN MITCHELL, was born Oct. 5, 1923 in Binghamton, NY. Joined the USMC Nov. 10, 1941. After boot camp was assigned to 11th Marines, 1st Div. at New River, NC.

Landed on Canal Aug. 7, 1942. Left for Australia in January 1943 (Ballarat). Participated in Asiatic-Pacific Theatre June 22, 1942 to Dec. 12, 1944. Returned to United States December 1944.

Received honorable discharge Oct. 5, 1945 (what a birthday present). He completed his education and joined Prudential Insurance Co. on May 26, 1947. Married to Lillian on April 26, 1950, she passed away Oct. 21, 1982. He has a son Steven, daughter-in-law Patty, granddaughter Jennifer, and grandson Matthew.

He lost a left lung Feb. 10, 1982, disability. Retired May 26, 1982 after 35 years with Prudential.

DANIEL MIZERAK, was born in Cherry Valley, NY on Aug. 15, 1922. Graduated from Cherry Valley Central School in 1940. Enlisted in USMC on March 5, 1941. Assigned to 1st Marine Div., Co. G, 2nd Bn., 1st Marines. Foreign service in Asiatic Pacific area from June 22, 1942 to July 7, 1944.

Participated in action against the Imperial Forces of Japan at Guadalcanal from Aug. 7, 1942 to Dec. 24, 1942. Was at Camp Goucester from Dec. 16, 1943 to March 1, 1944; Panama Canal Zone Feb. 22, 1945 to March 23, 1946.

Some memories of Co. G: the first American Marine planes landing on Henderson Field in August 1942; comrades (13) KIA on Aug. 21, 1942 during the Battle of Tenaru and his outlook on life was changed forever; the hunger in late August and September, existing on captured Japanese wormy rice, dysentery, mosquitoes, flies, infected bites, and malaria; the punctual noon bombing day after day; the shelling at night by ships standing off shore using their searchlights; the after dark listening posts across the Tenaru River; patrols, also over four months on the front lines without relief, the three, whole day air battles overhead in September, October, and November; the night, a ship blew up during an naval sea battle that turned night into day at their land positions; the nuisances, "Washing Machine Charley" took 1 1/2 hours, around midnight to drop one bomb, night after night and "Pistol Pete" took all day, to fire one 75mm shell on their ridge positions, G Co. galley took a direct hit, no casualties. It took a while to find and put him out of action.

The 1st Marine Div. was the only and the last to use the five round clip, bolt action, 1903 Springfield Rifle during the Guadalcanal Campaign.

His medals include the Presidential Unit Citation with two stars, Asiatic-Pacific, Good Conduct Medal with two stars plus three other medals and Rifle Expert.

Married to Beatrice Field Oct. 27, 1944. He has one daughter Eileen M. Leland, two sons Wayne and Brian, two grandchildren Lisa and Timothy, two foster daughters Pauline Putman and Judith Schlegel, and six grandchildren.

Employed by General Electric as machinist apprentice, tool and die maker, large motor and general rotor designer; Remington Rand as tool and product designer; State of New York, Dept. OGS, retired as assistant architect on April 29, 1988.

ROBERT J. MOBERG, was born July 28, 1915 in St. Paul, MN. Joined the USMC in October 1941 in Minneapolis, MN and was sent to boot camp at San Diego, CA. After boot camp he was assigned to G Co., 2nd Bn. and Regt., 2nd Div. at Camp Elliott.

A few weeks later he was transferred to Hqs. Co., 2nd Bn. Intelligence and attended Combat Intelligence School, Demolition and Sabotage School and also was an assistant in the Demolition and Sabotage School. A short time later he received his corporal stripes. On March 7, 1942 he married his hometown girlfriend in San Diego.

Landed in Tulagi, Solomon Islands on Aug. 7, 1942. On

Oct. 31, 1942 the 2nd Regt. was transferred to Guadalcanal. In February 1942 they were sent to Wellington, New Zealand at Camp McKaye's Crossing for R&R. In November 1943 landed on Red Beach in Tarawa.

After Tarawa was secured, the 2nd Div. was sent to the Big Island, HI For injuries received at Tarawa, he was sent to Pearl Harbor Hospital #128. From there he was transferred to Seattle Navy Hospital, then to San Diego R&R Center for reassignment.

Received a 30 day leave before reporting to Camp Perry, Williamsburg, VA. While there he was chief censor for incoming and outgoing mail for a General Court Martial Brig.

Three months later he was transferred to Camp Lejeune, NC for reassignment. Attended advanced Combat Intelligence School and after that was asked to attend Aerial Photo School (API). Had a reoccurrence of malaria and was sent to the Navy hospital at Camp Lejeune, NC. While there the war ended and he was discharged and sent back to St. Paul, MN.

He went to the St. Paul Fire and Marine Insurance Co. where he worked before enlisting in the Marine Corps. After 37 years, he retired. He has three children: Mary, Robert John Moberg II, and Bruce. Robert is a lieutenant colonel in the Marine Corps Reserve.

On Sept. 10, 1990, he left the USA for a two week visit to Guadalcanal. He revisited many places that he was at and some that he had heard about but had not seen. He had a wonderful time. He plans to attend the 50th anniversary of the Invasion of Guadalcanal if his health and money permits. At the present time he is enjoying good health.

JOHN M. MOBLEY, was born Sept. 20, 1920 in Kershaw, SC. He enlisted in the USMC in August 1940. Assignment following boot camp was with the 1st Brigade, sailing for Cuba. In 1941 he transferred to the 1st Regt. when the 1st Div. was formed.

Served and fought with this unit in the Guadalcanal Campaign, scouting operations with the forward echelon in Finschafen, New Guinea, and in the Cape Gloucester Campaign. Fought in the battle of the Tenaru River on Guadalcanal. Went on many patrols in the rain forests of "no mans land." At Cape Gloucester, after his regiment captured the airport, he took part in raids along the coast in Higgins boats and patrolled the inland jungles.

In 1945 he was platoon sergeant in the 8th Regt. on Saipan. When the war was over, his regiment occupied a suburb of Nagasaki, Japan.

Married Eileen Reeves and has two sons, Charles and David.

WILLIAM DAVID MONJAY, was born in Centraila, WA on Sept. 7, 1921. He graduated from Washington High School in Portland, OR in 1939. He was the student body president there. He attended Oregon State College on a basketball scholarship until the war broke out.

He enlisted in the USMC on Jan. 2, 1942. After completion of basic training, he was assigned to the Signal Bn. in San Diego. In March of 1944 he was transferred to the 8th Amphibian Tractor Bn. and in June shipped out for the South Pacific.

In August he participated in amphibious operations and training on Guadalcanal. On Sept. 14, 1944, as a member of Co. C, he participated in the amphibious assault and capture of Peleliu in the Palau Islands. On April 1, 1945, he participated

in the amphibious assault and capture of Okinawa Island. His father told me the amphibious tractor that he commanded carried Ernie Pyle, the famous war correspondent, onto the beach where he was killed by the Japanese machine gun fire.

In December he returned to San Diego aboard the USS *Nashville* and was discharged on Dec. 21, 1945 as a platoon sergeant.

He married Lillian A. Rediske of Tacoma, WA on Feb. 17, 1946. He has three children, William David Jr., Susan Lee Yahns, Beverly Anita Tuengel, and five grandchildren all living near Seattle, WA.

After his discharge he went to work for Western Electric as a telephone installer. Then he went to the West Coast Telephone Co. (which was purchased by General Telephone and Electric) as an installation supervisor, eventually becoming the manager of building administration. William D. Monjay died on Nov. 25, 1978 and is buried at Cypress Lawn Cemetery in Everett, WA. *Submitted by William David Monjay Jr., Sergeant, USAF.*

JOHN F. MONTINI, was born Jan. 25, 1921 in Massillon, OH where he has been a lifelong resident. He enlisted in USMC on Aug. 20, 1941 while attending college level classes in Klamath Falls, OR.

After training at Parris Island, SC, he was assigned to New River, NC, where he was serving when WWII broke out. He was sent as a rifleman to the South Pacific with the 1st Marine Div. to Samoa Island, then to Guadalcanal and served in the campaign there from August to December 1942.

He was the first to contract malaria at Guadalcanal and was sent to Bellerat, Australia to spend three months in a hospital with malaria fever. He remained in Australia until July 1943, when he was shipped back to the United States to Long Beach, CA Naval Hospital for a two month stay. From there he was shipped home to Massillon for a 45-day sick leave, until October 1943. From Massillon went to Philadelphia, PA Naval Hospital for a two month stay, then back to New River, NC for three months before being shipped back overseas in March 1944 to the Hawaiian Islands, where he joined the 2nd Marine Div.

He served in campaigns on Saipan and Tinian in the Marianas Islands in June 1944. He was stationed on Saipan until March 1945 and again saw combat beginning Easter Sunday, April 1, 1945, on Okinawa. He was on Okinawa until April 14 when he was again shipped back to the States. In August 1945 he went to Klamath Falls, OR where he attended college level classes until he was discharged in October 1945.

The entire time he was in the service he served as a rifleman. He attained the rank of private first class when he was discharged in October 1945.

Married to Mary Halco on Dec. 3, 1960. He has two daughters, Shirley Ewicka and Carol Carter, both of Massillon, OH and six grandchildren. He has lived in Massillon all his life. He retired in 1982 from Republic Steel Corp. where he was employed as a maintenance man in the machine shop for 43 years. He is a life member of the American Italian Club of Massillon and a life member of the DAV, Chapter 38.

EDSEL F. MOORE, was born Jan. 24, 1922 in Lawrence County, AL. Went to University of Alabama and also took ROTC.

Enlisted in USMC Jan. 30, 1942 as a regular. Went to boot camp at Parris Island, SC, then to New River, NC. Was assigned to Weapons Co., 5th Regt., 1st Div. He left New River and went through the Panama Canal to Wellington, New Zealand on the USS *Wakefield*. Landed on Guadalcanal Aug. 7, 1942, then to Brisbane and Melbourne, Australia; Millen Bay, New Guinea; Cape Gloucester, and New Britain. Came back to the U.S. on points on the *Roe Shombole* to San Diego then to Camp Lejeune, NC as a combat instructor. Discharged Jan. 31, 1946.

He attended the University of Alabama, the Atlanta Law School LLB and LLM degrees. He is a member of the Georgia Bar. Was elected to Alabama legislature in 1963, also obtained LLB degree from Jones Law School. Retired from the state of Alabama Judicial System Feb. 1, 1989.

Married Lucy V. Blackburn on May 27, 1955. They have two children Elizabeth and James. He is a member of VFW, American Legion, Masonic Lodge, and Baptist Church.

DESIRE MOREAU, (BUD), was born Oct. 13, 1924 in Duquesne, PA. Enlisted in USN May 13, 1942. Went to boot camp in Newport, RI; then aboard USS *O'Bannon* in late June 1942. Put ship into commission, plankowner.

Went to South Pacific after shakedown, made WT1/c. Served aboard the O'Bannon all through the war. Discharged in November 1945.

Married Alice McConville in August 1946. They have two sons, one granddaughter, and one grandson.

He went into auto repairs and started his own garage in 1955 and is still working part-time.

GERALD H. MORRISON, (PETE), was born Feb. 14, 1920 in Avard, OK. Enlisted in the USN in September of 1941. Orders sent him to the 8th Naval District U.S. Naval Hospital, Corpus Christie, TX. After a short stay there he was sent to the U.S. Naval Training Station, Norfolk, VA for boot training.

After boot training was completed he was assigned to the U.S. Naval Hospital, Jacksonville, FL. After a short period of time he was reassigned to C Co., 1st Med. Bn., 1st Marine Div. FMF. After a short period of training with the Marines the 1st Marine Div. was sent to the South Pacific via the Panama Canal. He was aboard the USS *McCawley* and after 30 some days at sea the division docked at Apia on the island of Upolu in British Samoa. After a period of training the division boarded ships and prepared to move on to Guadalcanal and the resulting action that followed. After being discharged he returned to Oklahoma and started back to college.

Married Geneva Davis in August of 1946. They have two sons and two grandson.

DON MOSS, "I have always been impressed by athletes who give everything to their sport. I admire their intensity, their ability to please others and make a good living at the same time. As a sports painter, I like to think that I do the same."

Cypress Point on the Monterey Peninsula is one of America's most spectacular golf links. Don Moss sketches and photographs the surf pounded cliff edged 15th green. From early morning to late afternoon, he shoots rolls of film at all angles, research for his oil painting of this sea lion and deer populated paradise.

Jimmy Connors, eyes flashing, grimaces in the intensity of his serves and volleys. Moss captures with machine-gun clicks of film Connor's mid-air two handed backhand he will later portray on canvas.

In his favorite of all sports, Moss skis Utah powder in fast smooth turns, abruptly stopping in an explosion of snow. His camera motor-drive catches the finest skiers in the U.S. carving rapidly toward him down the steep fall line. Back in the studio, he will recapture the excitement in depicting the action of the U.S. Demonstration Ski Team.

After the Marines in WWII, Don came to New York to work as a free lance artist. For over 30 years, his art has appeared regularly in *Sports Illustrated*. Moss has painted a dozen U.S. Postal Stamps, athletes in most sports, ski areas and golf courses around the country. The Moss studio built onto his 1810 Ridgefield, CT farmhouse, is a kaleidoscopic museum of his sports art. He is a Life Member of the Society of Illustrators, a Board Member of the National Art Museum of Sport and was elected "Sports Artist Of The Year, 1985" by the United States Sports Acaademy. His paintings hang in the major sports halls of fame, in the USAF art collection and are included in many books on sport and art. President Reagan invited him to the White House opening of the Smithsonian's "Champions of American Sport Exhibition" which featured three of Don's paintings.

ROBERT C. MUEHRCKE - Please refer to page 147.

WILLIAM C. MUELLER, was born in Chicago, IL on Aug. 15, 1919. He enlisted in the USN in October 1936.

After training at the Chicago Naval Armory (he was a member of the 21st Div. USN), he shipped out in March 1942 from Norfolk, VA aboard the USS *Colhoun* (old four piper converted to APD). He went from San Diego to Honolulu, to Midway, to Tulagi, then to Guadalcanal. The USS *Colhoun* was sunk at Guadalcanal on Aug. 31, 1942 three miles off Lunga Point. Mueller was picked up by LCVP.

He returned to San Diego in March 1943 to attend LCS School and was assigned to B-4-D Unit. He returned to the South Pacific until he was discharged Oct. 25, 1945.

Mueller has one son Robert and has resided in Atlanta for 30 years.

RAYMOND C. MULLIN, is a native of Catasauqua, PA. He enlisted in the USMC on Dec. 8, 1941; went through boot camp at Parris Island and trained with F Co., 2nd Bn., 7th Marines at New River, NC.

He departed from Norfolk, VA on April 10, 1942 for British Samoa. Left Samoa and arrived at Guadalcanal September 18 where he was wounded by mortar fire on November 4.

Evacuated by air to Espiritu Santo and then by the hospital ship *Solace* to the Fiji Islands. He returned to the states and served on guard duty at several posts until January 1945 when he joined the 4th Marine Div. at Maui, HI. He was discharged Nov. 7, 1945.

He graduated from East Stroudsburg State Teachers College (now university) with a B.S. degree in health and physical education. He also received a B.A. degree from New York University and a Doctor of Education degree from Lehigh University, Bethlehem, PA. He taught school for 34 years, 28 and half as a professor at Millersville University, Millersville, PA.

Dr. Mullin is active in several veterans organizations. He served as state commander of the VFW in Pennsylvania (1983-1984). He is also a member of the Masons in Millersville. For his many contributions to community activities he has received various awards and citations from civic, service and veterans organizations.

He is married to the former Laura Jean Tice and has two children. He and his wife reside in Millersville, PA.

DANIEL D. MYERS, T/SGT, was born April 4, 1918 in Stewartsville, NJ. He spent the years prior to the war as an auto mechanic. After enlisting he was assigned to Americal Div. 246th FA Bn., serving from Nov. 6, 1941 to May 23, 1945.

Went to basic training at Ft. Dix, NJ and shipped out on Task Force 6814 to Australia. Upon arrival at New Caledonia, he was given guard duty over huge nickel ingots at a nickel mine.

He served on Guadalcanal with the 2nd Marine Div. and received a Presidential Unit Citation with Bronze Star GO #67. In addition to a Presidential Unit Citation he also received a Certificate of Merit Medal, a Philippine Liberation Medal with Bronze Star, an Asiatic-Pacific Campaign Medal with three Bronze Stars, American Defense and Good Conduct Medal.

FRANK S. MYERS, joined the USN in 1940 after high school in Bell, CA. He trained in San Diego. Served aboard six different ships, four for transportation duty: *Tennessee* (BB-43); *Chevalier* (DD-451); *Radford* (DD-446); *Petrof Bay* (CVE-80); PC (C) 1127; and PC 1145.

After Pearl Harbor and Coral Sea, he went to East Coast on new construction destroyers. He joined convoy to Casablanca in November 1942, then went through Panama Canal to Solomons, Guadalcanal, Munda, Kolombangara, Vella-La Vella etc. Then to Tarawa, the Marshalls, Guam, Saipan, the Philippines, Okinawa and Kure Naval Base, Hiroshima Bay during the occupation of Japan.

Was discharged from Navy in 1946 and awarded the Presidential Unit Citation.

In civilian life he was in the entertainment, boxing, and trucking professions. Now lives on the Arizona Nevada line in Littlefield, AZ. He has no family left.

JESSE C. NEIGHBORS, JR., was born Aug. 20, 1924 at New Smyrna Beach, FL. Entered service Feb. 11, 1941; Miami, Fl Naval Reserve. Graduated San Diego Naval Training Center July 1941. Assigned USS *Crescent City* (APA-21).

He made the initial invasion of Guadalcanal, this was his first war experience. Had duty in Korea in 1953. Pusan and four other stations.

Discharged Navy 1951 and enlisted USAF 1951 Patrick AFB, Florida. Did air crash rescue.

Awards: Authorized seven Battle Stars on the South Pacific Ribbon.

Medically retired staff sergeant 1955-1961 (temporary). Permanent retirement due to heart (100% service connected) in 1973. Prior to permanent medical retirement he was an accountant after college.

Married to E. LaVerne Trellis of Miami, FL. They have two children, one granddaughter and four great grandchildren.

GILBERT G. NELSON, born May 8, 1922 in Rockford, IL and immediately abandoned by parents and subsequently raised by various foster homes and grandparents. Graduated from Rockford High School June 1941 and joined Marine Corps in Chicago, IL on Aug. 11, 1941. Boot training in San Diego and Advanced Inf. Camp Pendelton, CA.

First engaged in battle at Midway Island (Eastern) on June 4, 1942 with 3rd Defense Bn. attached to 1st Marine Div. He manned a 40mm and hopefully helped shoot down the Mitsubishi Zero that crashed on the island.

Returned to Pearl Harbor on July 9, 1942. Boarded troop ship *Betelgeuse* and about a month later landed on Guadalcanal on Aug. 7, 1942 at Lunga Point. On August 9 crossed over to Tulagi for reinforcements. Records show this but he has no memory of occurrence. Back on Guadalcanal August 10 and stayed until Feb. 13, 1943. He had the whole nine yards including malaria, dysentery, and something called dengue. Participated in one of the Bloody Ridge incidents and Alligator Creek and Matanikau.

Arrived New Zealand for "rest". Back on Guadalcanal Oct. 6, 1943. Landed with 3rd Marine Div. on Bougainville Nov. 1, 1943. Saw action at several engagements. San Francisco on June 1, 1944 and honorably discharged on Jan. 11, 1945 as a buck sergeant. He was twice wounded. His most memorable incident was on Guadalcanal when they were being harassed by a Jap field piece inland. He was out of his foxhole when he heard the shell coming in. He ran for his foxhole but the shell beat him to it. His sea bag was blown up, he wasn't. He thanks the Lord.

Married to Sally for 39 years. She died of cancer in 1983. Presently married to his new wife, Carolyn. They currently reside in Starke, FL. He has no children.

WILLIAM C. NEVILLE, was born Jan. 3, 1923 at Daisy, GA. Enlisted in Btry. A, 214 National Guard Sept. 18, 1940 at Augusta, GA. Active duty Nov. 25, 1940 at Camp Stewart, GA.

After training at Camp Stewart, Pearl Harbor was bombed. They were called to Southern California to set up (AA) Defense. Stayed there about a year. Disembarked from San Francisco on the *Mt. Vernon* and landed at New Zealand, stayed a short period. Next on to Neumia New Caledonia on his birthday 1943 disembarked at Lunga Bay. They relieved the Marine's on Fighter Strip No. 1. Was in a 37mm and 50 cal. Machine Co. Was later transferred back to Btry. A, they became the 250th Searchlight Bn., They became the first to work the Germany Air Force in night fighters defense and stopped "Washing Machine Charlie". Shipped out to New Zealand for (RR) on his 20th birthday. Next on to New Guinea for 14 months, then the Philippines. Rotated for home, discharged at Ft. McPhearson, Oct. 19, 1945.

Married Lorain Guin, they have three children: Irish, Marie, and Victor. He is presently married to the former Frances Reader, and currently they reside in Hephzibah, GA.

WILLIAM A. NICHOLS, born Dec. 28, 1921 in Spartanburg, SC. He enlisted in U.S. Marine Corp Jan. 19, 1940 serving until June 30, 1948 and held the rank of master sergeant.

He attended Radio Operations School, two radar schools and the Navy Electronic School. He served in the South Pacific, including the Guadalcanal Campaign, in Marine Sqdn. VMO-251.

He taught three years in the Navy Electronic Technician School.

After discharge, he attended George Washington University. He worked at the Naval Research Lab designing instruments and electronic systems for rocket and satellite programs for 12 years then did similar work at NASA's Goddard Space Flight Center. Before retiring in 1987 he worked in industry managing electronic and control design teams.

He married Erin Ellis, a University of Maryland graduate in 1943. Their 48th anniversary approaches. They have one daughter, Lynn and two grandsons, William Tice and Gavin Tice.

JOSEPH T. NIXON, was born on May 20, 1924 at Signal Mountain, TN. Enlisted in the Marines on Sept. 10, 1941. After boot camp at Parris Island, was assigned to Quantico, VA, then to New River, NC for duty with the 1st Bn., 11th Marines. Shipped out from Norfolk, VA in April of 1942. After staging in Western Samoa landed on Guadalcanal with the 11th Marines. Served through the Guadalcanal Campaign as a forward observer for 75mm pack howitzers. Spent most of his time with 1st and 2nd Bn., 7th Marines. Nixon was one of the survivors of Japanese Colonel Oka's attacks on the 2nd Bn., 7th Marines the night of Oct. 26, 1942.

After rest in Australia, he landed at Cape Gloucester with the Pioneer Bn. of the 17th Marines. He served through the New Britain Campaign, and after repeated malaria attacks was evacuated to Brisbane, Australia and then back to the U.S.

He was stationed at Camp Pendleton waiting for more overseas duty when the Japanese surrendered. Discharged Sept. 30, 1946.

Returned to Tennessee and married his childhood sweetheart, Mary Elizabeth Leath. After continuing his education at the University of Tennessee, he spent 35 years in the Radio and Television business in the Los Angeles area.

Currently teaching Radio and Television Performing at Los Angeles City College. He resides with his wife in La Crescenta, CA.

EMIL NOVAK, was born June 23, 1917 at Wing, ND. Enlisted U.S. Navy February 1936. Passed flight physical in 1939. Scheduled for call to pilot training after first enlistment ended in February 1940. Decided that a non-injury land crash is more conducive to long life than the open sea. Attended Cornell University 1940-1941. Passed Army Air Corps pilot training tests at Syracuse, NY in 1941. Commissioned as Second Lieutenant pilot May 1942 at Victoria, TX.

Completed 102 combat missions from Guadalcanal in the Bell P-39 Air Cobra November 1942 through May 1943 and the P-38 Lockheed Lighting June-December 1943.

Married Mary E. Beatty at Shaw AFB, Sumter, SC 1946. Retired as USAF lieutenant colonel January 1958 after 20 years military service.

Completed work for a physics-math degree at Indiana and Michigan State Universities in 1961. Concluded 23 more years with federal civil service in 1984.

He has two sons, graduates of U.S. Merchant Marine and USAF academies, one daughter, and three grandchildren.

SHERMAN J. O'BRIEN, JR, was born May 24, 1924 in Quincy, MA. Enlisted U.S. Navy Oct. 13, 1941. Graduating boot training U.S. Newport, RI.

Put USS *President Hayes* in commission December 1941 at Brooklyn Navy Yard. Down East coast through the Panama Canal. Trained 2nd Div. Marines out of San Diego on amphibious landing from ship and small boats. Made invasion of Guadalcanal and Tulagi Aug. 7, 1942. The *Hayes* shot down a couple of Jap planes D-Day. Landed 2nd Div. Marines. A bunch of "tough Marines" O'Brien is proud to have known them all. Next invasion Rendova. USS *McCauley* sunk in front of *Hayes* by Jap torpedo bombers. *President Hayes* USN would have been hit but, Captain F. W. Benson USN saved her by his expert navigation under enemy fire. Transferred to USS *Fuller* (APA-7). Next invasion Bougainville. *Fuller* hit by Jap 500 pound bombs.

Returned to States after emergency supply run, and a wartime marriage to Helen M. McGrail. Returned for invasions of Saipain, Tinian, Kwajalein, Eniwetock, Peliteu, Lingayen Gulf and Leyte and Luzon in the Philippines. Last invasion and the toughest was Okinawa.

O'Brien earned 12 Battle Stars during invasions. Retired from Lowell Post Office in 1981.

He is the founding father of Centralville Sportsman Club in Lowell, MA and Greater Lowell Fly Fishers and Salmon Unlimited of Greenland, NH. O'Brien has been married to Helen for 47 years and they have six children, and 14 grandchildren.

JOSEPH F. O'HARA, was born on Aug. 3, 1919 in Cleveland, OH. Enlisted Feb. 5, 1941 in the 37th Div., C Btry., 135th Field Arty.

Stationed at Camp Shelby, Indiantown Gap, New Zealand, Fiji, Guadalcanal, Mundai, Guadalcanal, Bougainville, Guadalcanal, and Ft. Sill, OK. Discharged with rank of sergeant on Sept. 23, 1945. Awards: American Defense Medal, Good Conduct Medal, South Pacific and one Battle Star for Munda and Bougainville. His most memorable experience is having Thanksgiving Dinner with the hospitalized men from Guadalcanal on Nov. 11, 1942. He married Jackie Kelch in 1949. They have four daughters, Karen, Shelia, Eileen and Rita, seven grandchildren.

He was a police officer in Cleveland, OH for 30 years and lived in California for 13 years. He retired and in 1976 and moved to Florida in 1989. He enjoys fishing and traveling.

KENNETH L. OLSEN, was born on Sept. 30, 1917. Enlisted U.S. Navy on May 24, 1938.

Served on board USS *Maryland*, USS *Fuller* (APA-7), USS *Sherbourne* (APA-205).

Participated in Puerto Rico, Iceland, Ireland, Scotland, Bougainville, Iwo Jima, Okinawa and Tokyo Bay.

He was discharged with rank of CMM.

He has one daughter, two sons and four granddaughters. He is an insurance agent.

JAY H. OPLINGER, born in Allentown, PA. Enlisted in February 1942 at age 18. Took basic training at Camp Wheeler, GA and shipped to Oahu in June 1942.

Assigned to Headquarters Co., 35th Inf., Recon Platoon. Participated in Guadalcanal, Vella La Vella, and Luzon Campaigns.

Spent hospital time in Guadalcanal, New Caledonia, Biak, and New Zealand for recurring attacks of malaria and yellow jaundice.

Shipped back to States June 1945 via hospital ship to Letterman General Hospital, San Francisco. Sent to Camp Pickett Convalescent Hospital, VA. Was discharged as sergeant October 1945.

Employed by Firestone Tire and Rubber Company, Pottstown, PA. Worked up from tire builder to traffic manager and was transferred to new plant in Perryville, MD where he was involved with opening and operations of the Firestone Plastics Company.

He is now retired, married with three sons, and four grandchildren. Resides in Bel Air, MD. He is a lifetime member of the 25th Infantry Division Association, and is a member of the VFW and American Legion, also the Guadalcanal Campaign Veterans.

FRED OSTERBRINK, born Nov. 3, 1913 Mattoon, WI. Enlisted Sept. 19, 1940 in 132nd Infantry National Guard, Tullahoma, TN. Discharged with rank of staff sergeant.

His memorable experience was when a Jap bullet hit a tree at Guadalcanal, he picked up the bullet, it was hot and he dropped it. Looked up in the tree for a Jap, but Col. Wright was shot from the Jap in the tree instead of Osterbrink.

He enjoys studying UFOs.

LLOYD N. OVERGAARD, was born on Sept. 18, 1918 Centerville, SD. Enlisted Aviation Ordnance on Jan. 28, 1942. Trained McChord Field, WA. Joined 5th Bomb Gp. in Hickam Field, HI in June 1942.

Later transferred to 11th Bomb Gp, 431st Sqdn., Santos New Hebrides, Dec. 25, 1942. Twenty-four men ordnance section sent to Henderson Field, Guadalcanal on detached service to service all B-17s stopping for bombs and armament.

Worked in engineering tent coordinating loading and changing bomb loads with Operations Headquarters as planes made short stops on search and strike missions from Santos Long flights.

Left March 15, 1943, all of them were malaria loaded, to USA for 30 days R&R and for reassignment back to Hickam Field. Transferred to Ordnance Supply Dept. Their mess tent and tent were blown up three days after they left. Only one of his many narrow escape experiences.

Guarded the atomic bombs in crates for a week before they were dropped. Did not know what was in them at the time. Was up for discharge the day after they dropped. Rank Staff Sergeant.

Married Mavis Brose, Arlington, SD on June 26, 1949 in Sioux Falls, SD. They have one son, twin daughters and seven grandchildren.

Retired after 45 years farming and cattle feeding on the same farm as his father that he took over after his father retired.

EARL DEXTER PADDOCK, was born in Pompey, NY on June 4, 1917, graduating from Fabius High School in 1935 in the middle of the Great Depression. He married Laura Howden in July 1938 and they had five children.

On March 4, 1944 he was drafted into the Army, took training at Ft. Dix, NJ, Camp Plauche, LA and Camp Gordon Johnson, FL. The army formed three Harbor Craft Companies because of the need for ship to shore installations on the re-taken South Pacific Islands. He was in the 363rd Harbor Craft and shipped out to Guadalcanal in December 1944. He also served in New Guinea and the Philippines. His work included cooking, shore duty on small boats and landing craft, and transporting supplies inland. While on the Canal his wife gave birth to twin boys. After the war was over in August 1945 he and his buddies waited six months in Manila for a ship to bring them home. After a 30 day ocean trip on the USS *Henry S. Foote* he was discharged from Ft. Dix with the rank of T-4. Seeing his eight month old twin sons was one of the highlights of his return. He soon became self-employed in the meat market he had owned and operated prior to being drafted. After 17 years in the meat market he entered the real estate business, from which he retired.

Dexter and his wife now keep themselves busy visiting their five living children - Esther Maybury in Preble, NY; Joyce Ranum in Great Falls, MT; Donald in Spokane, WA and Kenneth in Dryden, NY. Donald's twin, David, a first lieutenant in the army was killed June 7, 1968 in Vietnam while on his second tour of duty.

Dexter is a member of the American Legion, VFW, DAV, Dads of Foreign Service Veterans, and Guadalcanal Campaign Veterans. He is active in volunteer work for the American Cancer Society and Red Cross. His hobbies are gardening, swimming, ice skating and writing poetry, and antique cars.

VALERIAN "LARRY" PADRNOS, was born near Redfield, SD on April 12, 1918. Enlisted in the Marine Corps Jan. 5, 1942.

After training at the Marine base in San Diego and Camp San Luis Obispo, he was assigned to B-1-2-2 at Camp Elliott. Went ashore at 0740 on Florida Island, and later that day onto Guvatu. While en-route to Aola Bay on the night of October 9, the bow of the Higgins boat was ripped apart in a sudden

storm. Of 38 men, only 15 survived. While on Guadalcanal that November, Larry's company was under intense Naval bombardment. Days later, Larry was hit by one of "Pistol Pete" shell's near Matanikau River. Hospitalized, Larry was sent to Oakland, CA. Discharged in San Francisco on Jan. 15, 1946.

Retired from the Oakland Fire Dept. as a captain in 197? Larry and his wife, Phyllis, still reside in Oakland. They have seven children.

PRESTON S. PARISH, was born on Nov. 10, 1919 in Chicago, IL. Enlisted May 1941. Trained at Quantico, VA New River, NC.

April 1942 went overseas with the 7th Marine Regt. 1st Marine Div. enroute to Guadalcanal via British Samoa. After Guadalcanal remained with the 7th Marines serving in New Guinea, New Britain and Peleliu. February 1945 transferred to Naval flight training, released to inactive duty May 1946 as Major USMCR. Commenced work for American Flange and Manufacturing Company, New York City.

Married April 1948. Has five children and 14 grandchildren. In 1949 joined the Upjohn Company, retired in 1984, although still serve on its board.

In 1978 involved in founding of an aviation museum which has gained national recognition and which is now also the home of the Guadalcanal Campaign Veterans Association Museum.

JAMES E. PARROT - please refer to page 146

MELFORD F. PARKS, was born in Atlanta, GA on Sept. 5, 1923. Sworn into the Marine Corp in December 1941. Boot camp at Parris Island. Trained at Tent Camp, Jacksonville, NC. Left San Diego, CA in April 1942 aboard the USS *Harris*.

After spending a few months on Wallace Island, they were sent to Guadalcanal to help guard Henderson Field, K-3-7, then on to Melbourne, Australia and Camp Mount Martha.

Most memorable event: Driving for Col. Chesty Puller from Camp Mount Martha to town. The colonel would buy Dan Q. Rum while on visit to ship docks. Returned to Oakland Naval Hospital December 1943 with Elephantiasis. On to Camp LeJeune, NC. Discharged in 1945.

Married Mary Harris April 1948. They have two daughters, one son and six grandchildren.

JOHN PAVLOV, born in Lowellsville, OH near Youngstown, OH on Dec. 4, 1919. Enlisted USMC April 5, 1939. Boot camp at Parris Island, SC.

Served D-1-5 and D-1-7, then at Cuba, transferred to R-2-7th Regt., 1st Marine Div.

Served at British Samoa, Guadalcanal, New Guinea and Cape Gloucester. He was wounded on Guadalcanal. He was discharged on Oct. 12, 1945 with rank of platoon sergeant.

Worked for the U.S. Postal Service for 26 years August 1948 and retired on July 1, 1974. He has a son John W. Pavlov who served USMC during VC area - stateside only.

He would like to contact former Marines that remember him for a (B.S.) session.

JOSEPH PEDAJAS, was born on Nov. 25, 1920 in Chicago, IL. Enlisted in Army September 1940 and joined the U.S. Navy on Dec. 21, 1941. Served on board USS *Helena* (AM-156) and USS *Lackwana* (A-040). He remembers three sea battles on the USS *Helena*.

Received the Asiatic-Pacific Campaign Ribbon w/nine Battle Stars and the Navy Citation. He was discharged with the rank of BKR 2/c.

He is married and has three children and seven grandchildren. He is a retired railroad conductor.

DONALD W. PELTIER, was born in Mt. Clemens, MI June 7, 1925. Entered service January 1942 at trained at Great Lakes, IL. Transferred to San Diego February 1942. Sent to Pearl Harbor for temporary duty USS *Lexington* (CV-2) returned to San Pedro, CA. Assigned to USS *Boyd* (DD-544) for carrier support and rescue. Drew rescue duty at Tarawa. Ship was badly damaged with a loss of 17 crewmen. After repairs returned carrier to landing support. The USS *Boyd* was in 17 engagements with the Japanese.

She returned in March 1946 and was de-commissioned and mothballed. Peltier was the last sailor to leave the ship.

He was discharged in June 1946 and returned to Michigan with his new bride to raise five children. He retired in 1987 and resides in Portage, MI.

GEORGE H. PELVIT, joined the Navy on Jan. 5, 1937. After boot training went to the USS *Altair*, and from there to the USS *Cummings*. Discharged from the *Cummings*. Stayed out until Feb. 7, 1941. Then signed up for the USS *Meredith* (DD-434). This ship was on the raid on Tokyo. They were sunk Oct. 15, 1942, trying to get gas into Guadalcanal. Went to USS *Vestal* (AR-4) for nine months, then back to the States to put the USS *Salvo Island* (78) in commission at Bremerton, WA.

Made chief water tender lying in sick bay. They had a lot of close calls from Jap planes.

Discharged from Navy on Sept. 14, 1945. Returned to home state of North Dakota and married and began farming.

GORDON L. PERRY, was born April 9, 1925 in Dallas, TX. Enlisted in the Marine Corps Dec. 15, 1941. Boot camp was in San Diego and then he was sent to Camp Elliott and later to Camp Arthur where he celebrated his 17th birthday with many long hikes.

Landed on Florida Island, B.S.I. Aug. 7, 1942, then Gavutu, Tanambogo, and Tulagi. Went on raid to Aola Bay, Guadalcanal and returned to Tulagi. Left for Guadalcanal and stayed until January 1943. Left on the USS *President Jackson*, the same ship that landed them in August. Later was sent to New Zealand and after several bouts with malaria, was sent to U.S. Later he was assigned to a top secret project code name (X-Ray). This assignment was carried out in New Graunfels, TX at a bat cave. The bats were to be fitted with incendiary bombs to be used on Japan but, the project was later canceled.

He was then sent to Guam on the Special Weapons Co. 9th Marines until the war was over. He was discharged as a corporal Dec. 12, 1945. During 1951-1953, he was in Casablanca, Morocco as U.S. Air Force S/Sgt. Reserve.

Retired U.S. Naval Reserve as CPO and civil service (production control) at Kelly AFB, San Antonio, TX with 36 years service. He resides in San Antonio, TX with his wife Edna and daughter, Lenora.

GEORGE STANLEY PETERS, was born on Nov. 13, 1904 in Passiac, NJ. Married Louise Clara Hodges born Olmsted Falls, OH Oct. 16, 1904. Surgeon, commissioned lieutenant (Jg) Aug. 23, 1937 Reserve Medical Corp USN promoted Nov. 5, 1945 commander. Served in USS *Crescent City* (APA-21) Sept. 13, 1941 to Oct. 6, 1943.

Retired July 1, 1964.

Awards: Asiatic-Pacific Campaign Ribbon w/four Battle Stars, American Defense Medal w/one Star, Unit Commendation Ribbon, American Theatre Campaign Ribbon, World War Two Victory Medal, Naval Reserve Faithful Service.

He was a student Miami University, Ohio Wesleyan University (A.B. 1929), Temple University Medical (M. D. 1933). Served chief of surgery Montgomery VA Hospital: Chief of Staff and Surgery Fitt's Hill and Professional Center Hospital's Montgomery. Diplomate American Board Abdominal Surgery and International Board Surgery. Fellow of American College Surgeons - International College Surgeons - American Society Abdominal Surgeons - Pan Pacific Surgical Association - American Academy Family Physicians - American Occupational Medicine - Southeastern Surgical Congress and other professional organizations founder and owner University Medical Center Hospital, Montgomery. Subject of biographical record in several editions in *Who's Who in the South and Southwest* (15th Ed. 1976-1977) and listed in *Who's Who in America* (41st Edition 1980-1981), Library of Alabama Lives and *Who's Who in Alabama*. Mason, Knight Templar (Shriner, Jester). Men of Montgomery, Montgomery Area Committee of 100. Presbyterian, Phi Delta Theta. Served at various other Navy ship and shore stations.

WALTER PFAFFINGER, was born Sept. 10, 1912. He joined the Seabees and left Blue Earth, MN for the Great Lakes May 1, 1942. He was in the 6th Seabees Bn. and they left San Francisco July 21, 1942 and landed on Guadalcanal Aug. 30, 1942. They served on Guadalcanal until Jan. 5, 1943.

Awards: Presidential Unit Citation (Guadalcanal service).

He was overseas in the Southwest Pacific for 26 months the first trip overseas, getting back to the States in late September 1944.

On May 28, 1945 he left the States with the 6th Seabees for Okinawa landing on Okinawa July 15, 1945.

He served on Okinawa until early November 1945, going back to the States on points, he arrived back in the States in late November 1945 to be discharged.

ANDREW R. POLINY, was born Sept. 25, 1920 in Perth Amboy, NJ.

Enlisted in the USMC on Jan. 9, 1942 at 90 Church St. New York City. He went to boot camp in Parris Island, NC. He was involved on the initial attack on Guadalcanal where he served in the 1st Marine Div. He was wounded and sent to a

San Diego Naval Hospital for nine months, then shipped back to Guadalcanal, where he served then in the 6th Marine Div.

Many of his medals were not presented to him because his medical records were lost. He was presented a Sharpshooter Medal, Presidential Unit Citation, South Pacific Campaign Ribbon w/two Stars.

His rank was a private first class to corporal, being discharged as a private first class on Oct. 31, 1945. He served four years with the USMC.

He married Julia T. Harczuk from Carteret, NJ on Aug. 20, 1949 in St. Joseph's Church Carteret, NJ. They have five children. After being discharged he worked as a connector for Ironworkers of Northern New Jersey local 373 from PerthAmboy, NJ for 22 years. He gained the nickname "Sparrow" because of his precise skill on the iron.

He also started his own business with his brother which soon became the largest bait and tackle business on the East Coast.

He resided in Sayreville, NJ until his passing on Jan. 19, 1991. He was a Guadalcanal campaign director and corresponded to many fellow vets.

EDDIE E. POLLARD, was born in Ft. Worth, TX on June 3, 1925. Enlisted in Marine Corps Jan. 9, 1942, age 16. Sent to San Diego. Graduated boot camp Platoon 220.

Shipped out North Island June 18, 1942 on USS *Heywood* with 22nd Marines to Apia British Samoa. Transferred to F-2-7. Highest rank was corporal and was nicknamed "chicken" due to his age. 7th Regt. rejoined 1st Div. on Sept. 18, 1942 at Guadalcanal. Engaged in four different battles. Went to Melbourne and had malaria thrice and jaundice once. In 1943 went to New Guinea, Cape Gloucestor. After training more on Pavuvu landed on Peleliu 1944 and lasted eight days.

Most memorable event: while driving for what he thought was a foxhole on Guadalcanal during an air-raid he hit a tree-trunk. He knocked himself out and sustained injuries to eye and head, his face covered with blood.

Discharged Feb. 7, 1946 and re-enlisted Marine Air Corps August 1946 and sent to El Toro. Received medical discharge after re-injuring old injury in 1947. In 1945 he also served on USS *Wyoming*.

Married Jane Hurte February 1947 and has one daughter Patricia and one son George and four grandchildren. Pollard after discharge earned his B.A. degree and became an ordained minister.

CHARLES POLSKY, was born March 13, 1913 at Philadelphia, PA. He joined the Marines, serving at Parris Island and New River, NC. He served aboard the *American Legion*.

He enlisted in the Marines twice. He enlisted on Feb. 2, 1942 and served until March 20, 1943. He re-enlisted Oct. 18, 1943 and served until Oct. 20, 1944. He landed on Guadalcanal Aug. 7, 1942. He was in three battles on the island—Tenaru, Mataniku River and 10 patrols. He was discharged with the rank of private first class on March 20, 1943.

He is single and is a taxi cab driver.

BENJAMIN L. POWELL, JR., was born to a Quaker family from Greenville, NY; "Ben" was born April 7, 1922 in Springfield, MA. in 1923, the family moved to a tiny town in Pownal, VT. A merchant's son he was educated in nearby Hoosick Falls, NY.

Volunteered Dec. 8, 1941, after hearing of the attack on Pearl Harbor. Entered Marine Corps Jan. 6, 1942, Platoon #52; Parris Island to New River, NC. Via USS *San Francisco* to Wellington, New Zealand July 1942. Guadalcanal via USS *McCawley* Aug. 7, 1942. To Brisbane via USS *American Legion* Dec. 15, 1942. To Melbourne via USS *West Point* January 1943.

Hospitals in Melbourne and Ballarat. Back to San Diego for malaria May 1943. Bremerton Navy Yard August 1943. To Sun Valley Idaho Naval Hospital October 1943; to Chelsea Naval Hospital January 1944.

Boston Navy Yard, January 1944, under Colonel Pierce. Armed escort, prison chaser, gate, caisson, dock, padre and honor guard duty...sentry "old ironsides". He remembers well being sentry-orderly for Rear Admiral Robert Teobald, Commandant First Naval District, upon the Admirals return from a meeting, the Admiral asked him the score of the Boston Red Socks baseball game, he didn't know. From then on he paid attention to the Red Socks game; when asked again he was sure to know the score. Color Guard at Tenway, Statler and Copley Plaza Hotels, weddings, receptions and funerals. Guard freight rail shipments to ammo depots and allied war ships under Lt. Viand. Honor Guard for VIP's.

To New River December 1944, to Pendleton January 1945. Spent 1945 on Guam, Marianas H & S 9th Marines, while regiment on Iwo Jima. Built quonsets with the Seabees, working post exchange, commissary. During this time he found his brother, Sgt. David H. Powell with B-29 crew - General Curtis LeMay. David's plane was lost April 23 over Japan. After the loss of his brother, he supervised food dumps and in charge of walk-in freezors and coolers - night duty until end of war. Returned via Liberty ship *Comet*, Treasure Island, thence Camp LeJeune for honorable discharge, private, combat rifleman, supply clerk on Oct. 24, 1945.

When he sums up the war years, it is still a wonderment, traveled the Pacific on seven ships MS *John Ericson*, USS *McCawley*, USS *American Legion*, USS *West Point* (HMA.'s *Beaver* - Tug at Brisbade) USS *Lurline*, USS *Moormacdove*, USS *Comet*. Train-bus cross country six times. Traveled North-South both coasts four times. Five different large hospitals, many sick bays. Two major battles. Hospitals: Melbourne 4th General, Ballarat Australia Hospital, U.S. Naval Balboa Park; Bremerton Naval Hospital, Sun Valley Naval, Idaho, Chelsea Naval Hospital, Chelsea, MA.

After the war worked with his father in stores then into production control management; industrial engineering. Has three daughters and three sons with first marriage. Moved to Azusa, CA in 1964. Married Geraldine E. Andreski in 1973, a blue ribbon cook. He has eight grandchildren that are a joy. He enjoys music, volunteer work and sports.

VINCENT R. POWERS, born at Durbin, ND on March 8, 1919. Drafted into the U.S. Army on April 28, 1941 at Ft. Snelling, MN and then arriving at: Camp Clairbourne, LA on May 3, 1941 for basic training. San Francisco Cow Palace, Dec. 17, 1942; Umatilla Ordinance, Oregon, Dec. 25, 1941; Pendelton, Oregon, Dec. 28, 1941; Boise Idaho, Jan. 3, 1942; Ft. Ord, CA, March 10, 1942; Pier 42 San Francisco, CA, March 18, 1942 and boarded the USS *President Coolidge* ship. Sailed from San Francisco on March 18, 1942 at 1:00 p.m. Arrived at Melbourne, Australia, April 8, 1942. Arrived New Caledonia on April 19, 1942.

On Oct. 13, 1942 the 164th Infantry Regt. landed on Guadalcanal and were baptized with 15 and 16 inch shells as the Japs bombarded Henderson Field at night; as a result Powers and his buddy Rudy Pence got separated from their company and ate coconuts for a couple of days until they arrived back at the 3rd Bn. kitchen asking for water and were refused so they cocked their rifles and pointed them at the cook and said they wanted water and got it. They arrived back with Co. B and helped fight in the many battles; he and Rudy never took any prisoners because they knew about the Jap atrocities committed on the Americans. Once when their planes were to bomb and strafe the Japs in front of their lines they bombed and strafed them.

He saw the Japs float out to sea on the dead man float one after another out to sea in a straight line after the Battle of Point Cruz.

Many of his buddies were killed and he was fortunate to arrive safely back in the U.S. the middle of 1945 and immediately married his girlfriend on Feb. 28, 1945 and was discharged from an Army Camp in Wisconsin in August of 1945 after spending approximately three years overseas and four years, four months and four days in the service.

He then went to college on the G. I. Bill and graduated from the University of North Dakota in 1949.

He married Thelma Jorve on Feb. 28, 1945 and they have four sons: Jack, Ralph, Jay and Kim. He is retired and resides in Victor, MT.

FRANK J. PRIEBE, JR., was born June 26, 1922 in Springfield, MA. Moved to Hempstead, L.I., New York, 1927. Graduated from Hempstead High School 1941, worked days in an A&P Store and attended Hofstra College at night. Not registered with the draft board, volunteered for service in the U.S. Navy March 19, 1942.

Served in the Asiatic-Pacific Theatre 19 months with no R&R, Cub-Two 1st Echelon, ARU-145, PATSU 1-1. Served with Cub-Two in Hew Hebrides, Tulari, Guadalcanal, ARU-245 Guadalcanal, PATSU 1-1 Guadalcanal.

Awards: Bronze Star with Cub-Two for defense and capture of Guadalcanal, Bronze Star with ARU-145 for defense and capture of Bougainville.

Left the canal Aug. 4, 1944, checked into Alameda NAS, decommissioned PATSU 1-1 (being the senior yeoman; 2nd class) made up his own leave papers and reported to Green Cove Sprints, FL, VF-1 Fighting Squadron 1, Oct. 6, 1944.

The boloney hit the fan; Commander "Jumping Joe" Clifton (VF-1) heard his story and gave him a verbal tongue lashing in front of the administrative officers (and a wink) then assigned him as their flight yeoman and he worked off the USS *Guadalcanal* (what a coincidence).

He married the most beautiful WAVE on base, and was discharged on Oct. 8, 1945 Jacksonville NAS, with 83 points.

He was married for 48 years, his wife passed away on Dec. 17, 1985; they had two daughters, and one son. His son did two tours of Vietnam, and served seven years as an enlisted man (quartermaster). His son is still in the Navy with rank of lieutenant commander, with 27 years of service.

Preibe is a member of the American Legion, VFW, Guadalcanal Campaign Veterans. Retired from the Teamsters after 43 years of driving 18 wheelers at the age of 67.

ROBERT J. PUTNAM, native Denver, CO, graduate Denver Schools with four year scholarship to the University of Colorado. 1935 enlisted Pfc. Volunteer Marine Corps Reserve as officer candidate in 1st Platoon Leaders Class, boot camp San Diego summer 1935, additional summer training 1936-1937, called to active duty January 1941, graduated Basic School, Philadelphia Navy Yard June 1941, ordered to Parris Island Fleet Marine Force as platoon leader G-2-7, as captain

January 1942 - organized and trained Co. K, 3rd Bn., 1s[t] Marines (only officer for three months), landed with rein[-] forced rifle company Guadalcanal Aug. 7, 1942, mission t[o] take Mt. Austen. Company engaged in many major actions o[n] Guadalcanal - Tenaru, Matanikau - Bloody Ridge, etc.

Personally cited (Silver Star), company cited, battalion cited - same action, evacuated Dec. 16, 1942 to Australia. January 1943 ordered to Camp LeJeune, promoted to major-executive officer, 3rd Bn., 25th Marines; in and out hospitals 26 months for malaria and other tropical diseases incurred on Guadalcanal; 1945 Executive Officer Marine Barracks Charleston Navy Yard as lieutenant colonel, retired for combat disability March 1946, rank of Colonel at age of 31; moved to Asheville, NC with wife, Jeanne Reid Putnam of Charleston, SC. Two children; two grandchildren; retired 1980 manager chemical sales, Champion International. Took three year leave of absence 1953-1956 to lecture against Godless Communism.

In 1989 was awarded Commandant's Citation for "outstanding support of the Marine Corps and the nation reflecting great credit upon himself and the United States."

He has been a resident of Asheville for over 40 years.

BENJAMIN H. QUICK, was born April 1, 1917 at St. Aubert, MO. He entered service with the US Navy on Aug. 29, 1940. He served at USNTS, Great Lakes, IL. He also served aboard the USS *Chicago* (CA-29).

He served aboard several different ships: *Idaho*, *Chicago*, *Sonoma*, *Smallwood* and ARS 22. The ships were cruisers, minesweepers and sea tugs. He recalls the goodwill tour to Australia in 1941, the Battle of the Coral Sea, the Guadalcanal Campaign and the Battle of Savo Island.

He was discharged with the rank of machinist mate, first class on Aug. 29, 1946.

He married Vera. They have three children and five grandchildren. He retired March 27, 1982 from EEI, Inc. as a certified welder.

He has two brothers, Lester E. Quick and Lawrence (Larry) Quick. Lester joined the SeaBees about October 1936. He served for 32 years in the Pacific. Larry joined about June 1940 and served in the Atlantic until about 1945.

EDWARD G. QUINTON, was born on Nov. 24, 1929 in Cambridge, MA. Entered the U.S. Army in 1950 trained at Ft. Gordon, GA.

Sent to Japan with the U.S. Army Occupation Forces and ended up in Korea. Served 26 months between Japan and Korea.

Returned to the States in December 1953 and was honorably discharged on Jan. 31, 1954, at Ft. Devens, MA. Enlisted in the Massachusetts National Guard on Jan. 8, 1956, served 30 years before retiring on Dec. 2, 1987. Rank at time of discharge was sergeant first class.

Awards: Meritorious Service Medal, Army Commendation Medal, Occupation Medal (Japan), Humanitarian Service Medal, National Defense Service Medal, Korean Service Medal, Armed Forces Reserve Medal, Reserve Achievement

Medal, Army Service Ribbon, United National Service Medal, and numerous awards received during his service time.

Joined the Cambridge Police in 1960 and has 32 years of service.

Learned judo while on Occupation duty in Japan and has been with the sport for over 40 years. Served on the United States Olympic Committee and went to Japan for the Tokyo Olympics in 1964. Current holder of the 4th Degree Black Belt.

He resides in Cambridge, MA with wife, three sons and one daughter. He is a Life Member of Guadalcanal Campaign Veterans Association, member post 299 Veterans of Foreign Wars. His hobbies include judo, coin collecting, traveling. His most outstanding event in his military history was surviving the war.

Previous experiences: met a Japanese World War Pilot in 1950 who was shot down at Pearl Harbor. Was able to return to the canal twice, the first time in 1978 and meeting with Sir Jacob Vouza and Billy Bennett and last year with Lt. Col. Joseph Mueller, USMC (Ret.) where they found the place in the bush where a picture was taken of Marine commanders on Guadalcanal August 11, 1942, Reference Page 46 *Guadalcanal, The First Offensive.*

DONALD P. RACETTE, was born Putnam, CT on Feb. 9, 1923.

Enlisted in Navy Dec. 8, 1941 at Norwich, CT. Sworn in Jan. 2, 1942 at New Haven, CT. First duty USS *Wyoming*, then duty aboard USS *Lang* (DD-399).

Campaigns included Malta relief, Guadalcanal, Tulagi, New Georgia, Rendova, Vella La Vella, Kolobangara, Kula Gulf, Vella Gulf, Tarawa, Roi, Namur, Abraham (Kwajalein), Nauru, Caroline Raids, Saipan, Tinian, Kavieng. LSM #262 Philippines, Okinawa, Ie Shima, landed Japan for occupation. His battle-station aboard the ships was loader on twin 40 mm.

While at the canal, they picked up flyboys out of the drink and returned them to their carriers (*Wasp*, etc) Spent nights in Purvis Bay and on Jan. 22-24, 1963 shelled Japanese at Kokumbona.

Earned 11 Battle Stars and ended the war as SC 1/c. Discharged at Toledo, OH Dec. 21, 1945.

Married Dec. 22, 1945. Has one son and one daughter in Connecticut. He now resides on West Coast with wife Louella. His hobbies include photography, cartridge collecting and military history.

DAVID R. RAPLEY, born March 22, 1926 Hot Springs, AR. Enlisted in the USMC, Dec. 18, 1941, Minneapolis, MN. Boot training in Platoon 250, San Diego Marine Corps Training Base. Assigned to B Co., 1st Bn., 2nd Marines at Camp Elliott. Sent to the South Pacific on USS *President Jackson*. Invaded Florida Island in the Solomon Island chain on Aug. 7, 1942, 20 minutes before the landing on Guadalcanal, therefore being the first U.S. troops to invade Japanese occupied territory, starting the U.S. offensive in the Pacific. He also landed on Gavutu that same day. Then went to Tulagi before going to Guadalcanal October 30. He contracted malaria in December

and was evacuated to New Zealand, Jan. 15, 1943.

He returned to the U.S. on July 21, 1943 and was assigned guard duty at New Orleans, LA and Richmond, FL until being shipped back to the South Pacific, January 1945, to Guam with A Co., 1st Bn., 9th Marines.

Returned home to be discharged Dec. 19, 1945, at Great

Lakes Naval Training Station, Chicago, IL.

He married Betty Williams in 1949. They have a daughter Jane, a son Frank, and two grandsons, Kyle and William Cottrell. He has resided in Hot Springs, AR since being separated from the Marine Corps.

ROBERT S. RAY, was born on July 1, 1922 Noonday, Smith County, TX. Enlisted June 26, 1942. Co. A, 3rd Med. Bn., 3rd Marines. Stationed at: San Diego, CA, Camp Pendleton, New Zealand, Guadalcanal, Guam, Memphis, TN.

He remembers well nightly visits by "Washing Machine Charlie" on Guadalcanal. He also remembers firm friendships with some shipmates that are renewed at reunions biannually.

Discharged Oct. 13, 1945 as chief pharmacist's mate.

After returning from overseas (Guam), fall 1944, he was stationed at USHN, Memphis, TN, where he met and married Nancy Waits, a Corps WAVE from Kentucky. He mustered out of the Navy at Camp Wallace, TX on Oct. 13, 1945, worked until July 1946 when he re-entered college at the University of Colorado to complete his premedical education. He was accepted to medical school at UTMB, Galveston, TX in September 1949, and graduated in June 1954. He was hospitalized with TB twice in 1948 and 1951.

After internship at Brackenridge Hospital in Austin, TX, he practiced for one year in Corpus Christi, and then moved to Seguin, TX, where he was in family practice for the next 15 years. From Jan. 1, 1969 to Dec. 31, 1971, he was in radiology residency at UTMSSA and Bexar County Hospital in San Antonio, after which he returned to Seguin as staff radiologist at Guadalupe Valley Hospital, continuing to the present. Over the years, he established a "circuit" covering hospitals and clinics north, east, south, and west from Elgin to Three Rivers and Gonzales to San Antonio. Presently, most of his practice is in Floresville and Karnes City, and at several EMS clinics in San Antonio. He has done contract radiology for the U.S. Air Force since 1975: Randolph AFB Clinic from 1975 to 1980, and from September 1989 to present. He has been the contract radiologist at Kelly Air Force Base Clinic since April 1980.

He has three children: Bob, Sally and Greg. He was divorced in 1973 and remains single.

He lives on the sleepy west bank of the lazy Guadalupe River between New Braunfels and Seguin, TX, and wild horses couldn't drag him off his "reservation." He enjoys several hobbies, including photography, hunting, piano (lessons) and researching his family tree. His health is excellent, especially since quadruple bypass surgery in June 1989.

MILFORD N. REED, born Royal Oak, MI March 5, 1922. Enlisted Marine Corps Dec. 8, 1941.

After training at San Diego and Florida was assigned to VMSB-132 and was checked out by Major Sailer at North Island. Shipped out on *Lurline* Oct. 13, 1942 for New Caledonia. Departed Tontouta Airfield on R-4-D loaded with drums of gasoline en-route to Henderson Field, Guadalcanal. Arrived during air raid and was met by Bill Cohran driving an old Japanese truck. Upon arrival, Major Joe Sailer detached Reed to MAG-14. On Dec. 24, 1942, he was evacuated to Espirito Santo and assigned to Wing Headquarters. In October 1942 was evacuated to Army/Navy Hospital at Vila, Efate (Roses) for eye wound and later rotated stateside.

After recuperation and homeleave was assigned pilot pool at Cherry Point. On March 17, 1944 took detachment of

men for bombing training to IBM-Endicott, NY and a trip to India. Participated in training for "Project Danny" at Walnut Ridge, AR. Was discharged Oct. 11, 1945 at Jacksonville Naval Air Station, FL.

On Aug. 19, 1944, married his Marine Gunair Instructor Jean E. Frye, at Congaree Field. They have three children- son, Mark and daughters, Nancy and Judy and eight grandchildren.

After leaving Corps graduated from University of Minnesota and accepted a Commission as pilot in Air Force. Remained in Ready Reserve until retirement.

In 1952-1956, was extension agent for Federal Extension Service. In 1956 joined United States Department of State as foreign service officer and spent 20 years overseas. Retired and celebrating 46th wedding anniversary with Jean and family in Luray, VA.

LEONARD G. REH, JR., was born Nov. 20, 1923 in Pittsburgh, PA. Enlisted Aug. 8, 1941. Served on board USS *President Adams* (APA-19). He was discharged with rank of BM 1/c E-6.

He remembers Tulagi landing, the night battles and Jap air attacks. Awards: Navy Commendation, Good Conduct Medal, seven Battle Stars, Korean Service Award, Philippine Service Award.

He his married to Doris Mae and they have one son and three daughters. He is retired and is taking life easy and enjoying Las Vegas, NV.

MILTON E. REIM, was born in Billings, OK Oct. 23, 1924. He graduated from White Deer High, TX, attended West Texas State and graduated from the University of Missouri with a journalism degree.

He joined the U.S. Navy April 28, 1943, Lubbock, TX. He was stationed NTS San Diego, CA; Aviation Repair Unit Navy 145 Guadalcanal, Air Center Command; Navy Training School of Photography and Motion Picture Camera School, NAS Pensacola, FL; Photographic Sqdn. 2, NAS Norfolk, VA.

Awards: American Campaign Medal, World War II Victory Medal, Asiatic Pacific Campaign Ribbon. He was a photographers mate third class when honorably discharged at USN-PSC Shelton, VA March 5, 1946.

He married Bobbie Ferguson of Decatur, AL. He has two sons Martin and Russell and two granddaughters, all live in Texas. He was with newspapers in Alabama and editor of the Air University newspaper, Maxwell AFB, AL prior to joining NASA in Houston, TX as information officer for the space program. He retired from NASA in December 1979 and now resides in Brenham, TX. His hobbies include photography and traveling the USA.

HERBERT A. REIMERS, was born Nov. 13, 1923 in Benton Harbor, MI. Was drafted into the Army Feb. 3, 1943. Received his basic training at Camp Howes, TX as a squad leader in the 86th Inf. Division. He signed up to go overseas and joined the 40th Inf. Div. as a section sergeant in Cannon Co., and was made a tank commander of a M-7 Tank, their weapon was 105 howitzer. He took a nine man squad up into the mountains for about ten days, looking for a downed American pilot, they were not successful. He then spent seven months on the Island of New Britain then on to the Philippine Island of Luzon, Panay, Negroes, and Guamaris. He ended up in Pusan, South Korea.

He was discharged from the Army Dec. 17, 1945 as platoon sergeant.

Awards: Bronze Star w/three Battle Stars.

He married Irene Hintz in 1947 and they have three children and three grandchildren. He is a retired real estate broker and enjoys fishing, hunting, and life in general.

While in service he confiscated a Japanese flag from a Japanese soldier and 40 years later located the soldier and returned the flag. This past summer the grandson of the flag owner spent seven days with the Reimers. He plans to teach English in Japan. Reimer says that it is a "small world."

WILLIAM J. REINHART, was born on Feb. 5, 1920 in Philadelphia, PA. Enlisted in the Coast Guard Sept. 9, 1941 as apprentice seaman. Completed boot training at Algiers, LA Oct. 10, 1941. Transferred to Surf Station until March 15, 1942. Transferred to New River, NC for amphibious training until April 2, 1942. Assigned to USS *Fuller* April 3, 1942 as coxswain of landing craft. Participated in the first wave at Guadalcanal Aug. 9, 1942 and continued to supply Guadalcanal until transferred to USS *Hunter Liggett* Feb. 7, 1943. Participated in invasion of Bougainville Nov. 1, 1943. Transferred to Port Richmond Patrol Base after stateside leave March 16, 1944. Graduated from Aviation Maintenance School as AD3 March 1, 1945. Served in air stations both stateside and abroad.

Married Jacqueline Emery on Aug. 3, 1945. Has two sons, William and Charles. Retired from Coast Guard on July 1, 1962 as aviation maintenance officer. Took a position with McDonnel Douglas Aircraft Co. as a aircraft maintenance engineer. Retired from McDonnel Douglas Nov. 1, 1977 and moved to Florida.

JOSEPH J. REPKO, was born in Danbury, Ct on April 21, 1920. After working in a hat shop for a couple of years he joined the Marine Corps in September of 1940. After boot camp at Parris Island, he was shipped to Guantanamo Bay, Cuba and joined M Co., 2nd Bn., 7th Marines.

In the spring of 1941 he was sent to Tent City in New River, NC to join H Co., 2nd Bn., 1st Marines a new regiment.

He left San Francisco in June of 1942 on the *George F. Elliot* and landed at Wellington New Zealand. They landed on Guadalcanal Aug. 7, 1942. Then in Cape Gloucester and Peleliu.

He was discharged from the Marine Corp in February 1947.

He got back to the States in December 1944, and married a girl he met in high school. He resides in Brookfield, CT where he has been for the past 36 years, 12 miles from his birthplace.

CLINTON C. RICH, was born on Jan. 5, 1921 Syracuse, NY, Enlisted USN June 18, 1941 NRS Albany, NY. Units: Aviation Machinist Mate School, NAS Jacksonville, FL; Parachute Rigger School, Norfolk, VA. Stations served: Cub One - Guadalcanal Campaign, Acron (Red) Two, USNAS - Pensacola, Fl; USNAS-Bronson Field-Pensacola, FL; USNAS - Coco Sola Canal Zone, USNAS - Ft. Lauderdale, FL; Hedron, Fleet AirWing Eight CASU (F) Forty Seven FAETU PAC Ream Field, San Ysidro, CA, Guadalcanal Aug. 9, 1942 to Oct. 14, 1942. Evacuated to Hospital New Caledonia and then to Auckland, New Zealand Hospital as a result of multiple wounds from bomb fragments.

Awards: Purple Heart, Presidential Unit Citation w/ Bronze Star, Asiatic Pacific Medal w/one Star, American Defense Medal, World War II Victory Medal, American Campaign Medal, Good Conduct Medal w/one Star.

Discharged Nov. 13, 1947 U.S. Naval Training Center, San Diego, CA as parachute rigger 1st class.

Married to Josephine Kal of Norfolk, VA June 30, 1942. They have two sons, one daughter and eight grandchildren.

Presently retired from Bureau of Criminal Investigation New York State Police. Served 20 years.

STANLEY H. RICH, was born July 28, 1919 in Chicago, IL. Enlisted in the Marines May 1940. Trained in PLC 1940-1941 then called to active duty. Commissioned second lieutenant Lt. USMCR and served in the 1st Pioneer Bn., 1st Marine Div. from April 1941 through November 1944. Campaigns included Guadalcanal, Cape Gloucester and Peleliu.

Retired from active duty December 1945 with rank of captain.

Married Wells College sweetheart Janet Kitchell of Geneva, NY. They have three children and two grandchildren and two great grandchildren.

He owns and operates The MacIntosh Co. Glass Engravers in Lyons, NY.

CLYDE FRANCIS RINE, was born Aug. 23, 1917 in Glenmora, LA. Enlisted April 8, 1941. Served with A Btry., 245th FA Bn. Served in various islands in the Pacific including Guadalcanal, Philippines and Bougainville. He was discharged after four and one half years in the service. Served three and one half years in the Pacific. He was discharged as a Tech 4. He remembers arriving home on his birthday at Golden Gate.

Awards: Asiatic-Pacific Ribbon w/three Stars, World War II Victory Ribbon and Medal, Presidential Unit Citation Ribbon w/Guadalcanal Battle Star, Philippine Medal.

He has been married for 45 years and has two children, one son and one daughter and two grandchildren and one great grandchild.

He is a retired school crossing guard, auto and truck mechanic. He also has repaired lawn mowers and is just a general handyman.

DONALD WYMORE RITCHIE, was born Shelbyville, KY on Nov. 15, 1921. Graduated Shelbyville High School on May 25, 1938. Enlisted in the U.S. Navy June 17, 1939. After boot camp at Norfolk, attended Hospital Corps School at Portsmouth, VA. Graduated Dec. 8, 1939, and was assigned to Naval Hospital at Portsmouth. On Sept. 25, 1940 was transferred to the 1st Marine Div. WWII service as a member of Hq. Co., 1st Bn., 1st Marines, 1st Marine Div. included: Guadalcanal Aug. 7-Dec. 22,

1942. Eastern New Guinea September - December 1943, and Cape Gloucester, New Britain December 1943-April 1944.

Promoted to chief pharmacist mate on May 15, 1944, and to senior chief hospital corpsman on May 16, 1959, after serving on various ships and shore stations. Transferred to the Fleet Reserve on Aug. 3, 1959, and fully retired from the Navy on Nov. 1, 1968.

Awards: Presidential Citation (Guadalcanal), Good Conduct Medal (six awards), American Defense Medal, American Campaign, Asiatic-Pacific Campaign Ribbon w/four Stars, World War II Victory Medal, National Defense Service Medal.

Graduated Indiana University June 1964. Worked for the Kroger Co. 1964-1968, and for Community Hospital in Indianapolis from 1968 to retirement in 1981. He is single.

His memberships include: Indiana University Alumni Association, Fleet Reserve Association, Guadalcanal Campaign Veterans, Pentalpha Lodge of the F&AM, and the 1st Marine Division Association.

JOSEPH F. RITTMEYER, was born in Baltimore, MD on Oct. 20, 1923. Graduated from St. Martins Academy. Enlisted in Marine Corp at Baltimore on Dec. 30, 1941.

Boot camp at Parris Island, SC then to New River, NC. Shipped out of San Francisco on June 22, 1942. Returned to States June 19, 1944. Saw action at Tulagi and Guadalcanal. Wounded on Guadalcanal and sent to hospital in New Zealand. Rejoined outfit in Melbourne, Australia. Landed at Cape Gloucester Dec. 26, 1943. Returned to States June 19, 1944. He received the Purple Heart Medal.

He is married to Alice and has two children. He is retired and enjoys playing golf about five days a week.

CHARLES S. RIZZO, was born Sept. 10, 1914. Enlisted Jan. 21, 1941. Served with 147th Inf., 37th Div. from Camp Shelby, MS. He was a technician fifth grade. Participated at Guadalcanal, Iwo Jima and Emaru.

Awards: Combat Infantry Badge, three Combat Stars, American Defense Medal, Asiatic-Pacific Campaign Ribbon, Good Conduct Medal, Purple Heart, Bronze Star,

He was married in 1947 and has three children and nine grandchildren. He is retired and travels extensively.

ROBERT ROBINSON, was born at Dillsboro, NC on Sept. 15, 1919. He graduated from high school, Hamilton, WA in 1934 and enlisted in the United States Navy on Oct. 18, 1934. After recruit training at San Diego, CA, he served on board the USS *Altair*, a destroyer repair ship based at San Diego, CA until August 1940. He was then transferred to the USS *Meredith* (DD-434), where he served in the Atlantic, European and Pacific Theatres of operations. He was a survivor of the USS *Meredith*, which was sunk near Guadalcanal on Oct. 15, 1942. Of the 330 men on board only 97 were rescued.

He was then assigned to the USS *Russell* (DD-414) where he was commissioned ensign Sept. 15, 1944 and served the remainder of World War II. He then served in a number of intelligence billets until he retired as LCDR, USN in 1965.

He married Doris Rensink on Oct. 1, 1945 at Darrington, WA. They have three children: Arlayne Marie Monjay; James Robert Robertson; Holly Ann Robinson and four grandchildren.

He was employed as chief arson investigator Snohomish County, WA. He retired from that position in 1975 and resides in Marysville, WA.

His hobbies have been hunting, fishing, traveling and writing a book about the "Life, Death and Men of the USS Meredith (DD-434)" entitled *Shipmates Forever*.

GEORGE P. ROGERS, was born on Nov. 7, 1915 in Wetohatchie, AL. Enlisted USN Jan. 1, 1942. Served on board USS *Chippawar* and USS *Fuller*. He was a warrant machinist. Participated at Guadalcanal, Rendova, Bouganiville.

He is married and has two children and two grandchildren. He has been retired for ten years from his small business.

WILLIAM ROM, was born Ely, MN on Dec. 5, 1917. Navy rank lieutenant commander September 1940-May 1946. Served 13 months as USS *Maryland* "R" Div. officer. Cruised of Malaita in February 1943 warding off Japanese fleet attack of Guadalcanal. Left *Maryland* at Efate for Guadalcanal March 1943, seven months as Tulagi senior OD, two months Guadalcanal operations during Munda campaign. Later first lieutenant on carrier *Bismark Sea* (sunk at Iwo Jima). First lieutenant and cargo officer on attack transport USS *Navarro*. Delivered troops and hot cargo Okinawa April 1, 1945.

While touring Japan recently guide was "Hiro", trained as Kamikazi pilot to attack Okinawa ships but war ended before his final flight.

Wartime marriage to University of Washington coed Barbara Berlin. They have four children, (one doctor, two lawyers and one bush pilot), six grandchildren.

After war started Ely canoe trip outfitting business with 400 canoes in rental. Retired after 30 years but still running fly-in fishing camps in Canada and Minnesota.

SEYMOUR ROSENWASSER, was born April 21, 1915 at Brooklyn, NY. He studied art after high school and worked in three display studios in New York City.

He was drafted into the Army April 15, 1941. He had basic training at Ft. Bragg, NC. He was attached to the First Marines on Guadalcanal Nov. 12, 1942. He was with the American Division at Bougainville and the Philippines.

November 1942, he got lost near Pt. Cruz on Guadalcanal, his telephone line was cut just before his unit pushed forward. He went back to repair. When he returned to the front, he could not find the O.P.—they had moved forward. After running around for a while, he was told to get down by kneeling soldiers ready to move again. He finally found the O.P. and realized he was the only one *standing* in front of the line working for the O.P.

He was discharged with the rank of corporal on May 30, 1945.

He married Pearl and they have two children and four grandchildren. He is a retired (February 1990) jewelry store owner, Dobbs Ferry, NY. He studied watch repair at the Bulova Watch Company in Woodside, NY, where he met Gen. Bradley. He became chairman of the board.

He also remembers Nov. 12, 1942. At dawn, he went over the side, climbed down a couple of feet, then was ordered to stop and wait. He had to wait for the next Higgins boat. After a long wait, he finally got into the next boat. He landed on the beach after landing in the water.

JAMES D. ROTHERMEL, was born in Burton, TX, Aug. 20, 1918. Graduated from Brenham High School in 1938. Feb. 5, 1939 entered the National Youth Administration at Inks Dam, Burnet, TX through June 1940 taking training in drafting, construction painting, woodworking, machine shop and auto mechanics. July 1940 was employed as a construction painter at U.S. Naval Air Station, Corpus Christi, TX. March 24, 1942 enlisted in the Navy at Houston, TX as painter 3rd class reporting to Camp Allen, Norfolk, VA on June 18, 1942 assigned to the 14th U.S. Construction Bn. Aug. 6, 1942 moved to Davisville, RI constructing quonset huts and enlarging the base. On Aug. 22, 1942 left for Treasure Island, CA in preparation for overseas duty leaving Sept. 7, 1942 arriving in New Caledonia. While in Nouema built storage facilities and quonset huts for a hospital receiving station. They left Nouema for Guadalcanal arriving on Nov. 2, 1942. While at Guadalcanal they built roads, bridges, Carney Airfield for B-24s and 17s, operated a water purification station, operated a saw mill and built a tank farm to store aviation fuel. He was assigned to the painting and sign shop earning a second class painter rating. They left Guadalcanal on Nov. 8, 1943 for the good ole United States. The battalion was stationed at Camp Parks near Stockton, CA for 11 months then to Pearl Harbor for four months and a short stop over at Siapan. From Siapan to Okinawa landing Easter Sunday April 1, 1945 leaving Okinawa to the good old United States for separation being discharged Dec. 15, 1945 as painter first class.

After leaving the Navy earned a bachelors and masters degree in business administration education. Aug. 24, 1947 married Dorothy Ann Hodde. They have two sons and two grandchildren. His employment was in education for 29 years. Three years as a classroom instructor, 12 years as high school principal and 14 years as Dean of Business Administration Department at San Jacinto College, Pasadena, TX. Retiring Aug. 31, 1978 enjoying retirement by traveling and active in politics. In 1984 ran for Brenham City Council being re-elected for four terms and for the past two years serving as mayor-pro tem.

WALTER RUDAKIEWICZ, was born on Jan. 28, 1921. Enlisted in the Marine Corps on Feb. 3, 1942. After training at Parris Island was assigned to the beginning of the 1st Marine Div. (3-1-1).

Participated in action against the enemy at Guadalcanal, Cape Gloucester, New Britain, Peleliu Island. He was wounded at Peleliu Island. Had R&R at Melbourne, Australia. Discharged as corporal on Feb. 6, 1946.

Worked for Bethlehem Steel for 34 years and is now retired. He has one daughter Patricia Monahan and two wonderful grandchildren.

PAUL E. RUGERS, born Jan. 5, 1920 in Washington, D.C. and enlisted Jan. 6, 1941 in Washington, D.C. Served with Hq. Btry, 1st Bn., 214 CA (AA). Participated at Guadalcanal, New Caledonia, New Zealand. Discharged with rank of sergeant.

Married to Ellen, three children and four grandchildren. He is a retired U.S. Government investigator and past department commander, American Legion, Florida.

JOHN O. RUSSELL, was born on Aug. 13, 1922 in Webster County, KY. Enlisted Jan. 17, 1942. Served with the 37th Div., 145th Inf., Co. D. Stationed at Indiantown Gap, PA. Participated at Guadalcanal, Bougainville, New Georgia Island. Discharged with rank of staff sergeant.

Awards: Combat Infantry Badge, One Battle Star, Asiatic Pacific Theatre Ribbon and two Citations.

He married Grace Reynolds and has five children, 14 grandchildren and two great grandchildren. He is retired security officer for Exxon Company in Spartanburg, SC.

ANDREW ANTHONY SALEK, was born in Wilkes-Barre, PA on Feb. 9, 1924.

He enlisted in the U.S. Marine Corp on Feb. 2, 1942. He was assigned to the 1st Marine Div., B-1-5 and was among one of the first Marines to land on Guadalcanal. His unit received a citation on Feb. 4, 1943 for defending Tulagi, Gavutu, Tanambogo, Florida, Guadalcanal, British Solomon Islands and all enemy zone operations in the South Pacific Ocean. He was honorably discharged on Oct. 26, 1945 with rank of corporal.

He married Frances Sabulski of Wilkes-Barre, PA on June 26, 1949 and sometime after settled in Lyndhurst, NJ. He has two daughters employed by the Federal Bureau of Investigation.

In 1948, he began his career at the U.S. Postal Service. He received over 20 incentive awards. He completed numerous management training courses, including a course at the University of Oklahoma. He is now retired after achieving the position of superintendent of system operations at the New York Bulk and Foreign Mail Service in Jersey City, NJ.

Andrew has a home in the Pocono Mountains of Pennsylvania where he enjoys the outdoors and is an avid golfer.

PETER SARANTAPOULAS, was born in Johnson City, NY on June 22, 1923. Enlisted in the Navy Jan. 27, 1941. After boot camp at Newport, RI sent to Radio School in San Diego, CA. Was at Pearl Harbor on that day of Infamy Dec. 7, 1941 on board the USS *Argonne*. Returned to the mainland for assignment to new construction. Assigned to USS *George Clymer* and went ashore in North Africa Nov. 8, 1942 in the 4th wave, part of Navy radio beach party.

Returned to Norfolk, VA and sailed Panama Canal Christmas Day 1942 arriving Guadalcanal Feb. 6, 1943. Left Guadalcanal Feb. 9, 1943 arriving Wellington, New Zealand carrying Jap prisoner and survivors.

Stationed at NUY Radio Koli Point Guadalcanal March 1 through April 19, 1943 and again Dec. 23, 1943 through May 14, 1944. Veteran of Bougainville, Guam and Okinawa invasions carrying Marines.

Discharged from Navy Sept. 29, 1945 as radioman first class.

Married Gerladine Travis in 1948, and they have eight children.

He worked in communications WINR Binghamton, NY, NBC, New York and retired from ABC, New York after 25 years.

He now resides in Bardonia, NY.

WALTER SCHAD, was born Sept. 3, 1922 in Bronx, NY. Entered service Feb. 11, 1942. Served with C Co., 1st Antrac Bn., Dunedin, FL. He was discharged with the rank of corporal.

He received both the Navy and Marine Corps Medal.

He is married and has two sons, four grandchildren and one great grandchild.

He is president of Walt Schad and Son's Plumbing in New York.

EARL M. SCHAEFFER, was born April 25, 1922, Reading, PA. Enlisted in the Army July 1, 1940. Basic training at Camp Dix, NJ. Sent to Hickam Airfield T. H. Assigned 72nd Bomb Sqdn. Radio School at Wheeler Field, T. H. Gunnery School at Hickam.

Lived through Pearl Harbor attack, Battle of Midway and Solomon Islands Campaign. Flew 94 search and strike missions in B-18s and B-17s. Flew December 7 in B-18 searching for Jap Fleet. At Midway in B-17 where hit by ack-ack fire, knocking out electrical system to Bombay and Ball Turret and No. 2 engine and oxygen at waist guns. Many other exciting missions over Solomon Islands. Schaeffer remembers being very frightened of Ack-Ack Fire.

Discharged from Smoky Hill Air Base, Salina, KS May 26, 1945 with rank of technical sergeant. Returned to active duty Oct. 4, 1946. Stationed at Salina, KS; Biggs Field, El Paso, TX; Fairfax Field, Kansas City, KS; Wiesbaden (Y-80) Air Base, Germany; Furstenfeldbruck, Germany; Lowery Field, Denver, CO; Air Task Force 13, Taipie, Formoso; Lincoln AFB, Lincoln, NE; Semback AFB, Germany; Camp Perry; Wiesbaden, Germany and Keesler AFB, Biloxi, MS. Retired in the grade of master sergeant on Oct. 31, 1962 to Assaria, KS.

Awards: Silver Star, Distinguished Flying Cross w/one Oak Leaf Cluster, Air Medal w/three Oak Leaf Clusters, Presidential Unit Citation, Navy Presidential Unit Citation, Army Good Conduct Medal w/five Knots, Air Force Good Conduct Medal, American Defense w/one Star, Asiatic-Pacific Campaign Medal w/three Stars, American Campaign Medal, World War Two Victory Medal, World War Two Occupation Medal, Air Force Longevity Ribbon, Philippine Presidential Unit Citation.

Attended Brown Mackie College to learn accounting and business administration. Went to work at the Salina Planning Mill as office manager. After 22 years retired April 1986.

Married Rozella Olson June 1945. He has three sons: Steven, Robert and Gary and three grandchildren.

EDWARD J. SCHUELER, was born Oct. 27, 1919. Enlisted in the United States Navy Oct. 5, 1940. Served aboard the USS *Fuller* (APA-7) four and a half years.

Participated in transporting units of the 1st Marine Div. to Rejkyavik, Iceland. Transported American Expeditionary Force to Belfast, Ireland. initial landing at Guadalcanal, Salmon Islands. Reinforcement of Guadalcanal and consolidation of the Solomon Islands. Initial assault and reinforcement on Bougainville, Saipan, Marianas Island, Tinian, Peleliu Islands, Leyte, Philippine Islands, Leyte, Luzon at Lingayen Gulf, Okinawa, Ryukyus.

Awards: Good Conduct Medal, American Defense w/ Fleet Clasp, American Campaign Medal, Asiatic-Pacific Campaign w/one Silver Star and four Bronze Stars, World War Two Victory Medal, Philippine Liberation w/two Stars, Philippines Presidential Unit Citation.

Discharged from the U.S. Naval Hospital, San Leandron, CA July 24, 1945, carpenters mate first class.

Married Oct.. 26, 1940 to Mary Jane Sedgwick. They have four daughters and one son (deceased) and nine grandchildren.

He is past commander Winfield Scott V.F.W. Post 2193, past commander Maywood American Legion Post 133, past Seam Squarrel Military Order of Cooties, Ding-A-Ling Pup Tent 71, member 40/8 Legion.

He retired Jan. 22, 1982 as fire chief of Hines Fire Department.

FRED G. SCHULER, was born in Winchester, KS on Jan. 12, 1918. Enlisted in the Marine Corps Dec. 31, 1941.

After boot camp, in San Diego, he went to Camp Elliott for artillery training, where he was assigned to the 3 G10 2nd Div. Marine. After artillery training he was shipped out for the Pacific area aboard the USS *General Jackson*.

Landed on Solomon Islands on June 9, 1942 and stayed until Oct. 23, 1944. Action at Guadalcanal B.S. I. Aug. 7, 1942-Jan. 31, 1943 and Tarawa, Gilbert Islands Nov. 20-24, 1943. He had six attacks of malaria during the service.

Most memorable events: While on Tulagi, he saw John F. Kennedy on patrol. Later, some of his Marine buddies borrowed five gallons of torpedo juice from Kennedy's PT boat while it was docked. He also stood in the chow line with Cpt. James Roosevelt.

He returned to the States in 1946 and married Marzella Winn. They have six children and reside in Nortonville, KS.

HAROLD A. SCHUMACHER, was born in Portland, OR on Jan. 21, 1924. Enlisted in the Marine Corps June 8, 1941 in Seattle, WA 17 years old.

After training at San Diego went to Camp Elliott and shipped out Jan. 2, 1942 on the Monterey Liner with the 8th Marine Regt.

They were the first expedition force to leave in time of war. They landed in Pango Pango, Somoa. They left Somoa in October 1942 and landed in Guadalcanal Oct. 20, 1942. The Japanese bombed them from the air and sea.

In February 1943 they landed in New Zealand to train for the next campaign. October 1943 they proceeded to Tarawa. They were there three days and most his platoon 3 Co. L, 2nd Div., was wiped out. After securing the island, they were shipped out to Hilo, HI to build a new camp named, Tarawa.

Harold was shipped home to Camp Pendelton, CA. He was taught scout and sniper tactics and demolition. He shipped out to the Occupation of Japan in 1945 and there joined George Co. 5th Marines. In 1946 he was again shipped out to Peking, China, and there joined the 4th Regt. in the British Legation. They separated the Japs from the Chinese and shipped them home.

Discharged in June 1947. Harold met his wife, Sara Rodriguez, before going to Japan in 1945. They were married at the Little Church of Flowers, in Glendale, CA on May 17, 1947.

They have two daughters and four grandchildren. Harold worked for the post office 34 years. He has resided in Rosemead, CA for 43 years. Harold is retired and active as vice president of NARFE Chapter 9556 in Temple City, CA.

ALFRED SCHUSTER, was born in Chicago, IL on July 19, 1916. Joined the 28th Div., 14th Bn. USNR as a volunteer in 1933. He got his sea legs on the USS *Wilmette*. He was called out April 1941, to be trained as a winch operator on the AFI USS *Bridge* and the AF8 USS *Boreas*, refrigeration ships, was in the brig on the *Boreas*, in Pearl Harbor, the Sunday before the Japs it. The regulars referred to them as Feather Merchants. Served in the "Yacht Club" on the USS *Zeilin* (APA-3) for about three years. Rating BM 1/c and acting chief MAA. One of his duties as chief MAA was to assist in unloading their boats at Lingayen Beach and Iwo Jima.

After the war, he asked to ship over into the regular Navy and was told that after 11 years, he would have to start all over again, even as far as going back to boot camp. Left the "Yacht Club", as R.S. Thomas BM 1/c (L.T.M. - G.C.V.) once said. In September 1945 became a L.T.M. of the G.C.V. in 1989, and he met a lot of nice people.

Married Grace in 1939 and had two daughters and one son.

Worked at Crane Co. in Chicago 25 years and CTA 20 years as an electrician.

CHARLES E. SCOTT, was born Nov. 22, 1919 in White Bluff, Dickson County, TN. Enlisted in the Navy Dec. 15, 1941. Completed an abbreviated four week "boots" at San Diego, CA Jan. 12, 1942. Transported to Pearl Harbor via USS *Cresent City*. Disembarked and while on the pier was assigned to the USS *Saratoga* (CV-3). Later assigned to the flight deck plane handling Div. V-2.

With the completion of a drydock retro-fit at Bremerton, WA, the *Saratoga* joined the 7th Fleet that was in preparation for invasion of Guadalcanal. August 7 invasion was noted in his service record.

On Sept. 18, 1943 he left ship for training at Naval Technical Training Center 87th and Anthony, Chicago, IL. Completed training Jan. 31, 1944 with a specialist rate of AMMP 2/c. (aircraft propeller specialist).

With orders reading for the *Saratoga*, he began chasing it from port to port but was "snafued" by being given transportation from the receiving station, San Francisco to Pearl Harbor via a floating drydock being towed by a sea-going tug. Fourteen days later at Pearl the *Saratoga* was long at sea, therefore, his order were changed to NAS Ford Island. He was assigned to the A&R propeller repair shop.

Two memorable occasions outstanding were the crossing of the equator July 12, 1942 and witness the defeat of the shellbacks by the Pollywogs in the battle to hoist the "Jolly Roger" and from the *Saratoga* flight observed the Japs bombing the USS *Enterprise*.

Discharged Sept. 29, 1945 at Memphis, TN.

Retired after 38 years repairing office machines at Sperry Rand and from a local school board.

In 1950, married Marion Injeski. This union produced a treasured son and daughter. Scott now resides in Woodbine, MD.

JAMES W. SCRIVNER, was born on April 13, 1914 in Smith Grove, KY. He joined the U.S. Naval Reserve in Miami,

FL in May 1932. Called to active duty May 19, 1941. Boot camp in San Diego, they commissioned the USS *Crescent City* (APA-21) on Oct. 19, 1941. It carried 36 landing craft and two tank lighters. He left the ship on Dec. 13, 1944 as chief of A Div.-boat shop.

Made the invasions of Guadalcanal, Malaita, Bougainville, Guam, Peleliu, Leyte.

From Aug. 7, 1942 through Oct. 27, 1944 the *Crescent City* shot down seven planes and the crew earned ten medals and seven Bronze Stars. They arrived in California Dec. 13, 1944 30 days leave and back out to Leyte again until the end of the war. Back to Charleston, SC for discharge on Oct. 3, 1945. Back in Reserves until 1971.

He has two children and four grandchildren.

ROSS W. SETON, JR., was born May 10, 1921 in Perry, OK. Enlisted in the U.S. Coast Guard in July 1941. Boot camp at Port Townsend, WA. Served aboard the USS *Hunter Liggett* (PA-14) Guadalcanal, USS *Waters* (APD) Boat Pool #8, Munda, New Georgia, USS *Calaway* (PA-35), Emiru, USS *Centarus* (KA-17), Okinawa, Easter Sunday 1945. Discharged BM 2/c in June 1946.

Started trucking in 1946, contracting with the city of Los Angeles Bureau of Street maintenance until the present.

He has two daughters, Cindy, Sandy and one grandson.

SHEDD BROTHERS, after a tearful farewell to their parents in Hartford, CT, the three Shedd brothers, Robert, 20, Donald, 19, and Paul 18, went to Springfield, MA, to enlist in the Marines. After about six weeks of boot camp at Parris Island, they were assigned to 2nd Platoon, A Co., 1st Bn., 5th Marines, 1st Marine Div. at New River, NC.

After a long trip to New Zealand and the Fiji Islands, they arrived off Guadalcanal on Aug. 7, 1942. A and B Companies, 1st Bn., 5th Marines were to land two platoons each in the first wave. The 2nd Platoon with the three Shedd brothers was one of these. They never became involved in any of the vicious battles like the Tenaru or Bloody Ridge, but did their share of fighting sev-

Paul F. Shedd

Robert C. Shedd   *Donald C. Shedd*

eral times at the Matanikau River and west of there as well as much patrolling in many parts of the area.

On Oct. 18, 1942, A Co. was working on a new Regimen-

Paul, Donald and Robert Shedd

tal CP in the jungle west of Kukum when a flight of Japanese planes was hit by their fighters, causing them to jettison their bombs right on the work party who had no foxholes for protection. Twelve men were wounded and five were killed. Paul and Don were both wounded by shrapnel. Paul was evacuated to New Zealand, later to return to the company in Melbourne. He was soon sent to the States and then to Attu. Don was bandaged up and returned to duty, as were others of the company, leaving no record of their wounds.

Don and Bob left Guadalcanal on December 9 with the rest of the 5th Marines for rest and rebuilding in Australia. The two were on New Britain, where Bob was wounded. He was in the hospital on New Guinea for a month, then returned to the outfit in time for the capture of Talasea. Evacuated to New Caledonia. Returned to A-1-5 and finally returned to the States. He was probably the last of the original company to return to the States.

Paul, born in Rutland, VT on Jan. 14, 1924, married the former Betty Congdon. They have a daughter and two grandchildren. Don, born in Rutland, VT on Sept. 30, 1922, married the former Jean Stafford. They have a son, daughter and three grandchildren. Bob, born in Rutland, VT on Aug. 29, 1921, married the former Mary Lou West. They also have a son, daughter and three grandchildren.

All are planning to be in Washington, D.C. with the 1st Marine Div. Association reunion for the 50th Anniversary of the landing on Guadalcanal.

BERNARD J. SHEELER, was born April 30, 1922 at Pittsburgh, PA. He entered the service at Kingman, AZ on June 4, 1940. He served with the 1st Marine Division, M-3-7. He remembers his 10 years with the Ohio National Guard, Jan. 8, 1958 to Sept. 28, 1969. He was discharged with the rank of 1st Sgt./E8 on Sept. 28, 1969.

He married Lois Keller Sheeler. They have three children, two grandchildren. Employed with Ford Motor Company of Lima, OH as a machnist, V-8 crankshaft grinder.

LARRY C. SHEPHERD, born Sept. 2, 1911 at Lunenburg, MA, joined U.S. Navy on April 1, 1929. Served on several ships covering 11 years sea duty and nine years shore duty. Served 36 months overseas, 24 months in combat zones.

Most memorable experience was during a Jap held Guadalcanal bombing raid on July 8/9, 1942 and seeing the first ack-ack coming up with his name on it.

Flew a *Guinness Book* record breaking flight on the JRM Mariner *Caroline Mars* on Aug. 27/28, 1948 while with VR-2 at NAS Alameda.

Discharged from active duty on Dec. 7, 1948 and served additional eight years in fleet reserve as an aviation chief radio man. After discharge, served 24 years as a government inspector.

Married to Rosie on Sept. 19, 1936. Now spending time in mountain search and rescue with the county sheriff's posse.

WILLIAM S. SHIELDS, JR., was born July 23, 1917 at Thomson, GA. He entered the service with the Army on Nov. 25, 1940. He served at the following military stations and locations: Camp Stewart, GA, Benecia, CA, New Zealand, New Caledonia, Guadalcanal, New Guinea and Ft. Bliss, TX.

He was the first man out of his unit to be rotated back to the States on points. He was discharged June 8, 1945 with the rank of s/sgt.

He married Dorothy Jones of Thomson, Ga on Dec. 31, 1941. The have been married for more than 50 years. They

have three children and one grandchild. He worked as a power lineman with Georgia Power Company assisted in Supervisory Training Instruction, US Army Signal School, Ft. Gordon, GA. He retired July 23, 1982.

He has been active in the VFW for many years. He was the first All American Post Commander selected from the state of Georgia in 1964. Sine then, he has served through the chairs at his district and department, becoming state commander of the Georgia VFW in 1969-70. He has served on many national committees at the VFW and has served as national chairman of the community activities committee, Youth Activities Committee and was National Chairman of the VFW American Committee, 1976-77. He currently serves as Quartermaster; adjutant at VFW Post 7778 in Thomson, GA.

ROY JOSEPH SILVA "SMOKEY JOE", was born Sept. 13, 1924 in San Francisco. Raised on Dairy Ranch, San Joaquin Valley, CA (Merced County), until Navy enlistment.

Enlisted San Francisco Sept. 13, 1941. Special boot camp, Navy Reserve Air Training Center, Oakland Airport, due to overcrowding of San Diego and Great Lakes at that time.

Aerial Gunnery School NAS Alameda and Gun Pointers School 20mm Anti.

Served on USS *Enterprise* (CV-6) Air Group 6AMM 3/c, while recuperating from wounds received on Guadalcanal at Bremerton Naval Hospital, medical discharge June 27, 1943. Received belated promotion AMM 2/c March 1943. Served USS *Enterprise* as AC/mechanic and aerial gunner as well as gun pointer 20mm.

Received 1982 G.C.V.A. "Father Gehring-True Value Award".

Occupation as law enforcement since 1943, 42 years. Presently a forensic analyst, Polk County Sheriff's Department, Florida. He retired in June 1987.

Married Sydney C. Silva, they have four children (two deceased) from a former marriage, and five grandchildren.

He is the president and founder of Pacific War Veterans World War Two Association.

WALTER W. SINGLETERRY, was born July 27, 1916 in Red Oak, IA. Enlisted in the U.S. Navy June 13, 1934 and completed recruit training at San Diego, CA.

The first ship assignment was to the destroyer USS *Brooks* (DD-232), then to the USS *Humphreys* (DD-236), and in 1938 to the USS *Henley* (DD-391). He was assigned to the USS *Russell* (DD-414) when it was commissioned last in 1939 and earned nine battle stars by December 1943 when he was appointed warrant officer and served as electrical officer of the USS *Absd - 4* based at Manus until the end of WWII.

He was in China, Japan and Korea aboard the USS *Kermit Roosevelt* (ARG-16) and earned two Battle Stars for operations at Wonsan and Hungnam, Korea.

He has two daughters by his first wife, who is deceased, and lives in San Diego, CA with his second wife, Dorothy. They are co-ordinators for the annual reunion of the USS *Russell*.

RAYMOND R. SINKBEIL, was born in Zeeland, ND. Enlisted in the 164th Inf., North Dakota National Guard Unit on Jan. 2, 1941. He was called into active service Feb. 10, 1941. He then took basic infantry training at Camp Claiborne, LA.

Left San Francisco Harbor in March 1942 bound for Melbourne, Australia. After four days in Melbourne, the 164th was sent to New Caledonia, arriving there April 20, 1942 and became a part of the Americal Division.

Landed on Guadalcanal to reinforce the 1st Marine Div. on Oct. 13, 1942. What a reception they got! The Japanese bombed and shelled them shortly after they landed, and then that night, the Japanese Navy blasted the Henderson Airfield and surrounding area for four and one half years with two battleships (14 inch shells), one cruiser and seven destroyers! After five grueling months on the canal, they were shipped to the Fiji Islands in March 1943 for R&R.

Landed at Empress Augustus Bay, Bougainville Island, Northern Solomons on Chirstmas Day 1943. After the Battle for Bougainville was over (12 months later) the 164th was sent to Leyte, Philippine Islands landing there January 1945. Fought the Japs on Leyte; then on to Cebu Island (Central Philippines); and then on to Los Negros Island (Western Philippines).

Returned to the USA on the rotation system on June 28, 1945. Mustered out of service at Ft. Snelling, MN on July 6, 1945, after three years, three months and 11 days of foreign service. Participated in the Battle of Guadalcanal, Battle of Northern Solomons and Battle of the Southern Philippines.

Awards: Presidential Unit Citation w/Star, Asiatic-Pacific Theatre Service Medal, Philippine Liberation Ribbon w/Bronze Star and American Defense Service Medal.

Attended University of North Dakota under the GI Bill from September 1945 to 1949. Graduated with a B.S. degree in geology. Went to work for Continental Oil Company at Hutchinson, KS, where he met and married Helen Waldschmidt. They have a son, Gregg and a daughter, Charcita.

Retired from Conoco in May 1980 as a senior drilling superintendent and now resides in Lakewood, CO.

CLYDE SLOAN, was born Jan. 9, 1913 at Seattle, WA. He entered the USMC in February 1935. He served in the United States and at Shanghai, Cavite, Southern Pacific, Japan and Korea. He served on the USS *Tulsa* (Asiatic Fleet) 1936-1937.

They were hit by a typhoon in the Formosa Strait. A Navy Commander aboard as a passenger said it was the worst storm he had seen in 20 years of service. Paint scoured off to bare metal on the forward deckhouse by waves and spray crashing over the ships bow. With engines full ahead, the ship made no headway from about six bells of the evening watch to about eight bells the following morning.

He landed on Guadalcanal with the 1st Sep. Av.Engineer Bn., Nov. 10, 1942. They were attacked by about one dozen Japanese dive bombers during ship-to-shore unloading, followed by 25 twin-engine "Betty" bombers carrying torpedoes. One transport was damaged by a near miss, 17 of the 25 "Betty" bombers were shot down. They had to Bivouac in a coconut grove the first night ashore in the pitch dark. He kept waking up with his feet wet. At daybreak, he discovered that he had been trying to sleep on the sloping rim of a bomb crater half-full of water. Baptism of fire thoroughly completed with continued air attacks and naval gunfire during Nov. 11-15 battle of Guadalcanal.

He retired April 30, 1957 with the rank of captain. He married Nelle Eason, July 8, 1941 at Opelika, AL. They have three children and one grandchild. He was employed as a city police officer for Waldport, OR from 1962 to 1969; officer for Newport, OR from 1969 to 1974.

ANDREW A. SLOVINEC, was born Feb. 26, 1922 at Chicago, IL. He entered the service with the US Navy on Nov. 8, 1940. He served sea duty aboard the USS *New York*, USS *Duncan*, USS *Longshaw* and USS *Bennett*. He remembers the USS *Duncan* landing the first troops at Ellice Island. He participated in the battle of Guadalcanal, Battle of Savo Island and Cape Esperance. Sept. 15, 1942, the USS *Duncan* picked up 792 survivors of the stricken USS *Wasp* (CV-7).

On Dec. 3, 1943, he shot down a Japanese plane with 9 20mm shells. He served in the occupation and defense forces of Cape Torokivo.

He was twice married, has one child and four grandchildren. He is a carpenter on disability.

ARTHUR R. SMITH, was born in Beason, IL on March 13, 1918. Inducted into service April, 28, 1941, assigned to Co. G, 132nd Inf., Camp Forrest, TN. Sailed from New York on Jan. 23, 1942, landed at Melbourne, Australia Feb. 28. After arriving New Caledonia their regiment became a part of the Americal Div. Landed on Guadalcanal, Dec. 8, 1942 and committed to action on Mt. Austen. Sailed for Fiji on April 7, 1943 and while there transferred to 1008th Signal Co. August 1943 returned to Guadalcanal and was rotated to States in June 1944.

Married Helen Kollar in 1944 and will soon celebrate their 46th anniversary. They have three sons, Randall, Keith and Steven and daughter-in-laws Rebecca, Sharon and Rebecca, respectively. Seven grandchildren, Steven, Katie, Jessica, Annie, Jacob, Carrie and Robert.

Retired in 1978 as assistant fiscal officer, Veterans Administration Medical Center in St. Louis after 32 years service.

CLIFFORD WILLIAM SMITH, born Jan. 20, 1923 in Everett, MA. He entered the US Army and active service on Jan. 22, 1941. He was trained at Ft. Slocum, NY and shipped out for overseas duty and further basic training with the Hawaiian Division. He was with the 25th Inf. Div. when it was formed in October 1941. He was at Pearl Harbor during the attack. He was wounded in action at Guadalcanal and again very seriously in action in the Philippines and sent to the 63d evacuation hospital and was sent back to the States in June 1945. He was with the 25th Division in all its campaigns until he was wounded on May 15, 1945.

They were attacking the Japanese at the Gifu Strong Point on Guadalcanal in the Solomon Islands. They met with great resistance and had taken quite a lot of casualties, but the division and regiment were determined to take the objective at all costs, so they threw everything they had at the enemy. The Japanese were fighting for their very lives and so were our boys. Among the fusillade of machine gun, rifle fire, mortar shells and flying shrapnel, he was hit and fell wounded on Jan. 14, 1943. He was taken out of the jungle by native stretcher bearers to the 25th Division Field Hospital. Later, he was sent to the 39th General hospital in New Zealand. He then rejoined his outfit. Because of his wounds, he was sent to the 25th Re-Con Troop, Mechanized, of the same Division as a Reconnaissance Agent.

Everything went well except for a few narrow escapes that shook me and the rest of our regiment up. We lost a great many men. Replacements kept coming in all the time. Some men were killed or wounded and he lost many of his very good friends. They were on outpost with their halftracks and motorized vehicles dug in with just their guns exposed. On this night, they were severely attacked from all sides by the enemy. Shells were bursting all around and among them. They returned fire with everything they had. He knows they were giving a good account of themselves because of the enemy piled up around

their position. He received two machine gun bullets through his right hand and lost use of it, but continued firing his 50 calibre with his left hand—because of the butterfly trigger, he was able to keep firing. He was bleeding profusely, but could not stop or do anything about it because everything was happening fast. He knew that if he stopped [firing], they would be overrun.

All of the sudden, everything went blank for him. He was wounded in the head, chest, arms and legs with shrapnel. He doesn't understand how his buddies got him out of there. He awoke in the 63d Evacuation Hospital. He had a strong will to survive because no one in his outfit thought he would make it. As you can see, he did and was sent back home to the States.

He received the Silver Star for Gallantry in action, two Bronze Stars, two Purple Hearts, two Presidential Unit Citations, Combat Infantry Badge, Bronze Arrow Head, American Defense Medal with Clasp for Pearl Harbor, Asiatic Pacific Campaign Medal, Philippine Liberation Medal and the WW II Victory Medal.

He is a 100 percent disabled veteran, wartime service connected.

VERNON V. SMITH, was born in Kalamazoo, MI, son of Virgil and Jennie Smith, Oct. 6, 1923. Enlisted in the Army Feb. 1, 1943. He took training at Camp Sibert, AL.

He was a private for three months with the 119th Chemical Processing Company. Then he was transferred to the 128th Chemical Processing Company as a technician fifth grade Tumblerman for six months. Then shipped out from Camp Kilmer, NJ. They were on the troop ship for 41 days. By the time they had arrived at Guadalcanal he had his sealegs. For the rest of his Army career he was a military policeman; assisted the maintenance of military law at installations at Guadalcanal, acted as sergeant of the guard and commander of the guard, supervising the guard and security of installation.

Awards: World War Two Victory Medal, American Theatre Ribbon, Asiatic Pacific Theatre Ribbon w/four Overseas Service Bars, one Service Stripe, Good Conduct Medal.

He was discharged Feb. 1, 1946 from Ft. Sheridan, IL separation center.

His wife, Ann and he are retired from Western Michigan University. They have four children and eight grandchildren.

He has been with the Guadalcanal Campaign Veterans since May 1981. He says that you cannot find a better group of men.

JOHN J. SMOLKA, was born June 5, 1911 in Graceton, PA. Enlisted Marine Corps Sept. 28, 1940 Cleveland, OH.

After Parris Island assigned to Radio Operators School, Quantico. Graduated March 13, 1941. April 19, 1941 assigned to Hq. Co. 2nd Bn., 5th Marines, Communications, Quantico, C Barracks. New River Sept. 26, 1941. Left Norfolk May 19, 1942 USS *Wakefield*, Wellington, New Zealand June 14. (Flag Day). Guadalcanal (Tulagi) Aug. 7, 1942. Left the Canal on the John Adams Dec. 9, 1942 going to Brisbane on to Melbourne. Left Melbourne Oct. 10, 1943. Good Enough Island - Cape Glouchester on Christmas Day 1943. Went to Pavuvu Russells. Left Russells Nov. 4, 1944 on the Billy Mitchell for San Diego back to Quantico Co. G until discharge Sept. 11, 1945.

After Marines was a professional umpire for Minor Leagues for two years and then to radio announcing for 25 years in Georgia.

His most memorable experience is being recommended for the Silver Star Medal by Col. Chesty Puller.

He has never been married. He has two sisters living in Niles, OH, Ann Sukhey and Elizabeth Swindler.

WILLIAM EDWARD SNOW, was born in Altoona, PA on Dec. 4, 1920. He enlisted in the Pennsylvania National Guard in 1938. He enlisted in the U.S. Navy on Aug. 22, 1939. While on the USS *Fox* (DD-234) he did North Atlantic Neutrality Patrol. He was transferred to the destroyer USS *Cummings* (DD-365) at San Francisco, CA in January 1941. His most memorable experience was being a target for Japanese bombers and strafers while topside aboard the destroyer USS *Cummings* at Pearl Harbor on Dec. 7, 1941. He was a machinist mate second class. His ship was in the Navy Yard for repairs. They downed one dive bomber and assisted in the sinking of a submarine. He earned a Battle Star.

In March 1942 he commissioned the USS *McCalla* (DD-488). He participated in five battles and ten engagements earning five Battle Stars in the Solomon Islands. He was a plank owner of the USS *Napa* (APA-157) (attack transport) and earned one Battle Star for the Iwo Jima Invasion. He was honorably discharged on Oct. 20, 1945 as a chief machinist mate and joined the Naval Reserves.

Awards: American Campaign (with Foreign Service), American Theatre Ribbon, Good Conduct Medal w/one Star, Asiatic-Pacific Theatre w/one Silver and one Bronze Star, American Defense w/Clasp and Star, Commanding Officer Commendation from the USS *Cummings* and the USS *McCalla*.

He married Dorothy Lundmark and they have four children.

He retired as a utilities department supervisor from U.S. Steel, Fairless Works after 31 years service.

He is a member of the Pearl Harbor Survivors Association, Liberty Bell Philadelphia Capter #1, American Legion, Veterans of Foreign Wars, Tin Can Sailors, Inc., Guadalcanal Campaign Veterans and National Chief Petty Officers Association.

ROBERT W. SOMMERWERCK, was born in Baltimore, MD on April 19, 1910. Joined U.S. Naval Reserve Oct. 18, 1928 as fireman third class. Made many Summer training cruises during subsequent years. Called to active-duty Oct. 18, 1940 as watertender second class, Oct. 18, 1940. Following destroyer and transit guard duty in Panama returned to States and joined the USS *San Juan* (CL-54) in March 1942. The San Juan participated in the invasion of the Solomon's at Tulagi Aug. 7, 1942. After repairs in Australia the (CL-54) was involved in all major activity against the enemy. In November 1944 was promoted from chief petty officer to warrant machinist and assigned to USS *Vinton* (AKA-83) for continued duty in the Pacific to until end of war.

Separated from service Oct. 8, 1945. Returned to sales and sales promotion work in the wholesale field of major electrical appliances.

Following retirement in 1974 embarked upon professional acting career. To date has performed in more than 30 stage productions in addition over 70 films made for either television, theater or industry has done dozens of TV spots and a long list of print work for newspapers and magazines in the Baltimore/Washington area.

He is a member in good standing in SAG, AFTRA, and Actor's Equity.

Married for 50 years to childhood sweetheart Mitzi. He has served for nine years as the committee member for USS *San Juan* reunions.

FRANK J. SOUSA, JR., was born Sept. 24, 1923 in Bristol, RI.

Enlisted in U.S. Navy Jan. 13, 1942 served at Newport Training base to beginning of June 1942. Went aboard USS *O'Bannon* (DD-540) at commissioning as a plank owner. Remained aboard to November 1945. Shortly after their shake down cruise in Guantanamo Bay, Cuba he went to the Pacific until the end of the war. He earned eight Campaign Bars, including the Presidential Unit Citation, 17 Battle Stars and several commendations. Discharged November, 1945 with the rank of RDM2/c.

The USS *O'Bannon* was the most decorated destroyer during World War II. Its captain, Admiral MacDonald, was the most decorated Naval officer during World War II.

He and his wife, Gloria, have three daughters: Arline, Anne Marie and Francine. He retired as a building contractor and real estate broker.

CURTIS SPACH, (SPEEDY), born in Winston-Salem, NC on Nov. 15, 1919. Graduated from high school in 1938. Was listening to the radio when the Japs bombed Pearl Harbor. Passed the physical for the Marines on Jan. 13, 1942. He got in just as they were forming the 1st Marine Div.

Went overseas, July 22, to New Zealand. En-route to Guadalcanal they stopped for practice landings in the Fiji Islands. He went ashore in the 1st wave with L Co., 3rd Bn., 5th Regt. Was in every major battle and also a lot of jungle patrolling. He was in the 1st bayonet charge when his company captured Manitabau village. Left the island with the Div. on December 9 for Australia.

He attends most of the reunions of the 1st Marine Div. and the Guadalcanal Campaign Veterans.

He went back to the islands and the Canal and Australia in 1980. While on the canal he paid a visit to Sgt. Major Jacob Vouza one of the most famous native scouts.

He wants to urge everyone to attend every reunion, one can't express the joy of seeing your old pals again.

Discharged with rank of corporal.

He is married to Alice and he has two sons, Curtis III and Brian and two step-children, Roslyn and Rodney. He is retired.

LEWIS B. SPIVEY, was born at Fairmont, NC on July 11, 1922 in Robeson County. The Spiveys and Lewis family of Scott and have been in North Carolina since the late 1600s. He enlisted in the USMC on July 23, 1940. Basic training at P.I. Platoon 76. Assigned to Sea School Portsmouth, VA. Stationed on board the USS *Ranger* 1940-1941. Marine Barks Portsmouth Dec. 7, 1941. NOB & NAS 1942 Norfolk. Requested transfer to combat duty, transferred to Camp Elliott. Assigned to weapons Company 5th Marines, 1st Marines Div. October 1942. Participated in the Guadalcanal Cape Gloucester and Peleliu Campaigns. Was hit twice on Peleliu. Discharged Oct. 25, 1945. Active duty 1949-1950 during the Korean war. Received 2nd lieutenant commission in U.S. Army Reserve 1953.

He is a Life Member of 1st Marine Div. Association, DAV, VFW, member of Sons of the Revolution. Sons of Confederate Veterans - MOSB. Scottish American Military Society Clan MacLeod USA. Retired commandant of the Confederate States Marine Corps. Lt. Gen. in the Army of Tennessee CSA. Tennessee Colonel on the governor's staff.

Married Helen Faith Fox Aug. 31, 1942. They have three sons. Lacey Neal USMC 1966-1969 Vietnam Vet. 1st Marine Div., 5th Marines. John Eric and Lewis Bennet. They have five grandchildren and two great grandchildren.

He is retired from U.S. Civil Service since 1978.

JOSEPH F. SPROCK, was born in Philadelphia, PA. Aug. 18, 1920. Enlisted in the USNR Feb. 1, 1939. Active duty April 1, 1941. Served aboard USS *Hamilton* 141 and USS *Griffin* for a short time in early 1941. Assigned to USS *President Hayes* late 1941. Was a plank owner. Sailed to Pearl Harbor on two trips in February 1942 to bring back survivors of Pearl. Started training Marines April 1942. Sailed for Guadalcanal early July, making landing Aug. 7, 1942. Ascertained rate of Em 3/c while in Pacific. Also made landings at Rendova and Bougainville. Left President Hayes after second landing in Bougainville. Spent seven months in hospitals.

Discharged June 6, 1944. Continued working as an electrician remained of his time. Has been a mason for 20 years, VP northeast region of GCV, married to a fine lady and has seven children and seven grandchildren.

TOMMY C. STAMOS, was born in Stockton, CA and raised in Lodi, CA. He went to Lodi High School and Stockton College.

He joined Battery F, 164th FA, 40th Div., Oct. 9, 1939. He was inducted into full time service on March 3, 1942. He was sent to Camp San Luis Obispo. They became Battery C, 143rd FA, 40th Div. In June 1942, the 40th Division was sent overseas. He was left behind to train new recruits for three months, then he was sent to Camp Stoneman, then left Oakland for Pearl Harbor, HI, which took ten days. He was sent to Wheeler Field, assigned to Battery A, 64th FA, 25th Div. He was then sent to Guadalcanal, where the 64th FA was in combat. He was disabled in 1943 and sent to the 39th General Hospital in Auckland, New Zealand, then sent home to Hoff General Hospital in Santa Barbara. He was discharged in December 1943. He then joined the Merchant Marines in 1945. He sailed all over the Pacific, Persian Gulf, Ceylon, India, Japan, Wake Midway, Guam and the Philippines. He is a life member of DAV, VFW. He is also a member of the American Legion. He worked for Standard of California as an area salesman for 21 years. He started his own automotive parts business and retired in 1983.

He is active in veteran's groups, senior citizen groups and church. He is an elder at St. Andrew Lutheran Church in Stockton, CA.

CHARLES R. STEPHAN, was born Sept. 30, 1911 in Brooklyn, NY. Entered U.S. Naval Academy, June 1930 and commissioned, Ensign, USN May 31, 1934. Served on board USS *Colorado*, USS *Flusser*, USS *Raleigh*, USS *Woodworth* 1934-1944, DesDiv 01, USS *Iowa* in Korea. Military stations were TRAPAC, OPDEEVFOR, ORNAY OMDESRON 8. He achieved the rank of captain.

His memorable experiences include being on board USS *Raleigh* on Dec. 7, 1941 at Pearl Harbor, operations in Guadalcanal, The Slot, Rabaul, Kavieng, Bougainville, being CO on *Woodworth* (DD-460), the Philippines, executive officer of USS *Iowa* 1951-1952 in Korea.

Awards: Navy Cross, two Bronze Star Medals w/V.

Married Eleanor Stork on Feb. 14, 1937; they have four children: Yvonne, Joan, Charles (now a captain in USN), Robert; 13 grandchildren and eight great-grandchildren.

He was professor emeritus, Florida Atlantic University. Honorary Doctor of Engineering. He is retired. He is director and memberships chairman for the Legion of Valor of USA.

ROBERT RICHARD STEVENSON,

was born Jan. 19, 1909 in Lock Haven, PA. Enlisted service on July 1, 1942 with the Hopewill, VA Quartermaster Corp Training Camp. Served with U.S. Army Quartermaster Corp. He was technician fifth grade.

Memorable experience: He retrieved from the Lunga River a paper prepared by a Japanese officer stating that their fighter force was far superior than the Americans.

Awards: American Theatre of Operations, Good Conduct Medal, Asiatic-pacific Campaign Medal, Sharp Shooter Medal, CMTC.

Married Elsie Bendlin of West New York, NJ on Oct. 25, 1941 and they have celebrated their 50th wedding anniversary.

He is retired and enjoys puttering around his two acres of ground.

GEORGE A. STEWART, JR.,

was born in Cleveland, OH on July 1, 1922. Enlisted in the Marine Corps Dec. 15, 1941. Discharged on April 7, 1946.

Received his training at Parris Island, was assigned to K-3-5 1st Marine Div. January 1942 at Tent City, Jacksonville, NC. Was aboard the USS *Fuller* (APA-78) for landing on Guadalcanal on Aug. 7, 1942.

He was wounded on Oct. 7, 1942 on their advance to the Matanikau. He was a point-man with D.W. Whittington who was killed at the same time. After three months in the hospital in Auckland, he rejoined his outfit in Australia.

His most memorable event was when a group of U.S. Marines met General McArthur and Admiral Halsey before their invasion of Cape Glouchester, while in New Guinea, in late 1943.

Married Ann Phillips, he has have two daughters, Kathy and Barb, two sons Richard and James, they served in Navy and Marines in Vietnam, and two step-daughters Sue and Pattie. He has lived in Arizona for the past 15 years.

DAVID E. STILSON II,

was born on Aug. 8, 1923 in Montrose, PA. Enlisted in U.S. Marine Corps on June 17, 1941. Served in numerous post stateside and overseas locations. He achieved rank of sergeant.

Awards: Presidential Unit Citation w/one Bronze Star, Good Conduct w/Bronze Star, American Defense Medal, American Campaign, Asiatic-Pacific w/two Bronze Stars, World War Two Victory Medal, China Service Medal.

He is married to Joyce and they have a daughter Tracy Lynne. He is retired.

WILLIAM H. STONE,

was born on July 21, 1916 in Albertsville, AL. Graduated of University of Florida. ROTC commission.

Entered service as second lieutenant in the field artillery at Ft. Bragg, NC. Assigned to the 72nd Field Artillery Regiment. Regiment shipped to South Pacific in January 1942 to become a part of the newly formed Americal Div. Arrived on Guadalcanal Dec. 12, 1942 as part of the Americal. Was awarded the Bronze Star Medal while there. Outfit relieved from combat March 1, 1943. Sailed to Fiji for rest and replacements. Later took part in campaign on Bougainville for ten months. Was battery commander of Headquarters Btry. Div. Arty. and later BC of Battery B, 246th FA. After 33 months overseas, was transferred back to the U.S. Relived from active duty on Dec. 16, 1945.

Married to Karlene Thames June 1, 1939.

Was employed in the agricultural chemical business. He retired in February 1982. He and Karlene have two sons and three grandchildren.

FRANCIS S. STOVIAK,

was born on Jan. 10, 1922 in Uniontown, PA. Enlisted in the U.S. Marines on Dec. 29, 1941. Served at New River, New Caledonia, Australia, Mt. Martha, New Guinea, Cape Gloucester.

Achieved rank of second lieutenant and was discharged at Portmouth Virginia Naval Yard.

He remembers landing on Tulagia on Aug. 7, 1942 and a Jap attack of their troop carrier.

Awards: Purple Heart, Pacific Theatre, Cape Gloucester Campaign, Pioneer Bath, Guadalcanal Campaign.

Entered Cornell University and graduated in 1949. Married Reenie Buffet on March 4, 1949. They have two sons, John and Charles and two grandchildren, Morgan and Tyler.

He is self-employed as a manufacturing agent for Ford Service Industries. He is a member of the American Legion and Cornell Club.

ALBERT W. SUE,

was born on June 22, 1915 in Platteville, WI. Enlisted Marine Corps July 1934. After fighting sand fleas at Parris Island, SC, further training was at Quantico, VA in a base defense battalion, making two maneuvers on the USS *Antares* to Culebre, Puerto Rico.

In 1941 was assigned to the 1st Marines on their return to States from Cuba.

Was 1st Marines mess sergeant for the entire stay on Guadalcanal, Cape Gloucester, and Peleliu operations, returned Stateside on rotation, December 1944.

Was a plank owner at the Marine Corp Station, Kaneohe, Oahu. Retired at Camp LeJeune, NC, July 1958 as a CWO/3.

While on duty at the Naval Training Station, Great Lakes, IL was married to Mary Malavarsic Oct. 20, 1938. They have a son, Albert III, daughter, Suzanne and four

grandchildren and one great-grandson. They currently reside in Temecula, CA.

JOHN T. SUMNER,

was born in Omega, GA on Feb. 7, 1920. Enlisted in the Marine Corps Aug. 30, 1940. Trained at Parris Island, SC and joined a provisional company with more training in Guantanimo Bay, Cuba.

After returning to the States for three months for more training, he joined the 1st Marine Div. at Camp LeJeune, NC. He left Norfolk, VA in May 1942 and was shipped to New Zealand and landed on Guadalcanal on Aug. 7, 1942; then shipped to Brisbane, Australia on Dec. 9, 1942; then on to Ballarat, Australia for more training. Other operations were on Cape Gloucester, New Britain, Hollandia, Dutch New Guinea and then to Peleliu in the Palau Islands. During the fighting on Peleliu he was seriously wounded by a mortar shell and sent to the hospital at New Caledonia. He returned to the States at San Diego, CA for medical treatment the last of 1944 and then on to Pensacola, FL for more treatment. After a leave to visit family in Sparks, GA, he was transferred to Philadelphia, PA. He vividly remembers being at Washington, DC depot the day President Franklin D. Roosevelt's body arrived for burial. After Philadelphia he was transferred to Jacksonville, Florida Naval Air Station where he was honorably discharged on Aug. 16, 1945 with a 100% disability.

He married Louise Norman, Nov. 7, 1945, and they have one daughter and twin sons. They have resided in Tifton, GA since 1958.

ROBERT J. SWAFFORD,

was born in St. Joseph, MO on Oct. 26, 1923. Enlisted in Navy Feb. 26, 1941. After training at Great Lakes NTS was assigned to USS *Walke* (DD-416) in May 1941 at Charleston, SC. Served on *Walke* until she was sunk at Guadalcanal Nov. 15, 1942. After release from hospital on Tulagi, was assigned to COMAIRSOPAC on USS *Curtiss*. Other assignments were SCTC San Pedro, CA, APL 13, Navy Communications Unit 103, USS *Libra* (AKA-12), USS *PCS* 1413.

Discharged as signalman first class on Nov. 14, 1946 at San Diego, CA.

Married Margaret Violett in September 1947. They have one son, Roger and three daughters, Marian and twins Denise and Diane.

He was employed by Wire Rope Corp. of American in November 1952 and retired in March 1985.

He has been a lifetime resident of St. Joseph during the time he was in the service.

ROBERT S. THOMAS

ANDREW THOMPSON (JACK), was born on a farm Nov. 2, 1921 in Ednor, MD. Enlisted in Washington, D.C., 5th Bn. Marine Corp Reserve, October 1939. Called to active duty October 1940, stationed at Quantico, VA, Guantanamo Bay, Cub; Parris Island, SC; Camp LeJuene, NC; Wellington, New Zealand; Mount Martha, Australia and Russell Island Group. Unit: 1st Engineer Bn. and C Co., 1st Pioneer, 1st Marine Div.

Landed at Guadalcanal B.S.I., Aug. 7, 1942, Eastern New Guinea, October 26-Dec. 25 1942; Cape Gloucester, New Britain December 26-March 2, 1944. Peleliu Palau Island Sept. 15, 1944—Oct. 20, 1944.

Returned to Quantico, VA and was discharged Sept. 18, 1945. Held rank of staff sergeant.

Awards: two Presidential Unit Citations, World War Two Victory Medal, Asiatic Pacific Campaign Medal w/ four Bronze Stars, American Campaign Medal and American Defense Service Medal.

His most memorable experience is having the highest score in Rifle Range, (30 caliber rifle) of the year 1945, Quantico Marine Base, VA.

Retired from USDA, Beltsville, MD, 35 years government service including military.

Married to Phoebe Souder on Oct. 29, 1948. They have four children - two sons and two daughters.

HARRY C. TOEPFER, was born in New York City, July 26, 1922. Joined 32nd Div., United States Naval Reserves at Yonkers, New York July 1940. Called for active duty April 1941. Served on destroyers, North Atlantic, and then entered boot camp at Norfolk, VA. Was aboard the USS *President Adams* when war broke out, Dec. 7, 1941. On July 1, 1942 departed San Diego with elements of the 3rd Bn., 2nd Marines.

At one point they crossed the International Dateline and he made the statement that they were the "Unholy Four", because they skipped Sunday. Captain Dean insisted that it be written in the log and from that time on, the *Adams*, the *Hayes*, the *Jackson* and the *Crescent City* were referred to as the "Unholy Four".

Arrived Guadalcanal Aug. 7, 1942. The *Adams* was ordered to Gavuto the morning of August 8 to debark troops. Made subsequent trips to New Zealand and Australia ports with casualties, and returned to Guadalcanal with troops.

After leaving the *President Adams*, he commanded a small inter-island tanker at Pearl Harbor, and was later transferred to Force Quartermaster of the Pacific Fleet, under Admiral Chester Nimitz.

He was discharged October 1945. Worked on newspapers for 34 years.

Married, father of three, seven grandchildren. Retired and living in Clifton, NJ.

WILLIAM C. TRACY, was born on Feb. 15, 1919 in New York, NY. He enlisted in the U.S. Navy on Nov. 22, 1939 with the I-3-7 1st Marine Div.

He served on various Navy ships and stations. He was a chief pharmacist mate. He lost his assistant on Wallis Island and was the only medic taking care of a company consisting of 175 Marines. He also saw action at Guadalcanal.

He was with the Navy and in the Reserves for a total of 26 years.

Married Dorothy Braddock, Jacksonville, FL on Nov. 11, 1947. They have no children.

He retired from Jax Blood Bank and lost his pension so he went back to work for a national finance company for whom is still working.

His hobbies include golf and cooking. He has been chair person for I-3-7 Marine reunions for the past 11 years.

CHARLES W. A. TRAVIS, JR., was born on July 14, 1919, the son of the late Charles W. A. Travis, Sr. A World War II Navy Air Combat Veteran, he received four Bronze Stars, a Purple Heart, the Presidential Unit Citation and the Navy Commendation Medal while in action against the Japanese as a member of the Scouting Sqdn. Ringbolt, USS *Yorktown* (VS-64) and later with Torpedo Sqdn. One. He was a member of the Pearl Harbor Survivors Association, USS *Honolulu*, the

Guadalcanal Campaign Veterans Association, and was a life member of the Courtland Lodge NO. 32, Free and Accepted Masons, Peekskill, NY.

An instrumentation design engineer, he retired in 1973 from the U.S. Weather Bureau's Research Flight Facility. As a member of Project Story Fury, he had made over 100 flights into mature Atlantic hurricanes. He received the U.S. Department of Commerce's Special Achievement Award for developing specialized weather research instrumentation for use in hurricane and seeding experiments. A member of the Native Hurricane Rovers Protectorate, he began flying through hurricanes in the early 1950's while based at Morrison Field (Palm Beach International Airport) and continued until his retirement from government service.

Mr. Travis died unexpectedly on Feb. 8, 1991. A native of Peekskill, NY, he had been a resident of North Palm Beach, FL since 1960. *Submitted by his daughter, Patricia A. Travis.*

EARL O. TRIANTIS, was born April 27, 1924 in Akron, OH. Has resided in Chicago, IL since childhood.

Enlisted in the Army March 5, 1941 (just prior to 17th birthday), assigned to Co. C, 131st Inf. Took basic training at Camp Forrest, TN. At outbreak of war, was transferred to Co. C, 132nd Inf.

Left for the South Pacific January 1942, by way of New York, Panama, and Australia. Landed in New Caledonia March 1945 in the Liberation of the Philippines.

Was discharged at Ft. Sheridan, IL Sept. 1, 1945 with rank of Pfc.

Became a member of the Chicago Police Department in 1946, retiring from there in 1979, with over 33 years of service. Worked ten more years in private security; now fully retired.

Married Mary Lou Heide, of Chicago, in May 1952. They have one son, Robert.

DELLIE R. TRUELOVE, was born in Wake County, NC in 1923. Enlisted in the Marine Corps at Raleigh, NC. July 22, 1940. After boot camp at Parris Island, SC, he was sent to Cuba with A Btry., 1st Special Weapons Bn. Landed at Guadalcanal Aug. 7, 1942 after Guadalcanal was sent to Ballarat Australia. He participated in the Cape Gloucester, and Peleliu Campaigns, where he was wounded and was sent to the U.S. Naval Hospital at Guadalcanal, and was rotated back to the States. He was stationed at Marine Barracks U.S. Naval Retraining Command at Camp Perry, VA and in September 1945 was transferred to Marine Barracks U.S. Naval Base Charleston, SC and was discharged on July 24, 1946.

He met and married Helen Ines Smith and they have two sons Alan and Marck.

He worked with the Federal Fire Service at the U.S. Naval Weapons Station for 32 years.

He now resides in Goose Creek, SC where he has served for fire chief for 12 years.

RALPH L. TULLOCH, was born in Maryville, TN, April 5, 1923. Enlisted in the U.S. Marine Corps Jan. 23, 1942. Went through boot camp at Parris Island, SC. Assigned to Reg. Weapons Co., 7th Marines at tent camp, Camp Lejeune, NC. Shipped out to Samoa then to Guadalcanal in September 1942.

Hauled ammo and supplies three days and nights to the 1st and 2nd Bn., 7th Marines during the battles of Henderson Field and Mantanikau River, Oct. 24-26, 1942, resulting in a meritorious promotion.

Made the Marine Corps a career. Serving various duty stations with the 3rd Marine Div. and FMF Pac., also Parris Island and San Diego Recruit Depots and Quantico, VA.

Served in the Korean and Vietnam Wars. Retired as master sergeant in June of 1971.

Married Ruth C. Nelson of Omaha, NE, September 1946, they have three children. He now resides in Orlando, FL.

FRANK W. TURNER, was born in Glen Jean, WV on July 22, 1914. Enlisted in Marine Corps on June 2, 1939 in Washington, D.C. His reason for enlisting at that time was that war was in sight, and he preferred learning beforehand to protect himself.

After basic training at Parris Island, SC he was assigned to the Fleet Marine Force at Quantico, VA. While in Quantico, VA he went on maneuvers to the Virgin Islands, Viquces, Culeabra and Guantanamo Bay. He was assigned to the USS *Manley*, converted destroyer to scout vessel. He helped from the 1st, 5th, 7th, and 17th Regts., and the Pioneer Bn., all in the 1st Marine Div. He was in the original Guadalcanal landing, also at Cape Gloucester and Talesea on New Britain and Peleliu.

Received a battlefield commission to second lieutenant in USMCR on Guadalcanal, the swearing in officer was Col. Rowan, out under the palm trees. He attended the Royal Australian School of Camouflage at Sidney, Australia, and the Royal Demolition School at Koopka, Australia. He was promoted to major in the USMCR in 1952. He was also CO of the Shore Party Training School on Anslow Beach, SC.

He is married to the former Joan Aubil. They have one son, Richard, and three daughters: Elinor, Claire, and Diane, eight grandchildren. He has resided in Welch, WVA for the past 24 years.

JOHN GILES TURNER, JR. (JACK), was born in Burlington, Iowa Sept. 10, 1918. He graduated from Burlington High School and attended the University of Iowa.

He joined the Marine Corps Dec. 10, 1941 and served in the Pacific Theatre with the Regimental Weapons Co., 6th Regiment, 2nd Marine Div. from October 1942 until his honorable discharge in September 1945 with the rank of staff sergeant, communication.

Awards: Bronze Star and Campaign Stars for Guadalcanal, Tarawa, Saipan, Tinian and Okinawa. Among the Guadalcanal memories are of first days of combat; Washing Machine Charlie's nightly visits, many hours of malaria; the thrill of witnessing Wild Cats out-maneuver Zeros; and the serious shortage of food when supply ships were unable to dock. Their diet then, of necessity, consisted of french coconut, peanut butter and canned pineapple, which are all just now becoming palatable to him again.

He and his wife, Dawn, have three children: Kenneth, Candace and John III, and also have two grandchildren: David and Lauren. Before and after the war, he was employed by the Pennzoil Company, then became an automobile dealer in 1949 until his retirement in 1979 to the golf course. He currently resides in Laguna Niguel, CA with his wife of 46 years.

W. B. TUTTLE Col. USA (Ret.) was born in El Paso, TX on May 28, 1894. He attended public school at El Paso, TX and graduated from New Mexico Military Institute in 1914. He was appointed Regular Army by competitive examination in 1917. Was 1st Captain in ROTC.

He served three years with the Texas National Guard and 36 years with the Regular Army. During WW I he served as lieutenant to the captain, 3d U.S. Inf., Mexican Border Service. During WW II, he served 28 months in the South Pacific, commanding the 147th Inf. RCT (Independent). He also served 16 months in the European Theatre as Commander, 422d Inf., 106th Div. Among other posts, he served as Adjutant General, 78th Inf., Reserve Div., October 1934 to August 1935.

For his service to the country, he received the following military decorations: Legion of Merit with Oak Leaf Cluster, Bronze Star with Oak Leaf Cluster, Bronze Star (Navy) and the Combat Infantry Badge. He received a citation personally signed by Adm. William F. Halsey and

a seperate citation from Mr. James V. Forrestal, Secretary of the Navy. In addition, he received Battle Stars for the Guadalcanal, Bismark Sea, Northern Solomon Island, Northern France, Rhineland and Central Europe Campaigns.

He married Mae R. Tuttle. They have a son, William B. Tuttle, Jr. (Col., Inf. Graduate USMA (West Point), Class 1944) and daughter, Mrs. W. P. Yarbrough (Col. Yarbrough. Graduate USMA (West Point), Class 1936).

He organized reserve duty for PMS&T and Commandant Junior ROTC at Staunton Military College. He was deputy post commander of Carlisle Barracks, PA June 1946 to Jan. 1949.

Quoted as the "most outstanding leader among PMS&T's in Pennsylvania Military District: everything senior troop commander should be, held in high esteem by college head, faculty, cadet corps; was experienced Infantry Regimental Commander, holds Legion of Merit (OLC)." by Col. E. M. Sutherland, Chief, Pensylvania Military District. Maj. Gen. C. Andrus, Deputy Commanding General, 2d Army, Indorsing Officer: "Concur and add: Active, enthusiastic, experienced, fine sense of humor, excellent personality: superior professional qualifications together with personality served to make him superior PMS&T. Recommended for promotion to Brigadier General."

He retired July 31, 1953.

He was employed by the Pennsylvania Military College as assistant to the president, Aug. 1, 1953 to Aug. 31, 1954. He was also employed as Commandant of Cadets, Sept. 1954 to June 15, 1955. Resigned June 15, 1955.

ROY H. TYNER, was born in Libertyville, MO on April 29, 1918.

Enlisted in the U.S. Navy June 1935. Ships served on prior to 1942, *Holland, Sirius, Kalmia, Penobscot*. In 1942, assigned to USS *American Legion* (APA-17), South Pacific and Guadalcanal, then to boat pool Espiritu Santo. Returned to U.S. and assigned to USS *Munda* (CVE-104) rate at CBM.

Left Navy in 1947, joined Army. Sgt. first class, master sergeant to chief warrant officer. Captained U.S. Army ship in Korea 1952-1953 and on Dew Line Operation, Alaska 1954-1957.

Retired in 1957, various civilian jobs until 1974, then retired from civilian work. Purchased large sailing Trimaran just to go sailing and finally came ashore and quit sea. Now living in DeLand, FL in complete retirement, relaxing and traveling for pleasure throughout the U.S. and many foreign countries, including six trips back to New Zealand to renew and visit friends from 1942.

WILLIAM D. TYSON, born in Wrightsville, GA on Jan. 13, 1924, enlisted U.S. Marine Corps Sept. 24, 1941. After boot at Parris Island, SC and A School Jacksonville, FL joined MAG-14 at Camp Kearney, CA. Departed San Diego August 1942 aboard *Lurline*, transferred to Navy *Zeilin* at New Caledonia.

Arrived Guadalcanal November 1942. *Zeilin* hit by dive bombers while off loading. Departed Guadalcanal April 1943 for hospital Auckland, New Zealand. After short stint and R&R Victoria Park returned to Munda and Ondonga in New Georgia. 1946-1947 China, 1950-1951 Korea, 1954-1957 Hawaii, 1958 Europe, 1959-1960 Caribbean with various Stateside assignments in between. Retired September 1962 as master sergeant. After leaving Corps, self-employed in real estate and building. April

1991 semi-retired, enjoying excellent health and traveling. Currently planning to attend 50th Guadalcanal reunion.

Married Dora Hataway of Greenville, NC 1949. The have four children, all boys except two. No grand to date - just five ordinary crumb-crushing, curtain-climbing youngsters.

DAN UGRAN, was born on Feb. 14, 1920 in Youngstown OH. Entered service on Oct. 20, 1941 at Cleveland, OH. Boot camp at Parris Island, SC. Telephone School Quantico, VA Served with Special Weapons Btry., 11th Marines, E & D Btrys 2nd Bn., 11th Marines, 1st Marine Div. in the Pacific Theatre o Operations. He was discharged on Sept. 17, 1945 Quantico, V/ with rank of private first class.

Memorable experiences: Aug. 7, 1942 - Dec. 14, 1942 participated in capture and occupation of Guadalcanal. Dec. 25 1943 - Feb. 10, 1944 - participated in offensive and defensive action on Cape Gloucester, New Britain. March 6 to 15, 1944 participated in the offensive and defensive action of Talasea, New Britain. Sept. 15 to 30, 1944 - participated in offensive and defensive action on Peleliu, Palau Islands. Awards: Presidentia Unit Citation w/star, South West Pacific Theatre w/four stars and American Defense Medal.

Married Marjoire Baldwin on Oct. 11, 1946. They had five daughters and at present five grandchildren. He is retired and widower living in Akron, OH.

ROBERT E. VAN KEUREN, was born on Dec. 20, 194 in Wausau, WI. Joined the U.S. Marine Corps on Dec. 20, 194

following Pearl Harbor, because his father served in the Marine Corps in World War I. Was in on the original landing Solomon Islands. Served with 3rd Bn., M Co., 2nd Marines, landed on Gayuta Island on August 8 relieving the Marine paratroops who had landed the day before with over 50% casualties. They attacked a beach and island manned by Japanese Imperial Marines. Lost over 150 men and only had a 150 yard beachhead. Hardest 150 yard beachhead in the entire Pacific War. He salutes their accomplishment. Of course they had difficulty but they secured the entire island (seven acres) and also the island of Tonambogo (six acres) in only nine days (The Imperial Marines were the only forces sworn to die for the Emperor). They could only take nine prisoners out of 1300 men.

Disabled with a back injury, but refused a medical discharge and went with the battalion over to Guadalcanal Island. His unit received two Presidential Unit Citations for the Guadalcanal Campaign and the Battle of Bloody Ridge. He received an honorable discharge at the Marine Barracks, Washington, D.C. Sept. 29, 1945 with 87 points.

He was married one year later, Sept. 29, 1946 to a beautiful little South Carolina girl, Elizabeth Mattor. They have been married over 45 years and have two wonderful children Bob Jr. and Jeanie. He is retired.

WILLIAM VEALE, was born in Dunfermline, Scotland on July 14, 1923. He came to the U.S. in 1930. Joined Co. F, 103rd Engineers, 28th Div., Pennsylvania National Guard at the age of 14. Served from 1938 to 1941.

Joined the Marines Jan. 16, 1942 and went through boot camp in Platoon #114. Joined H-2-5 1st Marine Div. at New River, NC. Went to New Zealand and from there to Solomon Islands. Landed on Tulagi Aug. 7, 1942 after the Solomon Island Campaign went to Australia. Participated in the New Britain Campaign and was wounded March 6, 1944 at Talasea, New Britain.

Due to wounds and malaria was sent back to United States. Went back overseas and joined the 5th Marine Div. while in Hawaii, Japan surrendered. Went to Japan as occupation forces, stationed at Sasebo, Japan.

He was discharged Jan. 22, 1946.

Married Nov. 28, 1944 and had two children Bruce and Linda, four grandchildren and one great-grandchild.

Most memorable event was the first time he met master gunnery sergeant Lou Diamond at New River. The gunnery sergeant scared the hell out of Veale. Lou became a legend in the Marine Corps as the "best damn mortar man in the corp."

STEPHEN JOHN VITKA, was born in New Haven, CT. Was educated in New Haven Schools and George Washington University.

Joined U.S. Marine Corps, Jan. 5, 1926. Served on board USS *Florida*. Participated in Nicaraguan Revolution in 1927, the Chinese Civil War 1927-1930, Guantanamo Bay, Cuba in 1940 with the 1st Marine Div., New River, NC in 1941; Guadalcanal 1942 and was promoted to Marine gunner (warrant officer) also contracted malaria; Korean War 1950-1954 was promoted to captain. 1955-1956 on staff at U.S. Naval Prison, Portsmouth, NH. Retired July 31, 1956 from USMC as captain with 30 years service.

1958 was captain for the Dept. of Correction, NY. Commanded reformatory and was principal instructor, correction academy. In 1959-1961 was captain on staff, maximum security prison, Bronx, NY. Retired Dept. of Corrections June 2, 1961.

He has been past president of Rural Men's Republican Club: Chairman, Council of Republican Clubs: Selectman, Stamford, 1964-1967: Republican candidate for Connecticut General Assembly, 1966, 1978: Board of Representatives candidate 1975: Organized and member, Stamford Fair Rent Commission; 1970: Member, Patriotic Commission. Justice of Peace.

Organizer and past president, Stamford Veterans Council, 1965: Past commander; Stamford Memorial Post, VFW of U.S. Oscar Cowan Post, 3, American Legion: Commandant, Research Detachment and Fairfield County commandant, Marine Corps League: General Chairman, 1968 National Convention Marine Corps League at Bridgeport: Vice Commander, Chapter 13, DAV: Founder and past president (13 years) Western Connecticut Chapter, Retired Officers Association 1958: Organizer and past Treasurer, Connecticut Council of Chapters, Retired officers Association, 1979. Member; Military Order of World Wars; 1st Marine Div. Association, Marine Corps League, GCV Assoc.

PETER MICHAEL VIZZI, was born in Brooklyn, NY on April 17, 1922. Enlisted in the U.S. Navy on Jan. 3, 1942.

Served in the North Atlantic and in the Pacific. Was on the invasion of Guadalcanal on the USS *American Legion* (APA-17). Ship was credited for shooting down four Japanese aircraft during the Guadalcanal invasion. During the campaign they took on survivors and wounded from the heavy cruisers *Astoria*, *Quincy* and *Vincennes*. Made many runs at "Torpedo Alley" from Guadalcanal and Noumea in New Caledonia. Was at invasion of Bougainville. Served eight months at Navy base on Torokina Island Bougainville with another shipmate Andrew Black.

Was at invasion of Okinawa; his ship a that time was the USS *Pitt* (APA-223). Stayed in the Pacific until the occupation of Japan. They put troops ashore at Amori, Japan on the island of Honshu. The USS *Pitt* spent about one and one half years bringing troops home to muster out when the war was over. Was honorably discharged as gunners mate first class, USN on Dec. 14, 1946. Awards: WW II Victory Medal, American Campaign Medal, Asiatic Pacific Campaign w/four Bronze Stars, Navy Occupation Service (Asia); and China Service (extended).

Has a lifetime membership in the Guadalcanal Campaign Veterans. Also belongs to the Disabled Americans Veterans Commanders Club.

Married Olivia Isira Corona and they have two children Mary Esther Vizzi-Filippuzzi and Michelle Vizzi-Tolbert. Presently married to Lauerry Ruth Johnson Towne and has two step-children Dorina Towne-Davies and Theodore Carl Towne. He has three grandchildren and one great-grandchild. He is 69 years old, retired from the Pacific Bell Company, California and currently resides in Port Angeles, Washington.

WALTER J. WAGNER, was born Dec. 12, 1918 in Rutledge, PA. Entered the service October 1941; assigned to 394th Bomb Sqdn., 13th AR Force, 5th Bomb Gp.; stationed at Guadalcanal.

His memorable experiences include: dropping first 2,000 lb. bombs on Munda Air Base; and night attack on Ballale on July 16, 1943.

Discharged with the rank of sergeant. He was awarded the Distinguished flying Cross, and Air Medal with cluster.

Married to Jean and they have sons Walter Jr. and John, and four grandchildren. He sold his own manufacturing business and now works part-time in real estate.

EDWARD WALSH, (KNOBBY), was born April 5, 1920. Graduated from high school, joined the U.S. Navy in January 1942. Assigned to USS *Aaron Ward* (DD-483), stationed in the South Pacific.

His memorable experiences include: the invasion of Guadalcanal; night battle Nov. 11 to 15, the ship was damaged and sunk April 7, 1943; the invasion of Leyte Philippines Oct. 20, 1944.

Discharged November 1945 with the rank BM2/c. He received the Purple Heart for Guadalcanal.

Single, he has 11 Godchildren. Retired June 1982, bus driver, vice chairman Local 100 TWU.

RAYMOND J. WALSH, was born in Chicago, IL on Sept. 1, 1922. He graduated from Lane Tech High School in June 1940. Was in ROTC for four years, belonged to Officers Club.

Enlisted in USMC on June 11, 1942. Went through boot camp at San Diego in platoon 489, was assigned to MAR and SSI, FMAW.

Left the States in January 1943 aboard the *Lureline* to New Caledonia, then aboard the *Hunter Ligett* to Guadalcanal. While aboard the *Lureline* and on the islands did some entertaining with a German submarine commander.

Discharged Oct. 16, 1945 COG as a sergeant.

Married Lillian Whiteford on July 1, 1944. They have eight children and 13 grandchildren. They left Chicago in 1965 and are presently living in Albuquerque, NM.

WILSON P. WARNER, was born Nov. 23, 1919 in Locust Valley, NY. Joined the USMC on Feb. 3, 1942 for four years. Went to Parris Island for boot camp. Was in platoon 159 for about five weeks. From there went to Tent Camp, New River, NC and assigned to 1st Marines for a week or 10 days then transferred to 7th Marines.

Wasn't too long in New River before they went to Norfolk, VA then aboard USS *Heywood* (APA-6). They shoved off on or about April 10, 1942, destination unknown to them.

After a trip through the Panama Canal, they had a long zig zag trip in the Pacific and ended up in (Apia British Samoa), his platoon the third from G-2-7.

Had out-post duty on the island of Savaii. They left Samoa bound for the canal with a four stacker destroyer for escort.

The 2nd Bn. was aboard the APA-20 USS *Hayes*, the rest of the regiment and attached units were aboard the other president ships: *Adams*, *Jackson*, and *Cresent City*.

It appeared that the Japanese navy was aware they were headed for Guadalcanal to re-enforce the troops already there. Our Navy outsmarted theirs and they landed Sept. 18, 1942.

That night the Japs hit them with all they had and that included search lights and observation planes to spot the equipment and troops. But like all good Marine units, they made it through.

The 2nd Bn., 7th Marines were kept pretty busy in various situations to include going east to intercept a Japanese landing (part of more than a regiment plus a lot of supplies).

He got malaria while out on east end so spent about 10 days in the hospital, which included the Sunday the Japs thought they had the canal back. They even tried to land planes on Henderson Field that day.

He continued with G-2-7 until they left the canal for Melbourne, Australia and went to Mt. Marths, Australia.

Retired from the Marine Corps after 26 years with the rank gunney sergeant E7.

Married to Marcelene and they had two children Barbara and Peter. He is widowed, living in Locust Valley, NY, and retired from race horses.

GEORGE H. WARRINER, SR., was born in Port Kennedy, PA on Feb. 20, 1921. Enlisted in the USMC Feb. 2, 1942. After training at Parris Island was assigned to 1st Bn., 5th Marines, D Co., 1st Marine Div. at New River, NC.

Sailed from Norfolk, VA in May 1942 aboard the USS *Wakefield*. Arrived in Wellington, New Zealand on June 20, 1942. At the end of June at the dock of Aoteaquay they worked day and night unloading and loading ships in the cold rain.

Made overnight landing at Koro Island Fiji. He was on the USS *American Legion*.

Was in the first wave to hit Red Beach on Aug. 7, 1942. He was wounded and evacuated to America Samoa Hospital Mobile 3 by a Destroyer. Then after one month was shipped to San Diego Naval Hospital where he was treated and after eight months was discharged. Married to Helen Toby on Dec. 3, 1955. They have two daughters, Georgeana and Darlene, one son David, and eight grandchildren. He has resided in Conshohocken, PA for 35 years.

ROBERT A. WASTLER,

was born in Funkstown, MD on Nov. 17, 1921. He enlisted in the U.S. Army in Washington, DC on Nov. 5, 1940. Was sent to Ft. Slocum, NY, then on the USS *Leonard Wood* through the Panama Canal to San Francisco and Ft. McDowell on Angel Island, CA

Boarded the USS *St. Mahiel* on Jan. 23, 1941 at San Francisco, arriving at Honolulu, HI on Jan. 30, 1941. Assigned to Co. A, 35th Inf., 25th Inf. Div. at Schofield Barracks, HI. Was there when Pearl Harbor was bombed on Dec. 7, 1941. Patrolled the beaches at Barber Point until transferred to Regimental Hqs., S2 Recon. Plt., 35th Inf. in August 1942.

Participated in the battles for Guadalcanal (Hill 27, Gifu Strong Point), and the Northern Solomons, Vella La Vella, Munda, and New Georgia.

Was at the hospital in New Caledonia September 1943 with severe malaria. Returned Stateside on Dec. 7, 1943. Spent three months at O'Reilly General Hospital, Springfield, MO recuperating.

Reassigned as platoon sergeant at Ft. George Meade, MD (AGFRD Depot #1) to prepare the troops for service in the European Theater. After the European war ended, he was to be discharged (Demobilization) as he had 112 points (point system) but instead he was declared "essential" and sent to Camp Adair, OR (AGFRD Depot #4) to prepare and process replacement troops for the South Pacific. Finally returned to Ft. Meade, MD to be discharged Aug. 7, 1945.

Married to Evelyn Davis, whom he had grown up with, in January 1944. They lived in Washington, DC and Maryland until 1954 when they moved to Vancouver, WA. They have two children and three grandchildren.

GEORGE H. WEAVER,

was born Aug. 18, 1924 in Phoenixville, PA. Enlisted in USMC on Jan. 15, 1942 in Philadelphia, PA. He attended boot camp at Parris Island, SC. Attended Aviation Ordnance School at Jacksonville NAS.

Left for Camp Kearney, CA to join VMF 121. Left for New Caledonia on Sept. 1, 1942 and arrived on Sept. 28, 1942. Arrived at Guadalcanal on Nov. 11, 1942, ship was bombed in harbor. Took two near misses on night of Nov. 13, 1942 during an hour shelling from Japanese Navy.

Left mid-January for New Hebrides, New Zealand, and then stateside. Was serving second tour in Philippines when war ended.

Discharged as sergeant from Camp Lejeune, NC in November 1944.

Married the former Margaret Stoll. They have four children and six grandchildren. Retired after 36 years in construction. Now resides in Elkland, PA.

WEIFORD RUFUS WELLS,

was born Sept. 24, 1924 in Grand Crossing, Chicago, IL. Inducted into U.S. Army, Anti-Aircraft Artillery of C.A. Corps, March 1, 1943 in Chicago, IL.

Trained at Camp Wallace AAA Replacement Camp, TX as CW radio operator and infantry basic. Shipped overseas via Angel Island to Nomea, New Caledonia where he joined the Hq. Btry., 68th AAA Brigade. Moved up to Guadalcanal via

Espiritu Santo October 1943, then on to Bougainville June 1944.

Transferred to Btry. B, 736th AAA Gun Bn. in Treasury Islands. Shipped with this unit to Finschafen, New Guinea in February 1945 and to Northern Luzon, Philippines in July 1945.

Transferred to Hq. Btry. 104th AAA (AW) Bn. September 1945 and moved up to Shikoku Island, Matsuyama, Japan with the 24th Inf. Div. Having earned 60 points, returned to the States via 11th Redeployment Depot and Nagoya, Japan in December 1945, arriving Ft. Lawton, Seattle, Jan. 4, 1945.

His most memorable experience was returning to the USA and the trip across country in a crowded Great Northern Railroad coach train with below zero January weather and arriving back home in Chicago after three years.

Discharged Jan. 10, 1946 at Camp Grant, IL with the rank private first class. He served as radio, radar, telephone, teletype operator, and communication lineman. He received the Asiatic-Pacific Campaign Medal with one Bronze Star (Northern Solomons), Philippine Liberation Medal, Good Conduct Medal, World War II Victory Medal, four Overseas Bars, and a Ruptured Duck Lapel Button.

Married Leona Emma Thuro June 25, 1966 in St. Louis, MO. They have no children. He received a B.S. degree in mechanical engineering in June 1951 and became a registered professional engineer, State of Illinois in 1962. Worked in both private engineering business and government as a mechanical design engineer. Retired Jan. 3, 1985 from Puget Sound Naval Shipyard with over 25 years federal service.

Holds life memberships in ASME, ASHRAD, DAV, VFW, AMVETS, Purdue Alumni Association, and a PUFL in the American Legion.

His hobbies are amateur radio (KA7LBG), gardening, photography, wood working and carving, drawing and painting, reading, traveling and enjoying life.

RAYMOND P. WHITE,

was born Sept. 8, 1922 in Holliston, MA. Entered the service Feb. 10, 1942. Assigned to 1st Amphibian Tractor Bn., Co. C, 1st Marine Div.

Participated in action at Guadalcanal, Cape Gloucester, New Britain, and Peleliu Island.

Discharged May 9, 1946 with the rank of corporal. He received the Presidential Unit Citation with Ribbon Bar and two Bronze Stars, Peleliu Navy Unit Commendation, Good Conduct Medal, American Defense Service Medal, Asiatic-Pacific Campaign Medal, and the World War II Victory Medal.

Married to Shirley Davis White. They have three children, Kathleen Ann, Kevin, and Keith.

He works for himself in the profession of art work.

HARRY WIENS,

was born Nov. 26, 1918 near Munich, ND. He enlisted with Co. I, 164th Inf., Wahpeton, ND National Guard in November 1937.

The unit was federalized Feb. 10, 1941. They trained at Camp Claiborne, LA until Dec. 8, 1941. Thence to a cold Cow Palace, San Francisco. Left Christmas Eve when the regiment was scattered from California through Montana guarding dams, bridges, tunnels, airfields, etc. Personally had charge of guard station at railroad bridge crossing Lake Pend Oreille, Sandpoint, ID.

The regiment reassembled at Ft. Ord, CA, early March 1942. Absorbed additional men and boarded the *President*

Coolidge March 18, then zig-zagged 21 days to Melbourne, Australia, accompanied by the *Queen Elizabeth*, another liner, and the cruiser *Chester*, which all later split for Sydney. Delivered by *Santa Paula* to New Caledonia in mid-April. Unloaded ships, built ration dumps at Pieta, Dumbea. Guard duty at Dumbea pasture airfield. (Lt. Jarman's planes, including *Resurrection III*.) Was sergeant of the guard at Grand Docks, Noumea during the Battle of the Coral Sea. Manned beach defense positions nights, but no activity other than some shot-up PBY's returning to bay.

To Guadalcanal aboard the *Zeilin*, October 13, in time to sweat the Night of the Battleships while lying unsheltered amongst the coconut palms beside the airfield. Ten days later participant in Guadalcanal's largest land action, The Battle of Henderson Field, where the 164th proved conclusively the overwhelming superiority of a blazing M-1 when pitted against thrusting bayonets and slashing samuri swords. (164th was first to use the M-1 in battle.)

He was awarded the Bronze Star Medal for patrol activity on East-West Trail. That debris-strewn, skeleton-laden, grave-pocked retreat path of a defeated army is another story. To Fiji aboard the *Fuller* March 1, 1943. Back up to Bougainville aboard the *Cresent City*, landed Dec. 25, 1943. Continued patrol activity. Succumbed to tropical ills, evacuated by air to Guadalcanal, thence to Espiritu Santo, May 1944. Clung to bunk aboard *Morrow Bay* while it bucked in a stormy Pacific. Arrived at San Francisco, Letterman General Hospital July 4, 1944. Replacement training duty, Camp Maxey, TX until discharged September 1945.

Rejoined California National Guard, was recalled to overseas duty with the 40th Inf. Div., 160th Inf. for Korean Conflict. Retired from National Guard in 1966 as a master sergeant, Bn., Operations, HQ Co., 149th Armored, Salinas, CA, after participating in taming the Watts Riots and providing flood relief for Garberville, CA.

Married Margaret Bendel in 1949. They have two children, Mark and Shelley. Retired from the city of San Jose, CA Building Department, 1987 as supervising construction inspector. Lives in Scotts Valley, CA.

VIC WIER,

was born Victor Wierzbolowiez on a farm in Berrien County, MI on Feb. 12, 1923. He enlisted in the USMC Reserve Group on campus of Western Michigan University, Kalamazoo, MI in November 1942.

Attended boot training at Parris Island, SC and Aviation Gunner and Flight School, Jacksonville, FL in SBDs.

In August of 1944 he landed at Munda, New Georgia and joined the 1st Marine Aircraft Wing, Sqdn. VMSB-241 "Sons of Satan" and flew back and forth to Guadalcanal for new planes when available, spare parts, etc.

This MAG 24 group dive bombed and strafed Rabaul and Kavieng harassing the Jap headquarters there. They then island hopped Hollandia, Peleliu, Palau, Biak, Mortia, Emirau and to Leyte, Luzon, and ended up at Mindanao in the Philippines.

For close air support to the Army there he was awarded the Air Medal by Maj. Gen. L.E. Woods, USMC. The group received U.S. Navy and U.S. Army commendations.

Following discharge at Cherry Point, NC as a corporal he utilized the GI Bill and earned a B.S. degree at Western Michigan University; a master's degree at the University of Michigan and an educational specialist degree at Michigan State University.

He and his wife Lois were married in 1949 and have four children and nine grandchildren.

He served as high school principal for 33 years and retired June 1981. He joined GCV as an associate member in 1980 and served four terms as national treasurer of the Guadalcanal Campaign Veterans (1983 to 1991).

LORIN WILCOX (RED),

was born in Laona, NY on March 28, 1917. Enlisted in U.S. Army on July 13, 1938. He spent two years with 4th Coast Arty. in Balboa, Canal Zone and one year with 7th Coast Arty. at Ft. Hancock, NJ.

Was working in Atlanta, GA for Davey Tree Company when Japanese attacked Pearl Harbor.

He joined the Marines in Macon, GA on Jan. 27, 1942 and was assigned to C Btry., 11th Marines, 1st Marine Div., Tent City, NC. They spent six days loading ships at San Diego, CA before departing for the Pacific on a mission of war. After a short stop on Wallace Islands, was shipped out to Guadalcanal and landed Sept. 18, 1942. Left for Australia Jan. 12, 1943.

Discharged from Marines, Guard Bn., Navy Bldg. on Oct. 4, 1945 with the rank of corporal in both Army and Marines.

After the war returned to live in Australia for two years. Brought a baby kangaroo home and trained it to box. Worked the carnival circuit for several years during which it was used in the motion picture Million Dollar Mermaid, starring Esther Williams, Victor Mature, and Walter Pidgeon. Wilcox doubled for Mature and Jess White in boxing scenes.

"Red" and his wife "Pat" reside in Dunkirk, NY.

W. C. "JOSH" WILDER, was born April 11, 1923 in Alabama. He entered the USMC in August, 1942. He served at Parris Island, SC, Cherry Point, NC and Guadalcanal, Solomon Islands and Bougainville.

He recalls witnessing a huge number of American aircraft fighting Japs over Guadalcanal. He remembers the day and night Japanese attacks on Henderson Field. Many times U.S. equipment and planes were hit while on the ground. Many Japanese planes and pilots were downed, especially upon the arrival of the first F4U airplanes. He attained the rank of Tech/Sgt. and was discharged November 1945.

He remembers the active volcano on Bougainville—it was constantly spewing hot ash and fire, but never caused any damage that he knows of.

He returned to Guadalcanal in October 1988 and revisited Lunga Point, Bloody Ridge, Cape Esperance and Matankau. He stayed five days at Mendana Hotel. He saw the memorials and Fred Kona's Museum.

He married Millie Andrews on Aug. 19, 1945. They have three children and seven grandchildren. He retired as CEO (1989) from his own company. He attended MABS-1 46th Reunion and met many of his old fox hole buddies.

WALLACE W. (WALLY) WILLIAMS, was born Feb. 21, 1925. He enlisted in the US Navy July 1942. Boot Camp in San Diego, CA. He was transferred to the USS *Cushing* (DD-376) at Pearl Harbor. *Cushing* was sent to the South Pacific, where she was sunk in the Battle of Guadalcanal, Nov. 13, 1942. He spent two weeks on the 'canal' before transferring to Espiritu Santo for several months.

He was then sent Stateside and to school in Miami, FL. He transferred to Long Beach and became part of the crew for

construction of USS PC-788. He was transferred again to new construction for USS *Flint* (CL-97). He remained on *Flint* until the war ended.

He received his discharge in October 1945, but re-enlisted in 1948 and remained with the service until 1950. He was then discharged, only to join the US Naval Reserve. He transferred to Naval Aviation in 1949 and flew in P2V and P3 aircraft until his retirement Nov. 1, 1978 as chief petty officer.

He worked in marketing for Bell System from 1954 until 1982, when he retired. His wife, Marilyn, and he have two children and three grandchildren. They live in Palm Desert, CA.

JAY R. WILLETT, was born Oct. 1, 1923 at Superior, WI. He holds a masters degree in clinical social work.

He entered the USMC on Nov. 10, 1941, serving at San Diego, CA, Samoa, Guadalcanal and Tarawa.

He participated in patrols on Guadalcanal, retrieving dead bodies on Guadalcanal, liberty in New Zealand. He remembers being shot three times (neck, shoulder and arm) at Tarawa. He was decorated with the Purple Heart by Admiral Nimitz at the Naval Hospital in Hawaii. He was then limited to shore duty in the Horse Marine Detachment at Crane, IN.

He married Mary, but they divorced. He then married Virginia. He has five children and four grandchildren. He worked as director of Day Treatment Service at Ramsey County Mental Health Center. He retired May 31, 1985.

HERSCHEL J. WILSKY, was born Aug. 10, 1922 at Champaign, IL. He entered service with the US Marines in June 1941. He served at the following military stations and locations: San Diego, CA, Overseas, Camp LeJeune and Camp Pendleton. After boot camp at San Diego, CA, he went with 1-B-8 Marines to Camp Elliott, CA. They left San Diego one month after Pearl Harbor on Matson Liner *Lurline*. Pago Pago Samoa. They later landed on Guadalcanal Nov. 4, 1942. Some Japanese had landed the night before.

Shipped out of New Zealand with malaria and yellow jaundice. He recalls the air dog-fights, the malaria, huge night ship battles of Nov. 14-15—as seen from front line hills, scouting for deep patrols, including an ambush of a Japanese officer and private. He attained the rank of corporal and was discharged in September 1945.

He married Imogene Coffin. They have two children and three grandchildren. He retired from the University of Illinois Physical Plant as foreman of the brickmasons on March 1, 1988.

JOSEPH E. WOOD, CW04, USNR (Ret'd), born May 26, 1916 near Bay Minette, AL. Enlisted in the US Navy at Birmingham, AL, Jan. 12, 1936. Received boot training at N.O.B., Norfolk, VA. Commissioned the USS *Charleston* (PG-51) July 1936, at Charleston, SC. Reported for duty as flagship of Special Service Squadron, Panama Canal Zone, January 1937. Discharged Jan. 11, 1940 as EM3/C. Attended Coyne Electrical and Radio School, Chicago, IL. Employed by Hollingsworth and Whitney Company, paper and pulp manufacturers, Sept. 9, 1940 to Jan. 20, 1942. Enlisted in the US Naval Reserve Jan. 28, 1942 as EM2/C. Assigned to the USS *Fuller* (APA-7) which was assigned to amphibious forces in the South Pacific. Unloaded troops and supplies at Apia, Samoa; laid to at Pango Pango during the Battle of the Coral

Sea. Participated in Guadalcanal Campaign, Aug. 7, 1942, and Bougainville, November 1943. Promoted to CEM May 15, 1944; Warrant Officer W1, May 31, 1944. Participated in the invasion of Saipan, June 15, 1944. Reassigned to and commissioned the USS *Navarro* (APA-215) August 1944. Participated in the invasion of Okinawa April 1 (Easter Sunday) 1945 and occupation of Japan and China, 1945. Released to inactive duty, July 1946 as CW02. Re-employed by Hollingsworth and Whitney Company (now Scott Paper Company) as electrical maintenance supervisor. Retired in February 1979.

Organized four Naval Reserve units in Mobile, AL, serving as training officer for electrician and engineering rates. Promoted to CW03 in 1953 and CW04 in 1957. Transferred to CB Construction Bn. (Seabees) 6-23 in 1953, serving as training officer. Released to inactive duty February 1968. Retired from US Navy, June 1, 1976.

Community activities: Organized and was Scout Master of Boy Scout Troop 41. Organized Spanish Fort Volunteer Fire Department, serving as secretary. Organized Spanish Fort Men's Club, serving as president and secretary. Organized and was manager of the Spanish Fort Little League Baseball team. Elected Man of the Year in 1962. Member of the Spanish Fort United Methodist Church. Past Master, Spanish Fort Masonic Lodge. Past Grand Patron, Order of the Eastern Star, State of Alabama.

Joined FRA several years ago and was assigned to FRA Branch 22, Pensacola, FL. Joined Branch 76 (South Alabama) as a charter member in May 1989, instituted June 24, 1989. Married Izola Talley of Greenville, AL on Oct. 11, 1947. They have three children and two grandchildren.

WILLIAM A. WOOD, was born March 25, 1922 at Andover, MA. He received a Bachelor of Science in Civil Engineering.

He entered the Marine Corps on Aug. 8, 1940 and served with A Battery, Special Weapons Bn., 1st Marine Div.

They landed on Guadalcanal Aug. 7, 1942, disembarking from the *Libra*. The *Libra's* cooks served pancakes and sausage for breakfast. He had nine pancakes and then got ready to go over the side into an LCVP. His battalion provided light anti-aircraft defense around Henderson Field until they were relieved on Jan. 5, 1943. They are credited with shooting down 12 enemy aircraft. No wounds—just malaria.

Married to Peggy Wood (passed away Feb. 10, 1992). He has one child, three grandchildren and three great-grandchildren. He was a land surveyor and highway engineer and retired in January 1985.

ALBERT J. WORRICK, was born Dec. 16, 1920 at Fairbury, IL. He enlisted at Ft. Wayne, IN and was inducted into the USMC on Jan. 6, 1942. He graduated from Parris Island boot camp Feb. 8, 1942. He attained the rank of sergeant and was discharged Jan. 11, 1946.

He landed on Guadalcanal Aug. 7, 1942 with I Co., 3d Bn., 1st Marines, 1st Div. They departed Dec. 15, 1942.

His most memorable experience happened on the Teneru River, about one mile from the beach. They were under red alert, the planes near them were taking off in both directions. They were new to the Canal. A truck delivering pilots to the planes drove in front of an aircraft. The pilot of the aircraft lifted his wing to miss the truck—he was not up to flying speed for take off, so he ended up in a nearby jungle.

He sacrificed himself to save the other pilots. They got him out ok, but he was beat up pretty bad. Ambulance took him to the hospital. Never did hear how he came out.

He went back to the plane and took a machine gun out of the wing and 300 rounds of 50 calibre ammunition. He took the gun back to their implacement and tied it to a stump to give them more fire-power. The light 30 calibre was a good gun, but he thought the 50 calibre would help a lot—the Brass thought differently. He had to pack everything back to the plane. It took two days to take it out. To this day, he still wonders why he had to take it back when they needed the extra fire-power? His guess is that it was not GI issue.

He married Jean on June 10, 1944—she was in the Navy at the time. They have three daughters and one son, nine grandchildren and two great-grandchildren. They have resided in Lakewood, CA since 1947, retiring in December 1985.

They love the reunions. The GCV are the BEST!

DANIEL E. WRAY, JR., was born Feb. 21, 1923 at Steubenville, OH. He enlisted on Aug. 12, 1942 from Springfield, OH. He attended Boot Camp at Parris Island, SC with platoon 629 and qualified as an expert rifleman. He was transferred to Cherry Point, NC, and later to North Island Naval Air Station, San Diego, CA. Shipped out for the South Pacific Jan. 8, 1943 aboard the SS *Lurline*. Disembarked January 23 at New Caledonia to SS *Henry T. Allen* to Espiritu Santo. Embarked to SS *American Legion* to Guadalcanal and assigned to Marine Air Base Squadron 1, 1st Marine Aircraft Wing, which was in command of Henderson Field Operations. With MABS-1 served also a Ondonga and Munda before returning to Stateside Dec. 15, 1944. Was discharged at Cherry Point, NC Oct. 3, 1945.

Married Mary K. Schnell from Toledo, OH, Feb. 9, 1945 in New Bern, NC. They have two sons and two daughters and have resided in Troy, OH for over 40 years.

RICHARD B. WRIGHT, was born June 27, 1919 at Lowel, WA. He entered the service with the Army on Aug. 6, 1940. He was stationed at Camp Wolters, TX, Camp Shelby, MS and Indiantown Gap, PA.

He recalls landing in Tonga and the subsequent departure for Guadalcanal. He remembers the landing and combat and eventual defeat of Samoa. He was discharged with the rank of corporal on Feb. 21, 1945. He married Marie A. Walsh on April 15, 1944. They have two children and two grandchildren. He retired June 18, 1974 from the Puget Sound Naval Shipyard.

For his service during combat in WWII, he received the following awards/citations: Bronze Star Medal, Good Conduct Medal, American Defense Service Medal, American Campaign Medal, WW II Victory Medal, Combat Infantryman Badge and the Asiatic-Pacific Campaign Medal.

He is a woodcarver and likes photography. He also has a collection of antique tools.

ARVILLE E. YARBRO, was born in Ridgely, TN July 6, 1920. Enlisted in the Marine Corps Sept. 8, 1939.

After training at Parris Island, joined 3rd Defense Bn. at Hilton Head, SC. Shipped out to Pearl Harbor, April 1940; stayed until July 1942.

Landed on Guadalcanal Aug. 7, 1942, stayed until February 1943. Went to New Zealand for R&R.

He returned to United States Sept. 1943 for duty at Camp Elliott and Pedelton, CA. Went to Ordinance School at Quantico, VA, embarked overseas August 1945, was at Pearl Harbor at the end of the war. Discharged at Camp LeJeune, NC as gunnery sergeant.

Came home to Missouri, married Naomi Boyers Aug. 22, 1947. They have three children, Joy, Joan, Kenny and four grandchildren Carrie, David, Cassie, Neisha. He retired 1987 after farming for 40 years.

He is a member of Pearl Harbor Survivors Association and the Guadalcanal Campaign Veterans Association.

BENSON P. YERGER, was born in Stoneharbor, NJ on Aug. 9, 1922. Enlisted in the Marine Corps Dec. 8, 1941.

After training at Parris Island he was assigned to H&S Co., 4th Bn., 11th Marines at New River, NC. Shipped out for New Zealand May 1942 aboard the *Ericson* for a 22 day convoy to Wellington from San Francisco.

On arrival their company was transferred to the 5th Bn. from 55mm guns to 105 mm. They landed on Guadalcanal on Dept. 7, 19442 from USS *Hunter Liggett*. From that day to Dec. 15, 1942 he was one of the telephone and wire repair crew, with countless trips to the various artillery spotting positions, etc. to both lay and repair lines after the many shellings, bombings and firefights.

He left the canal on Dec. 15, 1942 aboard the USS *Hunter Liggett* for Brisbane, Australia. From there returned to the States aboard USS *West Point*. After much treatment for malaria at Camp Niland, CA he attained his corporal rating, then went to Elliott in the Provost Marshalls Office then to Pendelton with the Brig. Detachment. Thence to a six week transport Quartermaster School where upon graduating he was assigned to the USS *Circe* (AKA-25) and completed his enlistment aboard her in Yokohama, Japan, from there he was shipped back to Bainbridge, MD for discharge on Dec. 15, 1945.

He married Betty Roper in 1946 and they now live in a beautiful life care retirement community in Willow Street, PA.

CHARLES W. YOUNG, JR., was born in Trenton, NJ on May 22, 1920. He entered U.S. Army Nov. 3, 1941 at Fort Dix, NJ.

Trained at Fort Bragg, NC and was assigned to 72nd Field Artillery Regt.

Shipped out South Pacific, Brooklyn, NY on the liner *Uruguay* part of Task Force 6814. Sixty days later he arrived Noumea, New Caledonia. Became part of newly formed Americal Div. Arrived Guadalcanal Dec. 12, 1942 aboard USS *American Legion*. He had unlimited experiences. His most memorable was a January "Condition Black" when some of them served as reinforced infantry and the day from a forward OPI saw many planes, mostly zeroes and one cruisers downed in Iron Bottom Bay.

Early March shipped to Fiji Islands to recover and regroup. Some replacements were shipped to Bougainville and landed Christmas Day 1943.

Malaria, jungle rot and nerves caused his evacuation by plane to New Caledonia. He later returned to California for general recovery.

Re-assigned for limited service. Military district of Washington. Ordinance Office, Ft. Belvoir, VA. After three months Tropical Disease Hospital, NC, returned to Ft. Belvoir for discharge October 1945.

Married Blanche Babbit in December 1945 and they have one son and two grandchildren. He has resided near Trenton for 43 years.

IRVIN ZINS, was born on Dec. 28, 1923 in Cincinnati, OH. Entered service May 10, 1940 Co. D, 147th Inf. at Camp Shelby, Indiantown Gap.

He achieved rank of corporal and was discharged on July 13, 1945.

Awards: Combat Infantry Badge, Battle Stars for South Pacific and Good Conduct Medal.

While stationed at Indiantown Gap met his future spouse, Fern in the nearby town of Reading, PA. They have three children.

He is retired after being with Prudential for 30 years. He enjoys traveling, playing golf and bridge.

JAMES EDWARD PARROTT, was born Aug. 7, 1924 at El Paso, TX. He entered service with the U.S. Navy on Feb. 2, 1942. He served with Cub I on the Initial Invasion of Guadalcanal until the Solomon Islands were secured Feb. 23, 1943. He was part of Advanced Attack Force 58. He served with the U.S. Marine Corps in the Marianas until the end of WW II conflict. He was with a Korean liasion to land U.S. Navy Fleet until the end of the Korean War. He served aboard the USS *Zeilin* (APA-3) and USS *MaCalla* (DD-488).

On Tulagi, they were able to secure flour, sugar and baking soda.

He told the men he would make donuts. He used mineral oil to fry the dough. He didn't know there was no intestinal absorbtion of mineral oil, so they ate quite a few of the donuts—all ended up with oil spots on their butts every time they passed wind. He thought the men would never forgive him.

He was discharged with the rank of pharmacist 2d class. For his participation in combat, he received the followinf awards/medals: the American Campaign Medal with one Star, Asiatic-Pacific Service Medal with four Stars, Presidential Unit Citation for Korea and United States, Philippine Liberation Medal, National Defense Medal, Victory Medal, Korean Service Medal and Korean Service with two Stars.

He is a chiropractor, acupunturist and hypnotherapist residing in Oxnard, CA.

He married Marilyn Fowler on March 5, 1985 and they have three children: Joseph, Brynda Monique and Heidi Jacqueline.

Late Submissions

WILBERT P. KILVINGTON

HENRY KLIMECKI

LEA LUCERO

ROBERT C. MUEHRCKE, at age 16 enlisted in the Illinois National Guard's 132d Inf. Federalized on March 5, 1941 and trained at Camp Forrest. Then sent to the South Pacific as Task Force 6814, landed in Australia, occupied New Caledonia, became the Americal Division. Fought in the first offensive battles at Guadalcanal, recuperated from malaria in the Fiji Islands and fought at Bougainville. Sent to the Infantry School, commissioned and assigned at Okinawa to the First Platoon Company F, 383d Infantry destined to take famed Conical Hill.

In early August 1945 with a large number of points, he was sent home. He entered the educational pathway at the University of Illinois, received a B.S. and M.S. Degree. Graduated as Doctor of Medicine, interned at Cincinnati General, specialized in Nephrology at the British Post-Graduate School, University of London, and the University of Illinois Hospital.

He was past president of Heart Association of West Cook County, Chicago Society of Internal Medicine and Chicago Medical Society's Aux Plaines Branch.

He was a professor of medicine, Rush Medical College; Director of Medical Education at West Suburban Hospital Medical Center; Medical consultant to the Armed Services; chairman of the Guadalcanal-Solomon Islands War Memorial Foundation. Robert has 135 clinical and research articles and several books, including the award winner *Orchids in the Mud*, a military history of the 132d Inf. Regiment.

Three of seven sons are physicians. He resides with his wife, JoAnn in Oak Brook, IL.

Left, Bill Mueller. Right, Jack McClean (died aboard the USS Colhoun, sunk at Guadalcanal)

Last stateside liberty. A roving photographer took this picture at West Phila., 69th St.—A place called "Chez Vouz." They departed the next day for Norfolk, took on supplies, went through the Panama Canal bound for Noumea, New Caledonia. (Courtesy of Joe Gushinski)

1st Marine Division at Melbourne, Australia in 1943. (Courtesy of Glenn Mills)

U.S. Marine Air Force Maj. Smith, a pilot well remembered.

Featured is Hedy Lamarr. She was on a war bond tour at the Philadelphia Navy Yard. Troops were waiting for the USS Montpelier (CL-57) to be commissioned.

Administration Office on Guadalcanal. Front Row (L to R): Lt. Conkle, Lt. Hanscom, Lt. Comdr. Standich, Lt. Grant; Second Row (L to R): Loef Y2c, Wagner S1c, Hannigan SLc, Priebe Y2c, Rea Y3c, Leftwich CY; Third Row (L to R): Gonzales Bugmstr3c, Hodge Y3c, Andrews Y3c, Ratliff Y3c and Wilson Y2c. (Courtesy of Priebe, Jr.)

20mm Anti-aircraft gun position on Henderson Field, Guadalcanal. (Courtesy of W. A. Wood)

Nov. 10, 1943. Tulagi, Solomon Islands. (Courtesy of G. P. Rogers)

A Grumman F4F Wildcat on Henderson Field. (Courtesy of W. A. Wood)

Service Co., 147th Inf. at Emirau. Front Row: Ralph Bamber, Ralph Rigling, Joe Linneman, Roy Vaccarillo, Joe Kock, Arnold Nortman, Dan Jenns, Wilmer White and Carl Goldsberry. Back Row: Ralph Recher, Chris Seibert, Andrew Romisher, Alvin Crowder, Victor Billingsley.

First Division aboard the USS Libra on April 15, 1945. (Courtesy of A. S. Ciardi)

GUADALCANAL 50TH ANNIVERSARY INDEX

The following is an index of geographical locations, names, vessels and aircraft that appear within the narrative of this publication. The Personal Experience Stories are not indexed herein. The Veteran's Biographies are not indexed as they appear in alphabetical order following the Personal Experience Stories.

A

Aaron Ward 59, 60
Abe 59, 60
Abercrombie, Commander 64
Admiral Abe 60
Admiral (Rear) Willis, Lee 60
Admiralty Islands 29
Air Force 27
Air, Tinian Base 28
Alderman, John 51
Alligator Creek 30, 37, 38, 41, 42, 43, 46
Amberjack 51
Anderson 73
Chief Boatswain's Mate Ralph 40
Andrews 34
Aoba 29, 33, 36, 49
Aola 18, 37, 48
Arthur, Colonel John 67
Asia 17
Astoria 32, 33, 34, 35, 36
Atlanta 59, 60
Aubin, Bishop 48
Auckland 18
Australia 17, 18, 19, 20, 23, 32, 35, 36, 74
Avengers 29
Ayabe, General 68

B

B-17 51
Bagley 32, 33, 35
Ballard 47, 60
Barnett 21
Barton 59, 60
Basilone, Sergeant John 54
Bataan 36
Battle of Cape Esperance 50, 59, 75
Battle of Savo 75
Battle of the Eastern Solomons. 39
Battle of the Tenaru river 73
Bell, Commander F. 72
Bellow 53
Benham 61, 62
Bennet, Bill 66
Bill Wallace 38
Bloody Ridge 43, 46, 52, 53, 54, 55, 63, 75
Blue 32, 33, 35
Blunden, Seabee Commander J.P. 40, 50
Boise 49
Bonegi River 72, 73
Bonner, Corporal Al 67
Bougainville 17, 18, 29, 31, 33
Breijak, Corporal Chuck 30, 36, 39, 43, 46, 53
Bridson, Lieutenant 65
British Far East fleet 17
Bryant, Gun Captain 34
Buchanan 26, 27, 31
Burgess 49
Bush, Captain Charles 38
Byers, Gunner's Mate 34

C

C-47 51
Calhoun 26
Callaghan, Rear Admiral Daniel 59, 60
Callaghan 59
Canberra 32, 33, 35
Cape Esperance 17, 32, 41, 46, 47, 48, 49, 59, 61, 64, 65, 66, 71, 72, 73, 74
Captain Bode 32
Captain Greenman 34
Captain Jiro Katsumata 52
Captain Oda 52
Captain Stafford 48
Captain Torgerson 42
Central Pacific 19
Ceylon 23
Chamberlain, Marine Corporal 35
Champagne, Private Joe 53
Channel 61
Chesterfield 30
Chicago 32, 33, 35
China 18, 52
Chokai 23, 29, 32, 33, 34, 35, 51
Clemens, Martin 18, 19 26, 37, 38, 46, 48, 51
Clement, Caryl 35
Colonel Edson 41
Colonel Masunobi Tsuji 52
Colonel Oka 40, 42
Conger, Lieutenant Jack 55
Conoley, Major Odell 57
Corporal John Weiss 63
Corregidor 19, 36
Corwin, Private Robert 24, 26, 38, 39
Corwin, Quartermaster Nathaniel 34, 36
Corwin, Robert 21, 36
Cory, Lieutenant 37
Crane, Captain 28
Crane's Marines 31
Crutchley 32, 36
Crutchley, Admiral 23
Crutchley, Rear Admiral 32
Cuba 18
Cushing 59, 60
Custer, Sergeant 37

D

Daisy cutter 46
Datko, Chief Radioman 34
Davis, Captain 69
De Haven 73
de Klerk, Father 47, 48
del Valle, Colonel 54
Denley 49
Dick, Huerth 27
Dolloff, Gilbert 21, 51
Dolloff, Private Gilbert 26
Dolloff, Rifleman Gilbert 38, 39
Drum 34
Duncan 49

E

Eastern Force 35
Eastern New Guinea 17
Ed O'Neill 55
Edlin, Ray 38
Edson, Colonel 27, 41, 47, 74
Ellet 35
Elliott, Major 22
Enterprise 60
Espiritu Santo 19, 64

F

Faisi Harbor 40
Faisi Island 33
Falk, Doctor Victor 63
Few, Sergeant 37
Fiji 17, 74
Flecther 32
Fletcher 31, 35, 39, 59, 60, 64
Fletcher, Admiral 32
Fletcher, Vice Admiral 21
Florida Island 31
Fomalhaut 36
Foss, Captain Joe 63
France 50
Fubuki 49

Fujiwara, Lance Corporal 71
Fukada, Captain 71
Fukudome, Admiral 68
Fuller, Captain 54
Furimaya, Colonel 54, 55, 56
Furutaka 29, 33, 36, 49

G

Galloping Horse 68, 71, 72
Gaston 56
Gaston, Corporal 56
Gateby, Marine Lieutenant 36
Gavago Creek 58
Gavutu 26, 27, 28, 31
General Hyakutake 37
George, Colonel 74
George, Colonel Alexander 67
George F. Elliott 21, 31, 35
Getting, Captain 33
Ghormley 20, 32, 35, 46, 49
Ghormley, Vice Admiral Robert 18
Gifu 67, 71, 72, 73, 74
Gifu ridge 67
Goettge 24
Goettge, Lieutenant Colonel 36
Goto, Admiral 49
Grant, Corporal 56
Grayson 72
Green Island 29
Greenman 34
Gregory 40
Griffiths, General Samuel 21
Guam 19
Gurabasu 48
Gwin 61

H

Haiti 18
Hamikaze 73
Haruna 50
Harusame 59
Hawaiian Islands 19
Heilly 56
Heine, Lieutenant 40
Helena 49, 59
Helm 32, 35, 36
Henneken, Colonel 58
Hepburn, Admiral 35
Hersey, John 57
Heywood 19, 27
Hiei 58, 59, 60, 63, 75
Hill 148 27
Hill 208 27
Hill 281 27, 30
Hill 53 68, 69, 70
Hiroaki, Rear Admiral 58
Hirohito 68
Hobart 35
Honolulu 64, 65
Hoover, Captain 49
Horton, Dick 20, 26, 30, 41, 48
Hosokawa, Major 72
Hull 31
Hyakutake 23, 28, 37, 40, 41, 46, 47, 48, 49, 50, 52, 54, 55, 58, 62, 63, 65, 66, 70, 71, 72, 73, 75

I

I-1 65, 66
I-15 65
I-3 65
Ichiki, Colonel Kiyono 19, 37, 39, 40, 42, 43, 58, 73, 75
Ilu River 24, 26
Imamura, Commander General 66, 68, 73
Imamura, General Hitoshi 65

Imoto, Colonel 71, 72
Imperial Navy 23, 60
Inagaki, Major 71
Inoue, Admiral 23
Ishimoto 17, 19, 49

J

J.P. Blunden 46
Jackym, 2nd Lieutenant John 38
Jarvis 31, 36
Java 52
Jervis 33
Jintsu 39
John Ericsson 19
Johnson, Captain Richard S. 27, 42
Joncek 56
Jones, Corporal James 58, 68
Juneau 59, 60, 75

K

Kaiser, 2nd Lieutenant Bill 27
Kako 29, 33, 36
Kakombona 40
Kamimbo Bay 65, 66, 72, 73, 74
Kato, Captain 35
Katsumata, Captain 52, 53, 54
Kaufmann, Marine Signalman Arnold 19, 30, 51
Kavieng 23, 36
Kawaguchi, Major General Kiyotake 40, 41, 42, 43, 46, 47, 49, 52, 53, 55, 57, 66, 75
Kawanishi 24, 26
Kelet, Lieutenant 41
Kennedy 66
Kieta 18
Kikuraki 19
King, Admiral 18, 19, 20, 21, 35
Kinryu Maru 39
Kinugasa 29, 33, 36, 49, 51, 60
Kirishima 58, 59, 60, 61, 62
Kitts, Captain 65
Kiwi 65, 66
Kline 53
Knox, Frank 51
Koilotumaru 48, 49
Kokumbona 57, 63, 72
Koli Point 57, 58
Kondo, Admiral 60, 61, 62
Kongo 50
Konuma, Colonel 72
Koro Island 20, 23, 24
Koyangi, Captain 50
Kukum 30, 42, 43, 52, 58
Kukum village 41
Kurosaki, Captain 72, 73, 74
Kusaka 68

L

Laffey 59
Lamson 64, 65
Lardner 64, 65
Leiphart 55, 56
Lexington 32
Lieutenant Colonel Frank Goettge 20
Lieutenant Yasuo Obi 66
Lineweber, Lieutenant 49
Little 40, 41
Lofberg, Lieutenant Commander 40
London 18
Lunga 20, 25, 26, 32, 35, 36, 41, 48, 49, 51, 55, 67
Lunga Point 26, 30, 32, 37, 58, 64
Lunga River 30

M

MacArthur, Douglas   20
Maikaze   73
Makigumo   73
Makita, Lieutenant   53, 54
Malaita   17, 48
Malaya   52
Manchuria   52
Manila Bay   75
Marchant, Resident Commissioner   18, 30
Marchant, William   17
Marine Gene Keller   76
Martin Clemens   38, 41, 48, 51
Maruyama, Lieutenant General   52, 53, 54, 55, 56, 57, 65, 66, 75
Maruyama Trail   52, 53, 57
Mason, Captain   27
Mason, Paul   29, 31, 50
Matanikau River   19, 36, 40, 41, 46, 48, 52, 53, 55, 62, 68
Matsuyama, Rear Admiral   35
Maxwell, Lieutenant Colonel   24
Maya   51
McCandless, Lieutenant Commander   60
McCarthy, Bob   38
McCawley   32, 35
McFarland   51
McKee, Lieutenant   61
McLaughlin, Sergeant Bill   71
Meiyo Maru   29, 36
Melhorn, Lieutenant Charles   65
Meredith   51
Metapona river   58
Midway Island   19
Mikawa, Admiral   24, 28, 29, 31, 32, 35, 36, 40, 60, 75
Mikawa, Rear Admiral Gunichi   23
Miller, Major   28
Minamoto   57
Minneapolis   64, 65
Mission, Visale   25
Mitsubishi   66
Mitsubishi bombers   28
Mitsubishis   29
Miyazaki, General   72
Moa   66
Monssen   26, 27, 59, 60
Montgomery, Corporal   27
Moresby, Port   28
Morinda   18
Mount Austen   26, 30, 46, 52, 66, 67
Mugford   29
Myoko   51

N

Nagara   58, 59
Nagono, Admiral   68
Nakagome   53, 54
Nakaguma Colonel   46, 47, 48, 52
Nakajima, Commander Tadishi   28, 29
Nakayama, Lt.   41, 42
Nalimbu river   58
Nasu, Major General   47, 52, 53, 54, 55, 56
Naval Battle of Guadalcanal   60
Nelson, Colonel   67
New Britain   17, 29
New Caledonia   17, 20
New Georgia   66
New Guinea   17, 23, 24, 28, 40, 68
New Hebrides   18, 19, 23, 32, 35, 48, 51, 60, 63, 64
New Ireland   23, 29
New Orleans   64, 65
New River   18
New York Herald Tribune   22
New York Times   22
New Zealand   18, 19, 20, 21, 64, 65
Nicaragua   18
Nicholas   73
Nimitz, Admiral   51, 74
Nishino, Gen.   40, 41, 42, 47

Nishiyama, Major   71
Norfolk   19, 46
North Carolina   18, 21
Northampton   64, 65
Northern Force   32, 33, 35, 36

O

O'Bannon   59
Obi, Sub Lieutenant   70, 71, 72, 74
Ohmae, Commander   23, 35
Oite   37
Oka, Colonel   40, 41, 43, 46, 47, 52, 55, 56, 57, 67, 71
Okajima   67
Okajima, 1st Lieutenant   67, 71
Okamura, Lieutenant   25, 26
Okinoshima   17, 19
Oklahoma   32
O'Neill, Shopfitter Ed   58
OPERATION WATCHTOWER   20
Oyashio   64

P

Paige, Sergeant Mitchell   18, 46, 51, 55, 56, 58, 75
Patch, General   67, 68, 70, 72, 73
Patterson   36
Patteson   32, 33
Patuxent River   18
Pawlowski   56
Pearl Harbor   22, 23
Pensacola   64, 65
Philippines   19, 23
Pistol Pete   50, 76
Poha river   72
Point Cruz   47, 57, 58, 63, 66, 71, 72
Pollock, Lieutenant Colonel   38
Port Moresby   23
Portland   59, 60
Pratt, Commander   37
Preston   61
Private Tadeshi Suzuki   73
Puller   74
Puller, Colonel   53
Puller, Lieutenant Colonel Chester   46

Q

Quincy   26, 32, 34, 36

R

Rabaul   17, 18, 20, 21, 22, 23, 26, 28, 29, 32, 36, 37, 40, 41, 46, 47, 52, 55, 65, 66, 68, 73
Ralph Talbot   32, 33, 35
Ramada   48
Rapasia, Michael   35
Rear Admiral Aritomo Goto   17
Red Beach   24, 25, 26, 27, 31, 74
Riefkohl   33, 34
Riefkohl, Captain "Freddie"   32
Ringer, Captain   37
Roberts, Ray   38
Rogal, Corporal   49
Rogers, Major Otho   47
Rosendahl, Captain   64
Ruavatu   48

S

S-38   36
S-42   19
Sakai   29
Sakai, Saburo   28
Sakakibara, 1st Lieutenant   39
Saki   38
Salt Lake City   49
Samoa   18, 46
San Francisco   49, 59, 60
San Juan   26, 27, 35
Sano, Lieutenant General   58
Sapuro   28

Sapuru   20, 74
Saratoga   21, 22
Savo   49, 59, 60, 64
Savo Island   32, 35, 50, 55, 61, 72
Scott, Admiral   59
Scott, Rear Admiral Norman   49, 59
Sea Horse   68
Seabees   40
Sealark   61
Sealark Channel   32, 34, 36, 37, 48, 49, 50, 51, 54, 60, 64
Segi   66
Segilau   74
Segilau river   71, 72, 74
Seminole   55, 58
Sendai   61
Sergeant Ralph Briggs   53
Sexton, Tom   18, 19
Shea, Corporal John   38
Sherman, Captain F.   35
Shirai, 2nd Lieutenant   54
Shoji, Colonel Toshinari   53, 55, 57, 58
Shortland Islands   19, 39, 47
Shortlands   60, 62, 65, 74
Sinclair, Commander   33
Singapore   17
Sio, Alan   24
Sister Marie Therese   17
Skylark Channel   41
Smith, Chief Water Tender   34
Smith, Lieutenant Commander E.   63
Smith, Roy   42
Snell, Lieutenant E.   24
Solomon Island   19, 24, 49
Solomon Islands   17, 18, 23, 64
Sorenson   48, 49
Sorenson, Sergeant James   48
South Dakota   60, 61, 64
Southern Force   32, 33, 35, 36
Spanish-American War   75
Spaulding, Sergeant   37
Stafford, Captain   48
Stansberry   56
Star   56
Sterett   59
Stertet   59
Sugita, Colonel   58
Sugiyama   68
Sugiyama, Marshal   68
Sumiyoshi, Major General   52, 53
Suziki, Captain   56
Suzuki, Private Tadashi   39
Sweeny, Lieutenant Robert   31
Syoychi   68

T

Taivu Point   37, 39, 40
Takanani   64
Tanai, 1st Lieutenant   68
Tanaka   39, 40, 47, 60, 61, 62, 63, 64, 65, 75
Tanaka, Admiral Raizo   37
Tanaka, Rear Admiral   58
Tanambogo   26, 27, 28, 31
Tangarare   48
Tangarare Mission   47
Tasimboko   40, 41, 42, 43, 49, 52, 54, 55
Tassafaronga   40, 51, 52, 60, 62, 63, 64, 66, 71, 72
Taylor   57
Taylor, Lieutenant Commander   49
Tenaru River   30, 36, 38, 41, 63
Tenryu   29, 35
Terazuki   65
The Slot   32
The Sullivans   60
Therese, Marie   48
Therese, Sister   48
Therese, Sister Marie   20, 28
Tinian   29
Titi   73, 74
Tokyo   23, 28, 29, 37, 40, 57, 58, 63, 65, 68, 75

Tokyo Bay   65
Tokyo Express   40, 47, 48, 52, 58, 62, 66
Tomioka, Captain   68
Topper, Lieutenant Commander   34
Torgeson   74
Tregaskis, Richard   26, 31, 36, 39
Trevor   55
Truesdell   34
Truesdell, Commander   34
Truk   23
Tsuji   52, 53, 58
Tsuji, Colonel   53, 57, 65, 68
Tsukahara, Area Commander Admiral   4
Tulagi   17, 18, 19, 20, 23, 24, 26, 27, 28, 30, 32, 35, 41, 48, 49, 51, 55, 60, 65, 68, 73, 74
Turner, Admiral   35, 60
Turner, Admiral Richard Kelly   22

U

Umasami river   72, 73, 74
Umikaze   40

V

Vandegrift   20, 22, 23, 25, 30, 31, 32, 36, 38, 41, 42, 46, 47, 48, 49, 51, 54, 57, 58
Vandegrift, General Alexander   18
Verahue   73
Vice-Admiral Kusaka   68
Vincennes   32, 33, 34, 35, 36
Vireo   51
Visale Mission   17, 20, 28, 48, 74
Visaona, Nicholas   19, 25, 26, 48, 63
Vouza, Sergeant Major Jacob   38
Vunakanau   23

W

Wake Island   22
Walke   61
Walsh, Commander   33
Washing Machine Charlie   50, 51, 71
Washington   18, 60, 61, 62
Wasp   27, 35
Watanabe, Lieutenant Colonel   54
Webster, Machinist 2nd Class Lyle   51
Weiss   64
Wellington   21
Wellington Dominion   22
White   57
White River   71, 72
Wildcats   29
Williams, Major Robert   27
Wilson   32, 35, 73
Wilson, Corporal Dean   38
World War I   50
Wright, Admiral Carleton   64
Wright, Colonel   67

X

X-Ray   25

Y

Yamamoto   50
Yamamoto, Admiral   19, 39, 47
Yoke   25
Yorktown   19, 32
Young, Boatswains Mate   35
Young, Lieutenant   27
Yubari   29
Yudachi   59, 60
Yukikaze   60
Yunagi   29, 33, 36

Z

Zane   55
Zero   29, 55, 63, 73
Zero fighters   28
Zeros   29, 51
Zook, Signalman L.   60

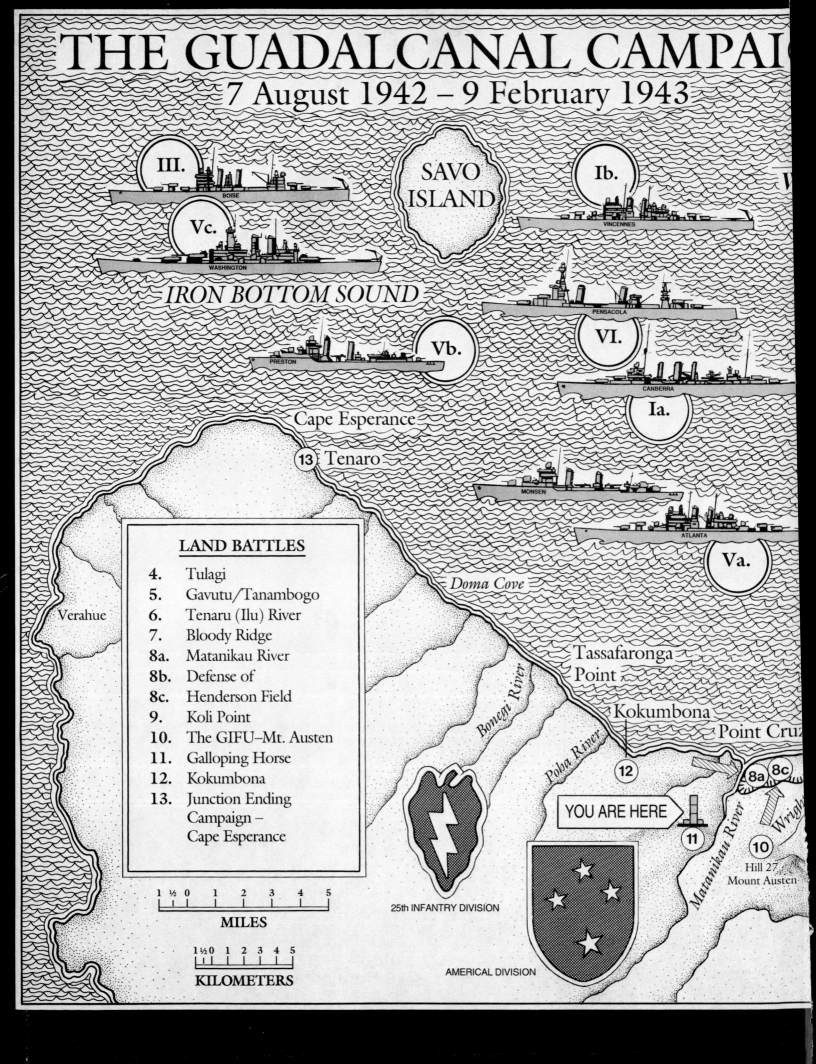

THE GUADALCANAL CAMPAI...
7 August 1942 – 9 February 1943

III.

Vc.

BOISE

WASHINGTON

SAVO ISLAND

Ib.

VINCENNES

PENSACOLA

VI.

CANBERRA

Ia.

IRON BOTTOM SOUND

Vb.

PRESTON

Cape Esperance

13 Tenaro

MONSEN

ATLANTA

Va.

LAND BATTLES

4. Tulagi
5. Gavutu/Tanambogo
6. Tenaru (Ilu) River
7. Bloody Ridge
8a. Matanikau River
8b. Defense of
8c. Henderson Field
9. Koli Point
10. The GIFU–Mt. Austen
11. Galloping Horse
12. Kokumbona
13. Junction Ending Campaign – Cape Esperance

Verahue

Doma Cove

Tassafaronga Point

Bonegi River

Kokumbona

Polo River

Point Cruz

12

8a 8c

YOU ARE HERE

11

Matanikau River

Wrigh...

10

Hill 27 Mount Austen

25th INFANTRY DIVISION

AMERICAL DIVISION

1 ½ 0 1 2 3 4 5
MILES

1 ½ 0 1 2 3 4 5
KILOMETERS